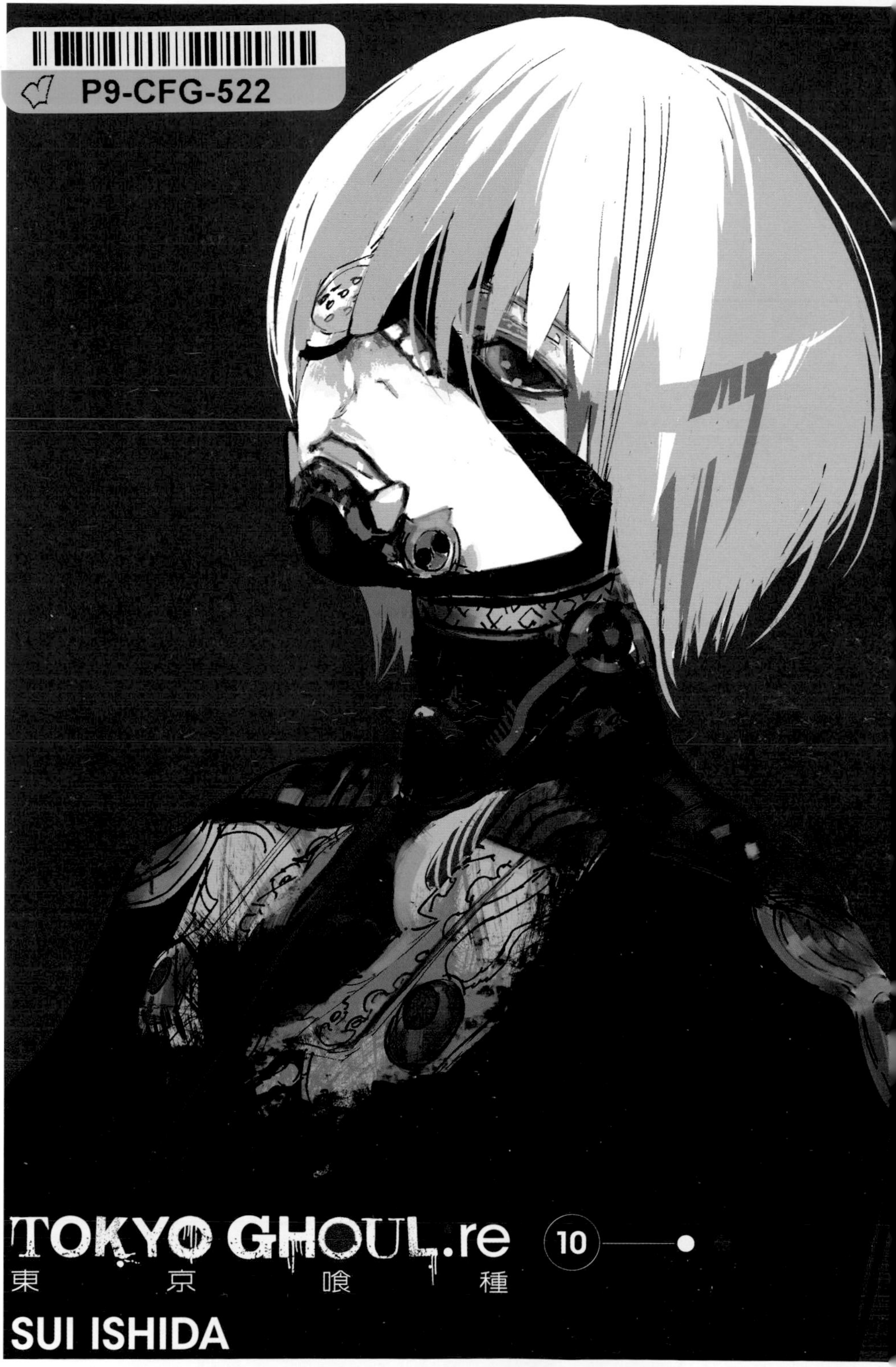

TOKYO GHOUL:re 10

東京喰種

SUI ISHIDA

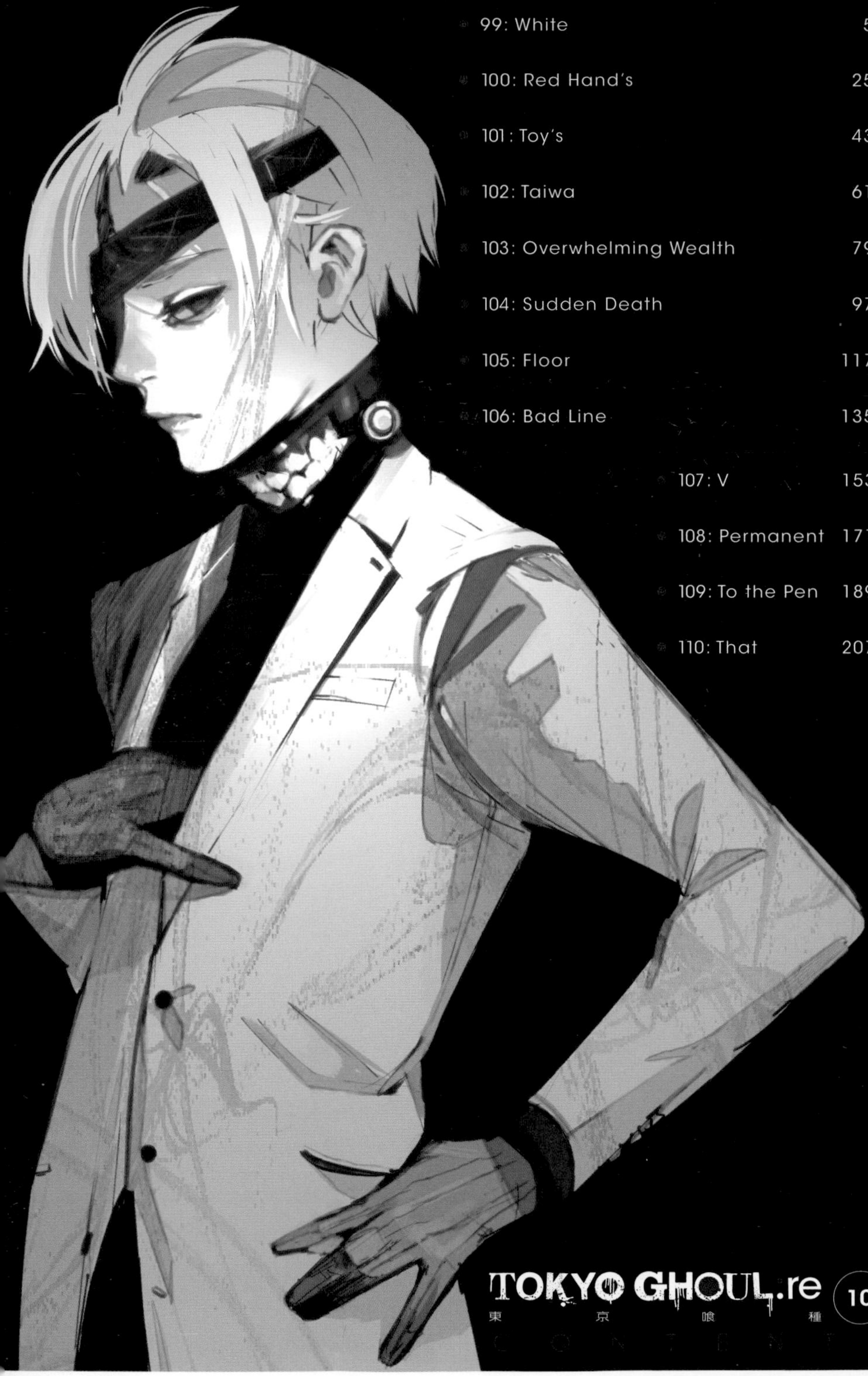

TOKYO GHOUL:re 10

東京喰種

CONTENTS

CCG Ghoul Investigators / Tokyo Ghoul :re

The CCG is the only organization in the world that investigates and solves Ghoul-related crimes. Founded by the Washu Family, the CCG developed and evolved Quinques, a type of weapon derived from Ghouls' Kagune. Quinx, an advanced, next-generation technology where humans are implanted with Quinques, is currently under development.

Mado Squad

Qs (Quinx) ● Investigators implanted with Quinques. They all live together in a house called the Chateau along with Investigator Sasaki.

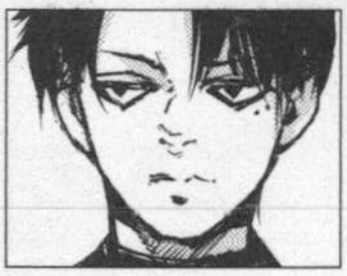

● Kuki Urie
瓜江久生
Rank 1 Investigator
New Quinx Squad leader and the most talented fighter in the squad. Demonstrating leadership after the death of Shirazu.

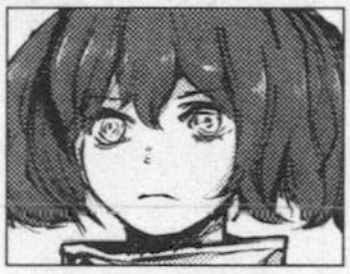

● Saiko Yonebayashi
米林才子
Rank 2 Investigator
Supporting Urie as Deputy Squad Leader while playing with her subordinates. Very bad at time management and a sucker for games and snacks.

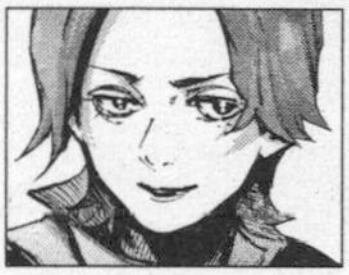

● Toma Higemaru
髯丸トウマ
Rank 3 Investigator
Discovered his Quinx aptitude before enrolling in the academy. Looks up to Urie. Comes from a wealthy family.

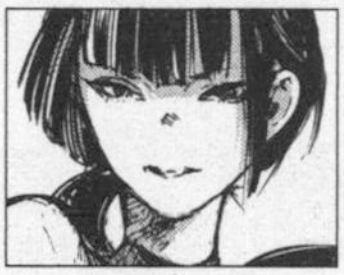

● Ching-li Hsiao
小静麗
Rank 1 Investigator
From Hakubi Garden like Hairu Ihei. Skilled in hand-to-hand combat. Came to Japan from Taiwan as a child.

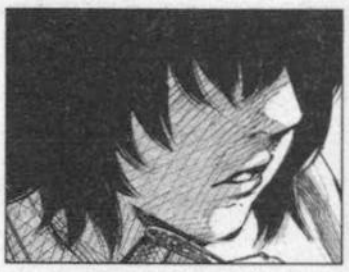

● Shinsanpei Aura
安浦晋三平
Rank 2 Investigator
Nephew of Special Investigator Kiyoko Aura. Unlike his aunt, who graduated at the top of her class, his grades were not that great.

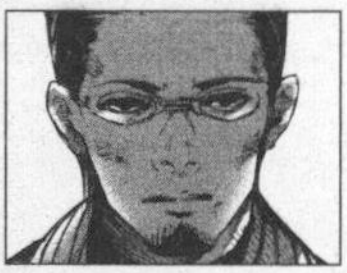

● Matsuri Washu
和修 政
Special Investitgator
Yoshitoki's son. A Washu Supremacist. Is skeptical of Quinxes. The only surviving member of the Washu family after the Rushima Operation.

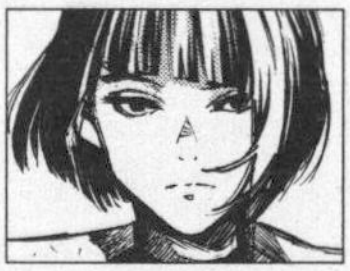

● Kori Ui
宇井 郡
Special Investigator
Promising investigator formerly with the Arima Squad. Became a special investigator at a young age, but has a stubborn side.

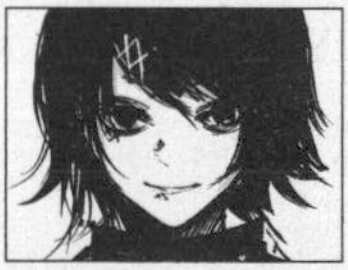

● Juzo Suzuya
鈴屋什造
Special Investigator
Promoted to Special Investigator at 22, a feat previously only accomplished by Kisho Arima. A maverick who fights with knives hidden in his prosthetic leg.

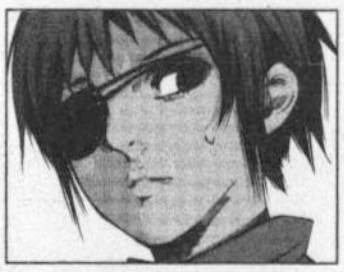

● Toru Mutsuki
六月 透
Rank 1 Investigator
Decided to become an investigator after his parents were killed by a Ghoul. Assigned female at birth, he transitioned after the Quinx procedure. Struggling with the lie he's been living with...

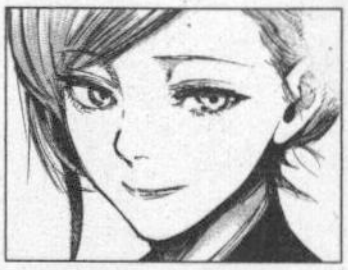

● Akira Mado
真戸 暁
Assistant Special Investigator
Mentor to Haise. Determined to eradicate Ghouls. Wounded aiding a Ghoul in the Rushima Operation. Currently being treated for injuries.

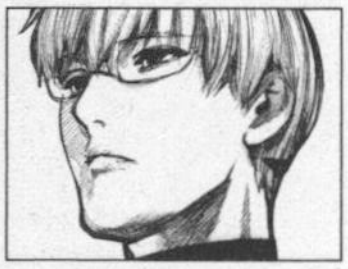

● Kisho Arima
有馬貴将
Special Investigator
An undefeated investigator respected by many at the CCG. Killed at Cochlea by the One-Eyed King.

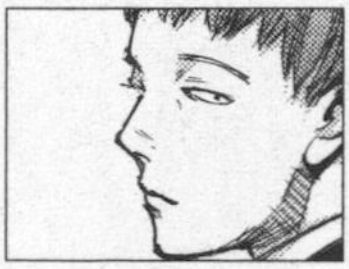

● Take Hirako
平子 丈
Senior Investigator
Kisho Arima's former partner. Took over Squad Zero at Arima's request and aided the One-Eyed King's escape before leaving the CCG.

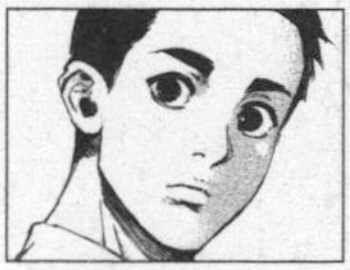

● Takeomi Kuroiwa
黒磐武臣
Rank 1 Investigator
Son of Special Investigator Iwao Kuroiwa. Has a strong sense of justice and has restrained Ghouls with his bare hands.

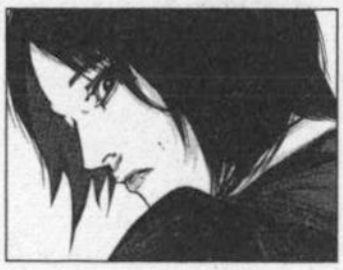

● Nimura Furuta
旧多二福
Rank 1 Investigator
Former subordinate of the late Shiki Kijima. Has many secrets.

T ● K Y ● G H ● U L

Tokyo Ghoul :re ● Ghouls

They appear human, but have a unique predation organ called Kagune and can only survive by feeding on human flesh. They are the nemesis of humanity. Besides human flesh, the only other thing they can ingest is coffee. Ghouls can only be wounded by a Kagune or a Quinque made from a Kagune. One of the most prominent Ghoul factions is the Aogiri Tree, a hostile organization that is increasing its strength.

Café :re

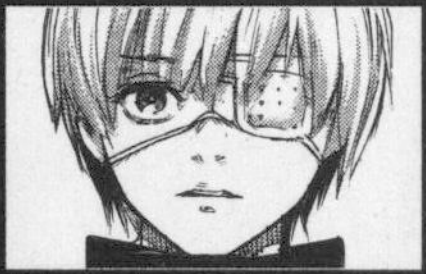

Ken Kaneki
金木 研
Mentored the Qs Squad as Haise Sasaki. A half-Ghoul who has succeeded Kisho Arima as the One-Eyed King.

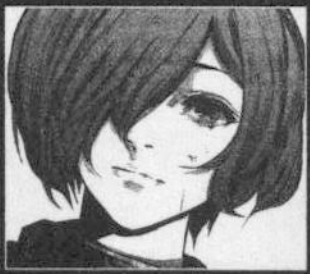

Touka Kirishima
霧嶋董香
Manager of Café :re. Wants to carry on the traditions of Anteiku.

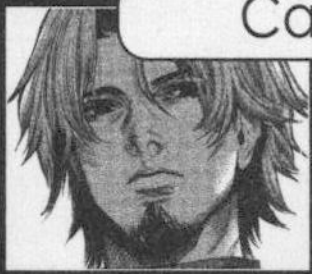

Renji Yomo
四方蓮示
:re barista. Infiltrated Cochlea with Touka.

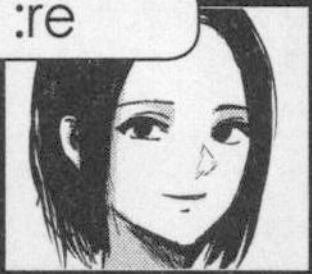

Kaya Irimi
入見カヤ
Ex-Anteiku employee.

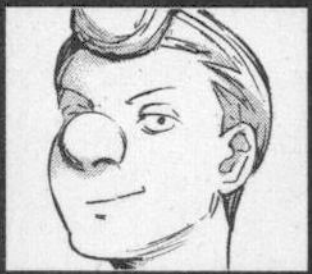

Enji Koma
古間円児
Ex-Anteiku employee.

Ex-Aogiri Tree

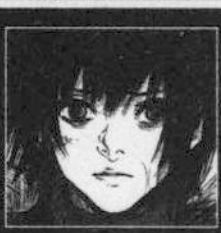

Ayato
アヤト
Touka's younger brother. A Rate SS Ghoul known as the Rabbit.

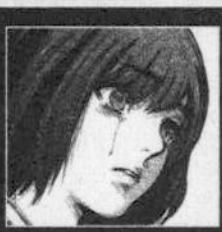

Hinami Fueguchi
フエグチ ヒナミ
Freed from Cochlea by Kaneki.

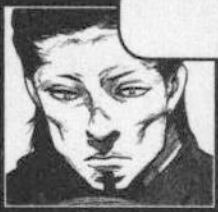

Banjo
バンジョー
Ayato's lieutenant. Treating Akira's wounds.

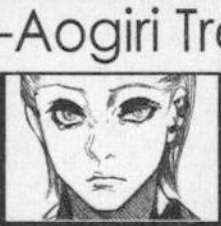

Naki
ナキ
Current leader of the White Suits. A Rate S, but frequently loses control.

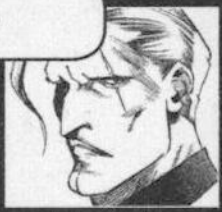

Shosei
承正
Member of the White Suits. Joined after being beaten by Naki.

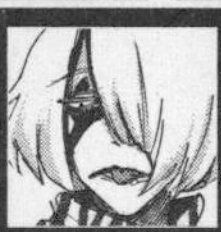

Hohguro
ホオグロ
Member of the White Suits. Joined after tying with Shosei.

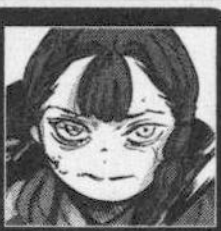

Miza
ミザ
Ex-leader of the Blades in the 18th Ward. A.K.A. Triple-Blade.

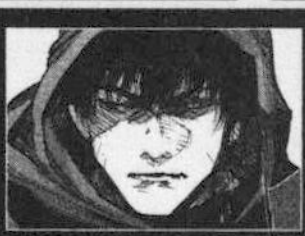

Kotaro Amon
亜門鋼太朗
Ex-CCG investigator. Failed subject of Kano's Ghoulification procedure. Known as Floppy. A glint of his old self still gleams in his eyes.

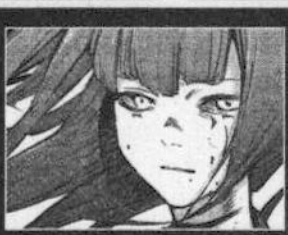

Kuro
クロ
Underwent Kano's Ghoulification procedure, like Ken Kaneki. Absorbed her twin sister Shirona into her body.

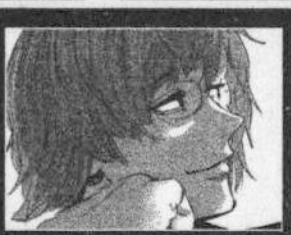

Nishiki Nishio
西尾 錦
The Ghoul known as Orochi. Tracking the Aogiri Tree.

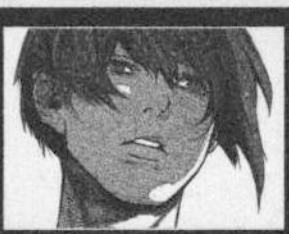

Shu Tsukiyama
月山 習
A Ghoul gourmand. Continues to pursue Ken Kaneki after the dissolution of his family's conglomerate.

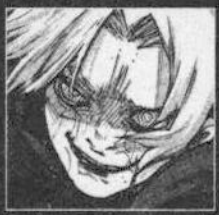

The Owl
オウル
Investigator Seido Takizawa's current form after Professor Kano implanted him with a Kakuho. Overwhelmingly powerful.

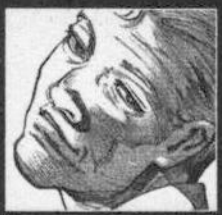

Akihiro Kano
嘉納明博
Medical examiner for the Aogiri Tree. Researching transplanting Kakuho into humans to create artificial half-Ghouls.

So far in :re

● K Y ● G H ● U L

The high-casualty Rushima Operation ends with Nimura Furuta wiping out the Washu family. Peace and quiet returns with the dissolution of the Aogiri Tree, but the CCG has begun to quietly collapse, revealing its dark secrets. Meanwhile, Ken Kaneki, who has regained his memory and succeeded Kisho Arima as the One-Eyed King, escapes Cochlea with the help of Squad Zero, led by Take Hirako. He takes shelter at Café :re, but...

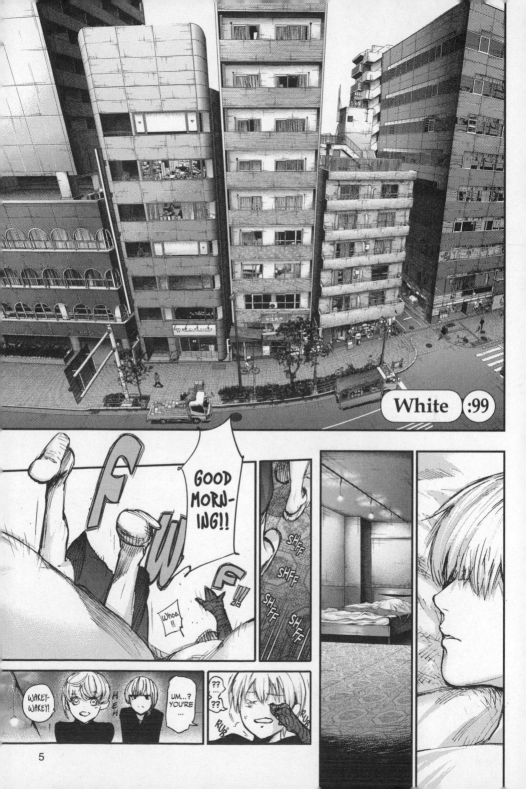

White :99

GOOD MORN-ING!!

FWAP!!

Whoa!!

SHFF
SHFF
SHFF
SHFF

WAKEY-WAKEY!

HEH

UM...? YOU'RE...

RUB
RUB

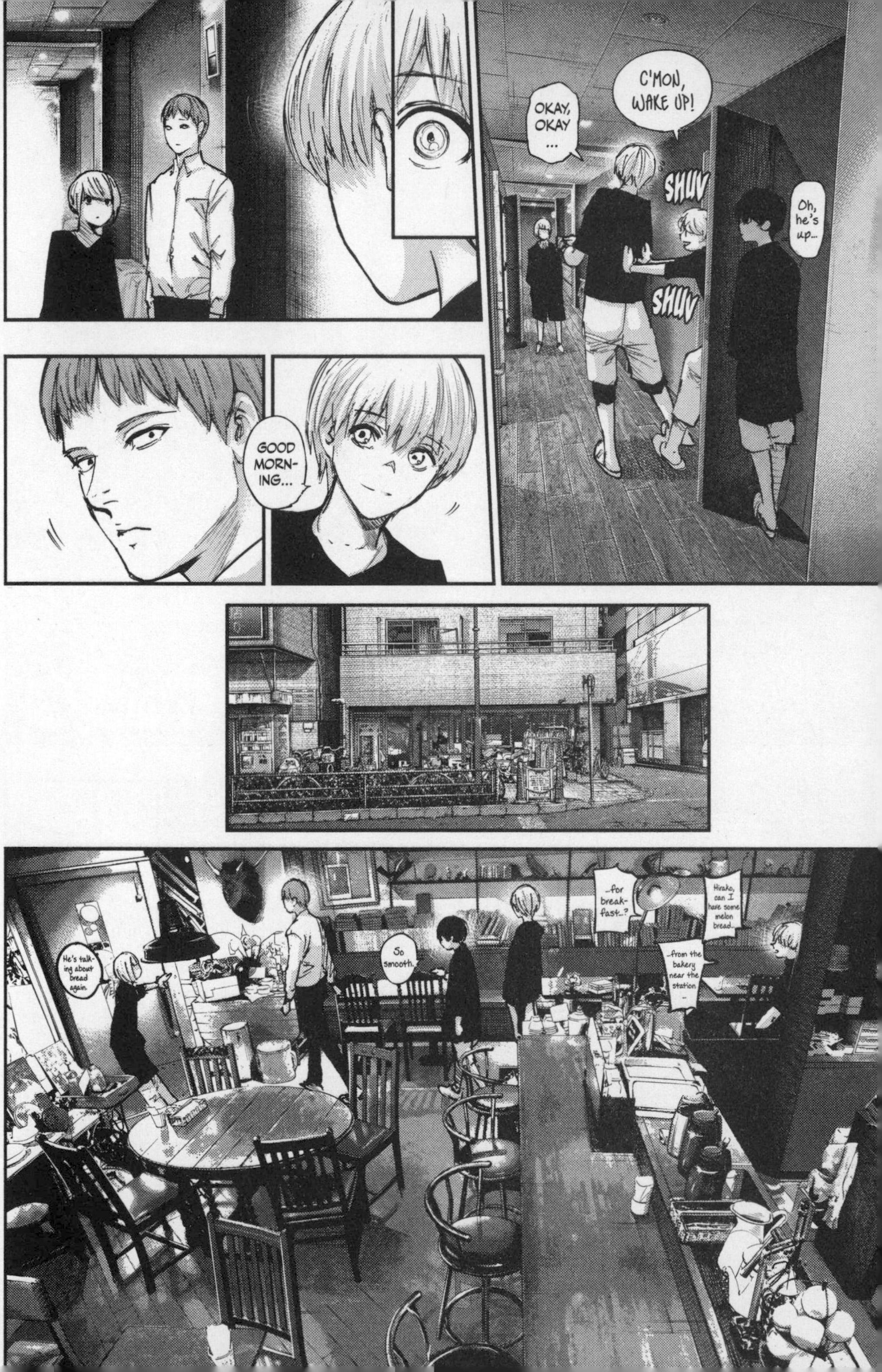
C'MON, WAKE UP!
OKAY, OKAY ...
SHUV
Oh, he's up...
SHUV
GOOD MORNING...
Hirako, can I have some melon bread...
...from the bakery near the station ...
...for breakfast...?
So smooth.
He's talking about bread again.

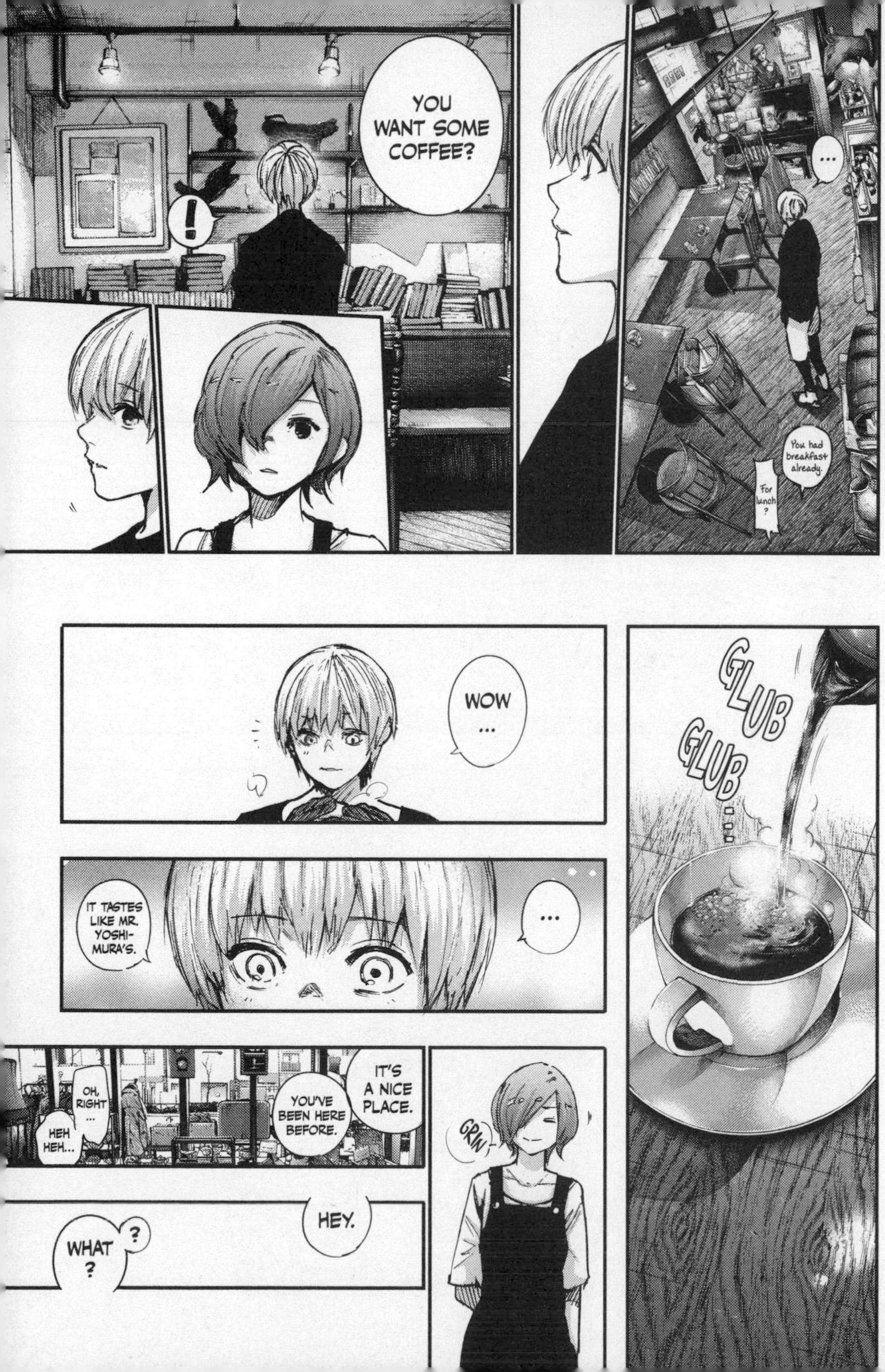
...
You had breakfast already.
For lunch?
YOU WANT SOME COFFEE?
!
GLUB GLUB
WOW ...
...
IT TASTES LIKE MR. YOSHIMURA'S.
GRIN
IT'S A NICE PLACE.
YOU'VE BEEN HERE BEFORE.
OH, RIGHT ...
HEH HEH...
HEY.
WHAT ?

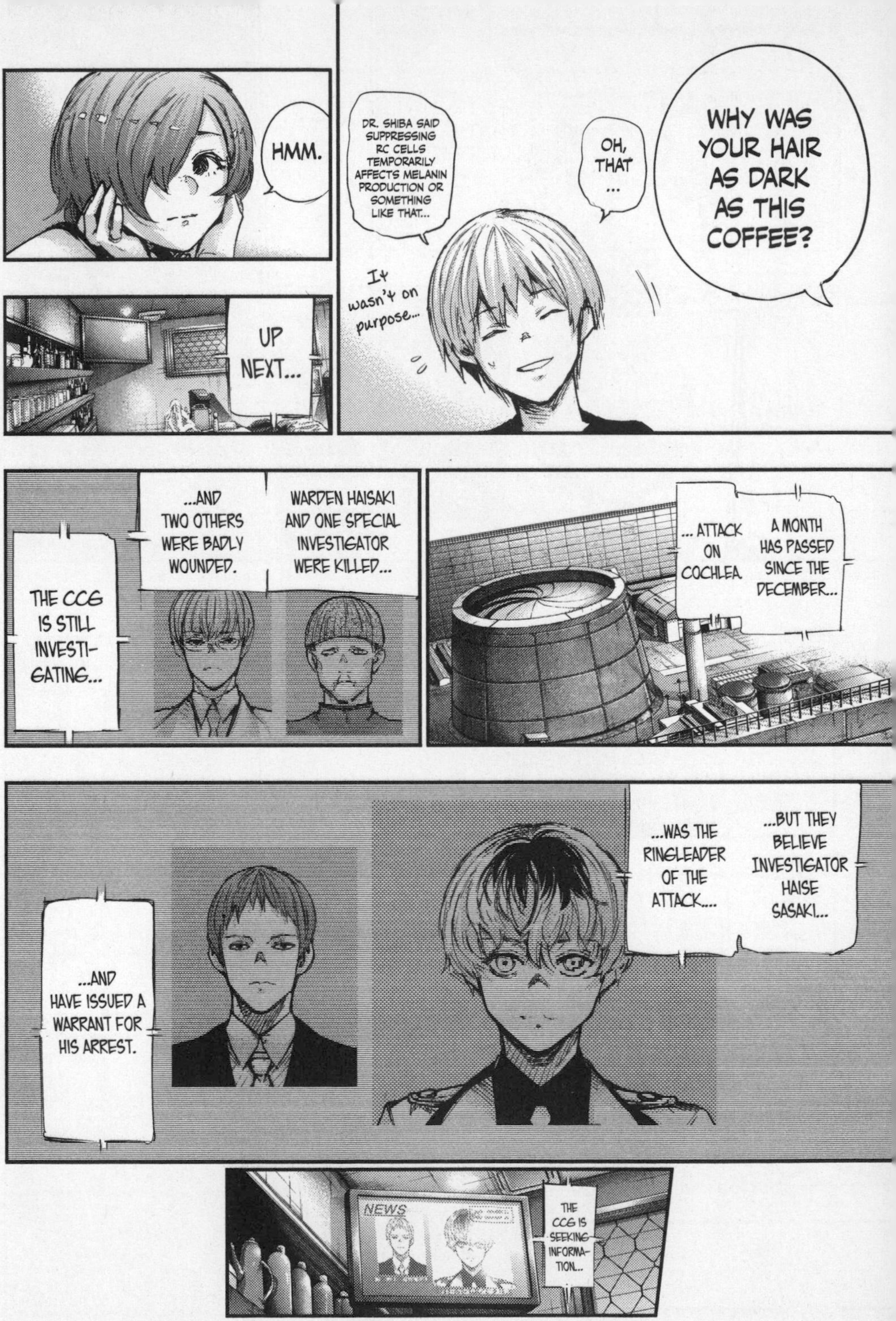
WHY WAS YOUR HAIR AS DARK AS THIS COFFEE?
OH, THAT ...
DR. SHIBA SAID SUPPRESSING RC CELLS TEMPORARILY AFFECTS MELANIN PRODUCTION OR SOMETHING LIKE THAT...
It wasn't on purpose...
HMM.
UP NEXT...
A MONTH HAS PASSED SINCE THE DECEMBER...
... ATTACK ON COCHLEA.
WARDEN HAISAKI AND ONE SPECIAL INVESTIGATOR WERE KILLED...
...AND TWO OTHERS WERE BADLY WOUNDED.
THE CCG IS STILL INVESTI-GATING...
...BUT THEY BELIEVE INVESTIGATOR HAISE SASAKI...
...WAS THE RINGLEADER OF THE ATTACK....
...AND HAVE ISSUED A WARRANT FOR HIS ARREST.
NEWS
THE CCG IS SEEKING INFORMA-TION...

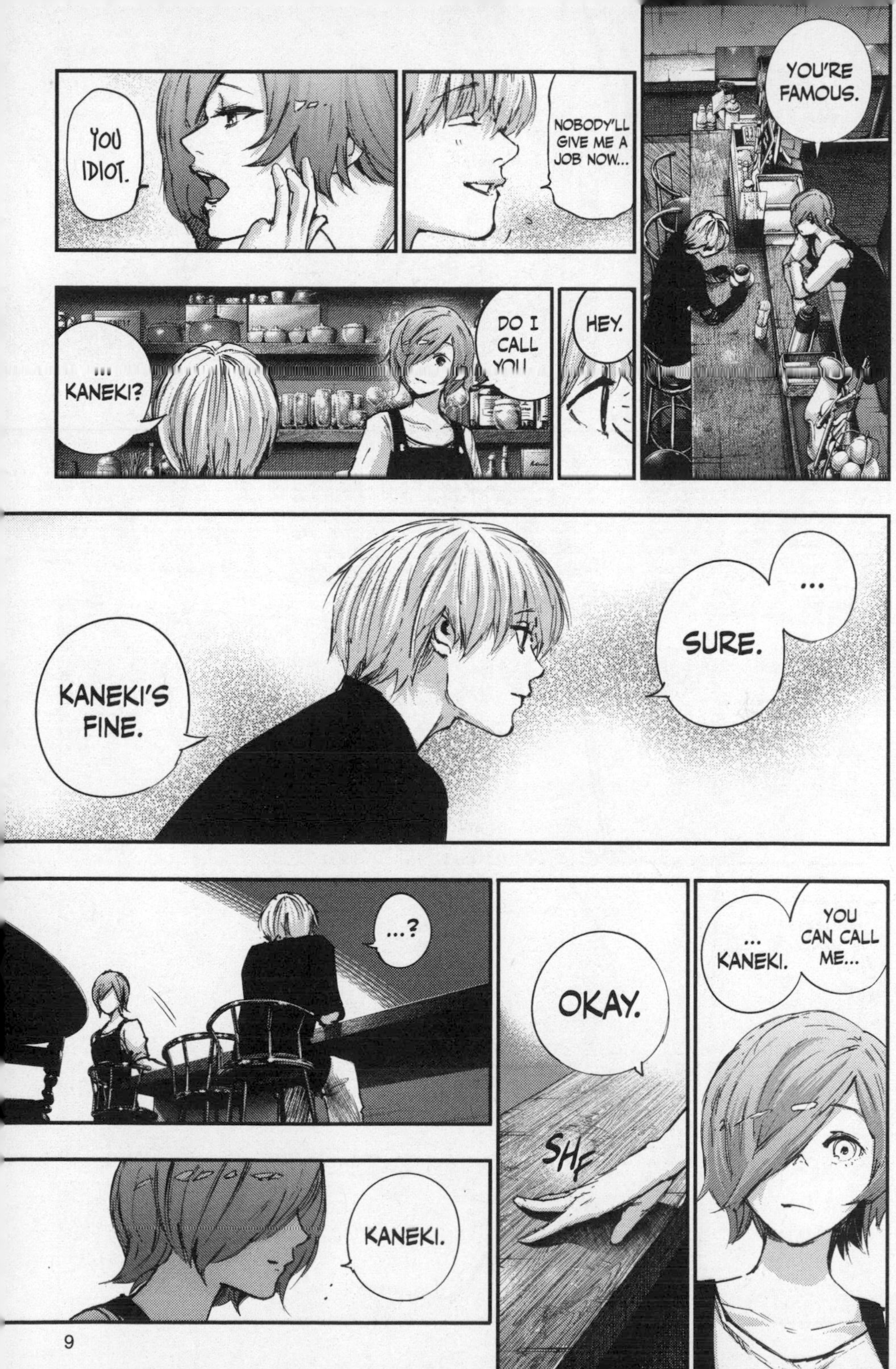
YOU'RE FAMOUS.
NOBODY'LL GIVE ME A JOB NOW...
YOU IDIOT.
HEY.
DO I CALL YOU
...KANEKI?
...
SURE.
KANEKI'S FINE.
YOU CAN CALL ME...
...KANEKI.
OKAY.
SHF
...?
KANEKI.

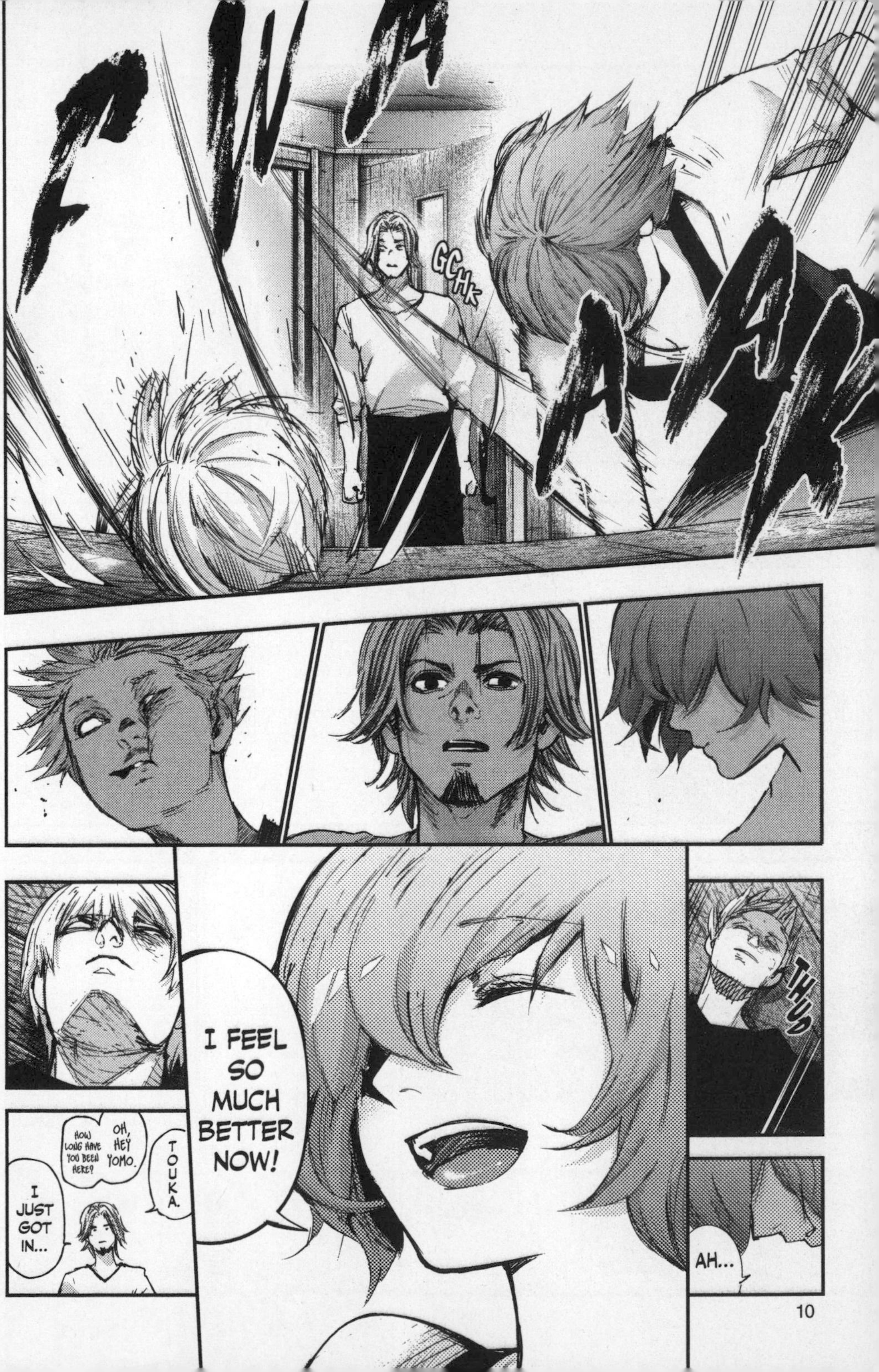
GCHK
THUD
I FEEL SO MUCH BETTER NOW!
AH...
TOUKA.
OH, HEY YOMO.
HOW LONG HAVE YOU BEEN HERE?
I JUST GOT IN...

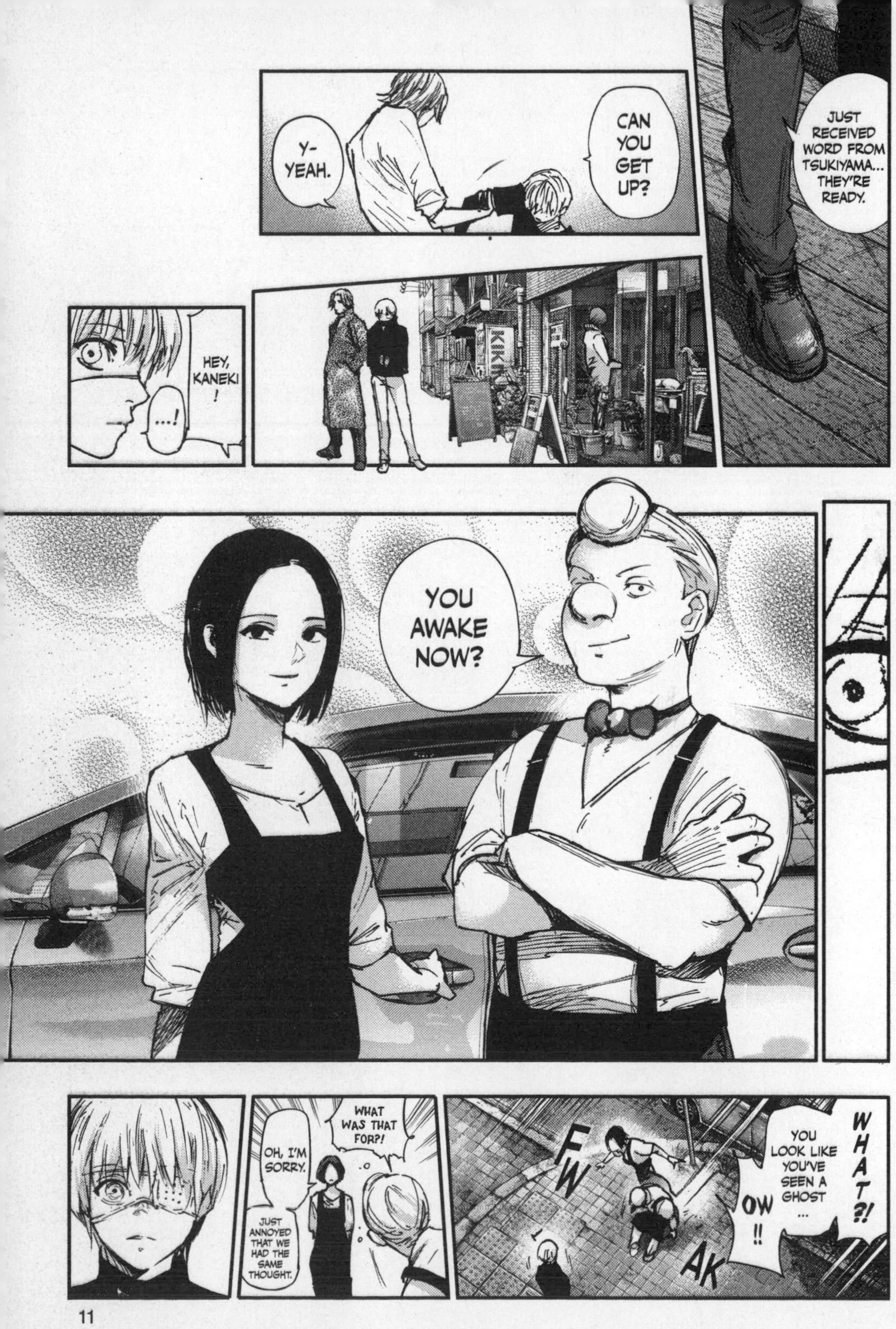
JUST RECEIVED WORD FROM TSUKIYAMA... THEY'RE READY.
CAN YOU GET UP?
Y-YEAH.
HEY, KANEKI!
...!
YOU AWAKE NOW?
WHAT?!
YOU LOOK LIKE YOU'VE SEEN A GHOST...
OW!!
FW
AK
WHAT WAS THAT FOR?!
OH, I'M SORRY.
JUST ANNOYED THAT WE HAD THE SAME THOUGHT.

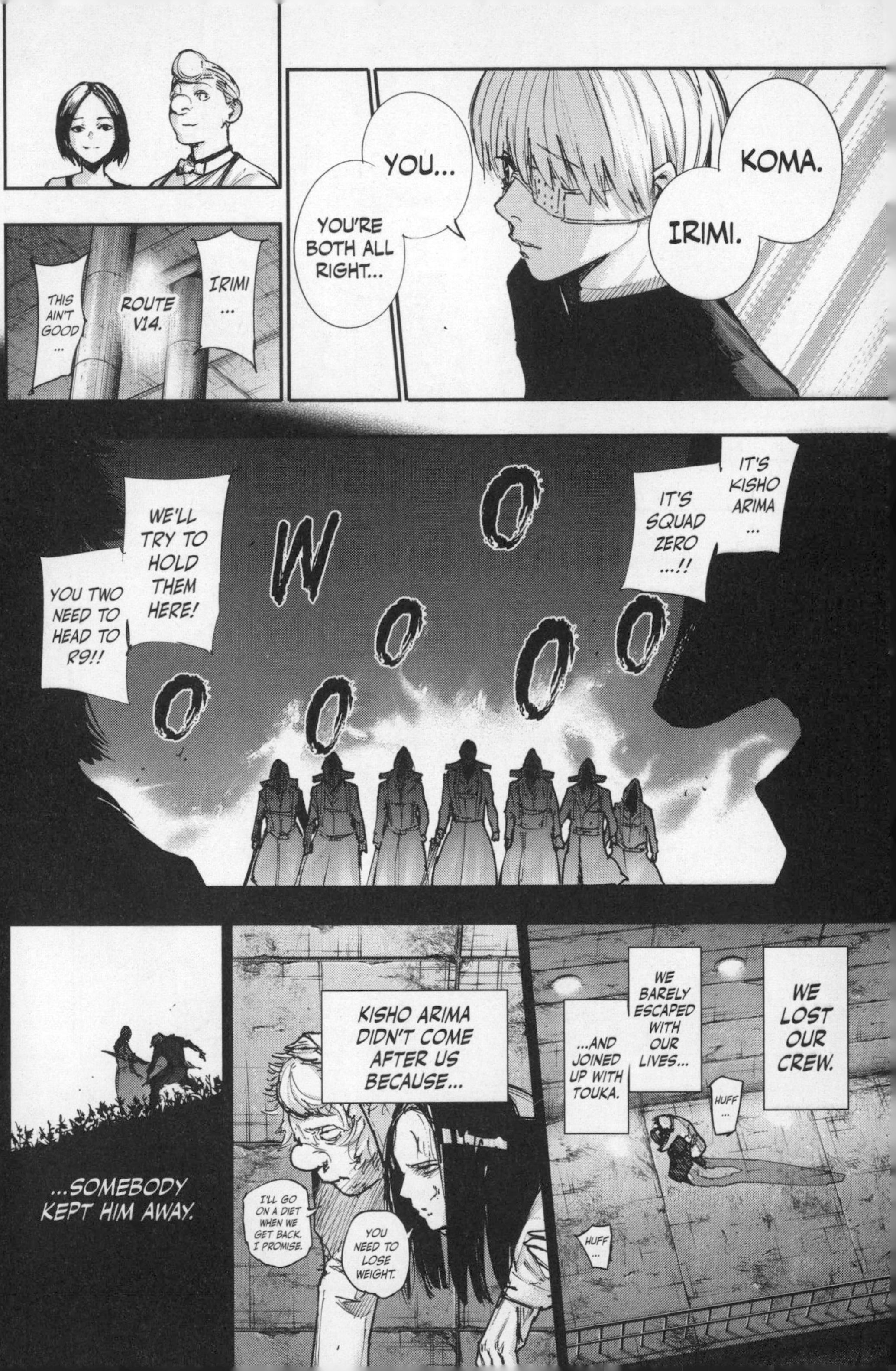
KOMA.
IRIMI.
YOU...
YOU'RE BOTH ALL RIGHT...
IRIMI ...
ROUTE V14.
THIS AIN'T GOOD ...
IT'S KISHO ARIMA ...
IT'S SQUAD ZERO ...!!
WOOOOOO
WE'LL TRY TO HOLD THEM HERE!
YOU TWO NEED TO HEAD TO R9!!
WE LOST OUR CREW.
WE BARELY ESCAPED WITH OUR LIVES...
HUFF ...
...AND JOINED UP WITH TOUKA.
KISHO ARIMA DIDN'T COME AFTER US BECAUSE...
HUFF ...
YOU NEED TO LOSE WEIGHT.
I'LL GO ON A DIET WHEN WE GET BACK. I PROMISE.
...SOMEBODY KEPT HIM AWAY.

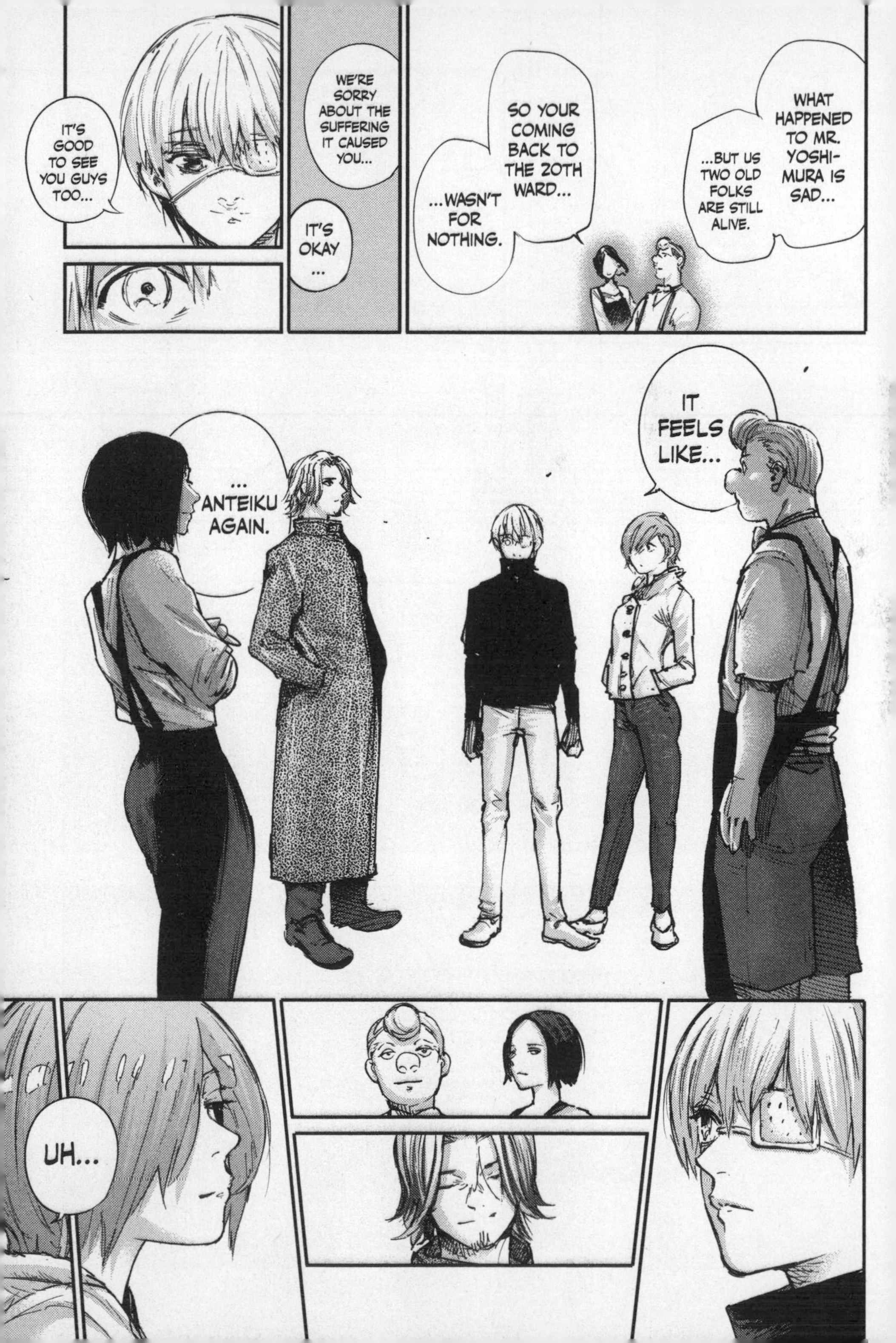
WHAT HAPPENED TO MR. YOSHIMURA IS SAD...
...BUT US TWO OLD FOLKS ARE STILL ALIVE.
SO YOUR COMING BACK TO THE 20TH WARD...
...WASN'T FOR NOTHING.
WE'RE SORRY ABOUT THE SUFFERING IT CAUSED YOU...
IT'S OKAY ...
IT'S GOOD TO SEE YOU GUYS TOO...
IT FEELS LIKE...
...ANTEIKU AGAIN.
UH...

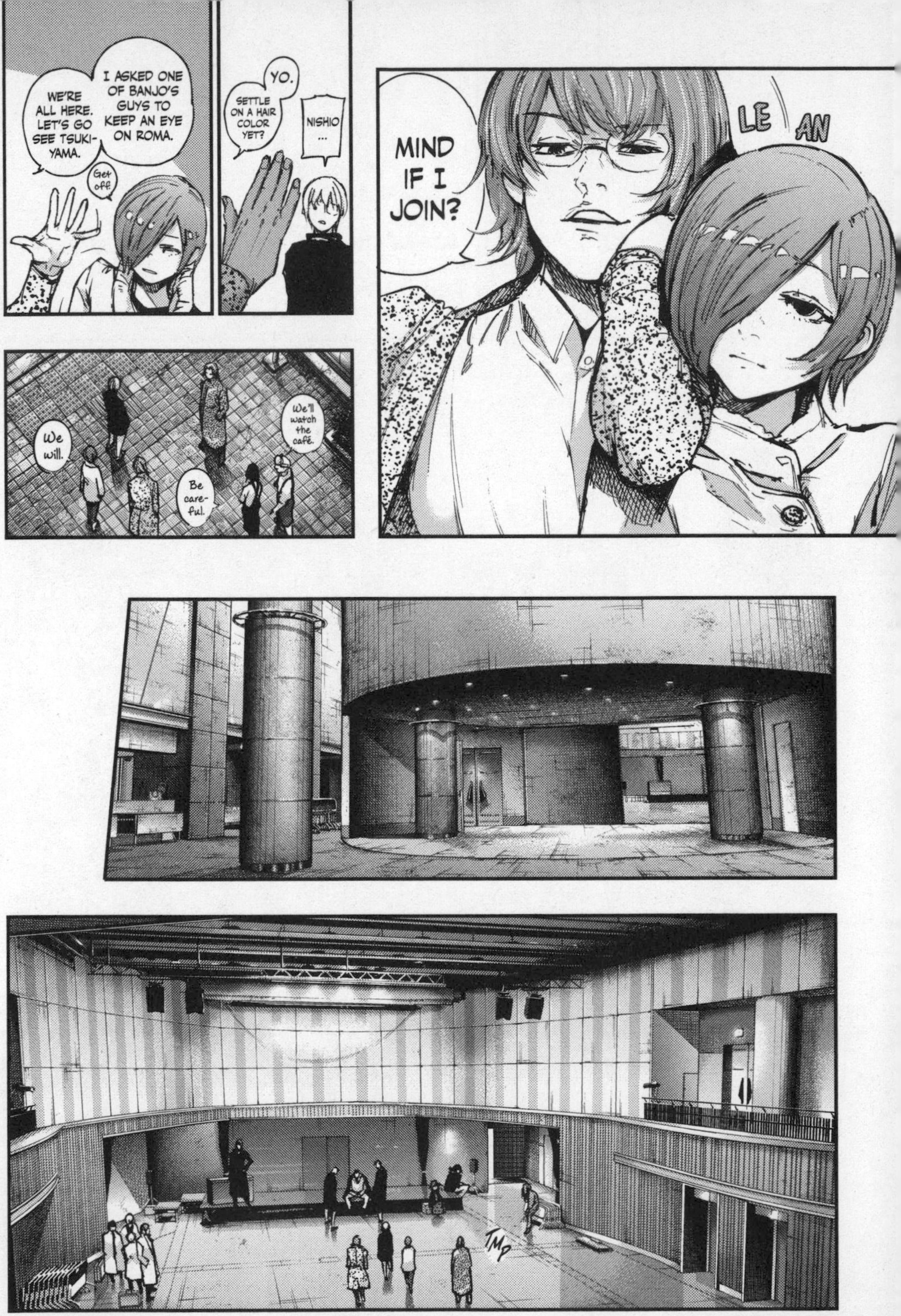
MIND IF I JOIN?
LE AN
YO.
SETTLE ON A HAIR COLOR YET?
NISHIO ...
I ASKED ONE OF BANJO'S GUYS TO KEEP AN EYE ON ROMA.
WE'RE ALL HERE. LET'S GO SEE TSUKI-YAMA.
Get off.
We'll watch the café.
Be care-ful.
We will.
TMP

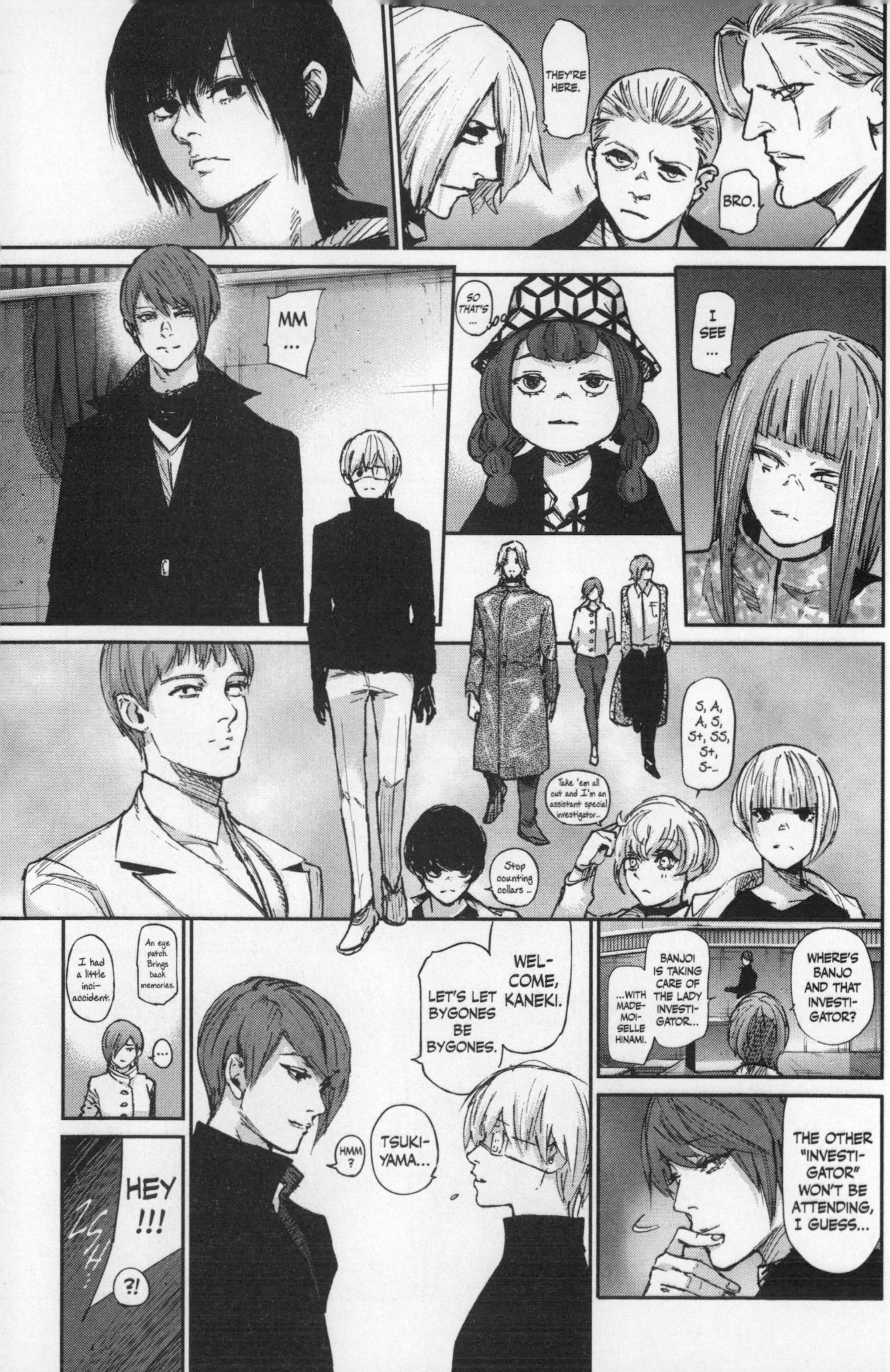

THEY'RE HERE.
BRO.
I SEE ...
SO THAT'S ...
MM ...
S, A, A, S, S+, SS, S+, S-...
Take 'em all out and I'm an assistant special investigator...
Stop counting collars ...
WHERE'S BANJO AND THAT INVESTI-GATOR?
BANJOI IS TAKING CARE OF THE LADY INVESTI-GATOR...
...WITH MADE-MOI-SELLE HINAMI.
THE OTHER "INVESTI-GATOR" WON'T BE ATTENDING, I GUESS...
WEL-COME, KANEKI.
LET'S LET BYGONES BE BYGONES.
TSUKI-YAMA...
HMM?
An eye patch. Brings back memories.
I had a little inci-accident.
...
HEY!!!
ZSH...
?!

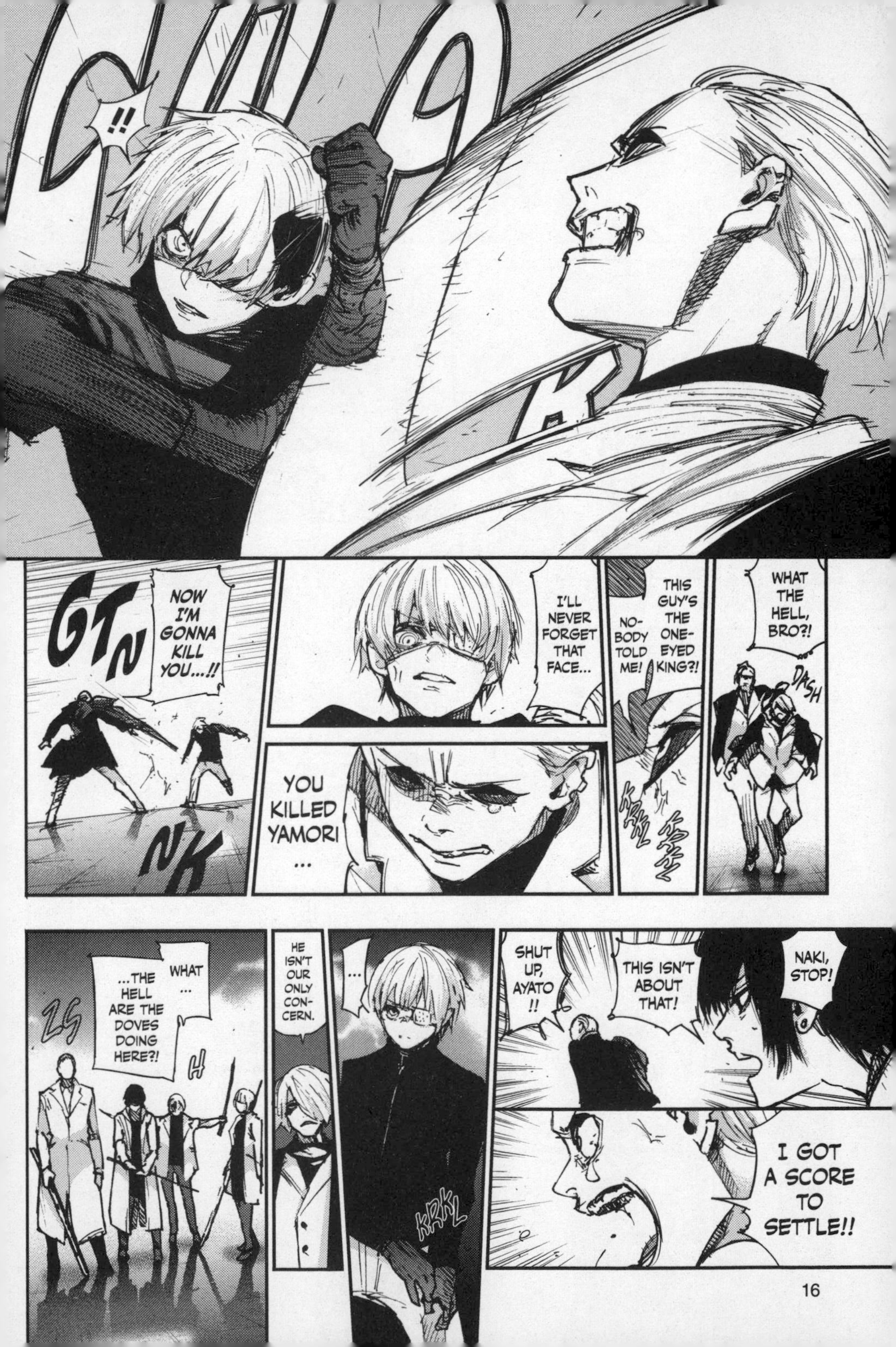
!!
WHAT THE HELL, BRO?!
DASH
THIS GUY'S THE ONE-EYED KING?!
NO-BODY TOLD ME!
KRKL
KRKL
I'LL NEVER FORGET THAT FACE...
YOU KILLED YAMORI ...
NOW I'M GONNA KILL YOU...!!
GTNNK
NAKI, STOP!
THIS ISN'T ABOUT THAT!
SHUT UP, AYATO !!
I GOT A SCORE TO SETTLE!!
...
KRKL
HE ISN'T OUR ONLY CON-CERN.
WHAT ...
...THE HELL ARE THE DOVES DOING HERE?!
ZSH

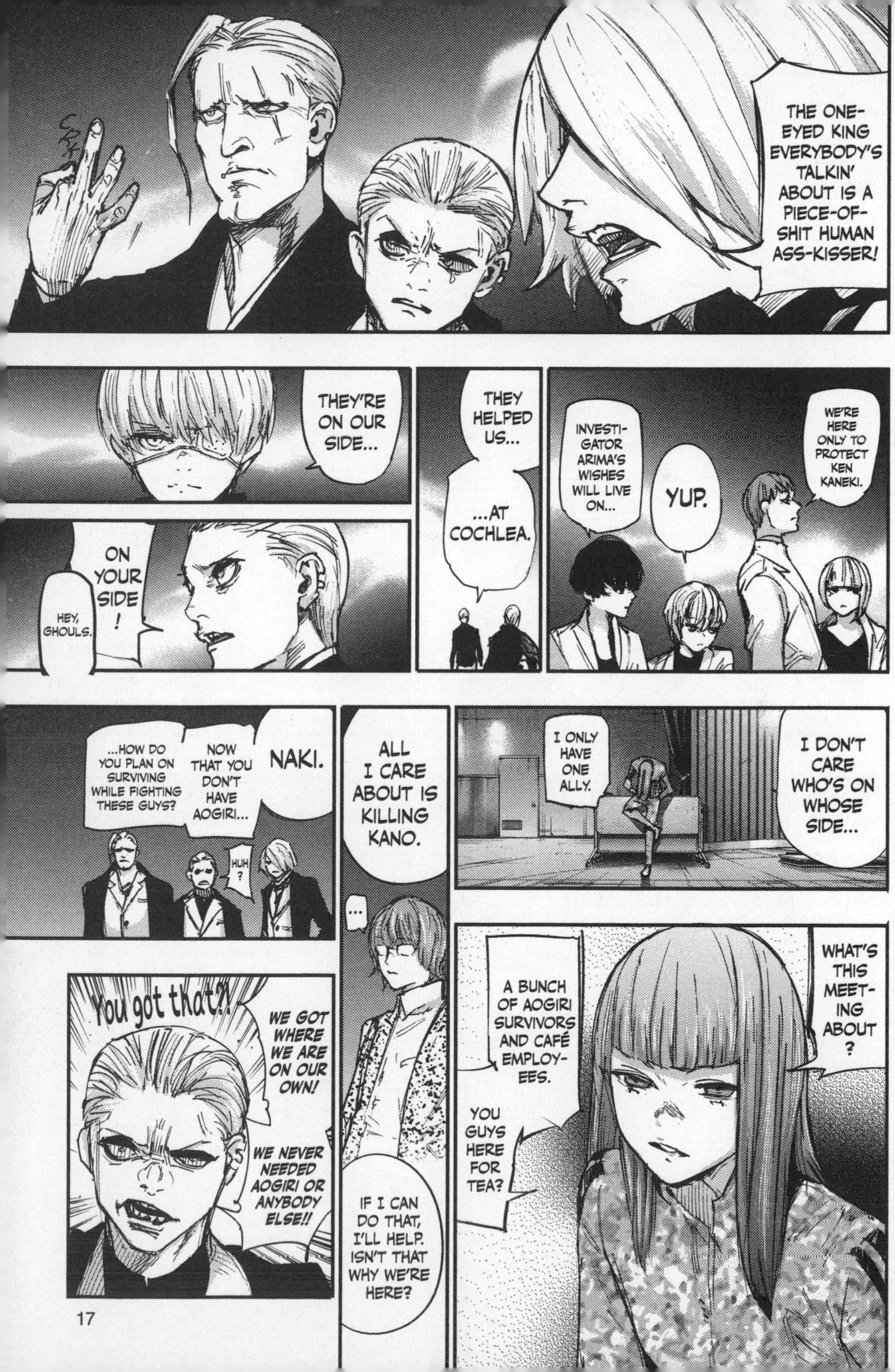

THE ONE-EYED KING EVERYBODY'S TALKIN' ABOUT IS A PIECE-OF-SHIT HUMAN ASS-KISSER!
WE'RE HERE ONLY TO PROTECT KEN KANEKI.
YUP.
INVESTIGATOR ARIMA'S WISHES WILL LIVE ON...
THEY HELPED US...
...AT COCHLEA.
THEY'RE ON OUR SIDE...
ON YOUR SIDE!
HEY, GHOULS.
I DON'T CARE WHO'S ON WHOSE SIDE...
I ONLY HAVE ONE ALLY.
WHAT'S THIS MEETING ABOUT?
A BUNCH OF AOGIRI SURVIVORS AND CAFÉ EMPLOYEES.
YOU GUYS HERE FOR TEA?
ALL I CARE ABOUT IS KILLING KANO.
...
IF I CAN DO THAT, I'LL HELP. ISN'T THAT WHY WE'RE HERE?
NAKI.
NOW THAT YOU DON'T HAVE AOGIRI...
...HOW DO YOU PLAN ON SURVIVING WHILE FIGHTING THESE GUYS?
HUH?
You got that?!
WE GOT WHERE WE ARE ON OUR OWN!
WE NEVER NEEDED AOGIRI OR ANYBODY ELSE!!

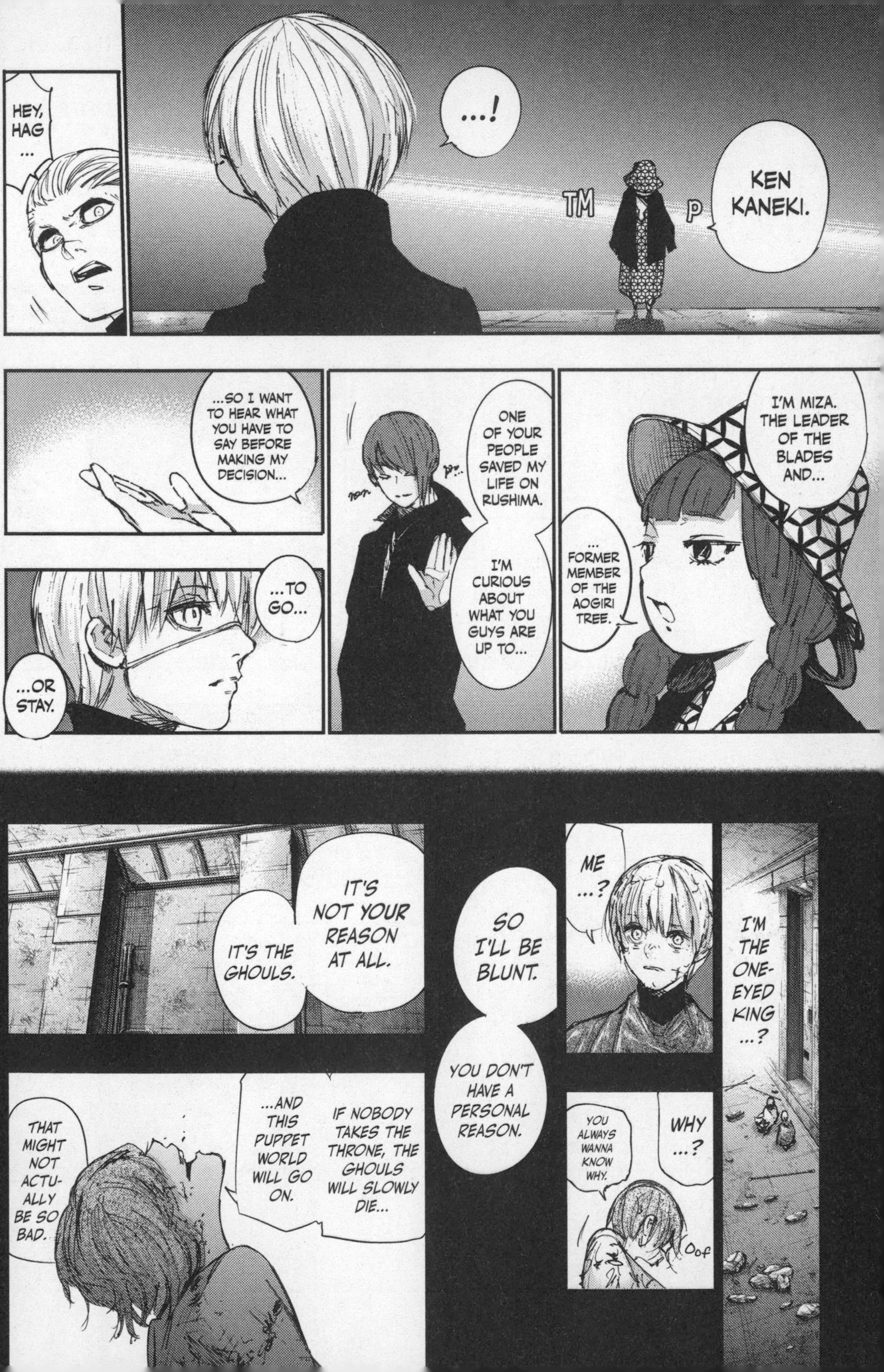
TMP
KEN KANEKI.
...!
HEY, HAG ...
I'M MIZA. THE LEADER OF THE BLADES AND...
...FORMER MEMBER OF THE AOGIRI TREE.
ONE OF YOUR PEOPLE SAVED MY LIFE ON RUSHIMA.
I'M CURIOUS ABOUT WHAT YOU GUYS ARE UP TO...
...SO I WANT TO HEAR WHAT YOU HAVE TO SAY BEFORE MAKING MY DECISION...
...TO GO...
...OR STAY.
I'M THE ONE-EYED KING ...?
ME ...?
WHY ...?
YOU ALWAYS WANNA KNOW WHY.
Oof
SO I'LL BE BLUNT.
YOU DON'T HAVE A PERSONAL REASON.
IT'S NOT YOUR REASON AT ALL.
IT'S THE GHOULS.
IF NOBODY TAKES THE THRONE, THE GHOULS WILL SLOWLY DIE...
...AND THIS PUPPET WORLD WILL GO ON.
THAT MIGHT NOT ACTUALLY BE SO BAD.

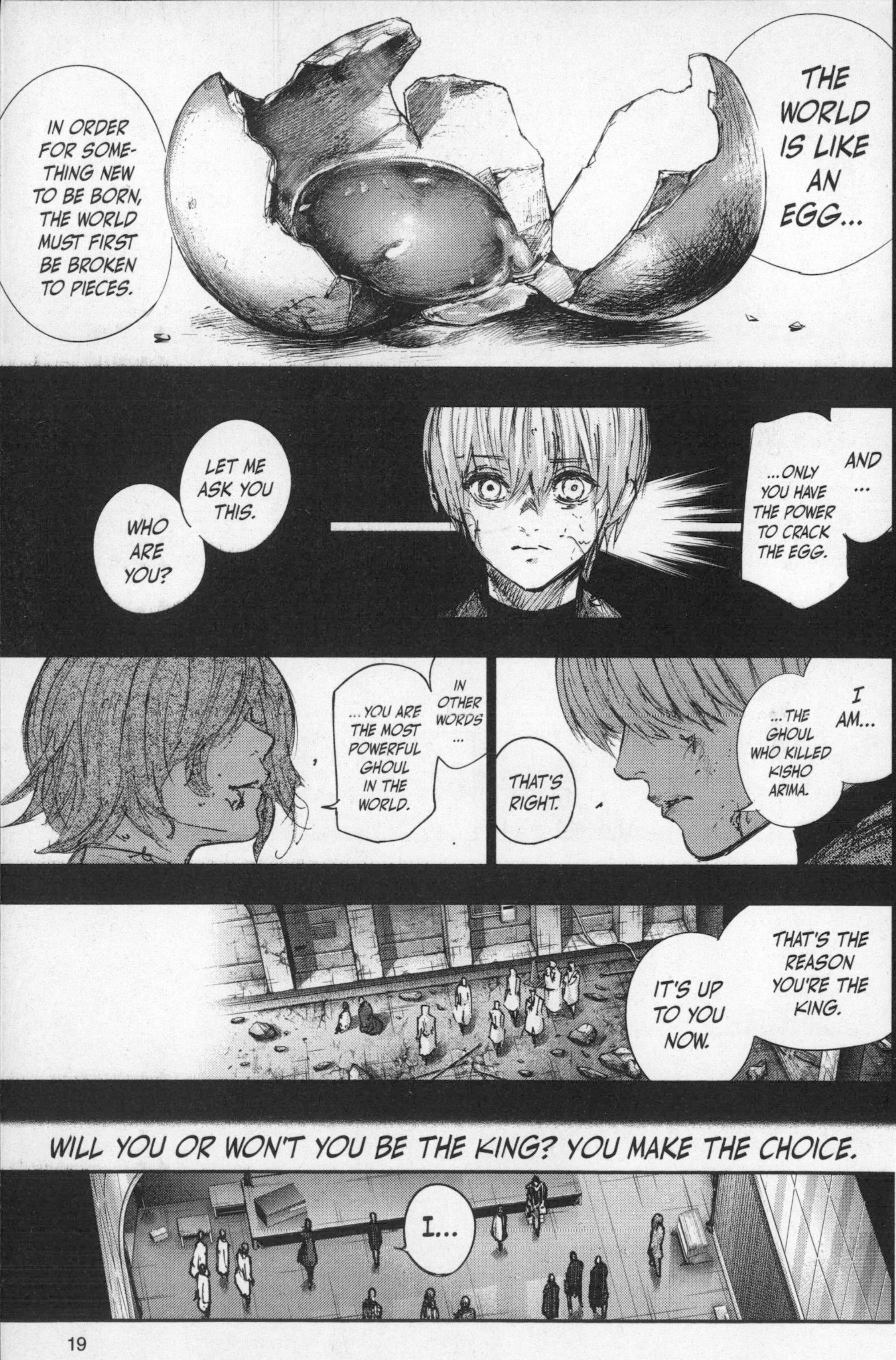
THE WORLD IS LIKE AN EGG...
IN ORDER FOR SOME-THING NEW TO BE BORN, THE WORLD MUST FIRST BE BROKEN TO PIECES.
AND...
...ONLY YOU HAVE THE POWER TO CRACK THE EGG.
LET ME ASK YOU THIS.
WHO ARE YOU?
I AM...
...THE GHOUL WHO KILLED KISHO ARIMA.
THAT'S RIGHT.
IN OTHER WORDS...
...YOU ARE THE MOST POWERFUL GHOUL IN THE WORLD.
THAT'S THE REASON YOU'RE THE KING.
IT'S UP TO YOU NOW.
WILL YOU OR WON'T YOU BE THE KING? YOU MAKE THE CHOICE.
I...

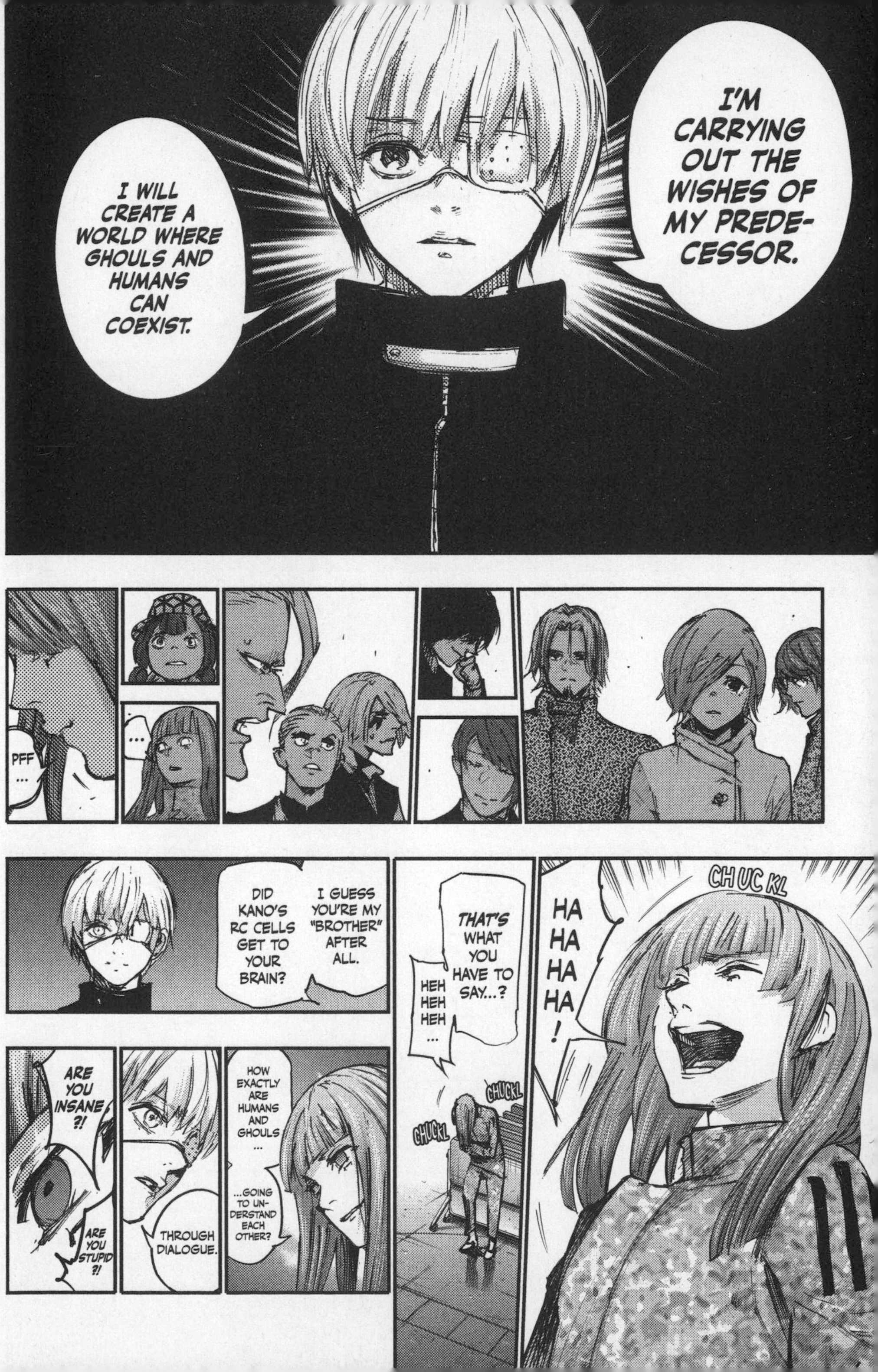
I'M CARRYING OUT THE WISHES OF MY PREDECESSOR.
I WILL CREATE A WORLD WHERE GHOULS AND HUMANS CAN COEXIST.
...
PFF ...
CHUCKL
HA HA HA HA!
THAT'S WHAT YOU HAVE TO SAY...?
HEH HEH HEH ...
CHUCKL
CHUCKL
I GUESS YOU'RE MY "BROTHER" AFTER ALL.
DID KANO'S RC CELLS GET TO YOUR BRAIN?
HOW EXACTLY ARE HUMANS AND GHOULS ...
...GOING TO UNDERSTAND EACH OTHER?
THROUGH DIALOGUE.
ARE YOU INSANE?!
ARE YOU STUPID?!

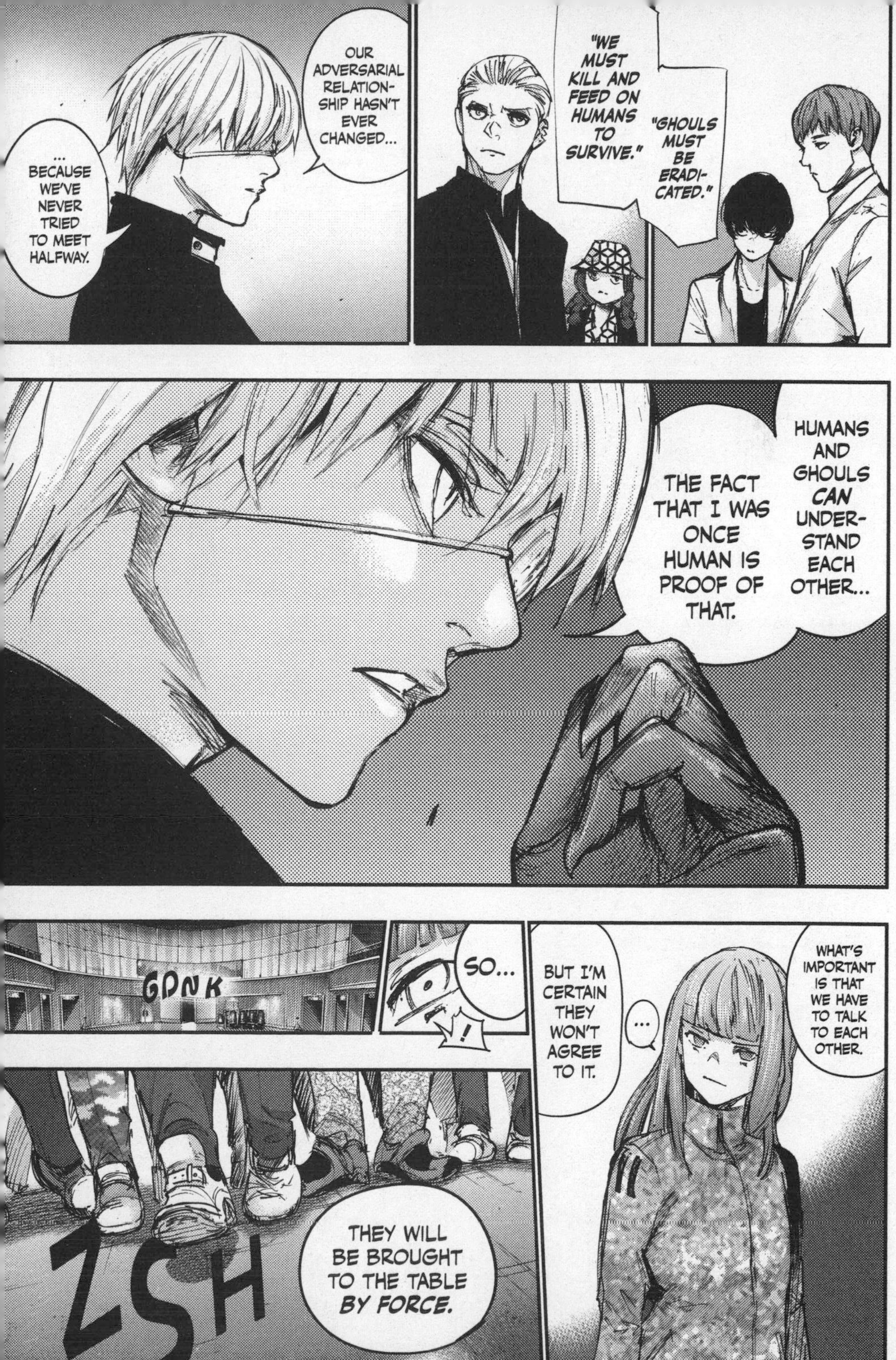
"GHOULS MUST BE ERADICATED."
"WE MUST KILL AND FEED ON HUMANS TO SURVIVE."
OUR ADVERSARIAL RELATIONSHIP HASN'T EVER CHANGED...
...BECAUSE WE'VE NEVER TRIED TO MEET HALFWAY.
HUMANS AND GHOULS *CAN* UNDERSTAND EACH OTHER...
THE FACT THAT I WAS ONCE HUMAN IS PROOF OF THAT.
WHAT'S IMPORTANT IS THAT WE HAVE TO TALK TO EACH OTHER.
...
BUT I'M CERTAIN THEY WON'T AGREE TO IT.
SO...
!
GDNK
THEY WILL BE BROUGHT TO THE TABLE *BY FORCE.*
ZSH

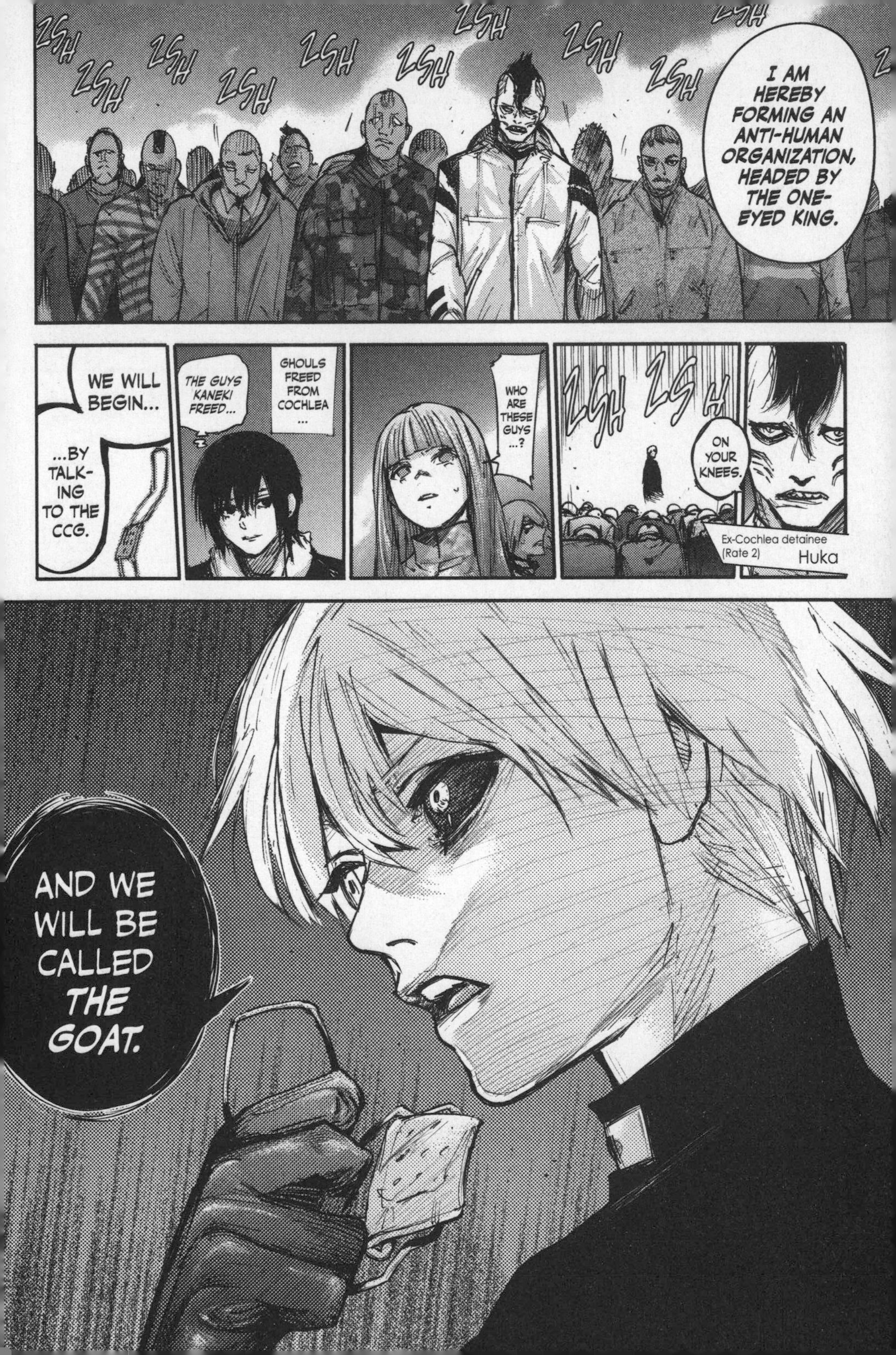
ZSH
I AM HEREBY FORMING AN ANTI-HUMAN ORGANIZATION, HEADED BY THE ONE-EYED KING.
ON YOUR KNEES.
Ex-Cochlea detainee (Rate 2) Huka
ZSH ZSH
WHO ARE THESE GUYS ...?
GHOULS FREED FROM COCHLEA ...
THE GUYS KANEKI FREED...
WE WILL BEGIN...
...BY TALKING TO THE CCG.
AND WE WILL BE CALLED THE GOAT.

Acrostic

Theme 1: Quinx

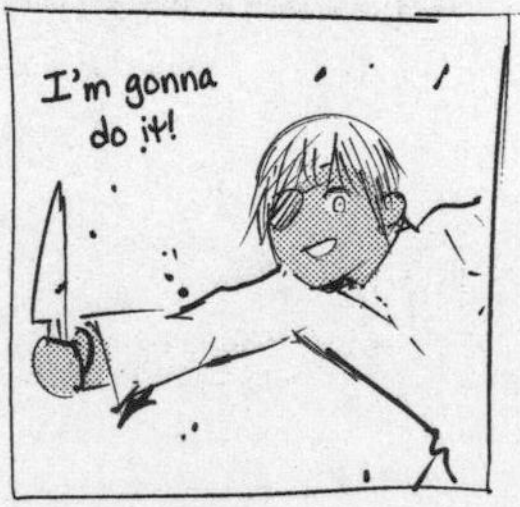
I'm gonna do it!

Q Quietly perverse colleague.

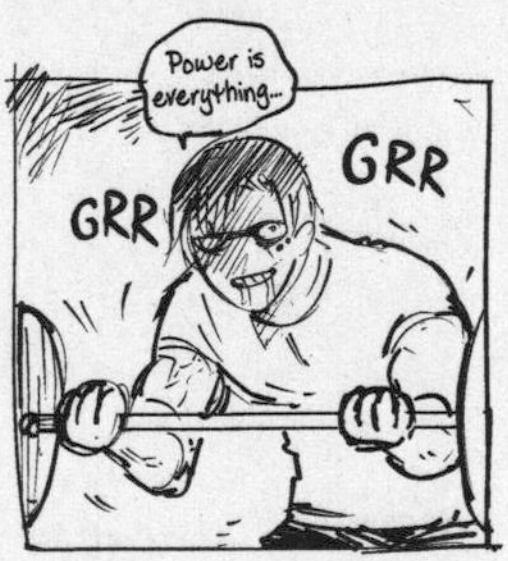
Power is everything...
GRR
GRR

U Utterly insidious machismo.

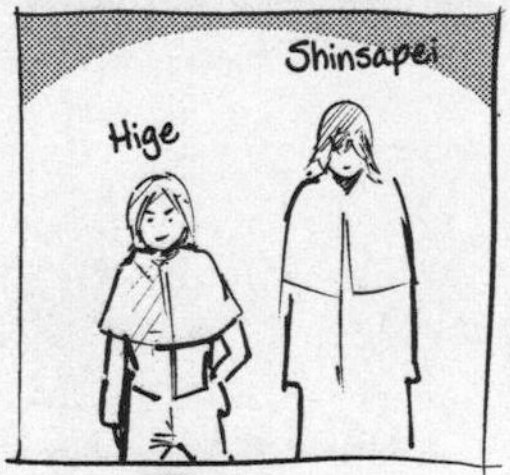
Shinsapei
Hige

I Indescribable pair.

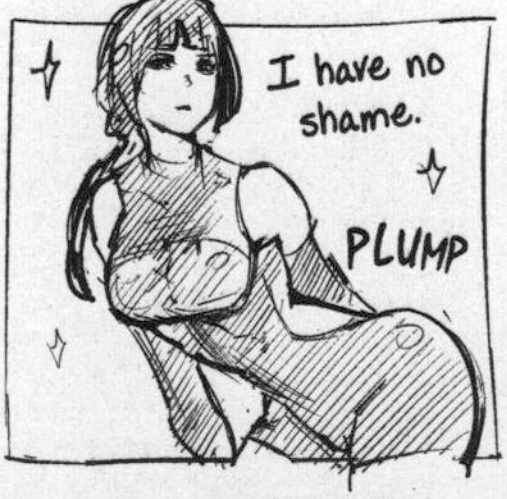
I have no shame.
PLUMP

N Nice and curvy.

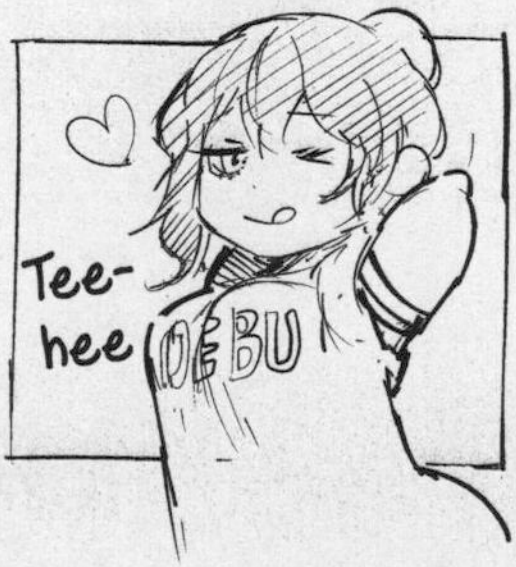
DEBU
Tee-hee

X Xennial hotness will be hosting this segment.

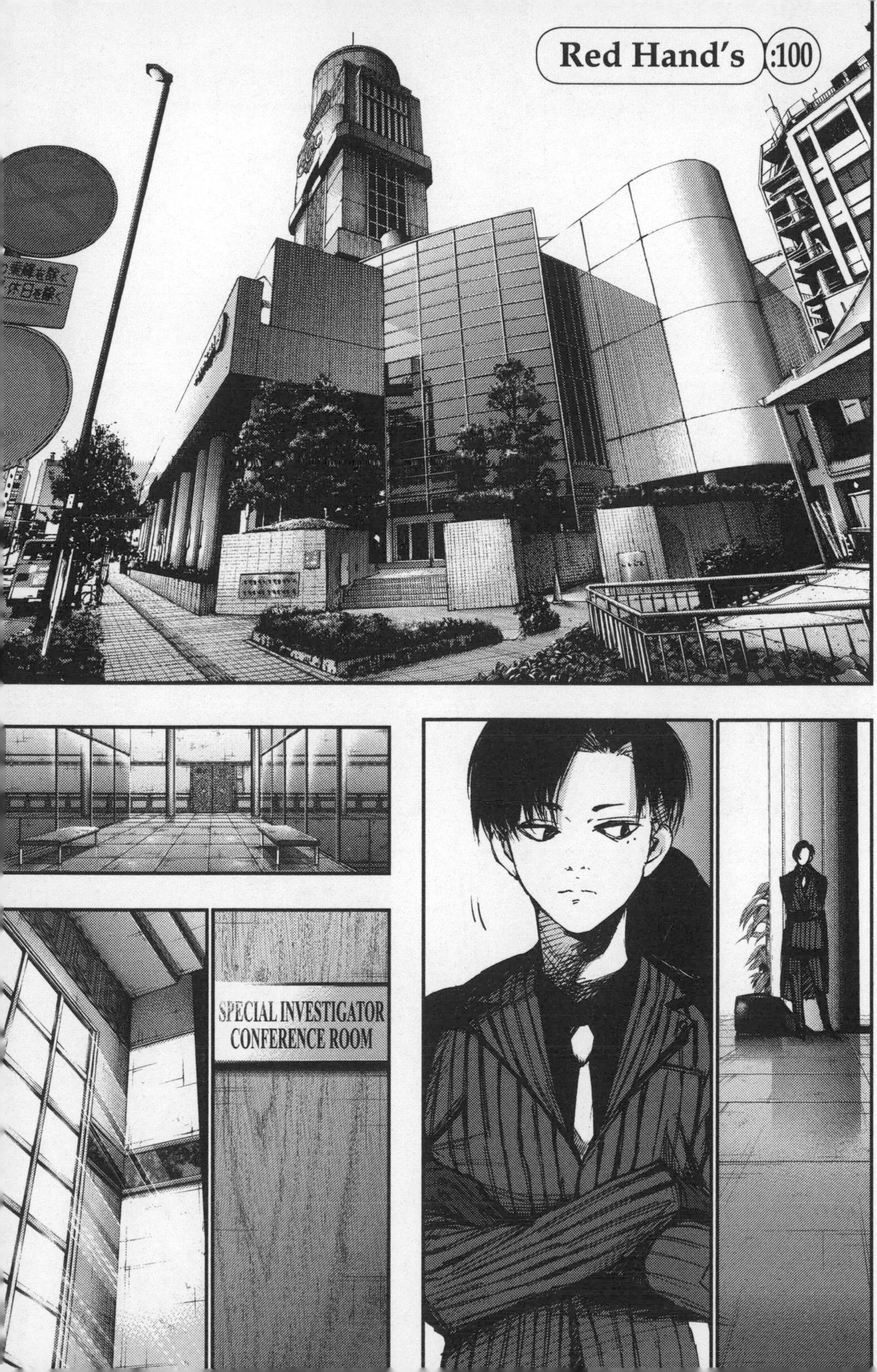
Red Hand's :100
SPECIAL INVESTIGATOR
CONFERENCE ROOM

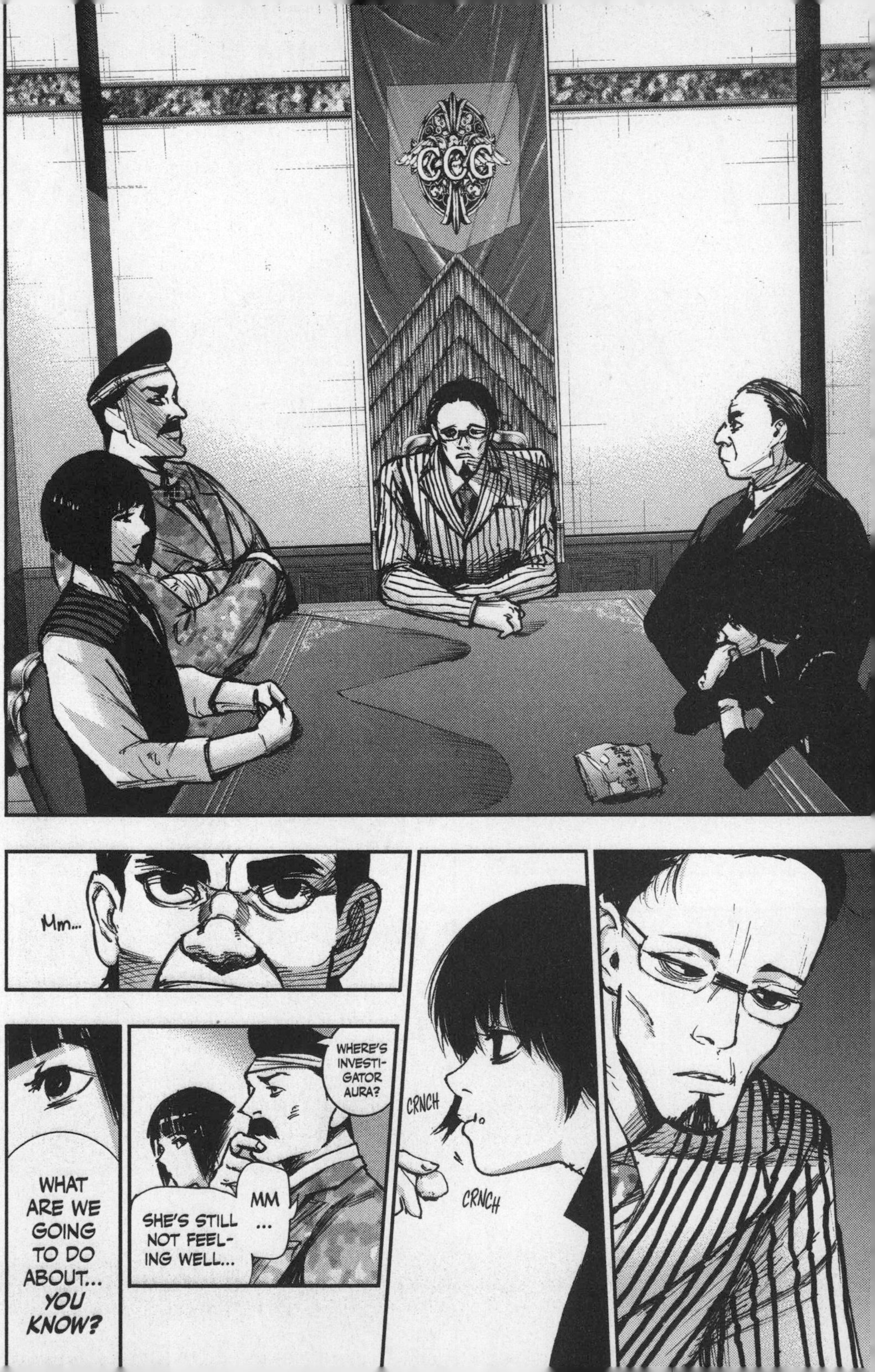
CCG
CRNCH
CRNCH
Mm...
WHERE'S INVESTIGATOR AURA?
MM...
SHE'S STILL NOT FEELING WELL...
WHAT ARE WE GOING TO DO ABOUT... *YOU KNOW?*

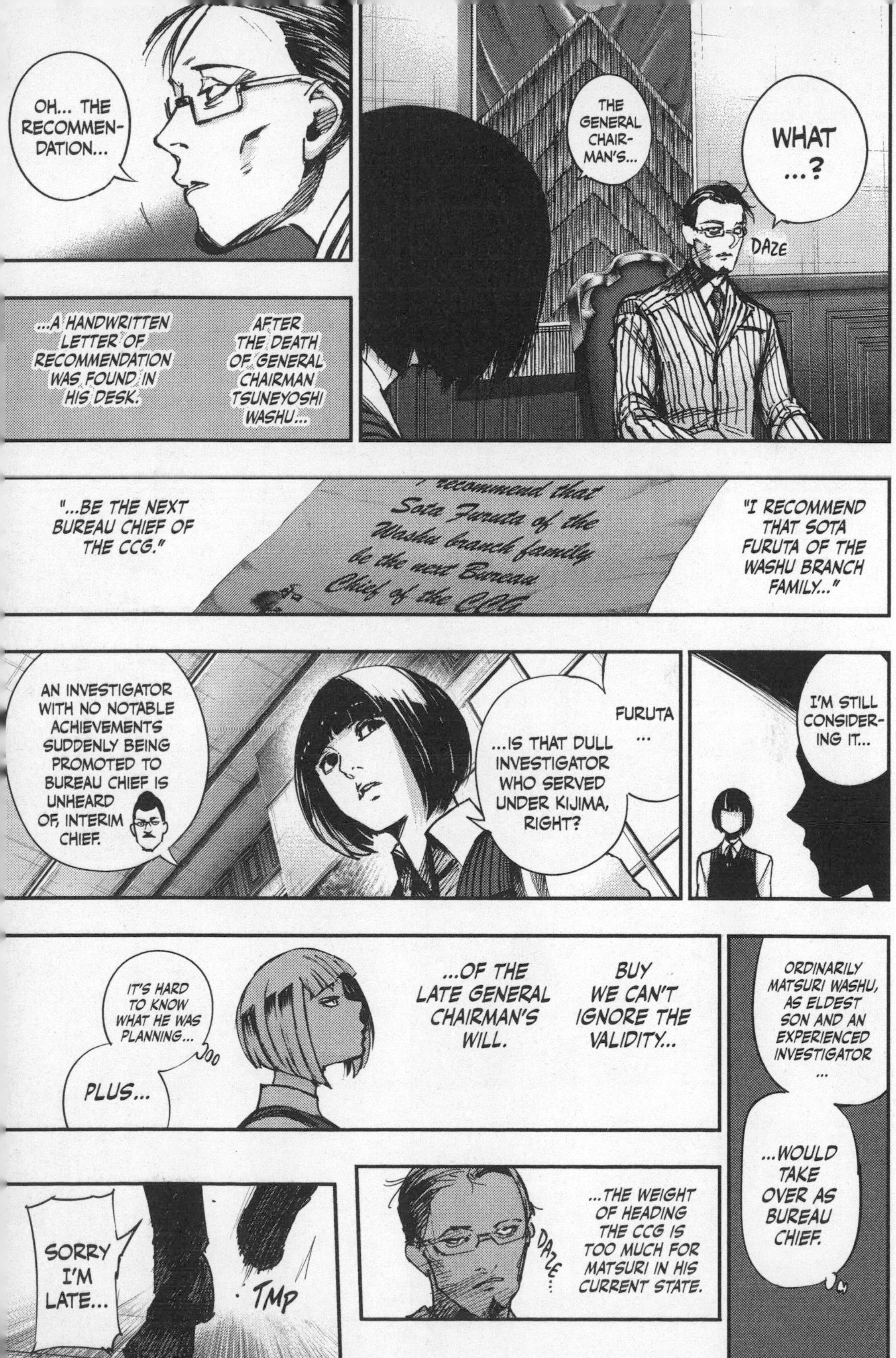
WHAT ...?
DAZE
THE GENERAL CHAIR-MAN'S...
OH... THE RECOMMEN-DATION...
AFTER THE DEATH OF GENERAL CHAIRMAN TSUNEYOSHI WASHU...
...A HANDWRITTEN LETTER OF RECOMMENDATION WAS FOUND IN HIS DESK.
"I RECOMMEND THAT SOTA FURUTA OF THE WASHU BRANCH FAMILY..."
recommend that
Sota Furuta of the
Washu branch family
be the next Bureau
Chief of the CCG
"...BE THE NEXT BUREAU CHIEF OF THE CCG."
I'M STILL CONSIDER-ING IT...
FURUTA ...
...IS THAT DULL INVESTIGATOR WHO SERVED UNDER KIJIMA, RIGHT?
AN INVESTIGATOR WITH NO NOTABLE ACHIEVEMENTS SUDDENLY BEING PROMOTED TO BUREAU CHIEF IS UNHEARD OF, INTERIM CHIEF.
ORDINARILY MATSURI WASHU, AS ELDEST SON AND AN EXPERIENCED INVESTIGATOR ...
...WOULD TAKE OVER AS BUREAU CHIEF.
BUY WE CAN'T IGNORE THE VALIDITY...
...OF THE LATE GENERAL CHAIRMAN'S WILL.
IT'S HARD TO KNOW WHAT HE WAS PLANNING...
PLUS...
...THE WEIGHT OF HEADING THE CCG IS TOO MUCH FOR MATSURI IN HIS CURRENT STATE.
DAZE...
SORRY I'M LATE...
TMP

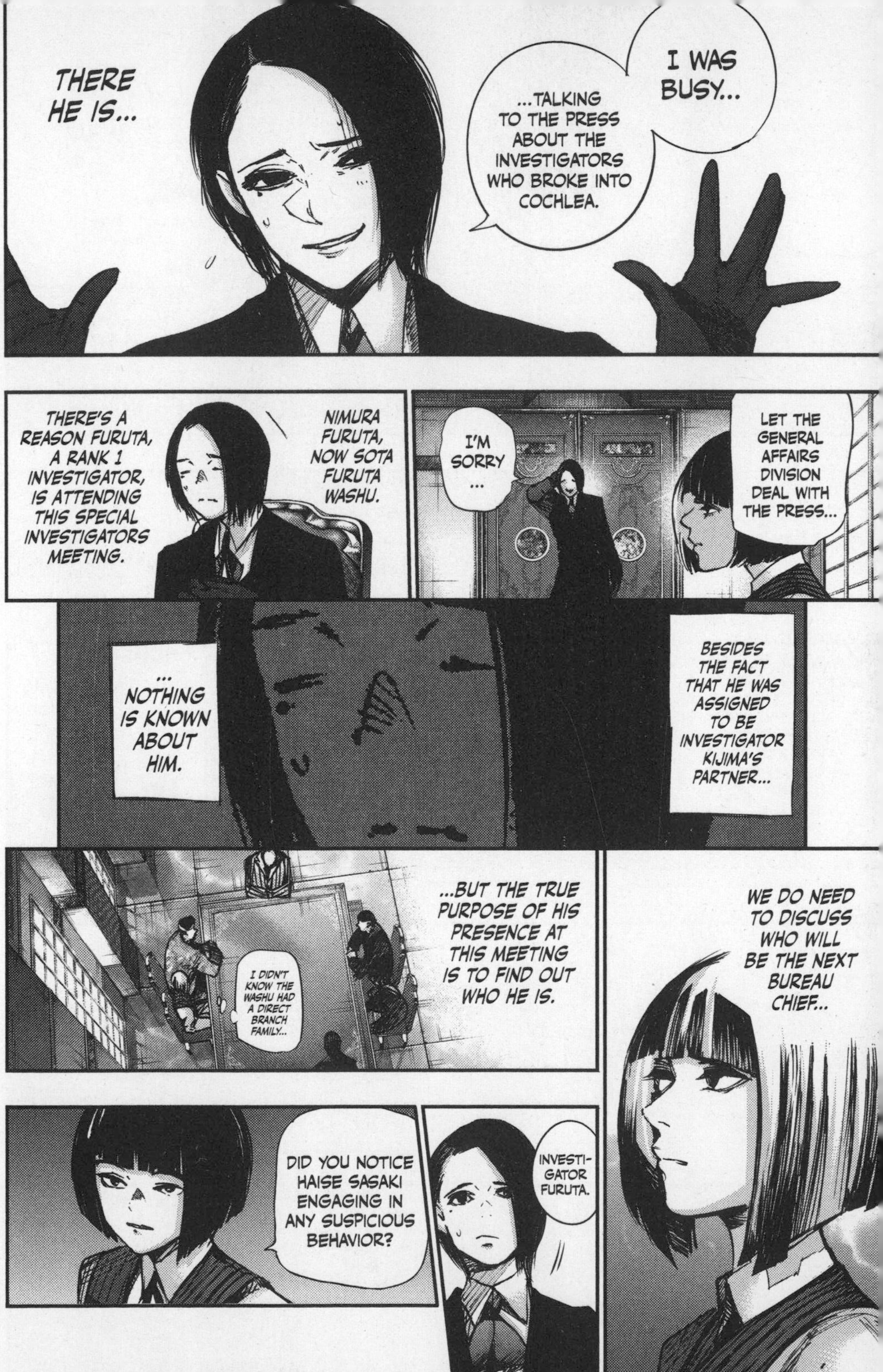
I WAS BUSY...
...TALKING TO THE PRESS ABOUT THE INVESTIGATORS WHO BROKE INTO COCHLEA.
THERE HE IS...
LET THE GENERAL AFFAIRS DIVISION DEAL WITH THE PRESS...
I'M SORRY ...
NIMURA FURUTA, NOW SOTA FURUTA WASHU.
THERE'S A REASON FURUTA, A RANK 1 INVESTIGATOR, IS ATTENDING THIS SPECIAL INVESTIGATORS MEETING.
BESIDES THE FACT THAT HE WAS ASSIGNED TO BE INVESTIGATOR KIJIMA'S PARTNER...
... NOTHING IS KNOWN ABOUT HIM.
WE DO NEED TO DISCUSS WHO WILL BE THE NEXT BUREAU CHIEF...
...BUT THE TRUE PURPOSE OF HIS PRESENCE AT THIS MEETING IS TO FIND OUT WHO HE IS.
I DIDN'T KNOW THE WASHU HAD A DIRECT BRANCH FAMILY...
INVESTI-GATOR FURUTA.
DID YOU NOTICE HAISE SASAKI ENGAGING IN ANY SUSPICIOUS BEHAVIOR?

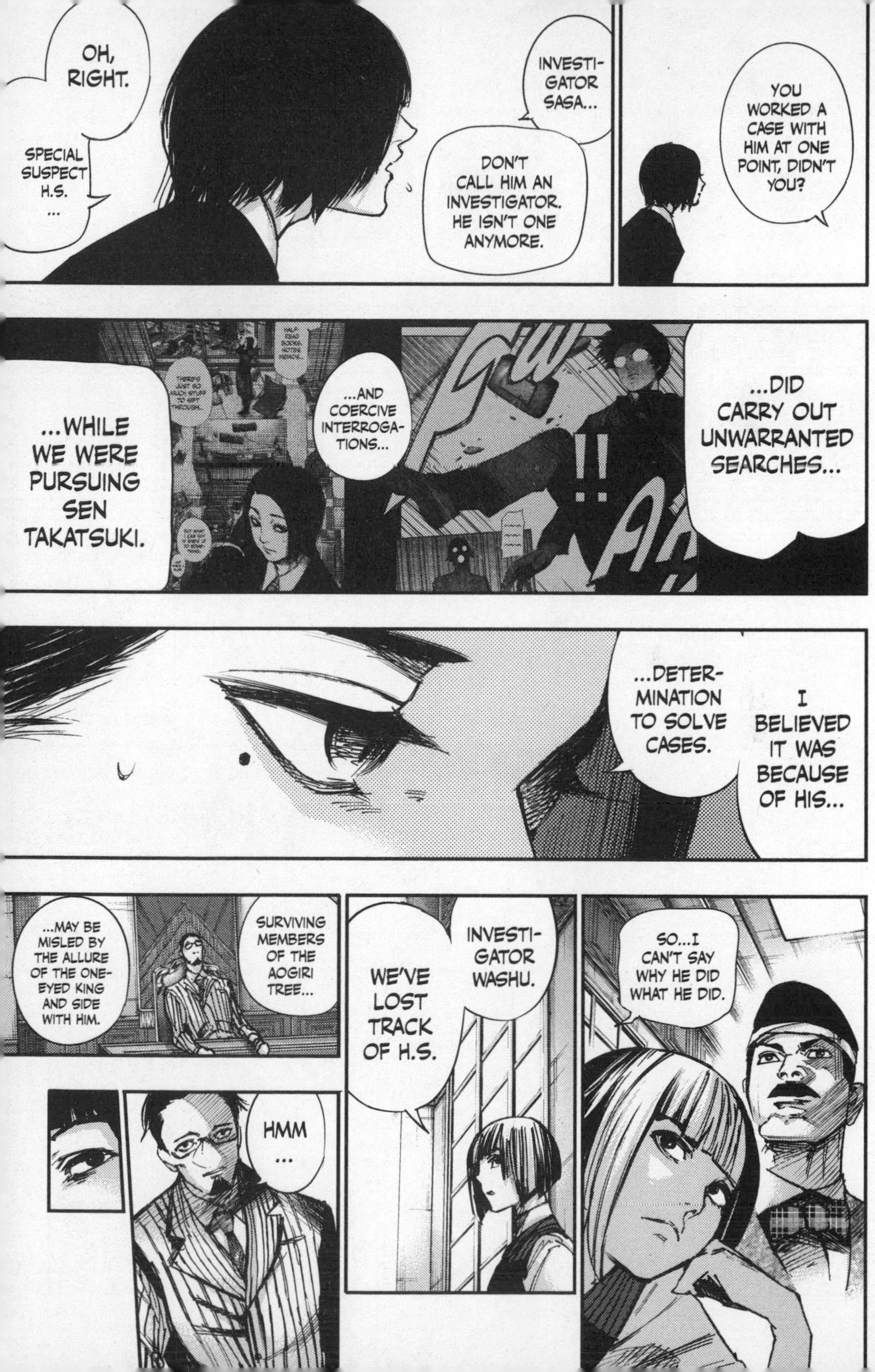
YOU WORKED A CASE WITH HIM AT ONE POINT, DIDN'T YOU?
INVESTIGATOR SASA...
DON'T CALL HIM AN INVESTIGATOR. HE ISN'T ONE ANYMORE.
OH, RIGHT.
SPECIAL SUSPECT H.S. ...
...DID CARRY OUT UNWARRANTED SEARCHES...
!!
...AND COERCIVE INTERROGATIONS...
...WHILE WE WERE PURSUING SEN TAKATSUKI.
I BELIEVED IT WAS BECAUSE OF HIS...
...DETERMINATION TO SOLVE CASES.
SO...I CAN'T SAY WHY HE DID WHAT HE DID.
INVESTIGATOR WASHU.
WE'VE LOST TRACK OF H.S.
SURVIVING MEMBERS OF THE AOGIRI TREE...
...MAY BE MISLED BY THE ALLURE OF THE ONE-EYED KING AND SIDE WITH HIM.
HMM ...

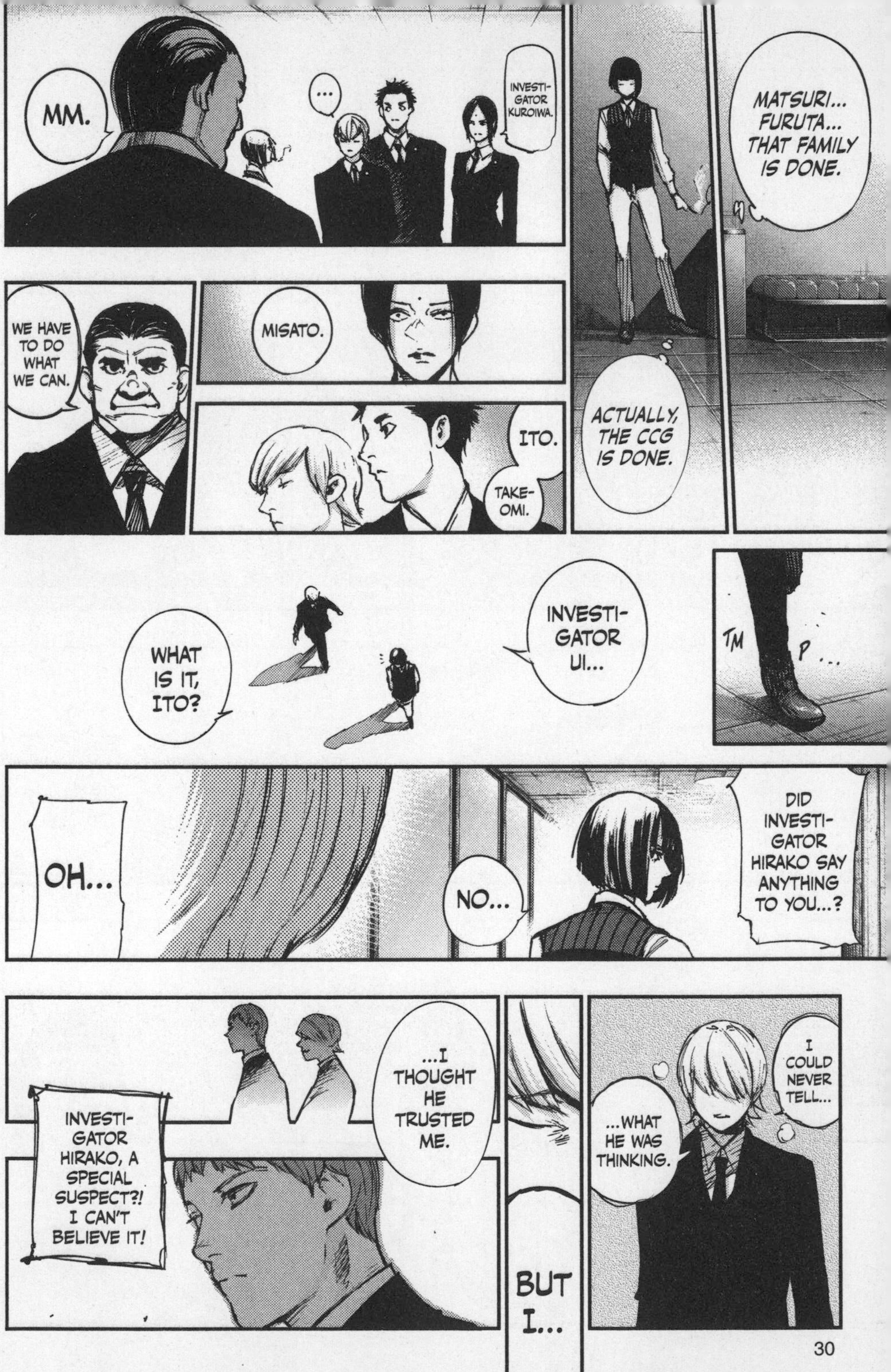
MATSURI... FURUTA... THAT FAMILY IS DONE.
ACTUALLY, THE CCG IS DONE.
INVESTIGATOR KUROIWA.
...
MM.
MISATO.
ITO.
TAKEOMI.
WE HAVE TO DO WHAT WE CAN.
TMP...
INVESTIGATOR UI...
WHAT IS IT, ITO?
DID INVESTIGATOR HIRAKO SAY ANYTHING TO YOU...?
NO...
OH...
I COULD NEVER TELL...
...WHAT HE WAS THINKING.
BUT I...
...I THOUGHT HE TRUSTED ME.
INVESTIGATOR HIRAKO, A SPECIAL SUSPECT?! I CAN'T BELIEVE IT!

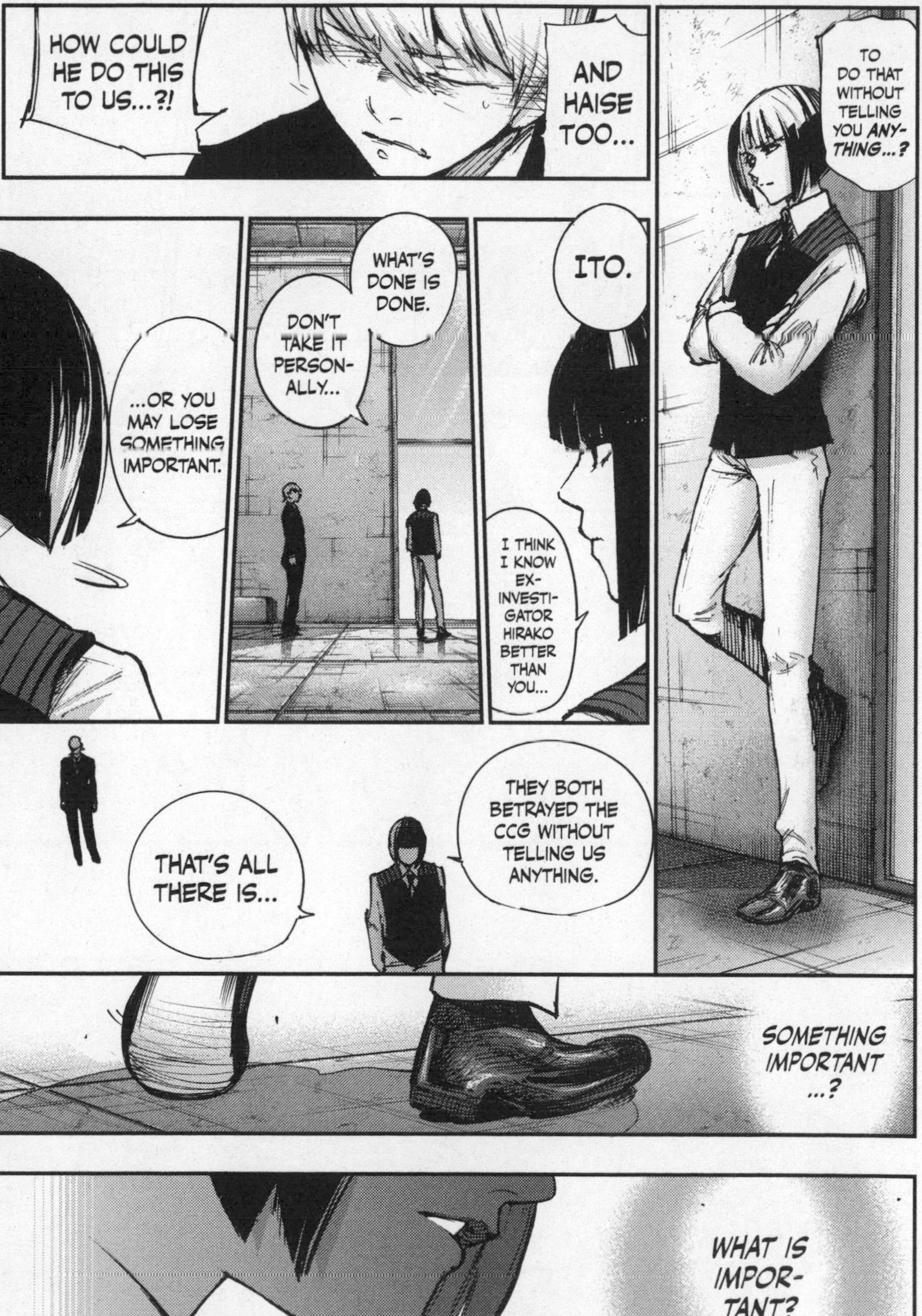
TO DO THAT WITHOUT TELLING YOU *ANYTHING*...?
AND HAISE TOO...
HOW COULD HE DO THIS TO US...?!
ITO.
I THINK I KNOW EX-INVESTIGATOR HIRAKO BETTER THAN YOU...
WHAT'S DONE IS DONE.
DON'T TAKE IT PERSONALLY...
...OR YOU MAY LOSE SOMETHING IMPORTANT.
THEY BOTH BETRAYED THE CCG WITHOUT TELLING US ANYTHING.
THAT'S ALL THERE IS...
SOMETHING IMPORTANT ...?
WHAT IS IMPORTANT?

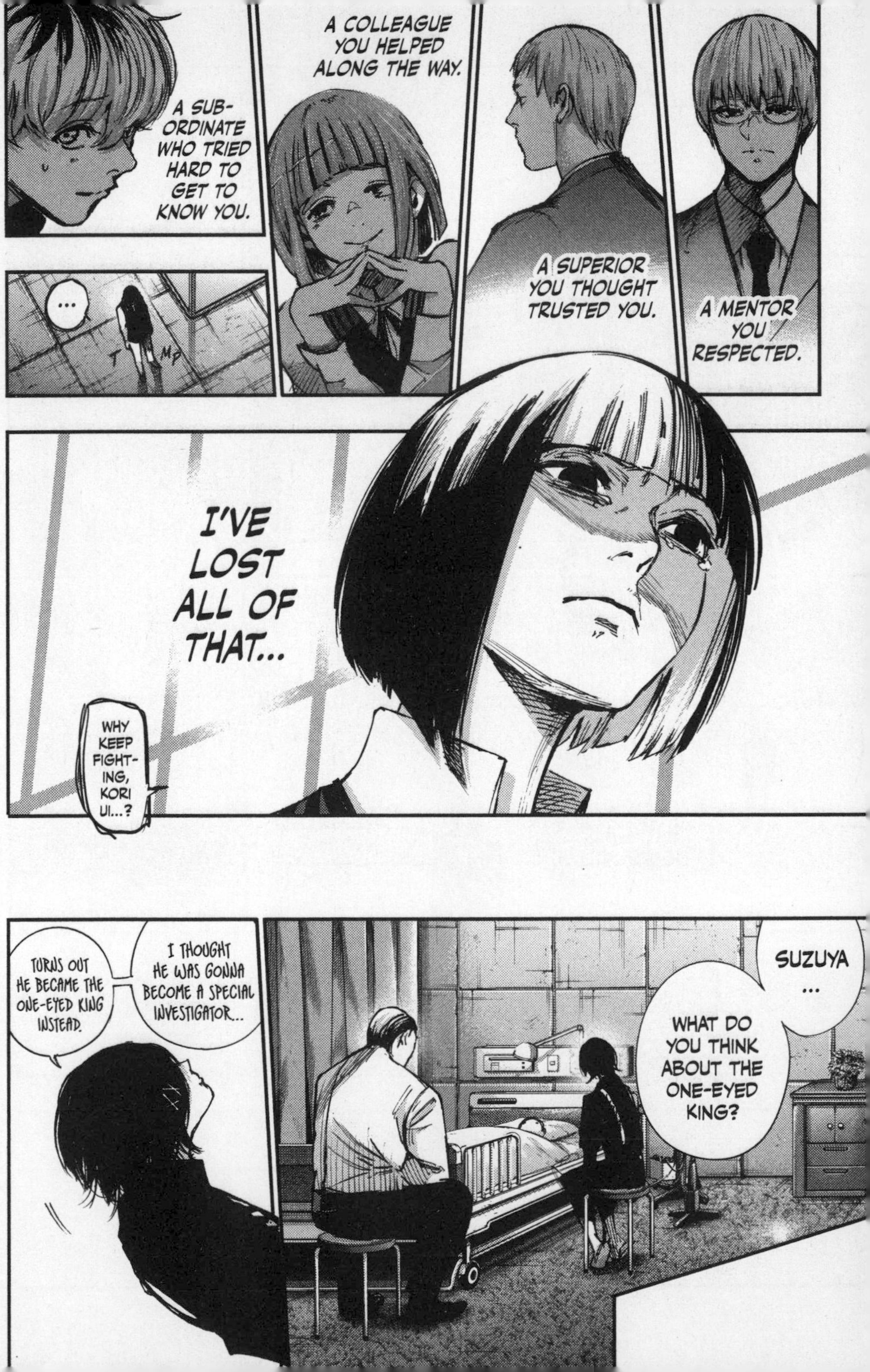
A MENTOR YOU RESPECTED.
A SUPERIOR YOU THOUGHT TRUSTED YOU.
A COLLEAGUE YOU HELPED ALONG THE WAY.
A SUB-ORDINATE WHO TRIED HARD TO GET TO KNOW YOU.
...
I'VE LOST ALL OF THAT...
WHY KEEP FIGHTING, KORI UI...?
SUZUYA ...
WHAT DO YOU THINK ABOUT THE ONE-EYED KING?
I THOUGHT HE WAS GONNA BECOME A SPECIAL INVESTIGATOR...
TURNS OUT HE BECAME THE ONE-EYED KING INSTEAD.

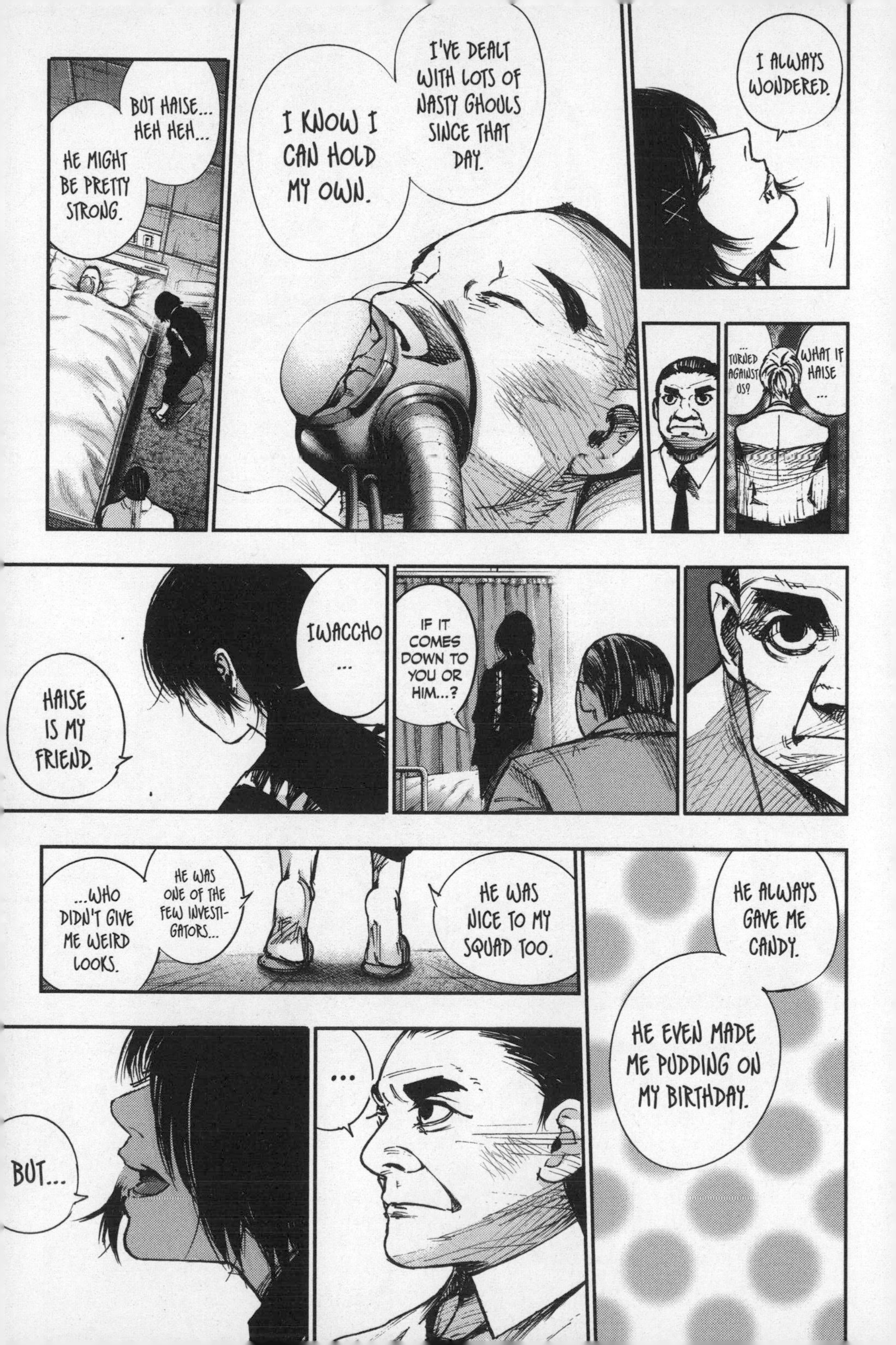
I ALWAYS WONDERED.
WHAT IF HAISE...
...TURNED AGAINST US?
I'VE DEALT WITH LOTS OF NASTY GHOULS SINCE THAT DAY.
I KNOW I CAN HOLD MY OWN.
BUT HAISE... HEH HEH...
HE MIGHT BE PRETTY STRONG.
IF IT COMES DOWN TO YOU OR HIM...?
IWACCHO...
HAISE IS MY FRIEND.
HE ALWAYS GAVE ME CANDY.
HE EVEN MADE ME PUDDING ON MY BIRTHDAY.
HE WAS NICE TO MY SQUAD TOO.
HE WAS ONE OF THE FEW INVESTI-GATORS...
...WHO DIDN'T GIVE ME WEIRD LOOKS.
...
BUT...

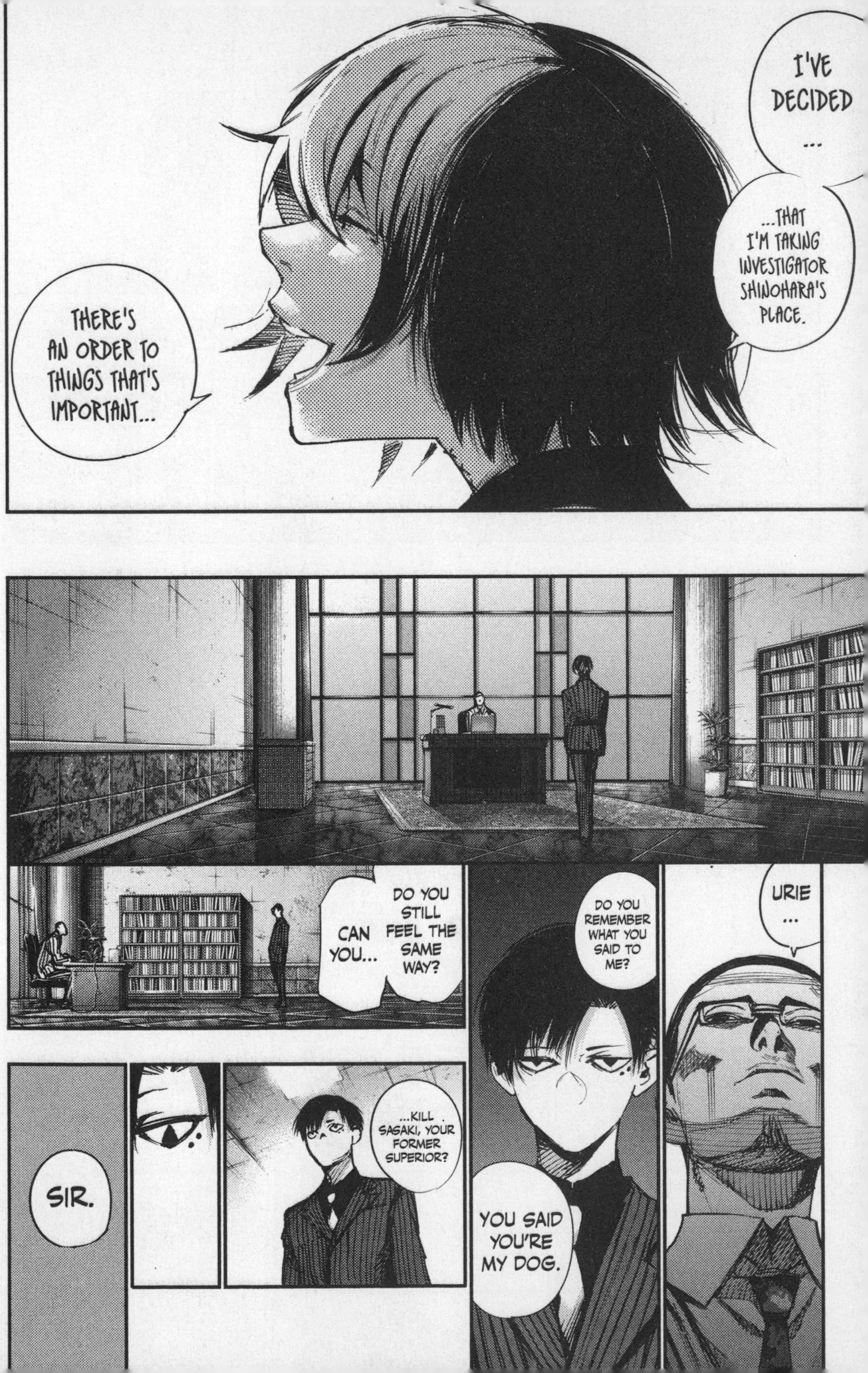

I'VE DECIDED ...
...THAT I'M TAKING INVESTIGATOR SHINOHARA'S PLACE.
THERE'S AN ORDER TO THINGS THAT'S IMPORTANT...
URIE ...
DO YOU REMEMBER WHAT YOU SAID TO ME?
YOU SAID YOU'RE MY DOG.
DO YOU STILL FEEL THE SAME WAY?
CAN YOU...
...KILL SASAKI, YOUR FORMER SUPERIOR?
SIR.

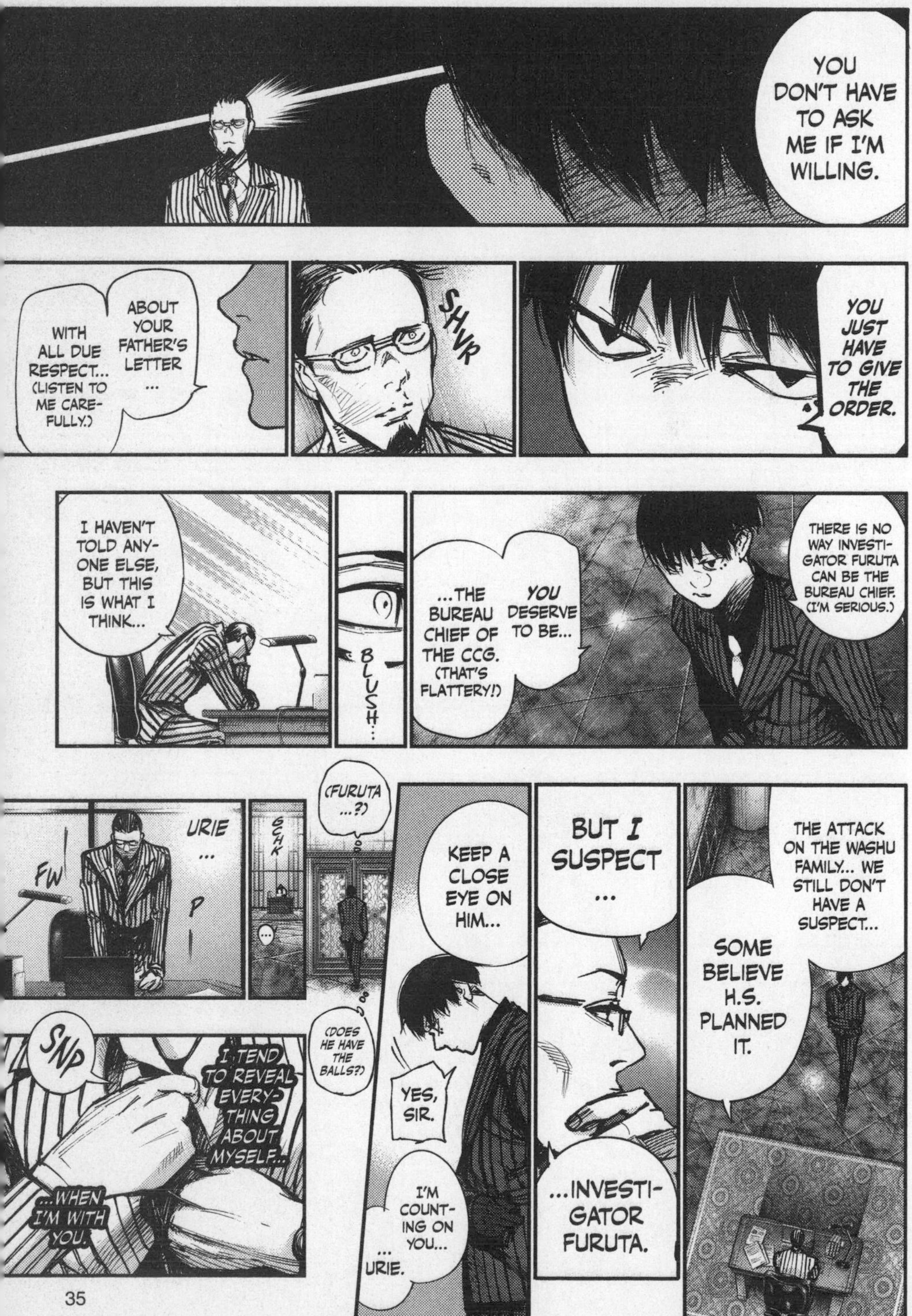

YOU DON'T HAVE TO ASK ME IF I'M WILLING.
YOU JUST HAVE TO GIVE THE ORDER.
SHVR
ABOUT YOUR FATHER'S LETTER ...
WITH ALL DUE RESPECT... (LISTEN TO ME CAREFULLY.)
THERE IS NO WAY INVESTIGATOR FURUTA CAN BE THE BUREAU CHIEF. (I'M SERIOUS.)
YOU DESERVE TO BE...
...THE BUREAU CHIEF OF THE CCG. (THAT'S FLATTERY!)
BLUSH...
I HAVEN'T TOLD ANYONE ELSE, BUT THIS IS WHAT I THINK...
THE ATTACK ON THE WASHU FAMILY... WE STILL DON'T HAVE A SUSPECT...
SOME BELIEVE H.S. PLANNED IT.
BUT I SUSPECT ...
...INVESTIGATOR FURUTA.
KEEP A CLOSE EYE ON HIM...
YES, SIR.
I'M COUNTING ON YOU...
... URIE.
(FURUTA ...?)
GCHK
...
URIE ...
P
FW
(DOES HE HAVE THE BALLS?)
SNP
I TEND TO REVEAL EVERYTHING ABOUT MYSELF...
...WHEN I'M WITH YOU.

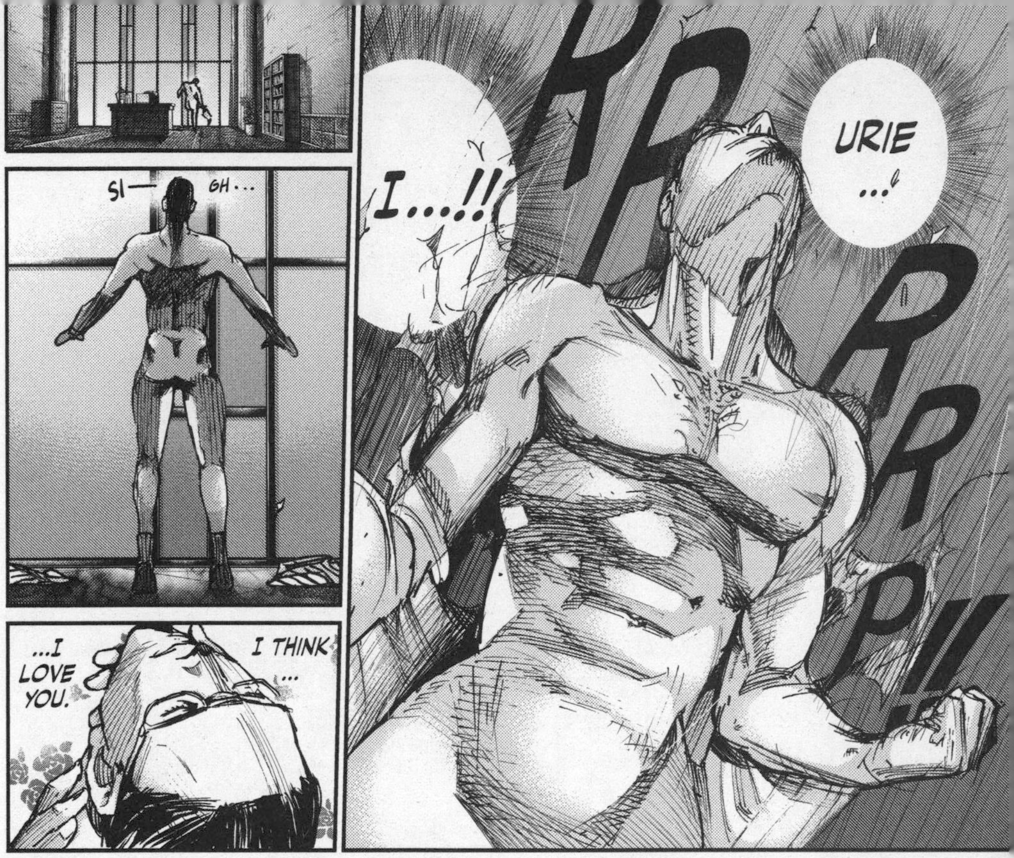
URIE ...!
RRRRP!!
I...!!
SI— GH...
I THINK ...
...I LOVE YOU.

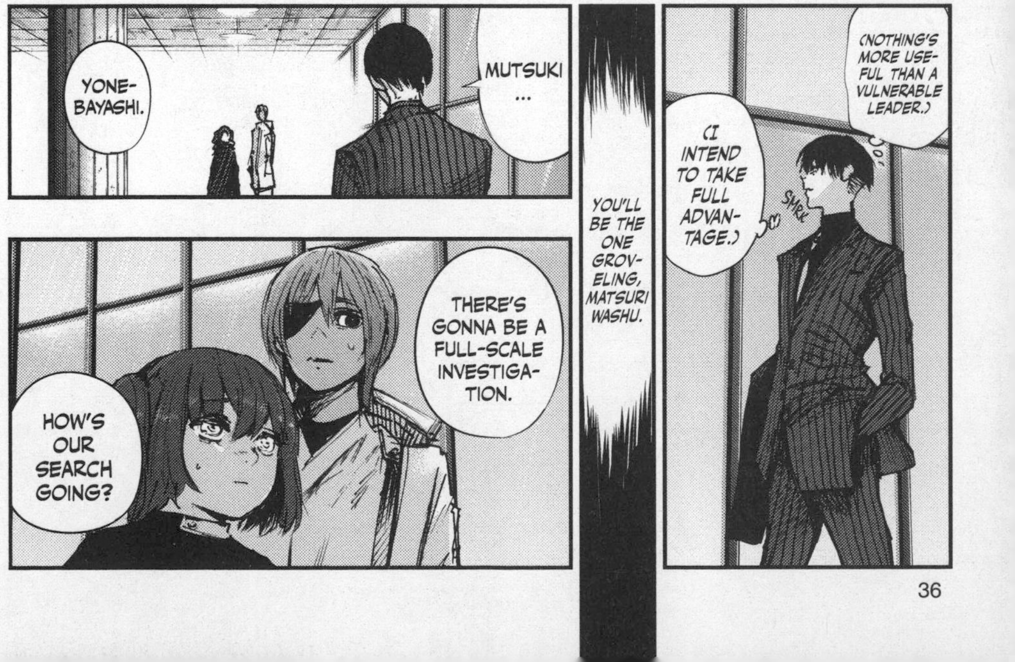
(NOTHING'S MORE USE-FUL THAN A VULNERABLE LEADER.)
SMRK
(I INTEND TO TAKE FULL ADVAN-TAGE.)
YOU'LL BE THE ONE GROV-ELING, MATSURI WASHU.
MUTSUKI ...
YONE-BAYASHI.
THERE'S GONNA BE A FULL-SCALE INVESTIGA-TION.
HOW'S OUR SEARCH GOING?

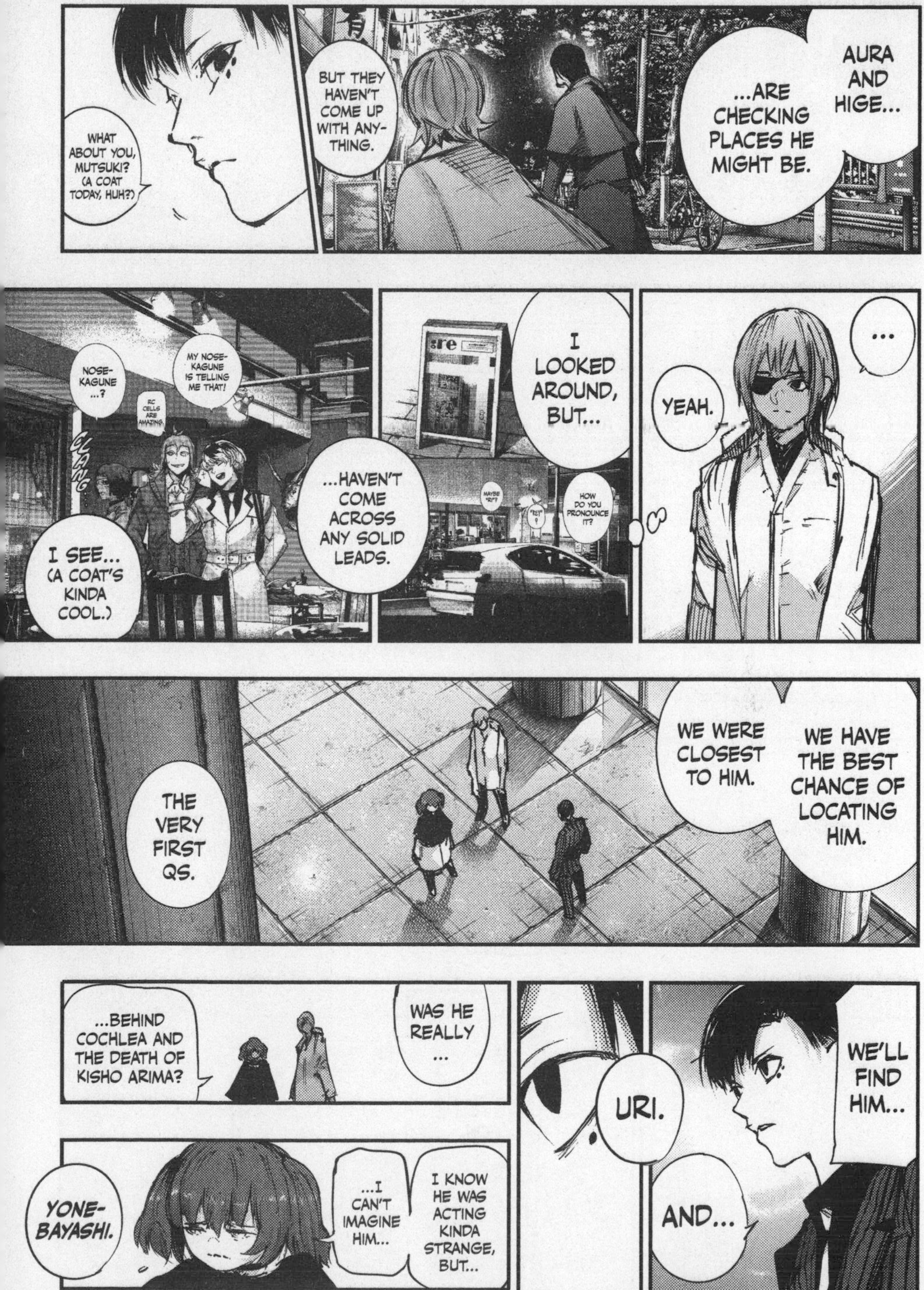
AURA AND HIGE...
...ARE CHECKING PLACES HE MIGHT BE.
BUT THEY HAVEN'T COME UP WITH ANYTHING.
WHAT ABOUT YOU, MUTSUKI? (A COAT TODAY, HUH?)
...
YEAH.
I LOOKED AROUND, BUT...
...HAVEN'T COME ACROSS ANY SOLID LEADS.
HOW DO YOU PRONOUNCE IT?
"REY"?
MAYBE "RI"?
:re
MY NOSE-KAGUNE IS TELLING ME THAT!
NOSE-KAGUNE...?
RC CELLS ARE AMAZING.
CLANG
I SEE... (A COAT'S KINDA COOL.)
WE HAVE THE BEST CHANCE OF LOCATING HIM.
WE WERE CLOSEST TO HIM.
THE VERY FIRST QS.
WE'LL FIND HIM...
URI.
AND...
WAS HE REALLY...
...BEHIND COCHLEA AND THE DEATH OF KISHO ARIMA?
I KNOW HE WAS ACTING KINDA STRANGE, BUT...
...I CAN'T IMAGINE HIM...
YONE-BAYASHI.

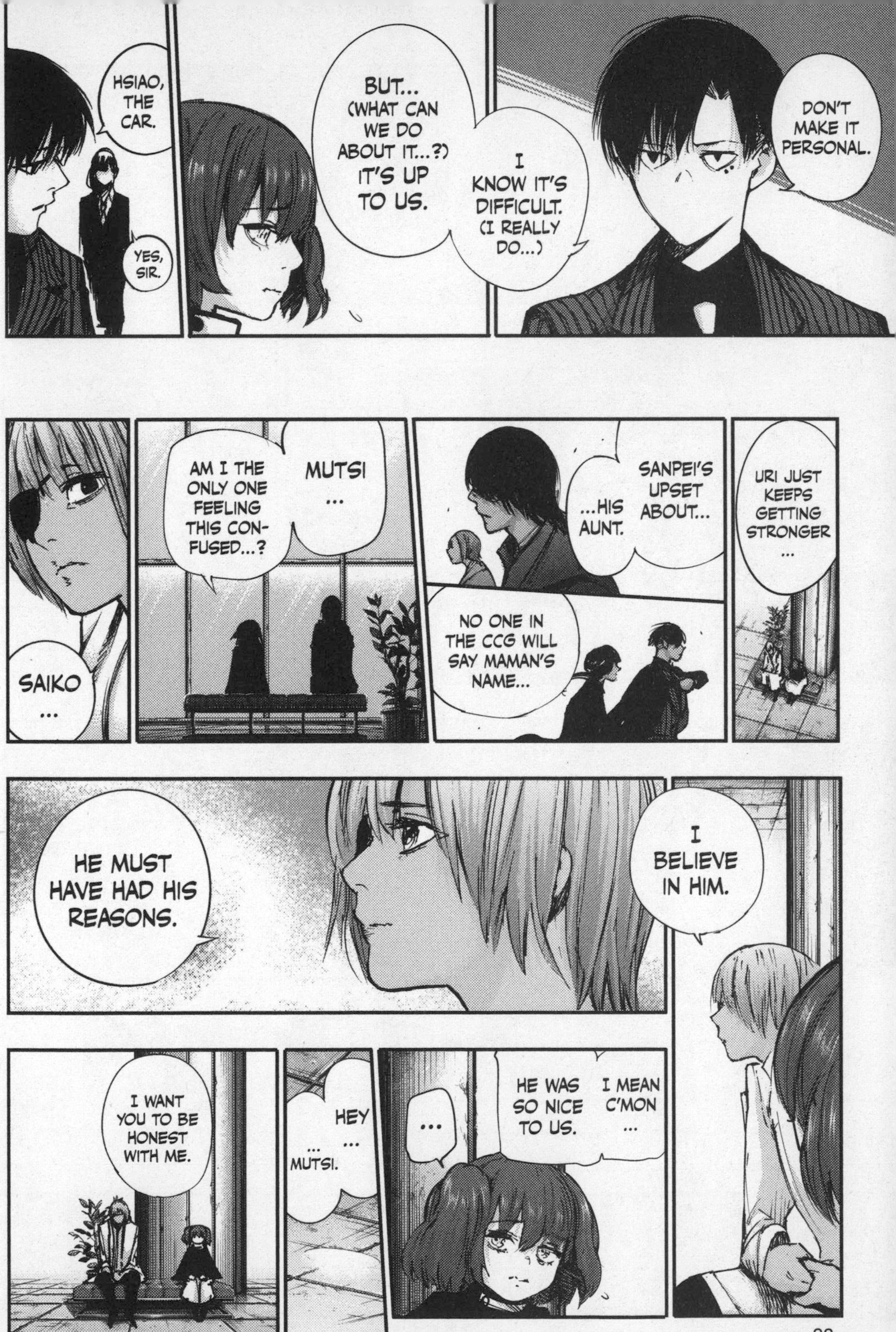
DON'T MAKE IT PERSONAL.
I KNOW IT'S DIFFICULT. (I REALLY DO...)
BUT... (WHAT CAN WE DO ABOUT IT...?) IT'S UP TO US.
HSIAO, THE CAR.
YES, SIR.
URI JUST KEEPS GETTING STRONGER ...
SANPEI'S UPSET ABOUT...
...HIS AUNT.
NO ONE IN THE CCG WILL SAY MAMAN'S NAME...
MUTSI ...
AM I THE ONLY ONE FEELING THIS CON-FUSED...?
SAIKO ...
I BELIEVE IN HIM.
HE MUST HAVE HAD HIS REASONS.
I MEAN C'MON ...
HE WAS SO NICE TO US.
...
HEY ...
... MUTSI.
I WANT YOU TO BE HONEST WITH ME.

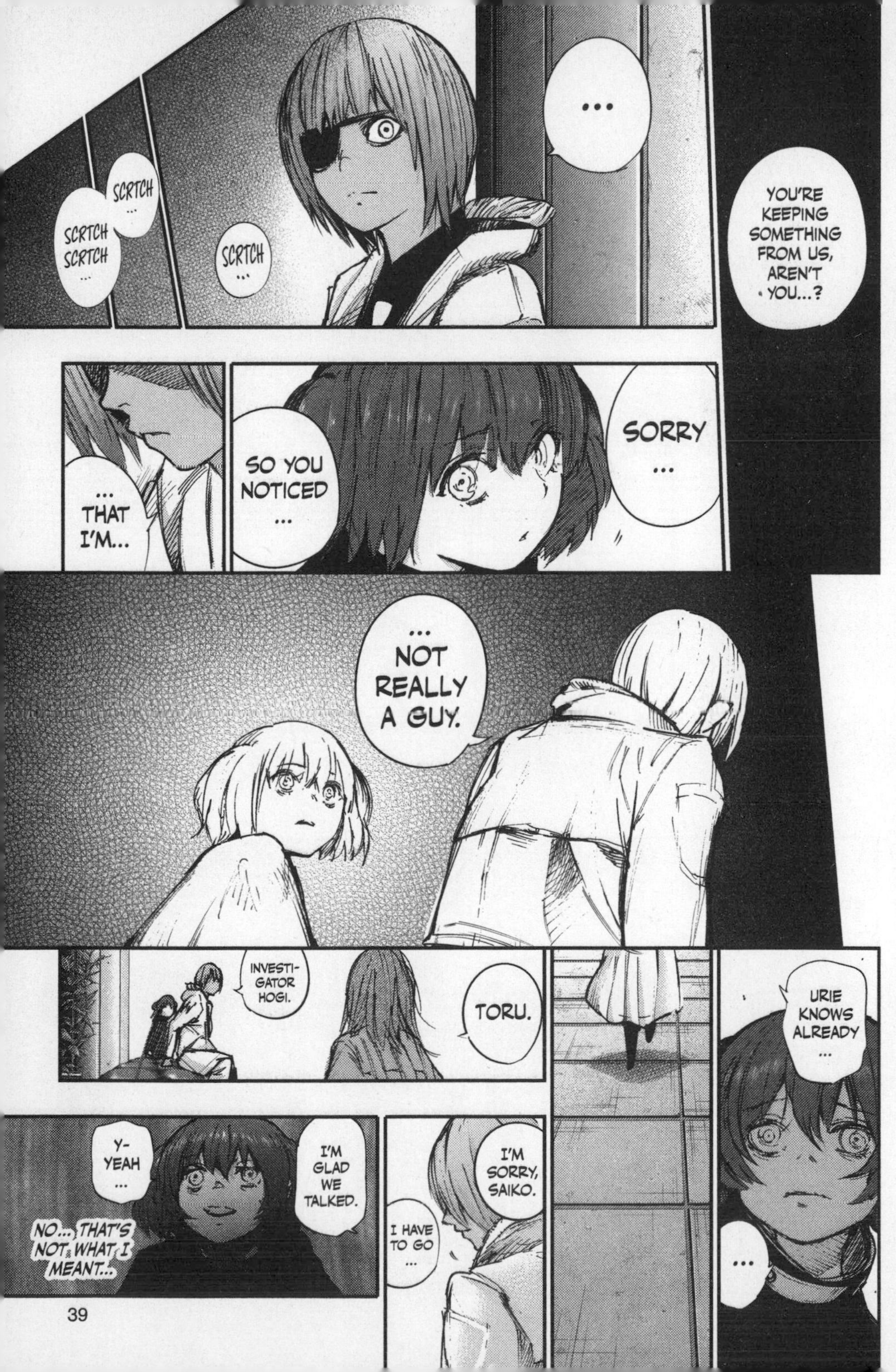
YOU'RE KEEPING SOMETHING FROM US, AREN'T YOU...?
...
SCRTCH ...
SCRTCH SCRTCH ...
SCRTCH ...
SORRY ...
SO YOU NOTICED ...
... THAT I'M...
... NOT REALLY A GUY.
URIE KNOWS ALREADY ...
...
TORU.
INVESTI-GATOR HOGI.
I'M SORRY, SAIKO.
I HAVE TO GO ...
I'M GLAD WE TALKED.
Y-YEAH ...
NO... THAT'S NOT WHAT I MEANT...

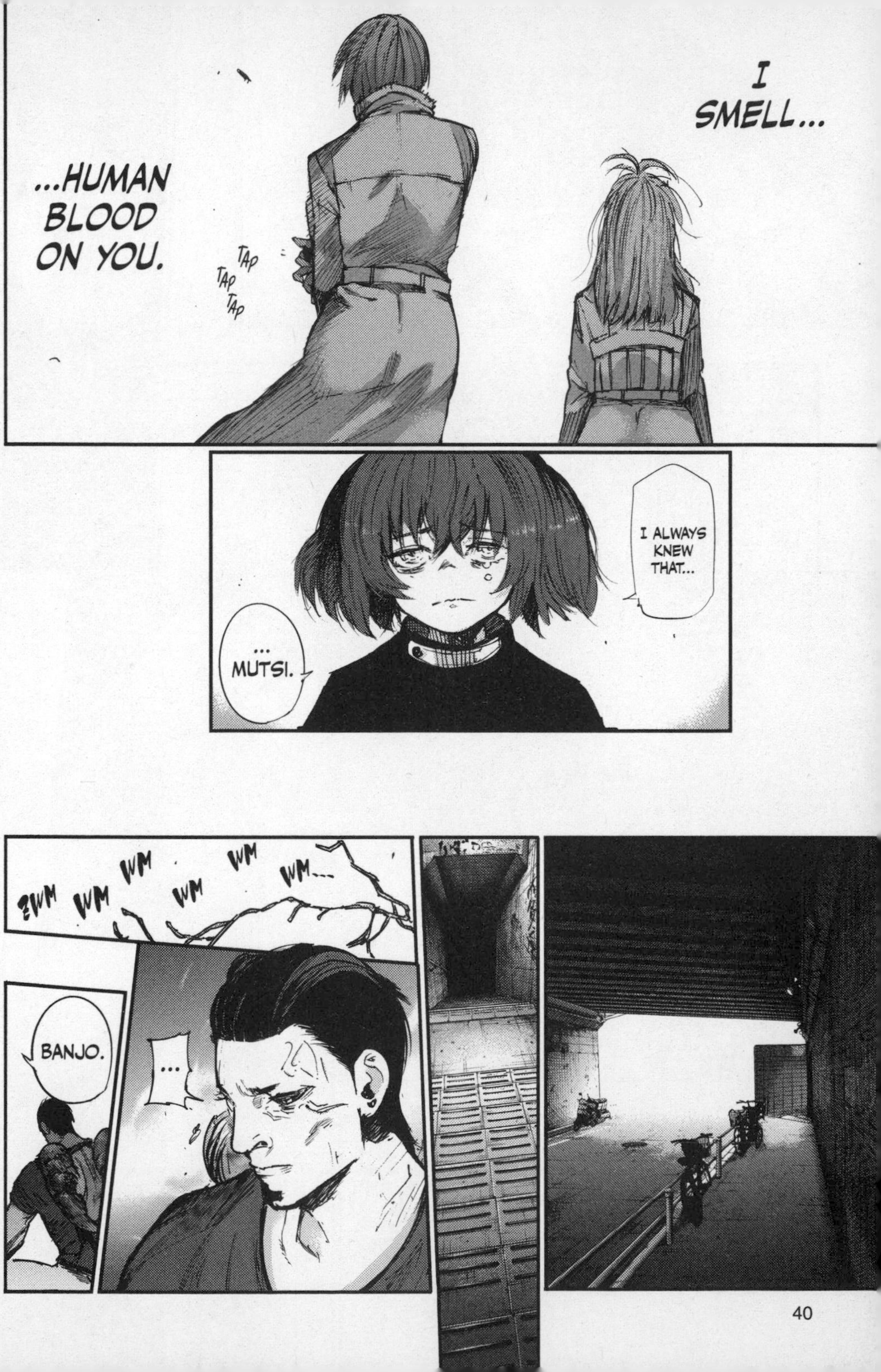

I SMELL...
...HUMAN BLOOD ON YOU.
TAP TAP TAP
I ALWAYS KNEW THAT...
... MUTSI.
WM...
WM
WM
WM
WM
ZWM
...
BANJO.

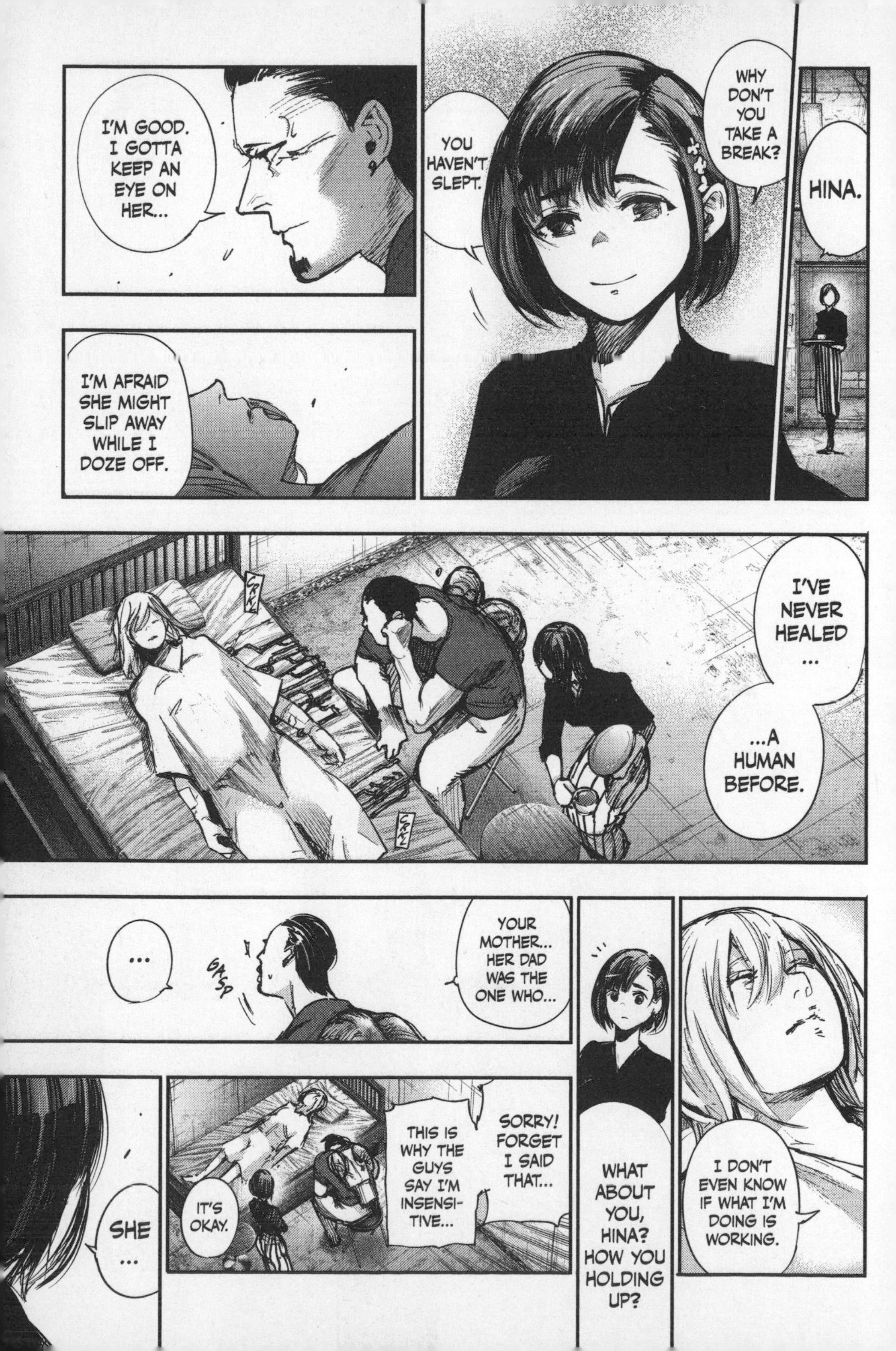
HINA.
WHY DON'T YOU TAKE A BREAK?
YOU HAVEN'T SLEPT.
I'M GOOD. I GOTTA KEEP AN EYE ON HER...
I'M AFRAID SHE MIGHT SLIP AWAY WHILE I DOZE OFF.
I'VE NEVER HEALED ...
...A HUMAN BEFORE.
CRK
CRK
I DON'T EVEN KNOW IF WHAT I'M DOING IS WORKING.
WHAT ABOUT YOU, HINA? HOW YOU HOLDING UP?
YOUR MOTHER... HER DAD WAS THE ONE WHO...
GASP
...
SORRY! FORGET I SAID THAT...
THIS IS WHY THE GUYS SAY I'M INSENSI-TIVE...
IT'S OKAY.
SHE ...

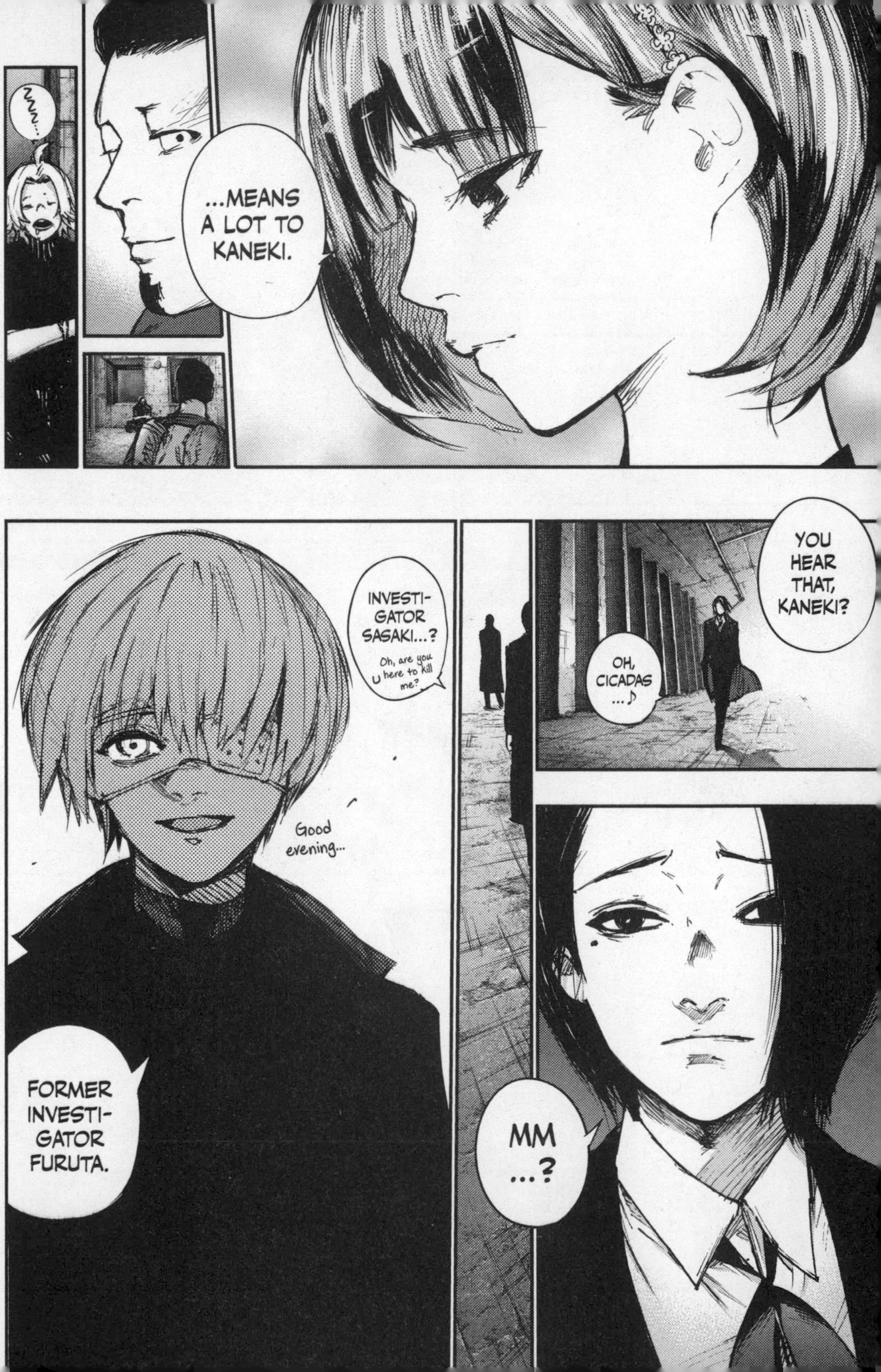
...MEANS A LOT TO KANEKI.
zzz...
YOU HEAR THAT, KANEKI?
OH, CICADAS ...♪
MM ...?
INVESTI-GATOR SASAKI...?
Oh, are you here to kill me?
Good evening...
FORMER INVESTI-GATOR FURUTA.

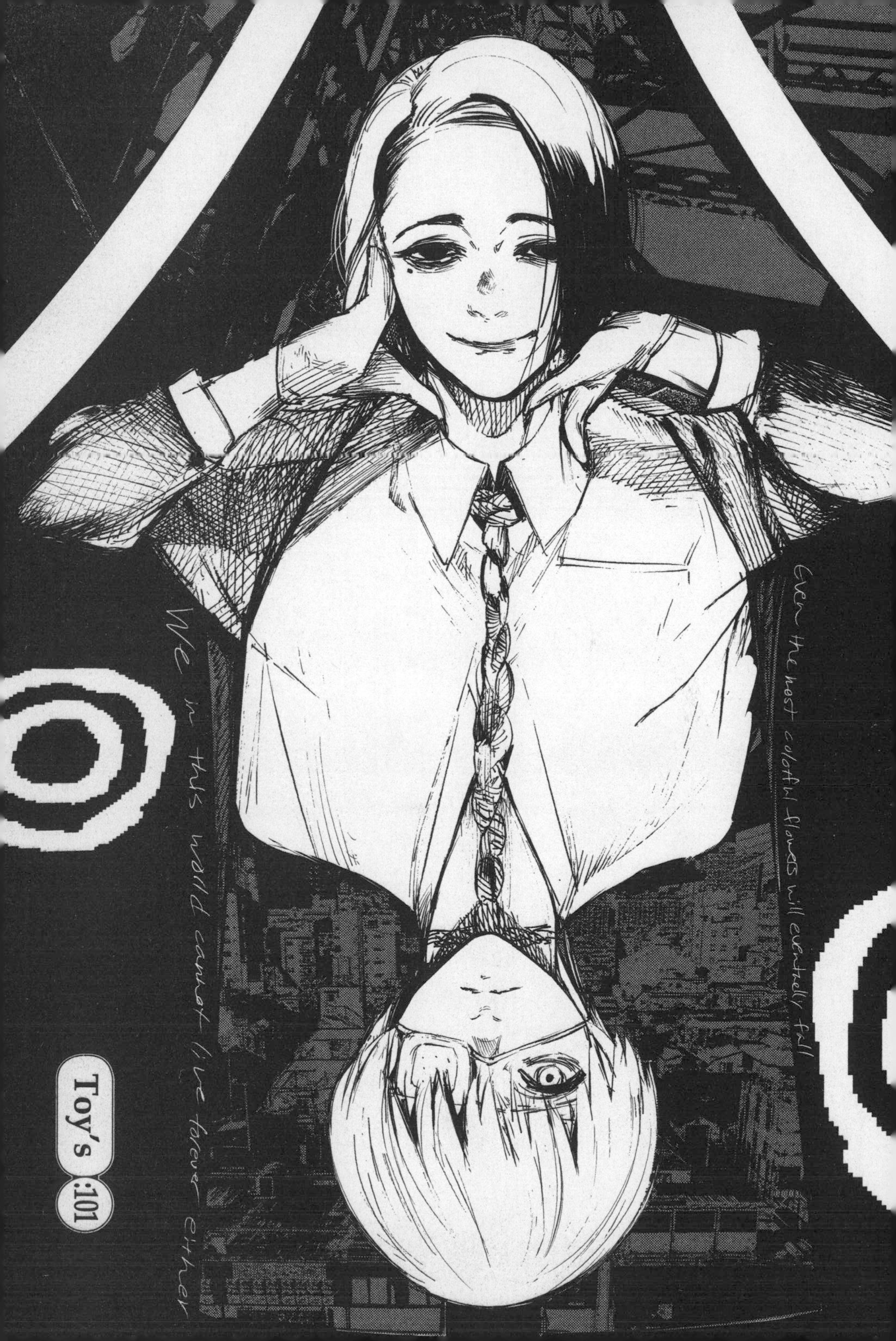

Even the most colorful flowers will eventually fall
We in this world cannot live forever either
Toy's :101

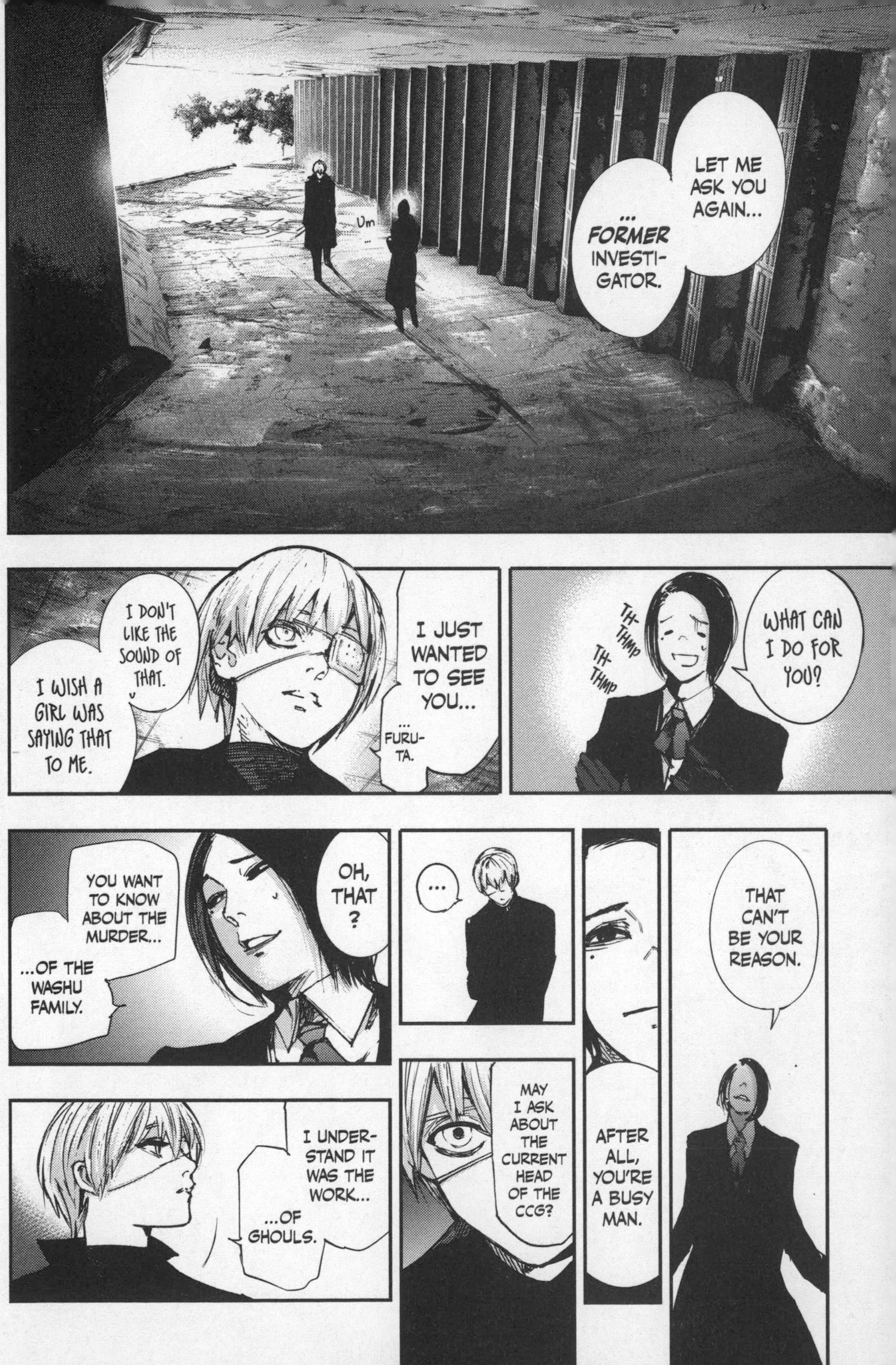

LET ME ASK YOU AGAIN...
...FORMER INVESTIGATOR.
Um ...
TH-THMP TH-THMP
WHAT CAN I DO FOR YOU?
I JUST WANTED TO SEE YOU...
...FURU-TA.
I DON'T LIKE THE SOUND OF THAT.
I WISH A GIRL WAS SAYING THAT TO ME.
THAT CAN'T BE YOUR REASON.
AFTER ALL, YOU'RE A BUSY MAN.
...
MAY I ASK ABOUT THE CURRENT HEAD OF THE CCG?
OH, THAT?
YOU WANT TO KNOW ABOUT THE MURDER...
...OF THE WASHU FAMILY.
I UNDER-STAND IT WAS THE WORK...
...OF GHOULS.

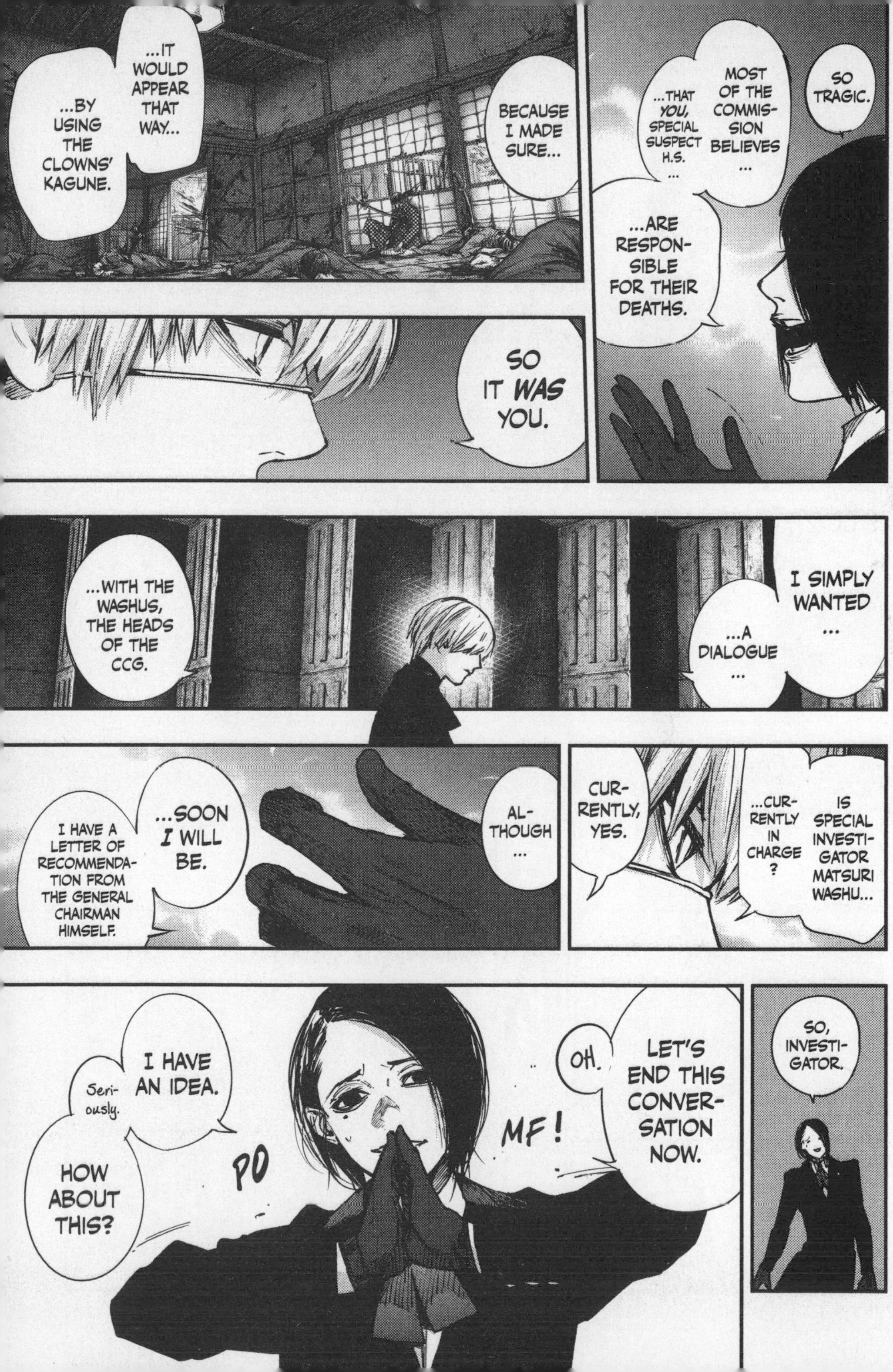
SO TRAGIC.
MOST OF THE COMMISSION BELIEVES...
...THAT YOU, SPECIAL SUSPECT H.S. ...
...ARE RESPONSIBLE FOR THEIR DEATHS.
BECAUSE I MADE SURE...
...IT WOULD APPEAR THAT WAY...
...BY USING THE CLOWNS' KAGUNE.
SO IT WAS YOU.
I SIMPLY WANTED...
...A DIALOGUE...
...WITH THE WASHUS, THE HEADS OF THE CCG.
IS SPECIAL INVESTIGATOR MATSURI WASHU...
...CURRENTLY IN CHARGE?
CURRENTLY, YES.
ALTHOUGH...
...SOON I WILL BE.
I HAVE A LETTER OF RECOMMENDATION FROM THE GENERAL CHAIRMAN HIMSELF.
SO, INVESTIGATOR.
LET'S END THIS CONVERSATION NOW.
OH.
MF!
I HAVE AN IDEA.
Seriously.
PO
HOW ABOUT THIS?

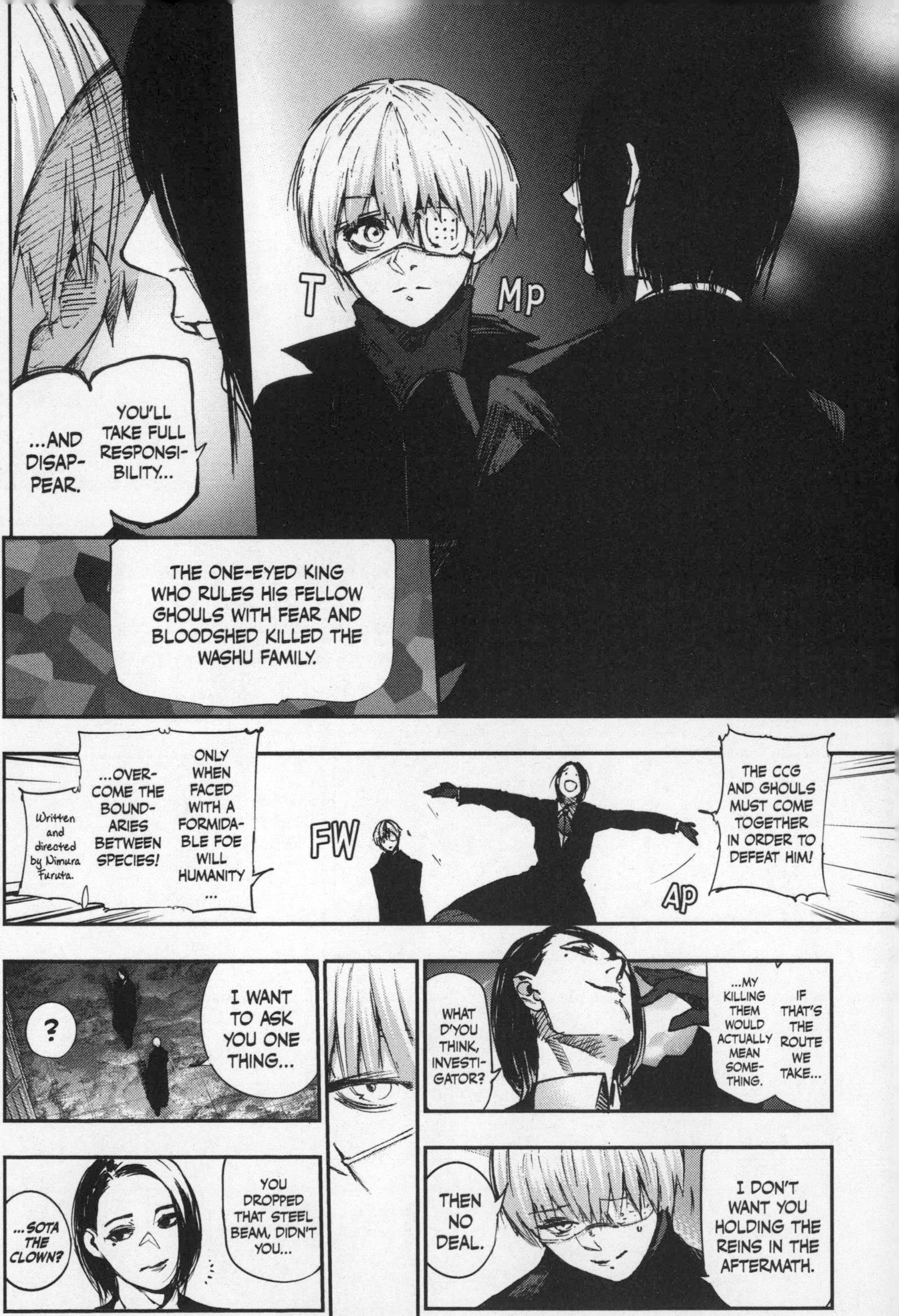
TMP
YOU'LL TAKE FULL RESPONSIBILITY...
...AND DISAPPEAR.
THE ONE-EYED KING WHO RULES HIS FELLOW GHOULS WITH FEAR AND BLOODSHED KILLED THE WASHU FAMILY.
THE CCG AND GHOULS MUST COME TOGETHER IN ORDER TO DEFEAT HIM!
AP
FW
ONLY WHEN FACED WITH A FORMIDABLE FOE WILL HUMANITY ...
...OVERCOME THE BOUNDARIES BETWEEN SPECIES!
Written and directed by Nimura Furuta.
IF THAT'S THE ROUTE WE TAKE...
...MY KILLING THEM WOULD ACTUALLY MEAN SOMETHING.
WHAT D'YOU THINK, INVESTIGATOR?
I DON'T WANT YOU HOLDING THE REINS IN THE AFTERMATH.
THEN NO DEAL.
I WANT TO ASK YOU ONE THING...
?
YOU DROPPED THAT STEEL BEAM, DIDN'T YOU...
...SOTA THE CLOWN?

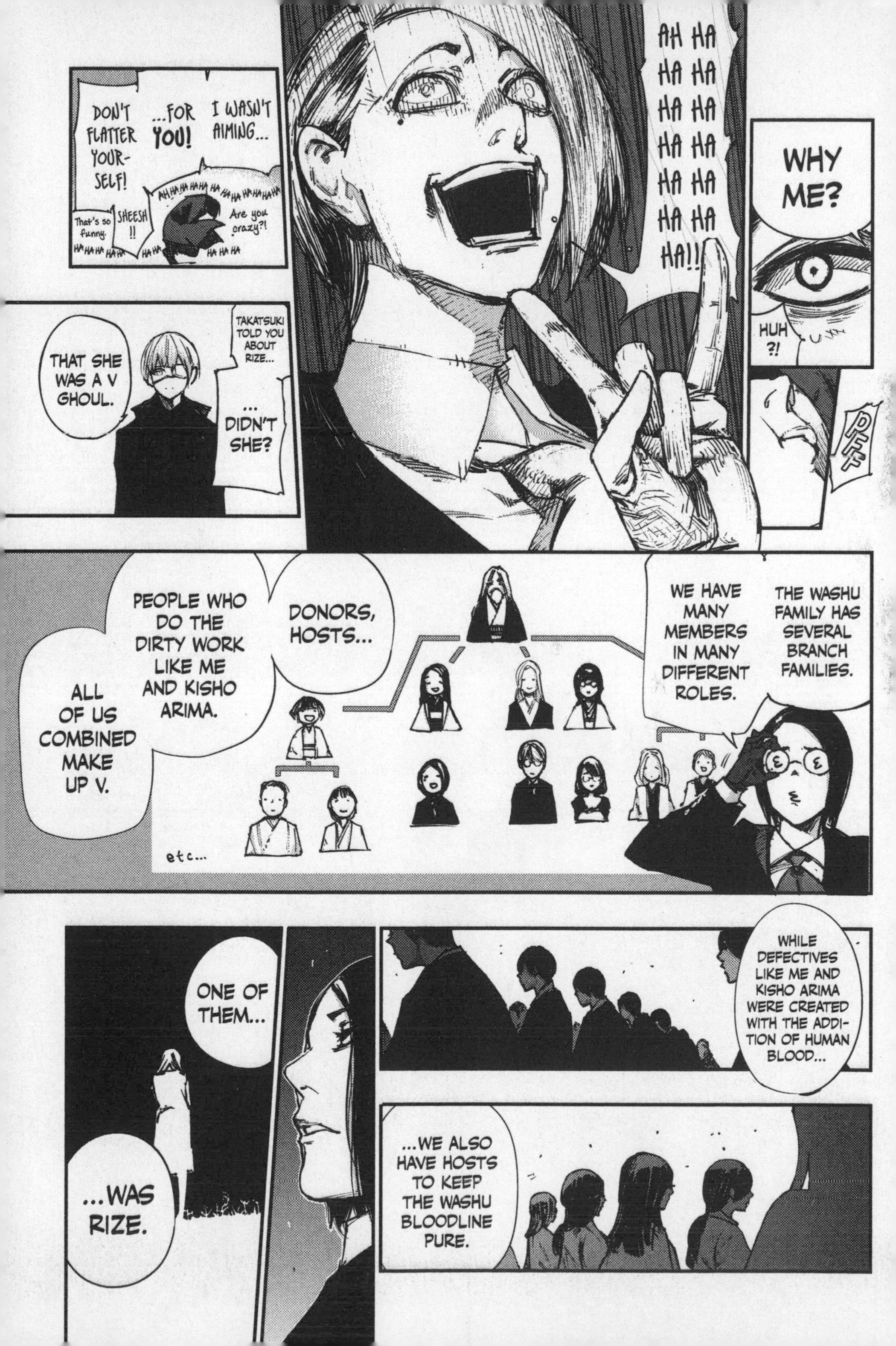
WHY ME?
HUH?!
PFFF
AH HA HA HA HA HA HA HA HA HA HA HA HA!!
I WASN'T AIMING...
...FOR YOU!
DON'T FLATTER YOURSELF!
AH HA HA HA HA HA HA HA HA HA HA
Are you crazy?!
SHEESH!!
That's so funny.
HA HA HA HA HA HA HA HA HA
TAKATSUKI TOLD YOU ABOUT RIZE...
...DIDN'T SHE?
THAT SHE WAS A V GHOUL.
THE WASHU FAMILY HAS SEVERAL BRANCH FAMILIES.
WE HAVE MANY MEMBERS IN MANY DIFFERENT ROLES.
DONORS, HOSTS...
PEOPLE WHO DO THE DIRTY WORK LIKE ME AND KISHO ARIMA.
ALL OF US COMBINED MAKE UP V.
etc...
WHILE DEFECTIVES LIKE ME AND KISHO ARIMA WERE CREATED WITH THE ADDITION OF HUMAN BLOOD...
...WE ALSO HAVE HOSTS TO KEEP THE WASHU BLOODLINE PURE.
ONE OF THEM...
...WAS RIZE.

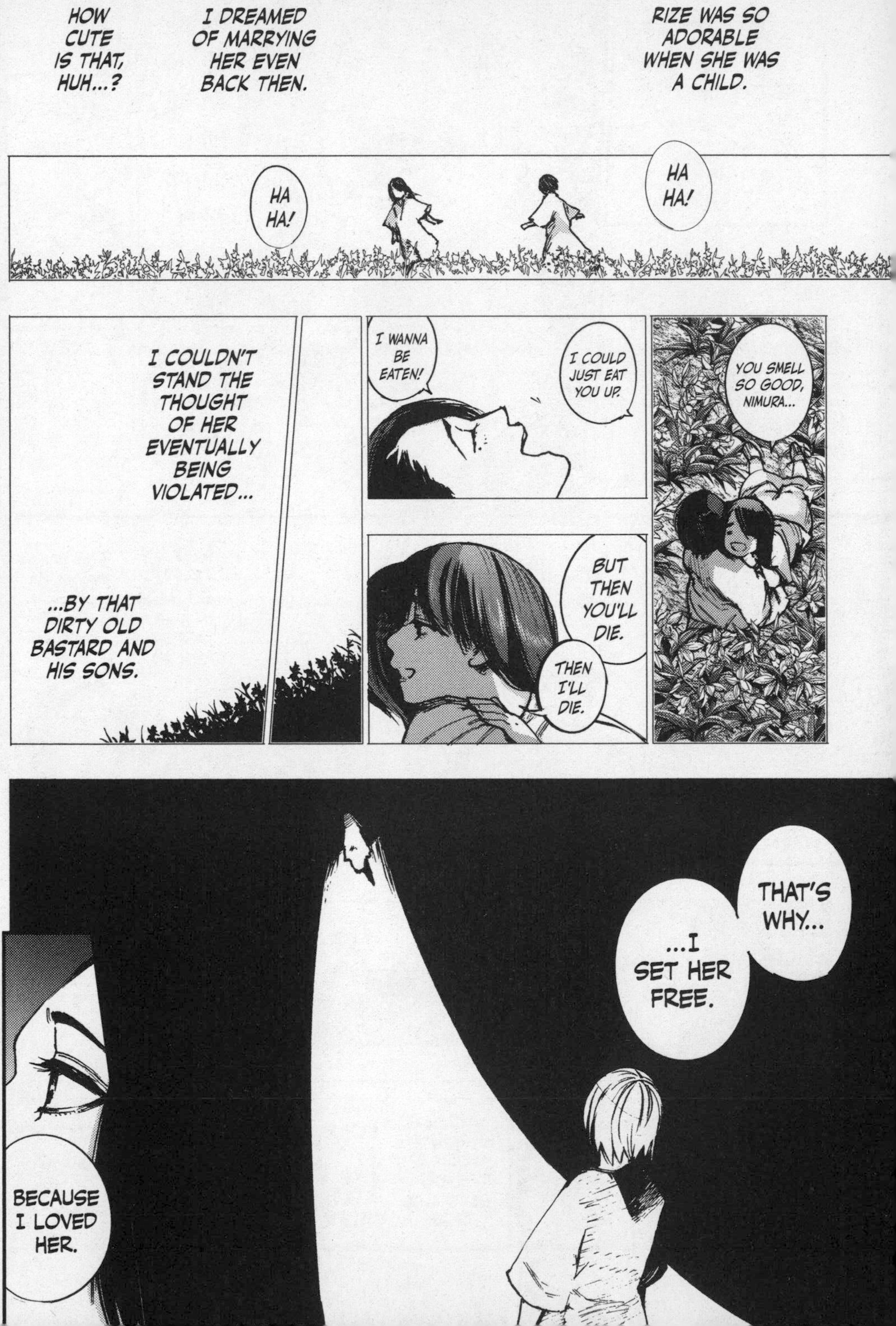
RIZE WAS SO ADORABLE WHEN SHE WAS A CHILD.
I DREAMED OF MARRYING HER EVEN BACK THEN.
HOW CUTE IS THAT, HUH...?
HA HA!
HA HA!
YOU SMELL SO GOOD, NIMURA...
I COULD JUST EAT YOU UP.
I WANNA BE EATEN!
BUT THEN YOU'LL DIE.
THEN I'LL DIE.
I COULDN'T STAND THE THOUGHT OF HER EVENTUALLY BEING VIOLATED...
...BY THAT DIRTY OLD BASTARD AND HIS SONS.
THAT'S WHY...
...I SET HER FREE.
BECAUSE I LOVED HER.

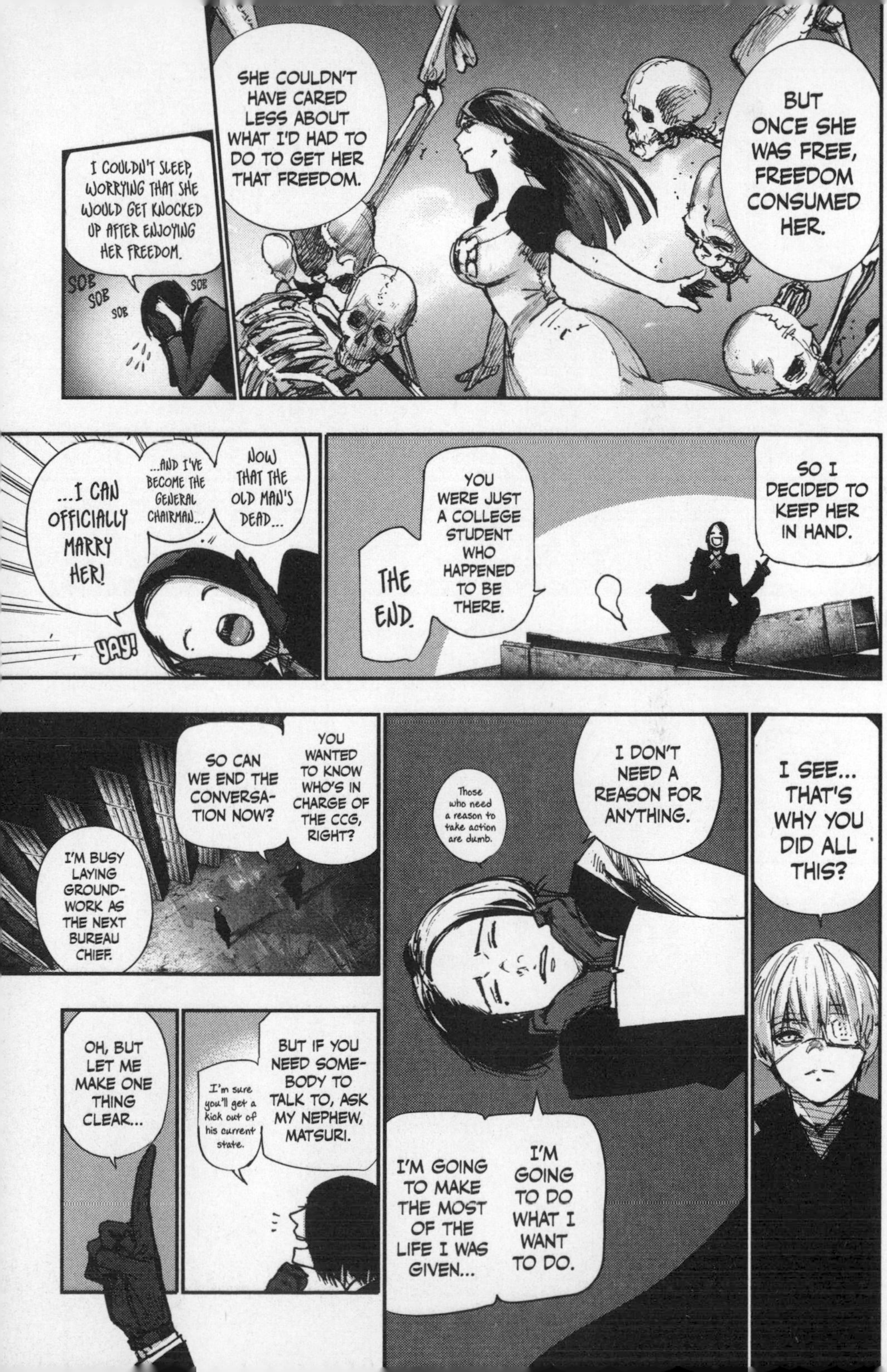
BUT ONCE SHE WAS FREE, FREEDOM CONSUMED HER.
SHE COULDN'T HAVE CARED LESS ABOUT WHAT I'D HAD TO DO TO GET HER THAT FREEDOM.
I COULDN'T SLEEP, WORRYING THAT SHE WOULD GET KNOCKED UP AFTER ENJOYING HER FREEDOM.
SOB SOB SOB SOB
SO I DECIDED TO KEEP HER IN HAND.
YOU WERE JUST A COLLEGE STUDENT WHO HAPPENED TO BE THERE.
THE END.
NOW THAT THE OLD MAN'S DEAD...
...AND I'VE BECOME THE GENERAL CHAIRMAN...
...I CAN OFFICIALLY MARRY HER!
YAY!
I SEE... THAT'S WHY YOU DID ALL THIS?
I DON'T NEED A REASON FOR ANYTHING.
Those who need a reason to take action are dumb.
I'M GOING TO DO WHAT I WANT TO DO.
I'M GOING TO MAKE THE MOST OF THE LIFE I WAS GIVEN...
YOU WANTED TO KNOW WHO'S IN CHARGE OF THE CCG, RIGHT?
SO CAN WE END THE CONVERSATION NOW?
I'M BUSY LAYING GROUNDWORK AS THE NEXT BUREAU CHIEF.
BUT IF YOU NEED SOMEBODY TO TALK TO, ASK MY NEPHEW, MATSURI.
I'm sure you'll get a kick out of his current state.
OH, BUT LET ME MAKE ONE THING CLEAR...

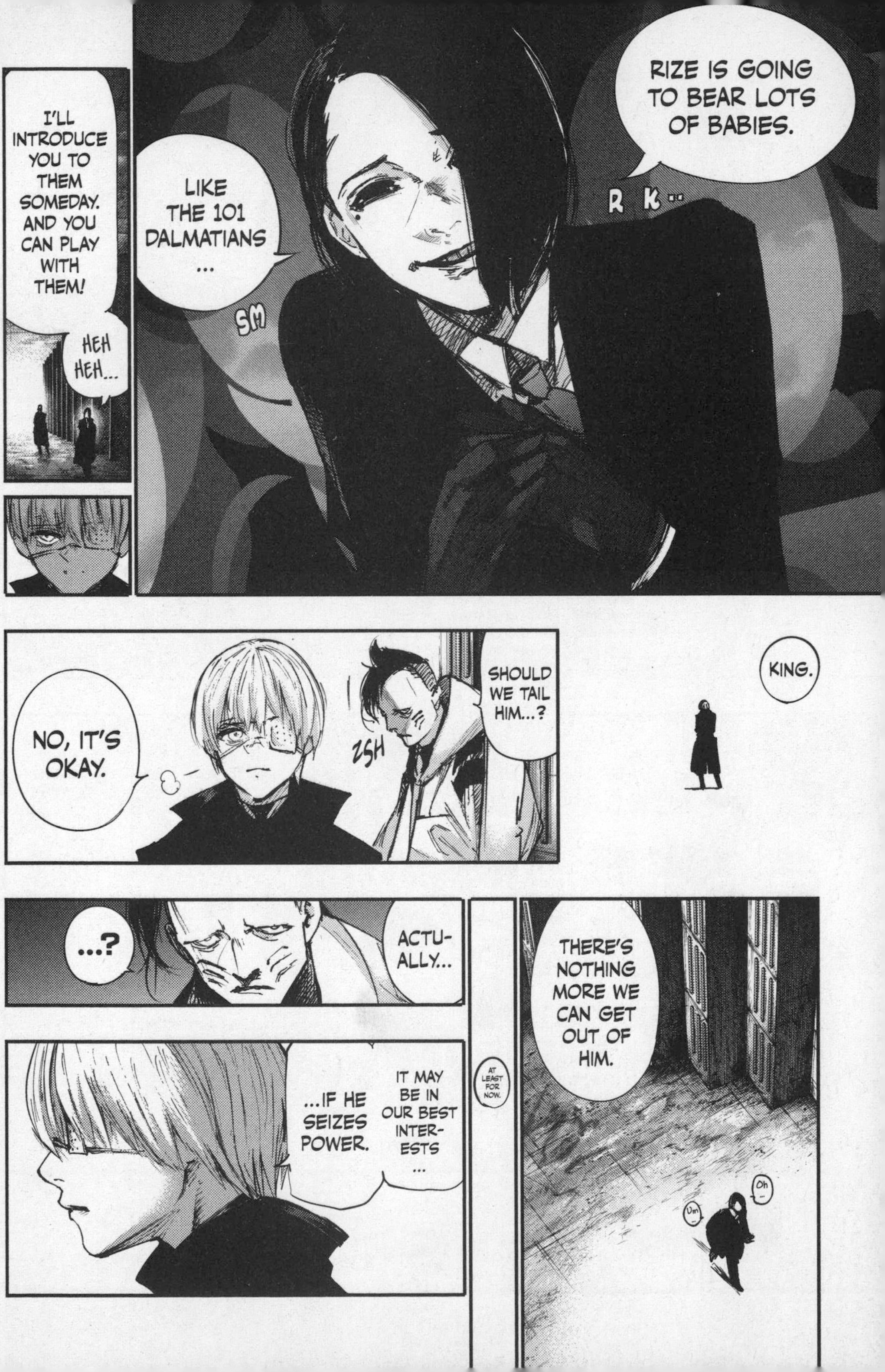
RIZE IS GOING TO BEAR LOTS OF BABIES.
R K...
LIKE THE 101 DALMATIANS ...
SM
I'LL INTRODUCE YOU TO THEM SOMEDAY. AND YOU CAN PLAY WITH THEM!
HEH HEH...
KING.
SHOULD WE TAIL HIM...?
ZSH
NO, IT'S OKAY.
THERE'S NOTHING MORE WE CAN GET OUT OF HIM.
Oh...
Um...
AT LEAST FOR NOW.
ACTU-ALLY...
...?
IT MAY BE IN OUR BEST INTER-ESTS ...
...IF HE SEIZES POWER.

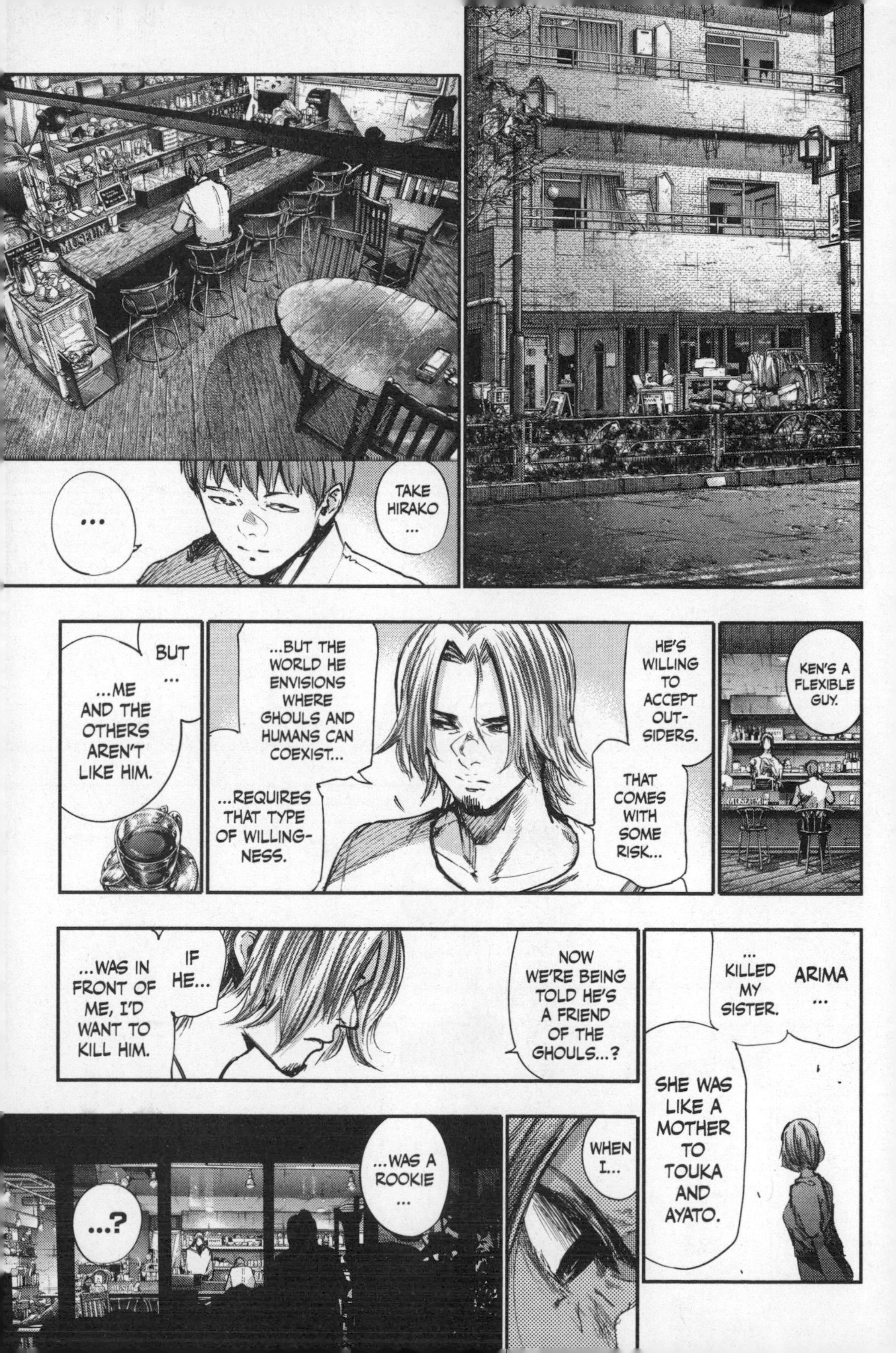
TAKE HIRAKO...
...
KEN'S A FLEXIBLE GUY.
HE'S WILLING TO ACCEPT OUT-SIDERS.
THAT COMES WITH SOME RISK...
...BUT THE WORLD HE ENVISIONS WHERE GHOULS AND HUMANS CAN COEXIST...
...REQUIRES THAT TYPE OF WILLING-NESS.
BUT...
...ME AND THE OTHERS AREN'T LIKE HIM.
ARIMA...
...KILLED MY SISTER.
SHE WAS LIKE A MOTHER TO TOUKA AND AYATO.
NOW WE'RE BEING TOLD HE'S A FRIEND OF THE GHOULS...?
IF HE...
...WAS IN FRONT OF ME, I'D WANT TO KILL HIM.
WHEN I...
...WAS A ROOKIE...
...?

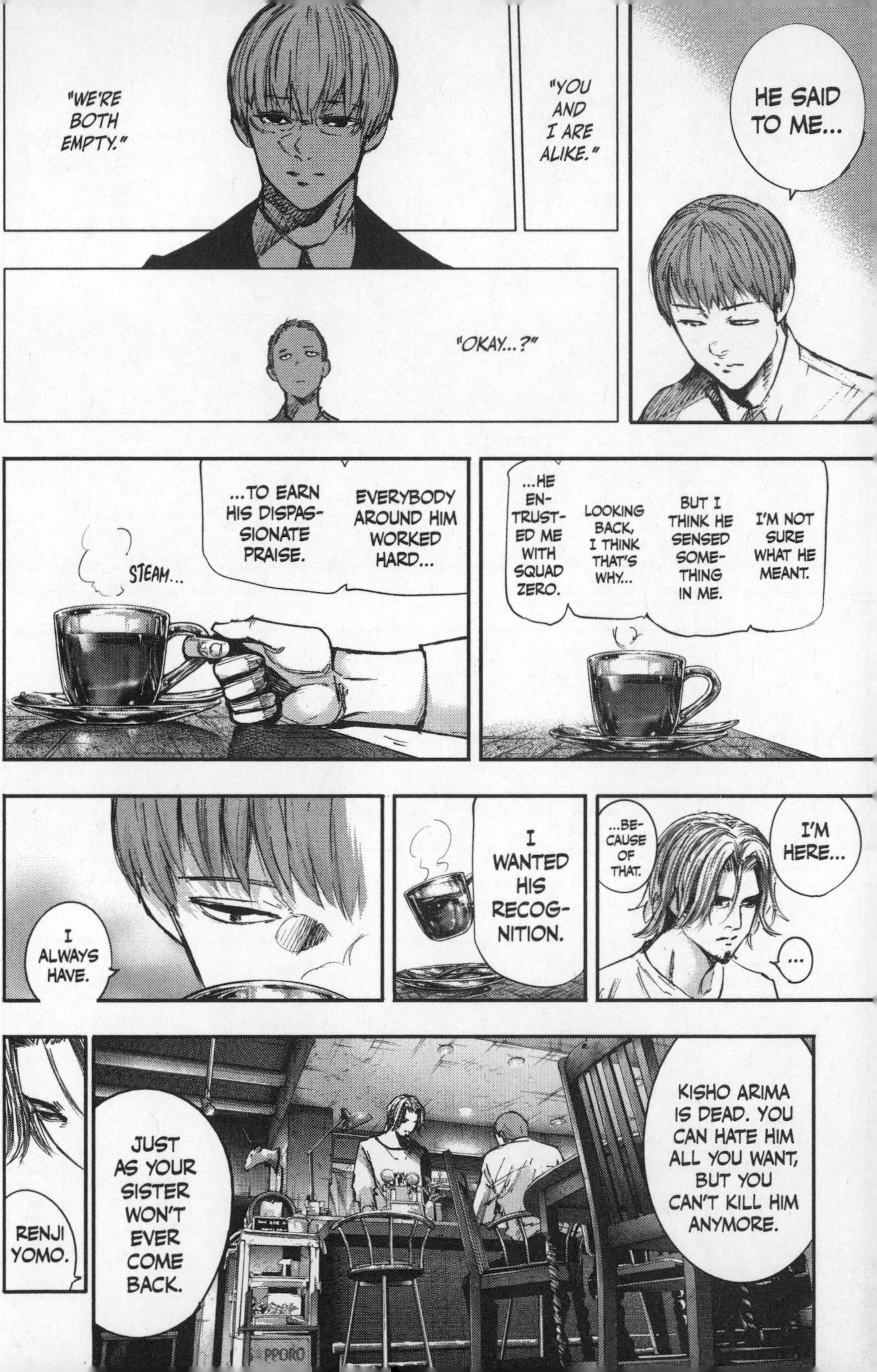
HE SAID TO ME...
"YOU AND I ARE ALIKE."
"WE'RE BOTH EMPTY."
"OKAY...?"
I'M NOT SURE WHAT HE MEANT.
BUT I THINK HE SENSED SOMETHING IN ME.
LOOKING BACK, I THINK THAT'S WHY...
...HE ENTRUSTED ME WITH SQUAD ZERO.
EVERYBODY AROUND HIM WORKED HARD...
...TO EARN HIS DISPASSIONATE PRAISE.
STEAM...
I'M HERE...
...BECAUSE OF THAT.
...
I WANTED HIS RECOGNITION.
I ALWAYS HAVE.
KISHO ARIMA IS DEAD. YOU CAN HATE HIM ALL YOU WANT, BUT YOU CAN'T KILL HIM ANYMORE.
JUST AS YOUR SISTER WON'T EVER COME BACK.
RENJI YOMO.

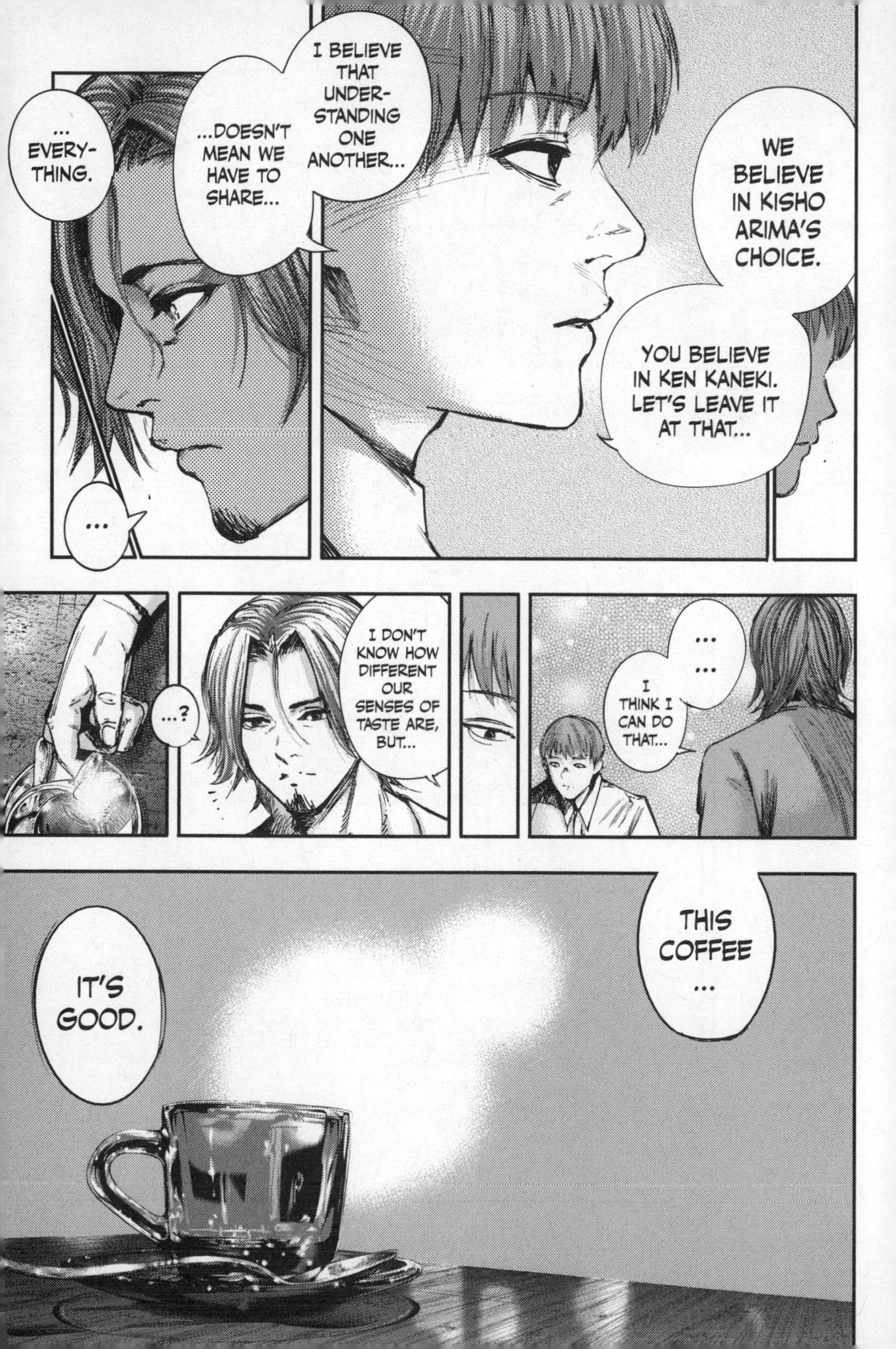
WE BELIEVE IN KISHO ARIMA'S CHOICE.
YOU BELIEVE IN KEN KANEKI. LET'S LEAVE IT AT THAT...
I BELIEVE THAT UNDER-STANDING ONE ANOTHER...
...DOESN'T MEAN WE HAVE TO SHARE...
... EVERY-THING.
...
... ...
I THINK I CAN DO THAT...
I DON'T KNOW HOW DIFFERENT OUR SENSES OF TASTE ARE, BUT...
...?
THIS COFFEE ...
IT'S GOOD.

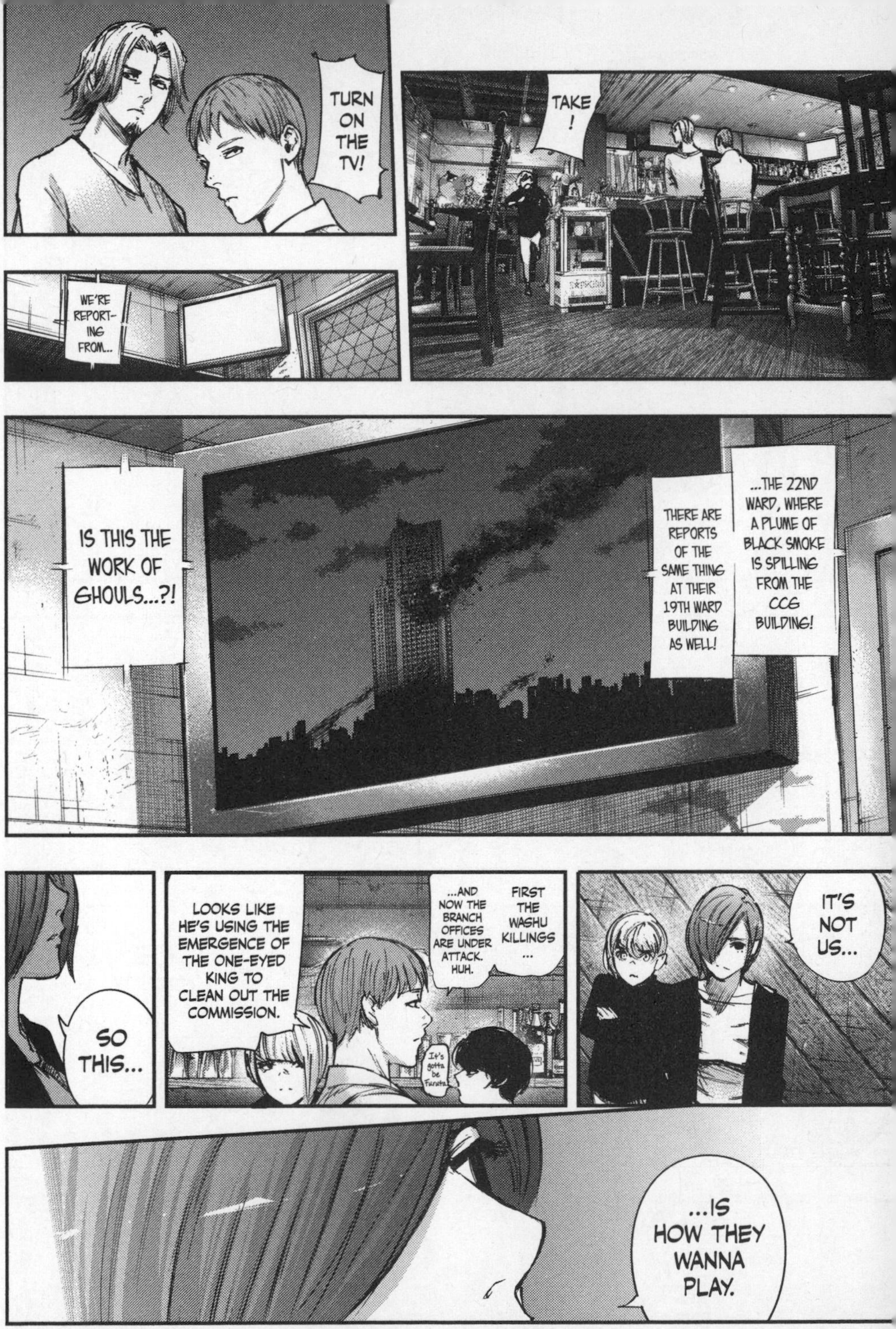
TAKE !
TURN ON THE TV!
WE'RE REPORTING FROM...
...THE 22ND WARD, WHERE A PLUME OF BLACK SMOKE IS SPILLING FROM THE CCG BUILDING!
THERE ARE REPORTS OF THE SAME THING AT THEIR 19TH WARD BUILDING AS WELL!
IS THIS THE WORK OF GHOULS...?!
IT'S NOT US...
FIRST THE WASHU KILLINGS...
...AND NOW THE BRANCH OFFICES ARE UNDER ATTACK. HUH.
It's gotta be Furuta.
LOOKS LIKE HE'S USING THE EMERGENCE OF THE ONE-EYED KING TO CLEAN OUT THE COMMISSION.
SO THIS...
...IS HOW THEY WANNA PLAY.

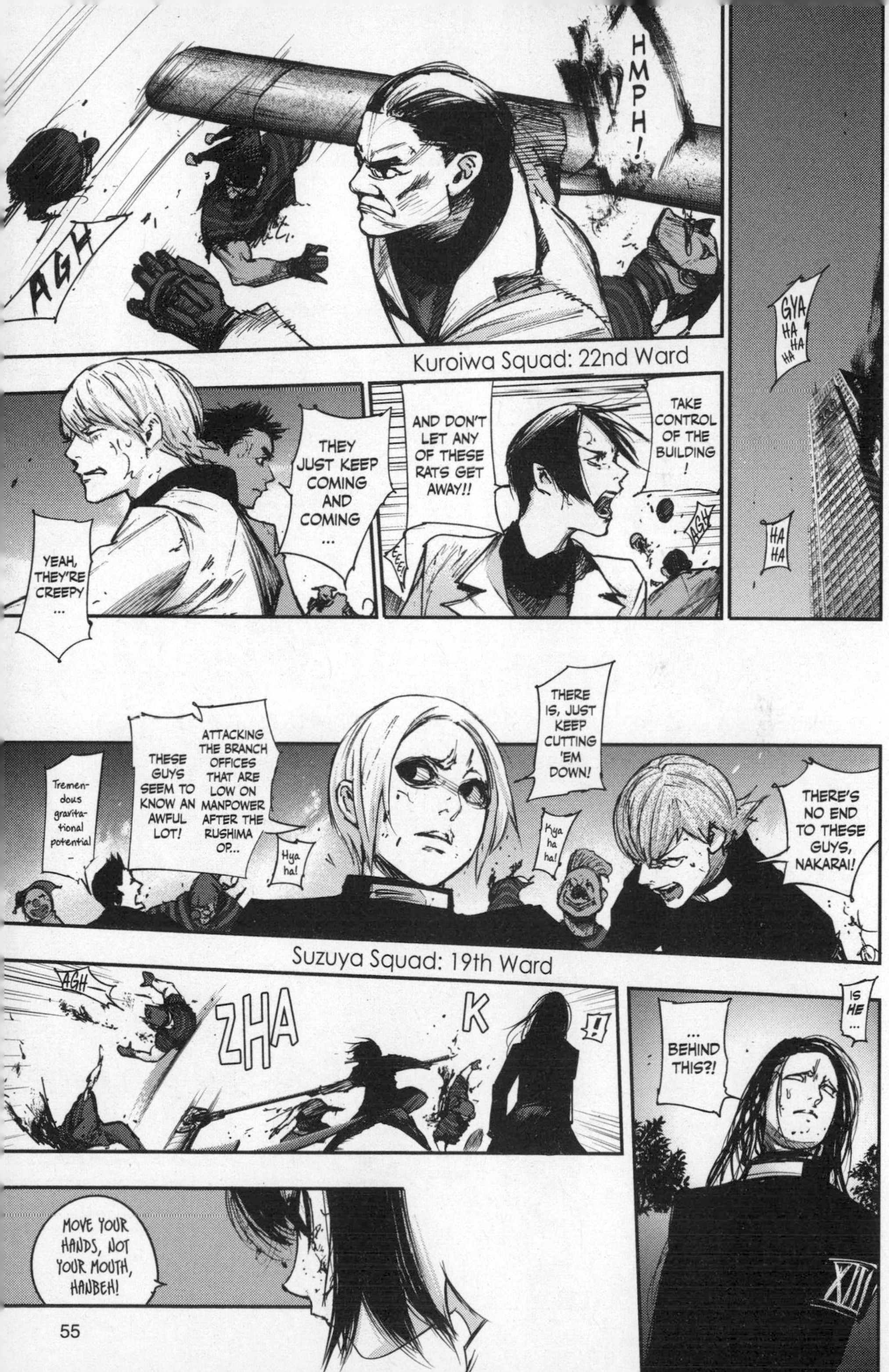
GYA HA HA HA
HA HA
HMPH!
AGH
Kuroiwa Squad: 22nd Ward
TAKE CONTROL OF THE BUILDING!
AND DON'T LET ANY OF THESE RATS GET AWAY!!
AGH
THEY JUST KEEP COMING AND COMING...
YEAH, THEY'RE CREEPY...
THERE'S NO END TO THESE GUYS, NAKARAI!
THERE IS, JUST KEEP CUTTING 'EM DOWN!
Kya ha ha!
ATTACKING THE BRANCH OFFICES THAT ARE LOW ON MANPOWER AFTER THE RUSHIMA OP...
THESE GUYS SEEM TO KNOW AN AWFUL LOT!
Hya ha!
Tremendous gravitational potential...
Suzuya Squad: 19th Ward
IS HE...
... BEHIND THIS?!
!
K
ZHA
AGH
MOVE YOUR HANDS, NOT YOUR MOUTH, HANBEH!

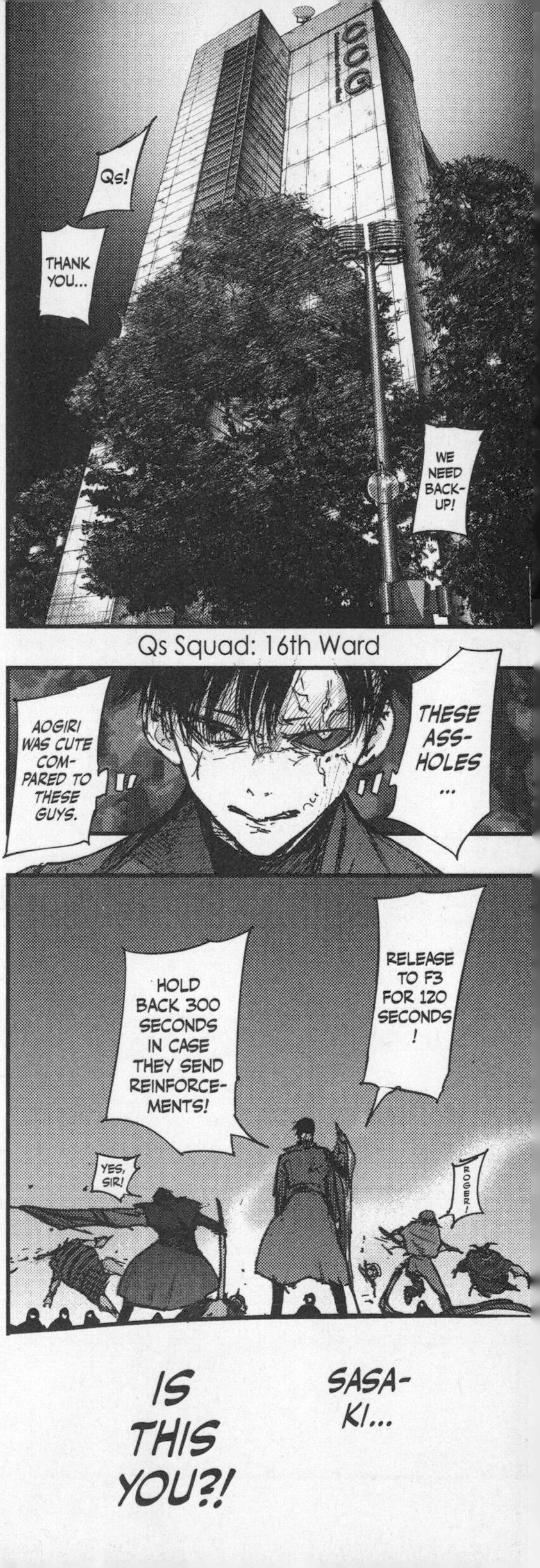
WE NEED BACK-UP!
Qs!
THANK YOU...
Qs Squad: 16th Ward
THESE ASSHOLES...
AOGIRI WAS CUTE COMPARED TO THESE GUYS.
RELEASE TO F3 FOR 120 SECONDS!
HOLD BACK 300 SECONDS IN CASE THEY SEND REINFORCEMENTS!
ROGER!
YES, SIR!
SASAKI...
IS THIS YOU?!

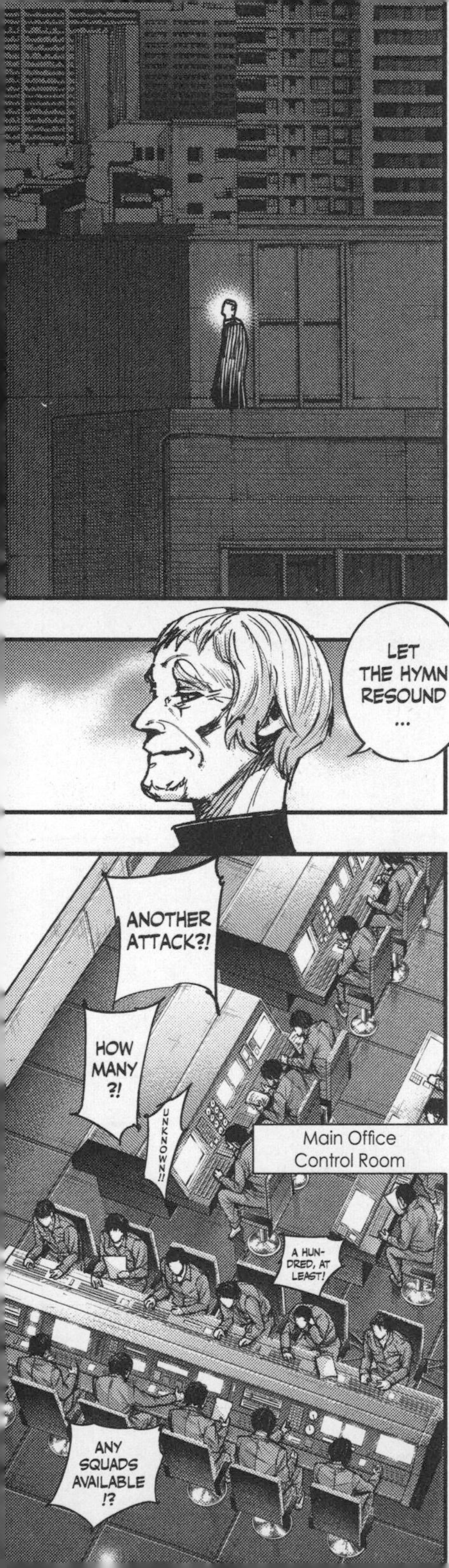
LET THE HYMN RESOUND...
ANOTHER ATTACK?!
HOW MANY?!
UNKNOWN!!
Main Office Control Room
A HUNDRED, AT LEAST!
ANY SQUADS AVAILABLE!?

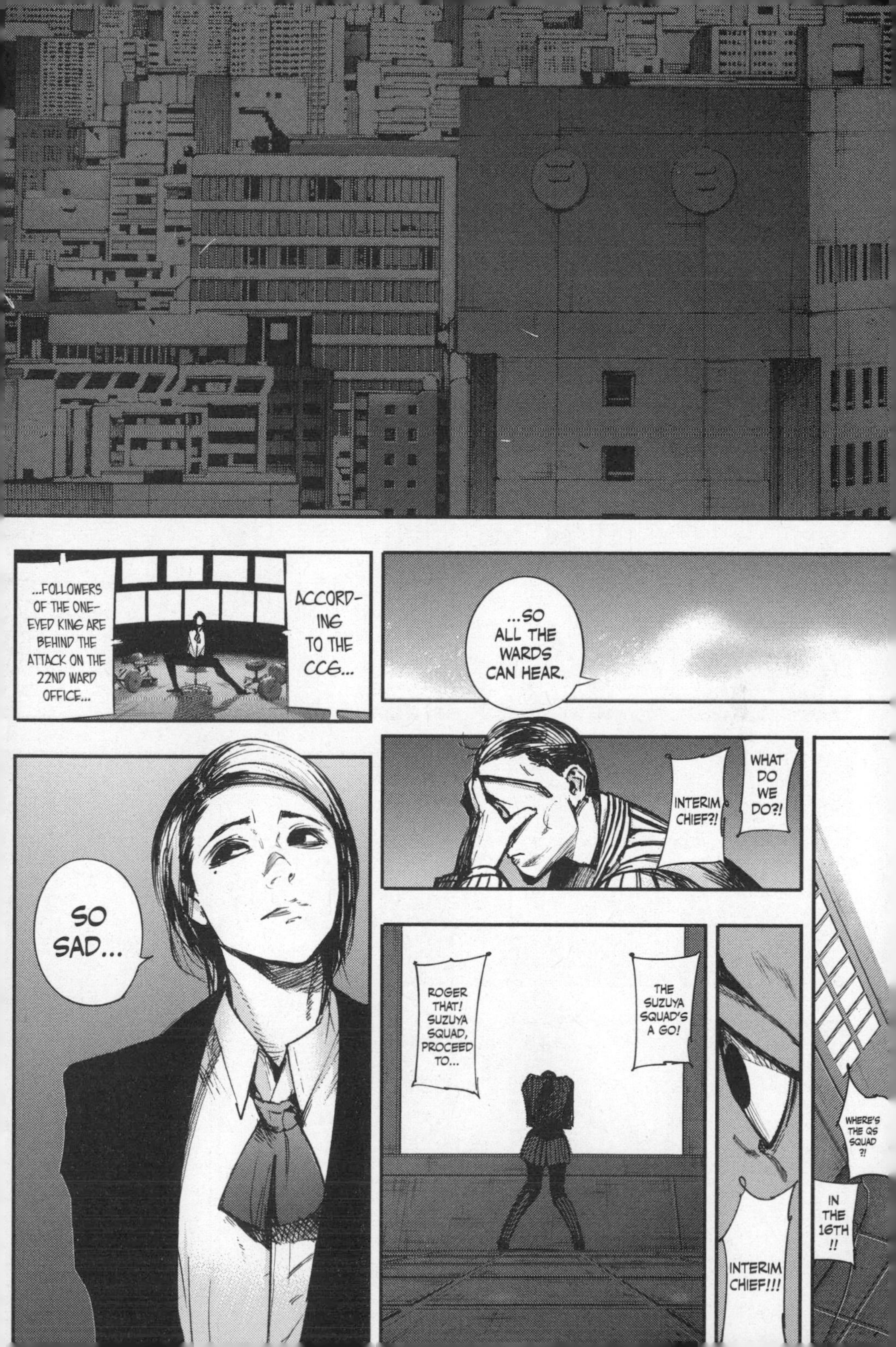
...SO ALL THE WARDS CAN HEAR.
ACCORD-ING TO THE CCG...
...FOLLOWERS OF THE ONE-EYED KING ARE BEHIND THE ATTACK ON THE 22ND WARD OFFICE...
WHERE'S THE QS SQUAD?!
IN THE 16TH!!
WHAT DO WE DO?!
INTERIM CHIEF?!
INTERIM CHIEF!!!
THE SUZUYA SQUAD'S A GO!
ROGER THAT! SUZUYA SQUAD, PROCEED TO...
SO SAD...

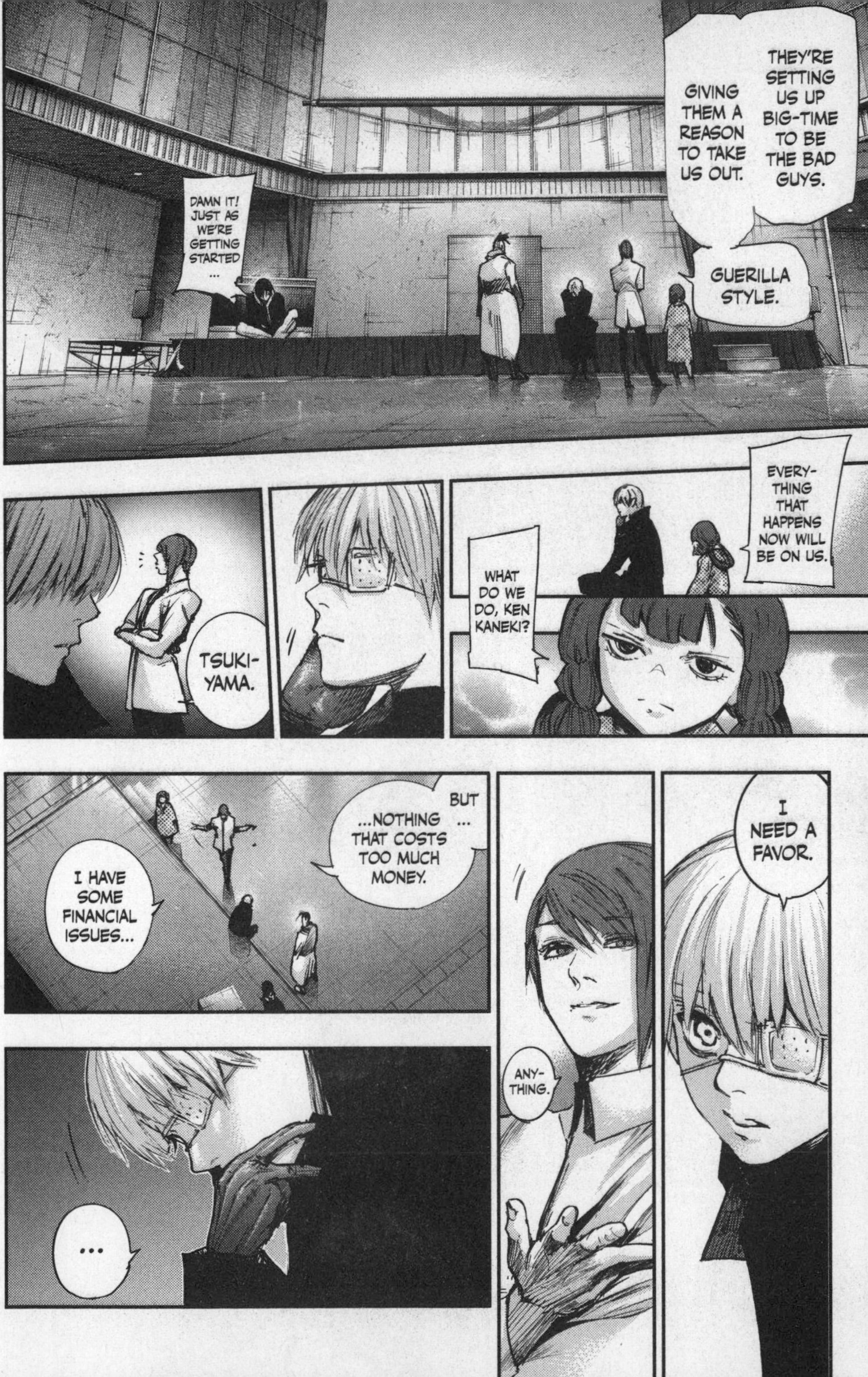
THEY'RE SETTING US UP BIG-TIME TO BE THE BAD GUYS.
GIVING THEM A REASON TO TAKE US OUT.
GUERILLA STYLE.
DAMN IT! JUST AS WE'RE GETTING STARTED ...
EVERY-THING THAT HAPPENS NOW WILL BE ON US.
WHAT DO WE DO, KEN KANEKI?
TSUKI-YAMA.
I NEED A FAVOR.
ANY-THING.
I HAVE SOME FINANCIAL ISSUES...
BUT ... ...NOTHING THAT COSTS TOO MUCH MONEY.
...

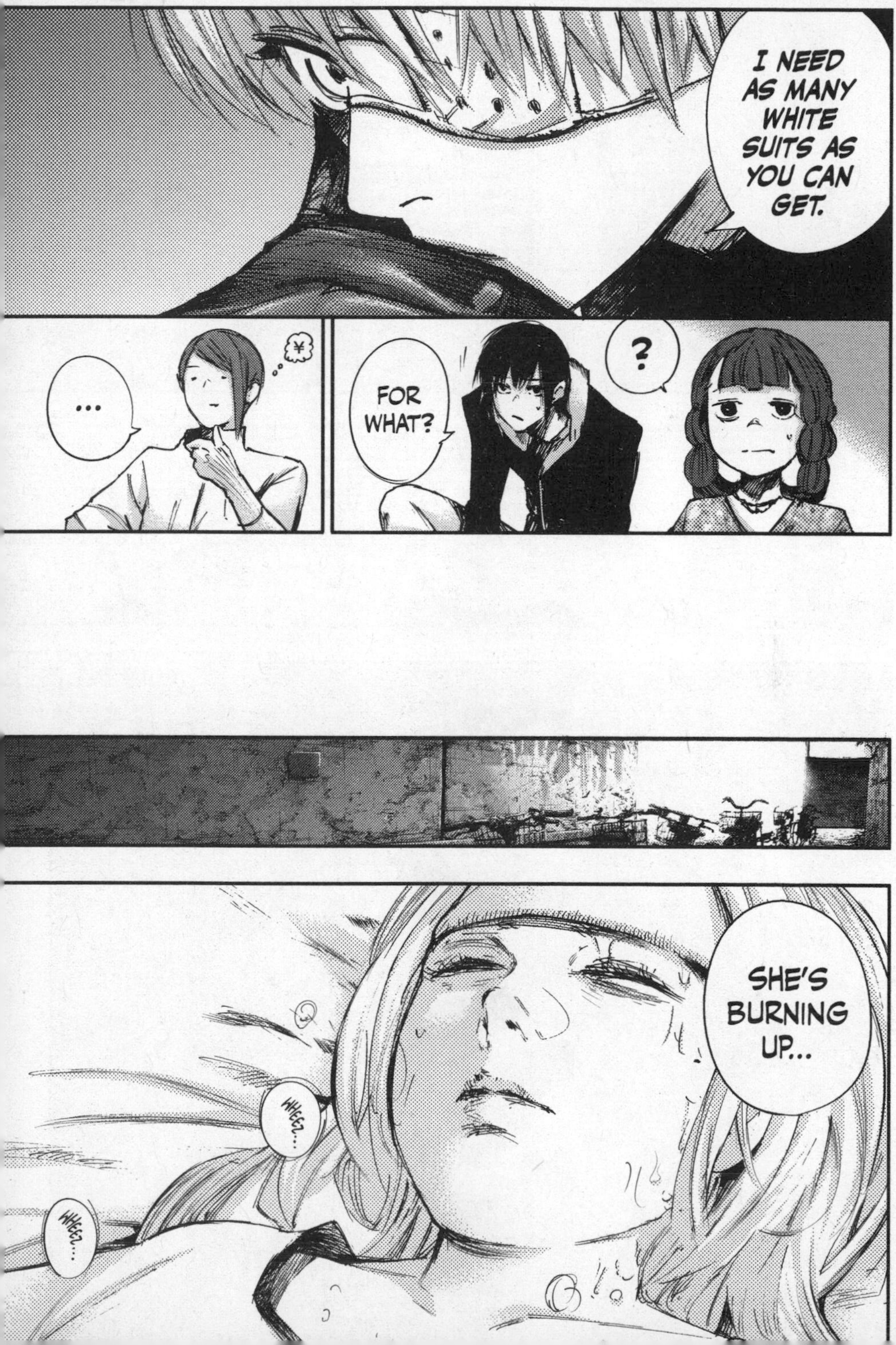
I NEED AS MANY WHITE SUITS AS YOU CAN GET.
?
FOR WHAT?
¥
...
SHE'S BURNING UP...
WHEEZ...
WHEEZ...

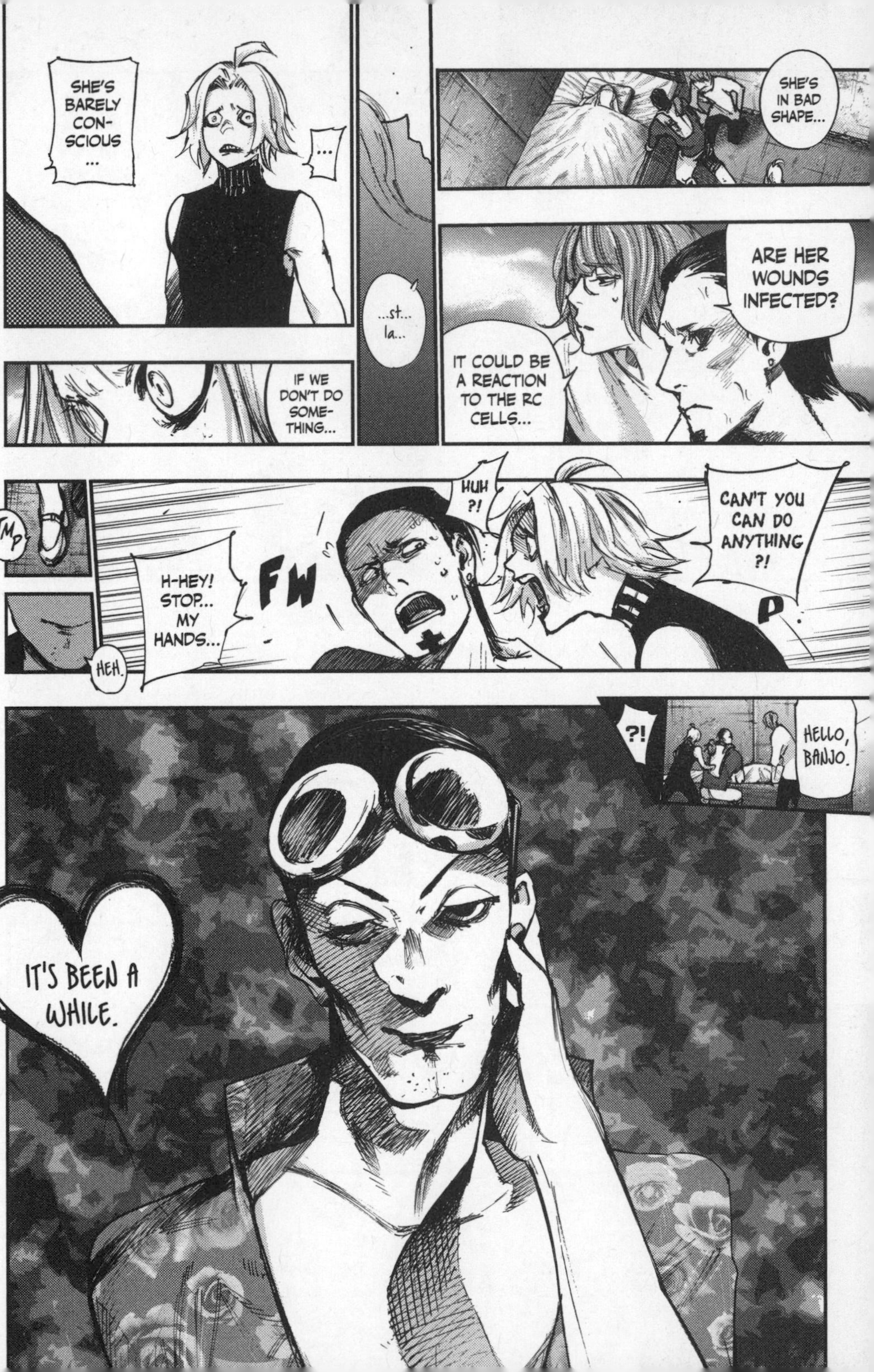
SHE'S IN BAD SHAPE...
ARE HER WOUNDS INFECTED?
IT COULD BE A REACTION TO THE RC CELLS...
...st... la...
SHE'S BARELY CON- SCIOUS ...
...
IF WE DON'T DO SOME- THING...
CAN'T YOU CAN DO ANYTHING ?!
P
HUH ?!
FW
H-HEY! STOP... MY HANDS...
TMP
HEH.
HELLO, BANJO.
?!
IT'S BEEN A WHILE.

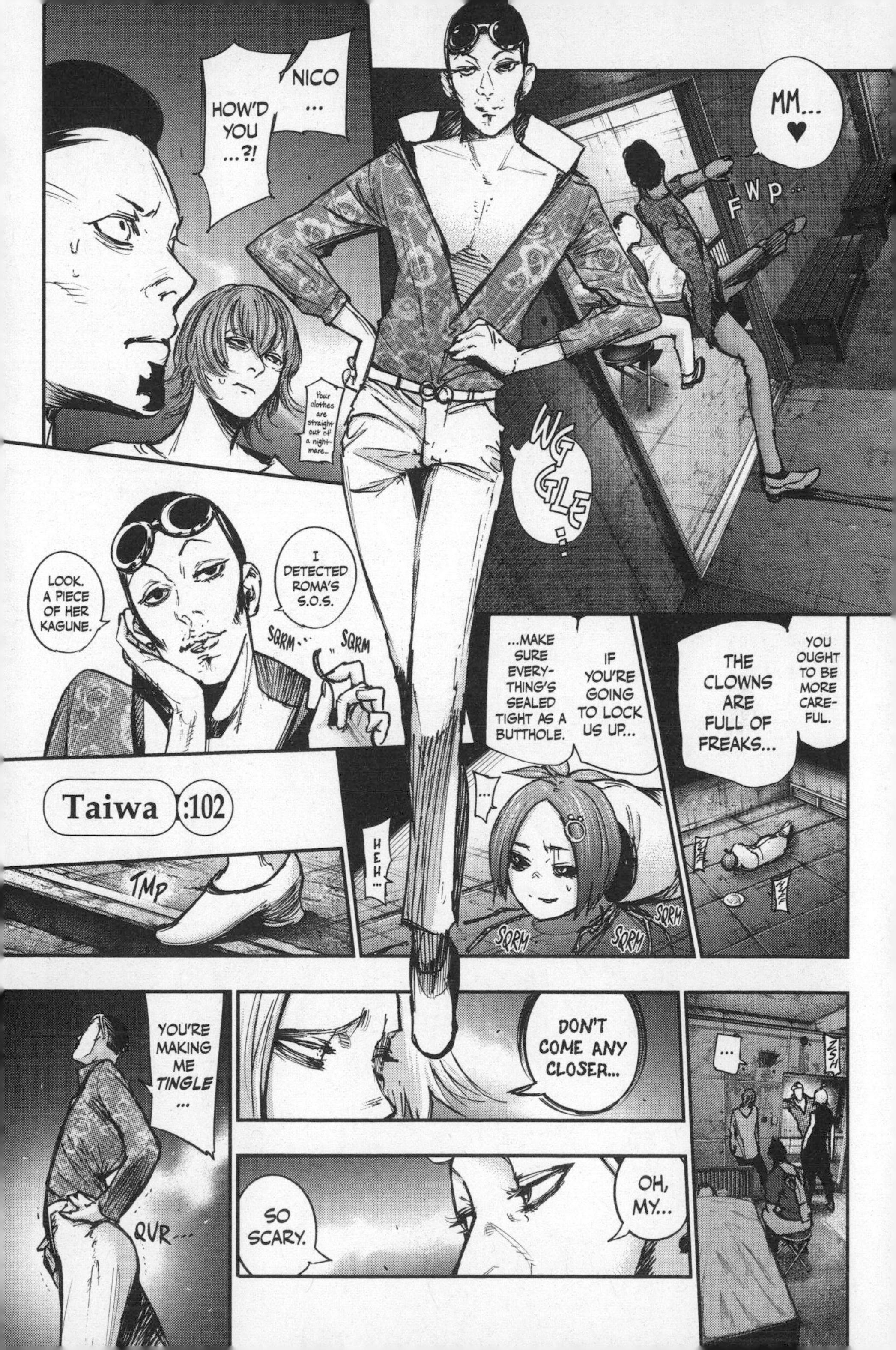
MM... ♥
FWP...
WGGLE...
NICO...
HOW'D YOU ...?!
Your clothes are straight out of a nightmare...
YOU OUGHT TO BE MORE CAREFUL.
THE CLOWNS ARE FULL OF FREAKS...
IF YOU'RE GOING TO LOCK US UP...
...MAKE SURE EVERYTHING'S SEALED TIGHT AS A BUTTHOLE.
...
HEH...
SQRM
SQRM
SQRM
I DETECTED ROMA'S S.O.S.
LOOK. A PIECE OF HER KAGUNE.
SQRM...
SQRM
Taiwa :102
TMP
...
ZSH
DON'T COME ANY CLOSER...
OH, MY...
SO SCARY.
YOU'RE MAKING ME TINGLE...
QVR...

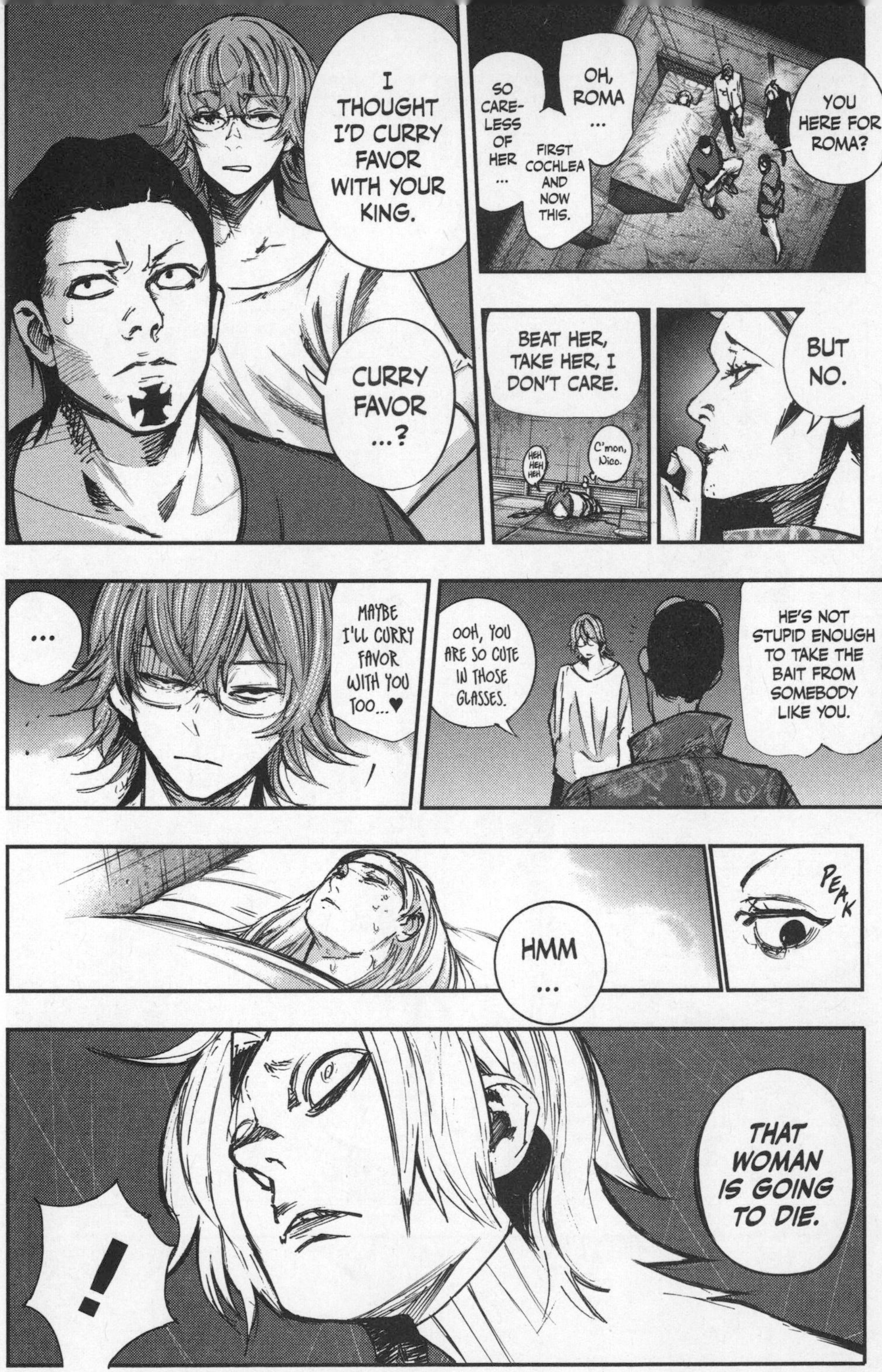

YOU HERE FOR ROMA?
OH, ROMA ...
SO CARE-LESS OF HER ...
FIRST COCHLEA AND NOW THIS.
BUT NO.
BEAT HER, TAKE HER, I DON'T CARE.
C'mon, Nico.
HEH HEH HEH
I THOUGHT I'D CURRY FAVOR WITH YOUR KING.
CURRY FAVOR ...?
HE'S NOT STUPID ENOUGH TO TAKE THE BAIT FROM SOMEBODY LIKE YOU.
OOH, YOU ARE SO CUTE IN THOSE GLASSES.
MAYBE I'LL CURRY FAVOR WITH YOU TOO...♥
...
PEAK
HMM ...
THAT WOMAN IS GOING TO DIE.
!

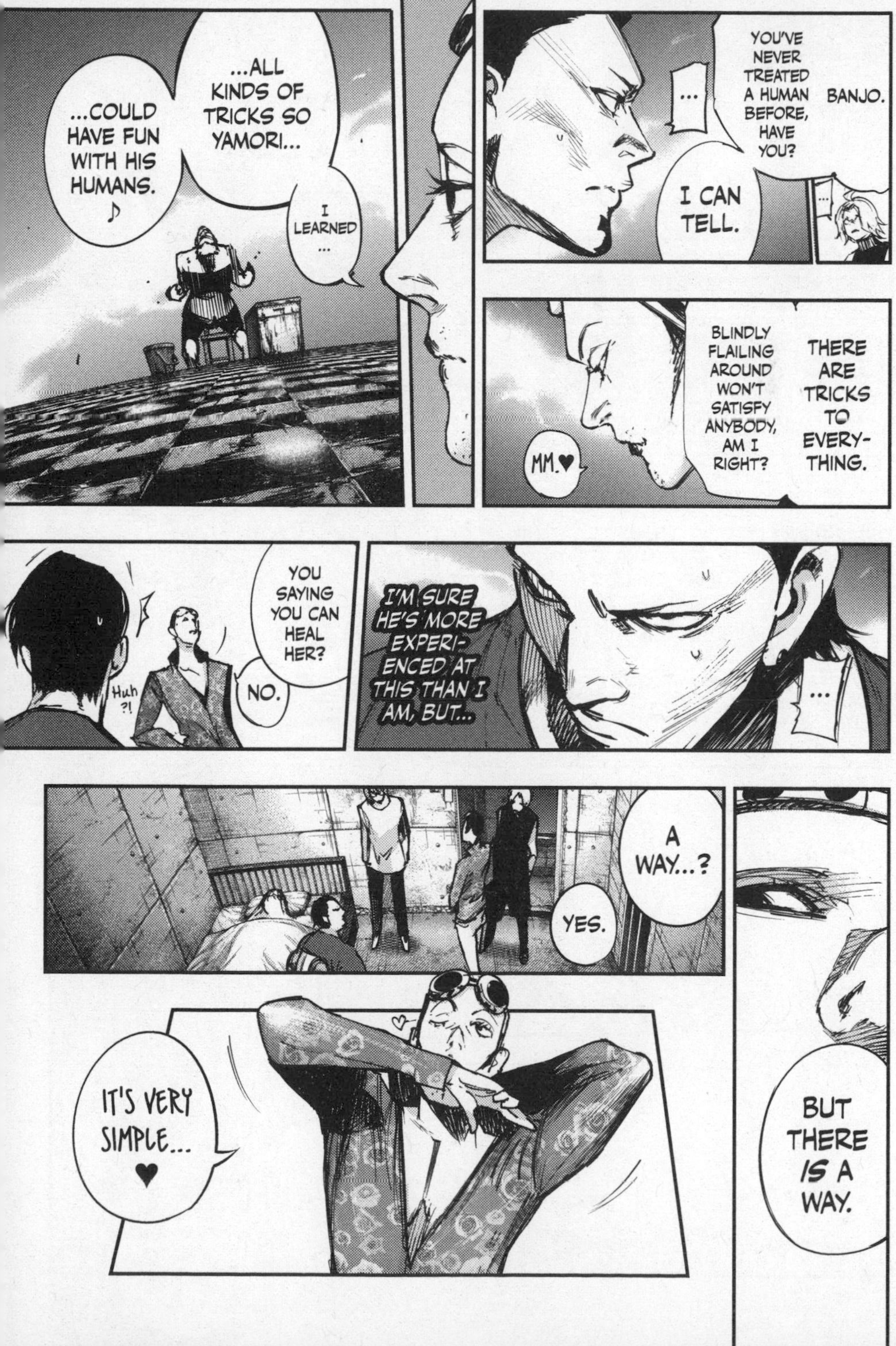

BANJO.
YOU'VE NEVER TREATED A HUMAN BEFORE, HAVE YOU?
...
I CAN TELL.
...
THERE ARE TRICKS TO EVERY-THING.
BLINDLY FLAILING AROUND WON'T SATISFY ANYBODY, AM I RIGHT?
MM.♥
I LEARNED...
...ALL KINDS OF TRICKS SO YAMORI...
...COULD HAVE FUN WITH HIS HUMANS. ♪
...
I'M SURE HE'S MORE EXPERI-ENCED AT THIS THAN I AM, BUT...
YOU SAYING YOU CAN HEAL HER?
NO.
Huh ?!
BUT THERE *IS* A WAY.
A WAY...?
YES.
IT'S VERY SIMPLE... ♥

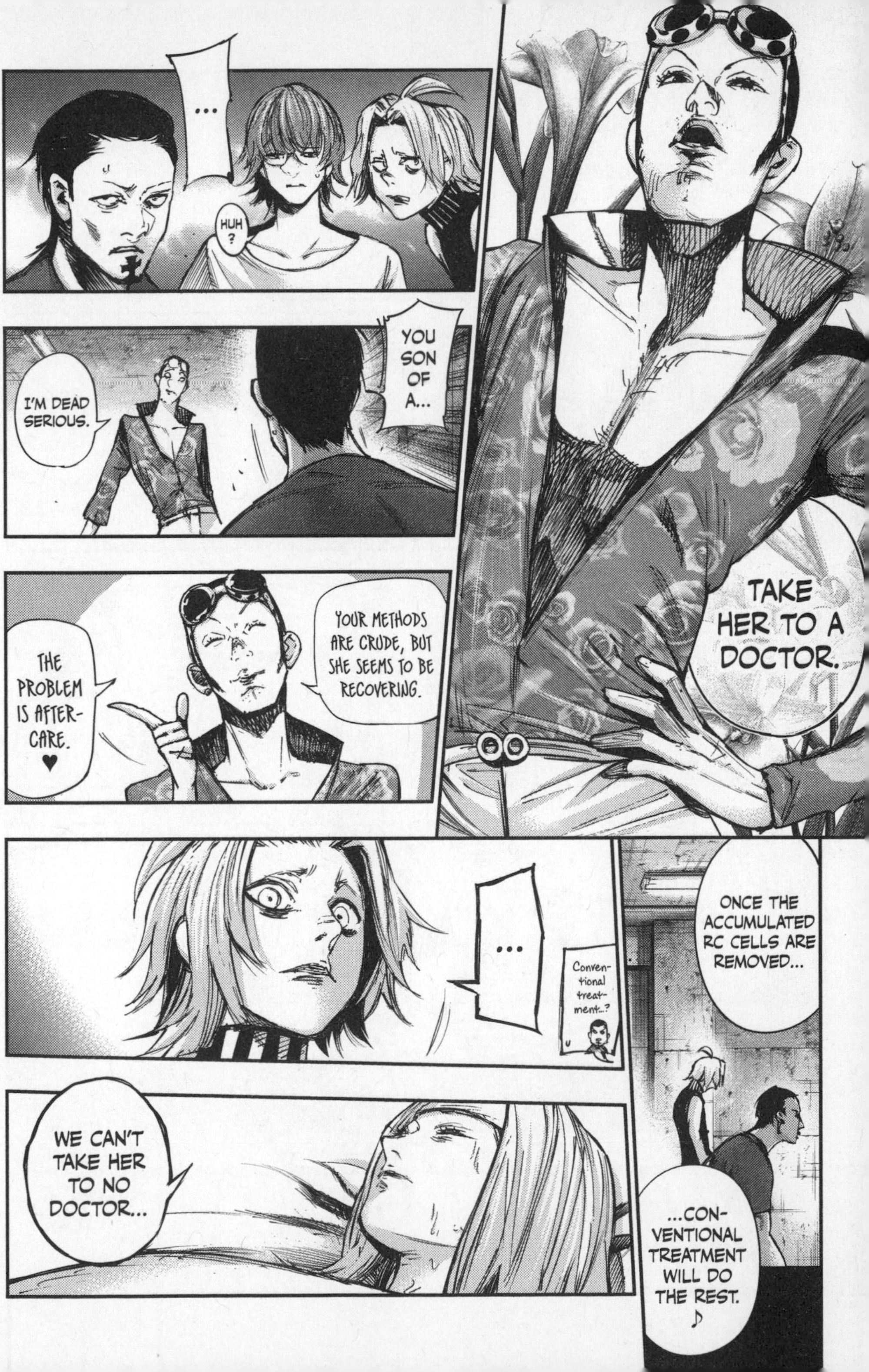
TAKE HER TO A DOCTOR.
...
HUH?
YOU SON OF A...
I'M DEAD SERIOUS.
YOUR METHODS ARE CRUDE, BUT SHE SEEMS TO BE RECOVERING.
THE PROBLEM IS AFTER-CARE. ♥
ONCE THE ACCUMULATED RC CELLS ARE REMOVED...
...CON-VENTIONAL TREATMENT WILL DO THE REST. ♪
...
Conven-tional treat-ment...?
WE CAN'T TAKE HER TO NO DOCTOR...

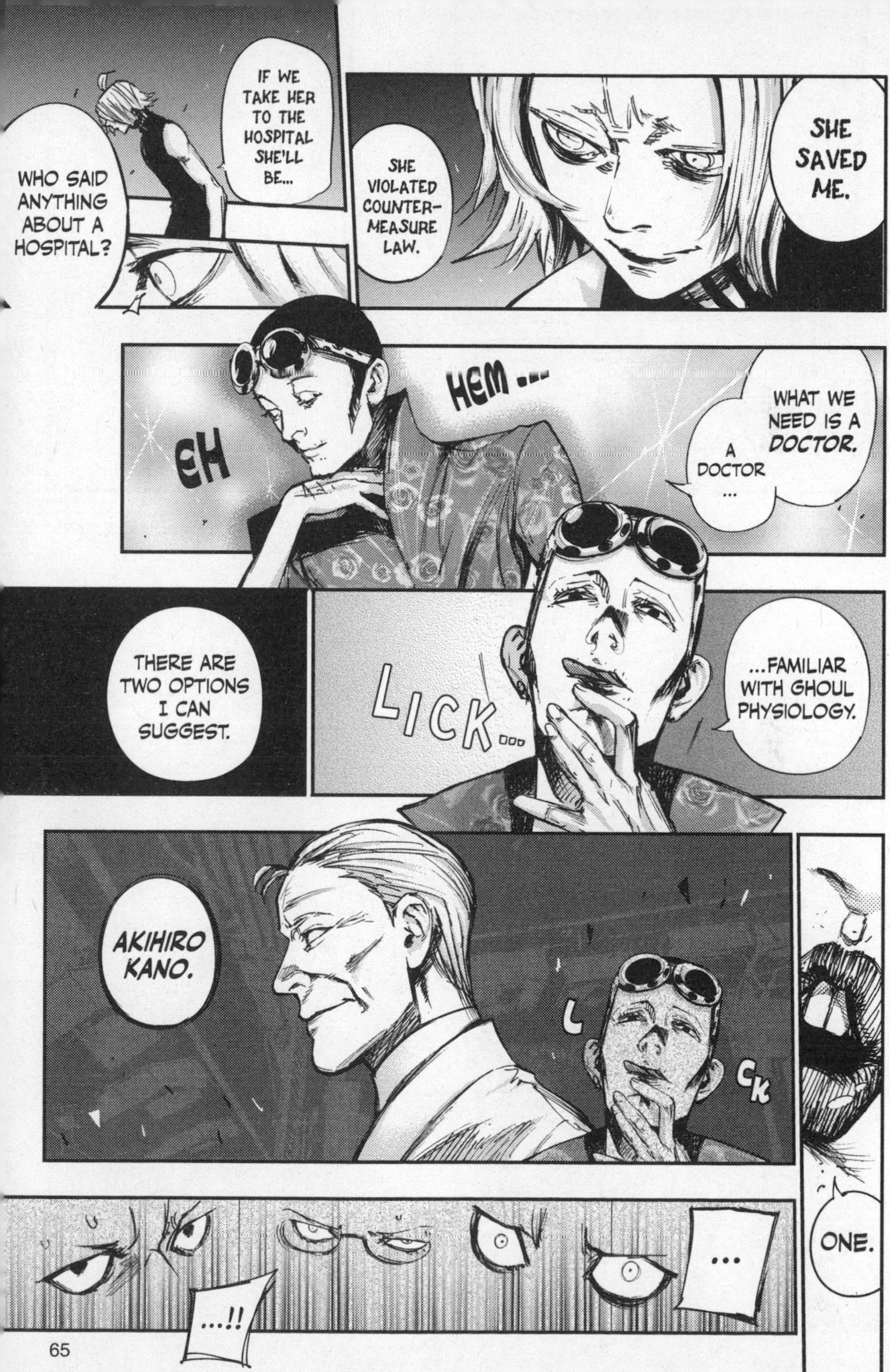
SHE SAVED ME.
SHE VIOLATED COUNTER-MEASURE LAW.
IF WE TAKE HER TO THE HOSPITAL SHE'LL BE...
WHO SAID ANYTHING ABOUT A HOSPITAL?
WHAT WE NEED IS A *DOCTOR.*
A DOCTOR ...
HEM ...
EH
...FAMILIAR WITH GHOUL PHYSIOLOGY.
LICK...
THERE ARE TWO OPTIONS I CAN SUGGEST.
ONE.
AKIHIRO KANO.
L
CK
...
...!!

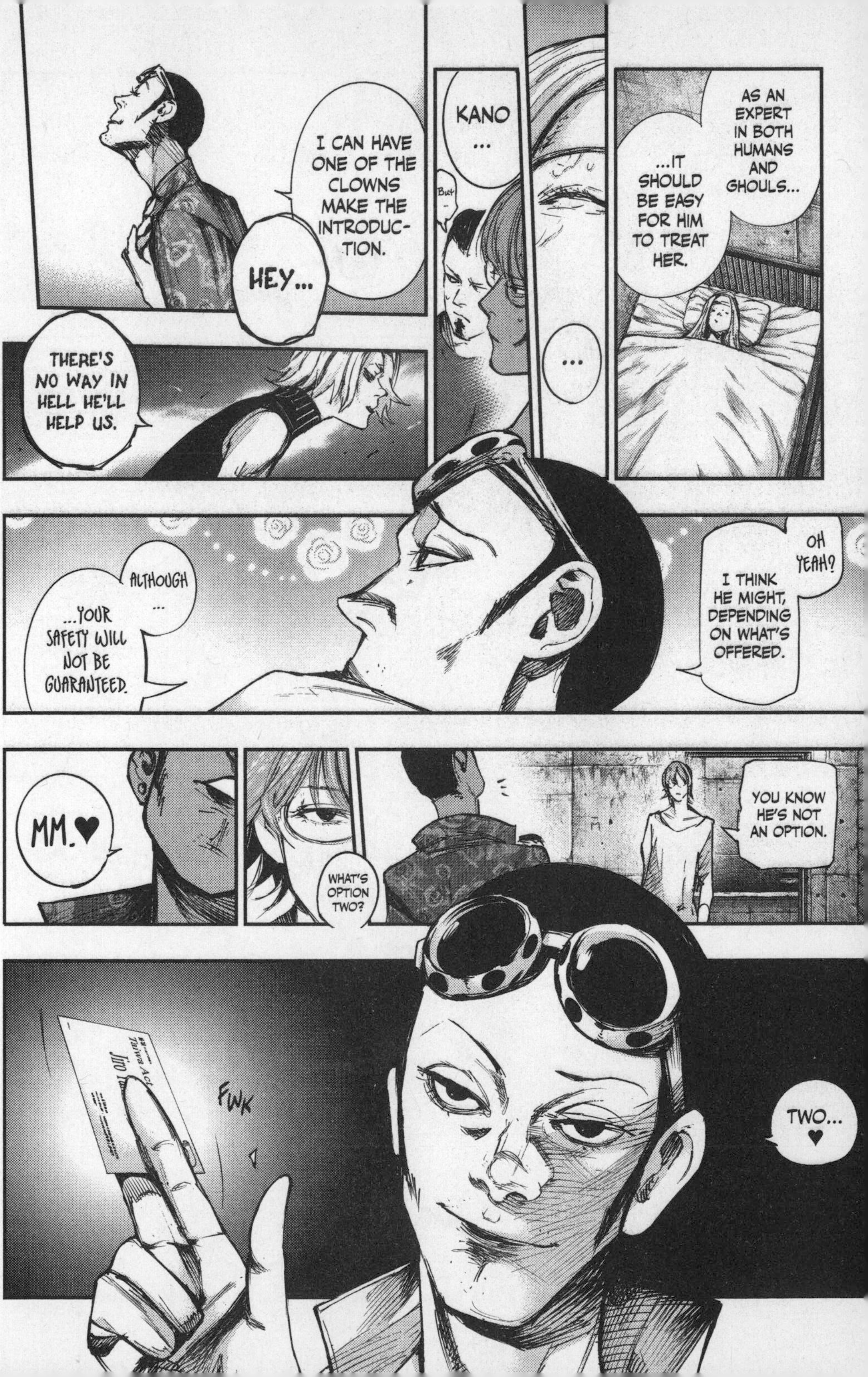
AS AN EXPERT IN BOTH HUMANS AND GHOULS...
...IT SHOULD BE EASY FOR HIM TO TREAT HER.
KANO ...
But ...
...
I CAN HAVE ONE OF THE CLOWNS MAKE THE INTRODUCTION.
HEY...
THERE'S NO WAY IN HELL HE'LL HELP US.
OH YEAH?
I THINK HE MIGHT, DEPENDING ON WHAT'S OFFERED.
ALTHOUGH ...
...YOUR SAFETY WILL NOT BE GUARANTEED.
YOU KNOW HE'S NOT AN OPTION.
WHAT'S OPTION TWO?
MM.♥
TWO... ♥
FWK

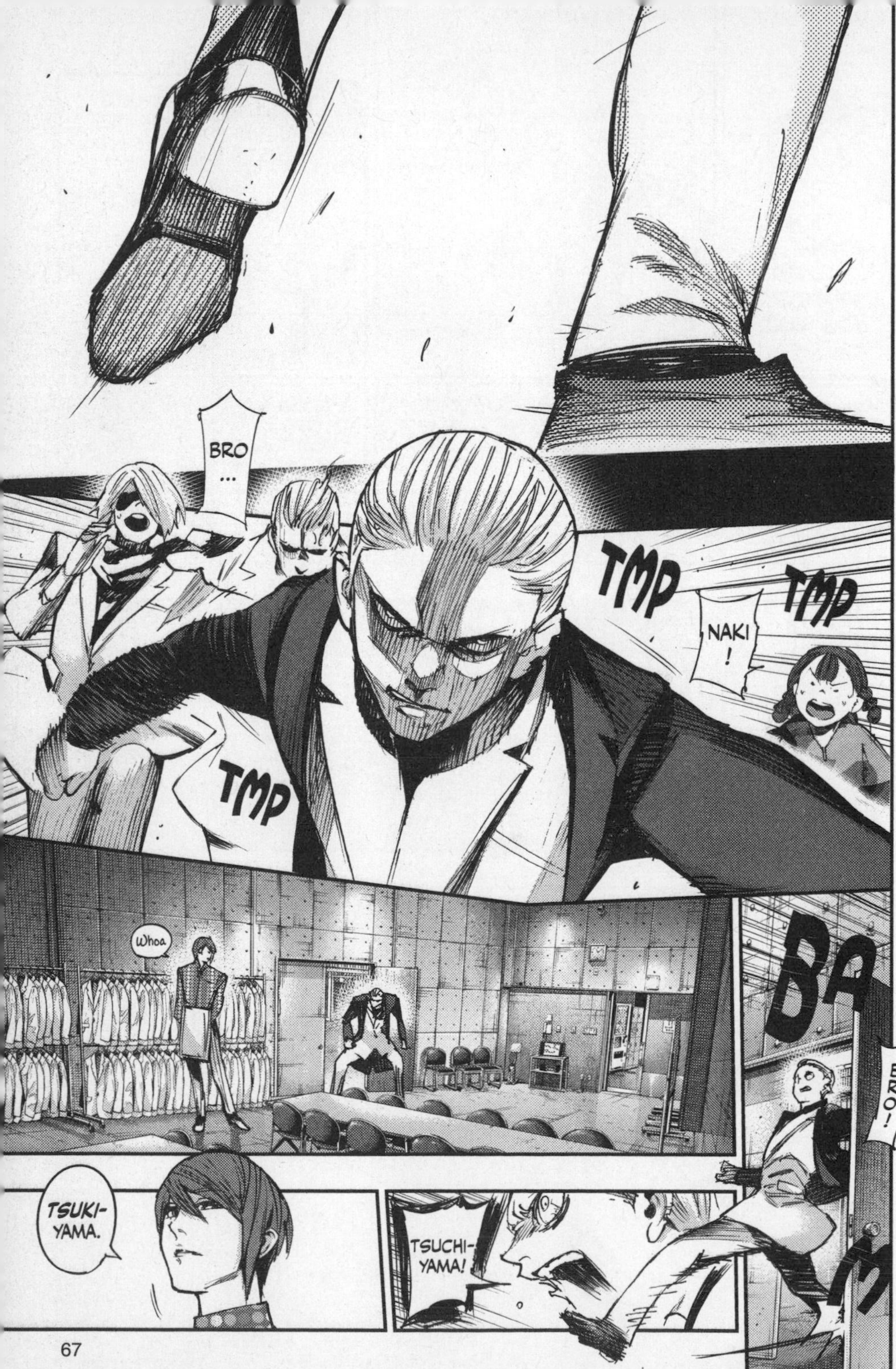
TMP
NAKI!
TMP
BRO...
TMP
BA
BRO!
M
Whoa
TSUCHI-YAMA!
TSUKI-YAMA.

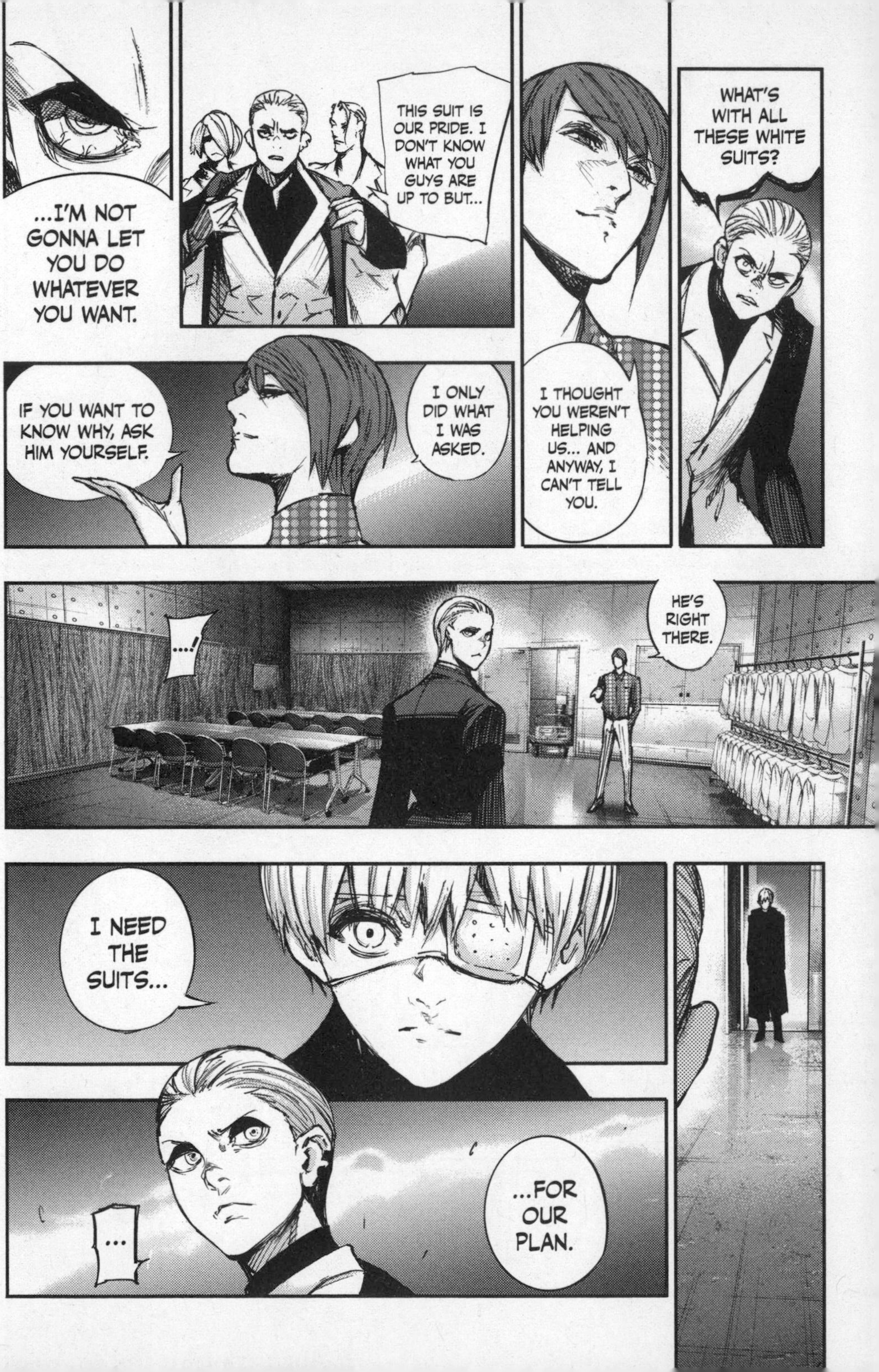
WHAT'S WITH ALL THESE WHITE SUITS?
I THOUGHT YOU WEREN'T HELPING US... AND ANYWAY, I CAN'T TELL YOU.
THIS SUIT IS OUR PRIDE. I DON'T KNOW WHAT YOU GUYS ARE UP TO BUT...
...I'M NOT GONNA LET YOU DO WHATEVER YOU WANT.
I ONLY DID WHAT I WAS ASKED.
IF YOU WANT TO KNOW WHY, ASK HIM YOURSELF.
HE'S RIGHT THERE.
...!
I NEED THE SUITS...
...FOR OUR PLAN.
...

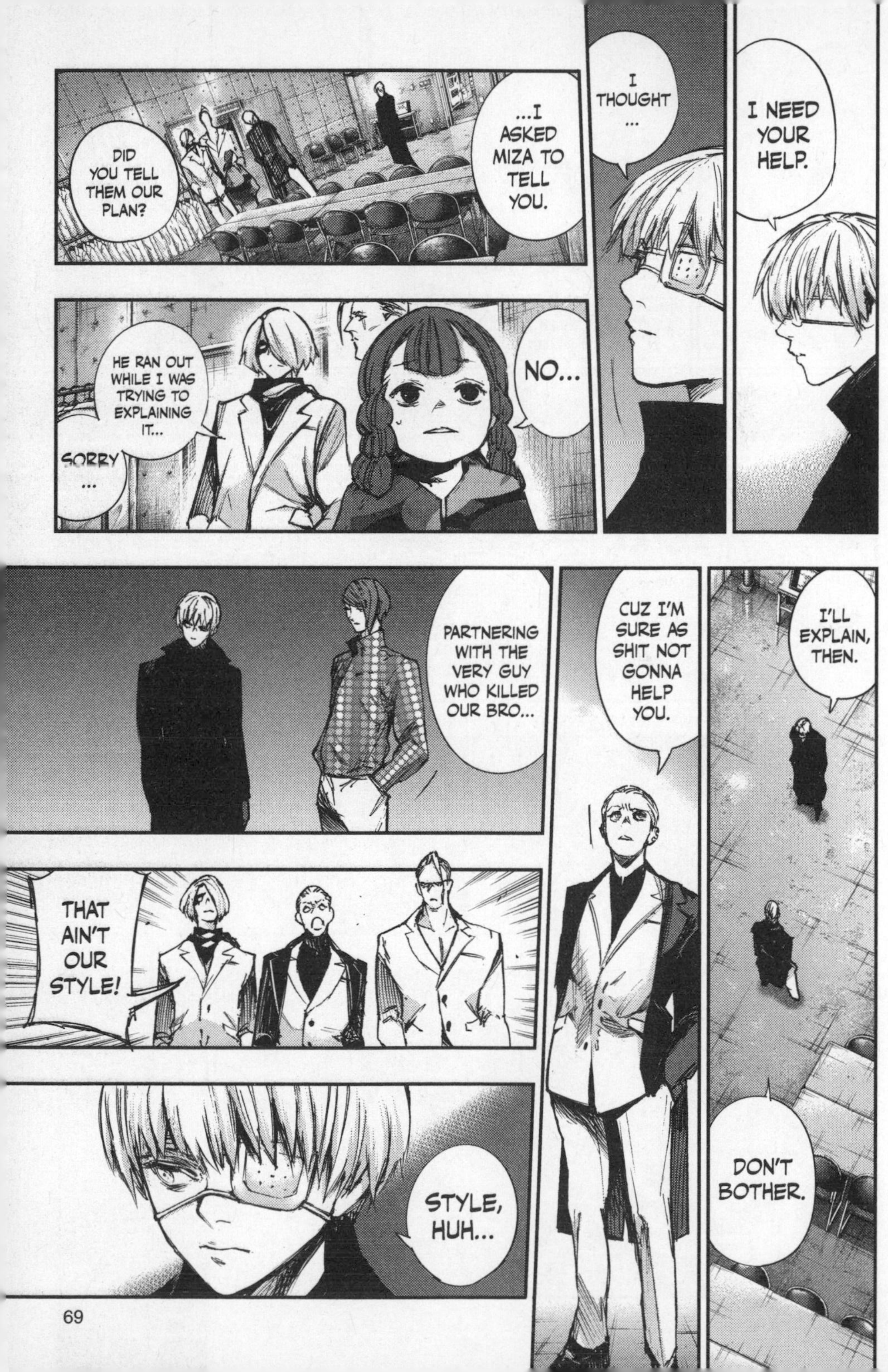
I NEED YOUR HELP.
I THOUGHT ...
...I ASKED MIZA TO TELL YOU.
DID YOU TELL THEM OUR PLAN?
NO...
HE RAN OUT WHILE I WAS TRYING TO EXPLAINING IT...
SORRY ...
I'LL EXPLAIN, THEN.
DON'T BOTHER.
CUZ I'M SURE AS SHIT NOT GONNA HELP YOU.
PARTNERING WITH THE VERY GUY WHO KILLED OUR BRO...
THAT AIN'T OUR STYLE!
STYLE, HUH...

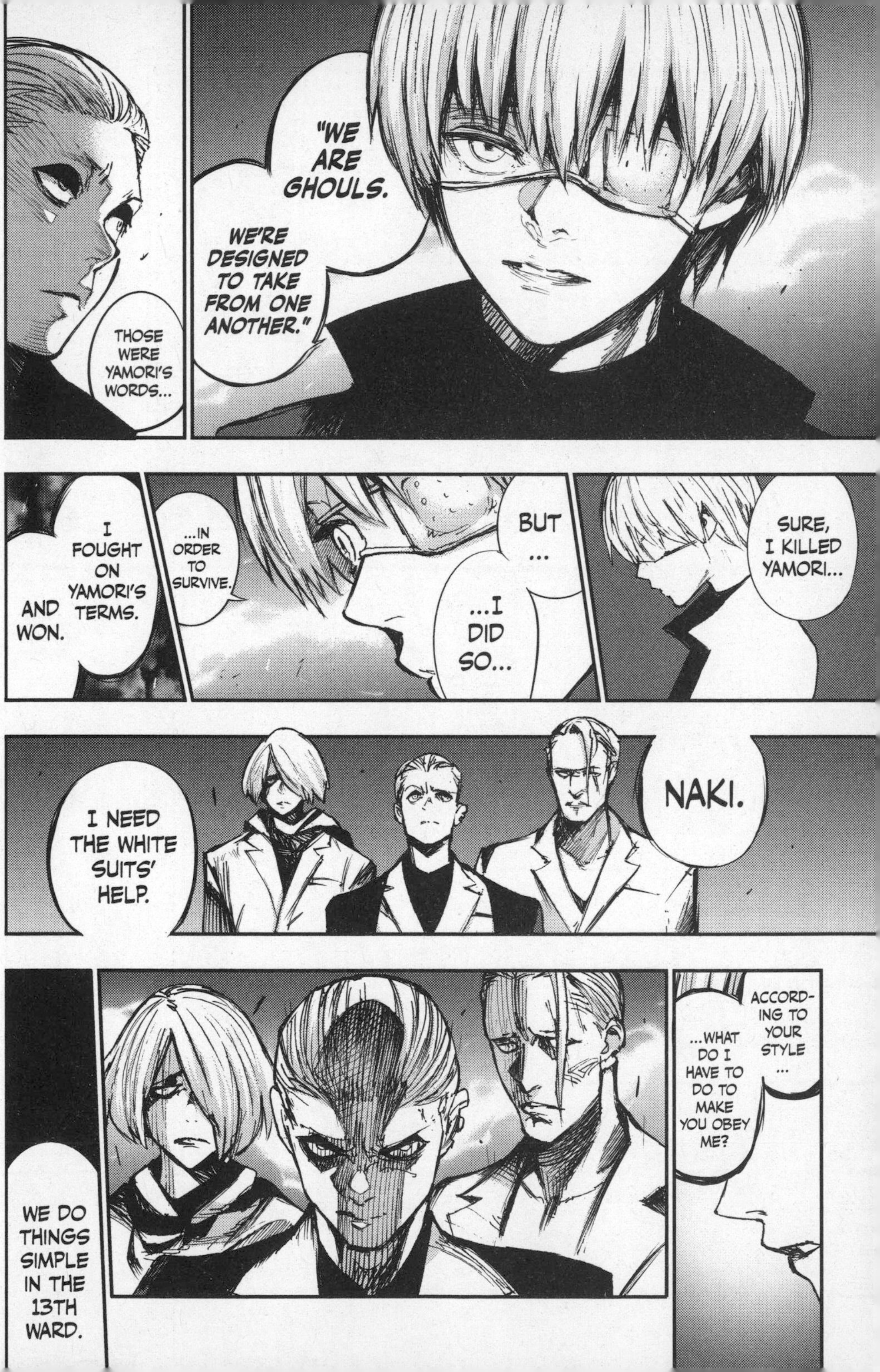
"WE ARE GHOULS.
WE'RE DESIGNED TO TAKE FROM ONE ANOTHER."
THOSE WERE YAMORI'S WORDS...
SURE, I KILLED YAMORI...
BUT ...
...I DID SO...
...IN ORDER TO SURVIVE.
I FOUGHT ON YAMORI'S TERMS.
AND WON.
NAKI.
I NEED THE WHITE SUITS' HELP.
ACCORD-ING TO YOUR STYLE ...
...WHAT DO I HAVE TO DO TO MAKE YOU OBEY ME?
WE DO THINGS SIMPLE IN THE 13TH WARD.

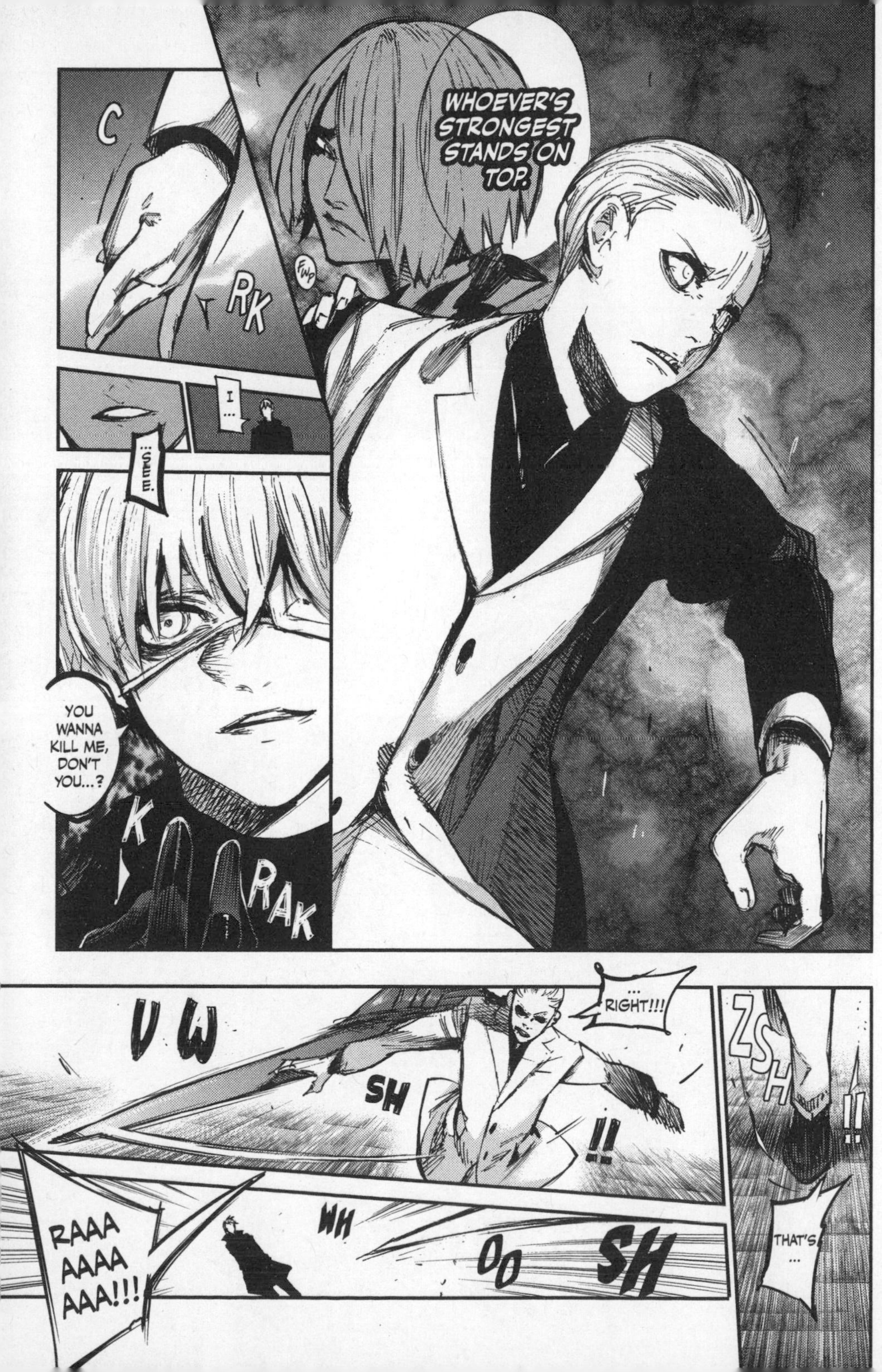
WHOEVER'S STRONGEST STANDS ON TOP.
FWP
C
RK
I ...
...SEE.
YOU WANNA KILL ME, DON'T YOU...?
K
RAK
ZSH
!!
THAT'S ...
... RIGHT!!!
VW
SH
!!
RAAA AAAA AAA!!!
WH
OO
SH

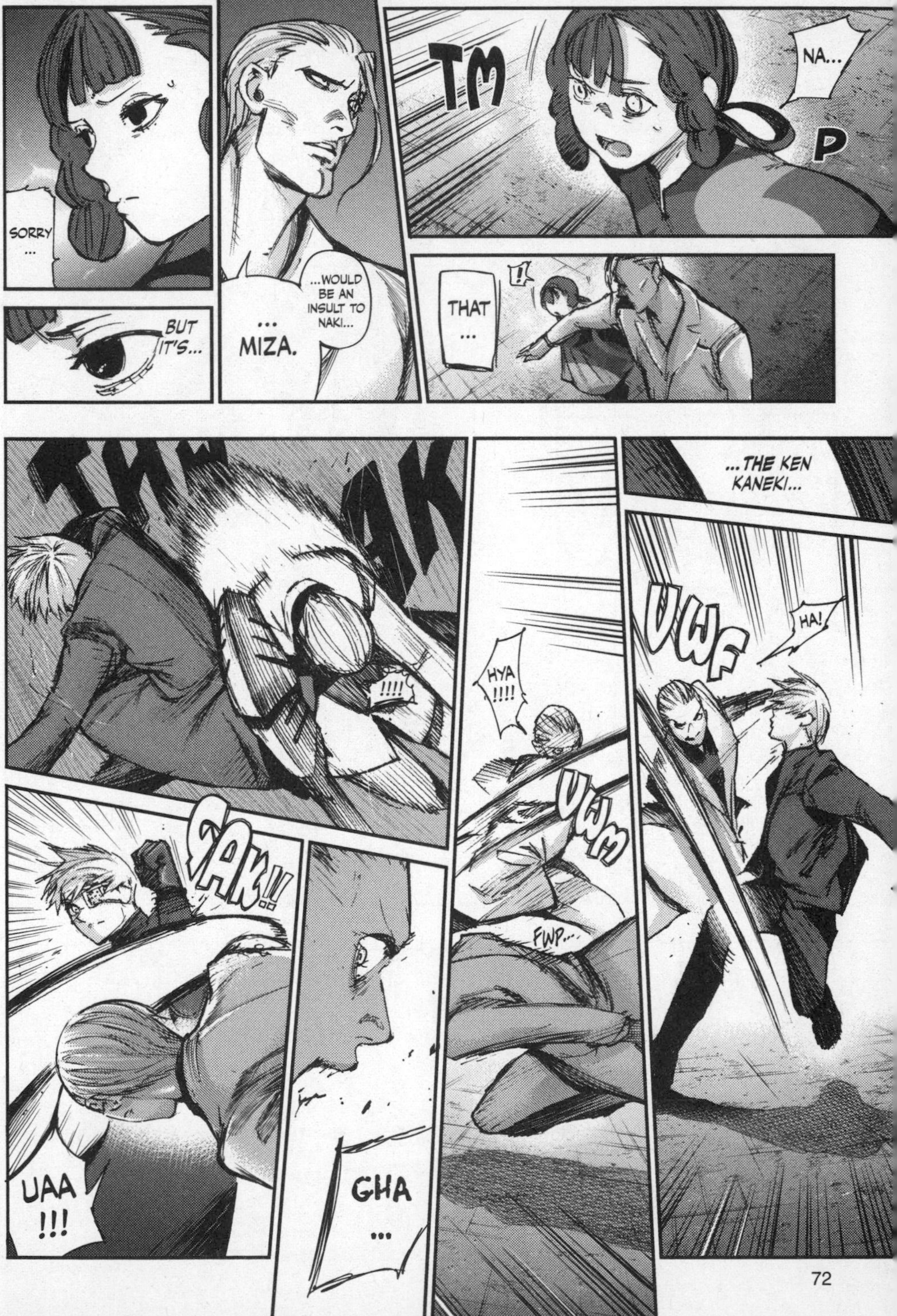
TM
NA...
P
THAT
...
!
...WOULD BE AN INSULT TO NAKI...
...
MIZA.
SORRY
...
BUT IT'S...
...THE KEN KANEKI...
UWF
HA!
HYA
!!!!
UWM
FWP...
THWAK
!!!!
GHA
...
GAK!!
UAA
!!!

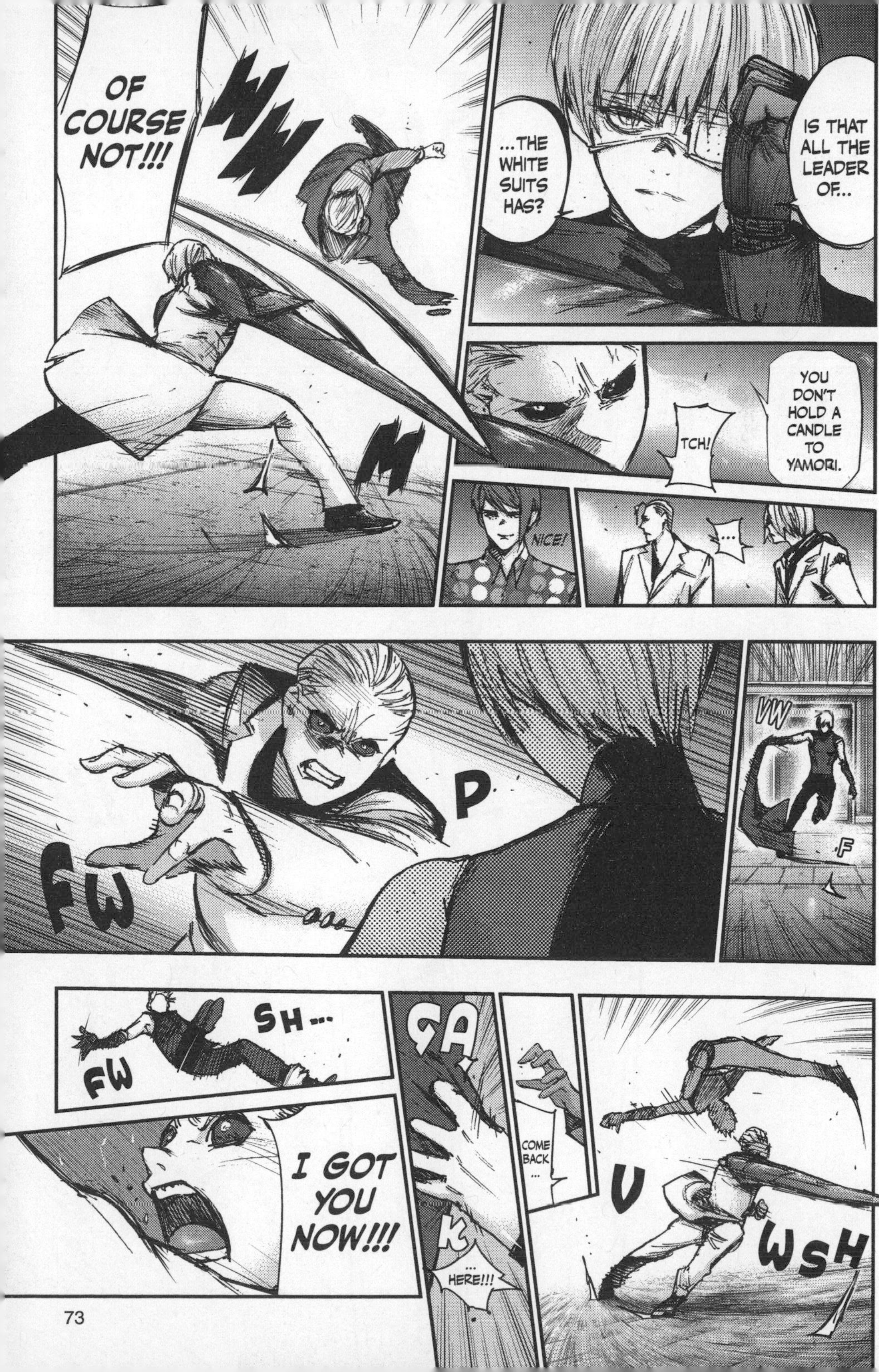

IS THAT ALL THE LEADER OF...
...THE WHITE SUITS HAS?
YOU DON'T HOLD A CANDLE TO YAMORI.
TCH!
...
NICE!
OF COURSE NOT!!!
WWW
M
VW
F
P
FW
U
WSH
COME BACK...
GA
K
...HERE!!!
SH...
FW
I GOT YOU NOW!!!

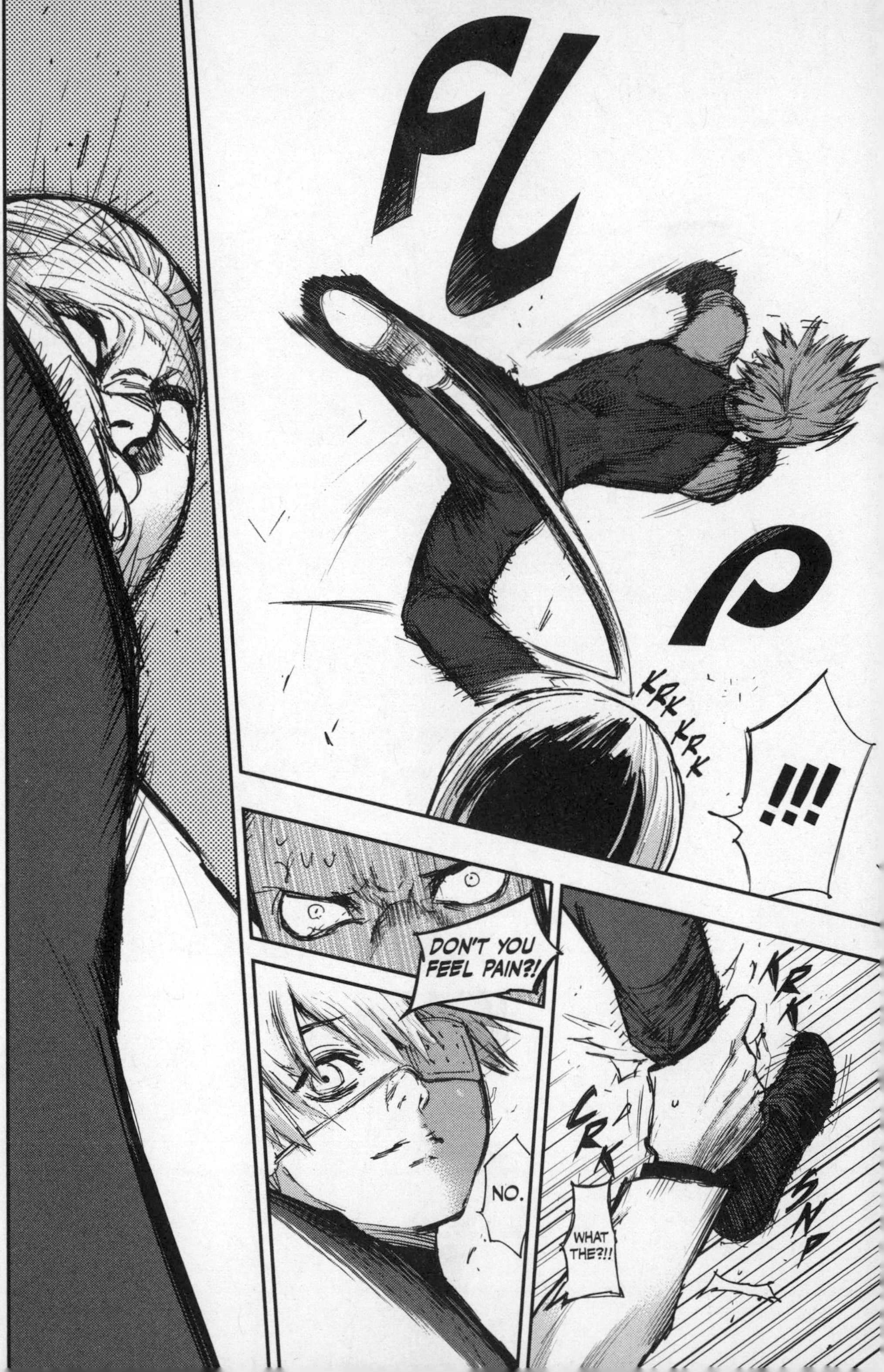
FLIP
KRK KRK
!!!
KRK
CRK
SNAP
WHAT THE?!!
DON'T YOU FEEL PAIN?!
NO.

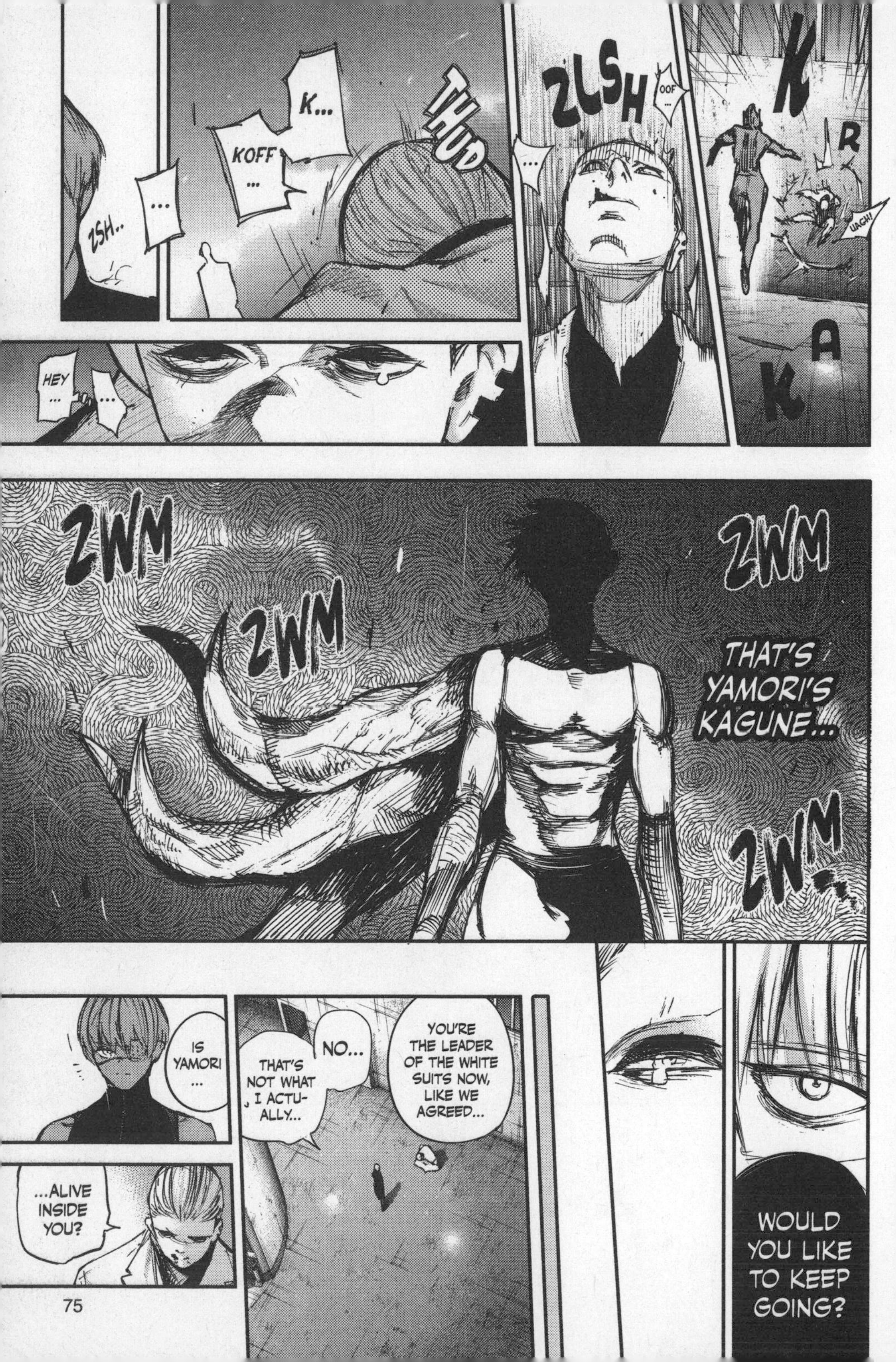

K
R
UAGH!
A
K
ZLSH
OOF ...
...
THUD
K...
KOFF ...
...
ZSH..
HEY ...
...
ZWM
THAT'S YAMORI'S KAGUNE...
ZWM
ZWM
ZWM
WOULD YOU LIKE TO KEEP GOING?
YOU'RE THE LEADER OF THE WHITE SUITS NOW, LIKE WE AGREED...
NO...
THAT'S NOT WHAT I ACTU-ALLY...
IS YAMORI ...
...ALIVE INSIDE YOU?

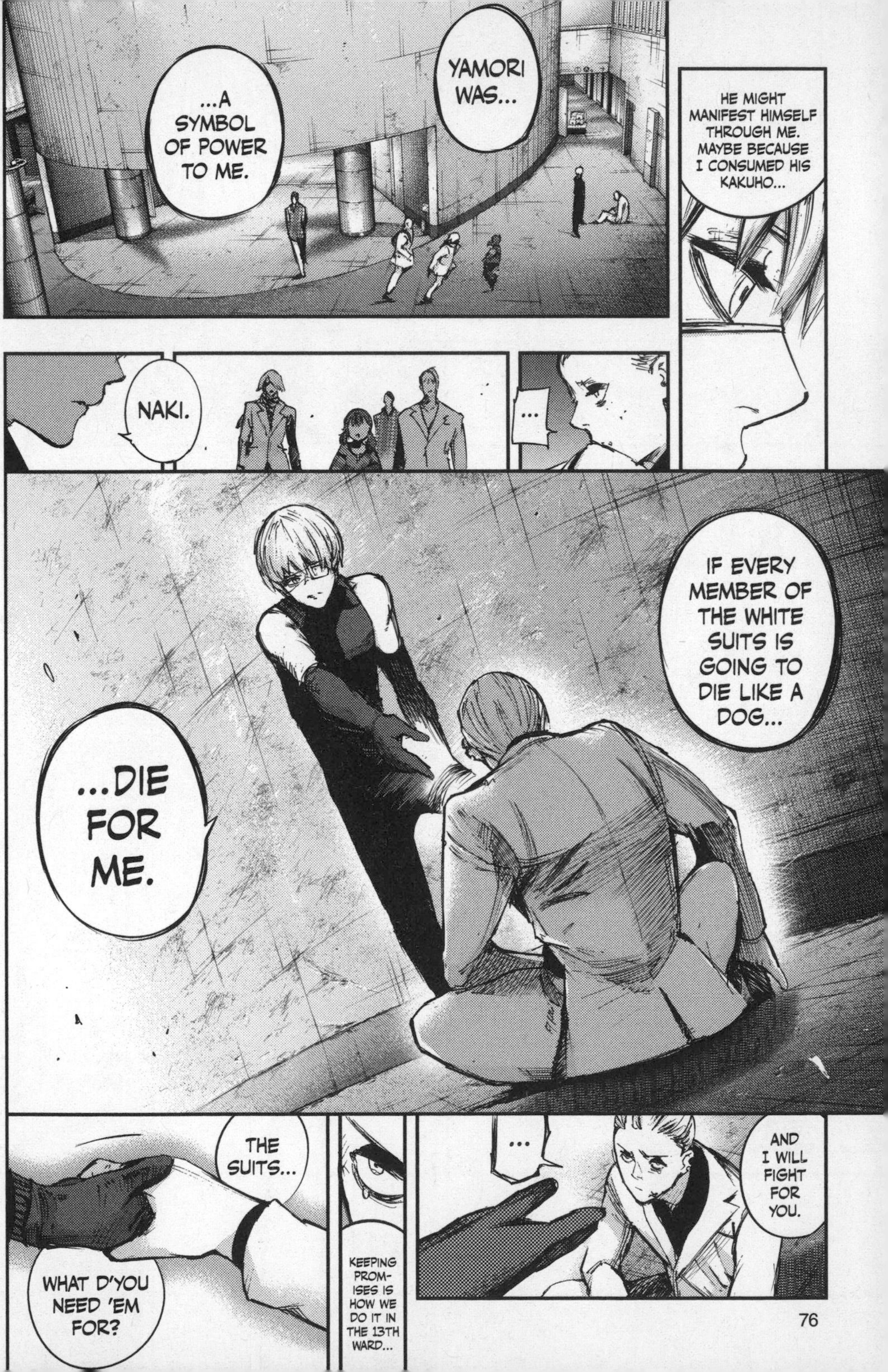
HE MIGHT MANIFEST HIMSELF THROUGH ME. MAYBE BECAUSE I CONSUMED HIS KAKUHO...
YAMORI WAS...
...A SYMBOL OF POWER TO ME.
...
NAKI.
IF EVERY MEMBER OF THE WHITE SUITS IS GOING TO DIE LIKE A DOG...
...DIE FOR ME.
AND I WILL FIGHT FOR YOU.
...
KEEPING PROM-ISES IS HOW WE DO IT IN THE 13TH WARD...
THE SUITS...
WHAT D'YOU NEED 'EM FOR?

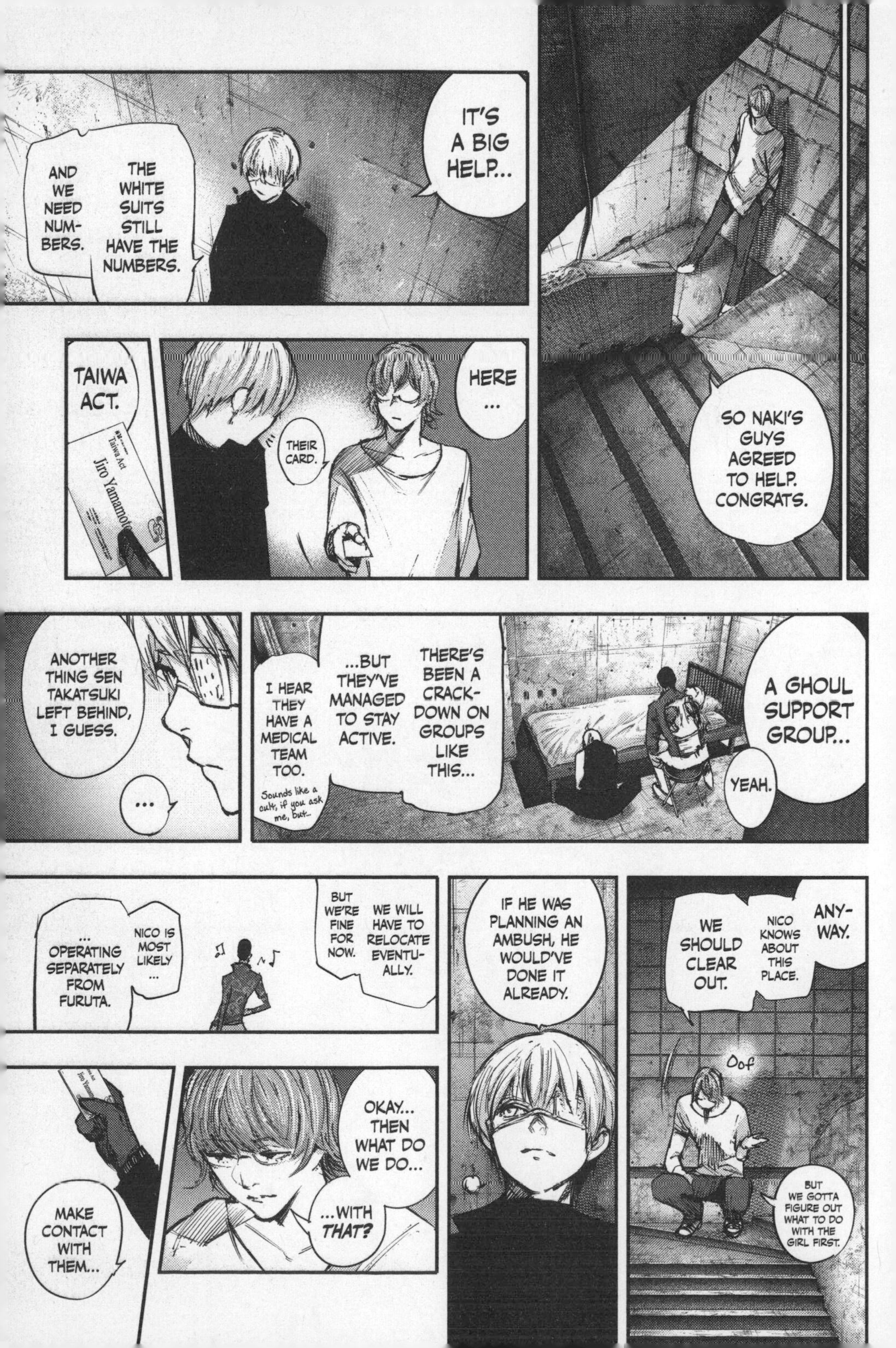
SO NAKI'S GUYS AGREED TO HELP. CONGRATS.
IT'S A BIG HELP...
THE WHITE SUITS STILL HAVE THE NUMBERS.
AND WE NEED NUM-BERS.
HERE...
THEIR CARD.
Taiwa Act
Jiro Yamamoto
TAIWA ACT.
A GHOUL SUPPORT GROUP...
YEAH.
THERE'S BEEN A CRACK-DOWN ON GROUPS LIKE THIS...
...BUT THEY'VE MANAGED TO STAY ACTIVE.
I HEAR THEY HAVE A MEDICAL TEAM TOO.
Sounds like a cult, if you ask me, but...
ANOTHER THING SEN TAKATSUKI LEFT BEHIND, I GUESS.
...
ANY-WAY.
NICO KNOWS ABOUT THIS PLACE.
WE SHOULD CLEAR OUT.
Oof
BUT WE GOTTA FIGURE OUT WHAT TO DO WITH THE GIRL FIRST.
IF HE WAS PLANNING AN AMBUSH, HE WOULD'VE DONE IT ALREADY.
WE WILL HAVE TO RELOCATE EVENTU-ALLY.
BUT WE'RE FINE FOR NOW.
NICO IS MOST LIKELY...
...OPERATING SEPARATELY FROM FURUTA.
OKAY... THEN WHAT DO WE DO...
...WITH THAT?
MAKE CONTACT WITH THEM...

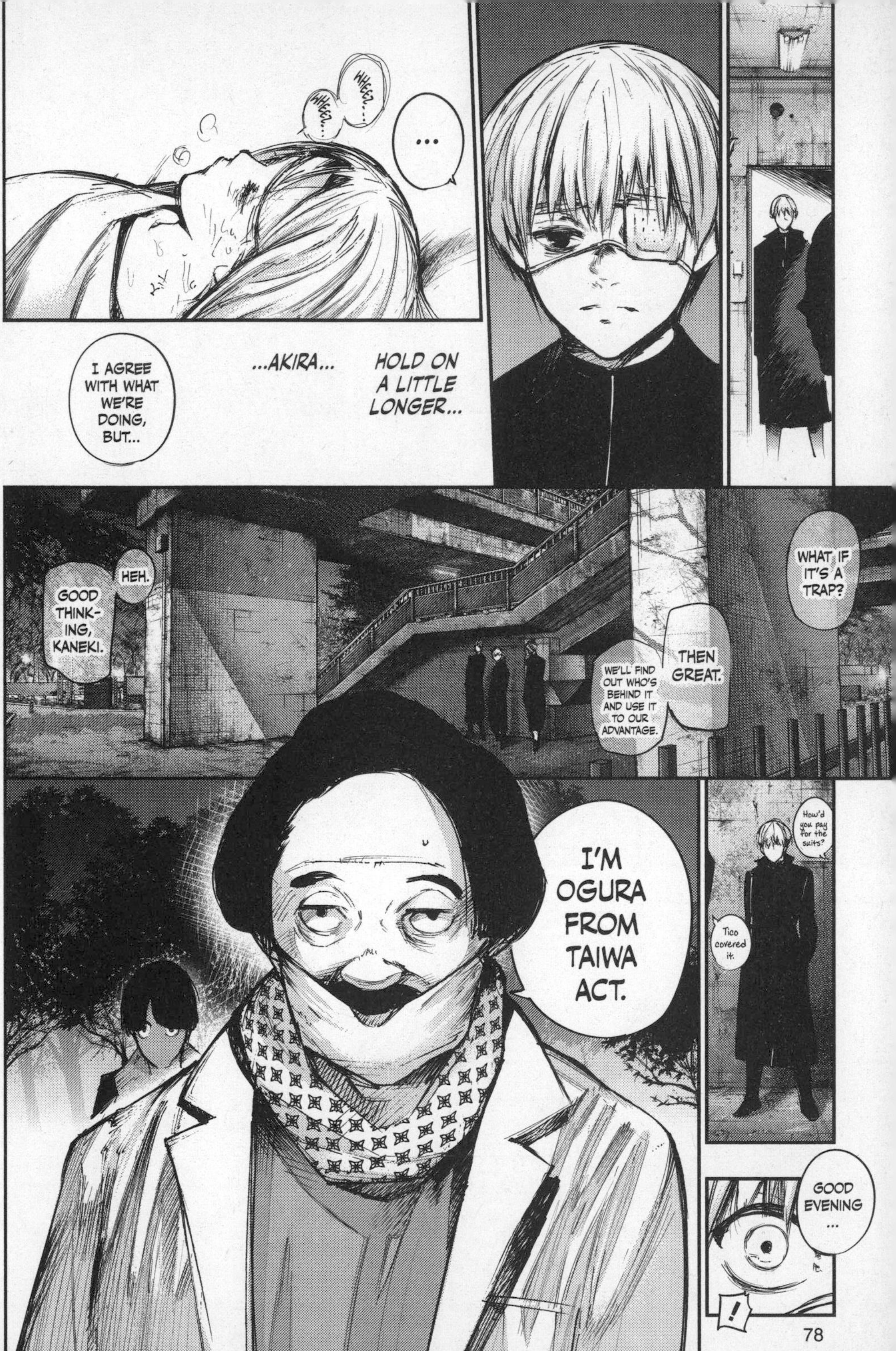
...
WHEEZ...
WHEEZ...
HOLD ON A LITTLE LONGER...
...AKIRA...
I AGREE WITH WHAT WE'RE DOING, BUT...
WHAT IF IT'S A TRAP?
THEN GREAT.
WE'LL FIND OUT WHO'S BEHIND IT AND USE IT TO OUR ADVANTAGE.
HEH.
GOOD THINKING, KANEKI.
How'd you pay for the suits?
Tico covered it.
GOOD EVENING...
!
I'M OGURA FROM TAIWA ACT.

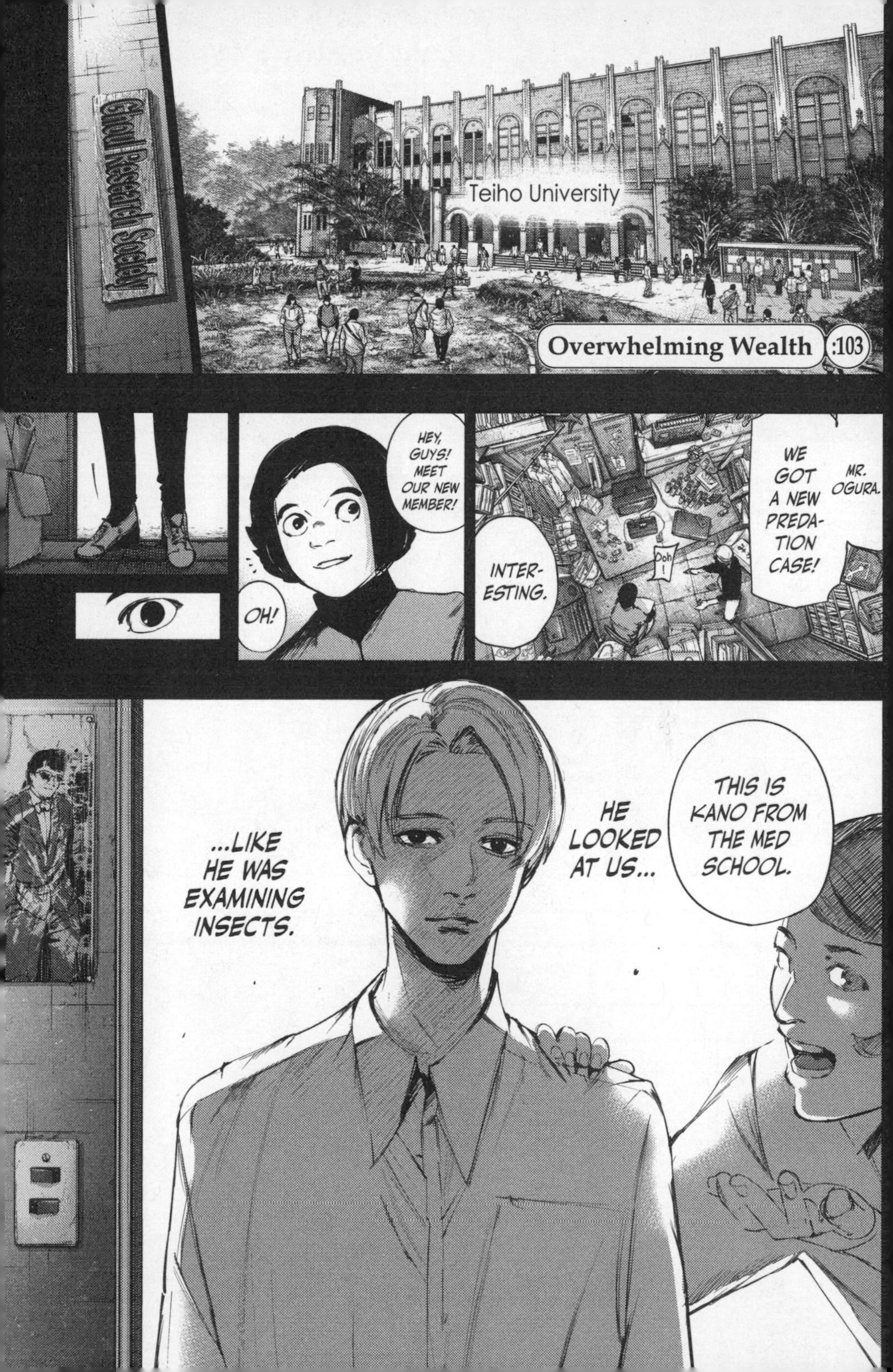
Teiho University
Overwhelming Wealth :103
Ghoul Research Society
MR. OGURA.
WE GOT A NEW PREDATION CASE!
Ooh!
INTERESTING.
HEY, GUYS! MEET OUR NEW MEMBER!
OH!
THIS IS KANO FROM THE MED SCHOOL.
HE LOOKED AT US...
...LIKE HE WAS EXAMINING INSECTS.

Overwhelming Wealth :103

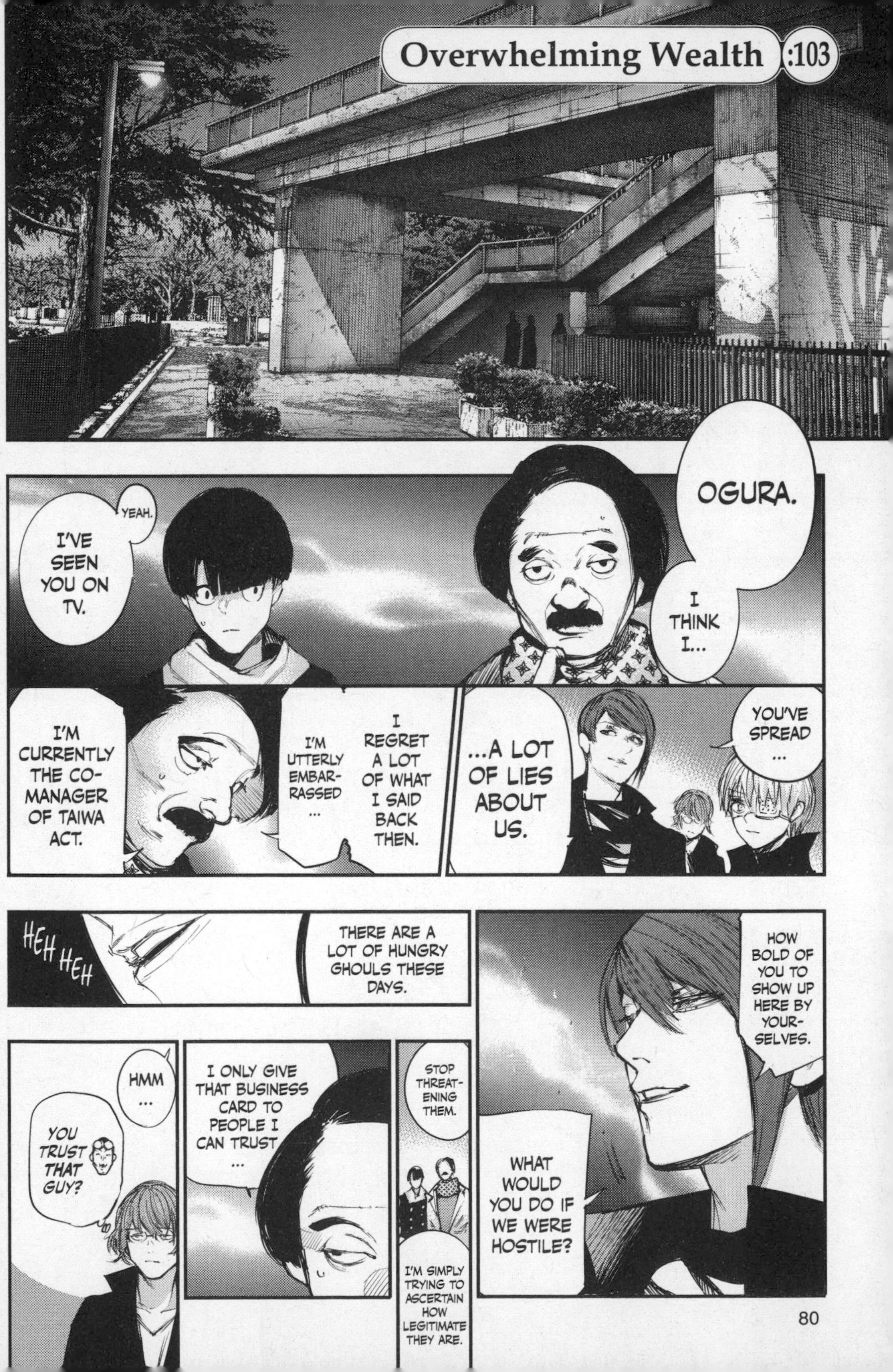

OGURA.
I THINK I...
YEAH.
I'VE SEEN YOU ON TV.
YOU'VE SPREAD ...
...A LOT OF LIES ABOUT US.
I REGRET A LOT OF WHAT I SAID BACK THEN.
I'M UTTERLY EMBARRASSED ...
I'M CURRENTLY THE CO-MANAGER OF TAIWA ACT.
HOW BOLD OF YOU TO SHOW UP HERE BY YOURSELVES.
WHAT WOULD YOU DO IF WE WERE HOSTILE?
THERE ARE A LOT OF HUNGRY GHOULS THESE DAYS.
HEH HEH
STOP THREATENING THEM.
I'M SIMPLY TRYING TO ASCERTAIN HOW LEGITIMATE THEY ARE.
I ONLY GIVE THAT BUSINESS CARD TO PEOPLE I CAN TRUST ...
HMM ...
YOU TRUST THAT GUY?

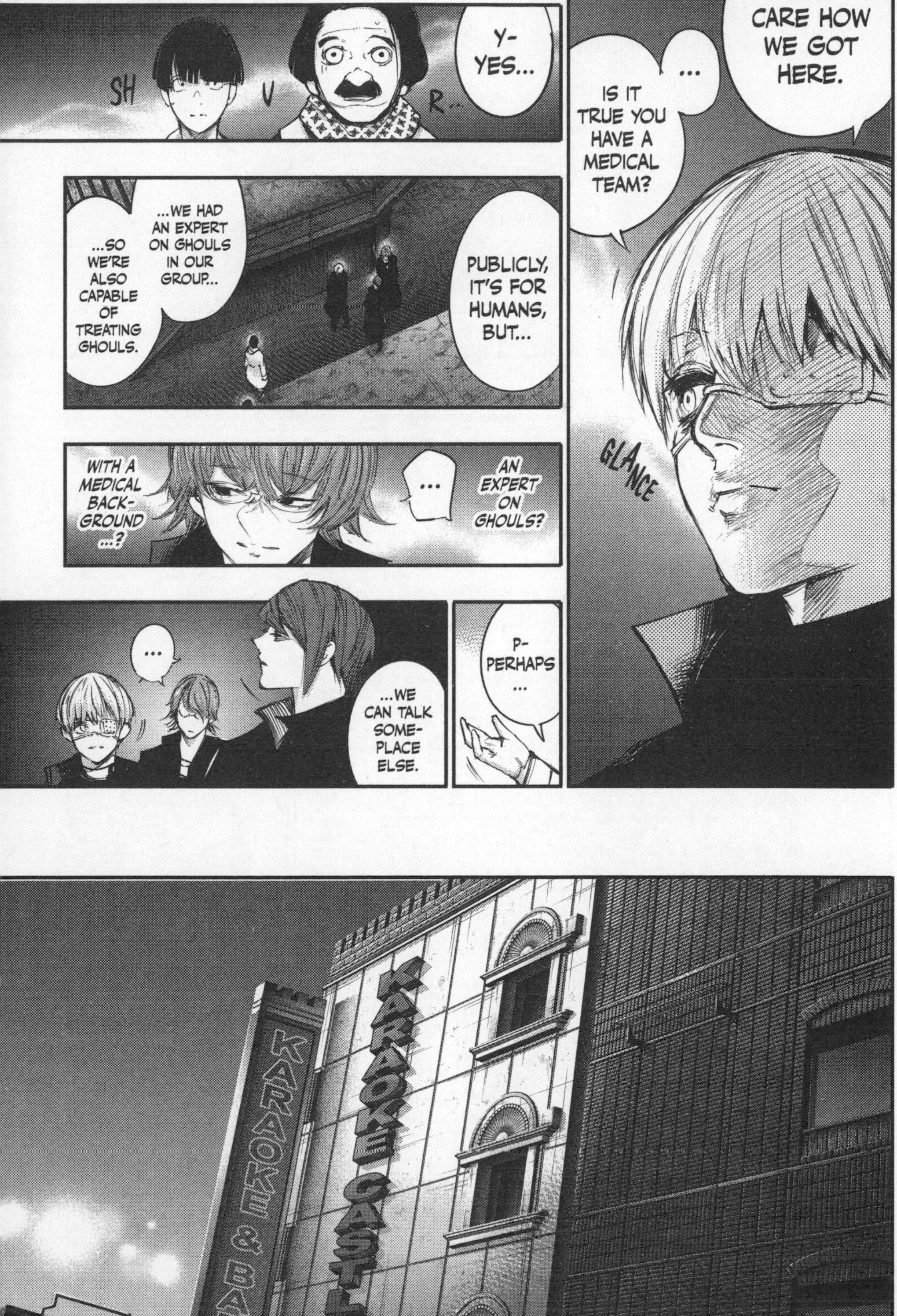
I DON'T CARE HOW WE GOT HERE.
...
IS IT TRUE YOU HAVE A MEDICAL TEAM?
GLANCE
Y- YES...
SHUVR...
PUBLICLY, IT'S FOR HUMANS, BUT...
...WE HAD AN EXPERT ON GHOULS IN OUR GROUP...
...SO WE'RE ALSO CAPABLE OF TREATING GHOULS.
AN EXPERT ON GHOULS?
...
WITH A MEDICAL BACK-GROUND ...?
P-PERHAPS ...
...WE CAN TALK SOME-PLACE ELSE.
...
KARAOKE CASTL
KARAOKE & BA

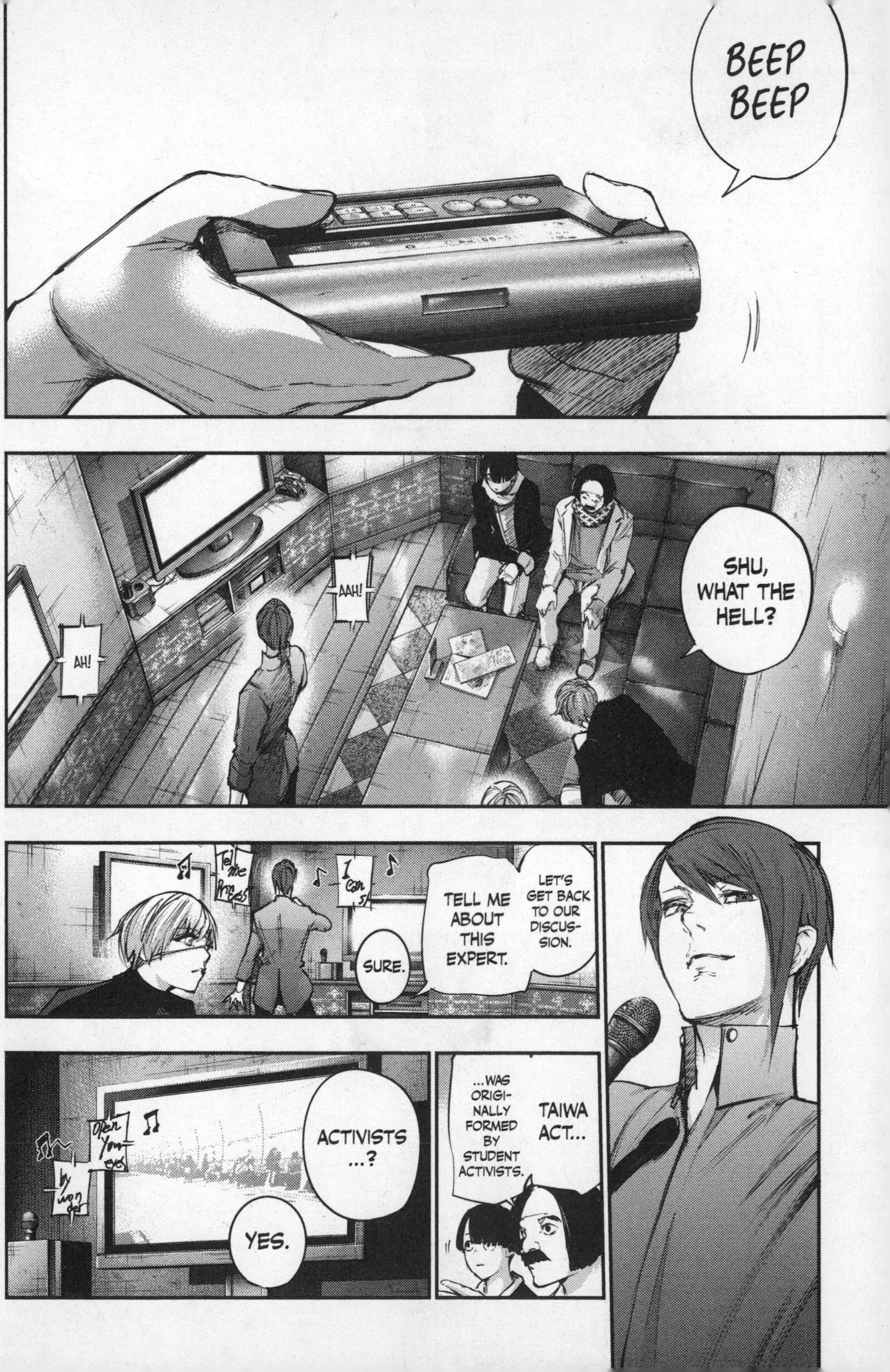
BEEP BEEP
SHU, WHAT THE HELL?
AAH!
AH!
LET'S GET BACK TO OUR DISCUSSION.
TELL ME ABOUT THIS EXPERT.
SURE.
TAIWA ACT...
...WAS ORIGINALLY FORMED BY STUDENT ACTIVISTS.
ACTIVISTS...?
YES.

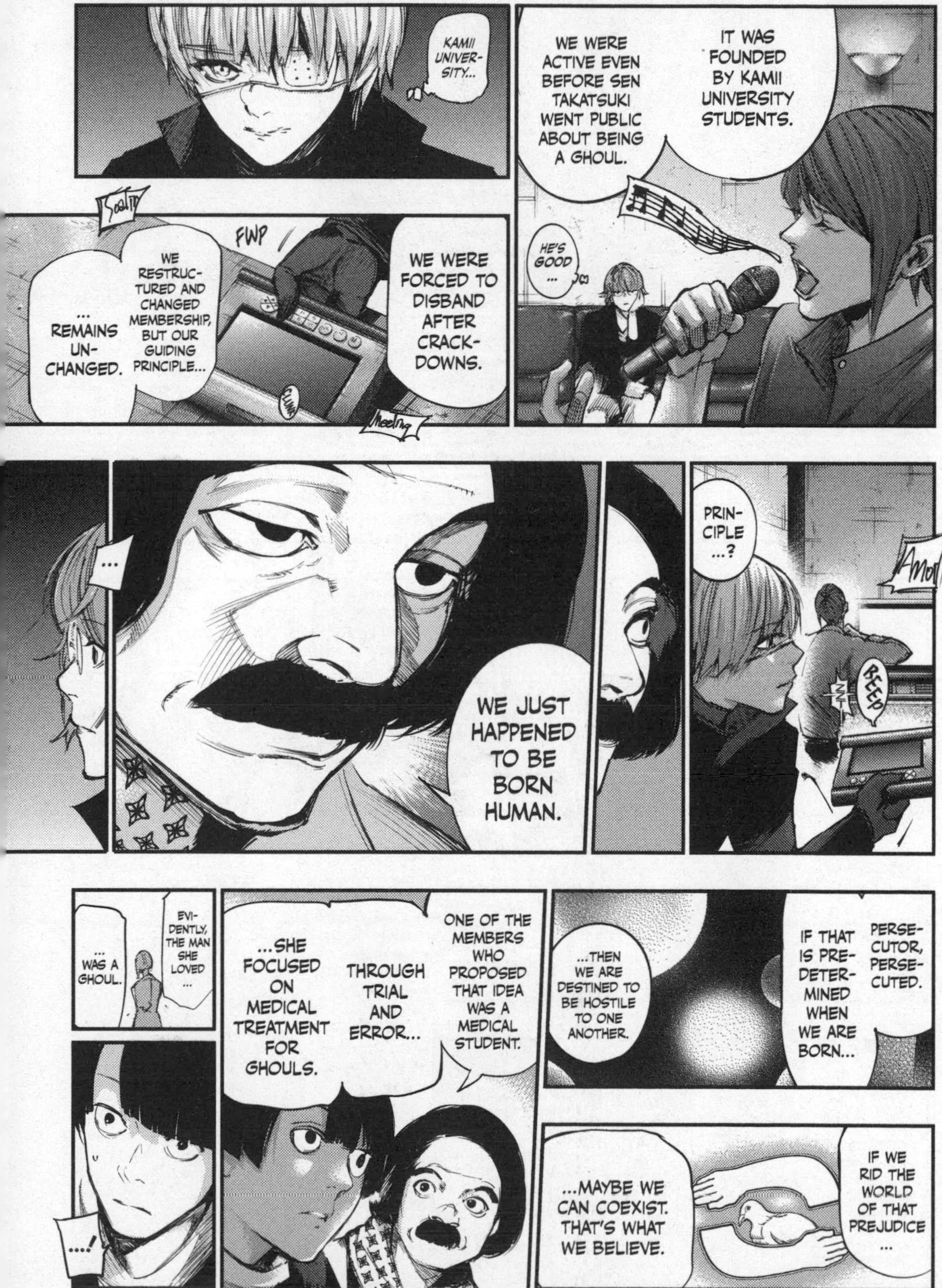
IT WAS FOUNDED BY KAMII UNIVERSITY STUDENTS.
WE WERE ACTIVE EVEN BEFORE SEN TAKATSUKI WENT PUBLIC ABOUT BEING A GHOUL.
KAMII UNIVERSITY...
HE'S GOOD...
WE WERE FORCED TO DISBAND AFTER CRACKDOWNS.
FWP
WE RESTRUCTURED AND CHANGED MEMBERSHIP, BUT OUR GUIDING PRINCIPLE...
...REMAINS UNCHANGED.
PRINCIPLE...?
BEEP
WE JUST HAPPENED TO BE BORN HUMAN.
...
PERSECUTOR, PERSECUTED.
IF THAT IS PREDETERMINED WHEN WE ARE BORN...
...THEN WE ARE DESTINED TO BE HOSTILE TO ONE ANOTHER.
IF WE RID THE WORLD OF THAT PREJUDICE...
...MAYBE WE CAN COEXIST. THAT'S WHAT WE BELIEVE.
ONE OF THE MEMBERS WHO PROPOSED THAT IDEA WAS A MEDICAL STUDENT.
THROUGH TRIAL AND ERROR...
...SHE FOCUSED ON MEDICAL TREATMENT FOR GHOULS.
EVIDENTLY, THE MAN SHE LOVED...
...WAS A GHOUL.
....!

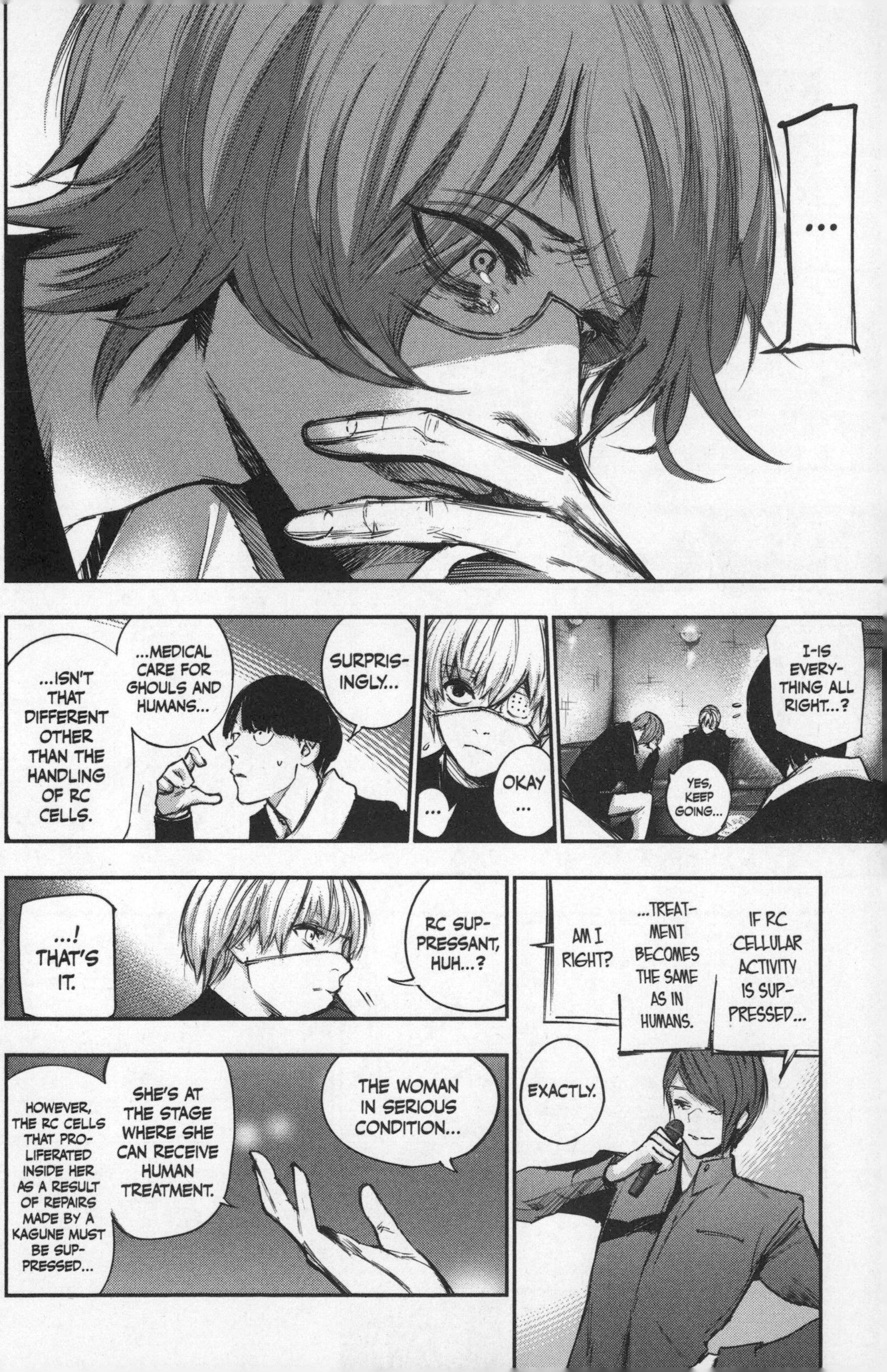
...
I-IS EVERY-THING ALL RIGHT...?
YES, KEEP GOING...
SURPRIS-INGLY...
OKAY ...
...
...MEDICAL CARE FOR GHOULS AND HUMANS...
...ISN'T THAT DIFFERENT OTHER THAN THE HANDLING OF RC CELLS.
IF RC CELLULAR ACTIVITY IS SUP-PRESSED...
...TREAT-MENT BECOMES THE SAME AS IN HUMANS.
AM I RIGHT?
EXACTLY.
RC SUP-PRESSANT, HUH...?
...! THAT'S IT.
THE WOMAN IN SERIOUS CONDITION...
SHE'S AT THE STAGE WHERE SHE CAN RECEIVE HUMAN TREATMENT.
HOWEVER, THE RC CELLS THAT PRO-LIFERATED INSIDE HER AS A RESULT OF REPAIRS MADE BY A KAGUNE MUST BE SUP-PRESSED...

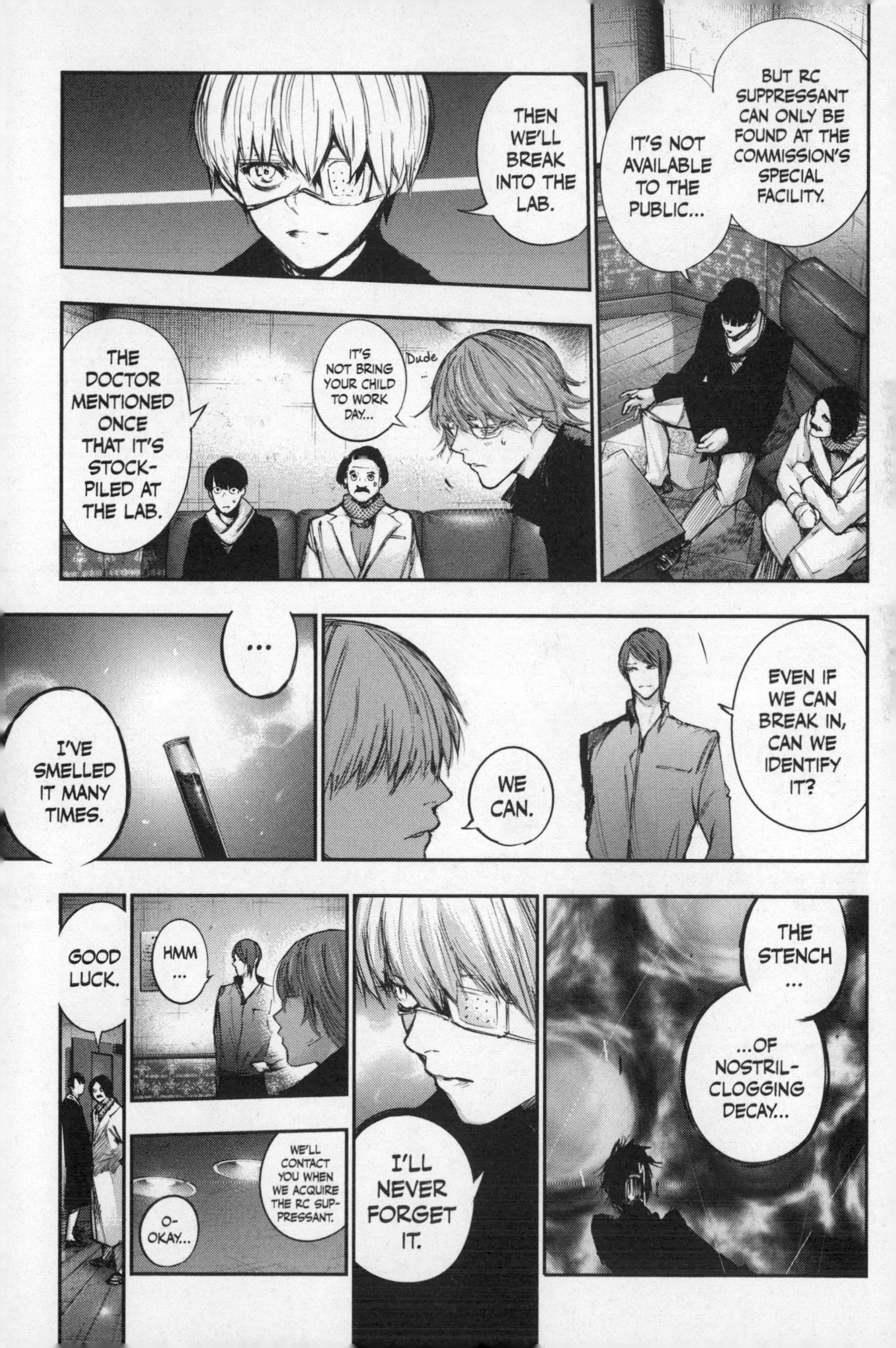
BUT RC SUPPRESSANT CAN ONLY BE FOUND AT THE COMMISSION'S SPECIAL FACILITY.
IT'S NOT AVAILABLE TO THE PUBLIC...
THEN WE'LL BREAK INTO THE LAB.
Dude ...
IT'S NOT BRING YOUR CHILD TO WORK DAY...
THE DOCTOR MENTIONED ONCE THAT IT'S STOCK-PILED AT THE LAB.
EVEN IF WE CAN BREAK IN, CAN WE IDENTIFY IT?
WE CAN.
...
I'VE SMELLED IT MANY TIMES.
THE STENCH ...
...OF NOSTRIL-CLOGGING DECAY...
I'LL NEVER FORGET IT.
HMM ...
WE'LL CONTACT YOU WHEN WE ACQUIRE THE RC SUP-PRESSANT.
O-OKAY...
GOOD LUCK.

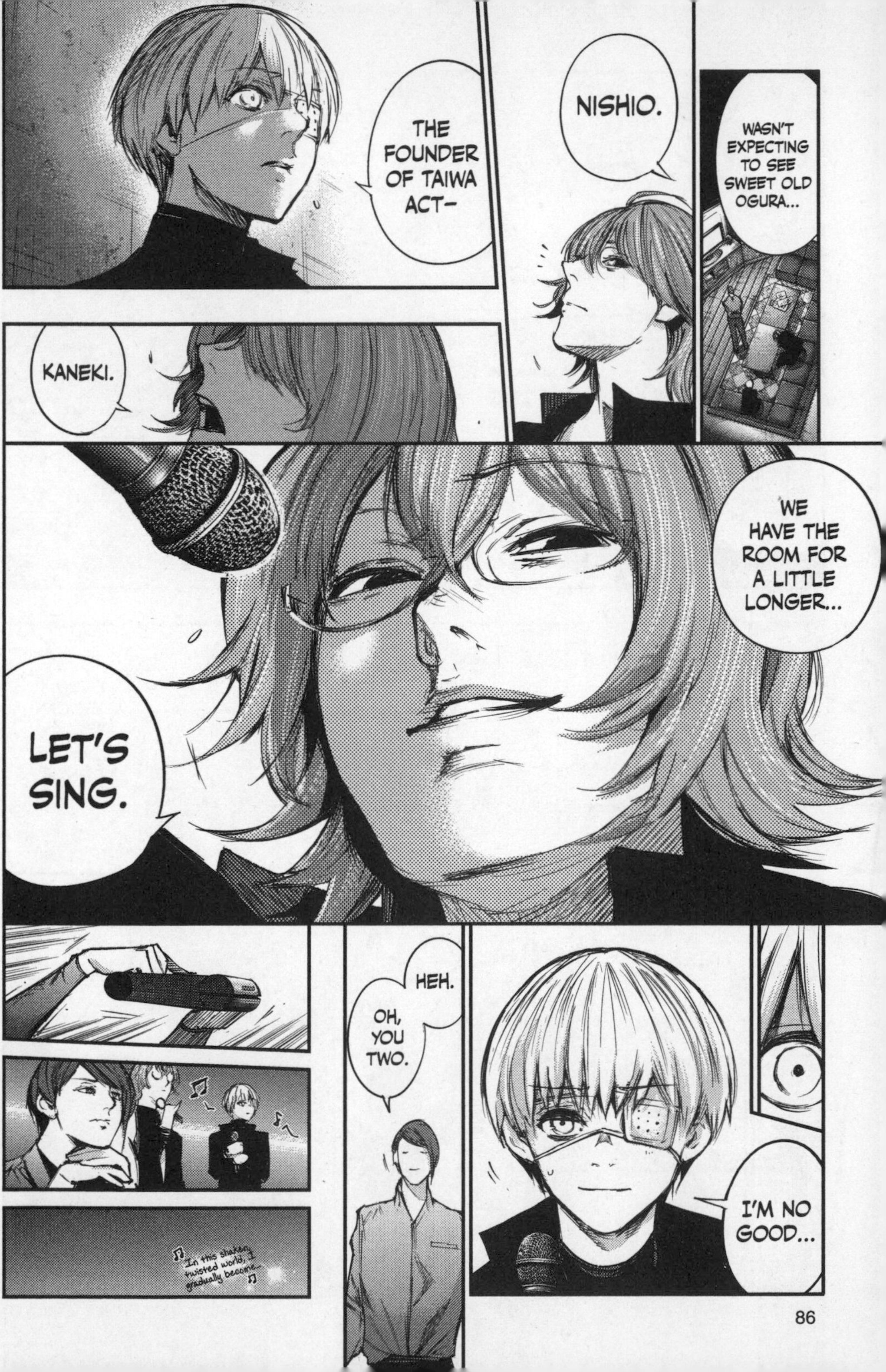
WASN'T EXPECTING TO SEE SWEET OLD OGURA...
NISHIO.
THE FOUNDER OF TAIWA ACT-
KANEKI.
WE HAVE THE ROOM FOR A LITTLE LONGER...
LET'S SING.
I'M NO GOOD...
HEH.
OH, YOU TWO.
In this shaken, twisted world, I gradually become...

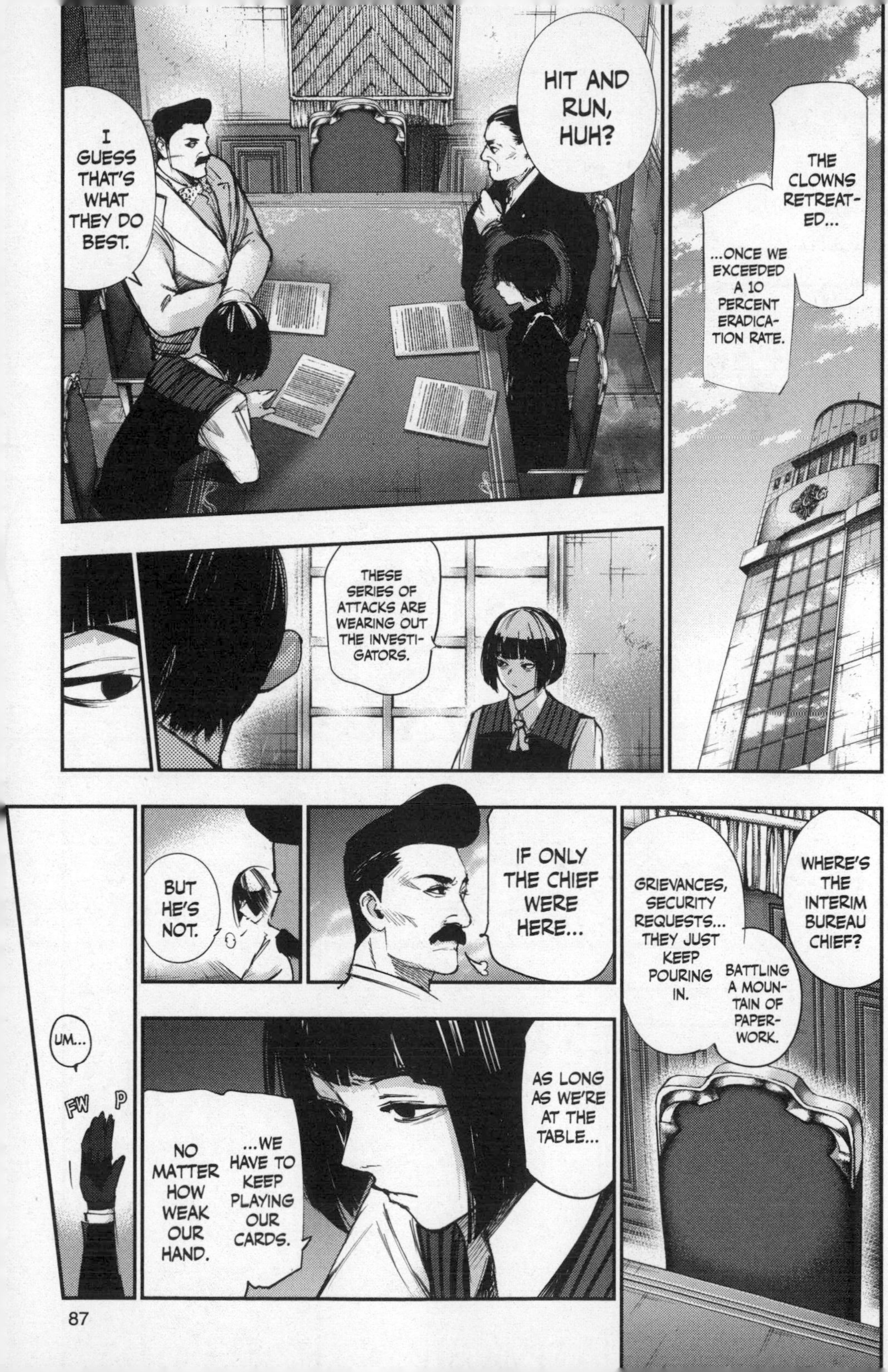
THE CLOWNS RETREATED...
...ONCE WE EXCEEDED A 10 PERCENT ERADICATION RATE.
HIT AND RUN, HUH?
I GUESS THAT'S WHAT THEY DO BEST.
THESE SERIES OF ATTACKS ARE WEARING OUT THE INVESTIGATORS.
WHERE'S THE INTERIM BUREAU CHIEF?
BATTLING A MOUNTAIN OF PAPERWORK.
GRIEVANCES, SECURITY REQUESTS... THEY JUST KEEP POURING IN.
IF ONLY THE CHIEF WERE HERE...
BUT HE'S NOT.
AS LONG AS WE'RE AT THE TABLE...
...WE HAVE TO KEEP PLAYING OUR CARDS.
NO MATTER HOW WEAK OUR HAND.
UM...
FWP

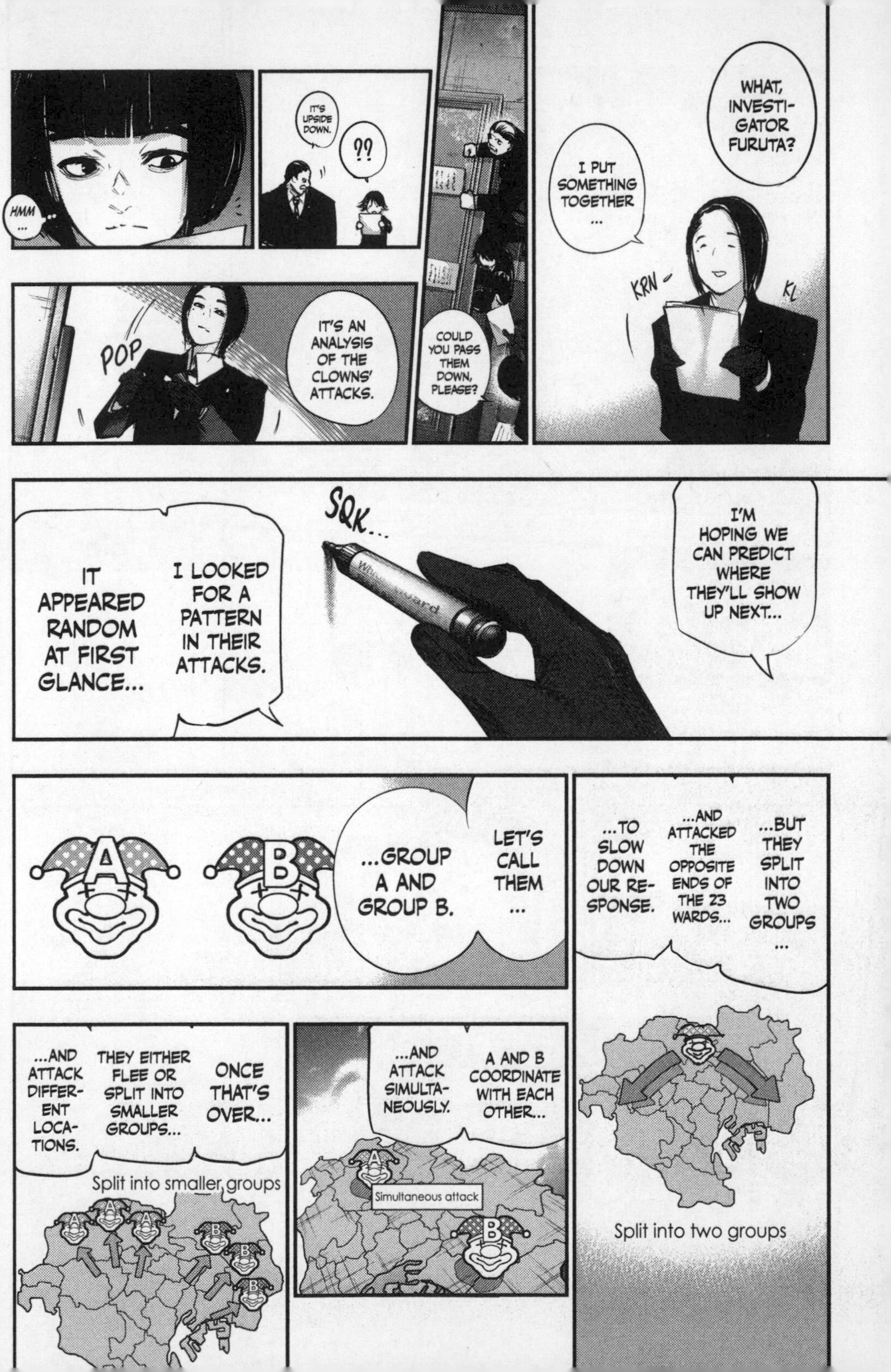
WHAT, INVESTIGATOR FURUTA?
I PUT SOMETHING TOGETHER...
KRN
KL
COULD YOU PASS THEM DOWN, PLEASE?
IT'S UPSIDE DOWN.
??
HMM...
IT'S AN ANALYSIS OF THE CLOWNS' ATTACKS.
POP
I'M HOPING WE CAN PREDICT WHERE THEY'LL SHOW UP NEXT...
SQK...
I LOOKED FOR A PATTERN IN THEIR ATTACKS.
IT APPEARED RANDOM AT FIRST GLANCE...
...BUT THEY SPLIT INTO TWO GROUPS...
...AND ATTACKED THE OPPOSITE ENDS OF THE 23 WARDS...
...TO SLOW DOWN OUR RESPONSE.
Split into two groups
LET'S CALL THEM...
...GROUP A AND GROUP B.
A
B
A AND B COORDINATE WITH EACH OTHER...
...AND ATTACK SIMULTANEOUSLY.
Simultaneous attack
ONCE THAT'S OVER...
THEY EITHER FLEE OR SPLIT INTO SMALLER GROUPS...
...AND ATTACK DIFFERENT LOCATIONS.
Split into smaller groups

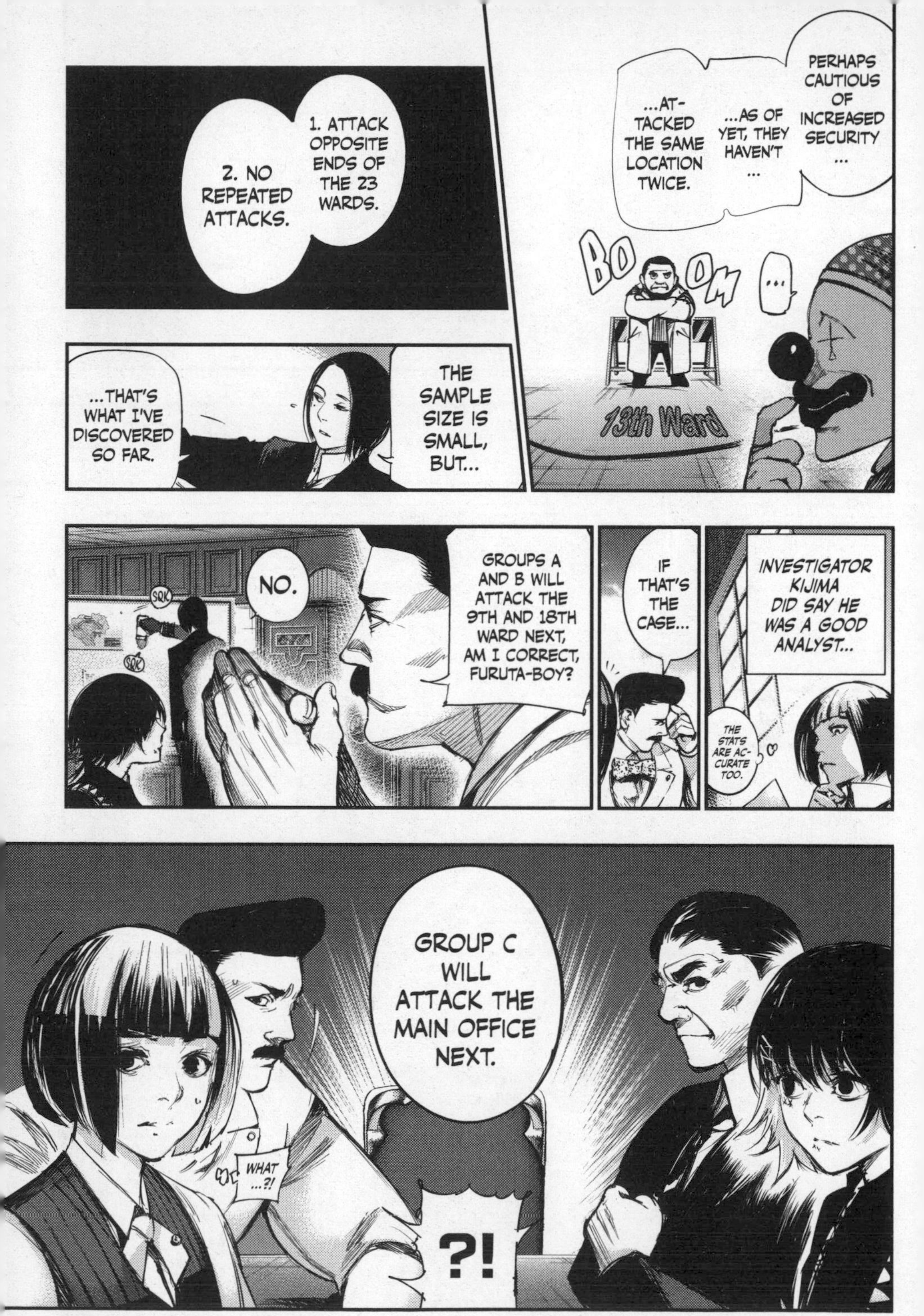
PERHAPS CAUTIOUS OF INCREASED SECURITY...
...AS OF YET, THEY HAVEN'T...
...ATTACKED THE SAME LOCATION TWICE.
BOOM
...
13th Ward
1. ATTACK OPPOSITE ENDS OF THE 23 WARDS.
2. NO REPEATED ATTACKS.
THE SAMPLE SIZE IS SMALL, BUT...
...THAT'S WHAT I'VE DISCOVERED SO FAR.
INVESTIGATOR KIJIMA DID SAY HE WAS A GOOD ANALYST...
THE STATS ARE ACCURATE TOO.
IF THAT'S THE CASE...
GROUPS A AND B WILL ATTACK THE 9TH AND 18TH WARD NEXT, AM I CORRECT, FURUTA-BOY?
NO.
SQK
SQK
GROUP C WILL ATTACK THE MAIN OFFICE NEXT.
WHAT...?!
?!

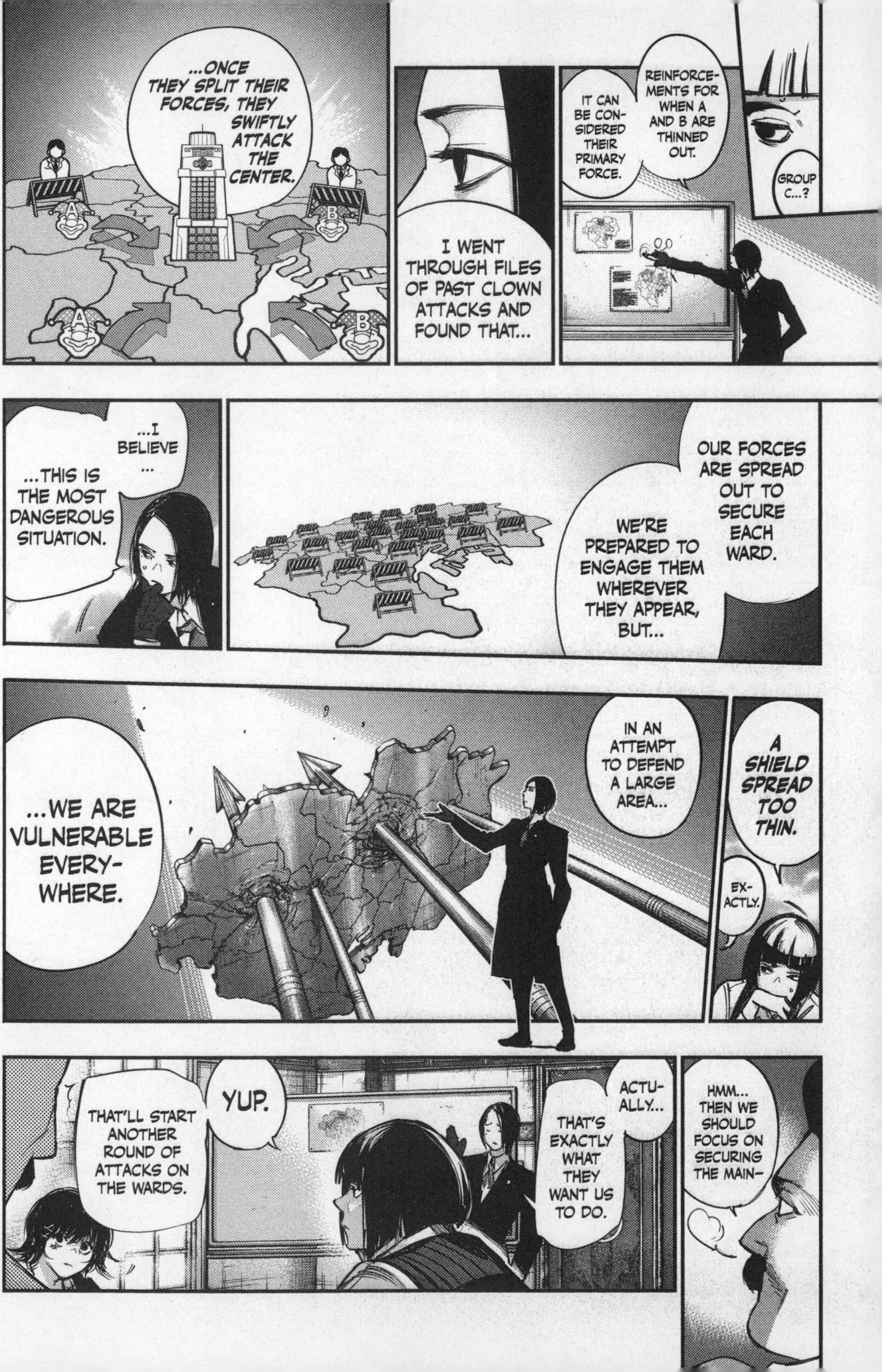
GROUP C...?
REINFORCEMENTS FOR WHEN A AND B ARE THINNED OUT.
IT CAN BE CONSIDERED THEIR PRIMARY FORCE.
I WENT THROUGH FILES OF PAST CLOWN ATTACKS AND FOUND THAT...
...ONCE THEY SPLIT THEIR FORCES, THEY SWIFTLY ATTACK THE CENTER.
OUR FORCES ARE SPREAD OUT TO SECURE EACH WARD.
WE'RE PREPARED TO ENGAGE THEM WHEREVER THEY APPEAR, BUT...
...I BELIEVE ...
...THIS IS THE MOST DANGEROUS SITUATION.
A SHIELD SPREAD TOO THIN.
EXACTLY.
IN AN ATTEMPT TO DEFEND A LARGE AREA...
...WE ARE VULNERABLE EVERYWHERE.
HMM... THEN WE SHOULD FOCUS ON SECURING THE MAIN-
ACTUALLY...
THAT'S EXACTLY WHAT THEY WANT US TO DO.
YUP.
THAT'LL START ANOTHER ROUND OF ATTACKS ON THE WARDS.

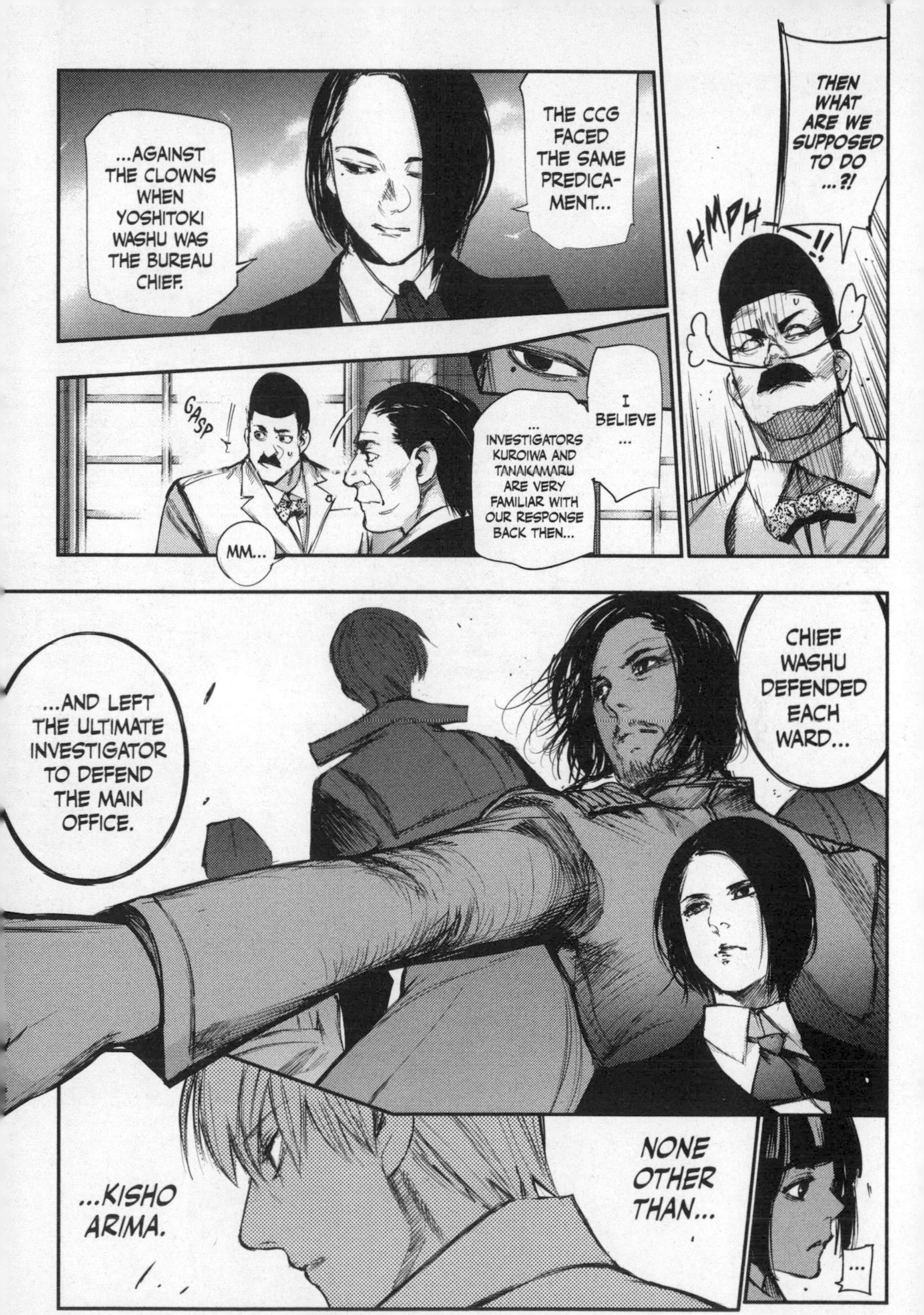
THEN WHAT ARE WE SUPPOSED TO DO ...?!
KMPH—!!
THE CCG FACED THE SAME PREDICAMENT...
...AGAINST THE CLOWNS WHEN YOSHITOKI WASHU WAS THE BUREAU CHIEF.
I BELIEVE ...
... INVESTIGATORS KUROIWA AND TANAKAMARU ARE VERY FAMILIAR WITH OUR RESPONSE BACK THEN...
GASP!
MM...
CHIEF WASHU DEFENDED EACH WARD...
...AND LEFT THE ULTIMATE INVESTIGATOR TO DEFEND THE MAIN OFFICE.
...
NONE OTHER THAN...
...KISHO ARIMA.

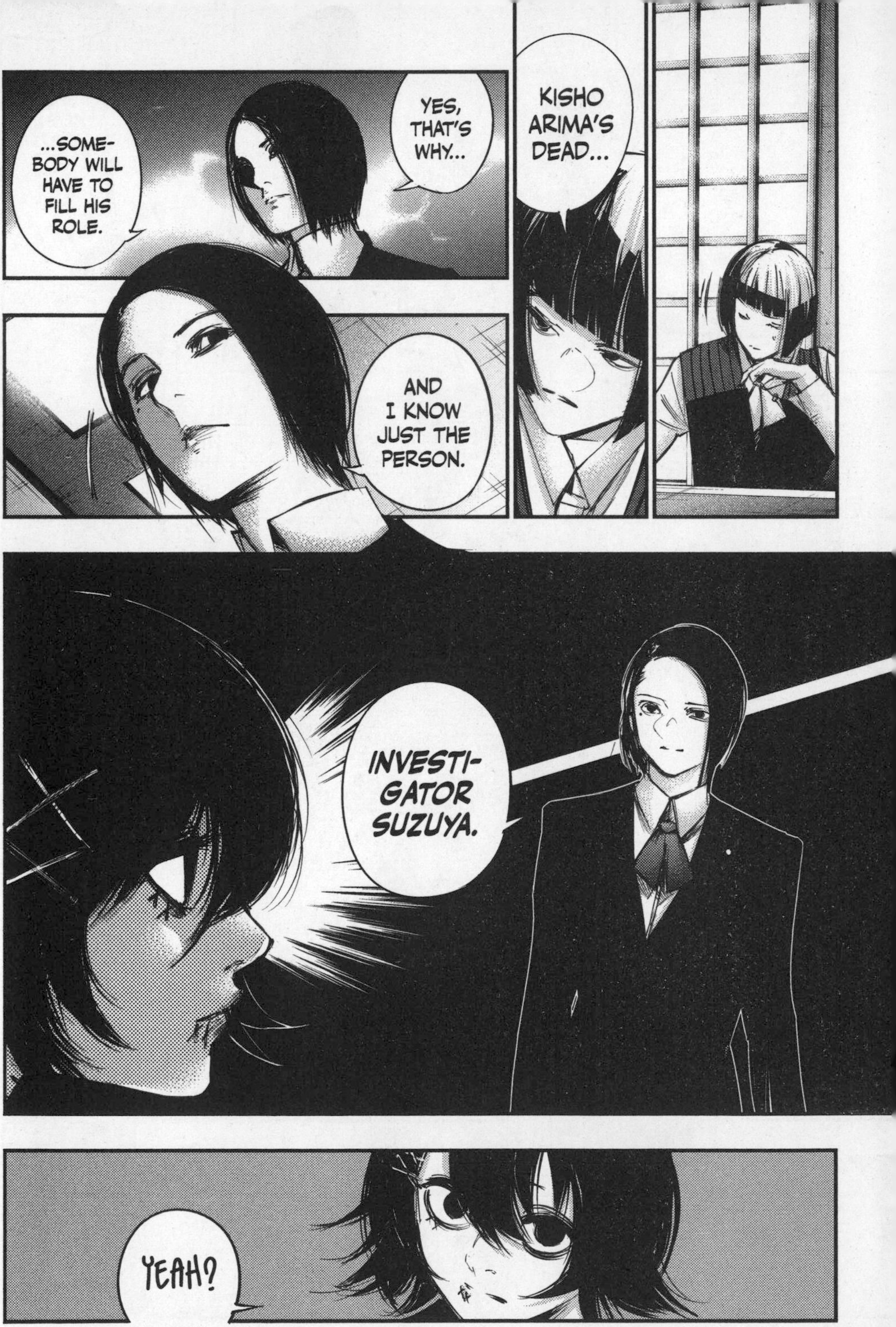
KISHO ARIMA'S DEAD...
YES, THAT'S WHY...
...SOMEBODY WILL HAVE TO FILL HIS ROLE.
AND I KNOW JUST THE PERSON.
INVESTIGATOR SUZUYA.
YEAH?

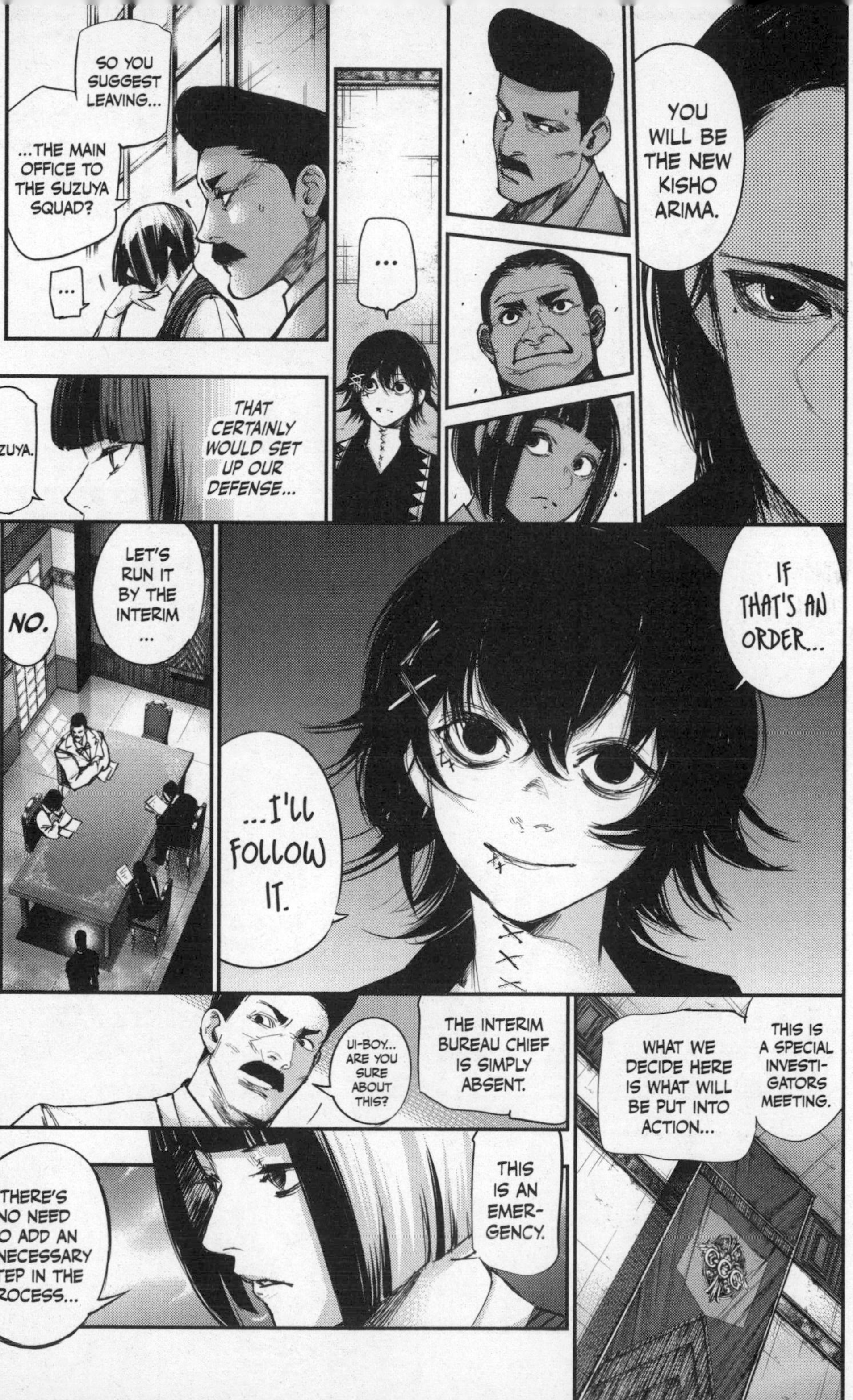
YOU WILL BE THE NEW KISHO ARIMA.
...
THAT CERTAINLY WOULD SET UP OUR DEFENSE...
SO YOU SUGGEST LEAVING...
...THE MAIN OFFICE TO THE SUZUYA SQUAD?
...
SUZUYA.
IF THAT'S AN ORDER...
...I'LL FOLLOW IT.
LET'S RUN IT BY THE INTERIM...
NO.
THIS IS A SPECIAL INVESTIGATORS MEETING.
WHAT WE DECIDE HERE IS WHAT WILL BE PUT INTO ACTION...
THE INTERIM BUREAU CHIEF IS SIMPLY ABSENT.
UI-BOY... ARE YOU SURE ABOUT THIS?
THIS IS AN EMERGENCY.
THERE'S NO NEED TO ADD AN UNNECESSARY STEP IN THE PROCESS...

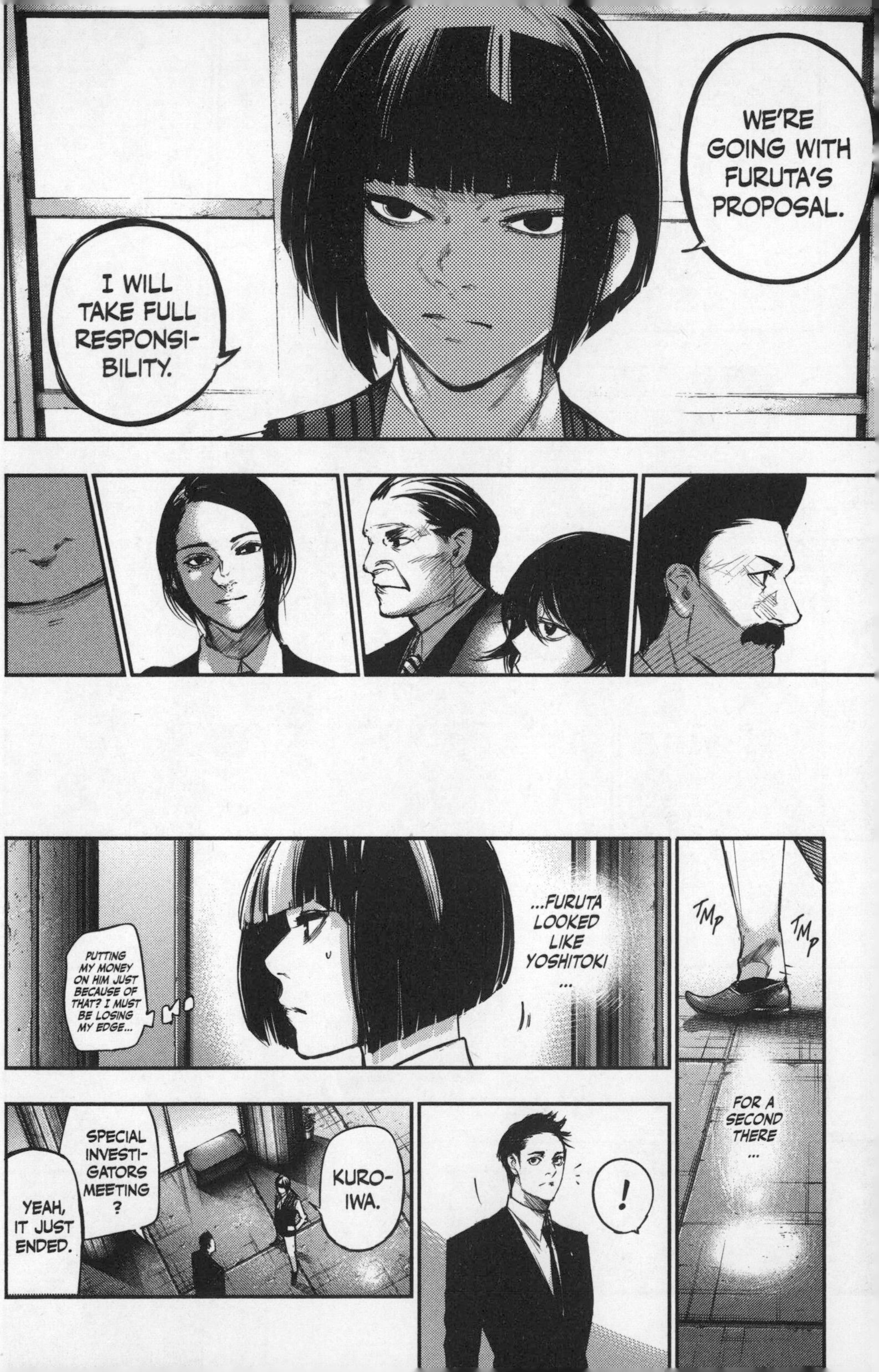
WE'RE GOING WITH FURUTA'S PROPOSAL.
I WILL TAKE FULL RESPONSI-BILITY.
TMP
TMP
FOR A SECOND THERE ...
...FURUTA LOOKED LIKE YOSHITOKI ...
PUTTING MY MONEY ON HIM JUST BECAUSE OF THAT? I MUST BE LOSING MY EDGE...
!
KURO-IWA.
SPECIAL INVESTI-GATORS MEETING ?
YEAH, IT JUST ENDED.

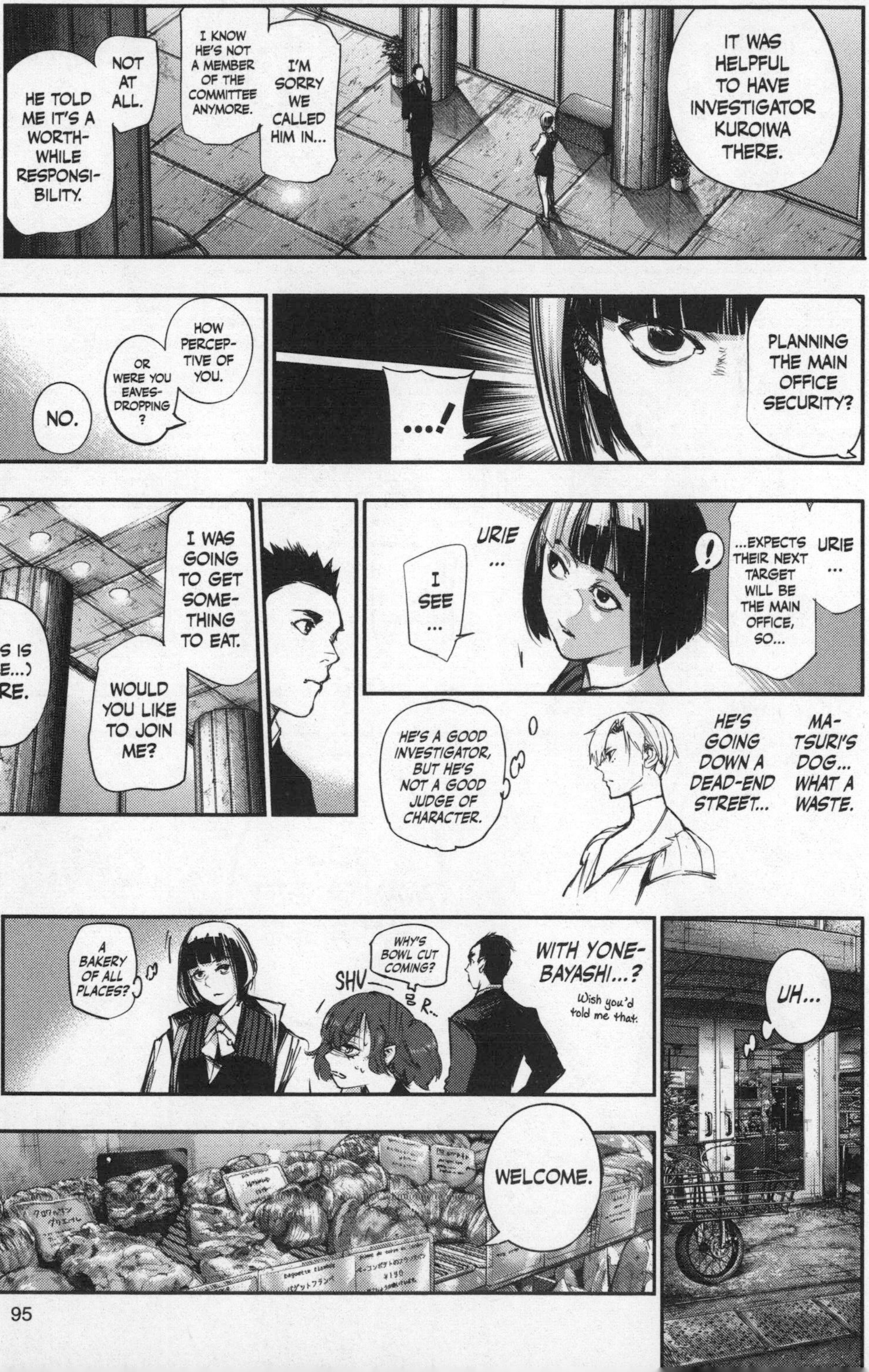
IT WAS HELPFUL TO HAVE INVESTIGATOR KUROIWA THERE.
I'M SORRY WE CALLED HIM IN...
I KNOW HE'S NOT A MEMBER OF THE COMMITTEE ANYMORE.
NOT AT ALL.
HE TOLD ME IT'S A WORTH-WHILE RESPONSI-BILITY.
PLANNING THE MAIN OFFICE SECURITY?
...!
HOW PERCEP-TIVE OF YOU.
OR WERE YOU EAVES-DROPPING?
NO.
URIE...
...EXPECTS THEIR NEXT TARGET WILL BE THE MAIN OFFICE, SO...
!
URIE...
I SEE...
MA-TSURI'S DOG... WHAT A WASTE.
HE'S GOING DOWN A DEAD-END STREET...
HE'S A GOOD INVESTIGATOR, BUT HE'S NOT A GOOD JUDGE OF CHARACTER.
I WAS GOING TO GET SOME-THING TO EAT.
WOULD YOU LIKE TO JOIN ME?
(THIS IS RARE...) SURE.
UH...
WITH YONE-BAYASHI...?
Wish you'd told me that.
WHY'S BOWL CUT COMING?
SHV
R..
A BAKERY OF ALL PLACES?
WELCOME.

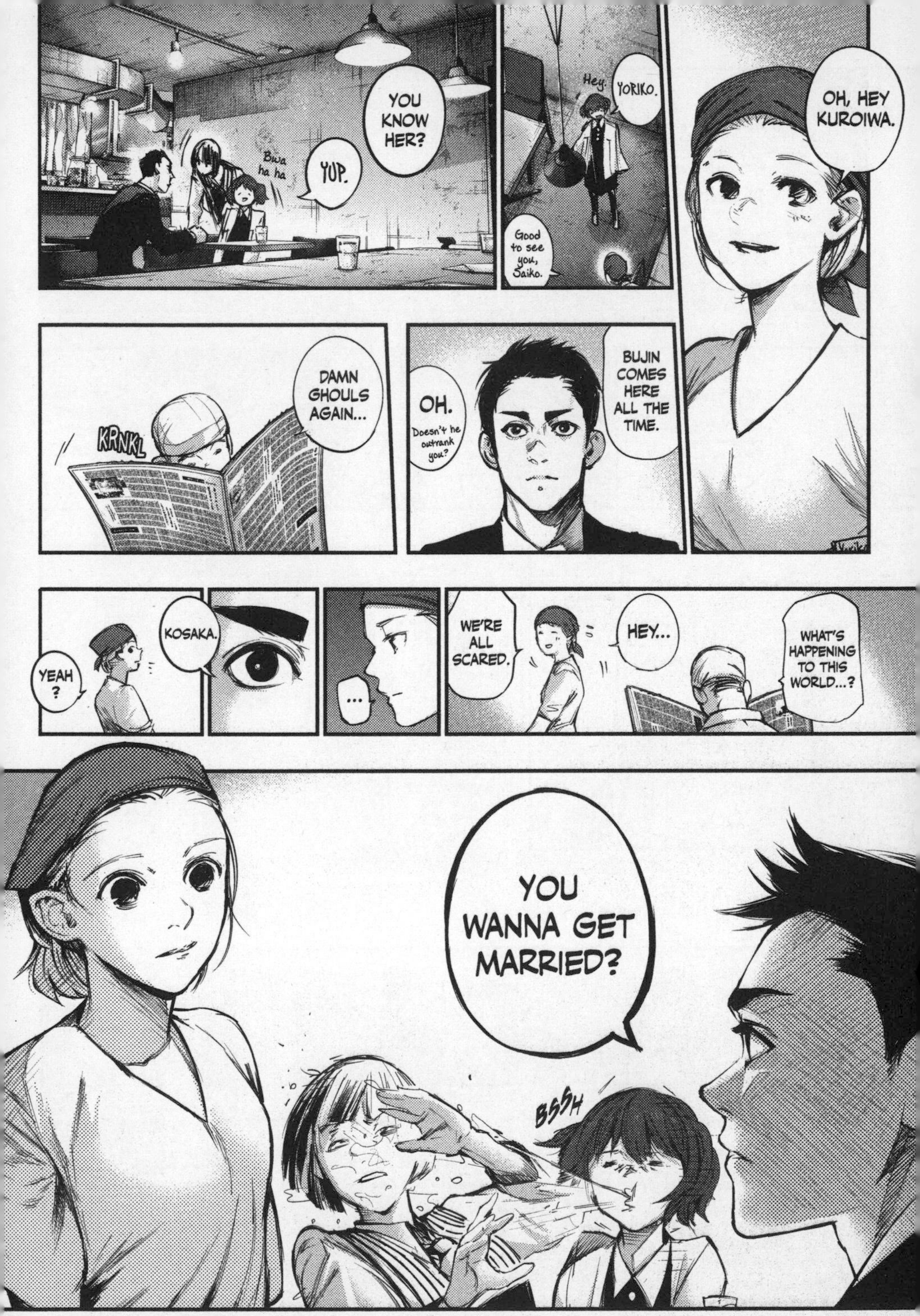
OH, HEY KUROIWA.
Hey.
YORIKO.
Good to see you, Saiko.
YOU KNOW HER?
YUP.
Bwa ha ha
BUJIN COMES HERE ALL THE TIME.
OH.
Doesn't he outrank you?
DAMN GHOULS AGAIN...
KRNKL
WHAT'S HAPPENING TO THIS WORLD...?
HEY...
WE'RE ALL SCARED.
...
KOSAKA.
YEAH?
YOU WANNA GET MARRIED?
BSSH

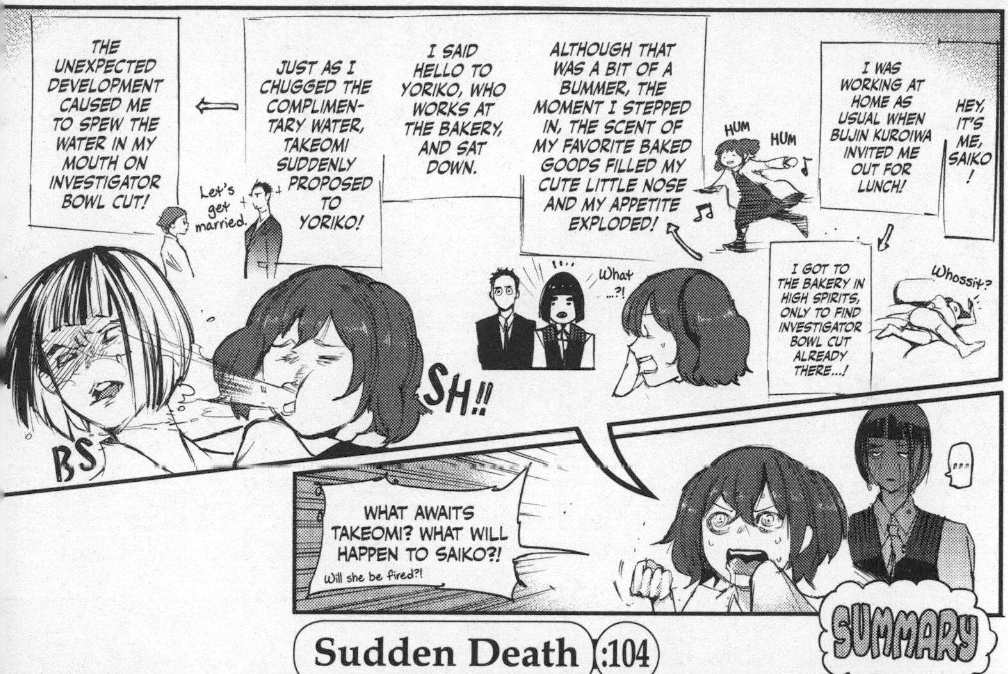
SUMMARY
HEY, IT'S ME, SAIKO!
I WAS WORKING AT HOME AS USUAL WHEN BUJIN KUROIWA INVITED ME OUT FOR LUNCH!
HUM HUM
ALTHOUGH THAT WAS A BIT OF A BUMMER, THE MOMENT I STEPPED IN, THE SCENT OF MY FAVORITE BAKED GOODS FILLED MY CUTE LITTLE NOSE AND MY APPETITE EXPLODED!
I SAID HELLO TO YORIKO, WHO WORKS AT THE BAKERY, AND SAT DOWN.
JUST AS I CHUGGED THE COMPLIMENTARY WATER, TAKEOMI SUDDENLY PROPOSED TO YORIKO!
Let's get married.
THE UNEXPECTED DEVELOPMENT CAUSED ME TO SPEW THE WATER IN MY MOUTH ON INVESTIGATOR BOWL CUT!
Whossit?
I GOT TO THE BAKERY IN HIGH SPIRITS, ONLY TO FIND INVESTIGATOR BOWL CUT ALREADY THERE...!
What ...?!
SH!!
BS
...
WHAT AWAITS TAKEOMI? WHAT WILL HAPPEN TO SAIKO?!
Will she be fired?!

Sudden Death :104

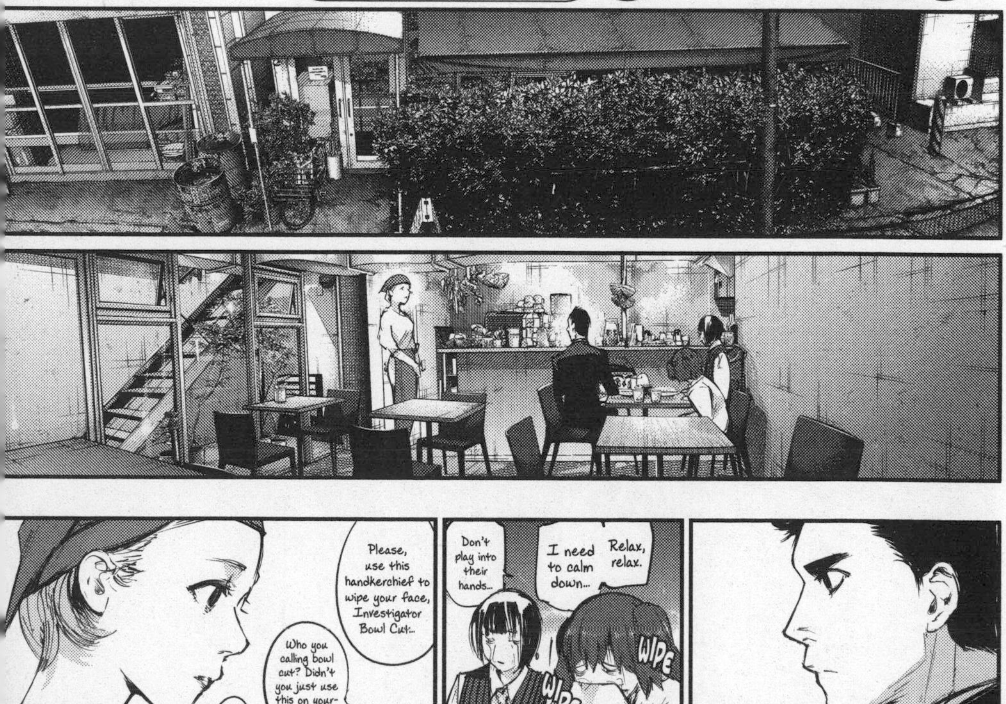
Relax, relax.
I need to calm down...
Don't play into their hands...
WIPE
WIPE
Please, use this handkerchief to wipe your face, Investigator Bowl Cut...
Who you calling bowl cut? Didn't you just use this on yourself?
Y...

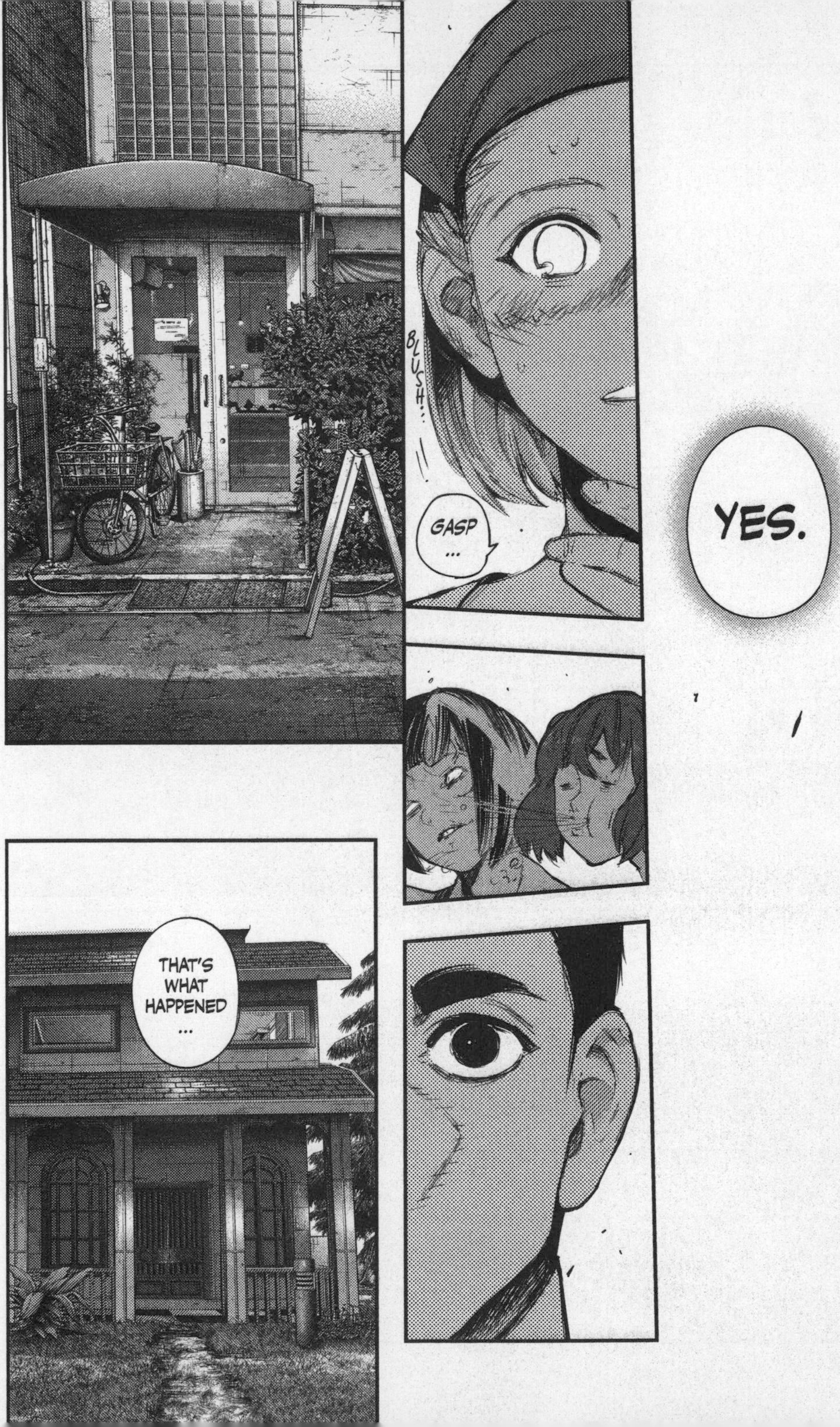
YES.
BLUSH...
GASP ...
THAT'S WHAT HAPPENED ...

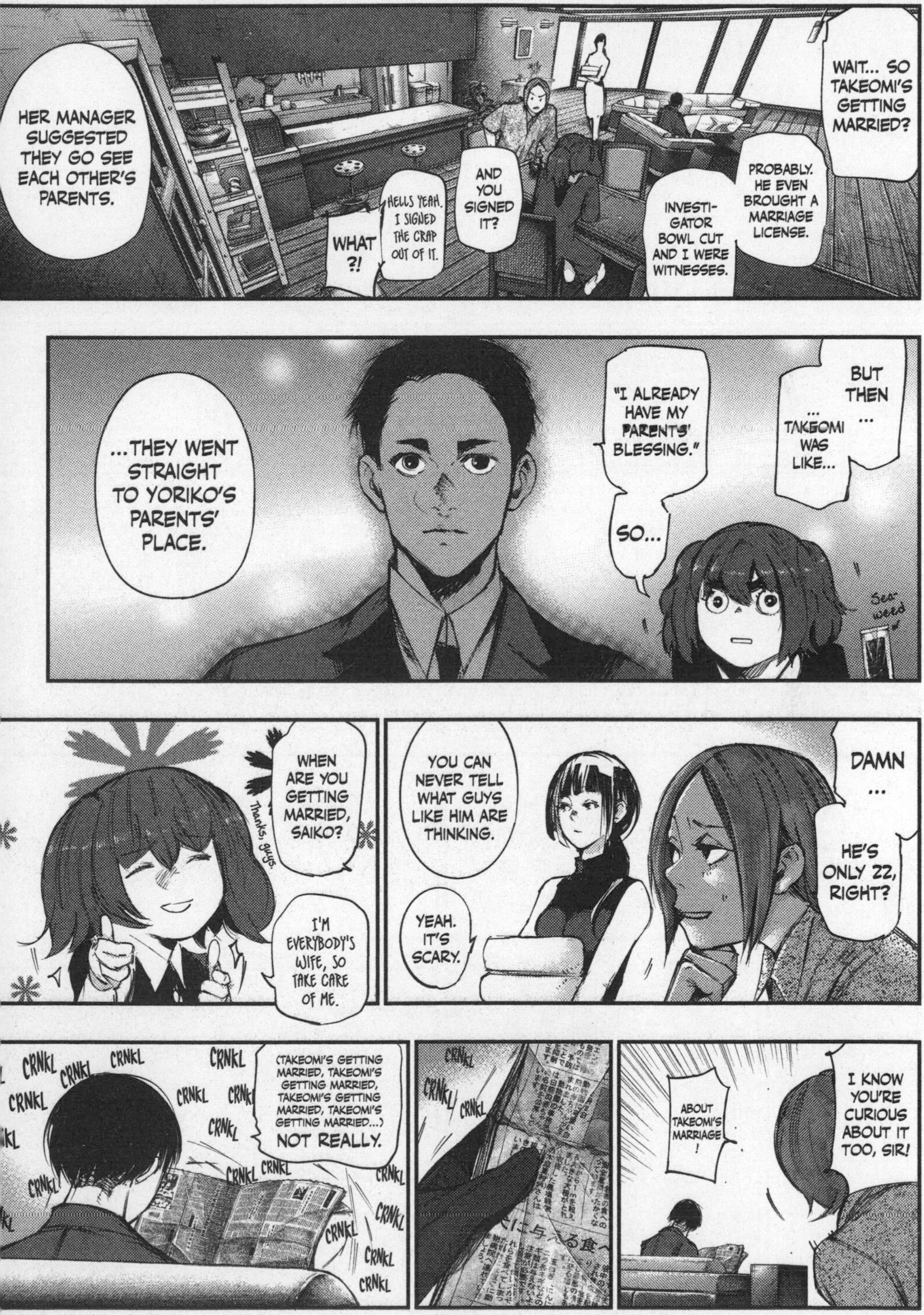
WAIT... SO TAKEOMI'S GETTING MARRIED?
PROBABLY. HE EVEN BROUGHT A MARRIAGE LICENSE.
INVESTIGATOR BOWL CUT AND I WERE WITNESSES.
AND YOU SIGNED IT?
HELLS YEAH. I SIGNED THE CRAP OUT OF IT.
WHAT?!
HER MANAGER SUGGESTED THEY GO SEE EACH OTHER'S PARENTS.
BUT THEN...
...TAKEOMI WAS LIKE...
"I ALREADY HAVE MY PARENTS' BLESSING."
SO...
...THEY WENT STRAIGHT TO YORIKO'S PARENTS' PLACE.
Seaweed
DAMN...
HE'S ONLY 22, RIGHT?
YOU CAN NEVER TELL WHAT GUYS LIKE HIM ARE THINKING.
YEAH. IT'S SCARY.
WHEN ARE YOU GETTING MARRIED, SAIKO?
Thanks, guys.
I'M EVERYBODY'S WIFE, SO TAKE CARE OF ME.
I KNOW YOU'RE CURIOUS ABOUT IT TOO, SIR!
ABOUT TAKEOMI'S MARRIAGE!
CRNKL CRNKL
CRNKL CRNKL CRNKL CRNKL CRNKL CRNKL CRNKL CRNKL CRNKL CRNKL CRNKL CRNKL CRNKL CRNKL CRNKL
(TAKEOMI'S GETTING MARRIED, TAKEOMI'S GETTING MARRIED, TAKEOMI'S GETTING MARRIED, TAKEOMI'S GETTING MARRIED...) NOT REALLY.

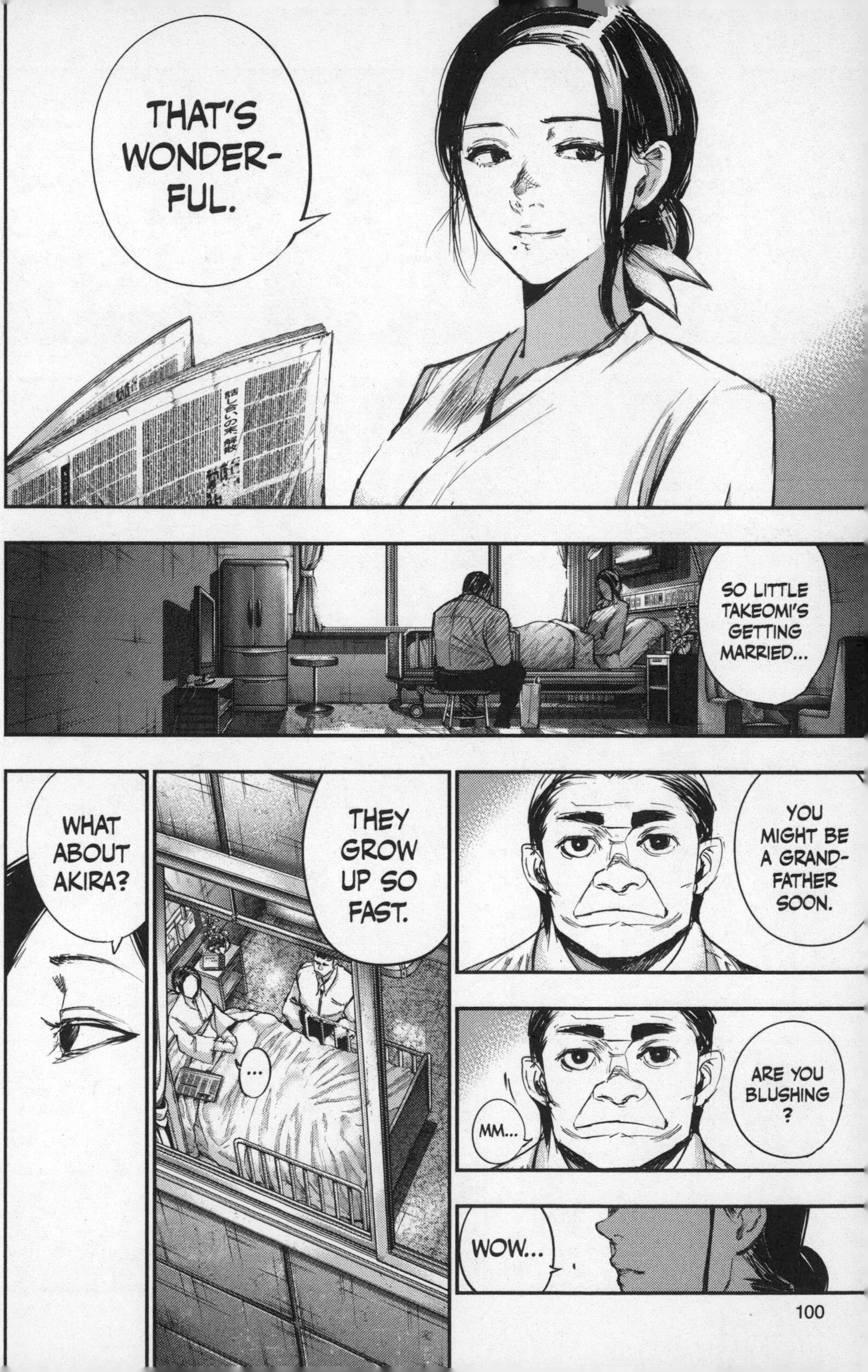
THAT'S WONDER-FUL.
SO LITTLE TAKEOMI'S GETTING MARRIED...
YOU MIGHT BE A GRAND-FATHER SOON.
ARE YOU BLUSHING?
MM...
WOW...
THEY GROW UP SO FAST.
...
WHAT ABOUT AKIRA?

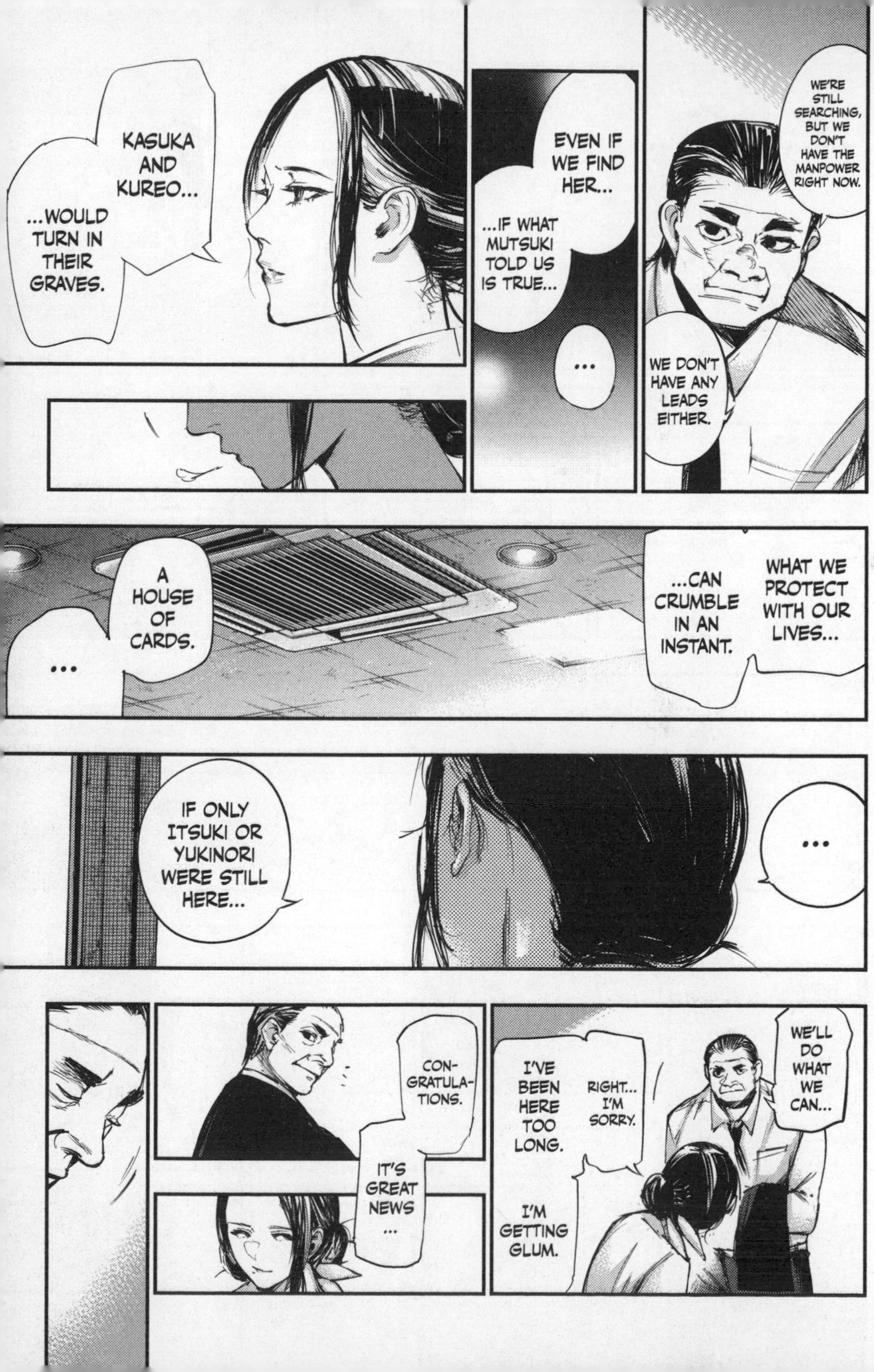
WE'RE STILL SEARCHING, BUT WE DON'T HAVE THE MANPOWER RIGHT NOW.
WE DON'T HAVE ANY LEADS EITHER.
EVEN IF WE FIND HER...
...IF WHAT MUTSUKI TOLD US IS TRUE...
...
KASUKA AND KUREO...
...WOULD TURN IN THEIR GRAVES.
WHAT WE PROTECT WITH OUR LIVES...
...CAN CRUMBLE IN AN INSTANT.
A HOUSE OF CARDS.
...
...
IF ONLY ITSUKI OR YUKINORI WERE STILL HERE...
WE'LL DO WHAT WE CAN...
RIGHT... I'M SORRY.
I'VE BEEN HERE TOO LONG.
I'M GETTING GLUM.
CON-GRATULA-TIONS.
IT'S GREAT NEWS...

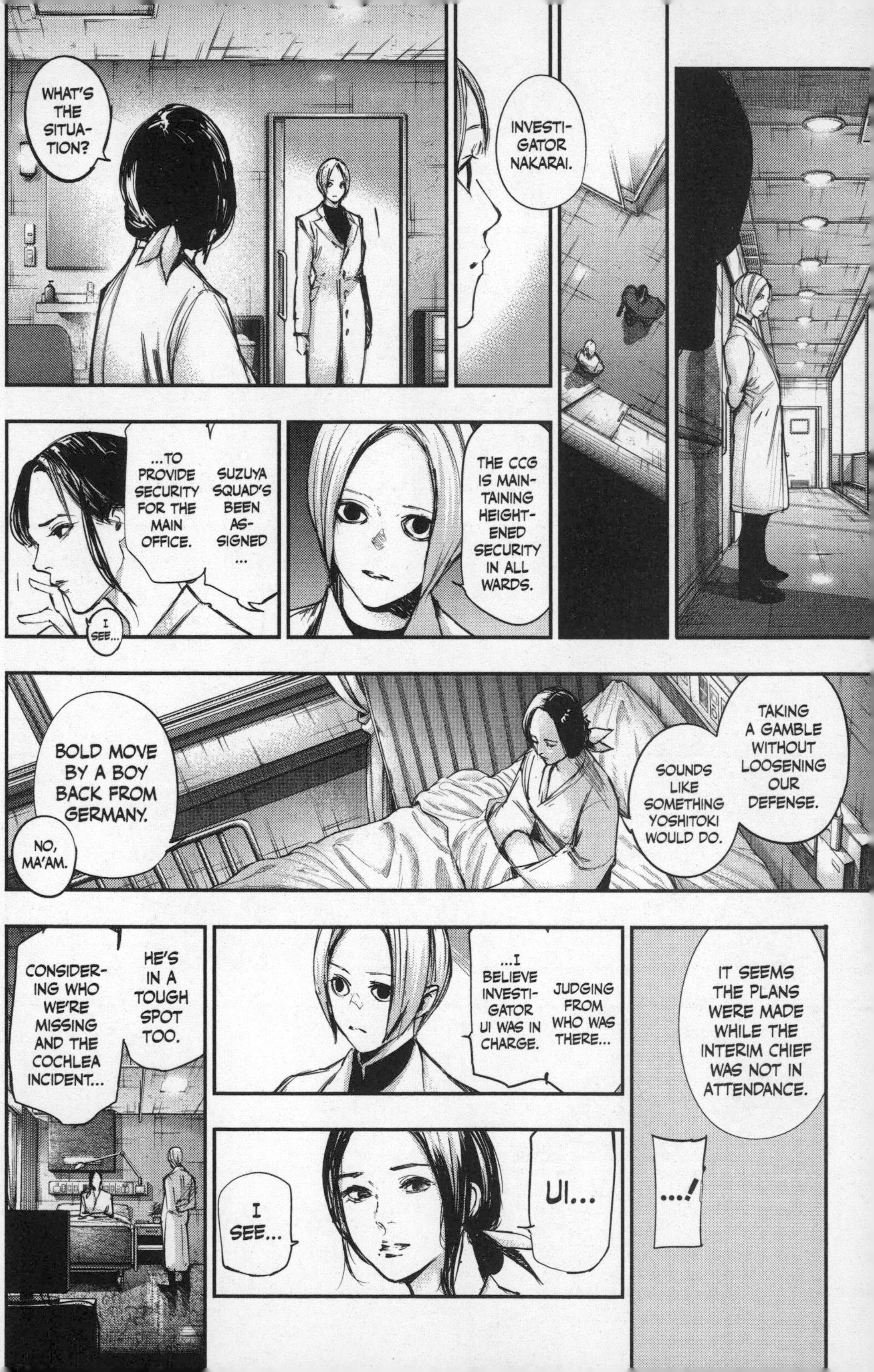
INVESTIGATOR NAKARAI.
WHAT'S THE SITUATION?
THE CCG IS MAINTAINING HEIGHTENED SECURITY IN ALL WARDS.
SUZUYA SQUAD'S BEEN ASSIGNED...
...TO PROVIDE SECURITY FOR THE MAIN OFFICE.
I SEE...
TAKING A GAMBLE WITHOUT LOOSENING OUR DEFENSE.
SOUNDS LIKE SOMETHING YOSHITOKI WOULD DO.
BOLD MOVE BY A BOY BACK FROM GERMANY.
NO, MA'AM.
IT SEEMS THE PLANS WERE MADE WHILE THE INTERIM CHIEF WAS NOT IN ATTENDANCE.
...!
JUDGING FROM WHO WAS THERE...
...I BELIEVE INVESTIGATOR UI WAS IN CHARGE.
UI...
I SEE...
HE'S IN A TOUGH SPOT TOO.
CONSIDERING WHO WE'RE MISSING AND THE COCHLEA INCIDENT...

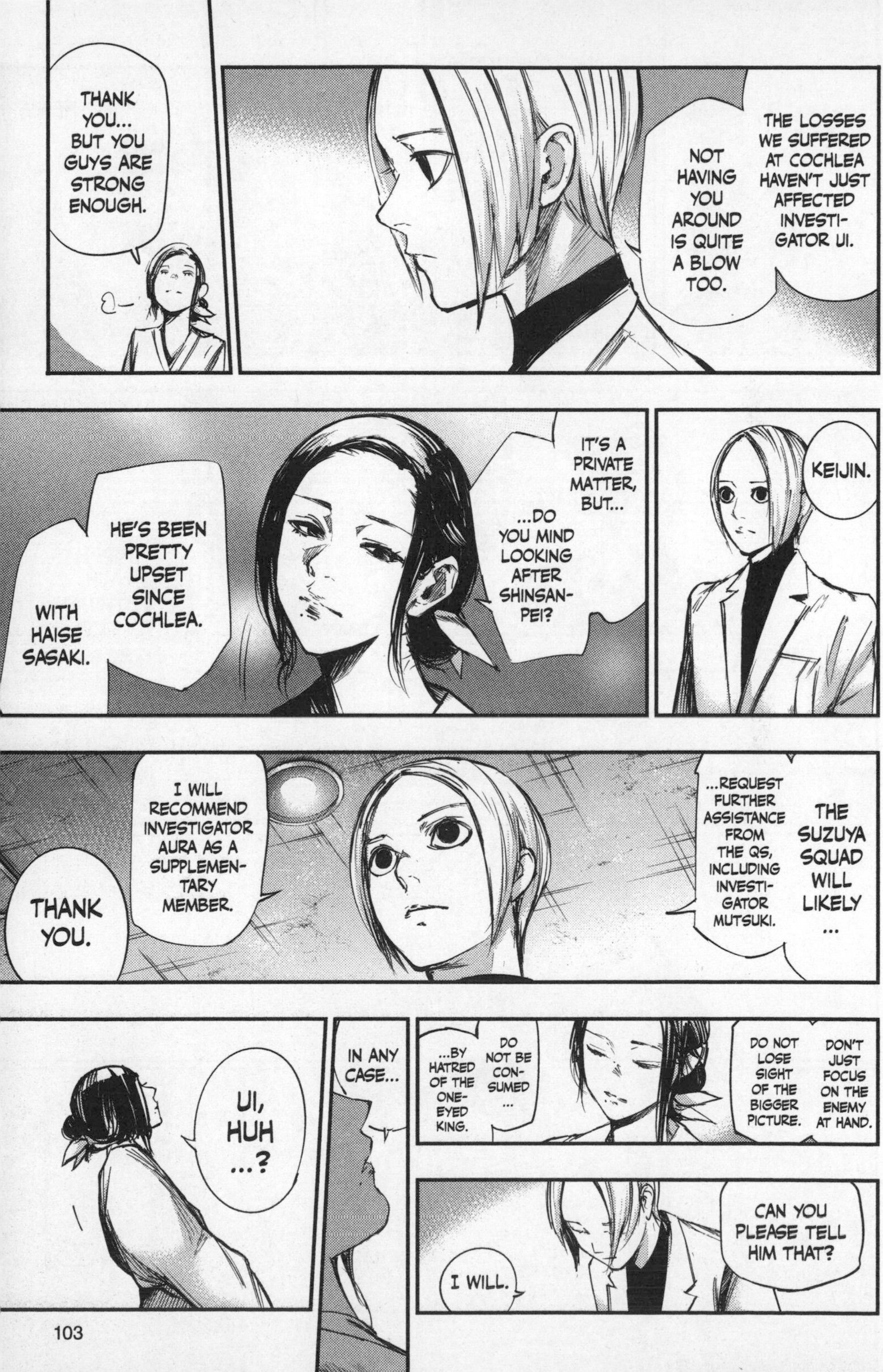
THE LOSSES WE SUFFERED AT COCHLEA HAVEN'T JUST AFFECTED INVESTI-GATOR UI.
NOT HAVING YOU AROUND IS QUITE A BLOW TOO.
THANK YOU... BUT YOU GUYS ARE STRONG ENOUGH.
KEIJIN.
IT'S A PRIVATE MATTER, BUT...
...DO YOU MIND LOOKING AFTER SHINSAN-PEI?
HE'S BEEN PRETTY UPSET SINCE COCHLEA.
WITH HAISE SASAKI.
THE SUZUYA SQUAD WILL LIKELY...
...REQUEST FURTHER ASSISTANCE FROM THE QS, INCLUDING INVESTI-GATOR MUTSUKI.
I WILL RECOMMEND INVESTIGATOR AURA AS A SUPPLEMEN-TARY MEMBER.
THANK YOU.
DON'T JUST FOCUS ON THE ENEMY AT HAND.
DO NOT LOSE SIGHT OF THE BIGGER PICTURE.
DO NOT BE CON-SUMED...
...BY HATRED OF THE ONE-EYED KING.
CAN YOU PLEASE TELL HIM THAT?
I WILL.
IN ANY CASE...
UI, HUH...?

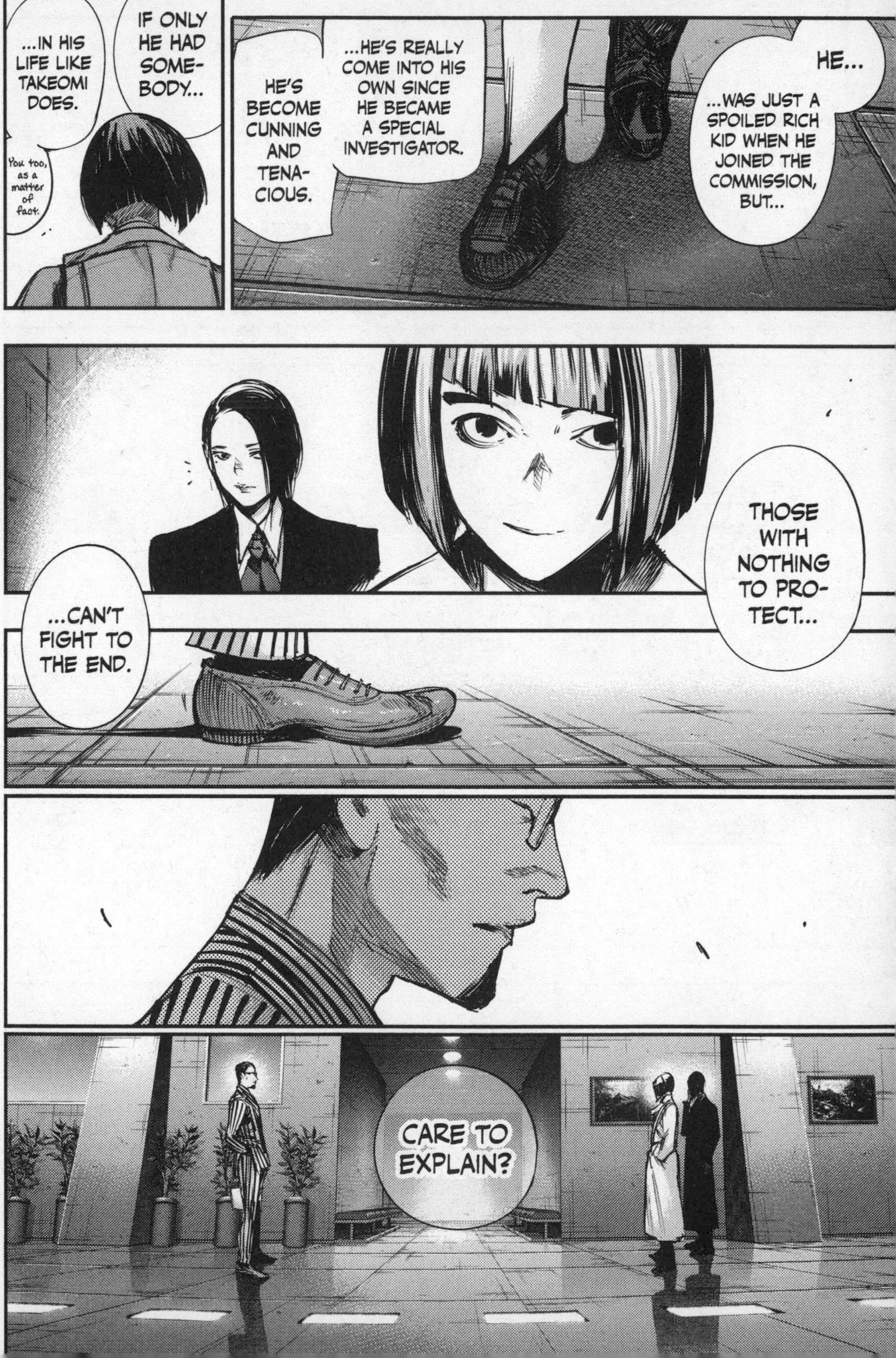
HE...
...WAS JUST A SPOILED RICH KID WHEN HE JOINED THE COMMISSION, BUT...
...HE'S REALLY COME INTO HIS OWN SINCE HE BECAME A SPECIAL INVESTIGATOR.
HE'S BECOME CUNNING AND TENACIOUS.
IF ONLY HE HAD SOMEBODY...
...IN HIS LIFE LIKE TAKEOMI DOES.
You too, as a matter of fact.
THOSE WITH NOTHING TO PROTECT...
...CAN'T FIGHT TO THE END.
CARE TO EXPLAIN?

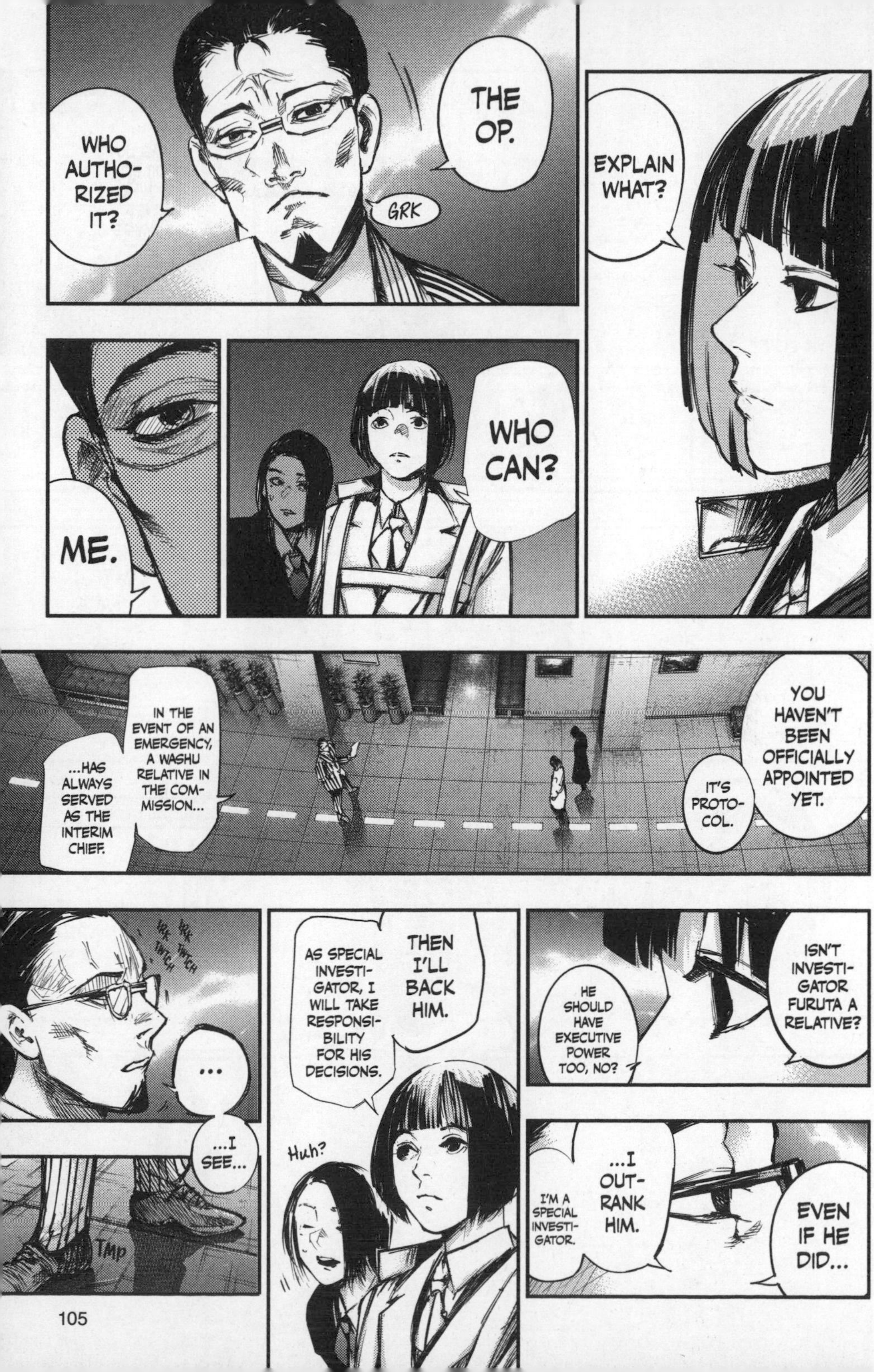
EXPLAIN WHAT?
THE OP.
GRK
WHO AUTHORIZED IT?
WHO CAN?
ME.
YOU HAVEN'T BEEN OFFICIALLY APPOINTED YET.
IT'S PROTOCOL.
IN THE EVENT OF AN EMERGENCY, A WASHU RELATIVE IN THE COMMISSION...
...HAS ALWAYS SERVED AS THE INTERIM CHIEF.
ISN'T INVESTIGATOR FURUTA A RELATIVE?
HE SHOULD HAVE EXECUTIVE POWER TOO, NO?
EVEN IF HE DID...
...I OUTRANK HIM.
I'M A SPECIAL INVESTIGATOR.
THEN I'LL BACK HIM.
AS SPECIAL INVESTIGATOR, I WILL TAKE RESPONSIBILITY FOR HIS DECISIONS.
Huh?
TWITCH TWITCH
...
...I SEE...
TMP

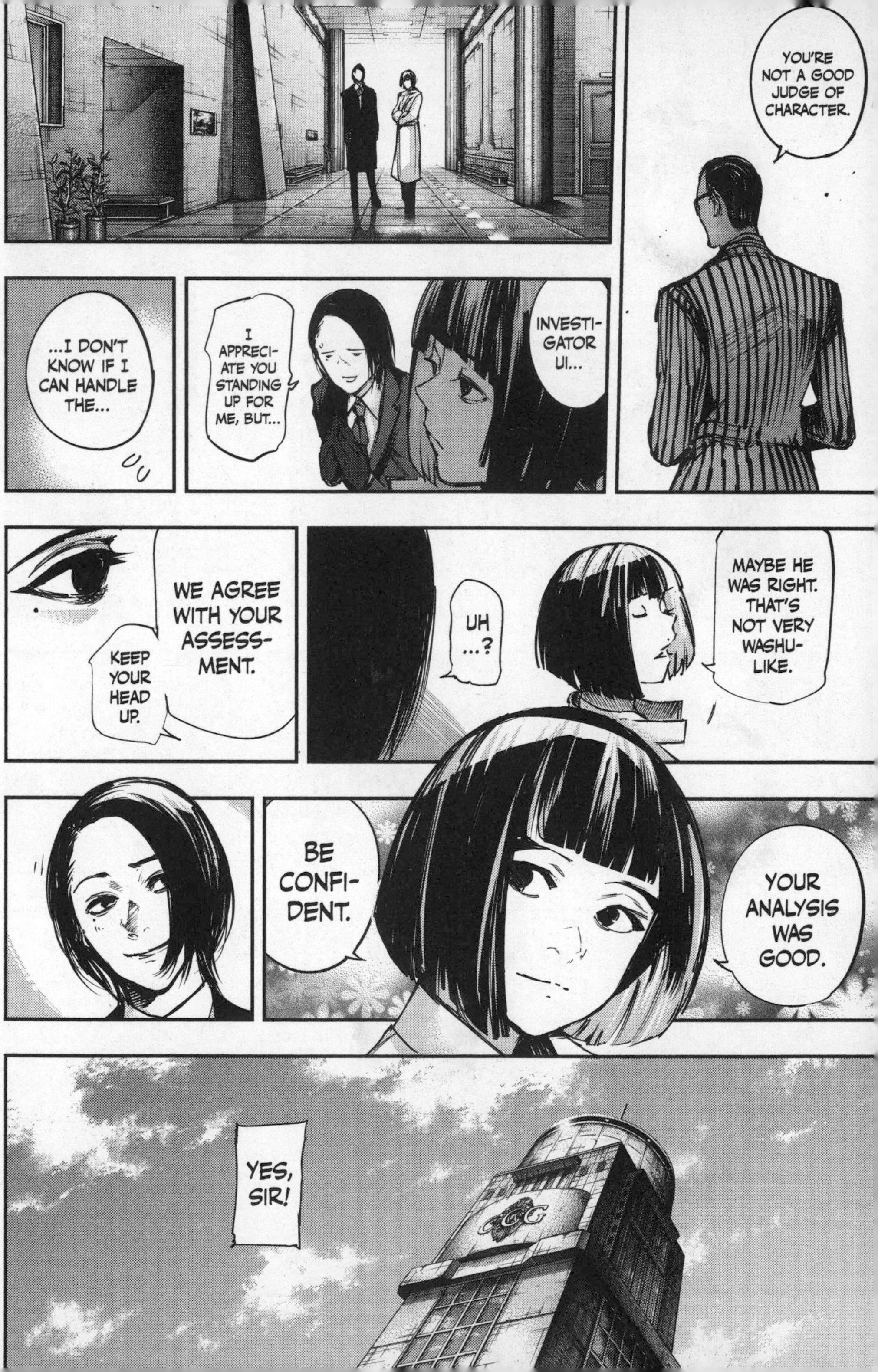
YOU'RE NOT A GOOD JUDGE OF CHARACTER.
INVESTIGATOR UI...
I APPRECIATE YOU STANDING UP FOR ME, BUT...
...I DON'T KNOW IF I CAN HANDLE THE...
MAYBE HE WAS RIGHT. THAT'S NOT VERY WASHU-LIKE.
UH ...?
WE AGREE WITH YOUR ASSESSMENT.
KEEP YOUR HEAD UP.
YOUR ANALYSIS WAS GOOD.
BE CONFIDENT.
YES, SIR!

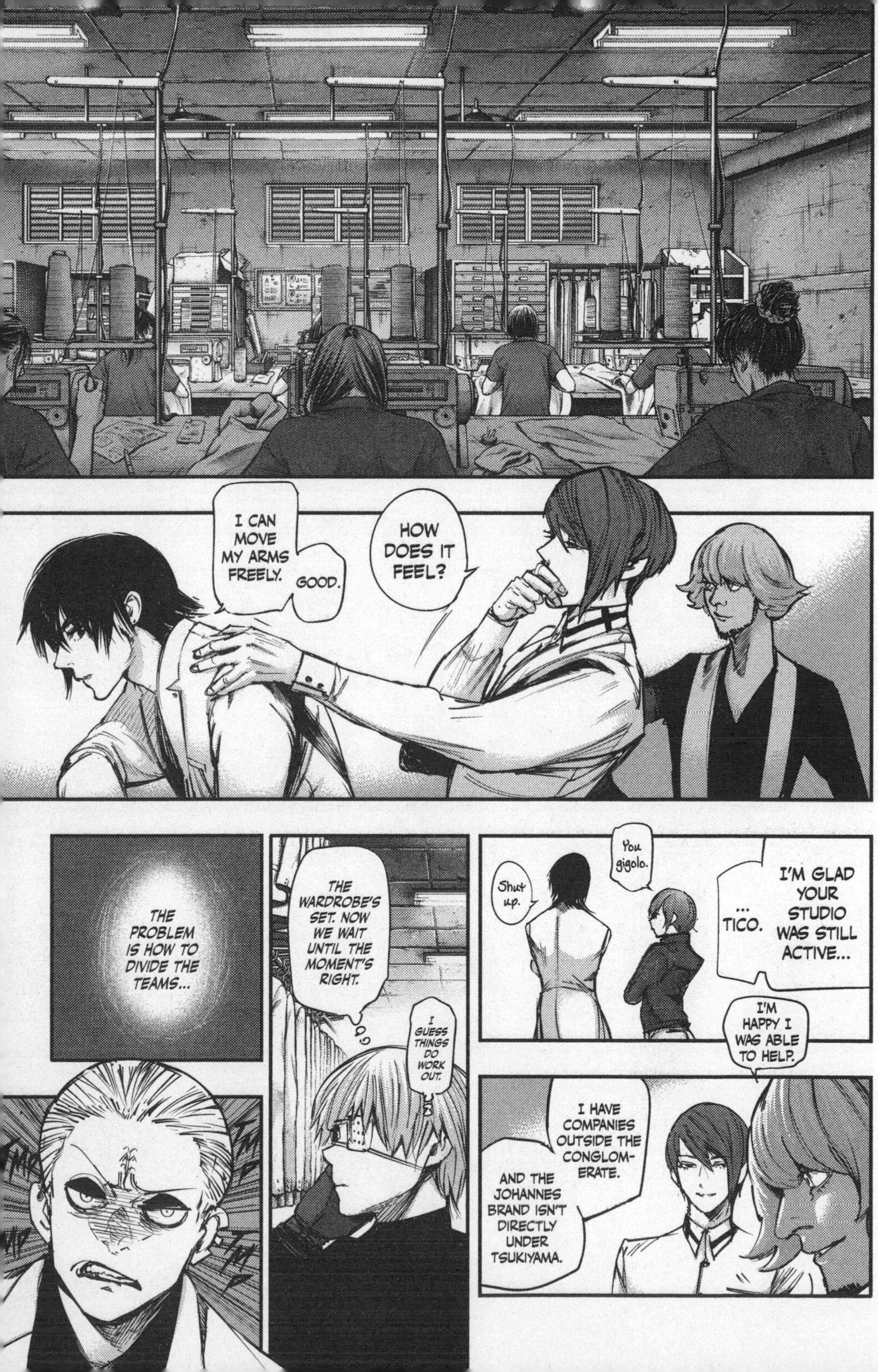
HOW DOES IT FEEL?
GOOD.
I CAN MOVE MY ARMS FREELY.
I'M GLAD YOUR STUDIO WAS STILL ACTIVE...
... TICO.
You gigolo.
Shut up.
I'M HAPPY I WAS ABLE TO HELP.
I HAVE COMPANIES OUTSIDE THE CONGLOM-ERATE.
AND THE JOHANNES BRAND ISN'T DIRECTLY UNDER TSUKIYAMA.
THE WARDROBE'S SET. NOW WE WAIT UNTIL THE MOMENT'S RIGHT.
I GUESS THINGS DO WORK OUT.
THE PROBLEM IS HOW TO DIVIDE THE TEAMS...
TMP

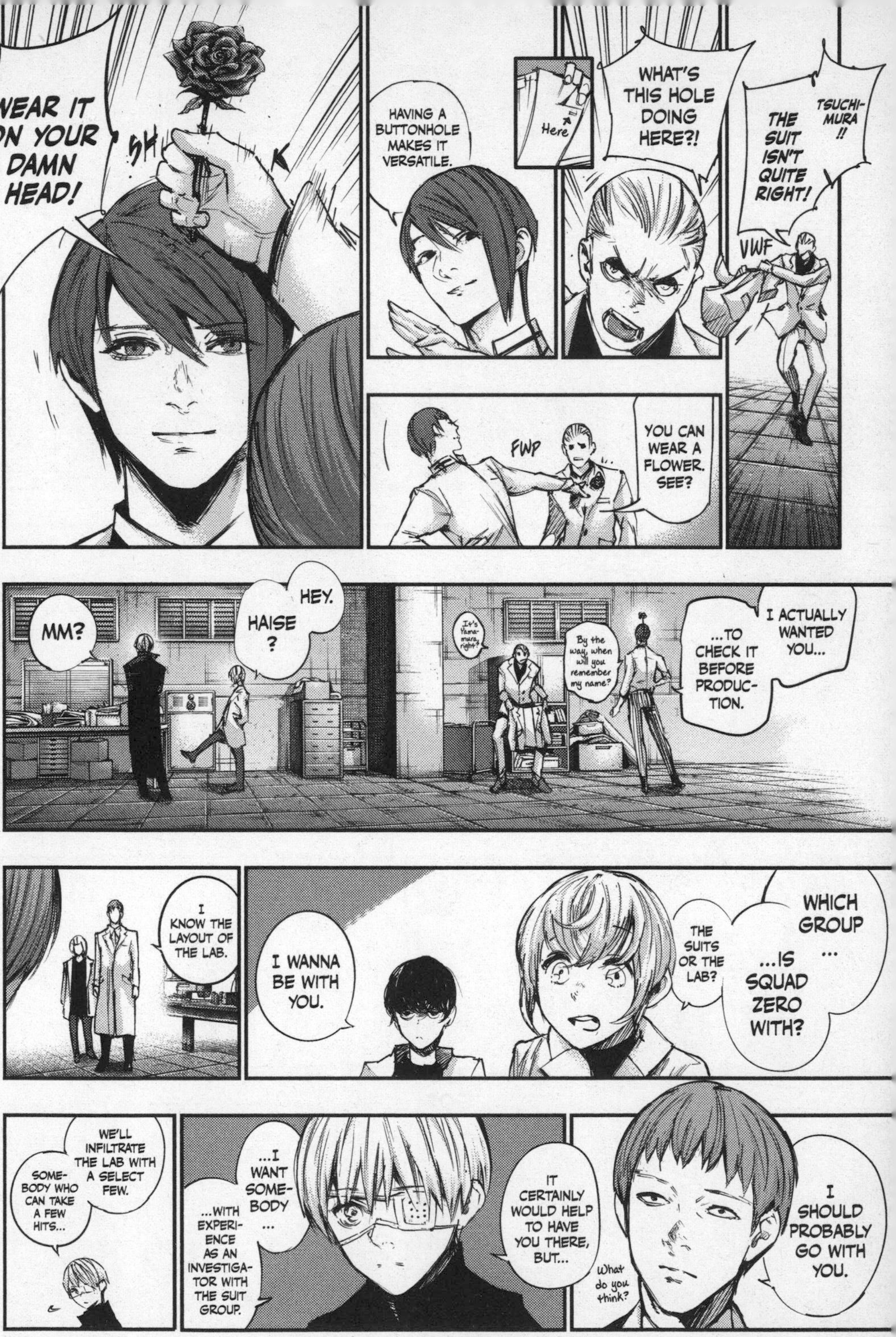
TSUCHIMURA!!
THE SUIT ISN'T QUITE RIGHT!
VWF
WHAT'S THIS HOLE DOING HERE?!
Here
HAVING A BUTTONHOLE MAKES IT VERSATILE.
YOU CAN WEAR A FLOWER. SEE?
FWP
WEAR IT ON YOUR DAMN HEAD!
SH
I ACTUALLY WANTED YOU...
...TO CHECK IT BEFORE PRODUCTION.
By the way, when will you remember my name?
It's Yamamura, right?
HEY. HAISE?
MM?
WHICH GROUP...
...IS SQUAD ZERO WITH?
THE SUITS OR THE LAB?
I WANNA BE WITH YOU.
I KNOW THE LAYOUT OF THE LAB.
I SHOULD PROBABLY GO WITH YOU.
What do you think?
IT CERTAINLY WOULD HELP TO HAVE YOU THERE, BUT...
...I WANT SOMEBODY...
...WITH EXPERIENCE AS AN INVESTIGATOR WITH THE SUIT GROUP.
WE'LL INFILTRATE THE LAB WITH A SELECT FEW.
SOMEBODY WHO CAN TAKE A FEW HITS...

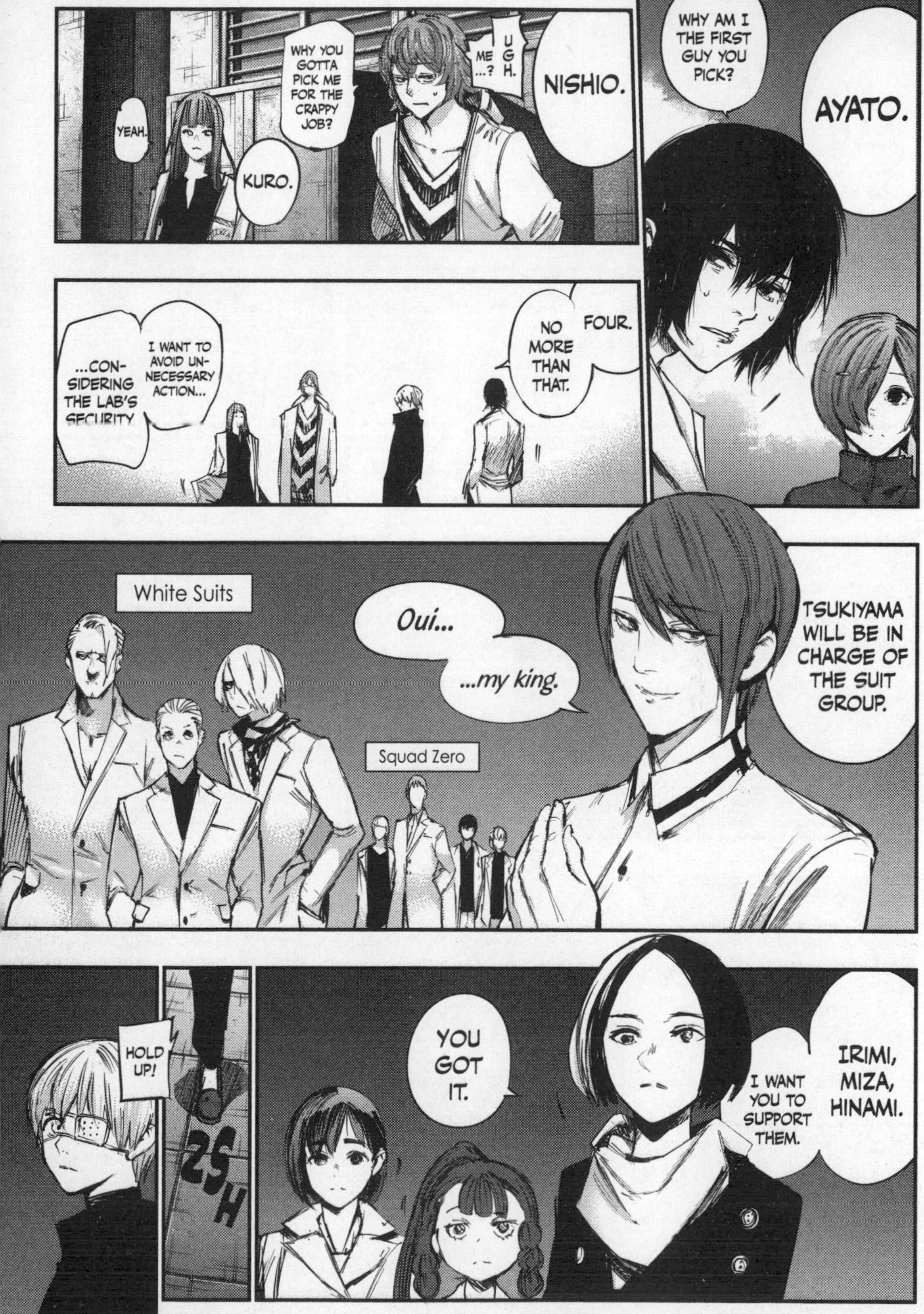
AYATO.
WHY AM I THE FIRST GUY YOU PICK?
NISHIO.
UGH.
ME...?
WHY YOU GOTTA PICK ME FOR THE CRAPPY JOB?
KURO.
YEAH.
FOUR.
NO MORE THAN THAT.
I WANT TO AVOID UNNECESSARY ACTION...
...CONSIDERING THE LAB'S SECURITY
TSUKIYAMA WILL BE IN CHARGE OF THE SUIT GROUP.
Oui...
...my king.
White Suits
Squad Zero
IRIMI, MIZA, HINAMI.
I WANT YOU TO SUPPORT THEM.
YOU GOT IT.
ZSH
HOLD UP!

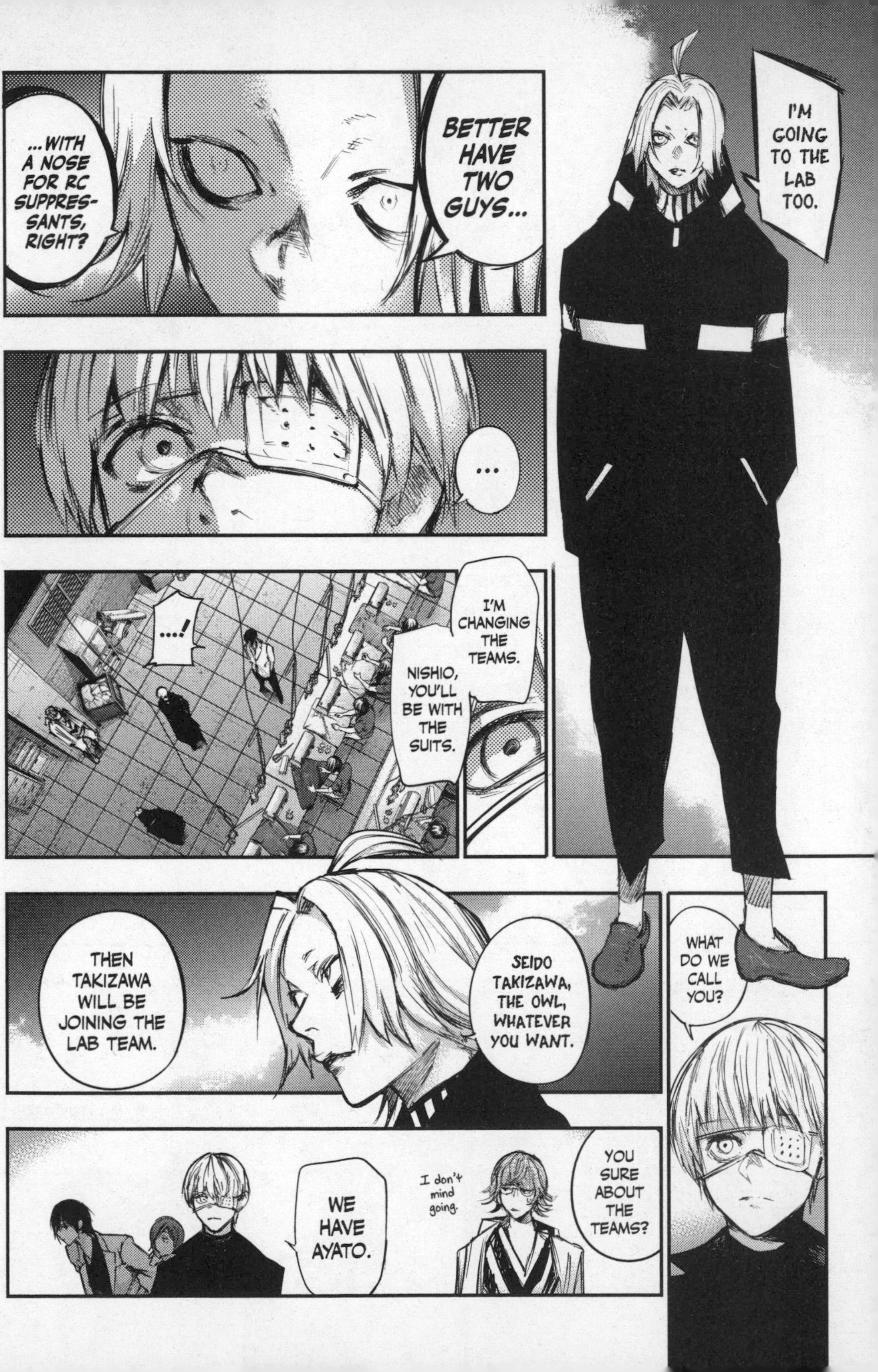
I'M GOING TO THE LAB TOO.
BETTER HAVE TWO GUYS...
...WITH A NOSE FOR RC SUPPRES-SANTS, RIGHT?
...
I'M CHANGING THE TEAMS.
NISHIO, YOU'LL BE WITH THE SUITS.
....!
WHAT DO WE CALL YOU?
SEIDO TAKIZAWA, THE OWL, WHATEVER YOU WANT.
THEN TAKIZAWA WILL BE JOINING THE LAB TEAM.
YOU SURE ABOUT THE TEAMS?
I don't mind going.
WE HAVE AYATO.

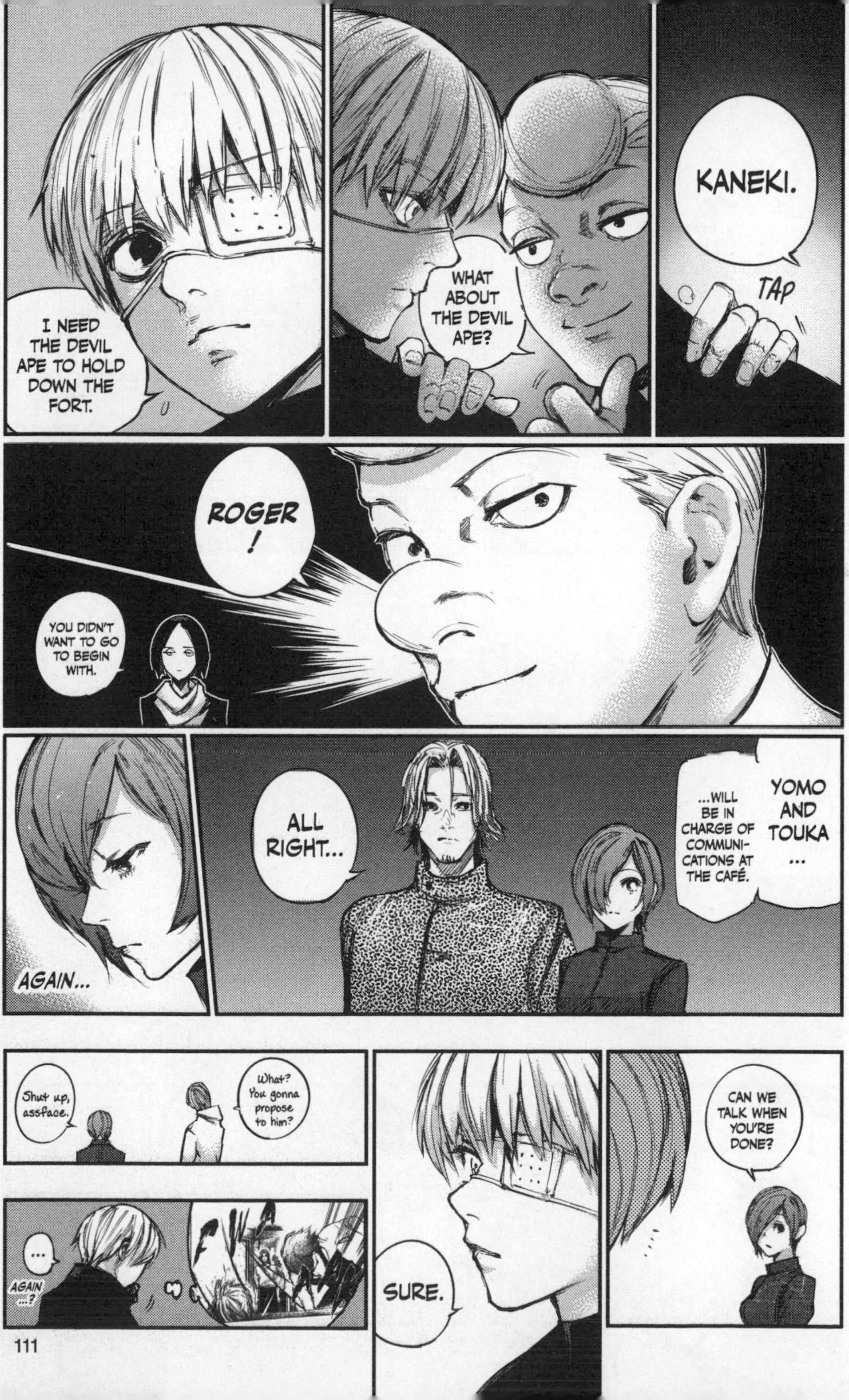
KANEKI.
TAP
WHAT ABOUT THE DEVIL APE?
I NEED THE DEVIL APE TO HOLD DOWN THE FORT.
ROGER!
YOU DIDN'T WANT TO GO TO BEGIN WITH.
YOMO AND TOUKA...
...WILL BE IN CHARGE OF COMMUNICATIONS AT THE CAFÉ.
ALL RIGHT...
AGAIN...
CAN WE TALK WHEN YOU'RE DONE?
...
SURE.
What? You gonna propose to him?
Shut up, assface.
...
AGAIN...?

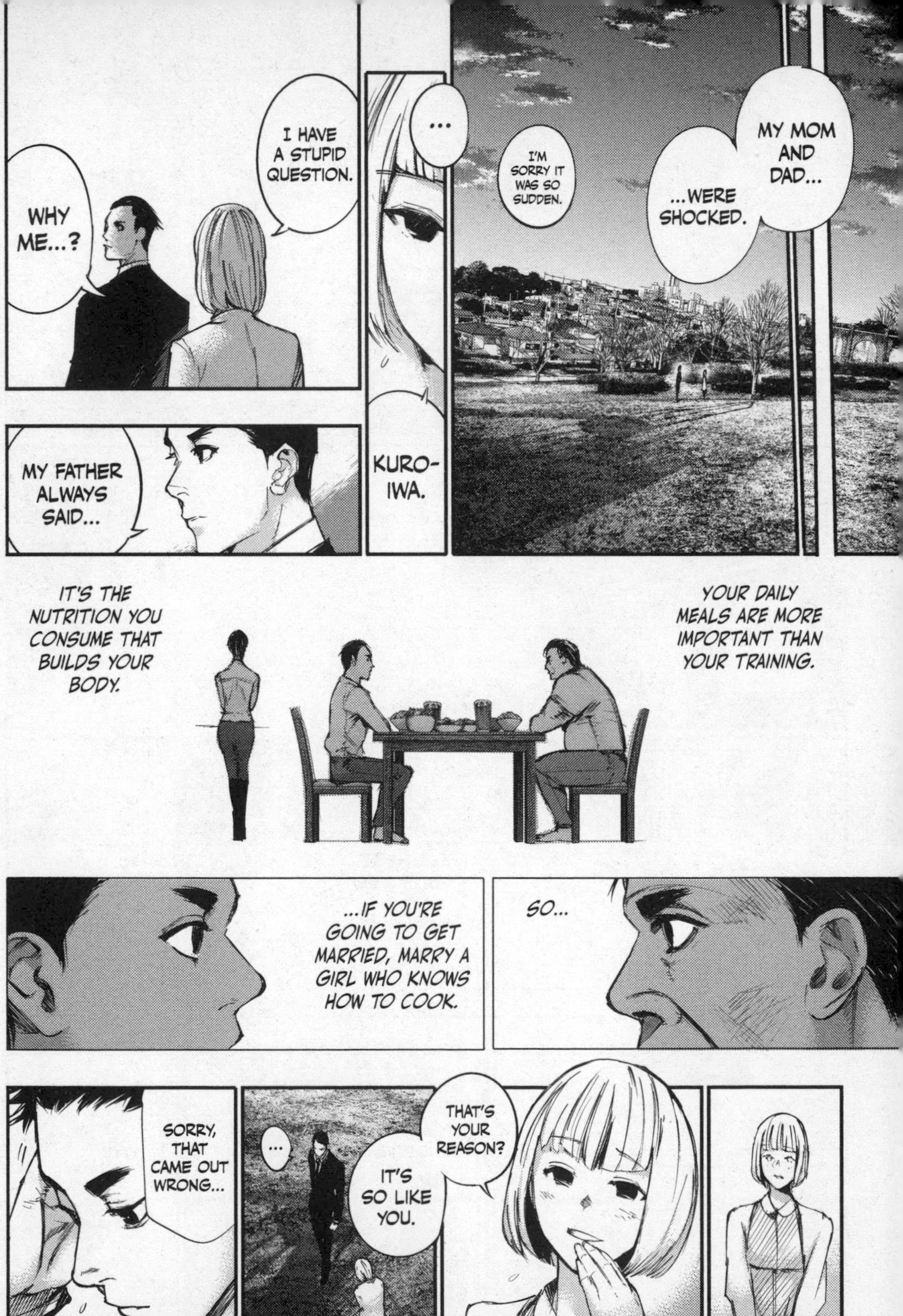
MY MOM AND DAD...
...WERE SHOCKED.
I'M SORRY IT WAS SO SUDDEN.
...
KURO-IWA.
I HAVE A STUPID QUESTION.
WHY ME...?
MY FATHER ALWAYS SAID...
YOUR DAILY MEALS ARE MORE IMPORTANT THAN YOUR TRAINING.
IT'S THE NUTRITION YOU CONSUME THAT BUILDS YOUR BODY.
SO...
...IF YOU'RE GOING TO GET MARRIED, MARRY A GIRL WHO KNOWS HOW TO COOK.
THAT'S YOUR REASON?
IT'S SO LIKE YOU.
...
SORRY, THAT CAME OUT WRONG...

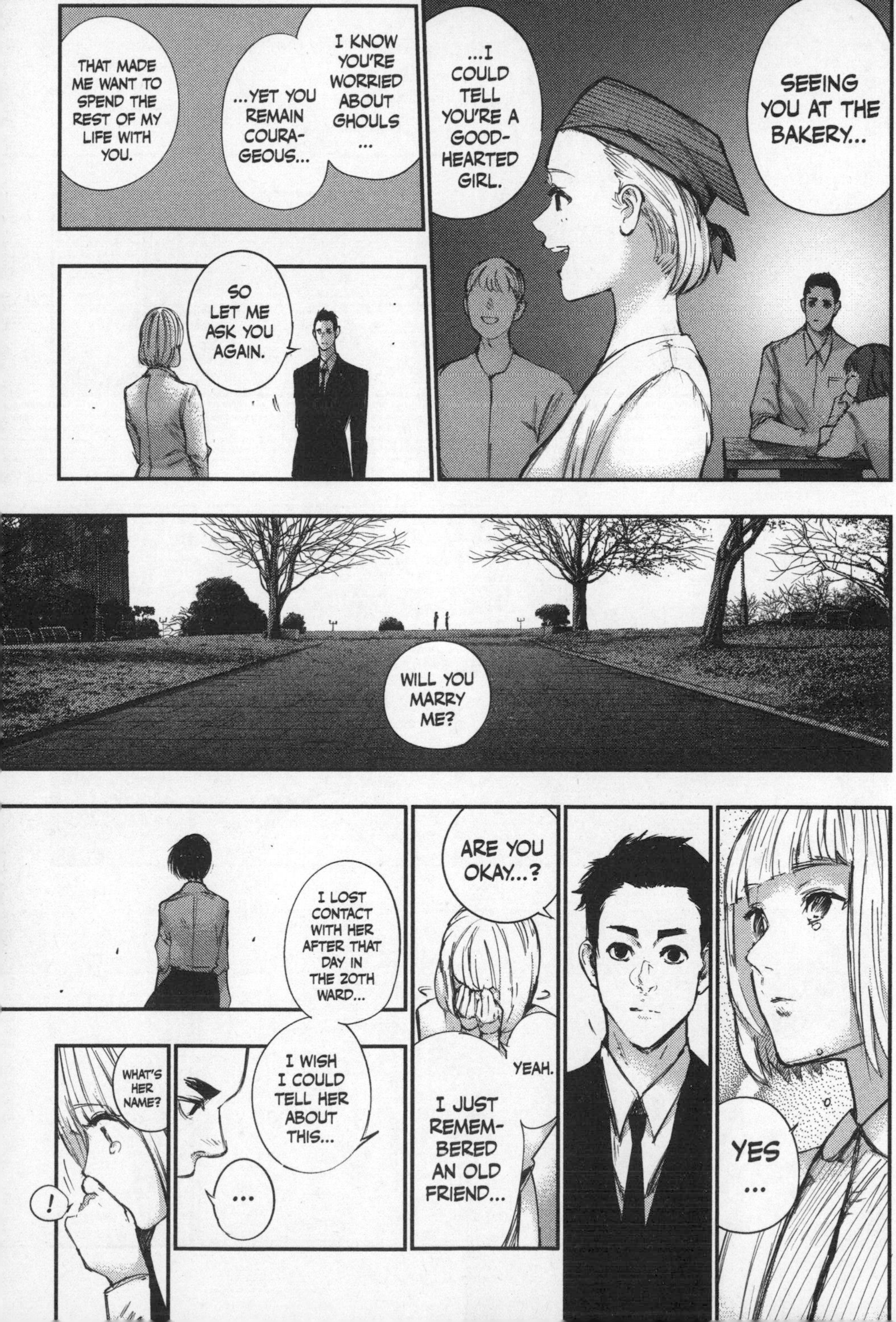
SEEING YOU AT THE BAKERY...
...I COULD TELL YOU'RE A GOOD-HEARTED GIRL.
I KNOW YOU'RE WORRIED ABOUT GHOULS...
...YET YOU REMAIN COURAGEOUS...
THAT MADE ME WANT TO SPEND THE REST OF MY LIFE WITH YOU.
SO LET ME ASK YOU AGAIN.
WILL YOU MARRY ME?
YES...
ARE YOU OKAY...?
YEAH.
I JUST REMEMBERED AN OLD FRIEND...
I LOST CONTACT WITH HER AFTER THAT DAY IN THE 20TH WARD...
I WISH I COULD TELL HER ABOUT THIS...
...
WHAT'S HER NAME?
!

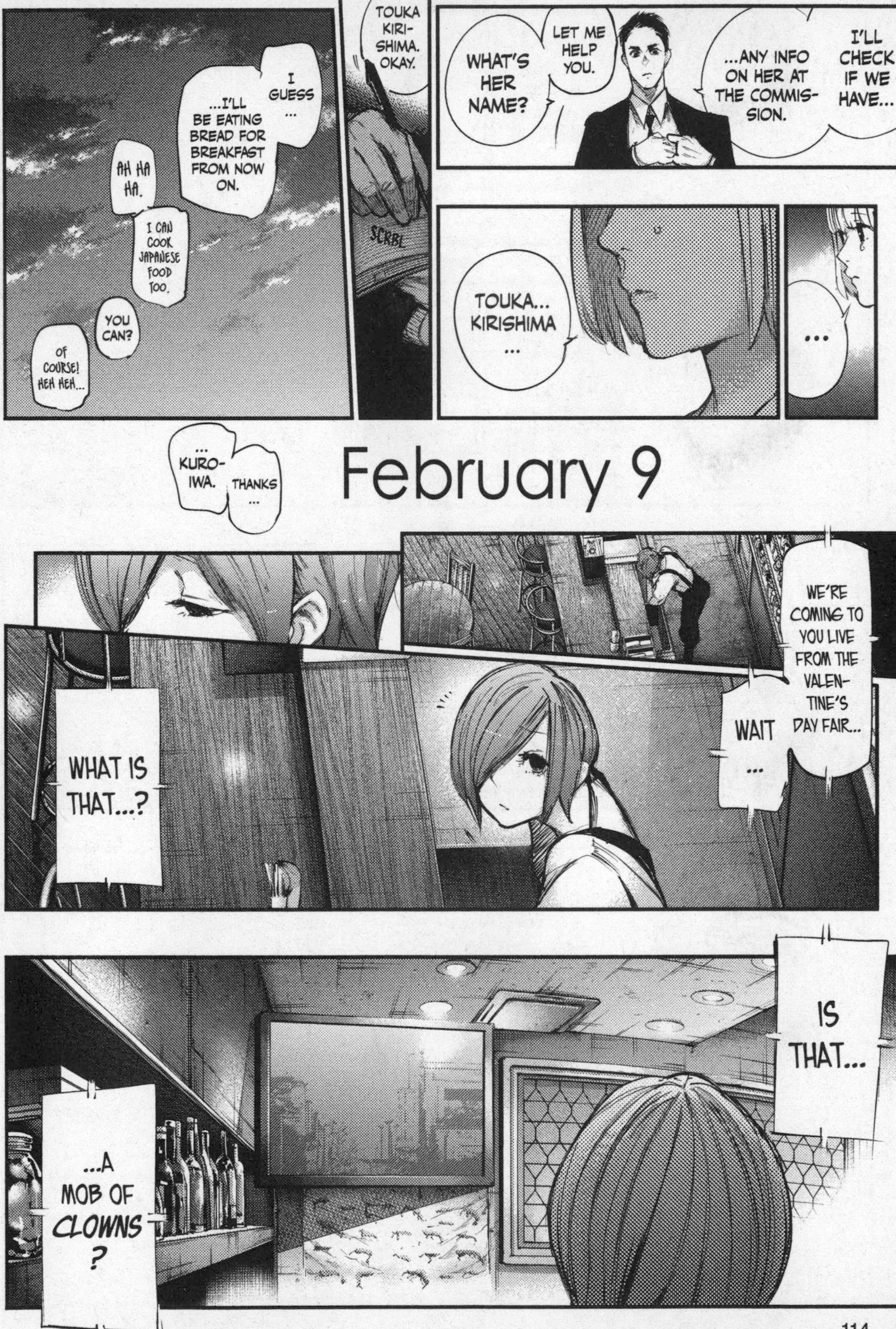

I'LL CHECK IF WE HAVE...
...ANY INFO ON HER AT THE COMMISSION.
LET ME HELP YOU.
WHAT'S HER NAME?
TOUKA KIRISHIMA. OKAY.
SCRBL
...
TOUKA... KIRISHIMA...
I GUESS...
...I'LL BE EATING BREAD FOR BREAKFAST FROM NOW ON.
AH HA HA.
I CAN COOK JAPANESE FOOD TOO.
YOU CAN?
OF COURSE! HEH HEH...
...KUROIWA.
THANKS...
February 9
WE'RE COMING TO YOU LIVE FROM THE VALENTINE'S DAY FAIR...
WAIT...
WHAT IS THAT...?
IS THAT...
...A MOB OF CLOWNS?

Acrostic

Theme 2: Tokyo Ghoul feat. Matsuri Washu

I will be your dog...
ZZZ
Urie...
ZZZ—

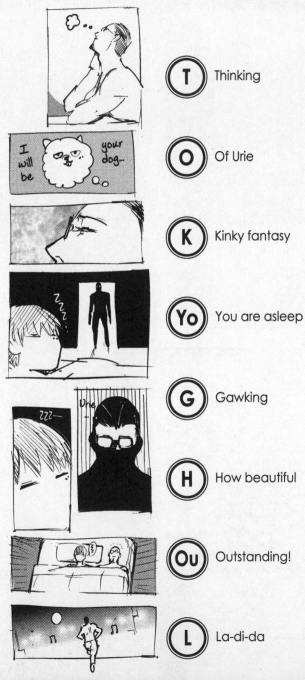

T Thinking

O Of Urie

K Kinky fantasy

Yo You are asleep

G Gawking

H How beautiful

Ou Outstanding!

L La-di-da

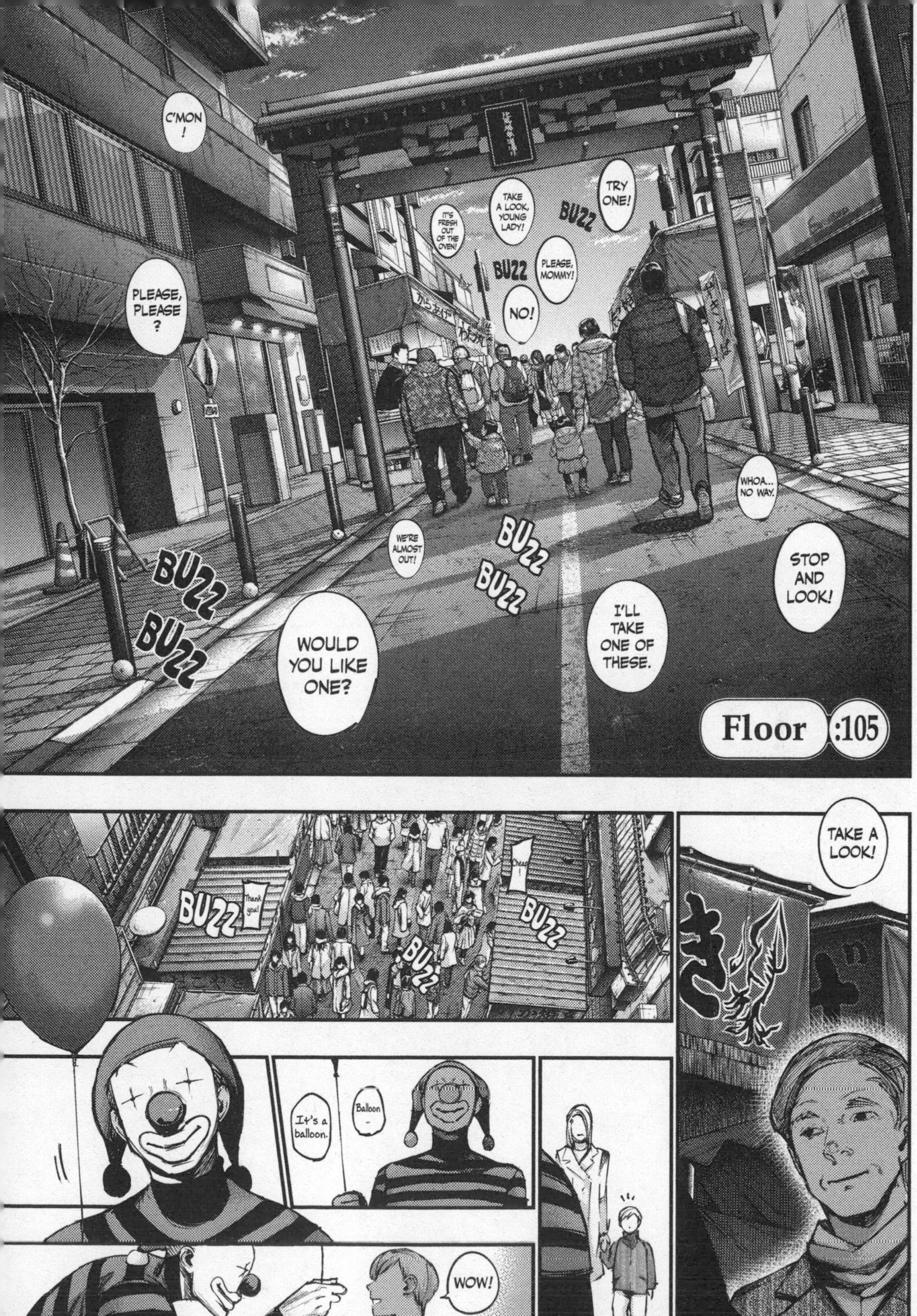
TRY ONE!
BUZZ
TAKE A LOOK, YOUNG LADY!
IT'S FRESH OUT OF THE OVEN!
PLEASE, MOMMY!
BUZZ
NO!
C'MON!
PLEASE, PLEASE?
WHOA... NO WAY.
STOP AND LOOK!
BUZZ BUZZ
WE'RE ALMOST OUT!
I'LL TAKE ONE OF THESE.
BUZZ BUZZ
WOULD YOU LIKE ONE?
Floor :105
TAKE A LOOK!
Cheap!
BUZZ
BUZZ
Thank you!
BUZZ
Balloon—
It's a balloon.
WOW!

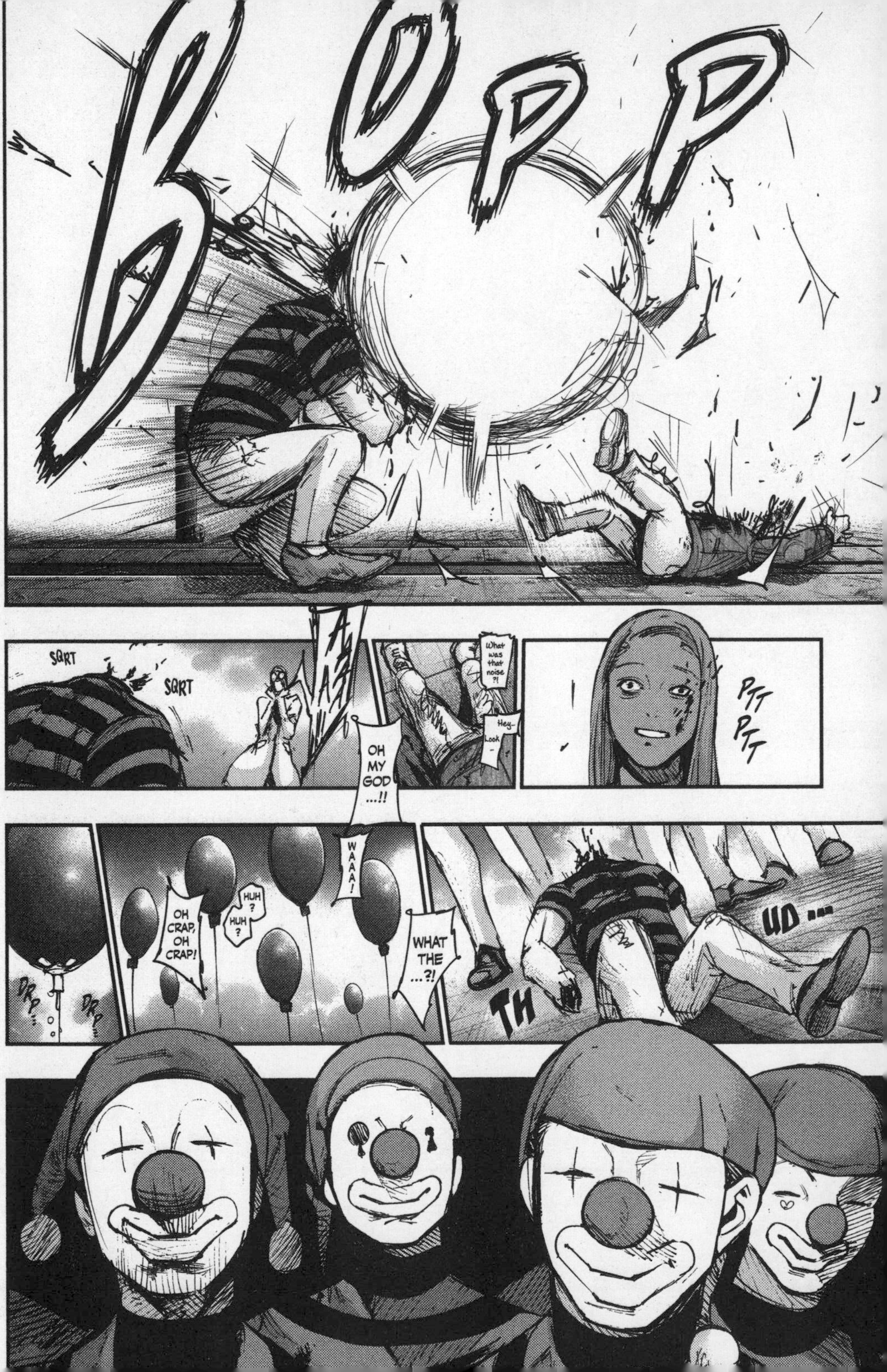
BOOP
!
PTT
PTT
What was that noise?!
Hey... Look...
OH MY GOD ...!!
SQRT
SQRT
UD...
TH
WHAT THE ...?!
WAAA!
HUH? HUH?
OH CRAP, OH CRAP!
DRP
DRP

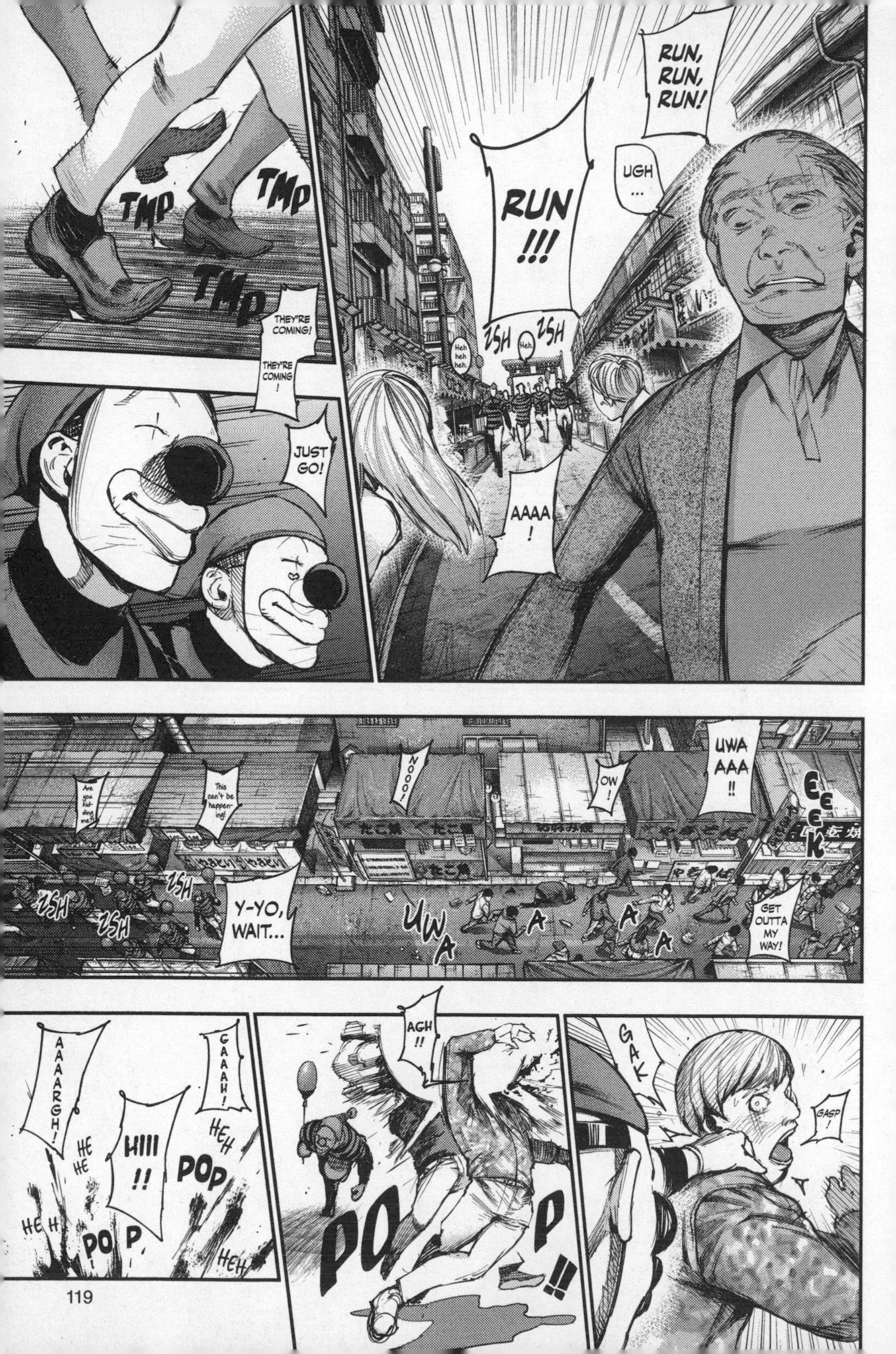
RUN, RUN, RUN!
UGH...
RUN!!!
Heh heh heh.
Heh.
ZSH ZSH
AAAA!
TMP TMP TMP
THEY'RE COMING! THEY'RE COMING!
JUST GO!
EEEK
UWA AAA!!
GET OUTTA MY WAY!
OW!
A A A
NOOOO!
UWA
Y-YO, WAIT...
This can't be happening!
Are you kidding me?!
ZSH ZSH ZSH
GAK
GASP!
AGH!!
POP!!
GAAAAH!
HIIII!!
AAAARGH!
HEH
HE HE
POP
HEH
POP
HEH

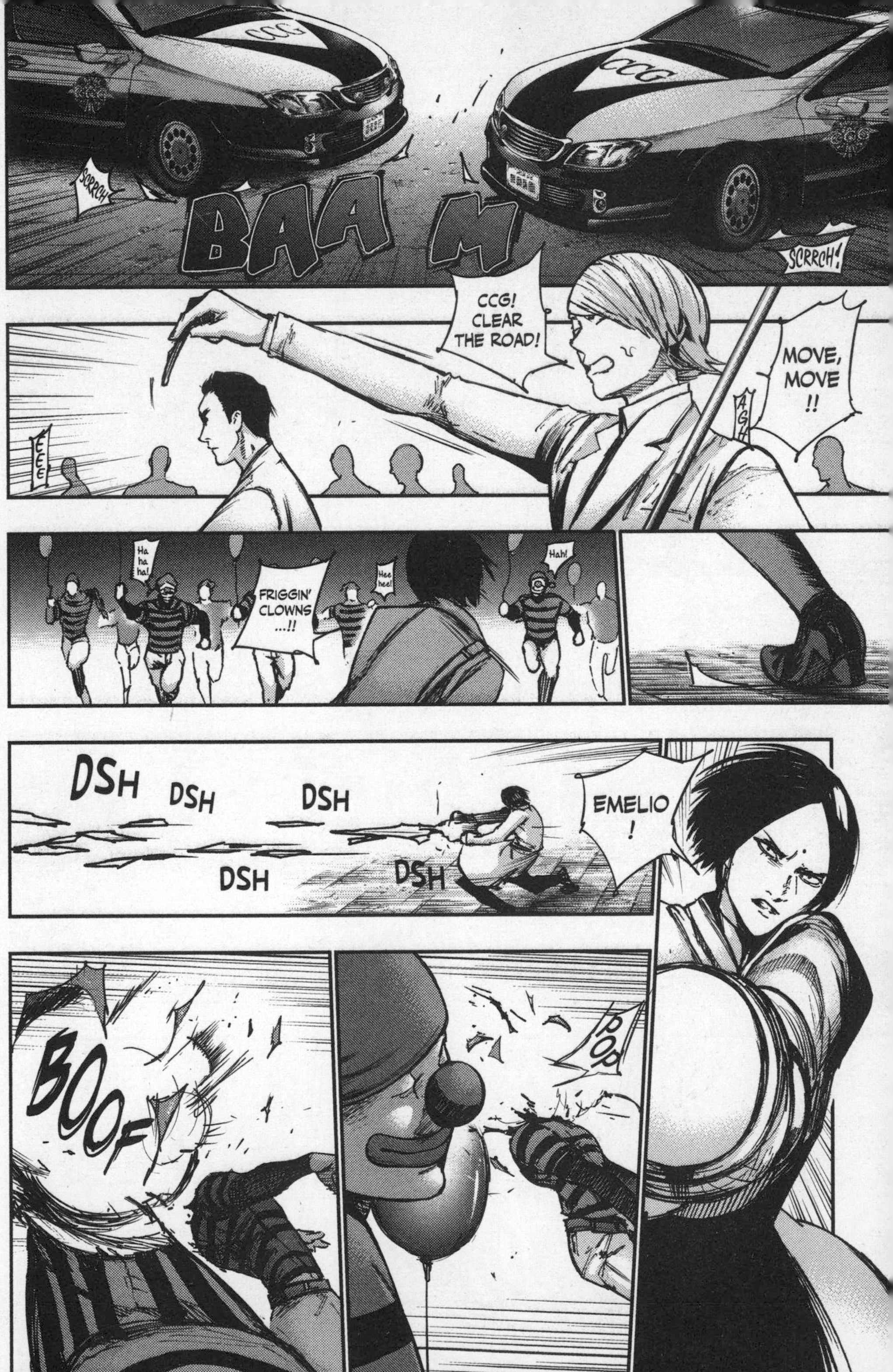
SCRRCH!
BAAM
SCRRCH
MOVE, MOVE!!
AGH
CCG! CLEAR THE ROAD!
EEE
Hah!
Hee hee!
FRIGGIN' CLOWNS...!!
Ha ha ha!
EMELIO!
DSH
DSH
DSH
DSH
DSH
POP
BOOF

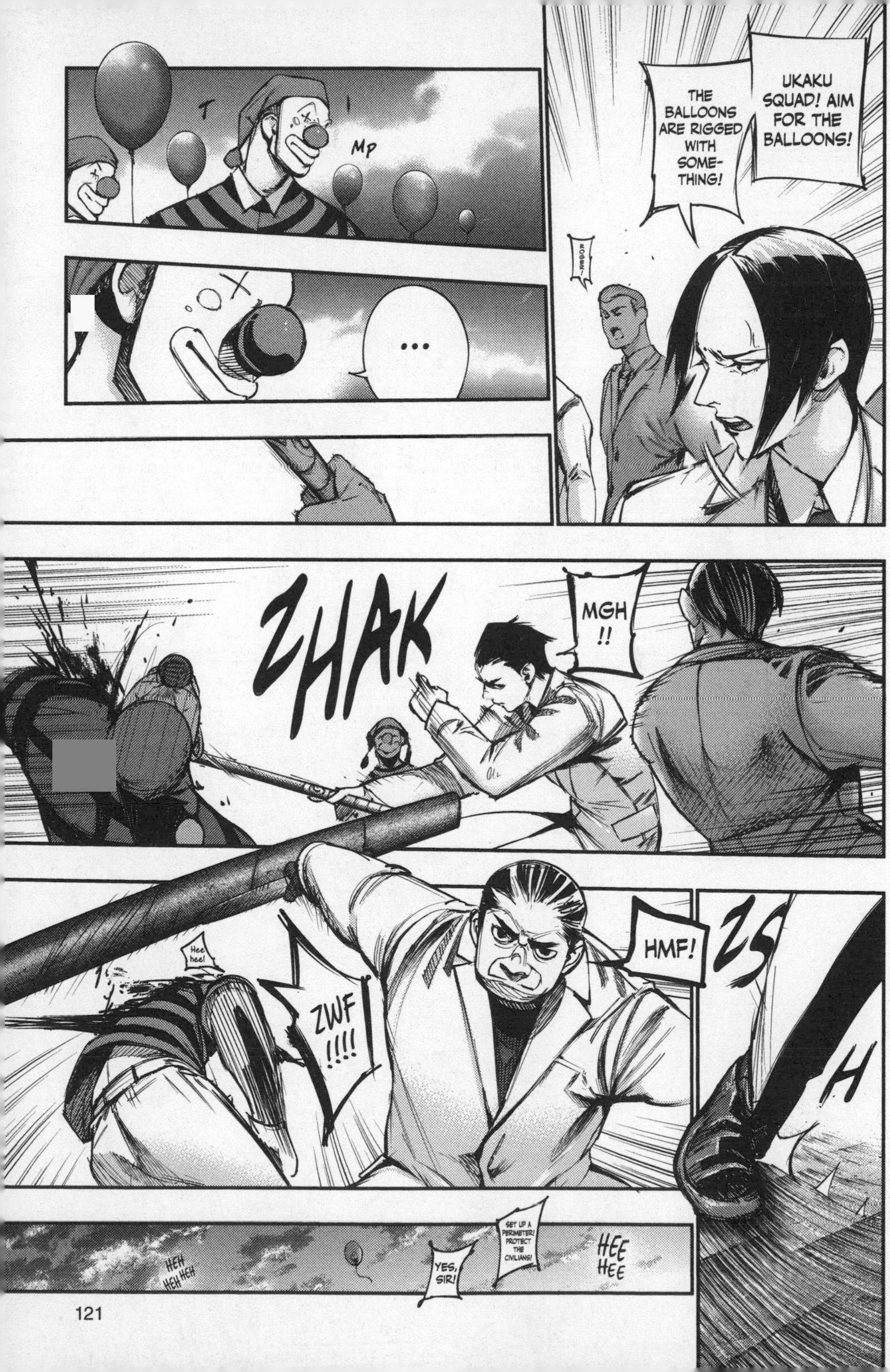
UKAKU SQUAD! AIM FOR THE BALLOONS!
THE BALLOONS ARE RIGGED WITH SOME-THING!
ROGER!
Mp
...
MGH !!
ZHAK
ZS
H
HMF!
ZWF !!!!
Hee hee!
HEE HEE
SET UP A PERIMETER! PROTECT THE CIVILIANS!
YES, SIR!
HEH HEH HEH

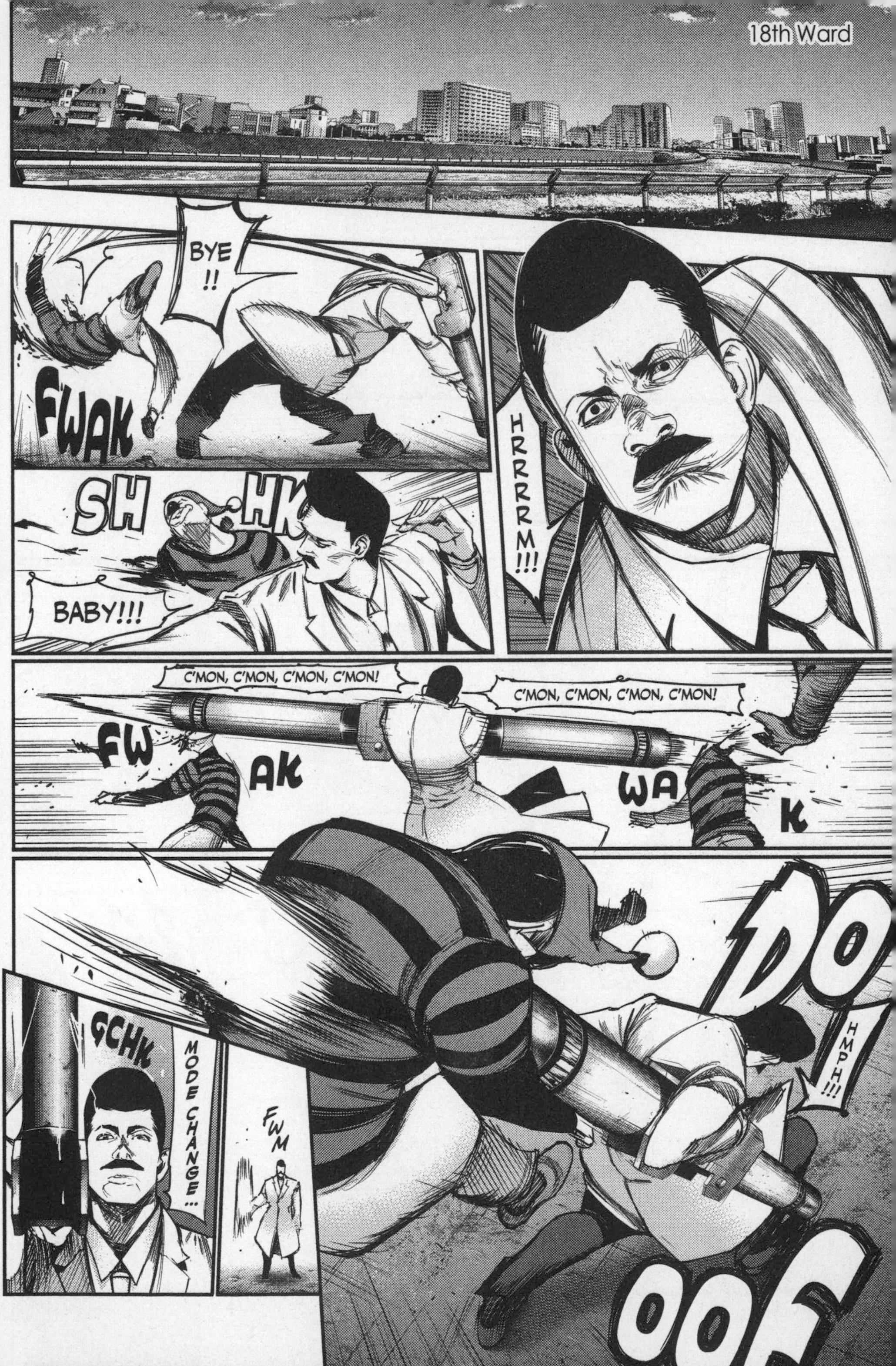
18th Ward
HRRRRM!!!
BYE!!
FWAK
SHHK
BABY!!!
C'MON, C'MON, C'MON, C'MON!
C'MON, C'MON, C'MON, C'MON!
WAK
FWAK
DOOOF
HMPH!!!
FWM
MODE CHANGE...
GCHK

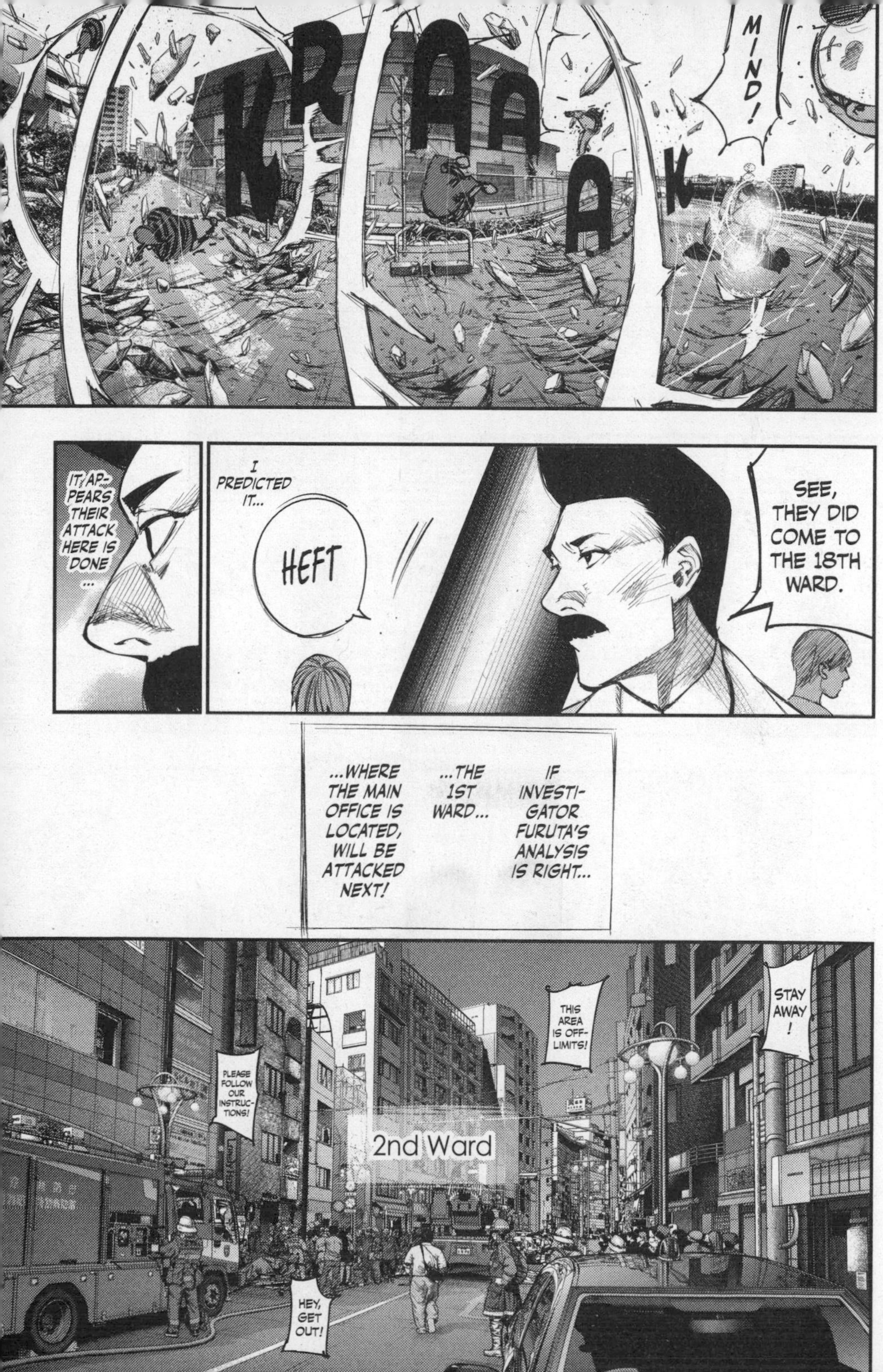
MIND!
KRAAAK
SEE, THEY DID COME TO THE 18TH WARD.
I PREDICTED IT...
HEFT
IT APPEARS THEIR ATTACK HERE IS DONE...
IF INVESTIGATOR FURUTA'S ANALYSIS IS RIGHT...
...THE 1ST WARD...
...WHERE THE MAIN OFFICE IS LOCATED, WILL BE ATTACKED NEXT!
STAY AWAY!
THIS AREA IS OFF-LIMITS!
2nd Ward
PLEASE FOLLOW OUR INSTRUCTIONS!
HEY, GET OUT!

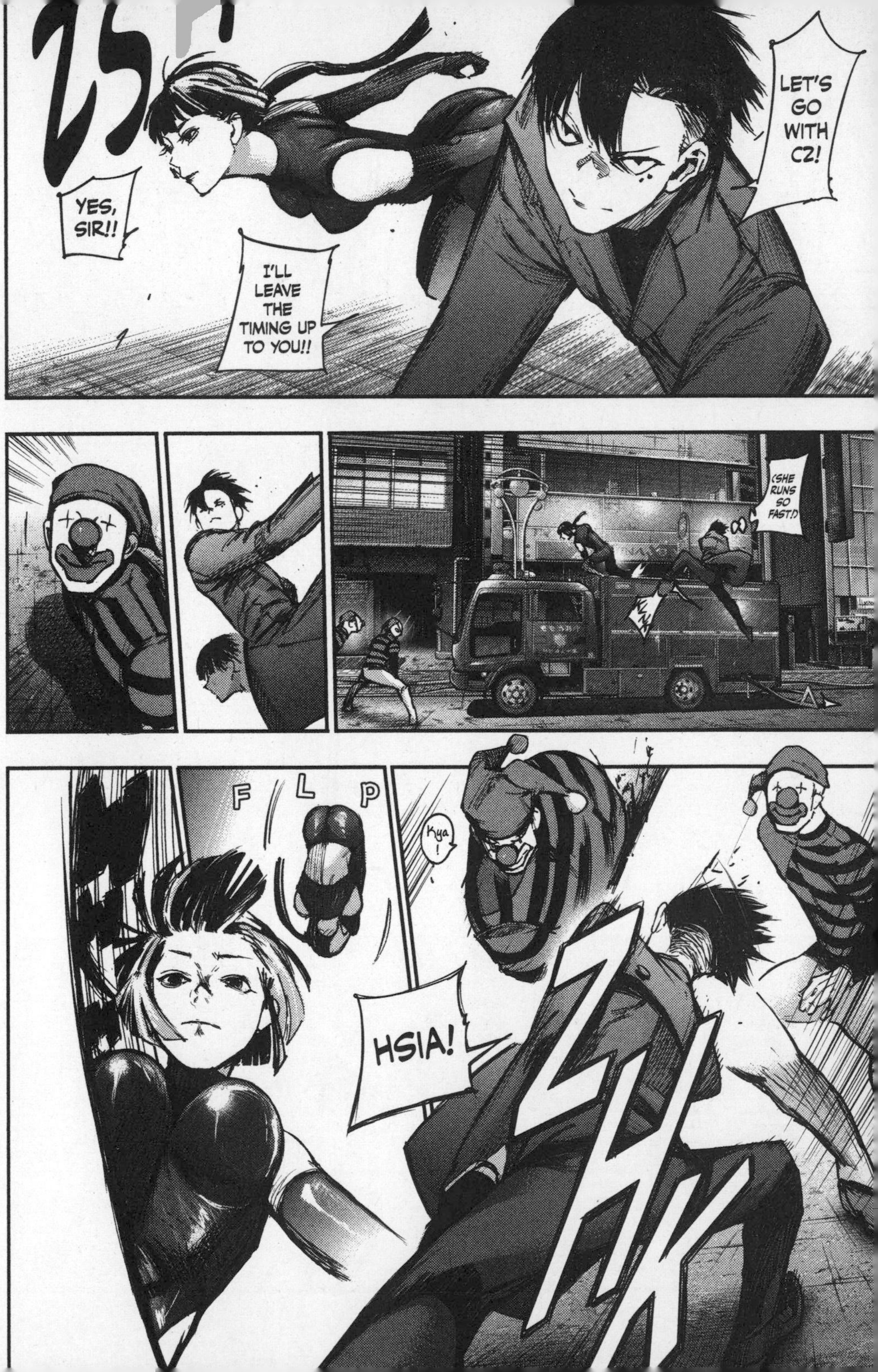
LET'S GO WITH C2!
I'LL LEAVE THE TIMING UP TO YOU!!
YES, SIR!!
(SHE RUNS SO FAST!)
Kya!
HSIA!
FLP

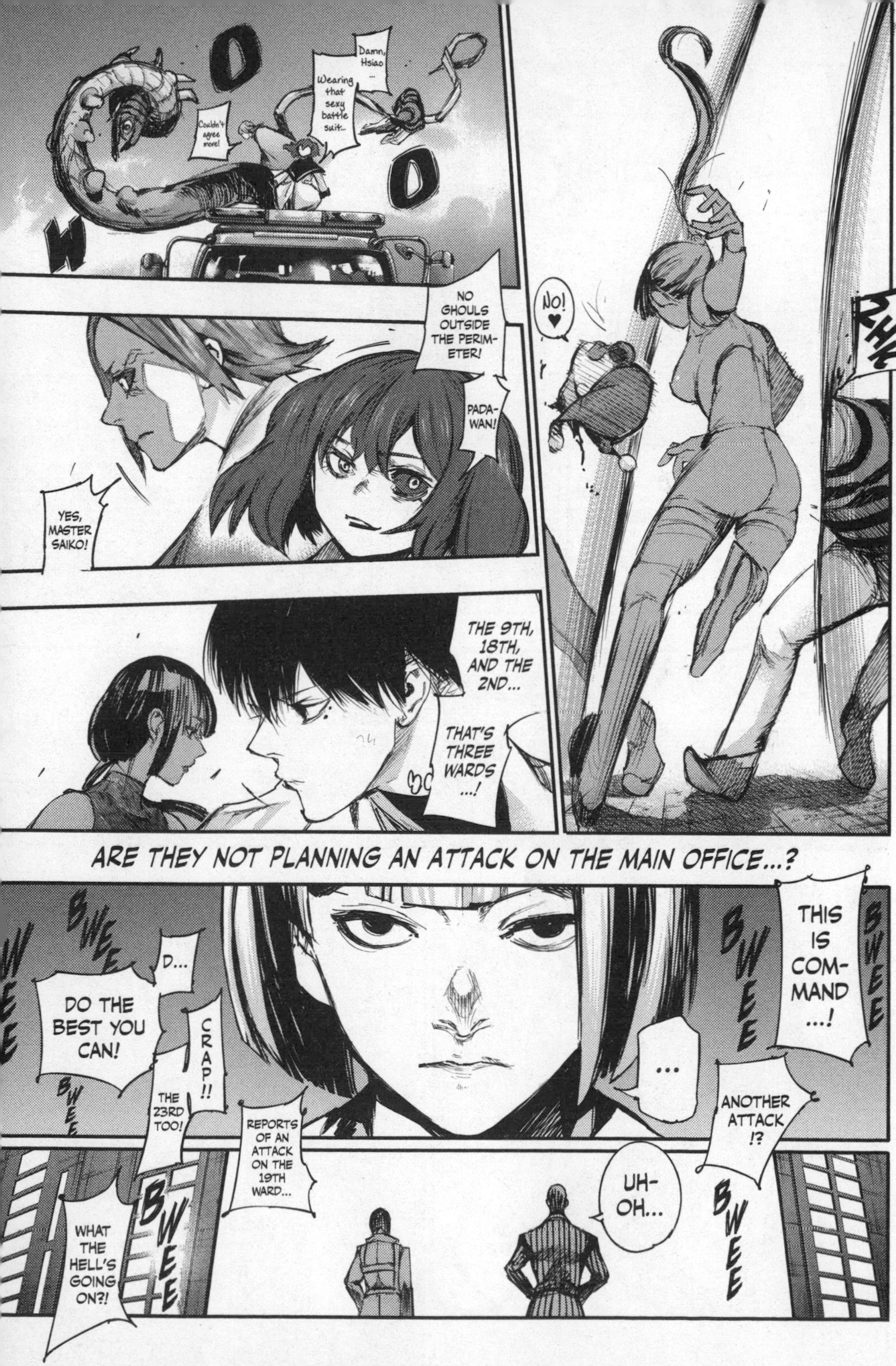

NO! ♥
SHK
Damn, Hsiao... Wearing that sexy battle suit...
Couldn't agree more!
NO GHOULS OUTSIDE THE PERIM-ETER!
PADA-WAN!
YES, MASTER SAIKO!
THE 9TH, 18TH, AND THE 2ND...
THAT'S THREE WARDS...!
ARE THEY NOT PLANNING AN ATTACK ON THE MAIN OFFICE...?
THIS IS COM-MAND...!
BWEE
...
ANOTHER ATTACK!?
BWEE
D...
DO THE BEST YOU CAN!
CRAP!!
THE 23RD TOO!
BWEE
UH-OH...
REPORTS OF AN ATTACK ON THE 19TH WARD...
BWEE
WHAT THE HELL'S GOING ON?!
BWEE

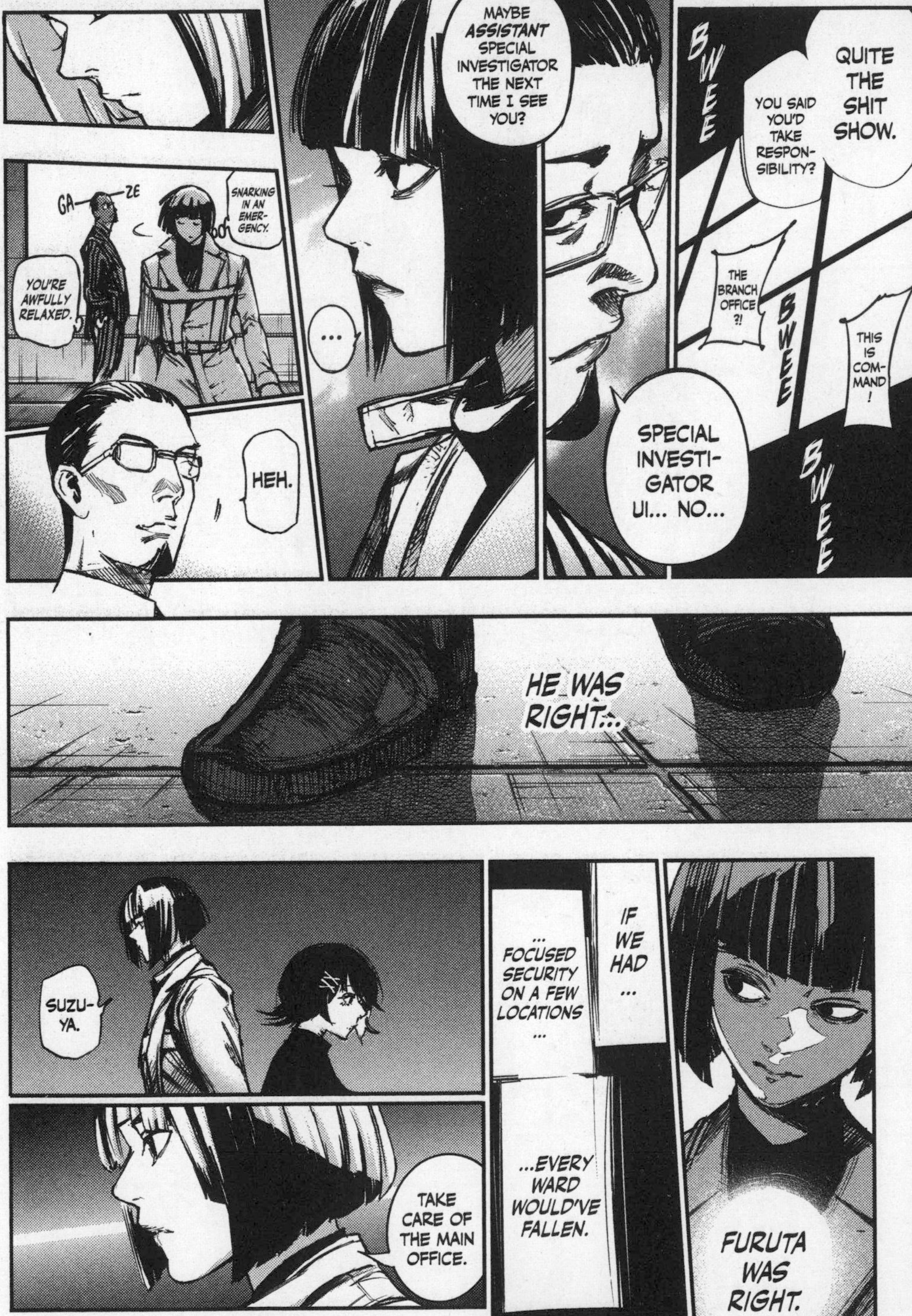
BWEE
QUITE THE SHIT SHOW.
YOU SAID YOU'D TAKE RESPON-SIBILITY?
THE BRANCH OFFICE?!
BWEE
THIS IS COMMAND!
BWEE
SPECIAL INVESTI-GATOR UI... NO...
MAYBE ASSISTANT SPECIAL INVESTIGATOR THE NEXT TIME I SEE YOU?
...
GA-ZE
SNARKING IN AN EMER-GENCY.
YOU'RE AWFULLY RELAXED.
HEH.
HE WAS RIGHT...
FURUTA WAS RIGHT.
IF WE HAD...
...FOCUSED SECURITY ON A FEW LOCATIONS...
...EVERY WARD WOULD'VE FALLEN.
SUZU-YA.
TAKE CARE OF THE MAIN OFFICE.

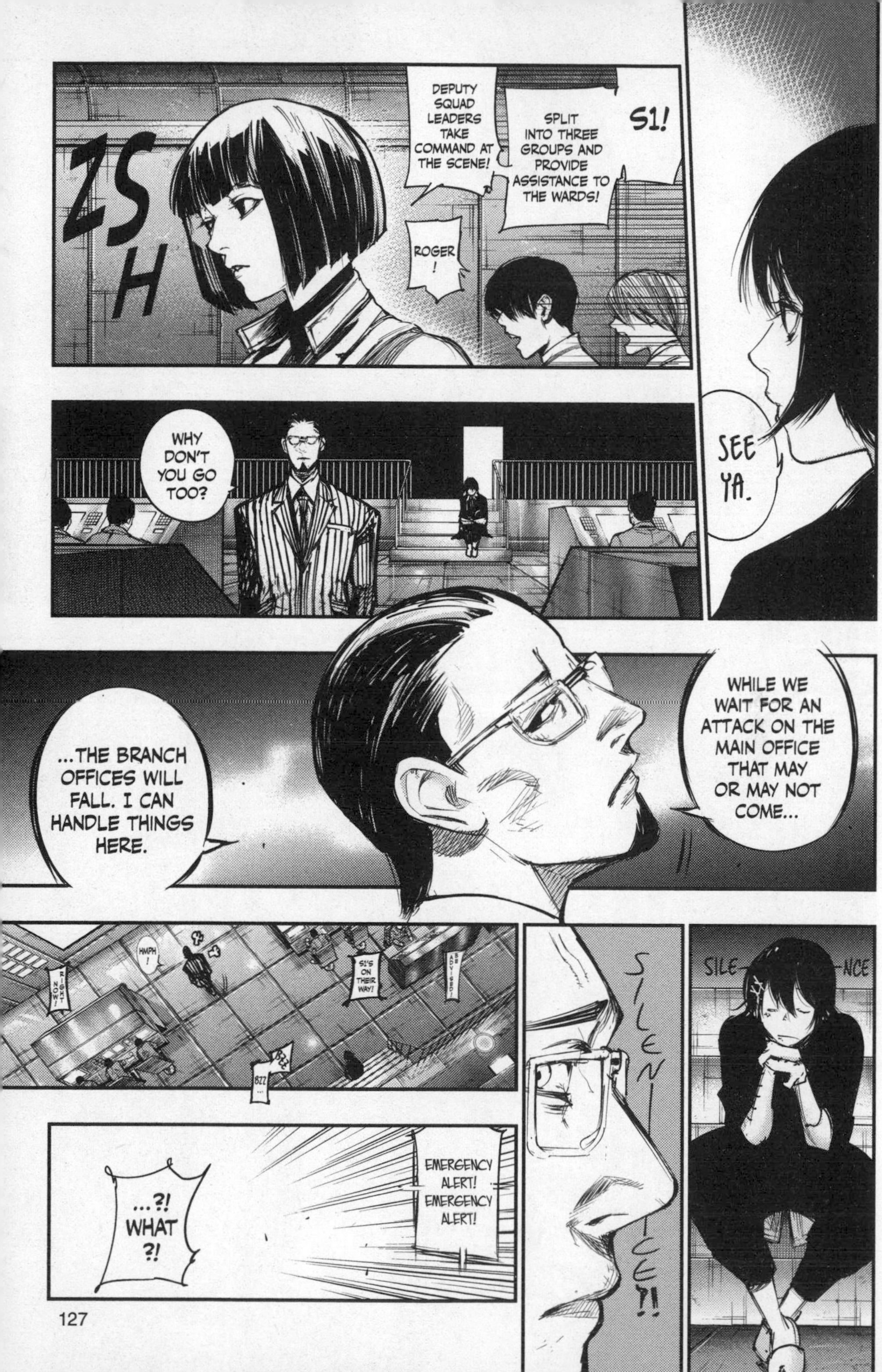
SEE YA.
S1!
SPLIT INTO THREE GROUPS AND PROVIDE ASSISTANCE TO THE WARDS!
DEPUTY SQUAD LEADERS TAKE COMMAND AT THE SCENE!
ROGER!
ZSH
WHY DON'T YOU GO TOO?
WHILE WE WAIT FOR AN ATTACK ON THE MAIN OFFICE THAT MAY OR MAY NOT COME...
...THE BRANCH OFFICES WILL FALL. I CAN HANDLE THINGS HERE.
SILE- NCE
SILENCE?!
BE ADVISED!
S1'S ON THEIR WAY!
HMPH!
RIGHT NOW!
BZZ
BZZ...
EMERGENCY ALERT! EMERGENCY ALERT!
...?! WHAT?!

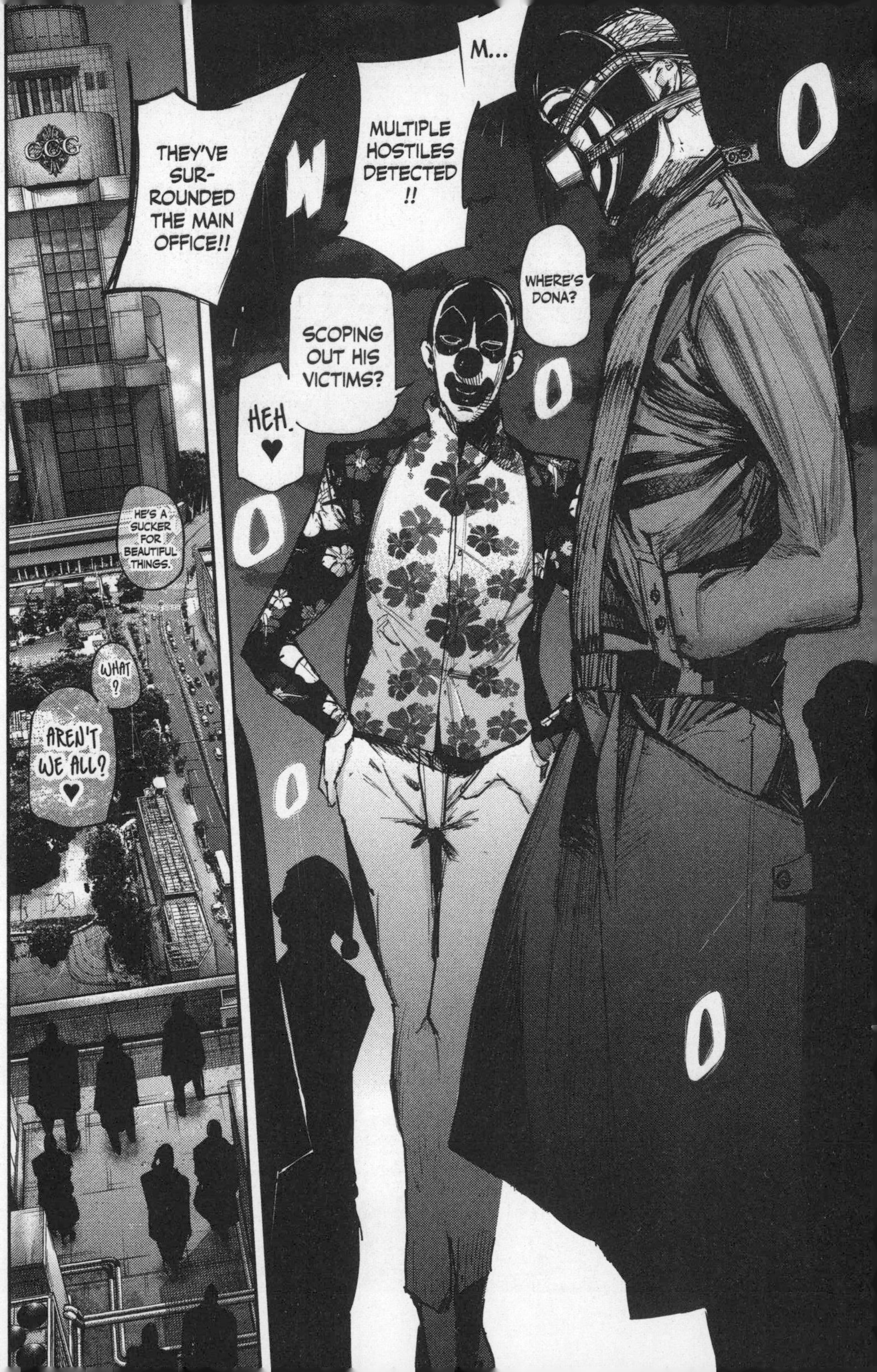
M...
W
O
MULTIPLE HOSTILES DETECTED !!
THEY'VE SUR-ROUNDED THE MAIN OFFICE!!
WHERE'S DONA?
O
SCOPING OUT HIS VICTIMS?
HEH. ♥
O
O
O
CCG
HE'S A SUCKER FOR BEAUTIFUL THINGS.
WHAT?
AREN'T WE ALL? ♥

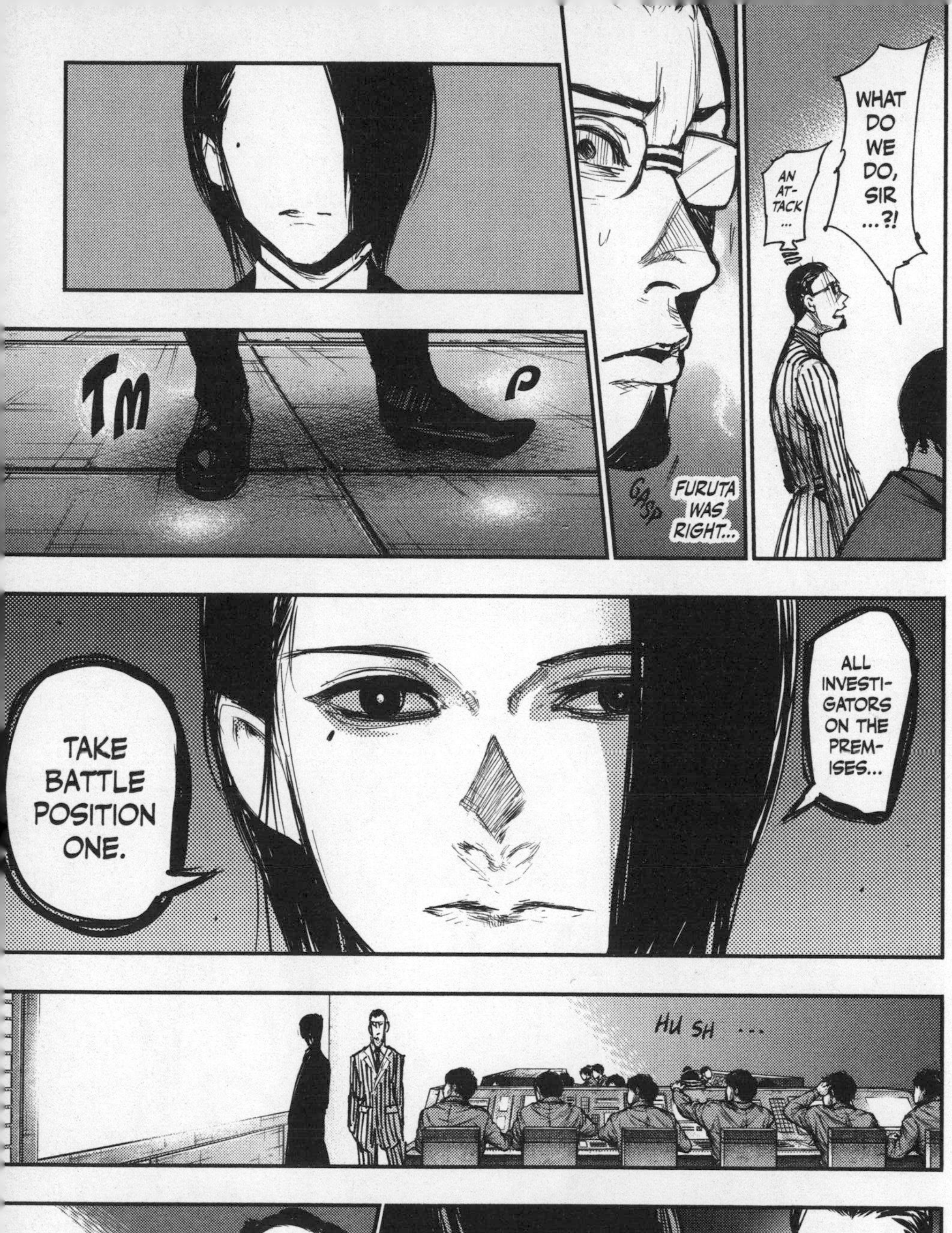
WHAT DO WE DO, SIR ...?!
AN AT-TACK ...
GASP
FURUTA WAS RIGHT...
TM P
ALL INVESTI-GATORS ON THE PREM-ISES...
TAKE BATTLE POSITION ONE.
HU SH ...
WHAT?

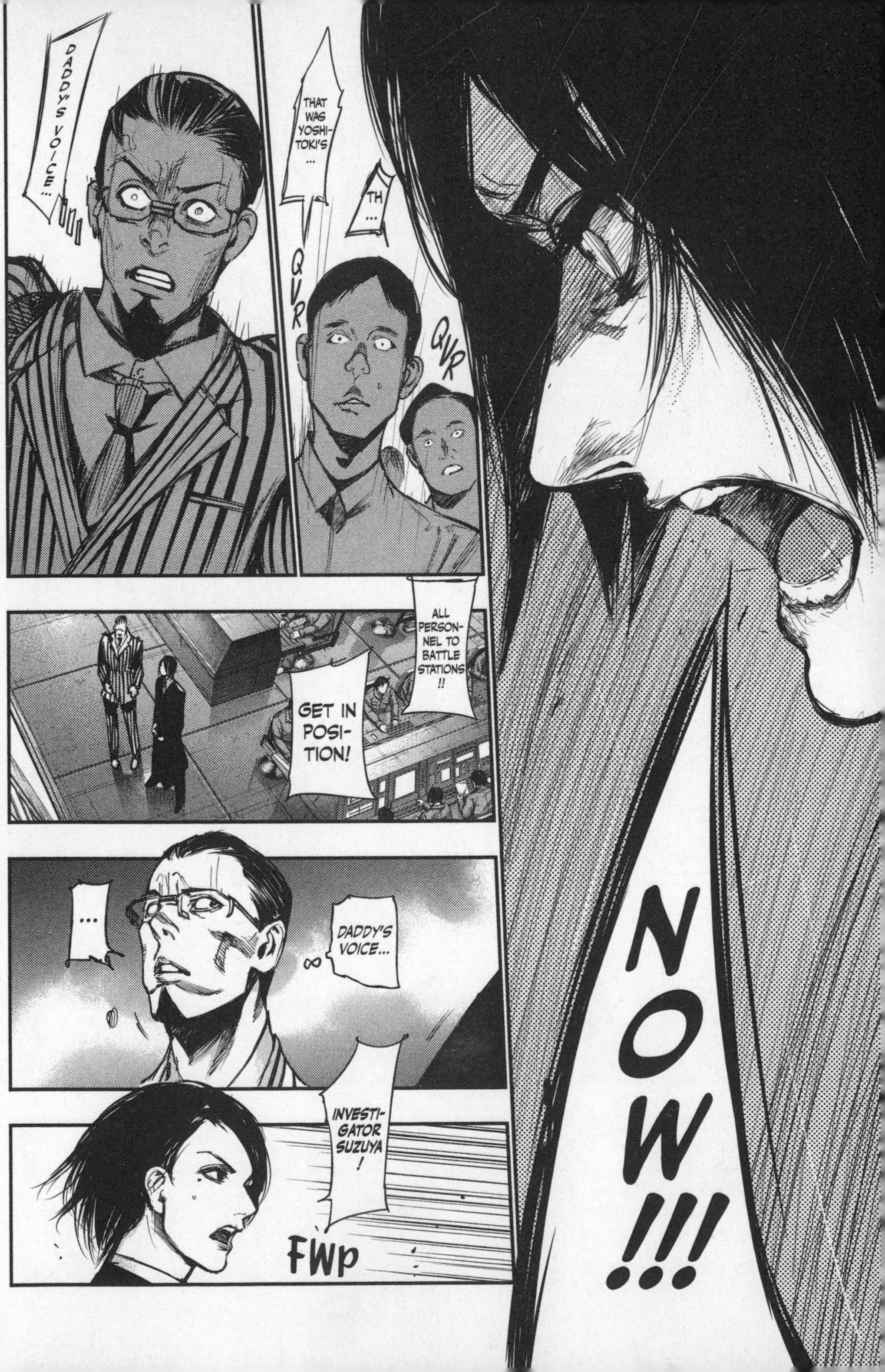
NOW!!!
THAT WAS YOSHI-TOKI'S ...
TH ...
QVR
QVR
DADDY'S VOICE...
ALL PERSON-NEL TO BATTLE STATIONS !!
GET IN POSI-TION!
DADDY'S VOICE...
...
INVESTI-GATOR SUZUYA !
FWp

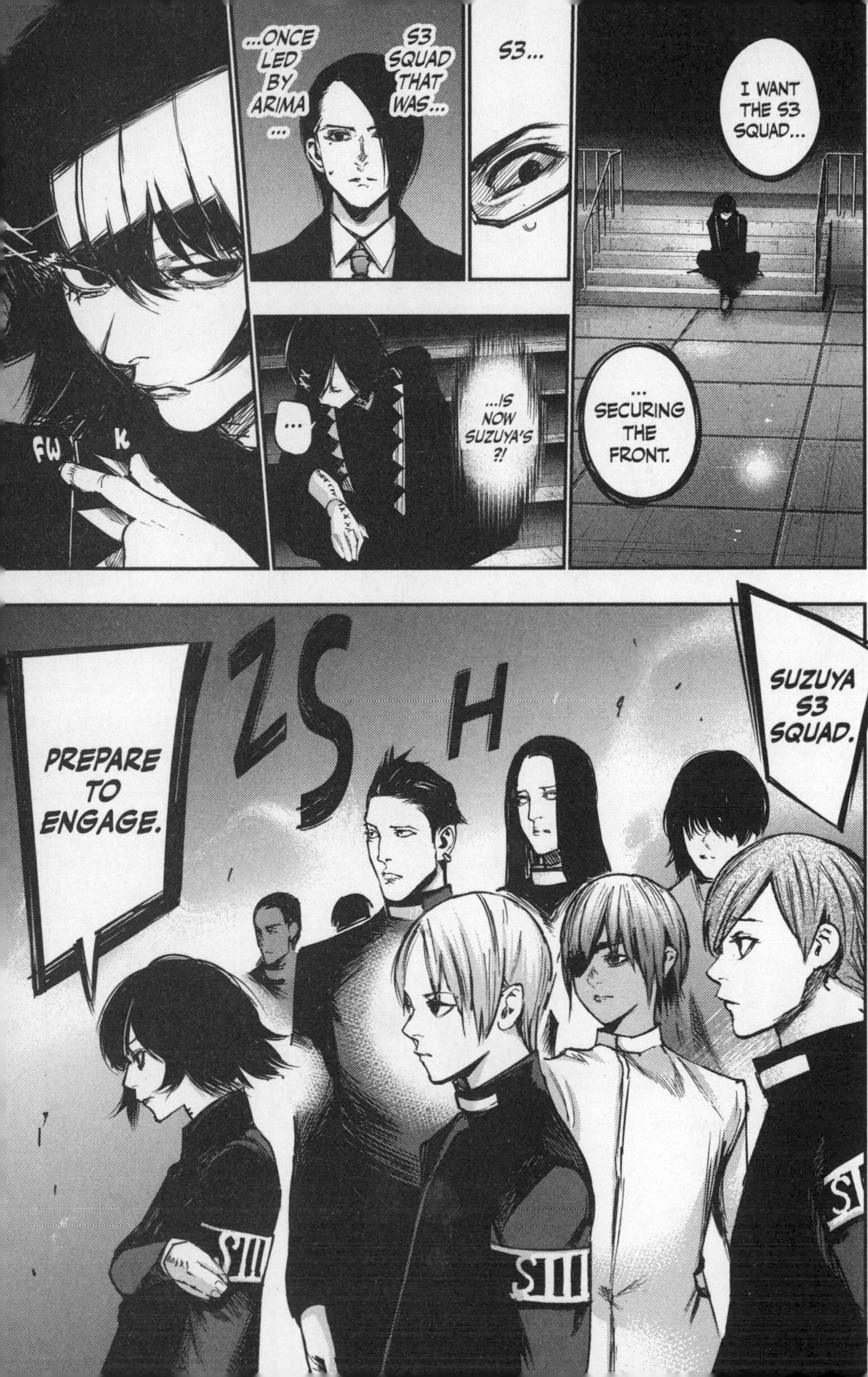
I WANT THE S3 SQUAD...
...SECURING THE FRONT.
S3...
S3 SQUAD THAT WAS...
...ONCE LED BY ARIMA ...
...IS NOW SUZUYA'S ?!
...
FW K
SUZUYA S3 SQUAD.
ZSH
PREPARE TO ENGAGE.

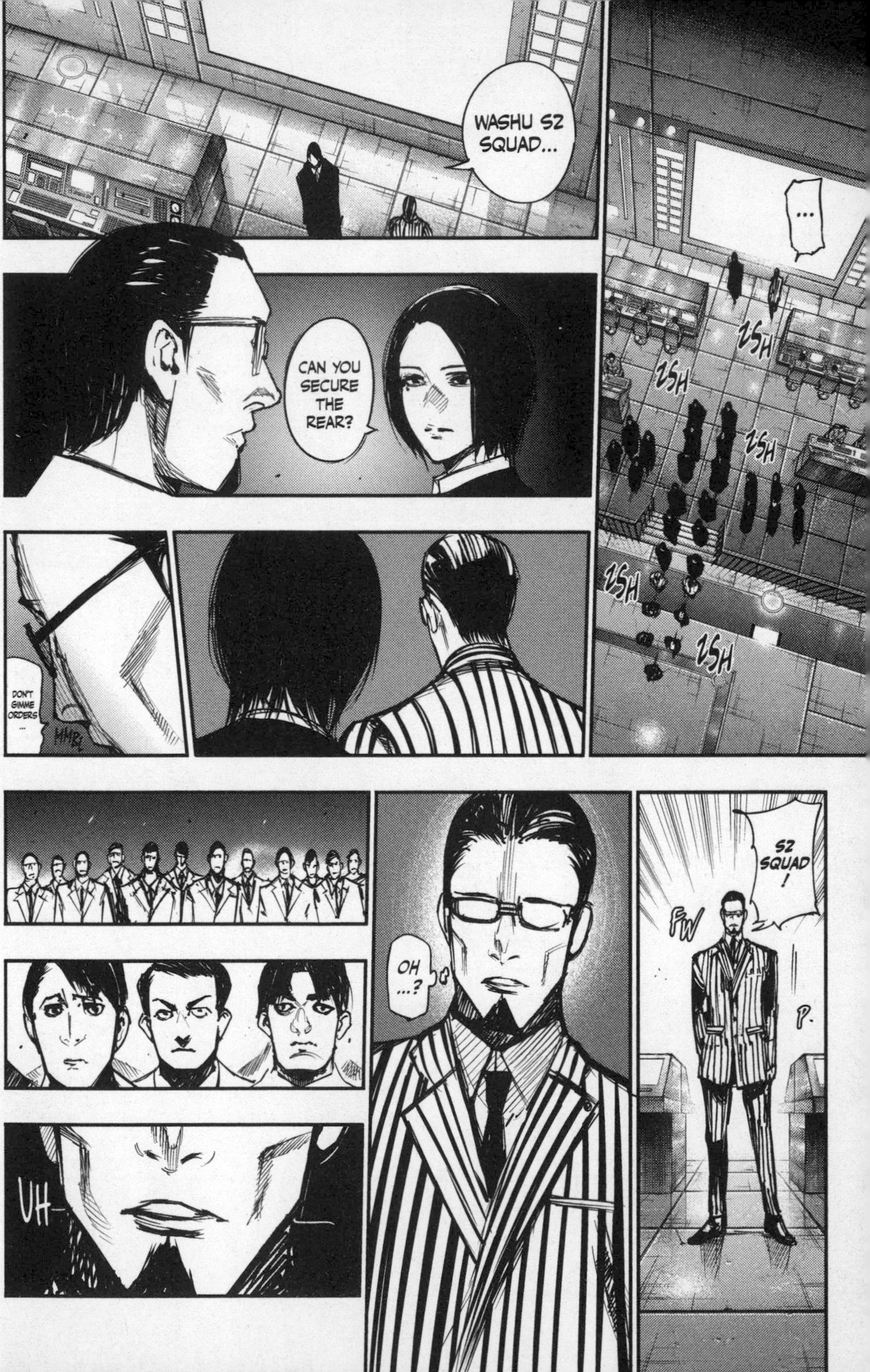

...
ZSH
ZSH
ZSH
ZSH
ZSH
WASHU S2 SQUAD...
CAN YOU SECURE THE REAR?
DON'T GIMME ORDERS...
MMRL
S2 SQUAD!
FW
P.
OH ...?
UH—

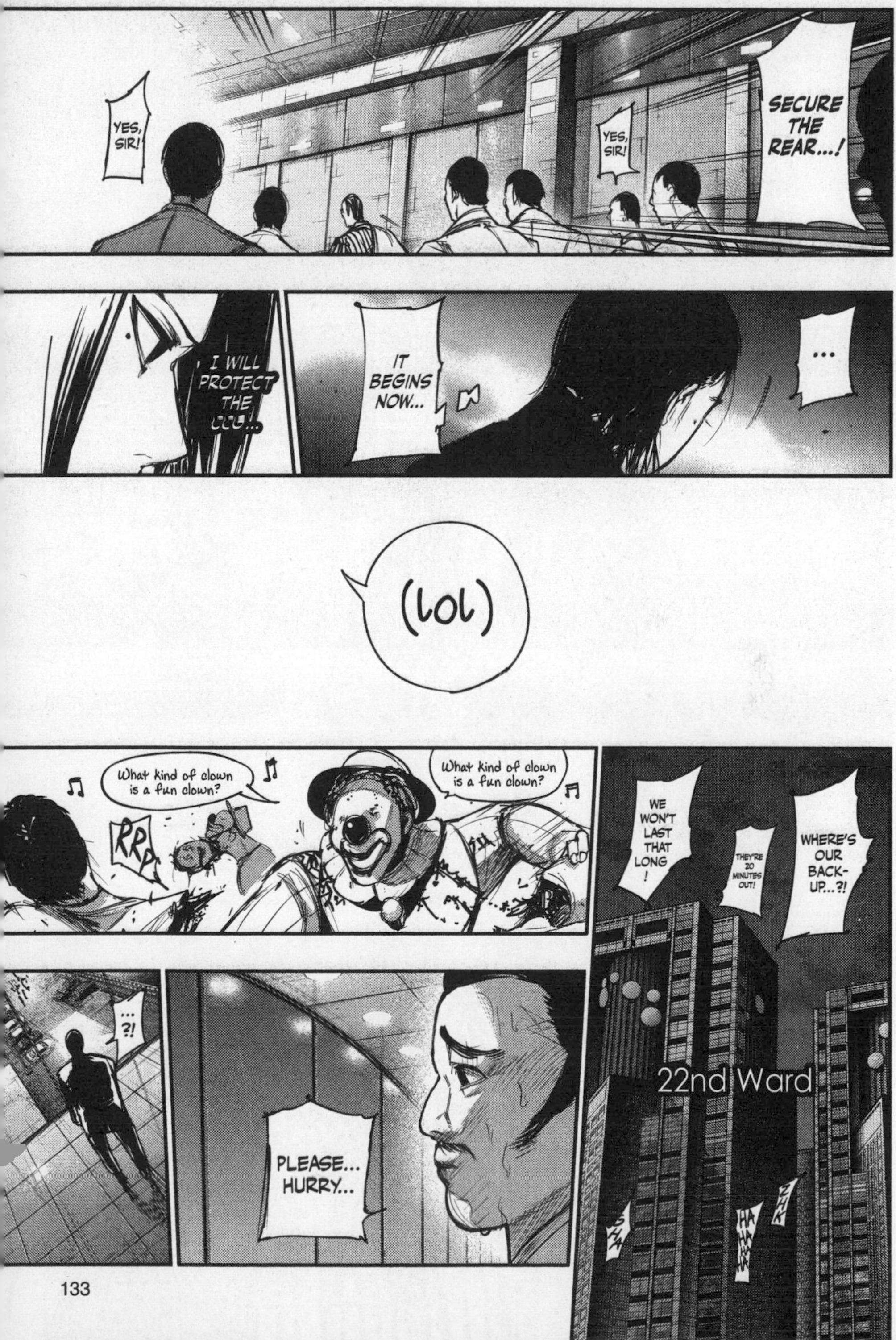
SECURE THE REAR...!
YES, SIR!
YES, SIR!
...
IT BEGINS NOW...
I WILL PROTECT THE CCG...
(lol)
WHERE'S OUR BACK-UP...?!
THEY'RE 20 MINUTES OUT!
WE WON'T LAST THAT LONG!
22nd Ward
What kind of clown is a fun clown?
What kind of clown is a fun clown?
RRP
PLEASE... HURRY...
...?!

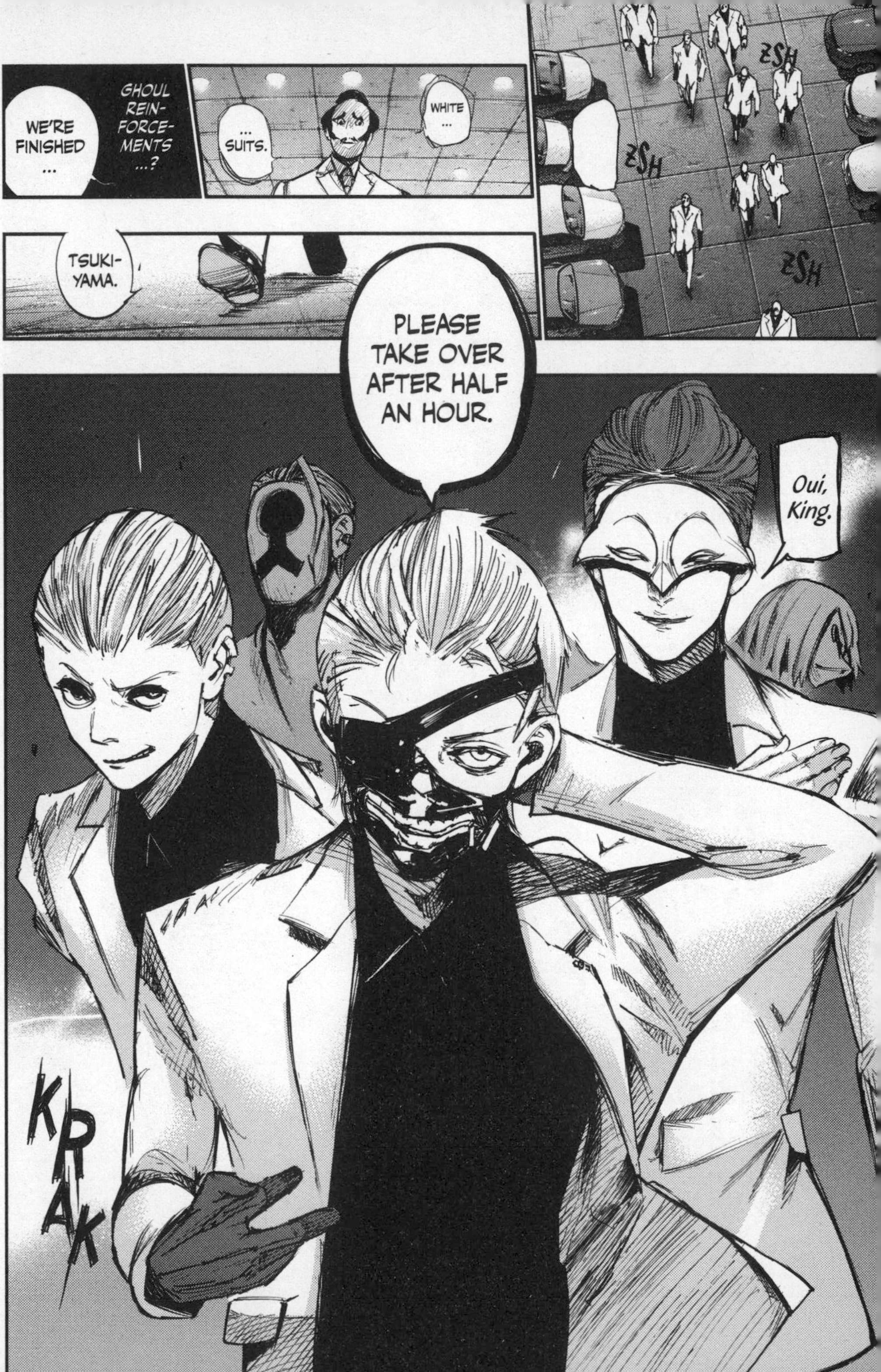
ZSH
ZSH
ZSH
WHITE ...
... SUITS.
GHOUL REIN-FORCE-MENTS ...?
WE'RE FINISHED ...
TSUKI-YAMA.
PLEASE TAKE OVER AFTER HALF AN HOUR.
Oui, King.
KRAK

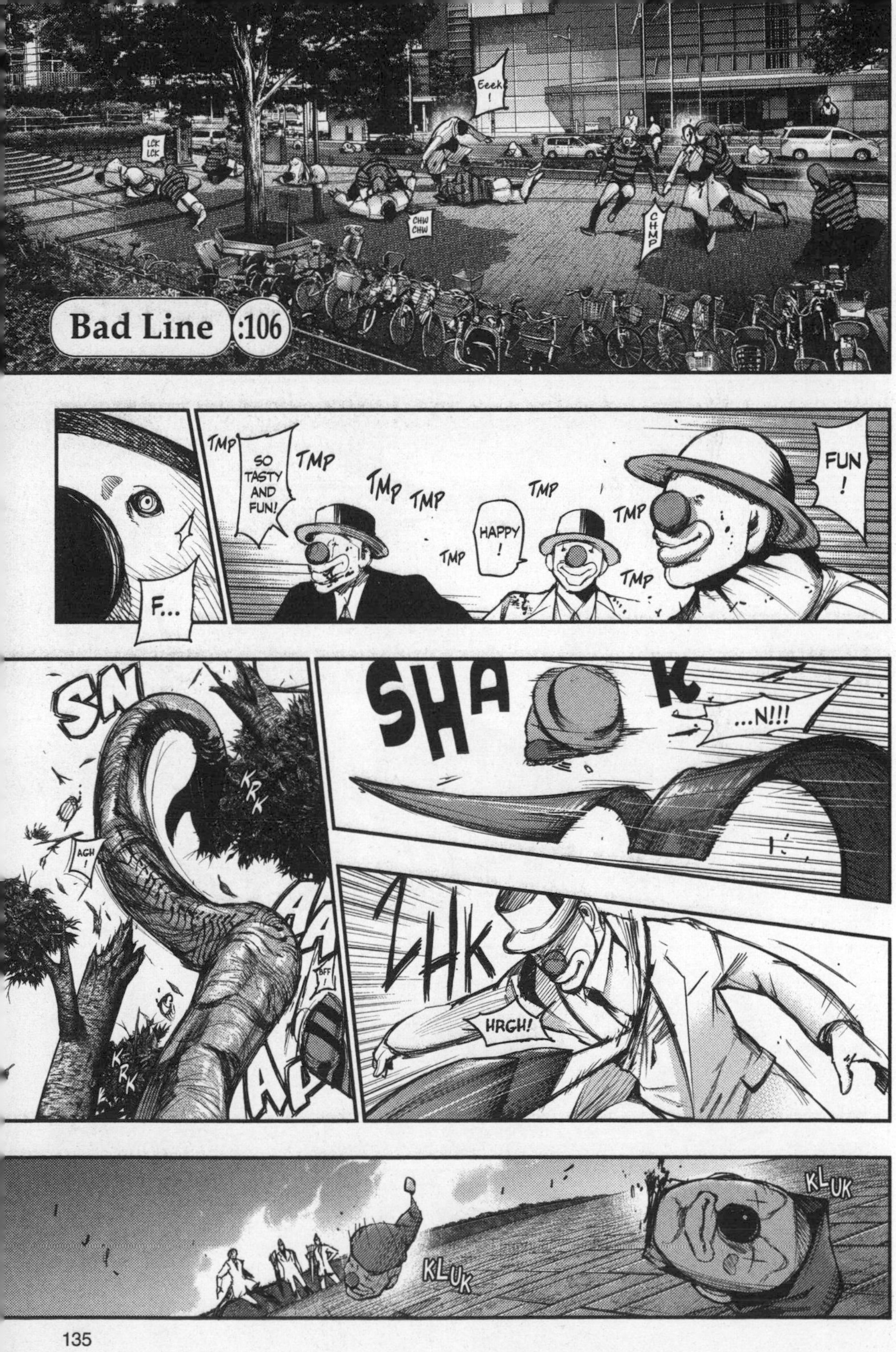
CHMP
Eeek!
CHW CHW
LCK LCK
Bad Line :106
FUN!
TMP
TMP
HAPPY!
TMP
TMP
TMP
TMP
SO TASTY AND FUN!
TMP
F...
SHA K
...N!!!
ZHK
HRGH!
SN
KRK
AGH!
AA
BFF!
KRK
AA
KLUK
KLUK

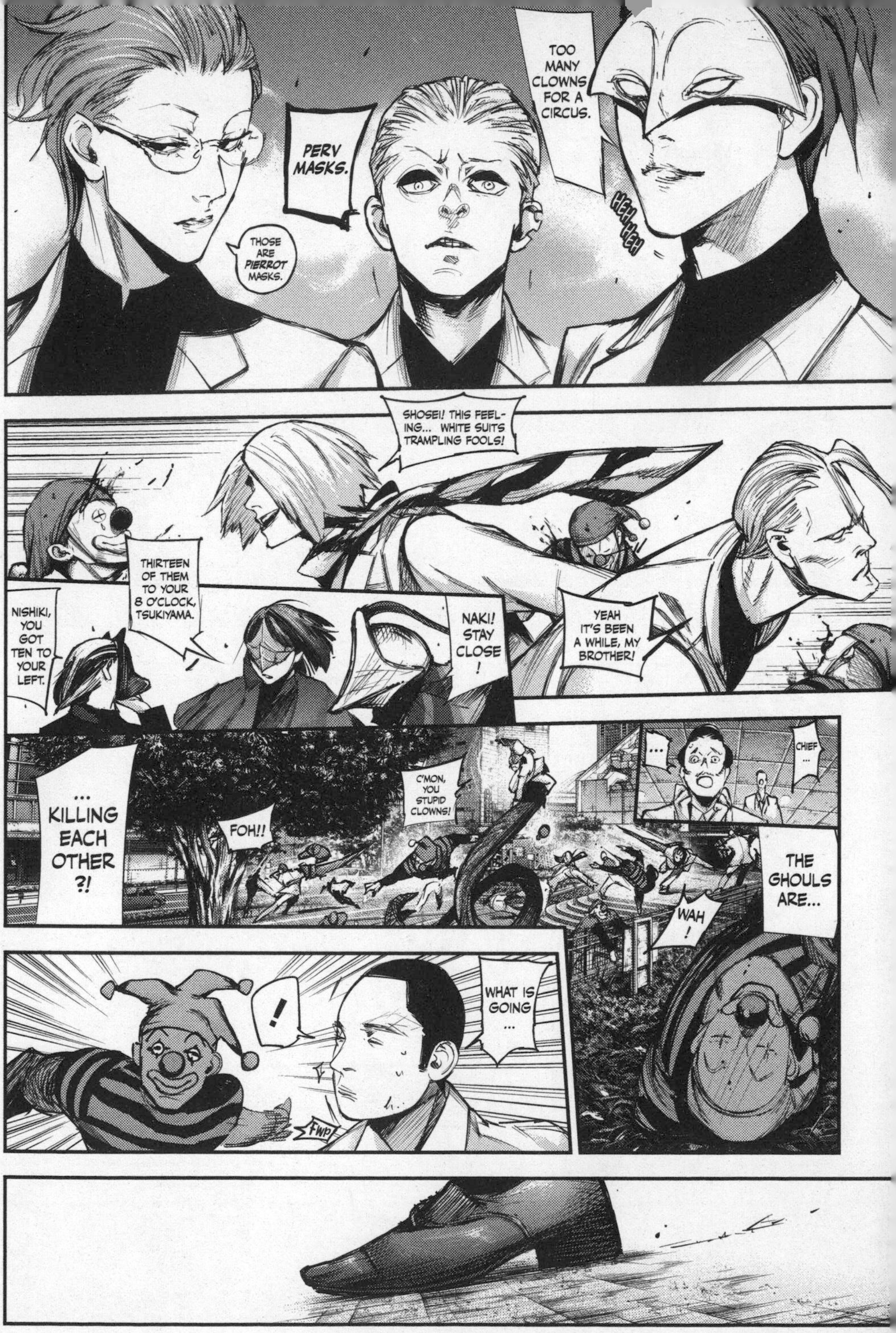
TOO MANY CLOWNS FOR A CIRCUS.
HEH HEH
PERV MASKS.
THOSE ARE PIERROT MASKS.
SHOSEI! THIS FEEL-ING... WHITE SUITS TRAMPLING FOOLS!
YEAH IT'S BEEN A WHILE, MY BROTHER!
NAKI! STAY CLOSE!
THIRTEEN OF THEM TO YOUR 8 O'CLOCK, TSUKIYAMA.
NISHIKI, YOU GOT TEN TO YOUR LEFT.
CHIEF...
...
THE GHOULS ARE...
WAH!
C'MON, YOU STUPID CLOWNS!
FOH!!
...KILLING EACH OTHER?!
WHAT IS GOING...
!
FWP

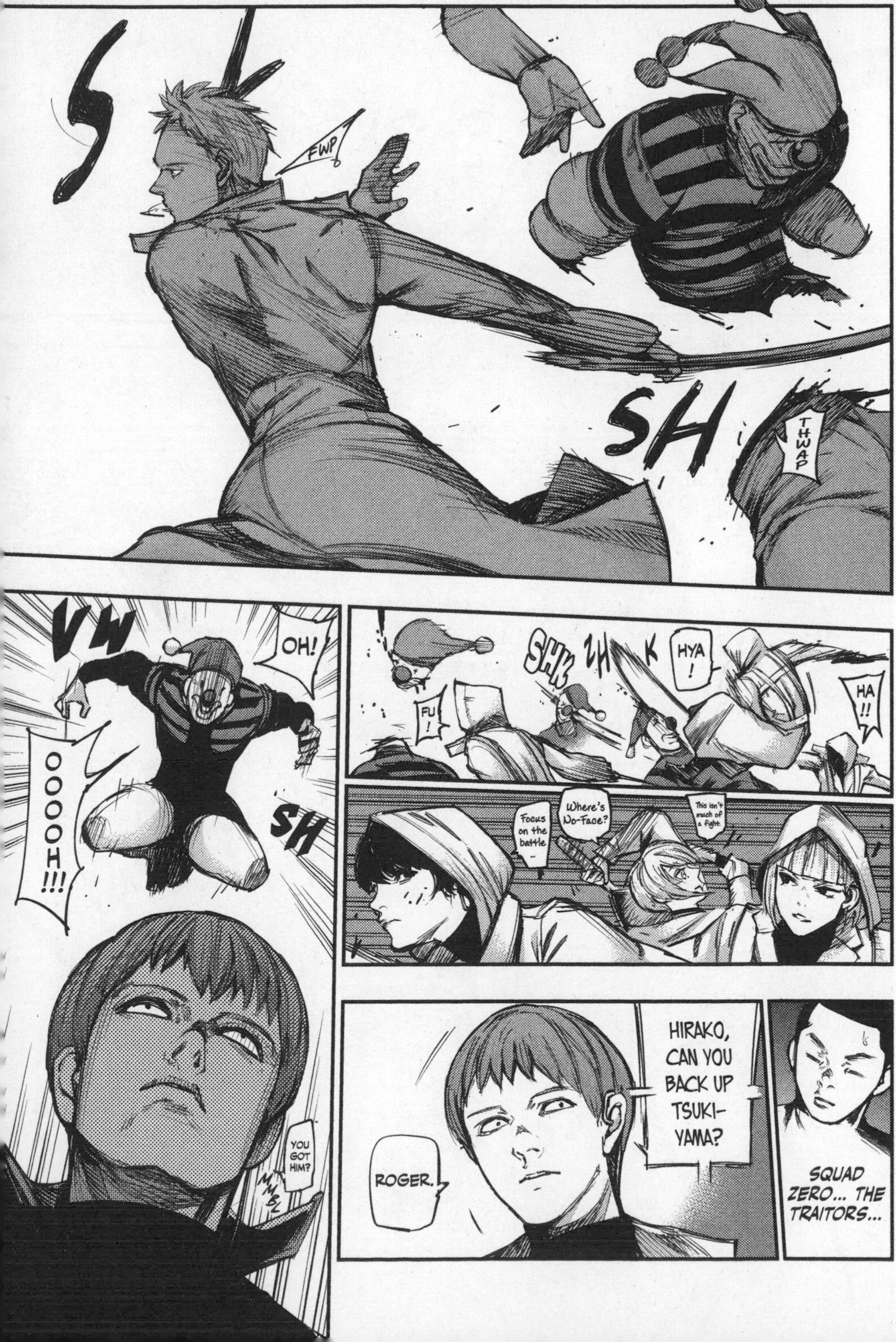
THWAP
SH
FWP
HA!!
HYA!
K
ZH
SHK
FU!
This isn't much of a fight.
Where's No-Face?
Focus on the battle...
SQUAD ZERO... THE TRAITORS...
HIRAKO, CAN YOU BACK UP TSUKIYAMA?
ROGER.
OH!
VW
OOOOOH!!!
SH
YOU GOT HIM?

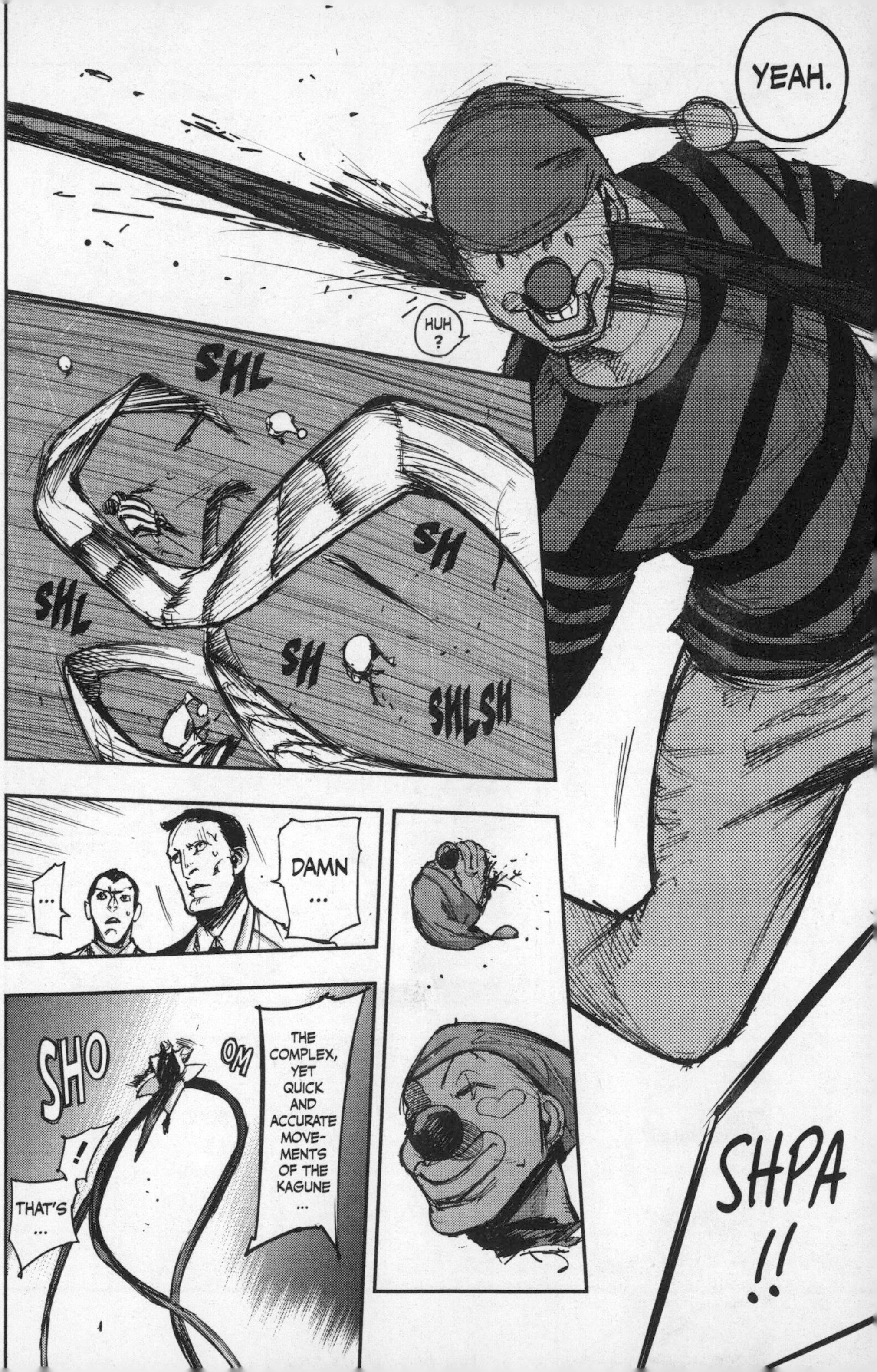
YEAH.
HUH ?
SHL
SH
SHL
SH
SHLSH
DAMN ...
...
SHPA !!
THE COMPLEX, YET QUICK AND ACCURATE MOVE-MENTS OF THE KAGUNE ...
SHO OM
!
THAT'S ...

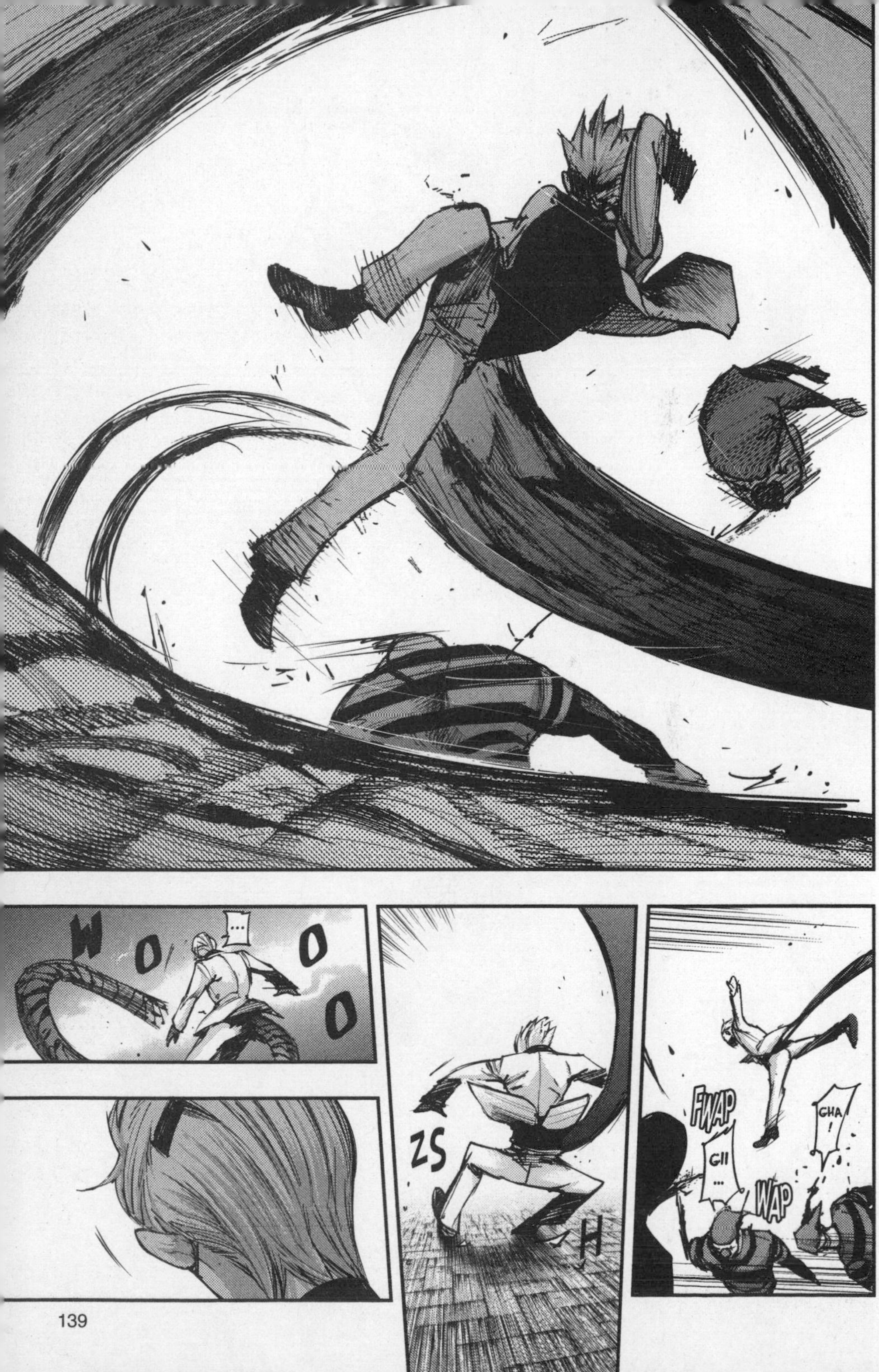
FWAP
GII ...
GHA !
WAP
ZS
H
...
WOOO

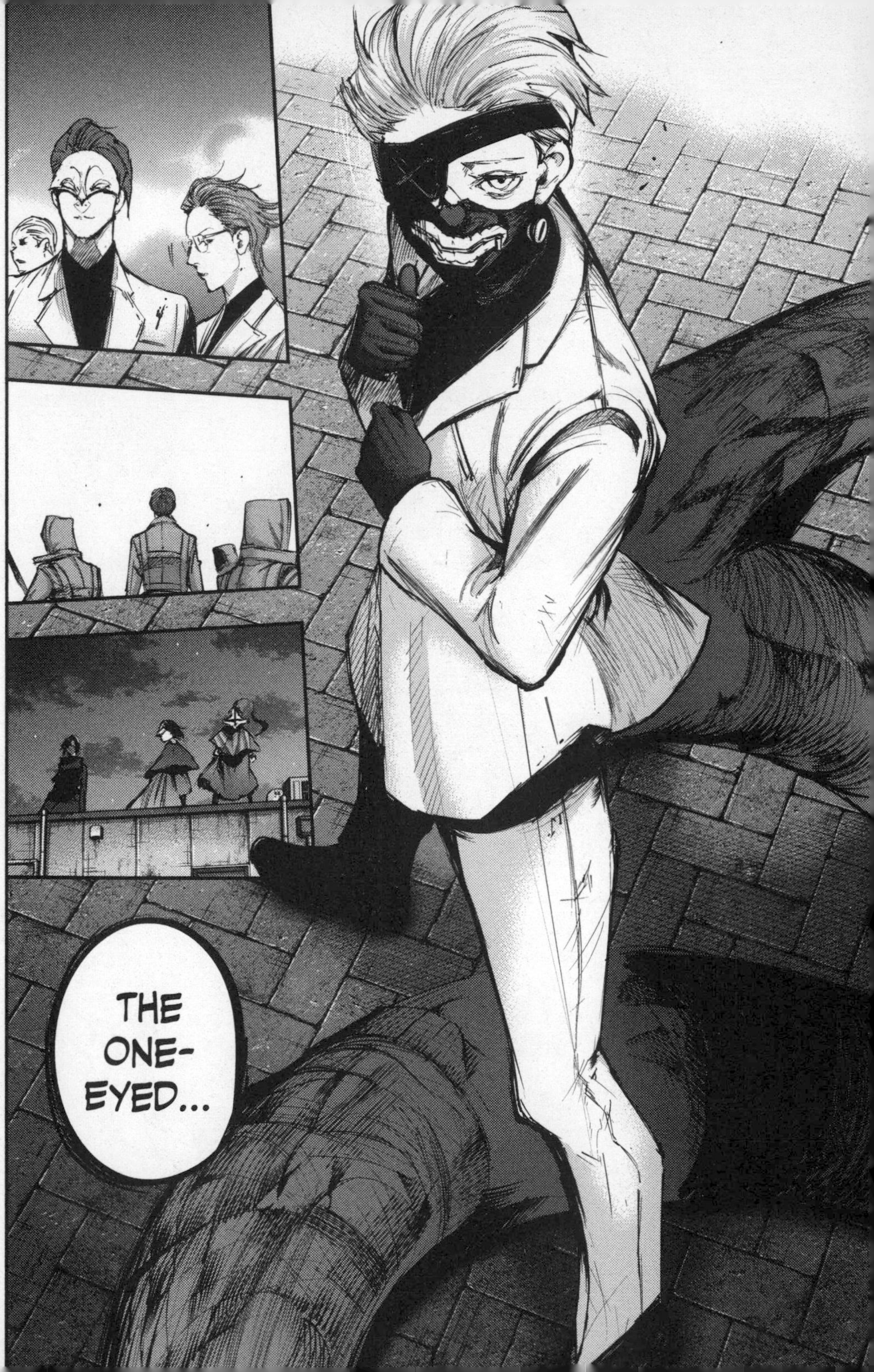
THE ONE-EYED...

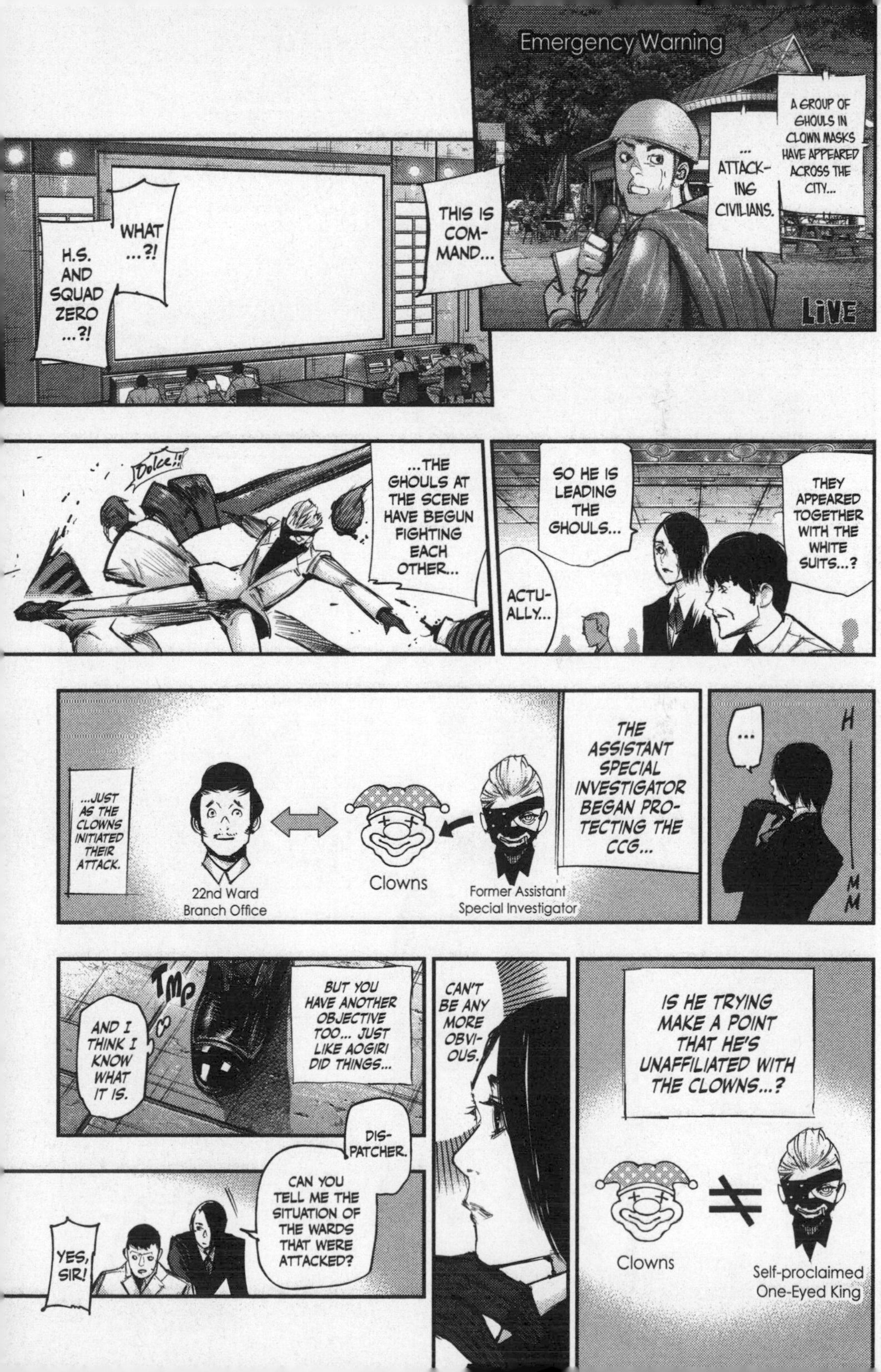
Emergency Warning
A GROUP OF GHOULS IN CLOWN MASKS HAVE APPEARED ACROSS THE CITY...
... ATTACKING CIVILIANS.
LIVE
THIS IS COMMAND...
WHAT ...?!
H.S. AND SQUAD ZERO ...?!
THEY APPEARED TOGETHER WITH THE WHITE SUITS...?
SO HE IS LEADING THE GHOULS...
ACTUALLY...
...THE GHOULS AT THE SCENE HAVE BEGUN FIGHTING EACH OTHER...
Dolce!!
H—MM
...
THE ASSISTANT SPECIAL INVESTIGATOR BEGAN PROTECTING THE CCG...
...JUST AS THE CLOWNS INITIATED THEIR ATTACK.
22nd Ward Branch Office
Clowns
Former Assistant Special Investigator
IS HE TRYING MAKE A POINT THAT HE'S UNAFFILIATED WITH THE CLOWNS...?
Clowns
Self-proclaimed One-Eyed King
CAN'T BE ANY MORE OBVIOUS.
BUT YOU HAVE ANOTHER OBJECTIVE TOO... JUST LIKE AOGIRI DID THINGS...
TMP
AND I THINK I KNOW WHAT IT IS.
DISPATCHER.
CAN YOU TELL ME THE SITUATION OF THE WARDS THAT WERE ATTACKED?
YES, SIR!

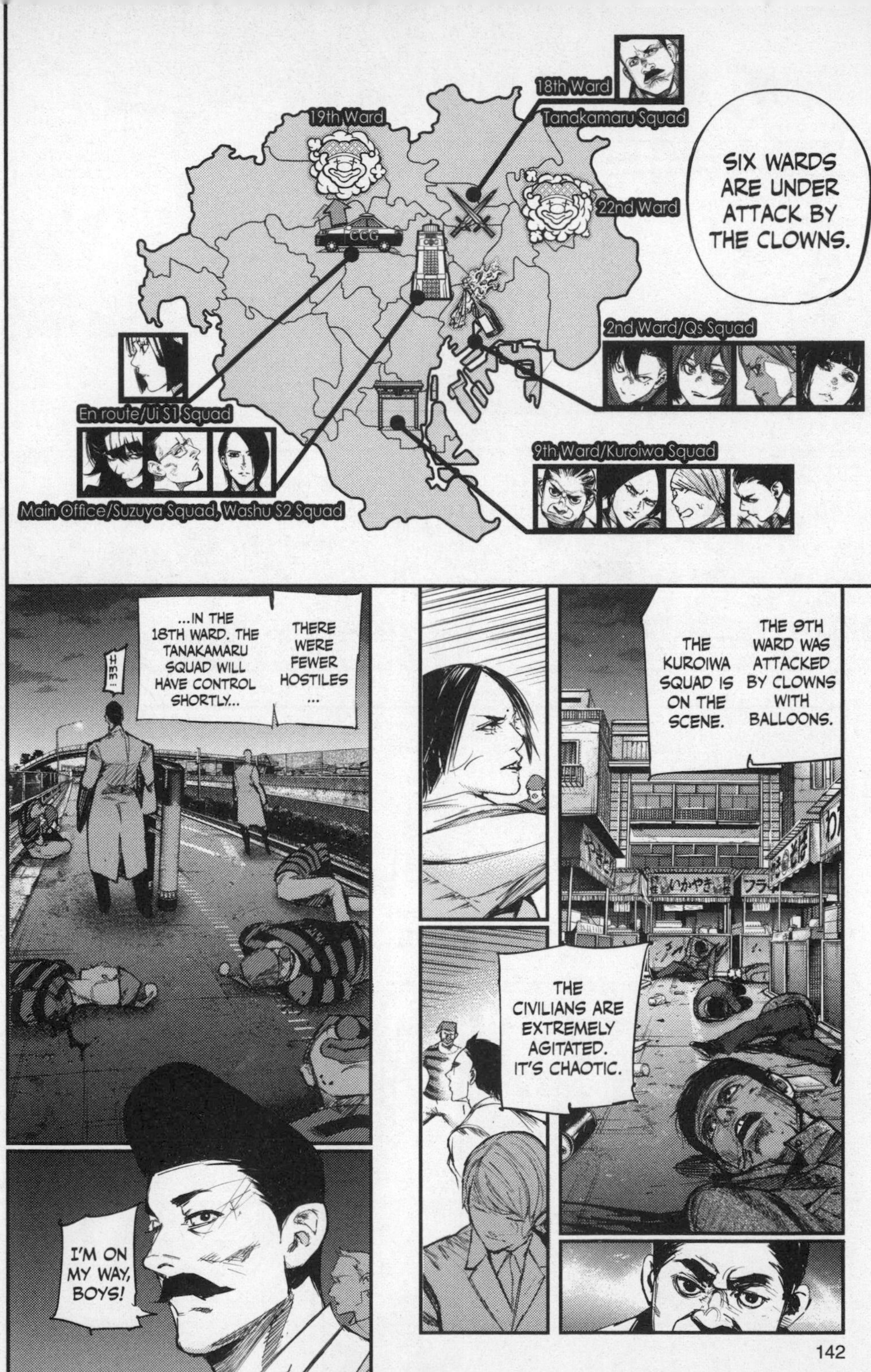
SIX WARDS ARE UNDER ATTACK BY THE CLOWNS.
18th Ward
Tanakamaru Squad
19th Ward
22nd Ward
2nd Ward/Qs Squad
En route/Ui S1 Squad
9th Ward/Kuroiwa Squad
Main Office/Suzuya Squad, Washu S2 Squad
THE 9TH WARD WAS ATTACKED BY CLOWNS WITH BALLOONS.
THE KUROIWA SQUAD IS ON THE SCENE.
THE CIVILIANS ARE EXTREMELY AGITATED. IT'S CHAOTIC.
THERE WERE FEWER HOSTILES...
...IN THE 18TH WARD. THE TANAKAMARU SQUAD WILL HAVE CONTROL SHORTLY...
I'M ON MY WAY, BOYS!

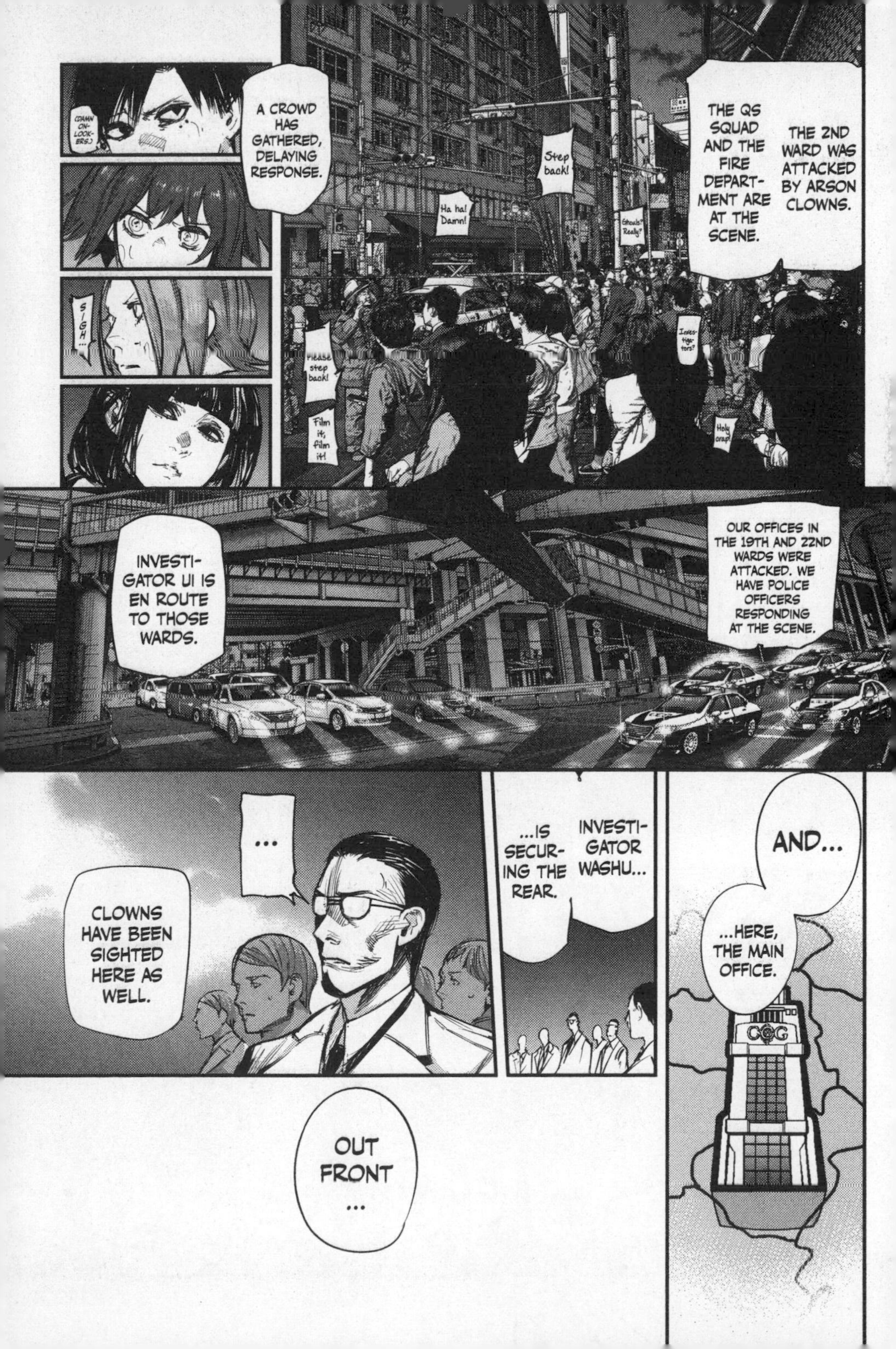
THE 2ND WARD WAS ATTACKED BY ARSON CLOWNS.
THE QS SQUAD AND THE FIRE DEPARTMENT ARE AT THE SCENE.
Step back!
Ghouls? Really?
Ha ha! Damn!
Investigators?
Please step back!
Film it, film it!
Holy crap!
A CROWD HAS GATHERED, DELAYING RESPONSE.
(DAMN ON-LOOKERS.)
SIGH...
OUR OFFICES IN THE 19TH AND 22ND WARDS WERE ATTACKED. WE HAVE POLICE OFFICERS RESPONDING AT THE SCENE.
INVESTIGATOR UI IS EN ROUTE TO THOSE WARDS.
AND...
...HERE, THE MAIN OFFICE.
INVESTIGATOR WASHU...
...IS SECURING THE REAR.
...
CLOWNS HAVE BEEN SIGHTED HERE AS WELL.
OUT FRONT ...

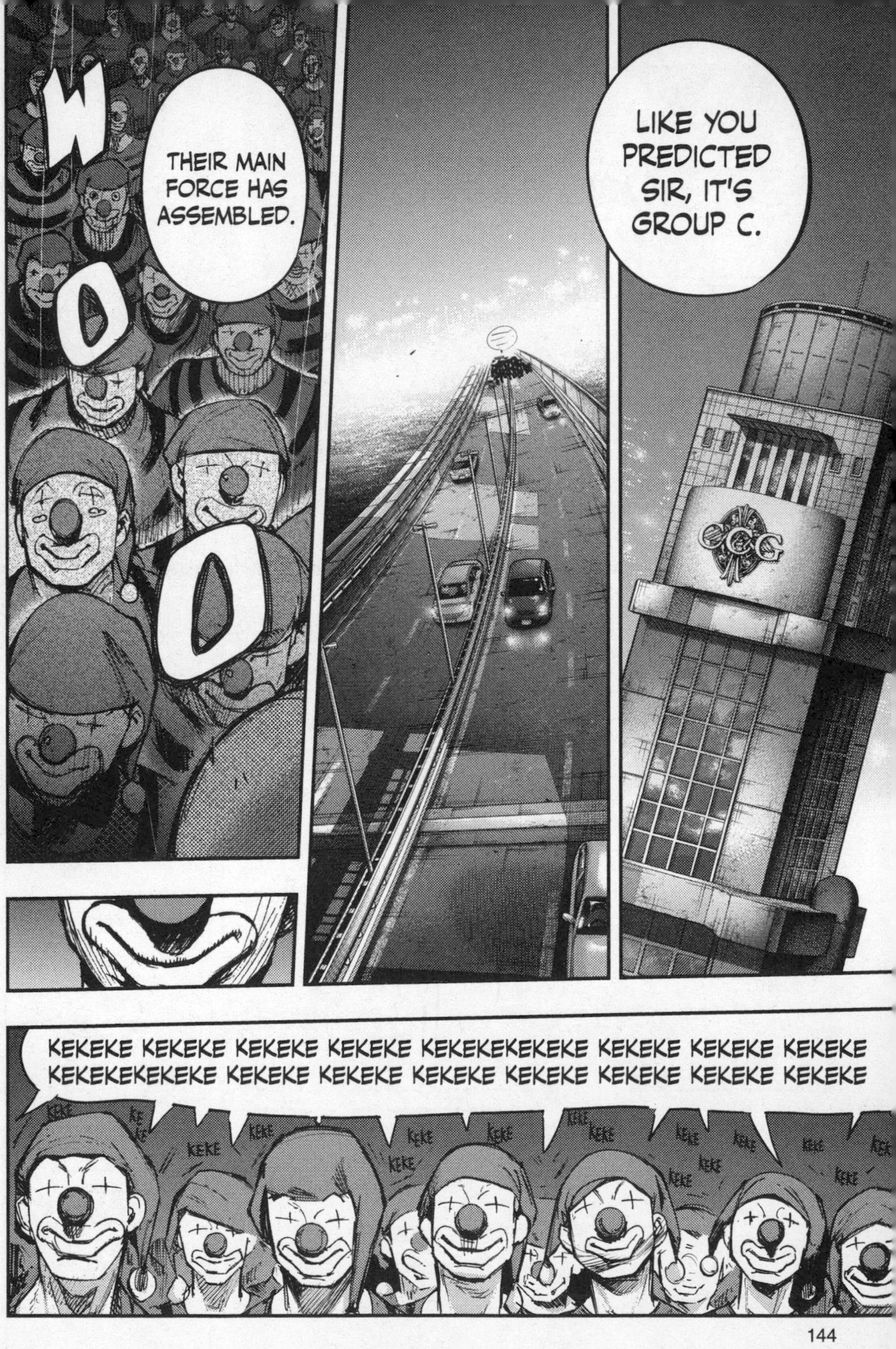
LIKE YOU PREDICTED SIR, IT'S GROUP C.
THEIR MAIN FORCE HAS ASSEMBLED.
WOO
KEKEKE KEKEKE KEKEKE KEKEKE KEKEKEKEKEKE KEKEKE KEKEKE KEKEKE KEKEKEKEKEKE KEKEKE KEKEKE KEKEKE KEKEKE KEKEKE KEKEKE KEKEKE

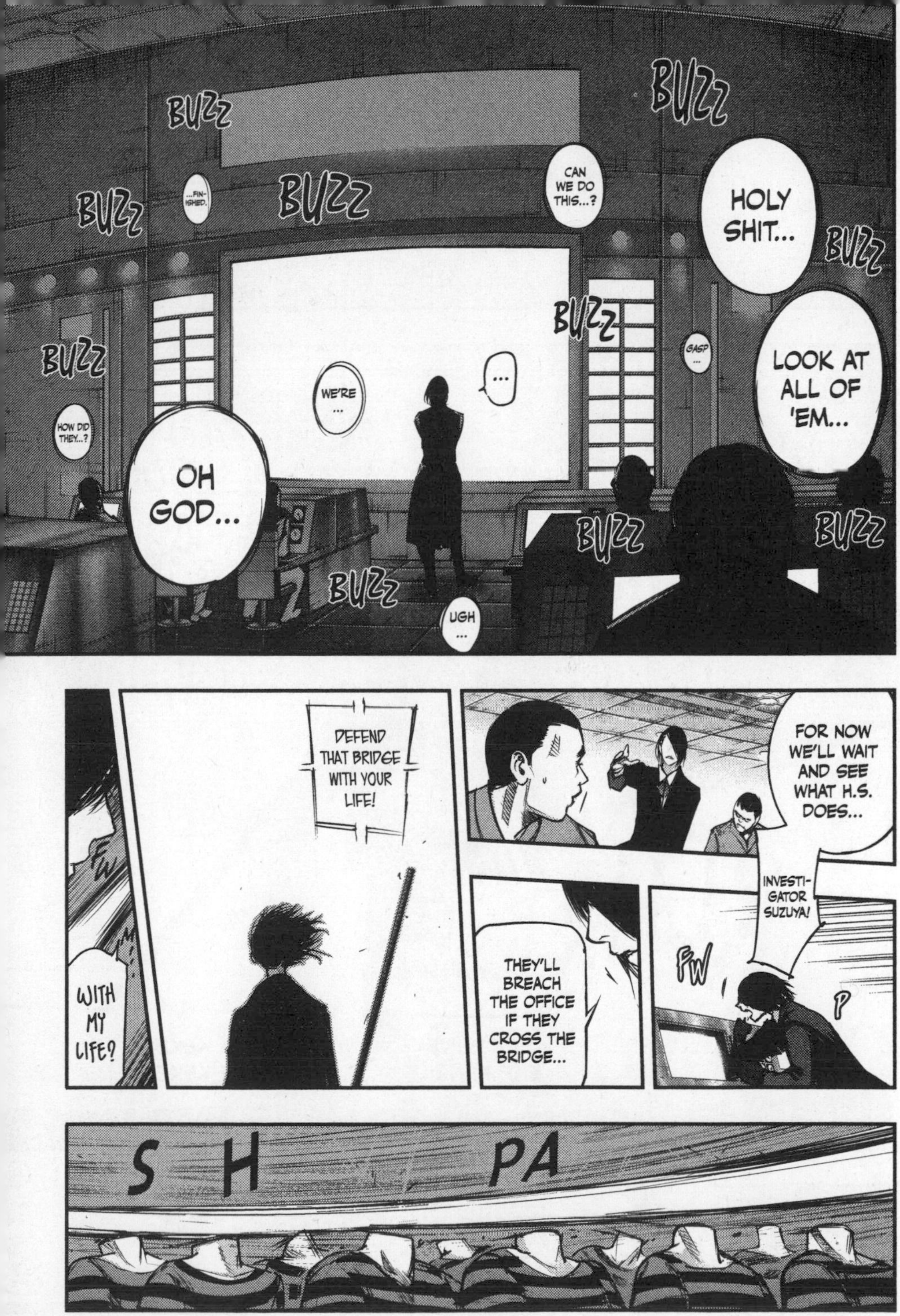
BUZZ
HOLY SHIT...
BUZZ
CAN WE DO THIS...?
BUZZ
...FIN-ISHED.
BUZZ
BUZZ
LOOK AT ALL OF 'EM...
GASP...
BUZZ
...
WE'RE...
BUZZ
HOW DID THEY...?
OH GOD...
BUZZ
BUZZ
BUZZ
UGH...
FOR NOW WE'LL WAIT AND SEE WHAT H.S. DOES...
INVESTI-GATOR SUZUYA!
FW
P
THEY'LL BREACH THE OFFICE IF THEY CROSS THE BRIDGE...
DEFEND THAT BRIDGE WITH YOUR LIFE!
FW
WITH MY LIFE?
S H PA

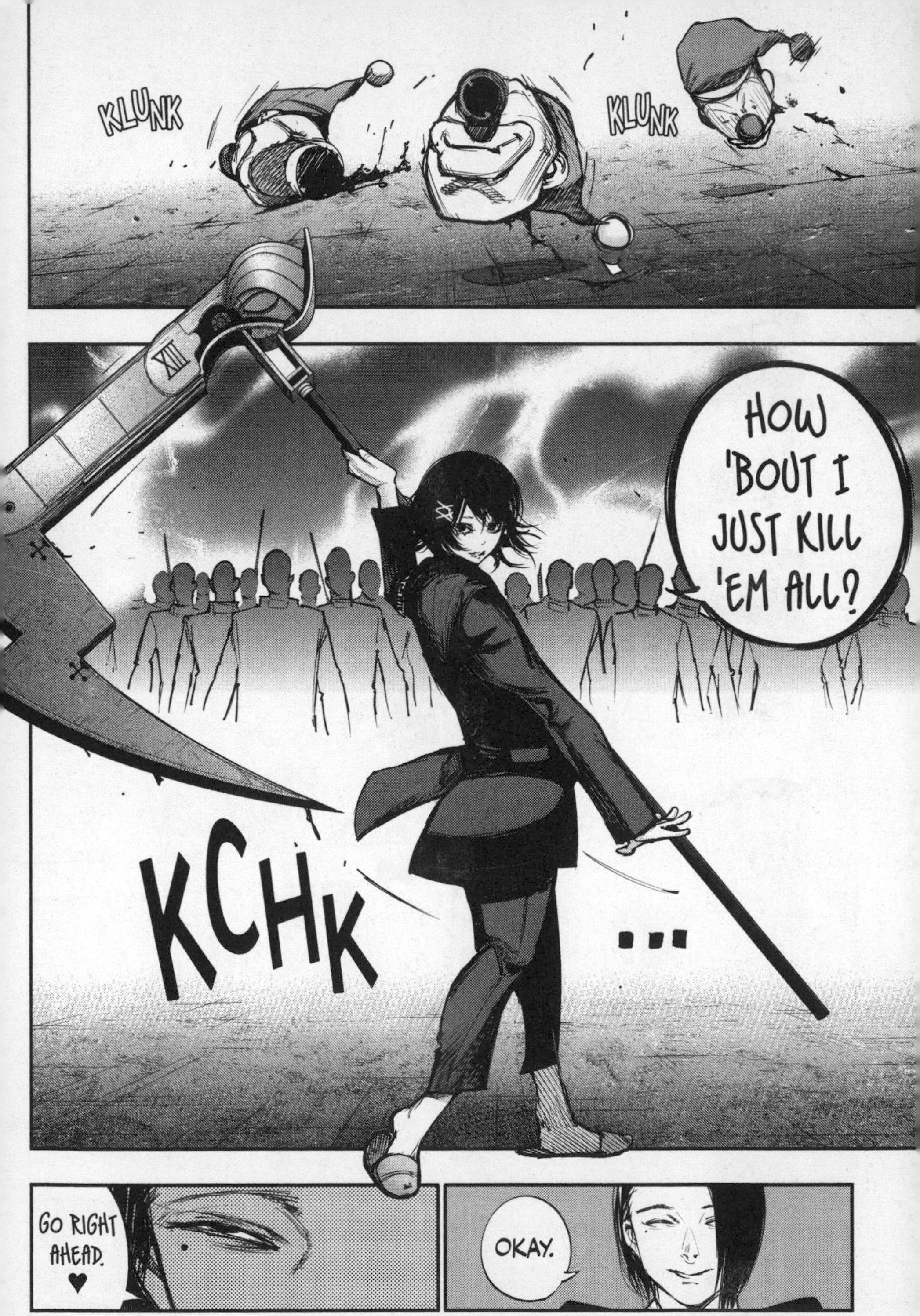
KLUNK
KLUNK
HOW 'BOUT I JUST KILL 'EM ALL?
...
KCHK
OKAY.
GO RIGHT AHEAD. ♥

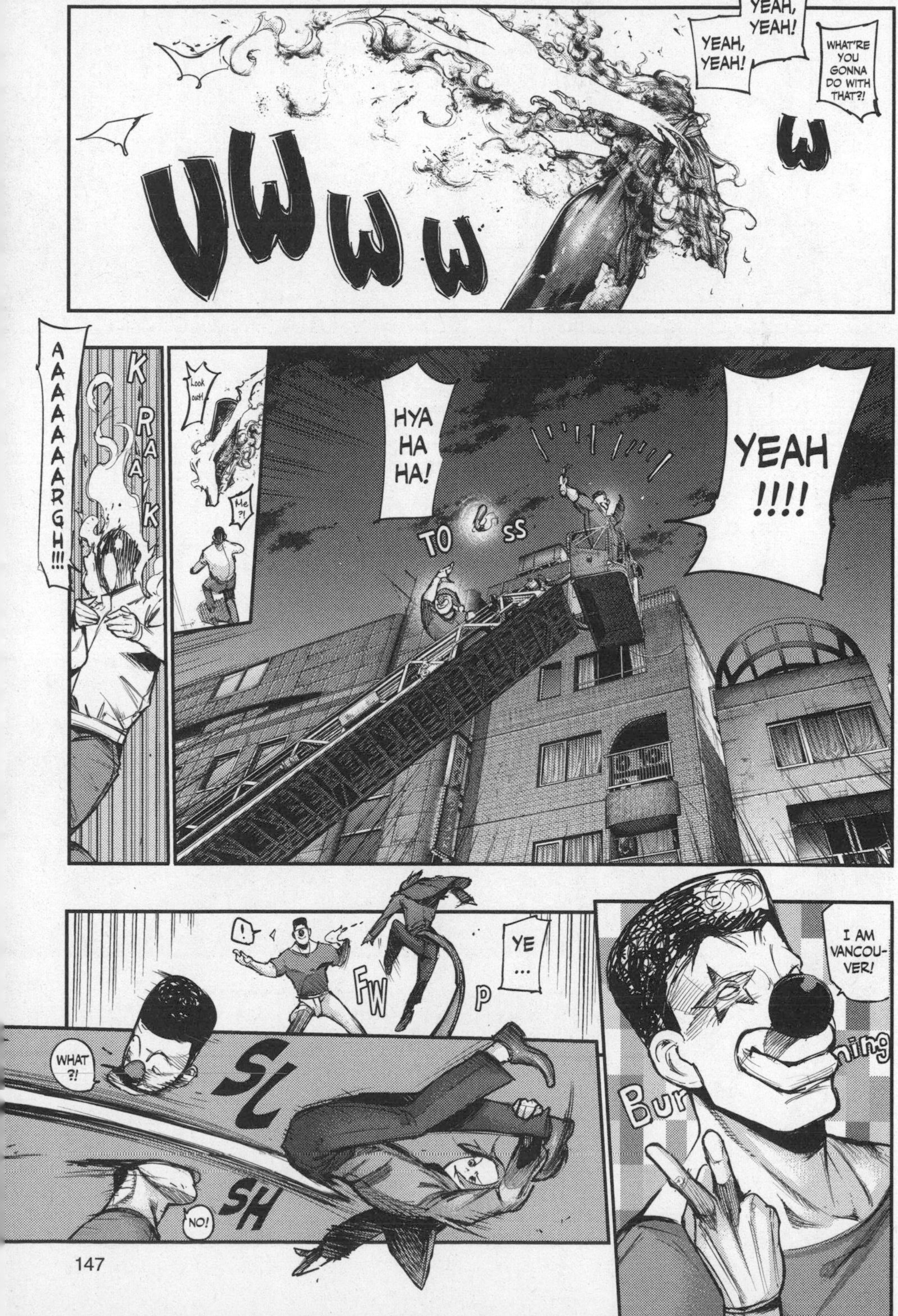
WHAT'RE YOU GONNA DO WITH THAT?!
YEAH, YEAH!
YEAH, YEAH!
VWWWWW
W
YEAH !!!!
HYA HA HA!
TOSS
Look out!
Me?!
KRAAK
AAAAAAAAARGH!!!
I AM VANCOU-VER!
Burning
YE ...
!
FWP
SL
SH
WHAT?!
NO!

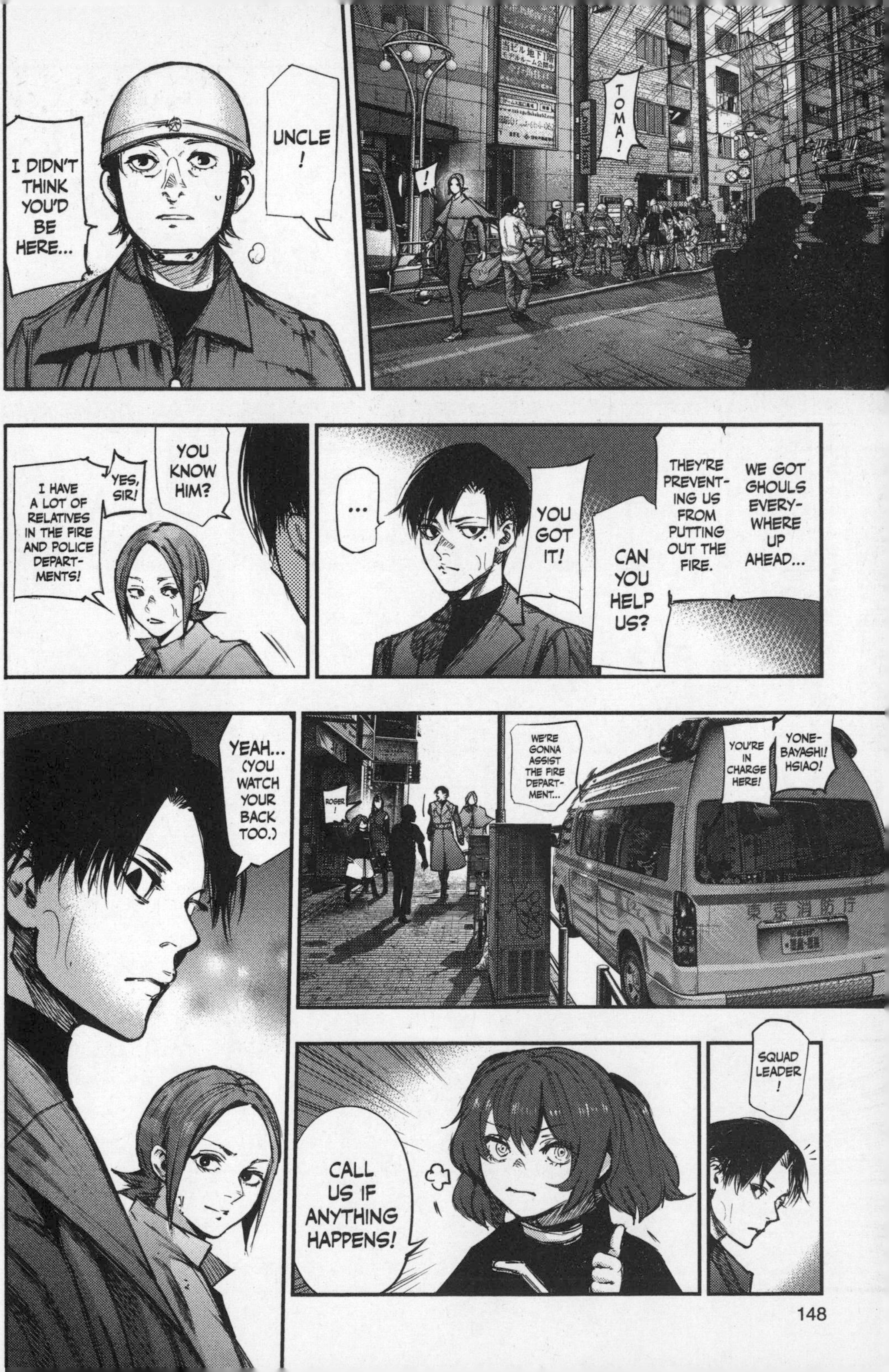
TOMA!
!
UNCLE!
I DIDN'T THINK YOU'D BE HERE...
WE GOT GHOULS EVERY-WHERE UP AHEAD...
THEY'RE PREVENT-ING US FROM PUTTING OUT THE FIRE.
CAN YOU HELP US?
YOU GOT IT!
...
YOU KNOW HIM?
YES, SIR!
I HAVE A LOT OF RELATIVES IN THE FIRE AND POLICE DEPART-MENTS!
YONE-BAYASHI! HSIAO!
YOU'RE IN CHARGE HERE!
WE'RE GONNA ASSIST THE FIRE DEPART-MENT...
ROGER!
SQUAD LEADER!
CALL US IF ANYTHING HAPPENS!
YEAH... (YOU WATCH YOUR BACK TOO.)

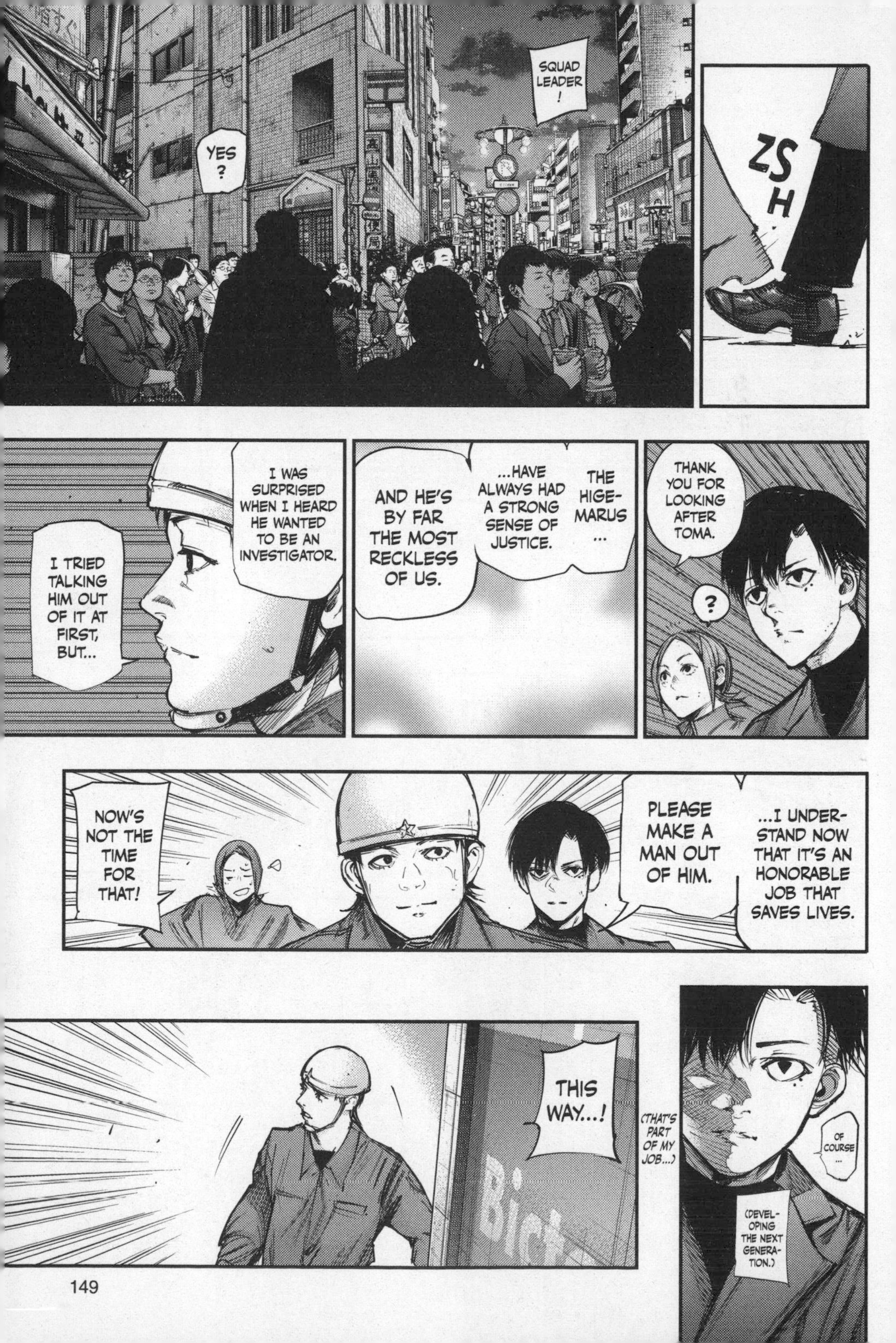

ZSH
SQUAD LEADER !
YES ?
THANK YOU FOR LOOKING AFTER TOMA.
?
THE HIGE-MARUS ...
...HAVE ALWAYS HAD A STRONG SENSE OF JUSTICE.
AND HE'S BY FAR THE MOST RECKLESS OF US.
I WAS SURPRISED WHEN I HEARD HE WANTED TO BE AN INVESTIGATOR.
I TRIED TALKING HIM OUT OF IT AT FIRST, BUT...
...I UNDER-STAND NOW THAT IT'S AN HONORABLE JOB THAT SAVES LIVES.
PLEASE MAKE A MAN OUT OF HIM.
NOW'S NOT THE TIME FOR THAT!
OF COURSE ...
(THAT'S PART OF MY JOB...)
(DEVEL-OPING THE NEXT GENERA-TION.)
THIS WAY...!

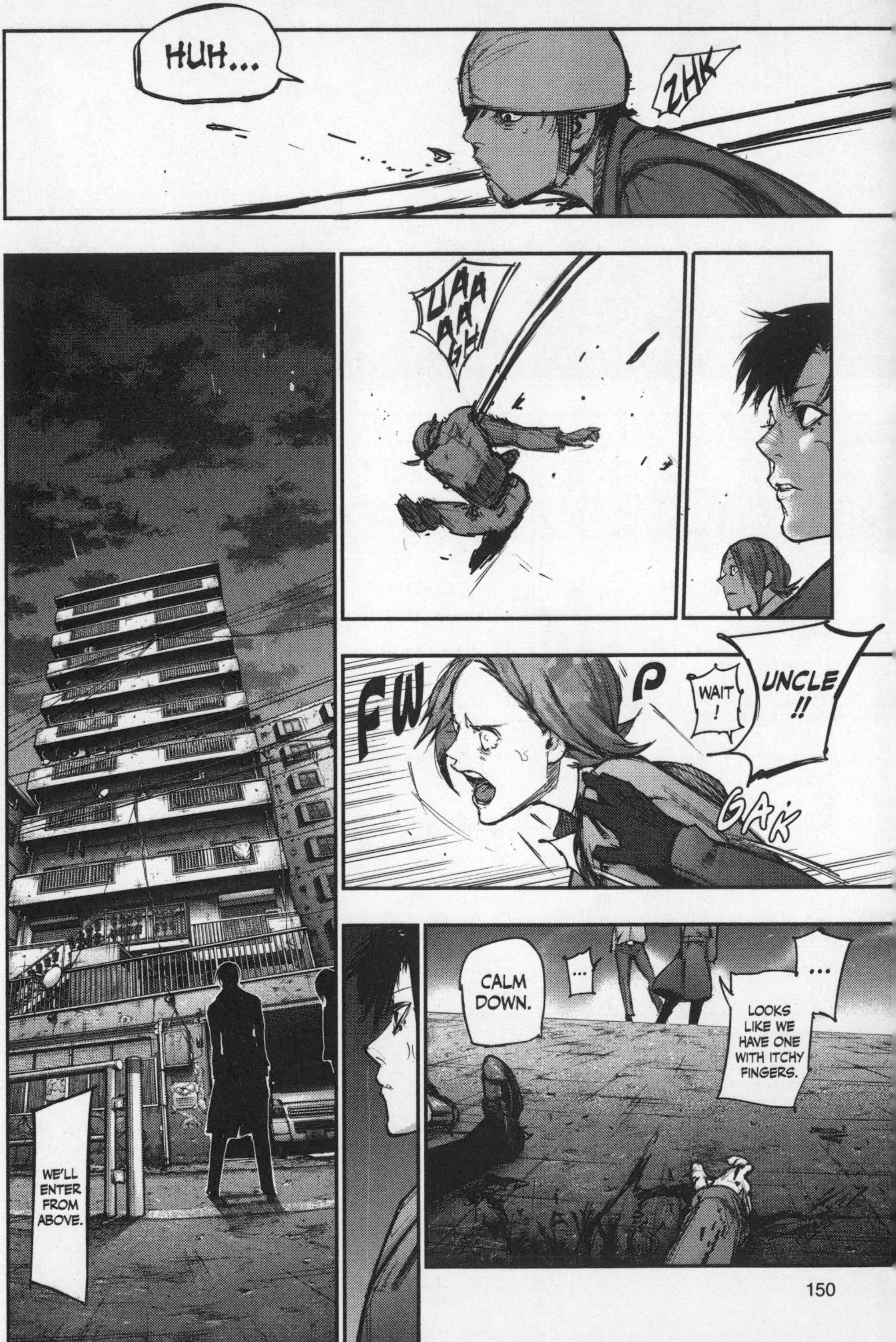
ZHK
HUH...
UAAAAGH
UNCLE!!
WAIT!
GAK
FW
...
LOOKS LIKE WE HAVE ONE WITH ITCHY FINGERS.
...
CALM DOWN.
WE'LL ENTER FROM ABOVE.

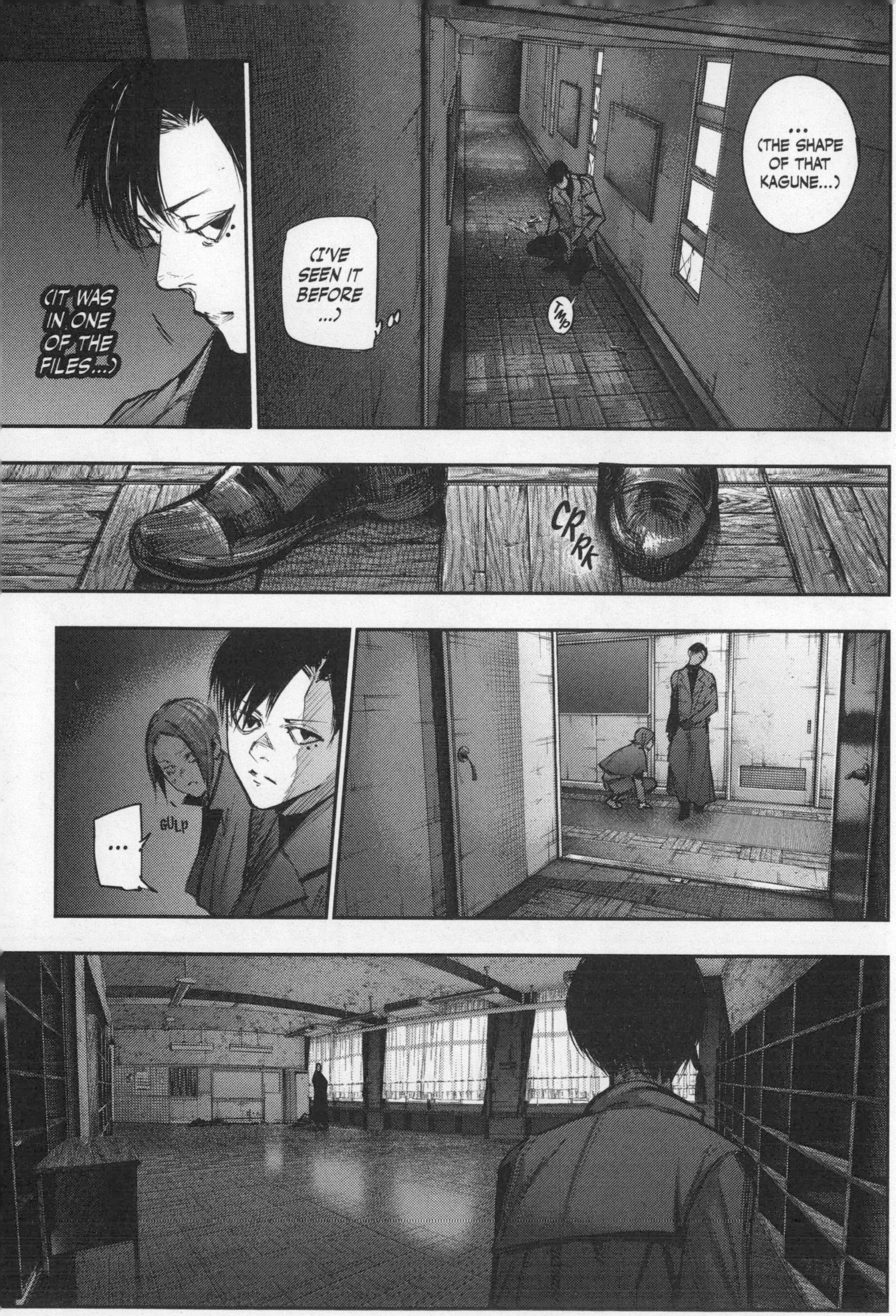
... (THE SHAPE OF THAT KAGUNE...)
TMP
(I'VE SEEN IT BEFORE ...)
(IT WAS IN ONE OF THE FILES...)
CRRK
GULP
...

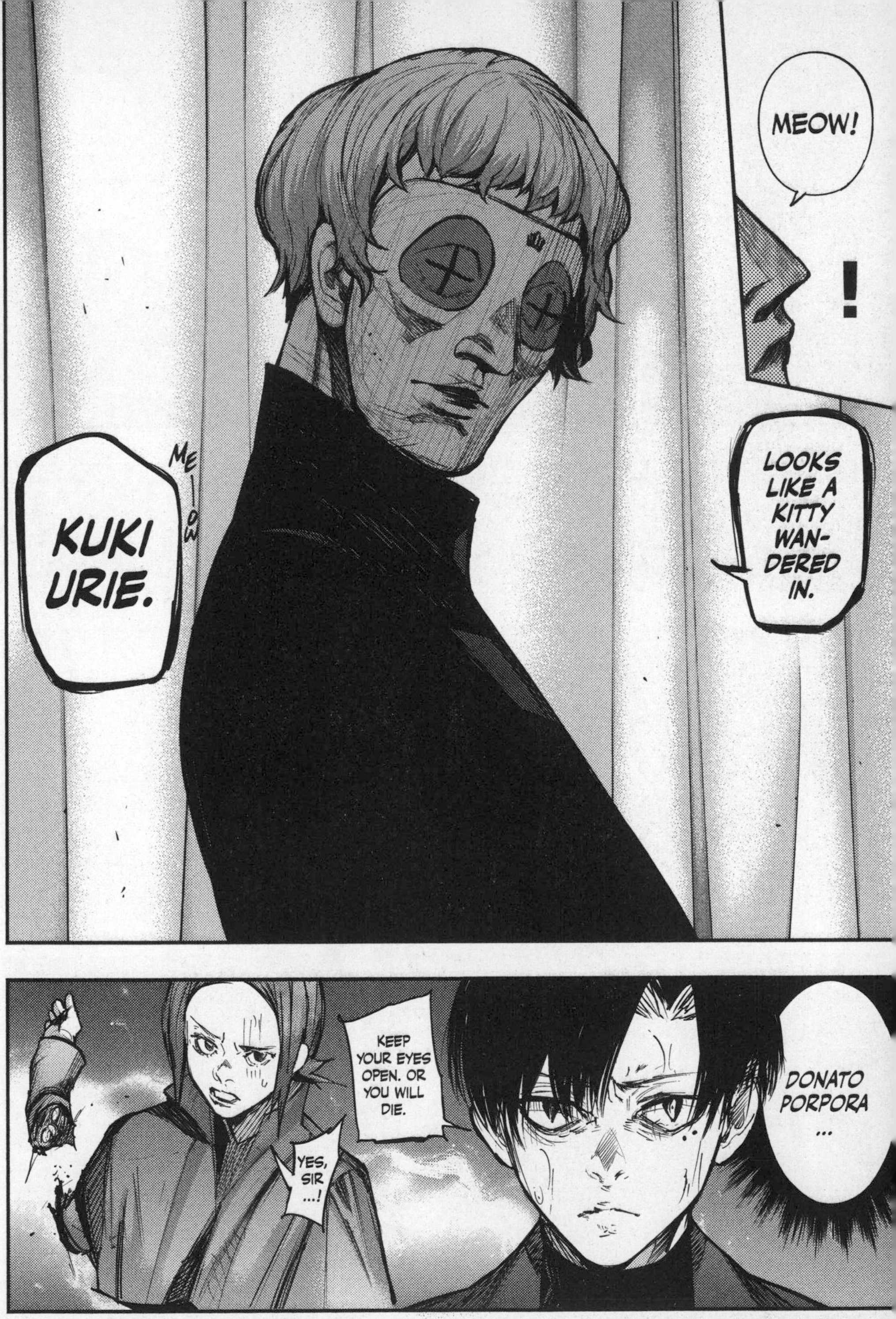
MEOW!
!
LOOKS LIKE A KITTY WAN-DERED IN.
KUKI URIE.
MEOW
DONATO PORPORA ...
KEEP YOUR EYES OPEN. OR YOU WILL DIE.
YES, SIR ...!

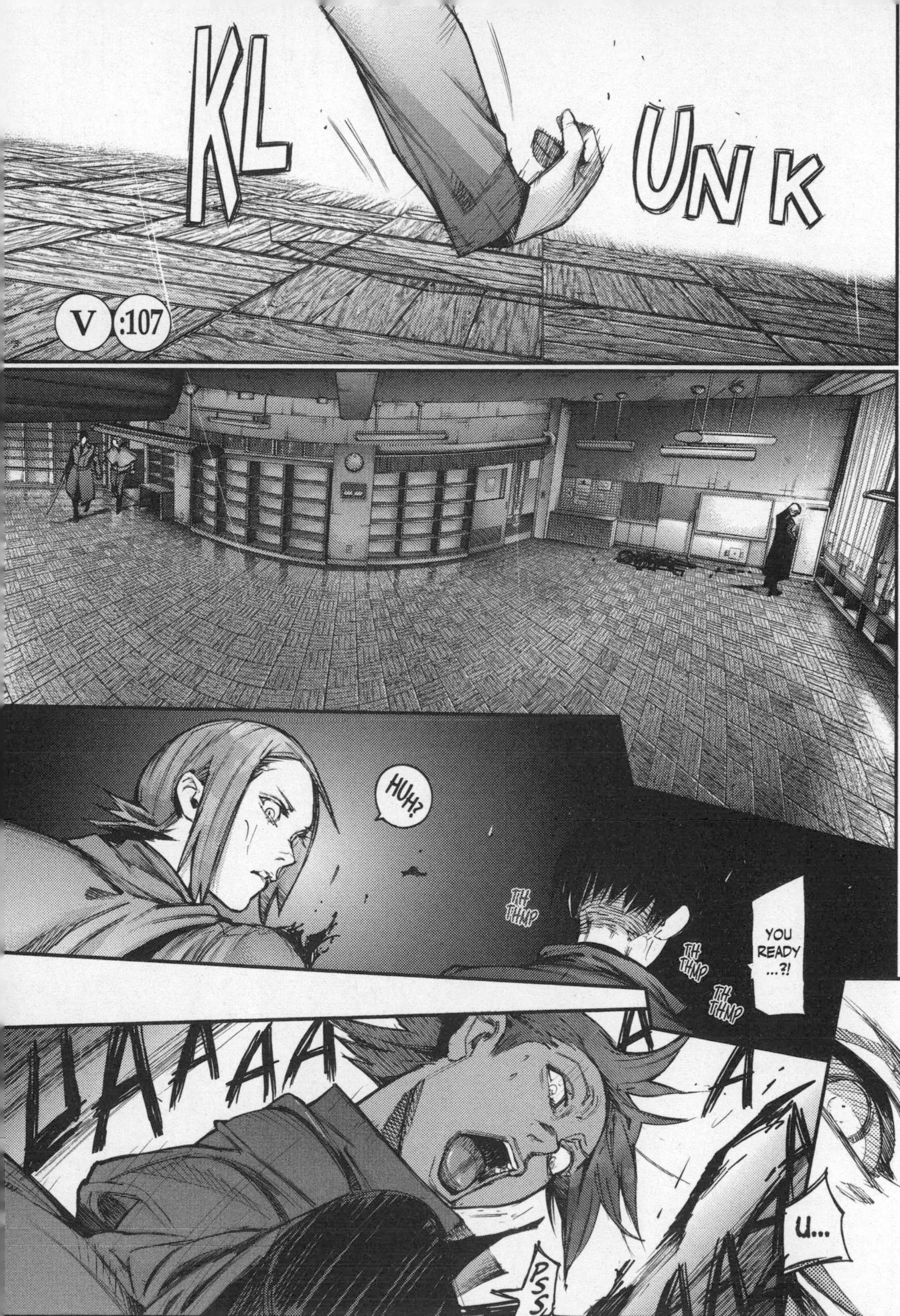
KLUNK
V :107
HUH?
TH THMP
TH THMP
TH THMP
YOU READY ...?!
U...
UAAAAAAAAA
PSSH

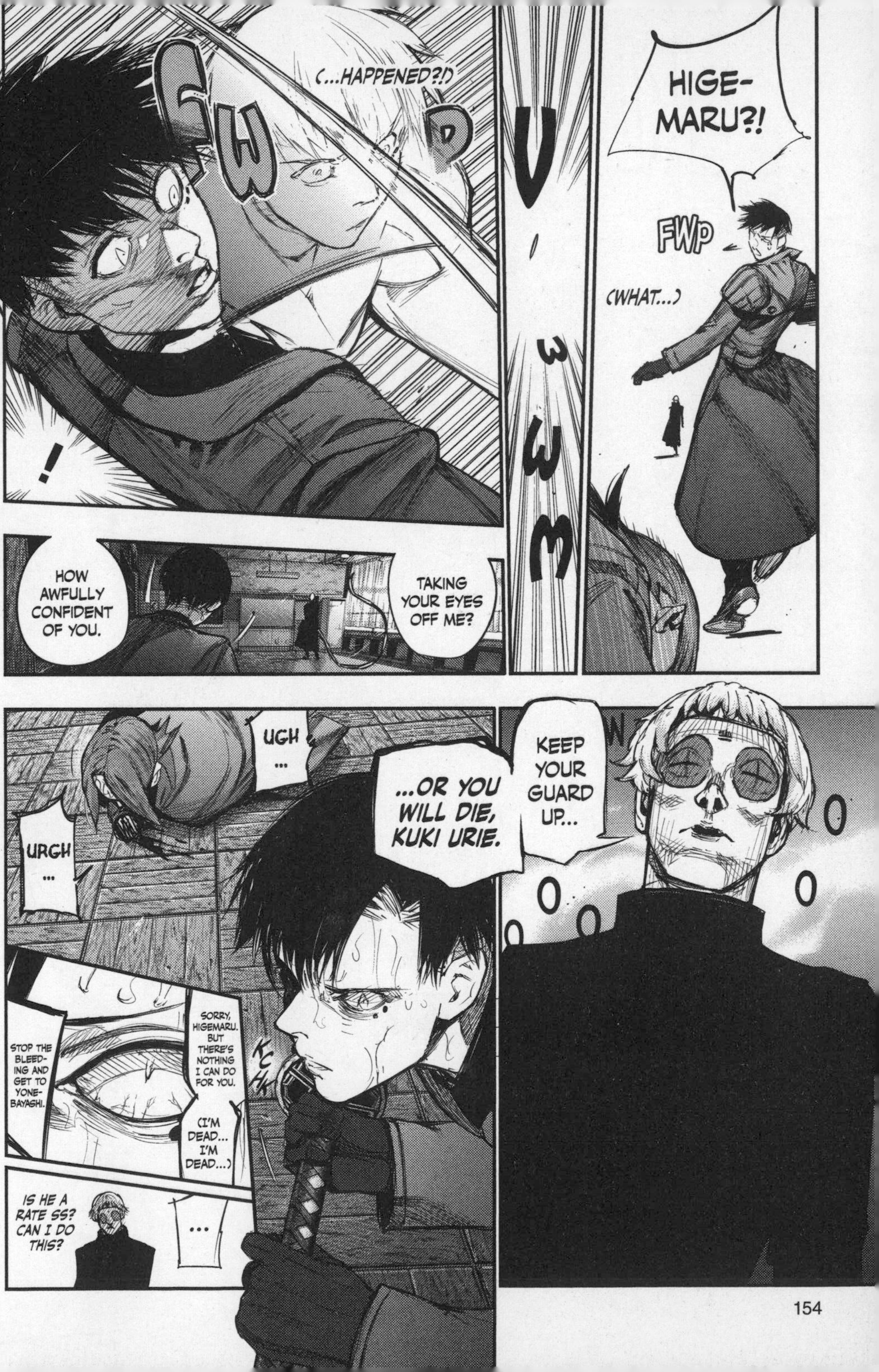
HIGE-MARU?!
FWP
(WHAT...)
(...HAPPENED?!)
!
TAKING YOUR EYES OFF ME?
HOW AWFULLY CONFIDENT OF YOU.
KEEP YOUR GUARD UP...
...OR YOU WILL DIE, KUKI URIE.
UGH ...
URGH ...
SORRY, HIGEMARU. BUT THERE'S NOTHING I CAN DO FOR YOU.
STOP THE BLEEDING AND GET TO YONE-BAYASHI.
(I'M DEAD... I'M DEAD...)
KCHK
...
IS HE A RATE SS? CAN I DO THIS?

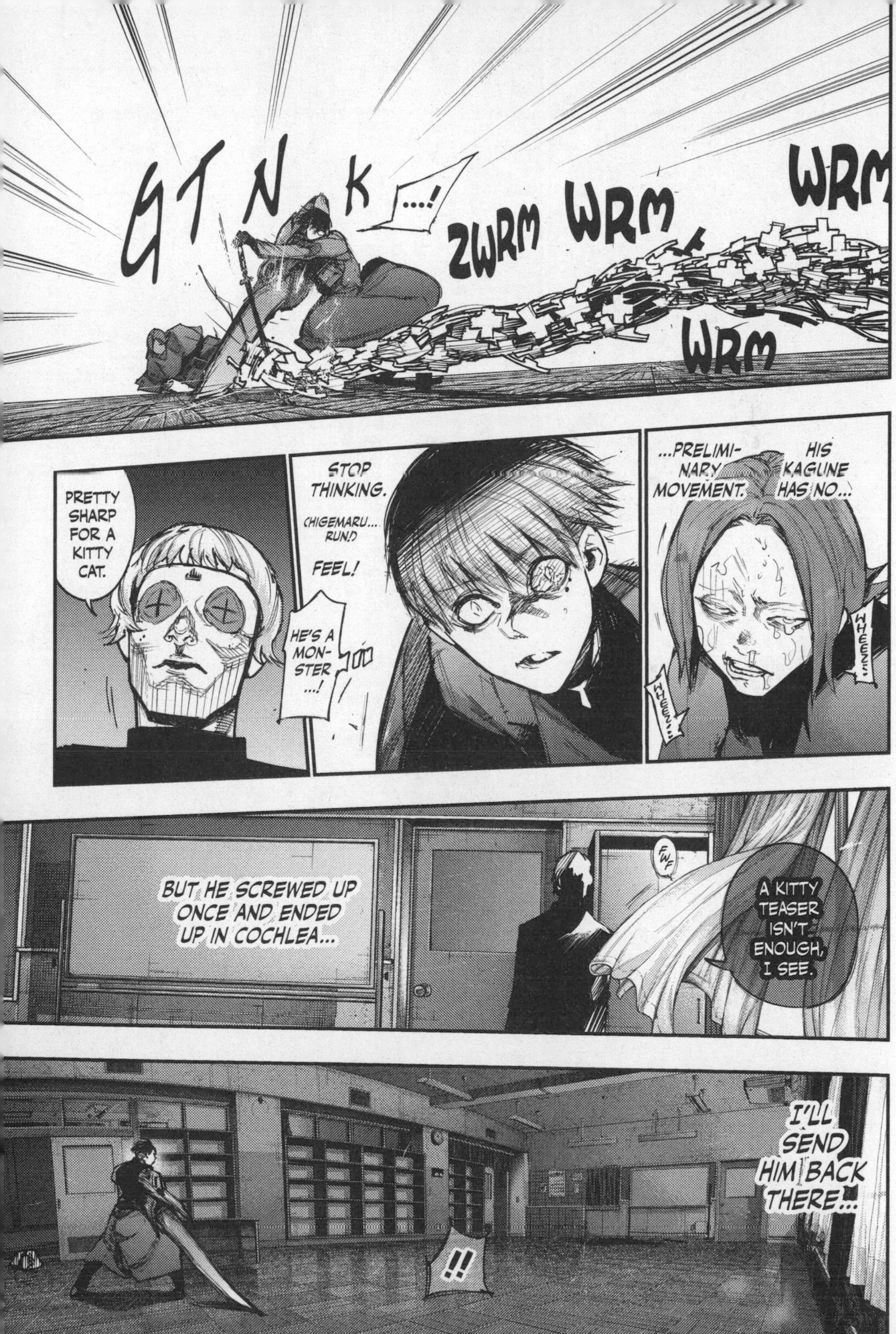
WRM
WRM
ZWRM
...!
GTNK
WRM
HIS KAGUNE HAS NO...
...PRELIMINARY MOVEMENT.
WHEEZ...
WHEEZ...
STOP THINKING.
CHIGEMARU... RUN!?
FEEL!
HE'S A MONSTER...!
PRETTY SHARP FOR A KITTY CAT.
A KITTY TEASER ISN'T ENOUGH, I SEE.
FWF
BUT HE SCREWED UP ONCE AND ENDED UP IN COCHLEA...
I'LL SEND HIM BACK THERE...
!!

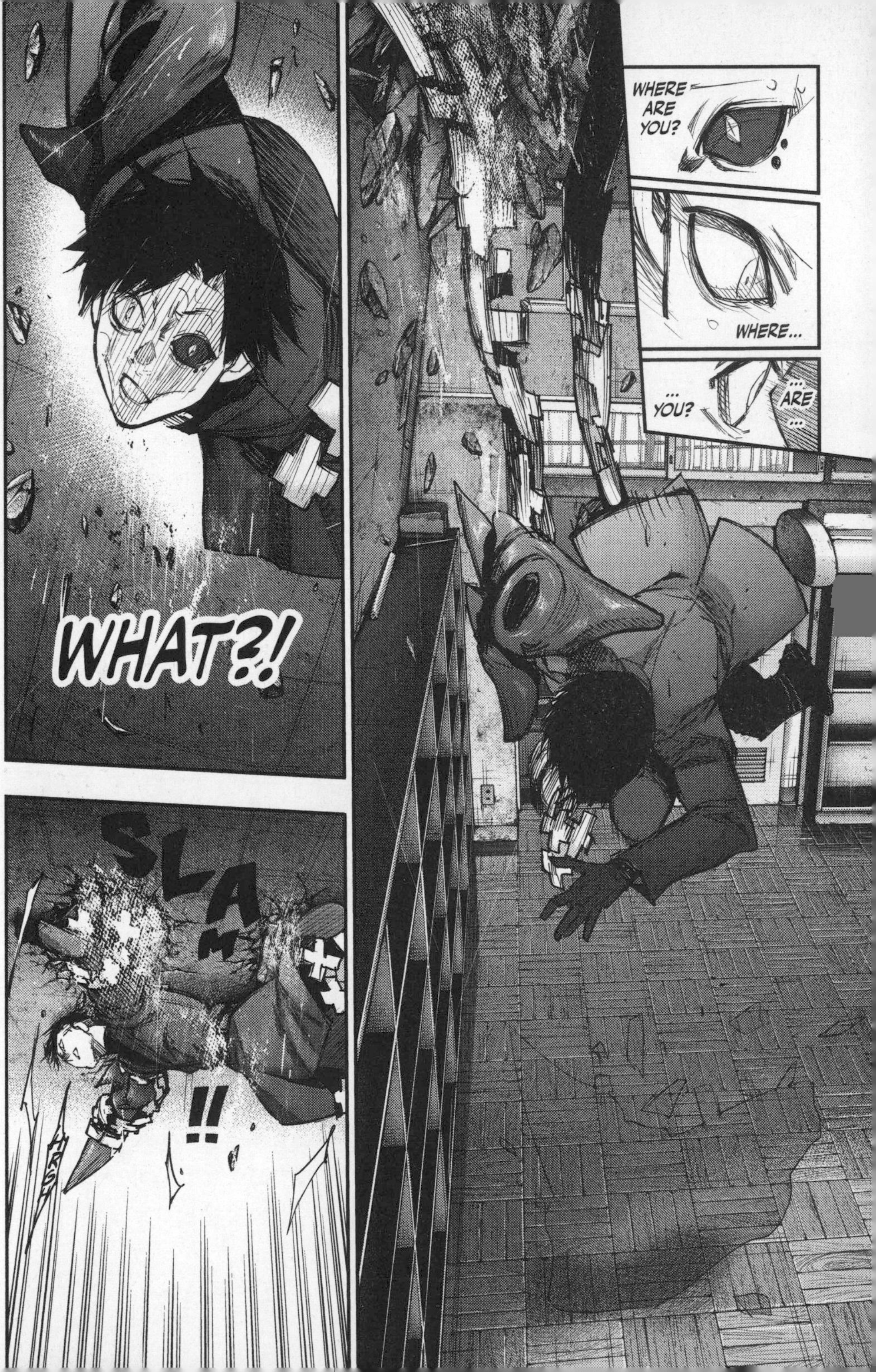
WHERE ARE YOU?
WHERE...
...ARE...
...YOU?
WHAT?!
SLAM
HRSH
!!

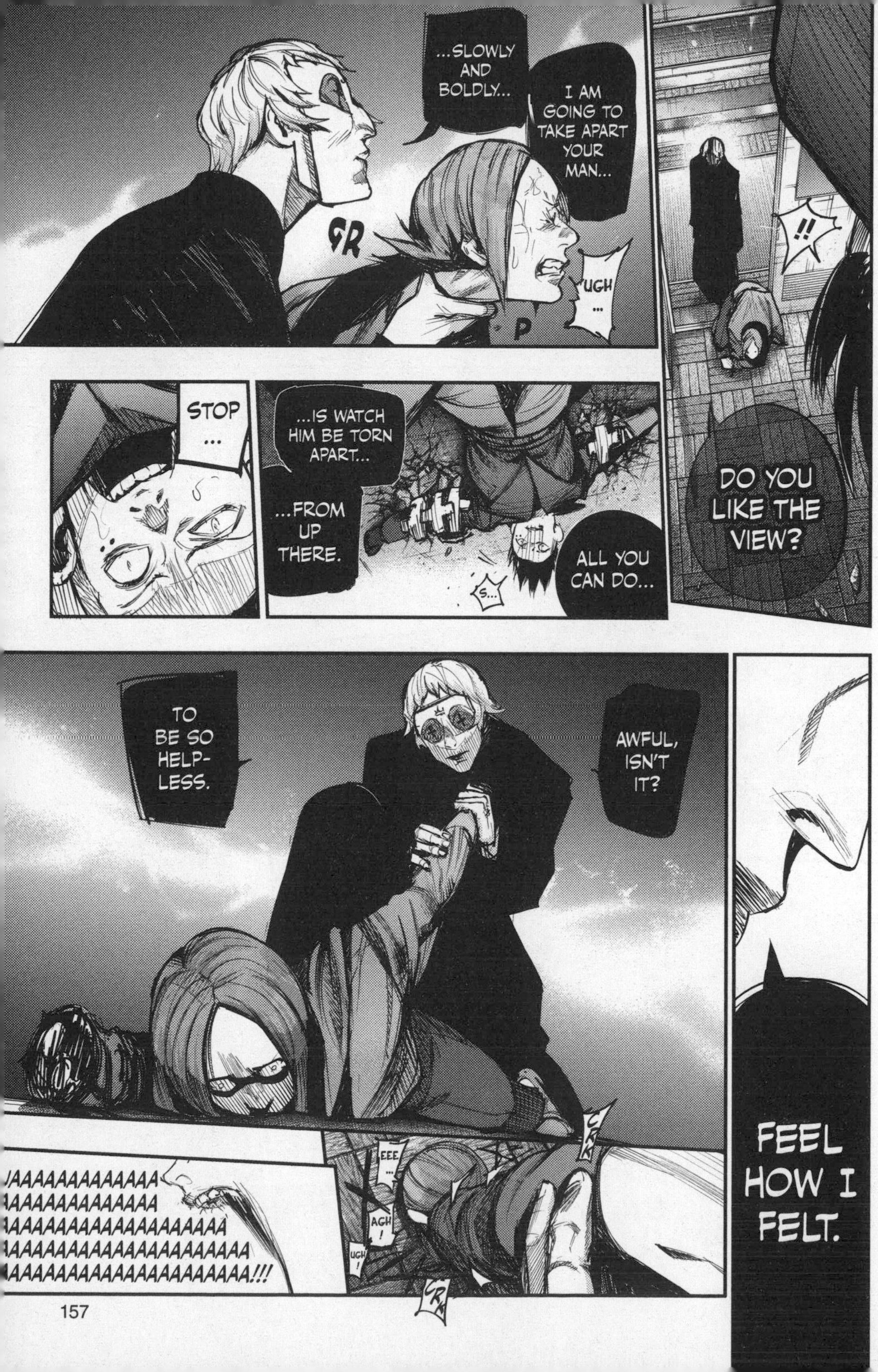
!!
DO YOU LIKE THE VIEW?
I AM GOING TO TAKE APART YOUR MAN...
...SLOWLY AND BOLDLY...
GR
UGH...
P
ALL YOU CAN DO...
S...
...IS WATCH HIM BE TORN APART...
...FROM UP THERE.
STOP...
FEEL HOW I FELT.
AWFUL, ISN'T IT?
TO BE SO HELP-LESS.
CRK
EEE...
AGH!
UGH!
CRK
AAAAAAAAAAAAAAAAAAAAAAAAAAAAAAAAAAAAAAAAAAAAAAAAAAAAAAAAAAAAAAAAAAAAAAAAAAAAAAAAAAAAAAAAAAAAAAAAAAAAAAAAAAA!!!

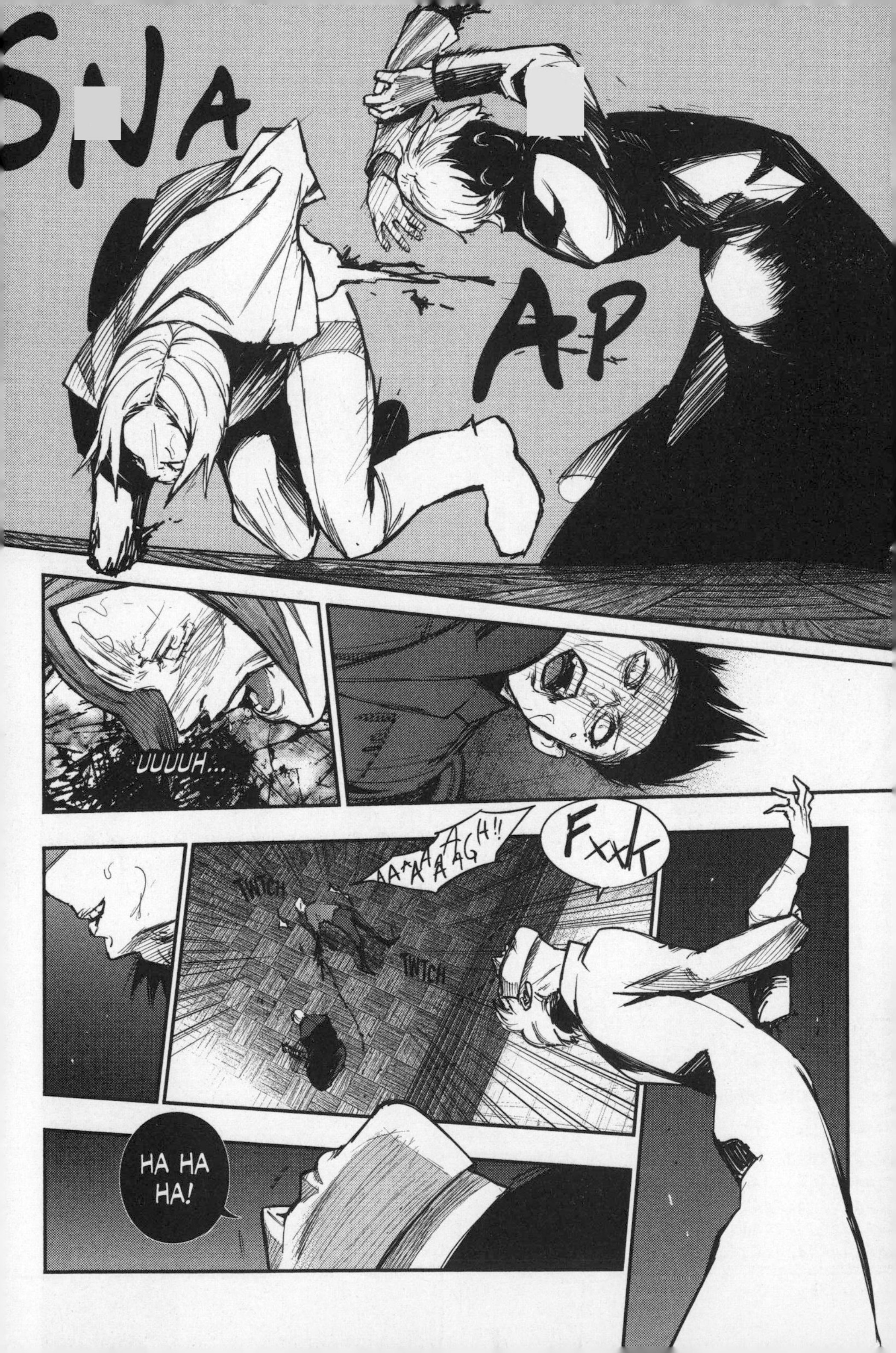
SNA
AP
UUUUH...
FXXK
AAAAAAAAGH!!
TWITCH
TWITCH
HA HA HA!

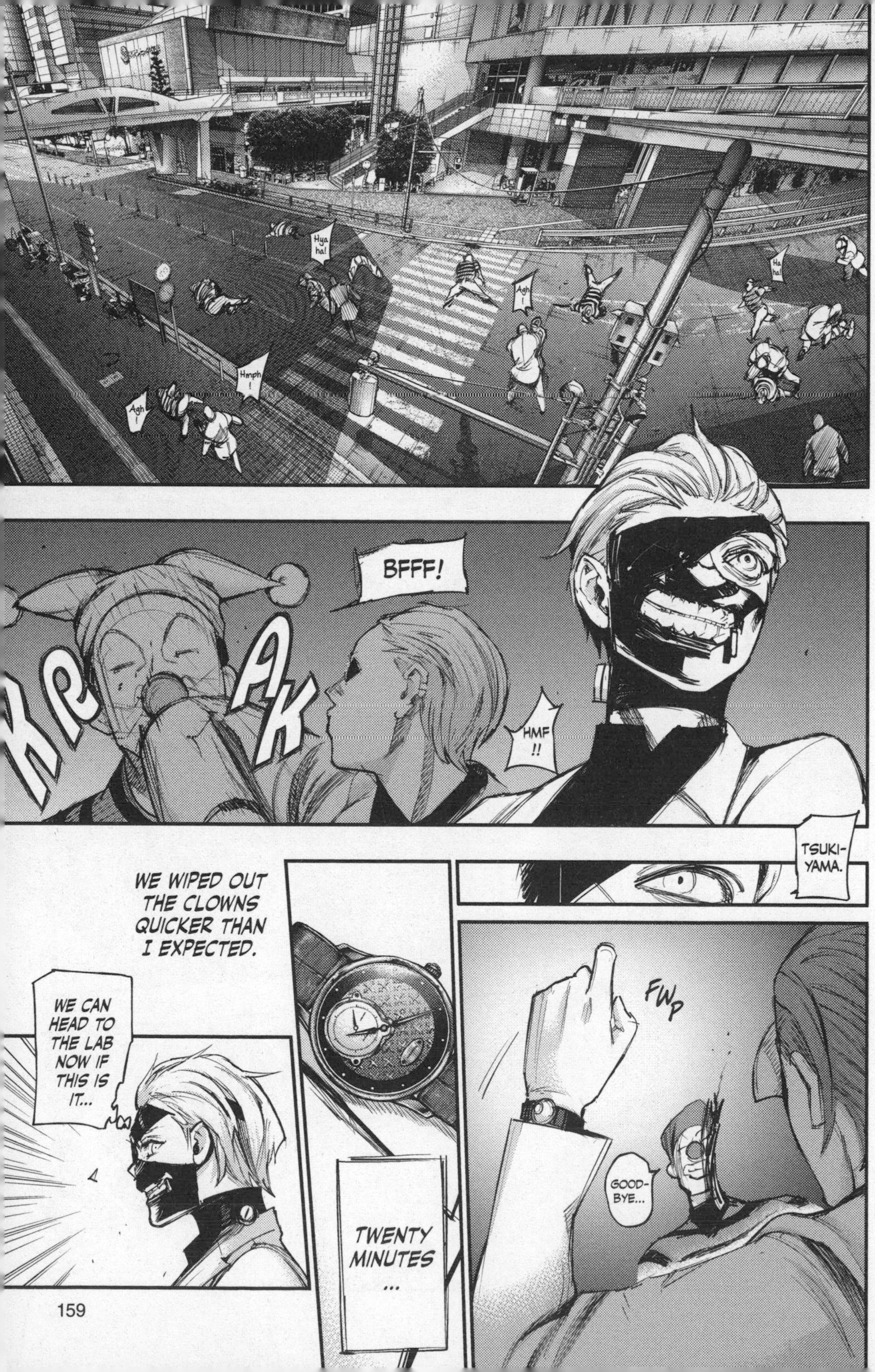
Ha ha!
Agh!
Hya ha!
Hmph!
Agh!
BFFF!
HMF!!
KRAK
TSUKI-YAMA.
FWP
GOOD-BYE...
TWENTY MINUTES...
WE WIPED OUT THE CLOWNS QUICKER THAN I EXPECTED.
WE CAN HEAD TO THE LAB NOW IF THIS IS IT...

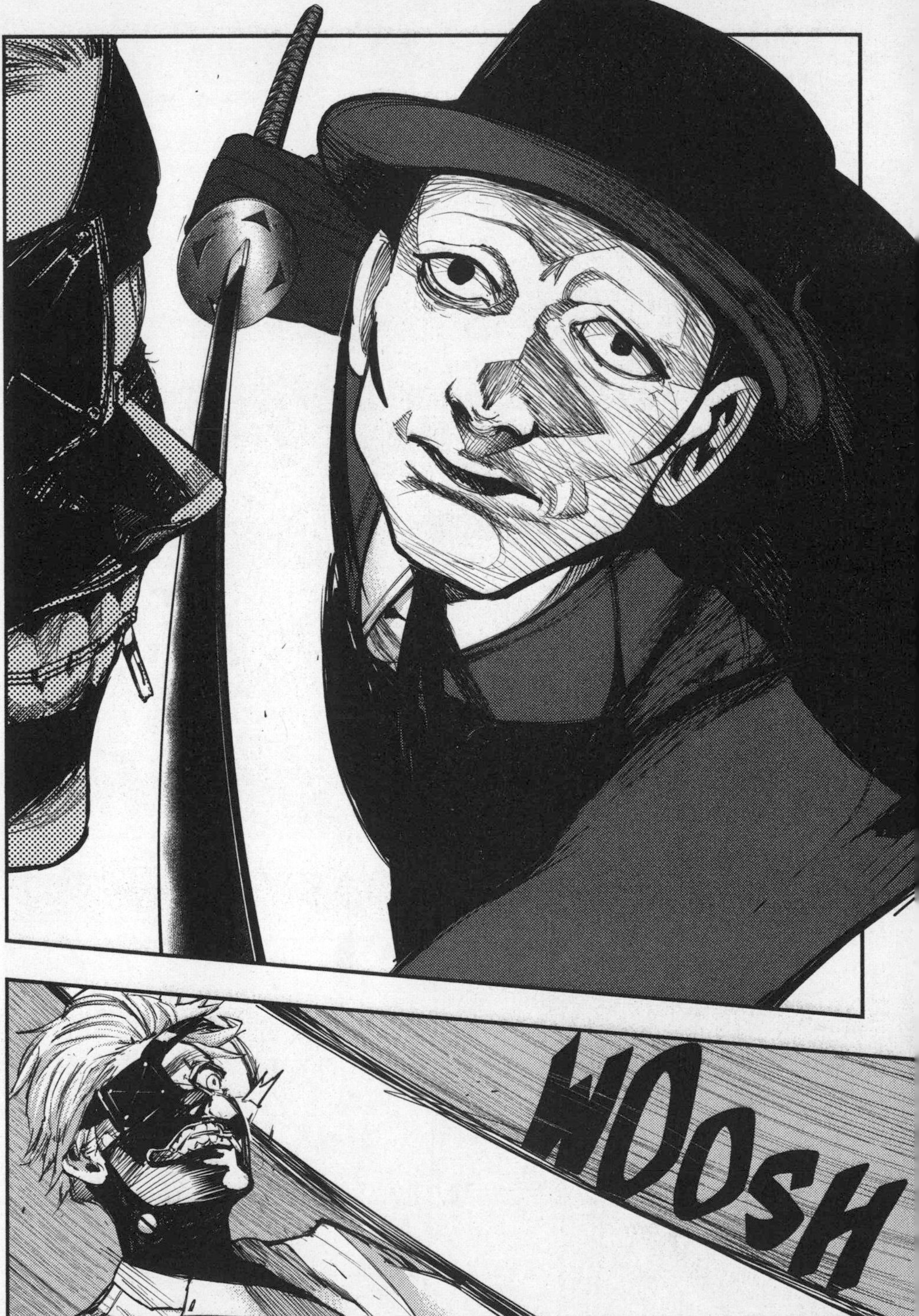
WOOSH

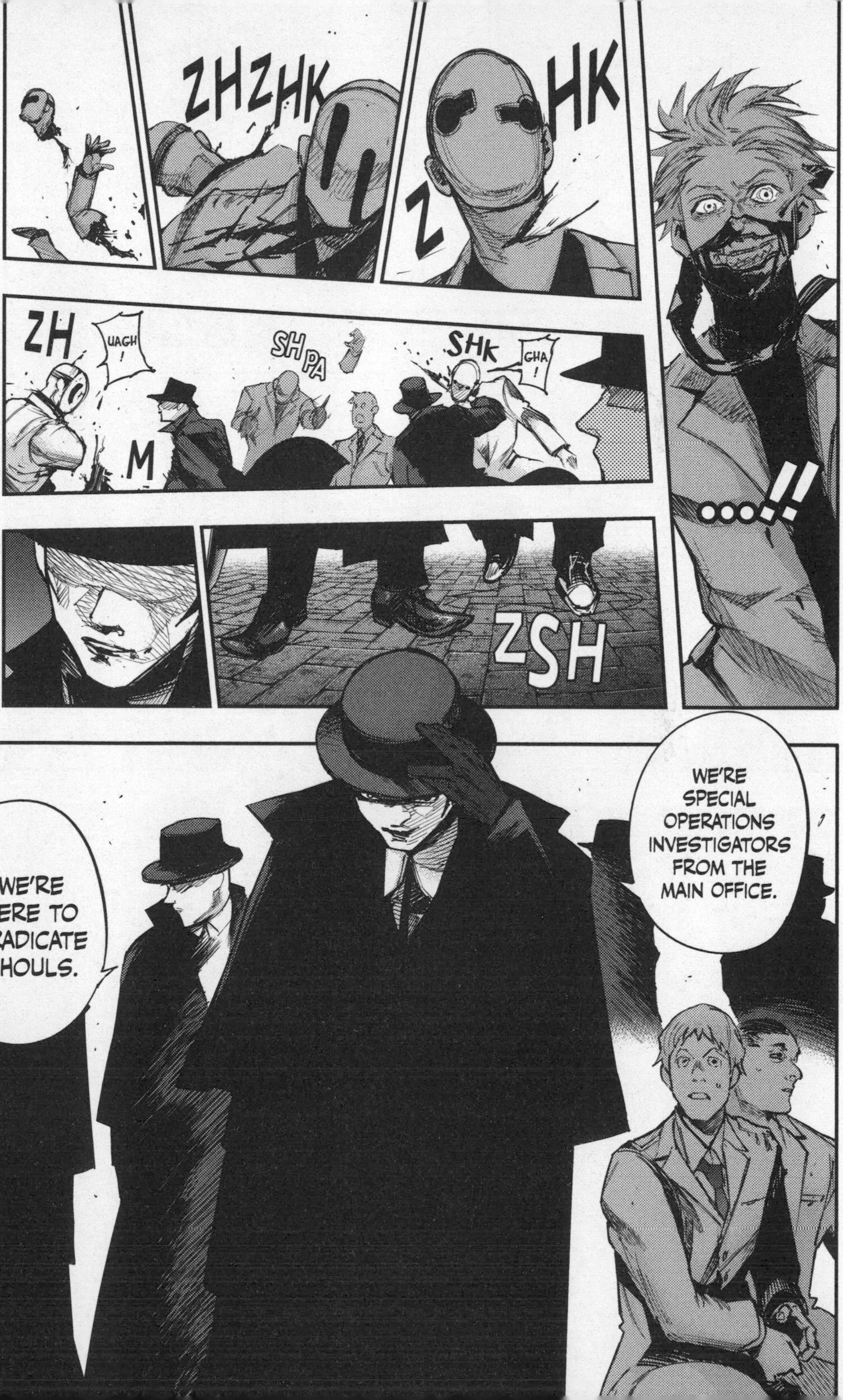
...!!
HK
Z
ZHZHK
GHA!
SHK
SHPA
UAGH!
ZH
M
ZSH
WE'RE SPECIAL OPERATIONS INVESTIGATORS FROM THE MAIN OFFICE.
WE'RE HERE TO ERADICATE GHOULS.

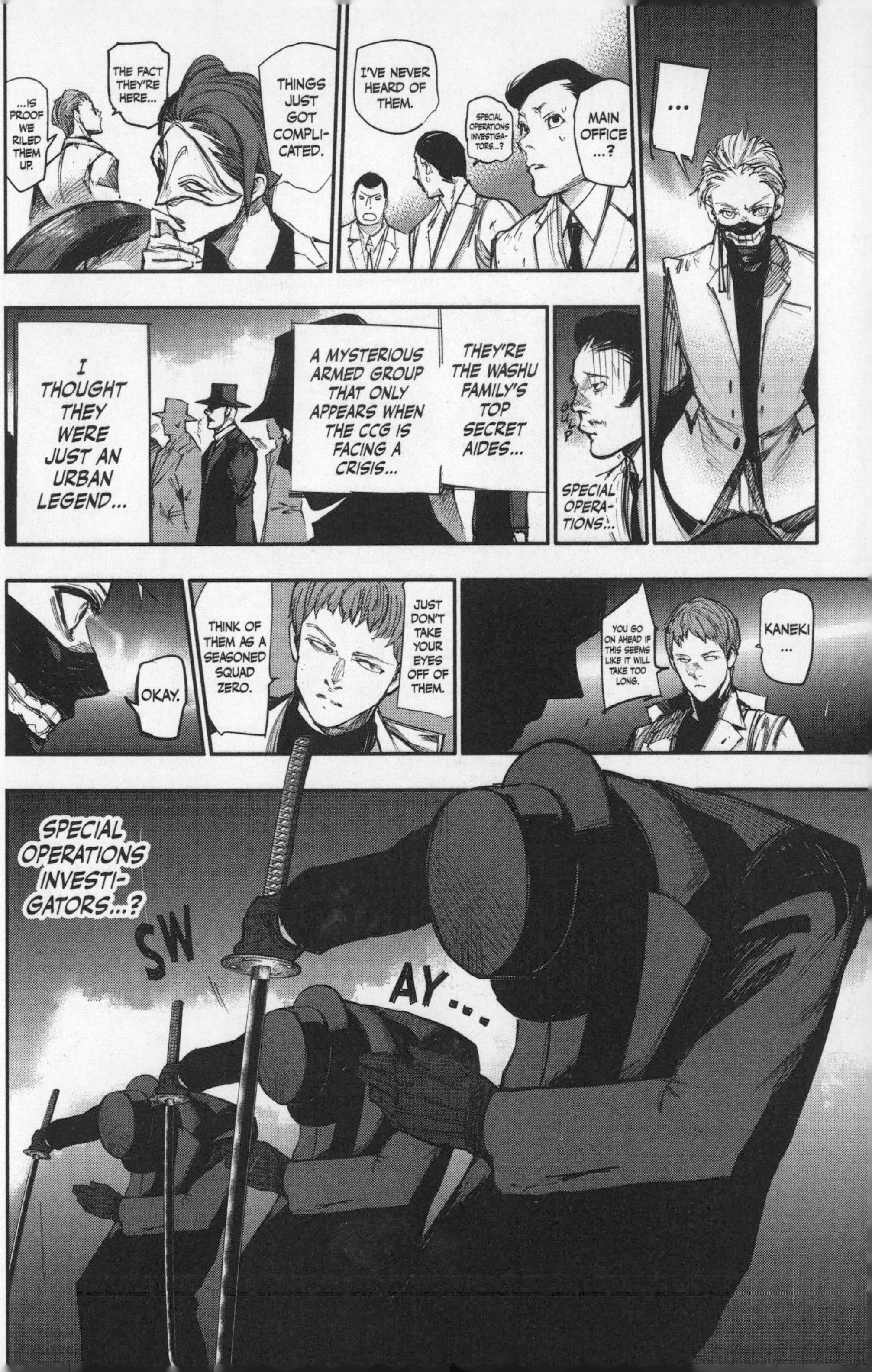
...
MAIN OFFICE ...?
SPECIAL OPERATIONS INVESTIGATORS...?
I'VE NEVER HEARD OF THEM.
THINGS JUST GOT COMPLICATED.
THE FACT THEY'RE HERE...
...IS PROOF WE RILED THEM UP.
GULP
SPECIAL OPERATIONS...
THEY'RE THE WASHU FAMILY'S TOP SECRET AIDES...
A MYSTERIOUS ARMED GROUP THAT ONLY APPEARS WHEN THE CCG IS FACING A CRISIS...
I THOUGHT THEY WERE JUST AN URBAN LEGEND...
KANEKI ...
YOU GO ON AHEAD IF THIS SEEMS LIKE IT WILL TAKE TOO LONG.
JUST DON'T TAKE YOUR EYES OFF OF THEM.
THINK OF THEM AS A SEASONED SQUAD ZERO.
OKAY.
SPECIAL OPERATIONS INVESTIGATORS...?
SWAY...

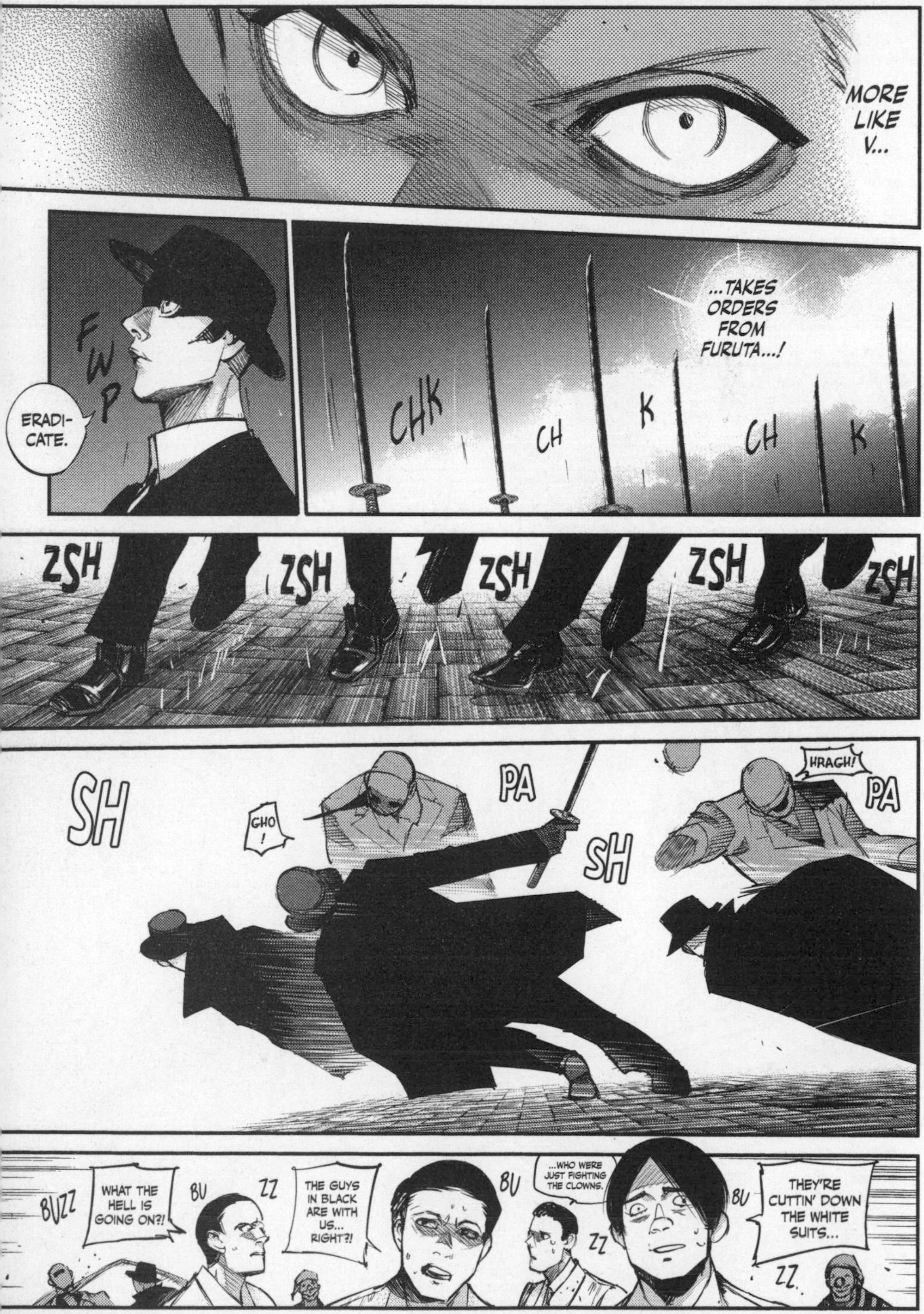
MORE LIKE V...
...TAKES ORDERS FROM FURUTA...!
CHK
CH
K
CH
K
FWP
ERADI-CATE.
ZSH
ZSH
ZSH
ZSH
ZSH
PA
HRAGH!
PA
SH
GHO!
SH
BU
ZZ
THEY'RE CUTTIN' DOWN THE WHITE SUITS...
ZZ
...WHO WERE JUST FIGHTING THE CLOWNS.
BU
ZZ
THE GUYS IN BLACK ARE WITH US... RIGHT?!
ZZ
BU
WHAT THE HELL IS GOING ON?!
BUZZ

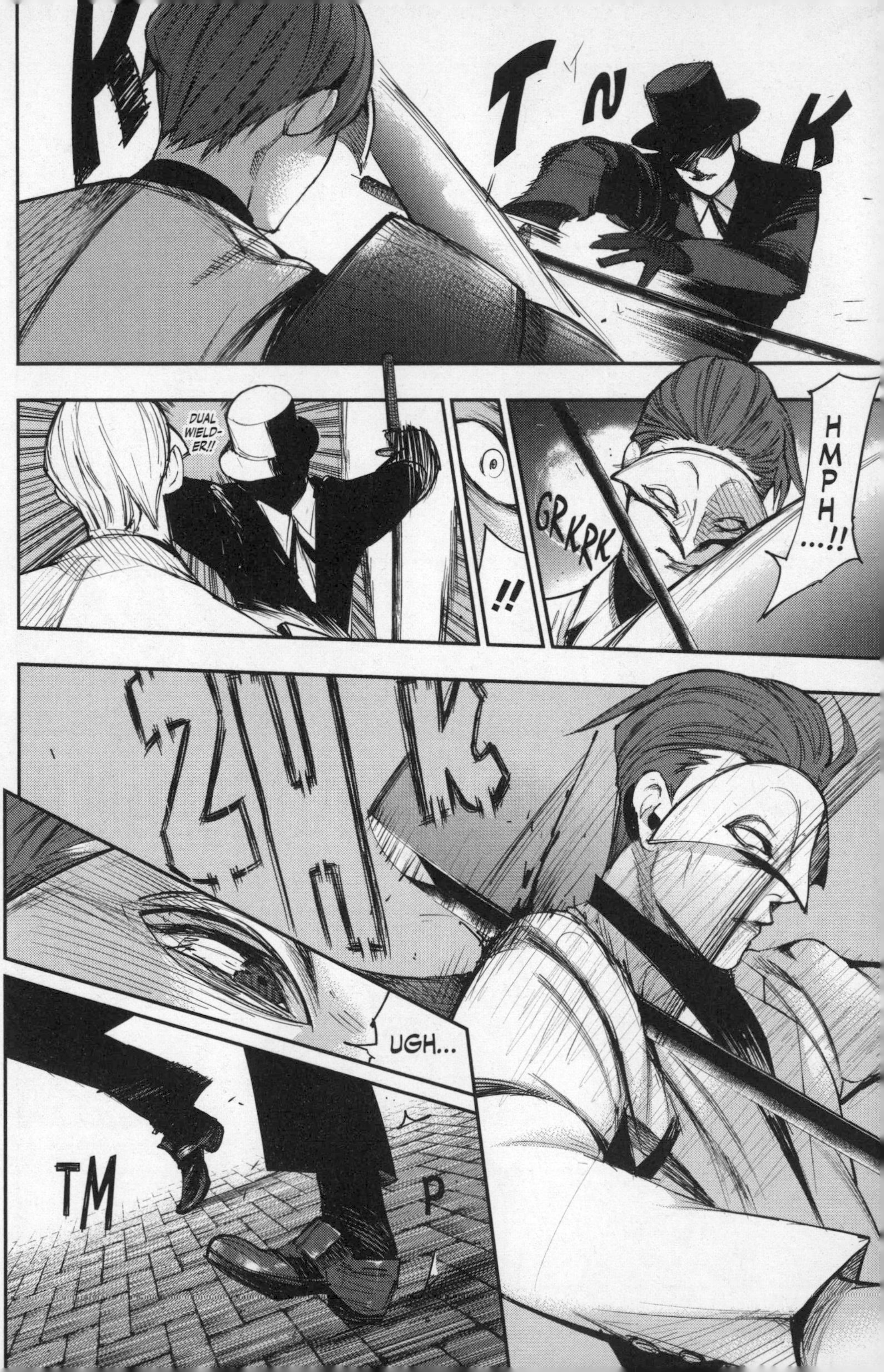
KTNK
HMPH...!!
GRKRK
!!
DUAL WIELD-ER!!
ZSHK
UGH...
TMP

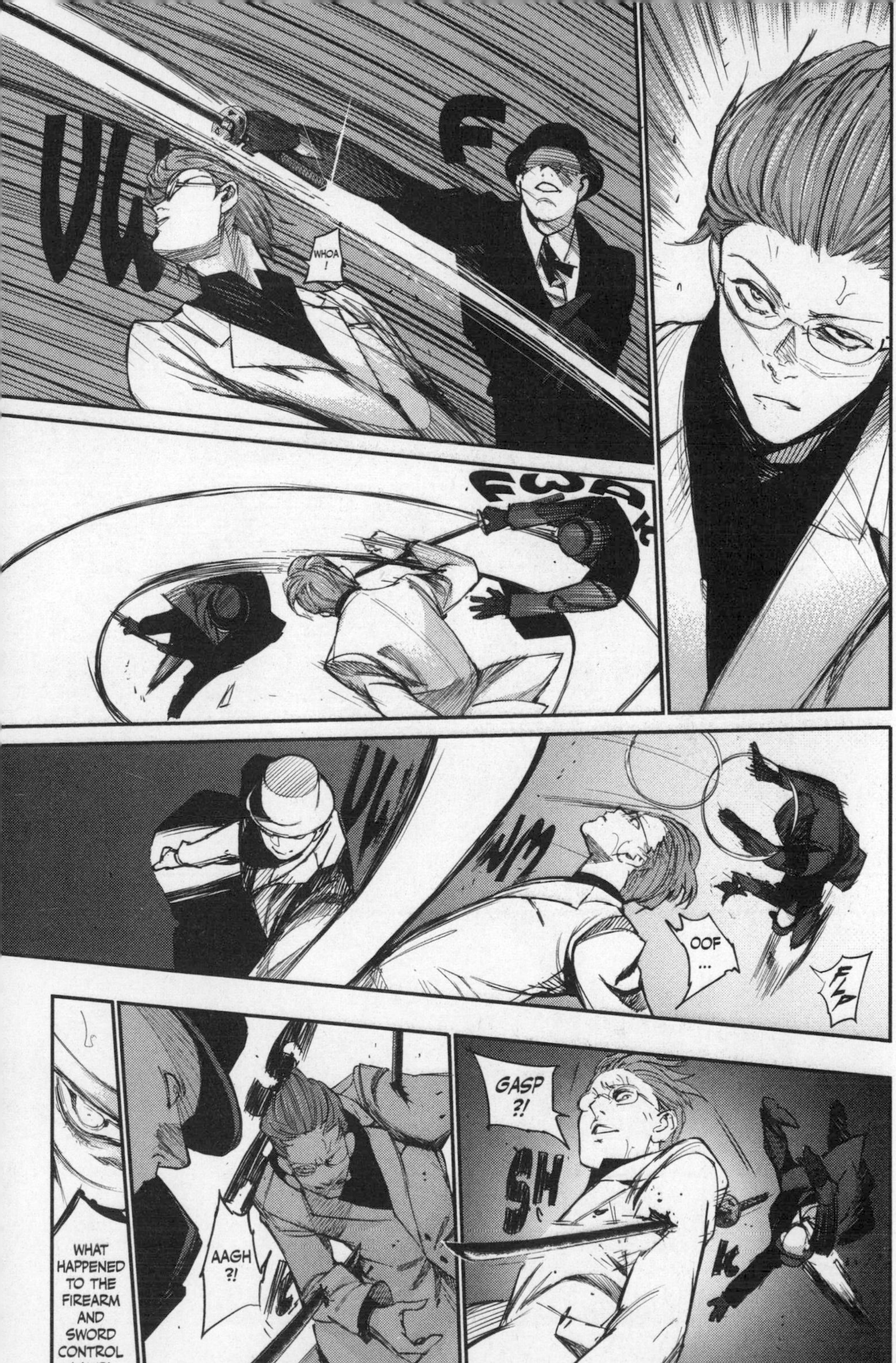

F
WHOA !
FWAK
OOF ...
FLP
GASP ?!
SH
AAGH ?!
WHAT HAPPENED TO THE FIREARM AND SWORD CONTROL LAW?!

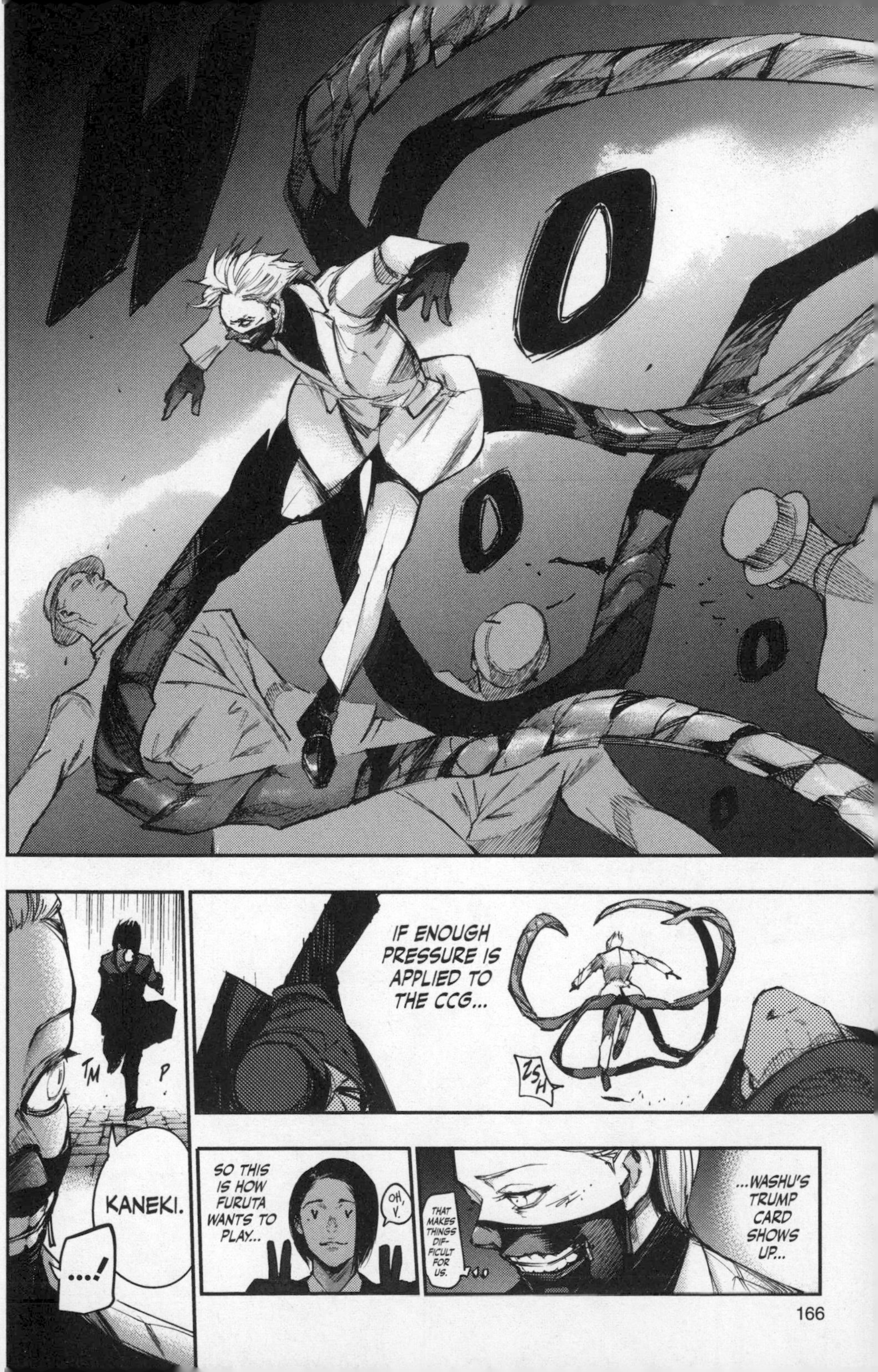
IF ENOUGH PRESSURE IS APPLIED TO THE CCG...
ZSH
...WASHU'S TRUMP CARD SHOWS UP...
SO THIS IS HOW FURUTA WANTS TO PLAY...
OH, V.
THAT MAKES THINGS DIF-FICULT FOR US.
TMP
KANEKI.
...!

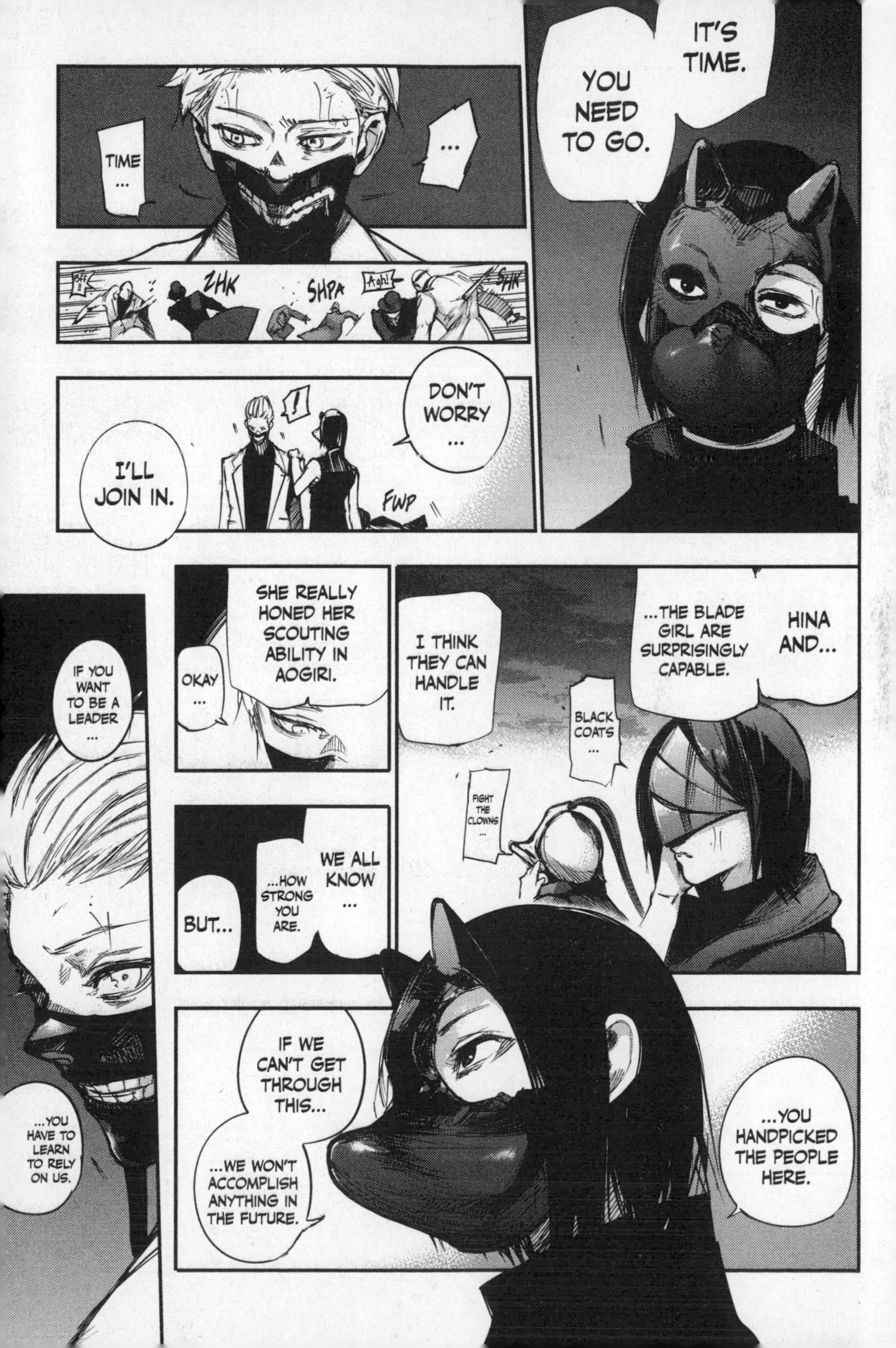
IT'S TIME.
YOU NEED TO GO.
...
TIME ...
SHK
Agh!
SHPA
ZHK
DON'T WORRY ...
!
I'LL JOIN IN.
FWP
HINA AND...
...THE BLADE GIRL ARE SURPRISINGLY CAPABLE.
I THINK THEY CAN HANDLE IT.
BLACK COATS ...
FIGHT THE CLOWNS ...
SHE REALLY HONED HER SCOUTING ABILITY IN AOGIRI.
OKAY ...
WE ALL KNOW ...
...HOW STRONG YOU ARE.
BUT...
...YOU HANDPICKED THE PEOPLE HERE.
IF WE CAN'T GET THROUGH THIS...
...WE WON'T ACCOMPLISH ANYTHING IN THE FUTURE.
IF YOU WANT TO BE A LEADER ...
...YOU HAVE TO LEARN TO RELY ON US.

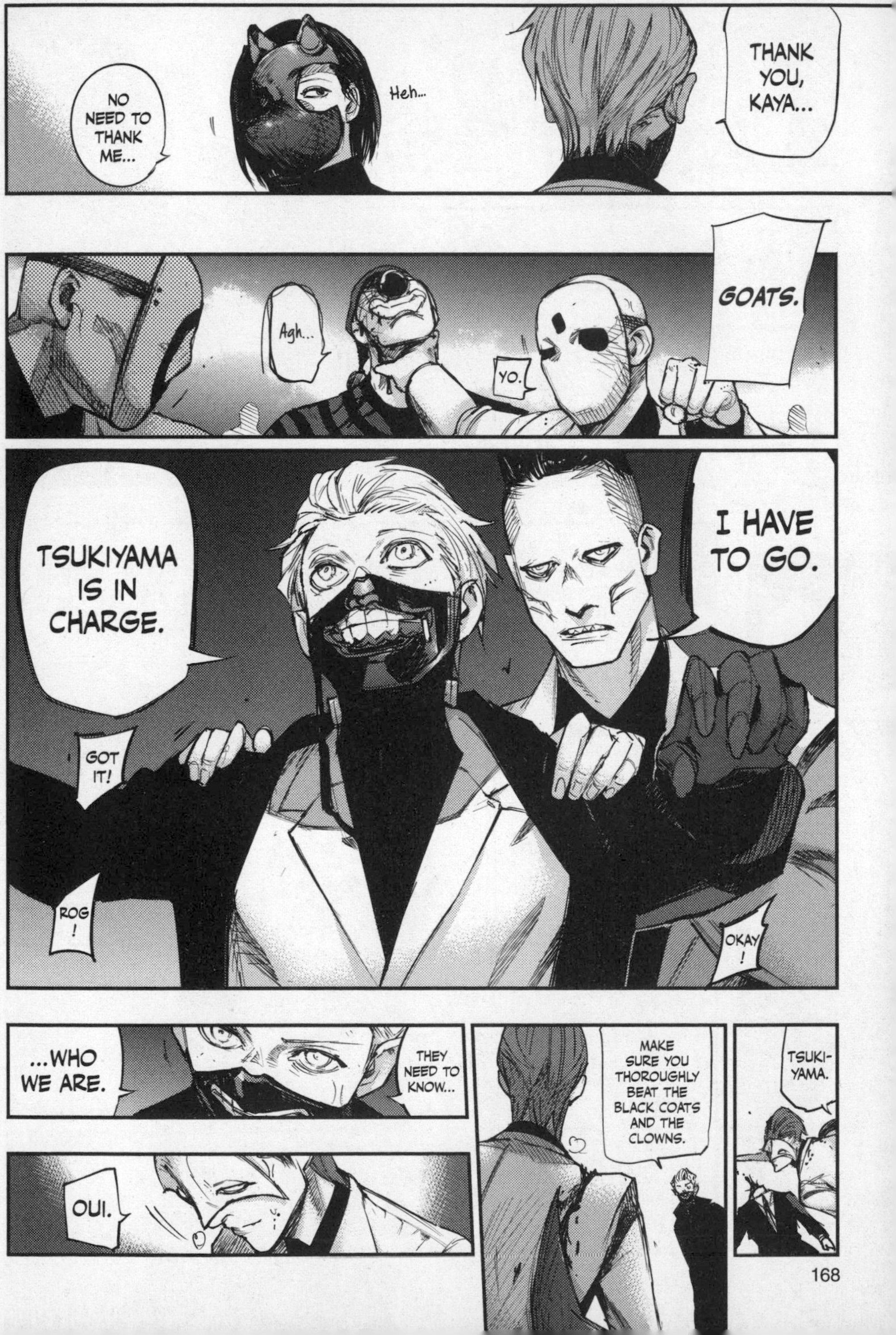
THANK YOU, KAYA...
Heh...
NO NEED TO THANK ME...
GOATS.
YO.
Agh...
I HAVE TO GO.
TSUKIYAMA IS IN CHARGE.
GOT IT!
OKAY!
ROG!
TSUKI-YAMA.
MAKE SURE YOU THOROUGHLY BEAT THE BLACK COATS AND THE CLOWNS.
THEY NEED TO KNOW...
...WHO WE ARE.
OUI.

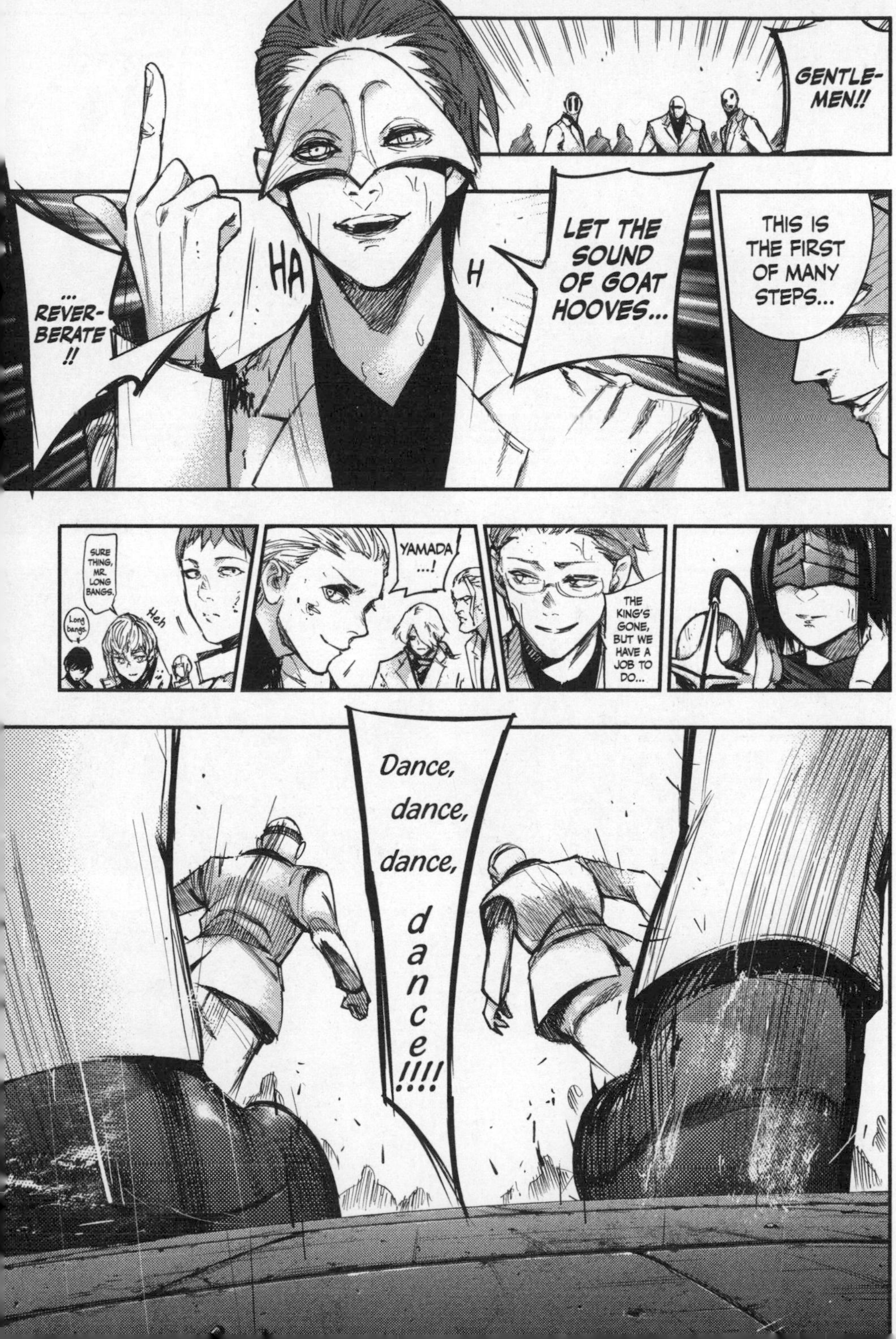
GENTLE-MEN!!
THIS IS THE FIRST OF MANY STEPS...
LET THE SOUND OF GOAT HOOVES...
HA
H
...REVER-BERATE!!
THE KING'S GONE, BUT WE HAVE A JOB TO DO...
YAMADA ...!
SURE THING, MR. LONG BANGS.
Heh
Long bangs.
Dance, dance, dance, dance!!!!

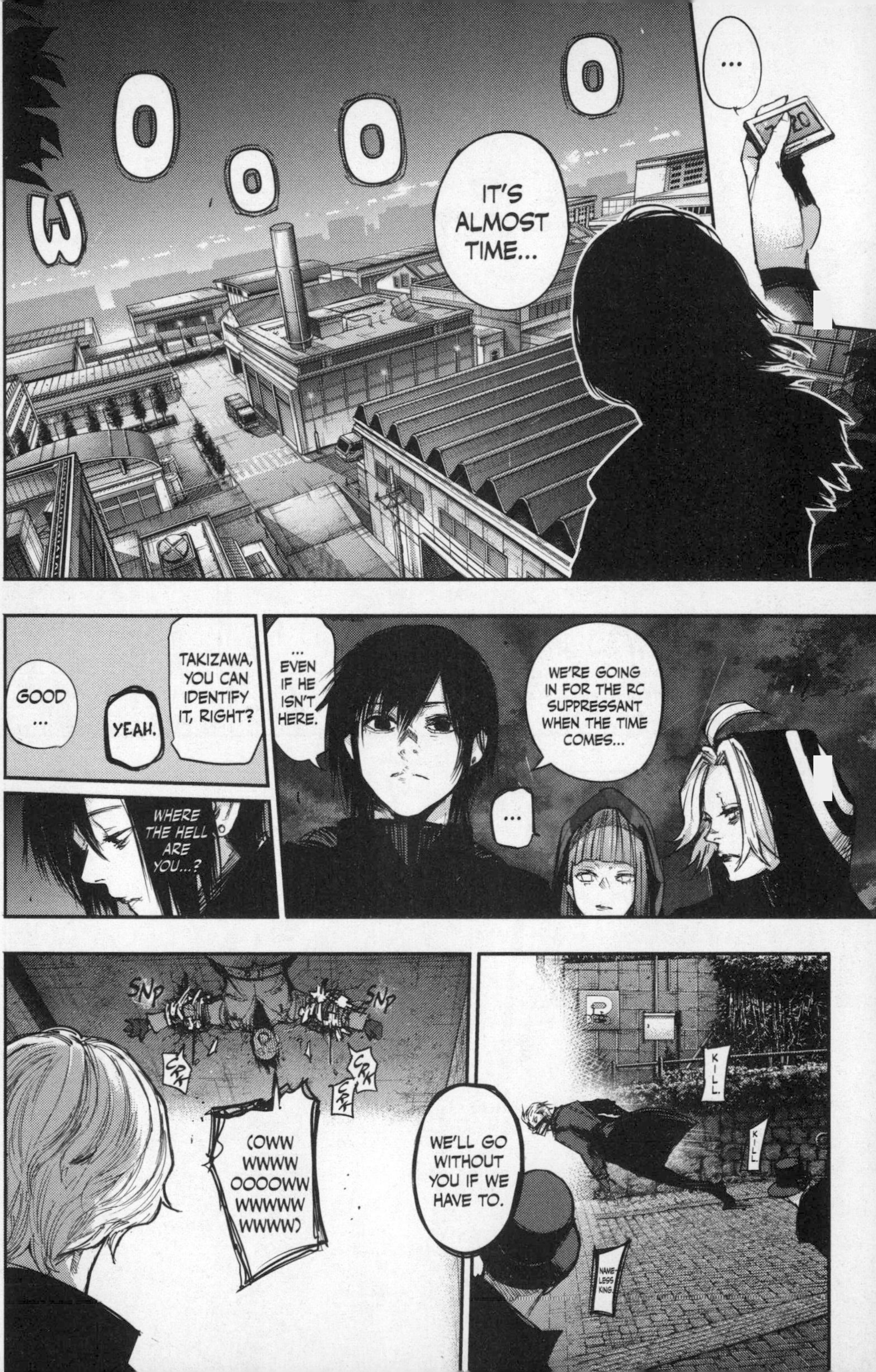
...
IT'S ALMOST TIME...
WOOOO
WE'RE GOING IN FOR THE RC SUPPRESSANT WHEN THE TIME COMES...
...
... EVEN IF HE ISN'T HERE.
TAKIZAWA, YOU CAN IDENTIFY IT, RIGHT?
YEAH.
GOOD ...
WHERE THE HELL ARE YOU...?
KILL.
KILL.
NAME-LESS KING.
WE'LL GO WITHOUT YOU IF WE HAVE TO.
SNP
SNP
CRK
CRK
CRK
(OWW WWWW OOOOWW WWWWW WWWW)

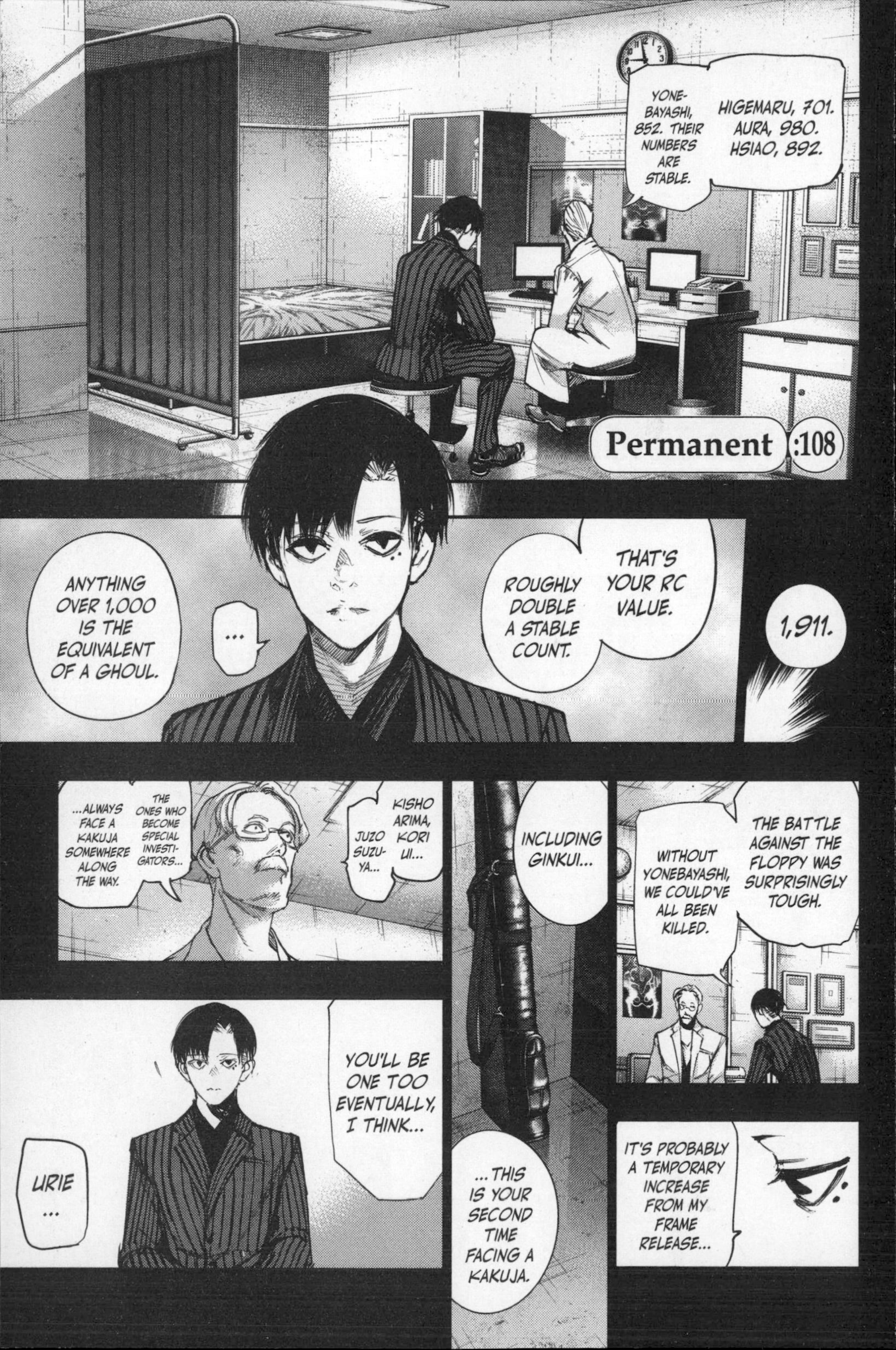
HIGEMARU, 701. AURA, 980. HSIAO, 892.
YONE-BAYASHI, 852. THEIR NUMBERS ARE STABLE.
Permanent :108
1,911.
THAT'S YOUR RC VALUE.
ROUGHLY DOUBLE A STABLE COUNT.
...
ANYTHING OVER 1,000 IS THE EQUIVALENT OF A GHOUL.
THE BATTLE AGAINST THE FLOPPY WAS SURPRISINGLY TOUGH.
WITHOUT YONEBAYASHI, WE COULD'VE ALL BEEN KILLED.
IT'S PROBABLY A TEMPORARY INCREASE FROM MY FRAME RELEASE...
INCLUDING GINKUI...
...THIS IS YOUR SECOND TIME FACING A KAKUJA.
KISHO ARIMA, KORI UI...
JUZO SUZUYA...
THE ONES WHO BECOME SPECIAL INVESTI-GATORS...
...ALWAYS FACE A KAKUJA SOMEWHERE ALONG THE WAY.
YOU'LL BE ONE TOO EVENTUALLY, I THINK...
URIE ...

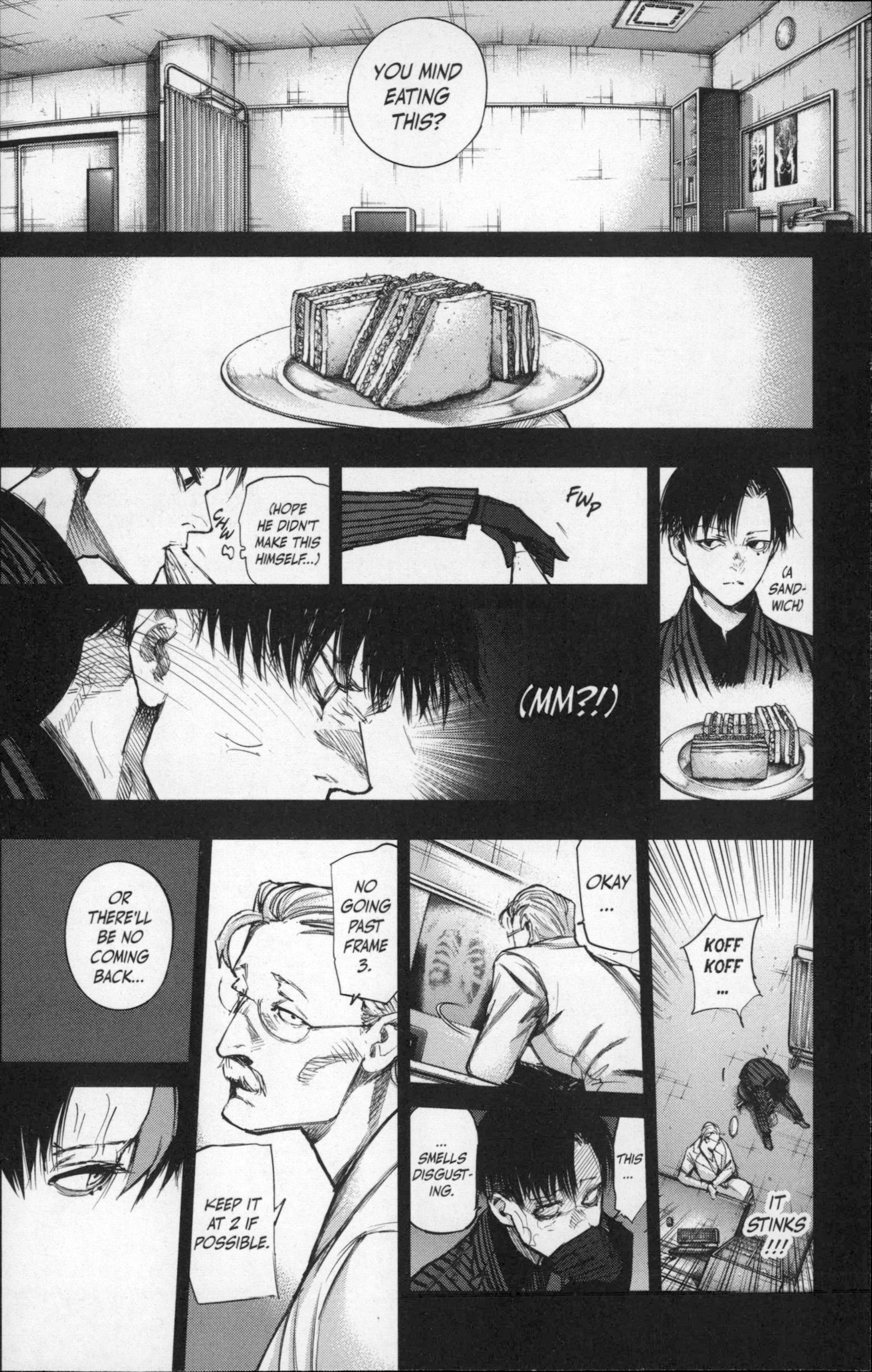
YOU MIND EATING THIS?
(A SANDWICH)
FWP
CHW
(HOPE HE DIDN'T MAKE THIS HIMSELF...)
(MM?!)
KOFF KOFF ...
IT STINKS!!!
OKAY ...
THIS ...
... SMELLS DISGUSTING.
NO GOING PAST FRAME 3.
KEEP IT AT 2 IF POSSIBLE.
OR THERE'LL BE NO COMING BACK...

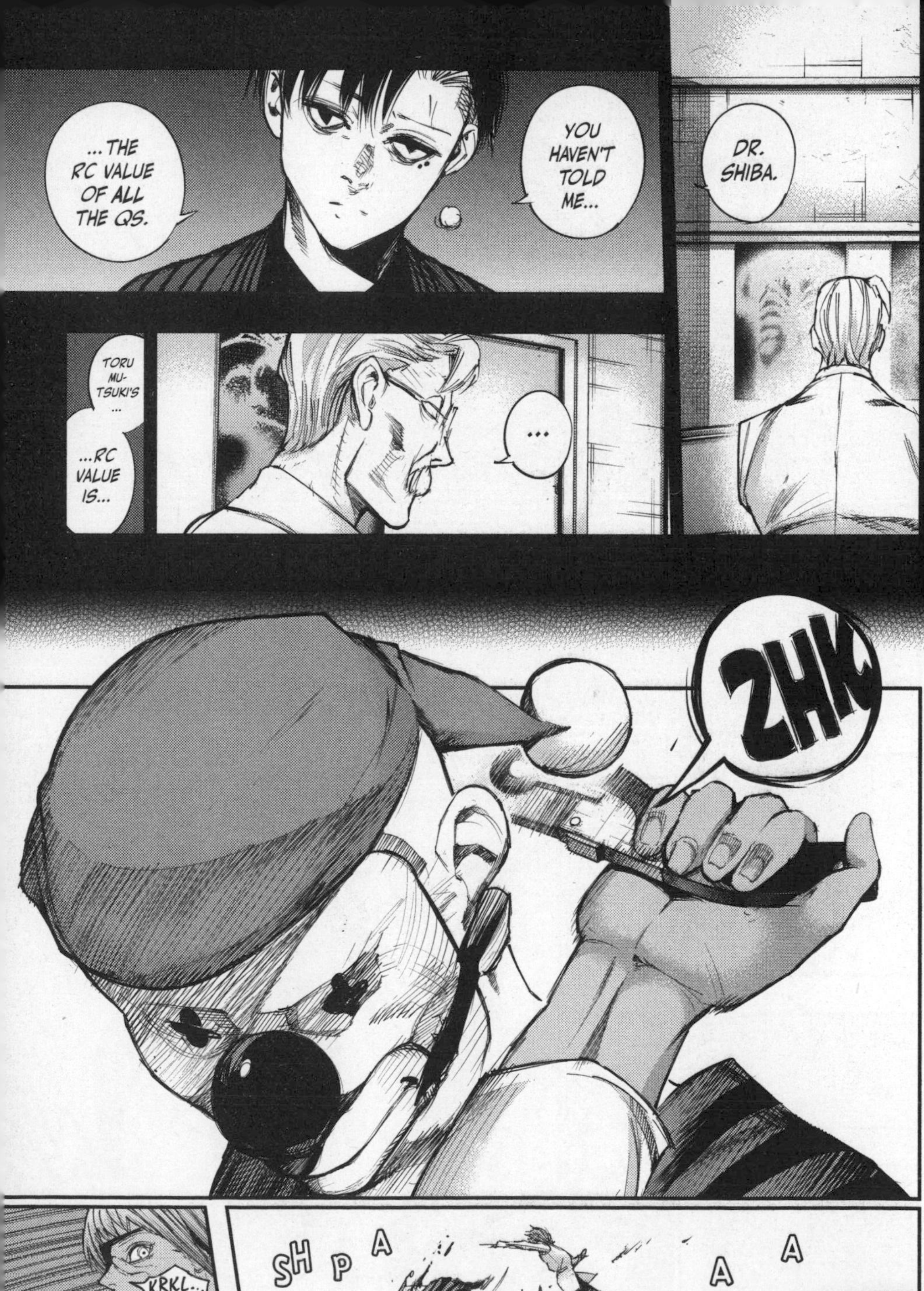
DR. SHIBA.
YOU HAVEN'T TOLD ME...
...THE RC VALUE OF ALL THE QS.
...
TORU MUTSUKI'S...
...RC VALUE IS...
ZHK
SHpA A A
KRKL...

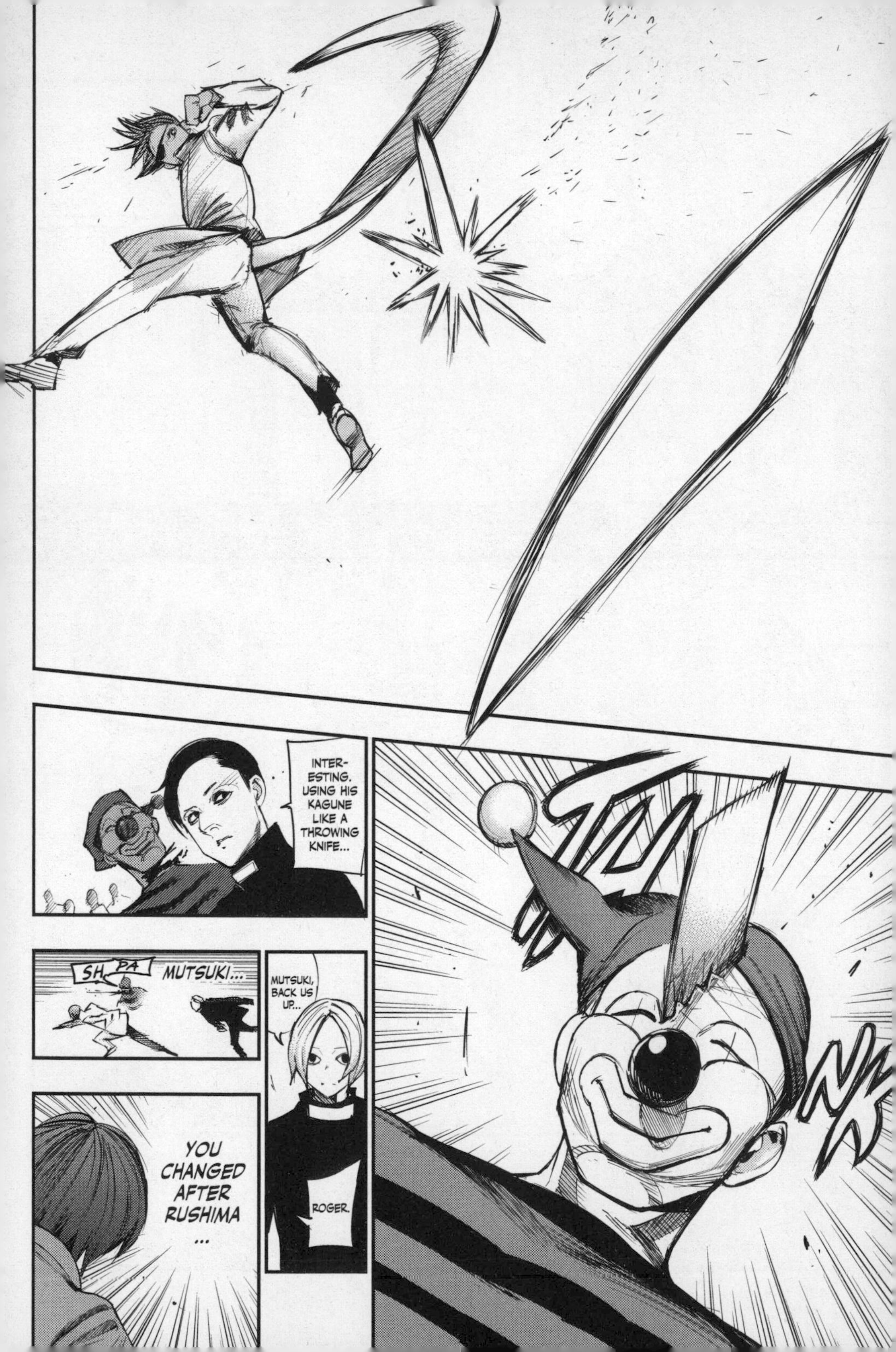
INTER-
ESTING.
USING HIS
KAGUNE
LIKE A
THROWING
KNIFE...
MUTSUKI,
BACK US
UP...
ROGER.
SH PA
MUTSUKI...
YOU
CHANGED
AFTER
RUSHIMA
...

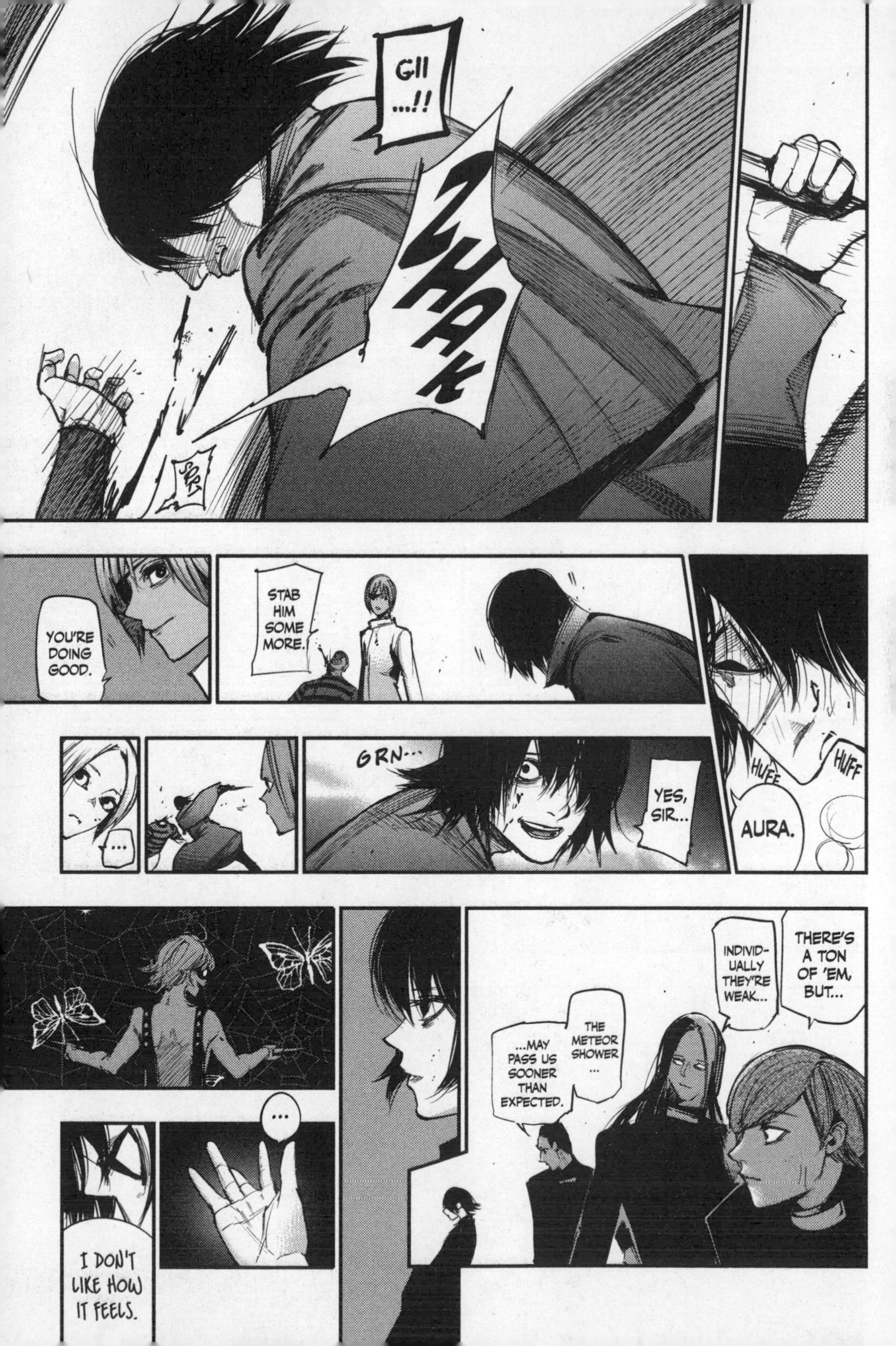
GII ...!!
ZWHAK
HUFF
HUFF
AURA.
STAB HIM SOME MORE.
YOU'RE DOING GOOD.
YES, SIR...
GRN...
...
THERE'S A TON OF 'EM, BUT...
INDIVIDUALLY THEY'RE WEAK...
THE METEOR SHOWER...
...MAY PASS US SOONER THAN EXPECTED.
...
I DON'T LIKE HOW IT FEELS.

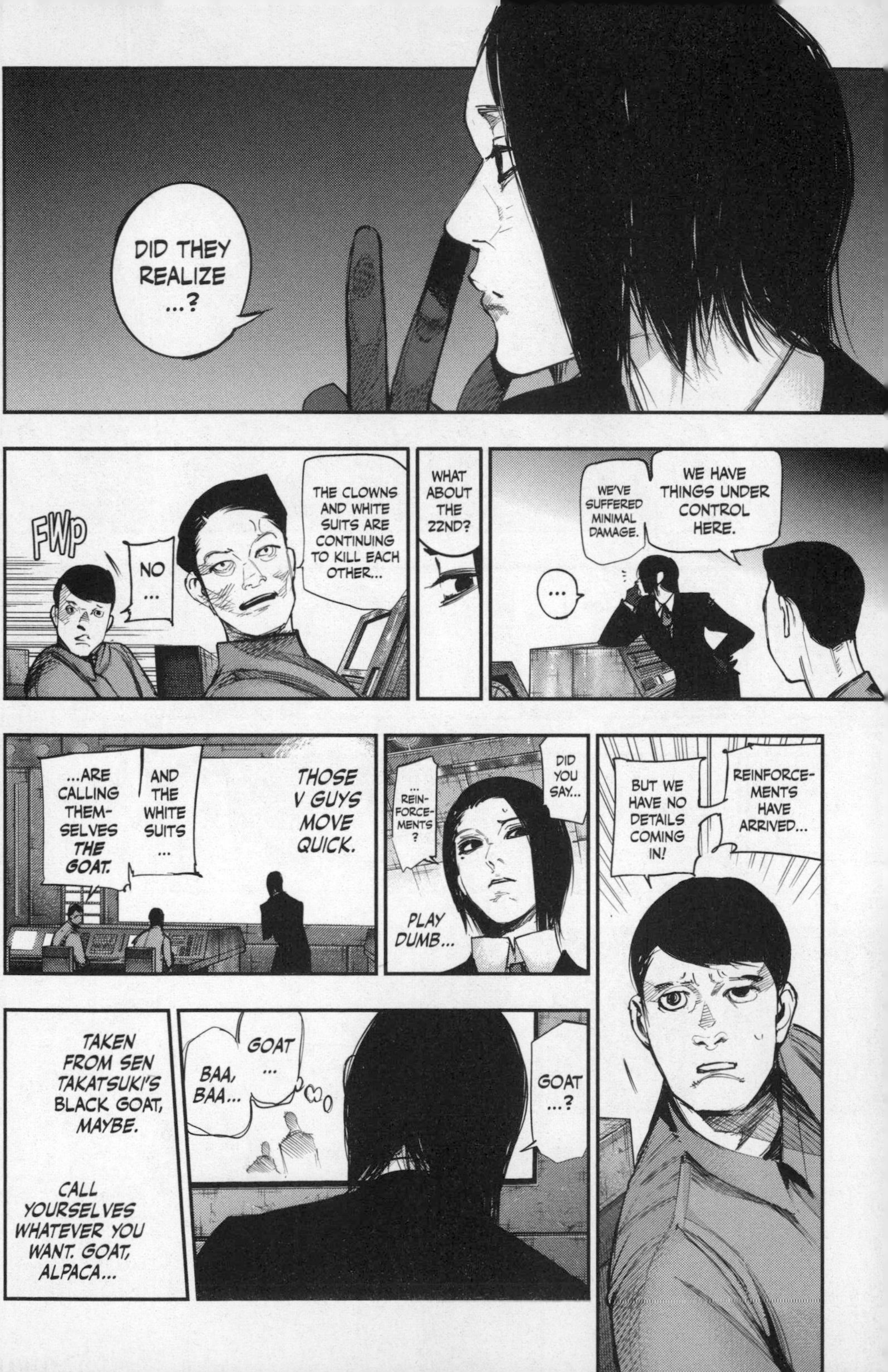
DID THEY REALIZE ...?
WE HAVE THINGS UNDER CONTROL HERE.
WE'VE SUFFERED MINIMAL DAMAGE.
...
WHAT ABOUT THE 22ND?
THE CLOWNS AND WHITE SUITS ARE CONTINUING TO KILL EACH OTHER...
NO ...
FWP
REINFORCE-MENTS HAVE ARRIVED...
BUT WE HAVE NO DETAILS COMING IN!
DID YOU SAY...
... REIN-FORCE-MENTS ?
PLAY DUMB...
THOSE V GUYS MOVE QUICK.
AND THE WHITE SUITS ...
...ARE CALLING THEM-SELVES THE GOAT.
GOAT ...?
GOAT ...
BAA, BAA...
TAKEN FROM SEN TAKATSUKI'S BLACK GOAT, MAYBE.
CALL YOURSELVES WHATEVER YOU WANT. GOAT, ALPACA...

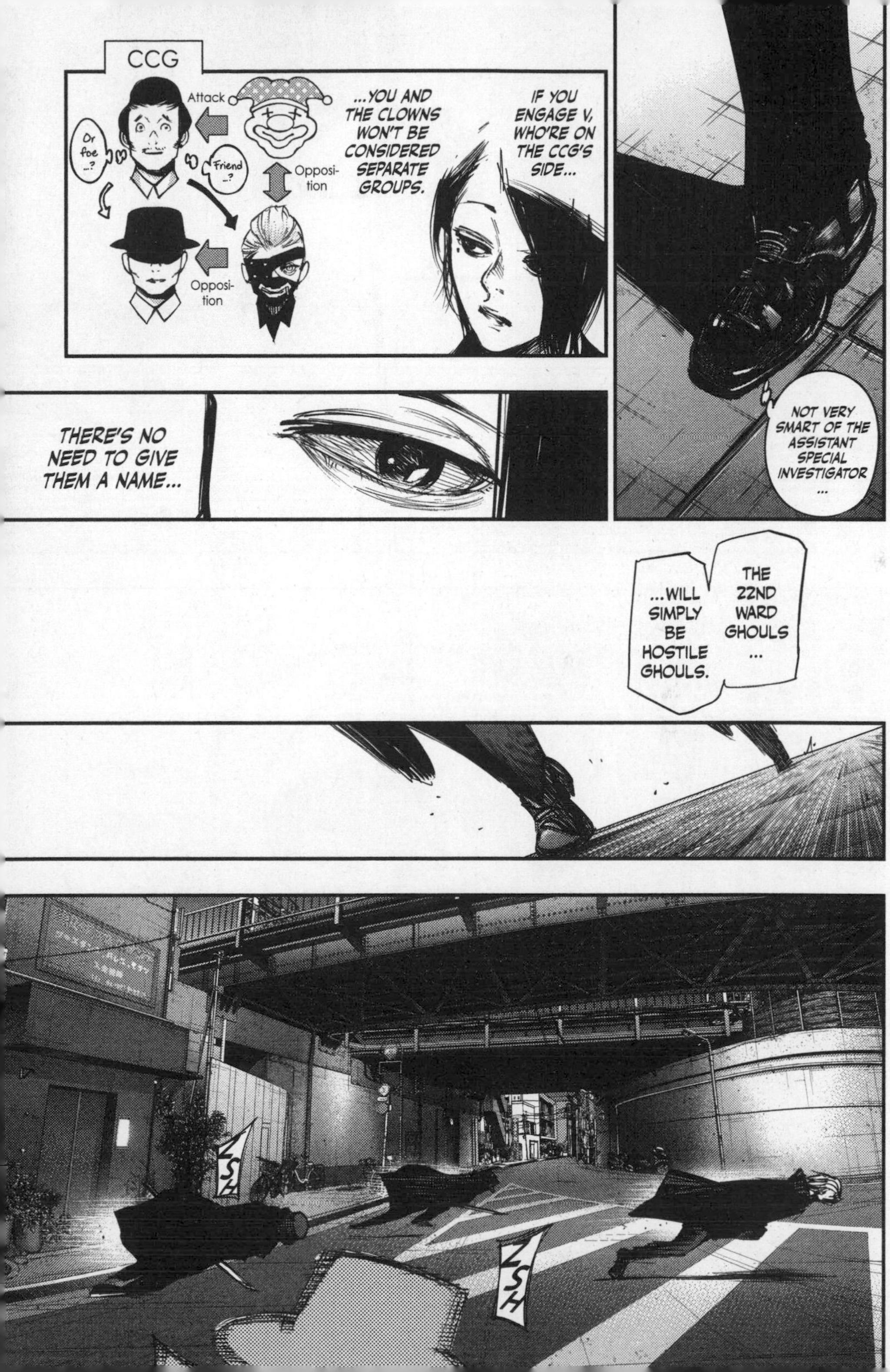
NOT VERY SMART OF THE ASSISTANT SPECIAL INVESTIGATOR ...
IF YOU ENGAGE V, WHO'RE ON THE CCG'S SIDE...
...YOU AND THE CLOWNS WON'T BE CONSIDERED SEPARATE GROUPS.
CCG
Attack
Or foe ...?
Friend ...?
Opposition
Opposition
THERE'S NO NEED TO GIVE THEM A NAME...
THE 22ND WARD GHOULS ...
...WILL SIMPLY BE HOSTILE GHOULS.
ZSH
ZSH

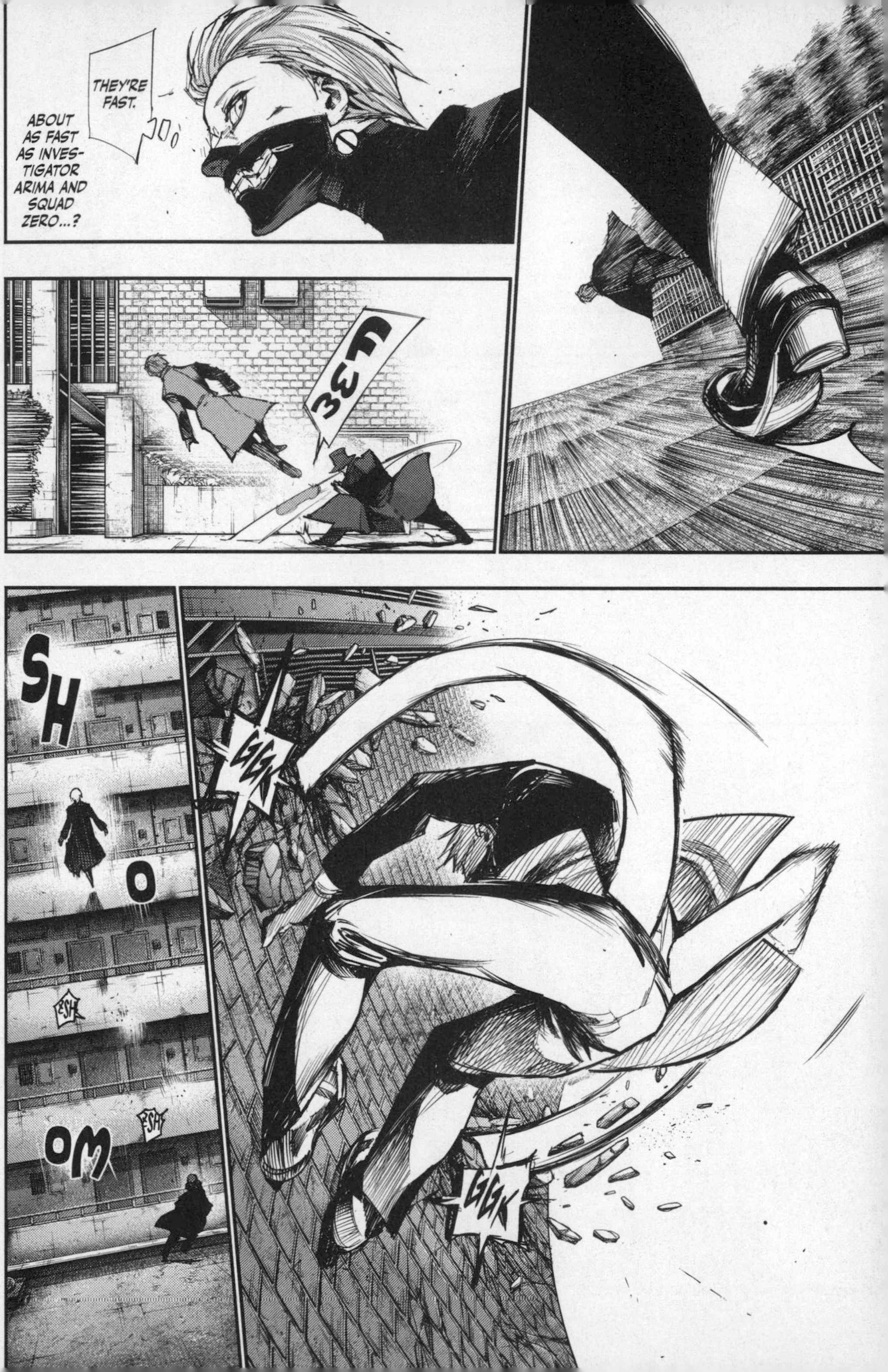
THEY'RE FAST.
ABOUT AS FAST AS INVESTIGATOR ARIMA AND SQUAD ZERO...?
SHOOM

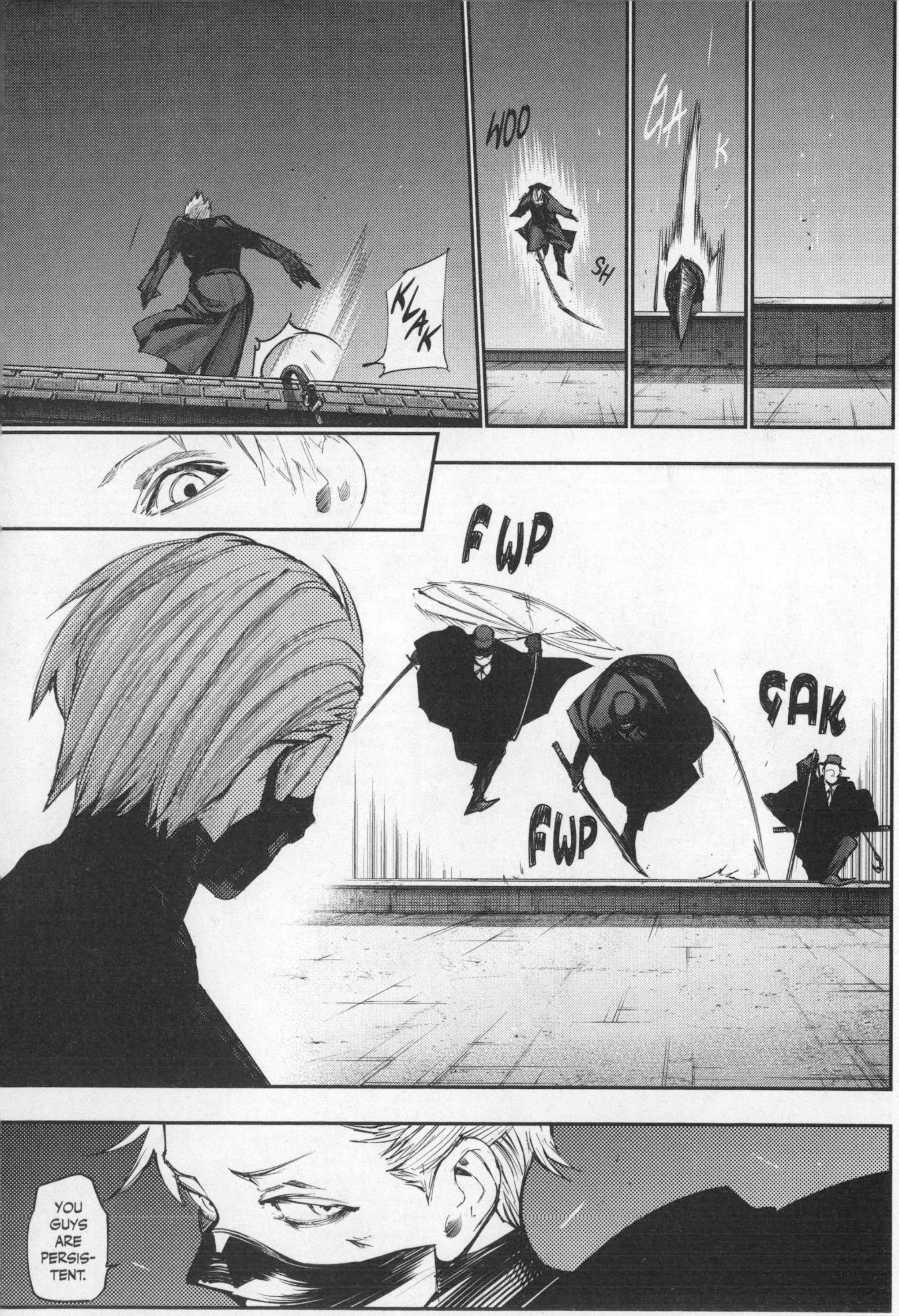
GAK
WOO
SH
KLAK
FWP
GAK
FWP
YOU GUYS ARE PERSIS-TENT.

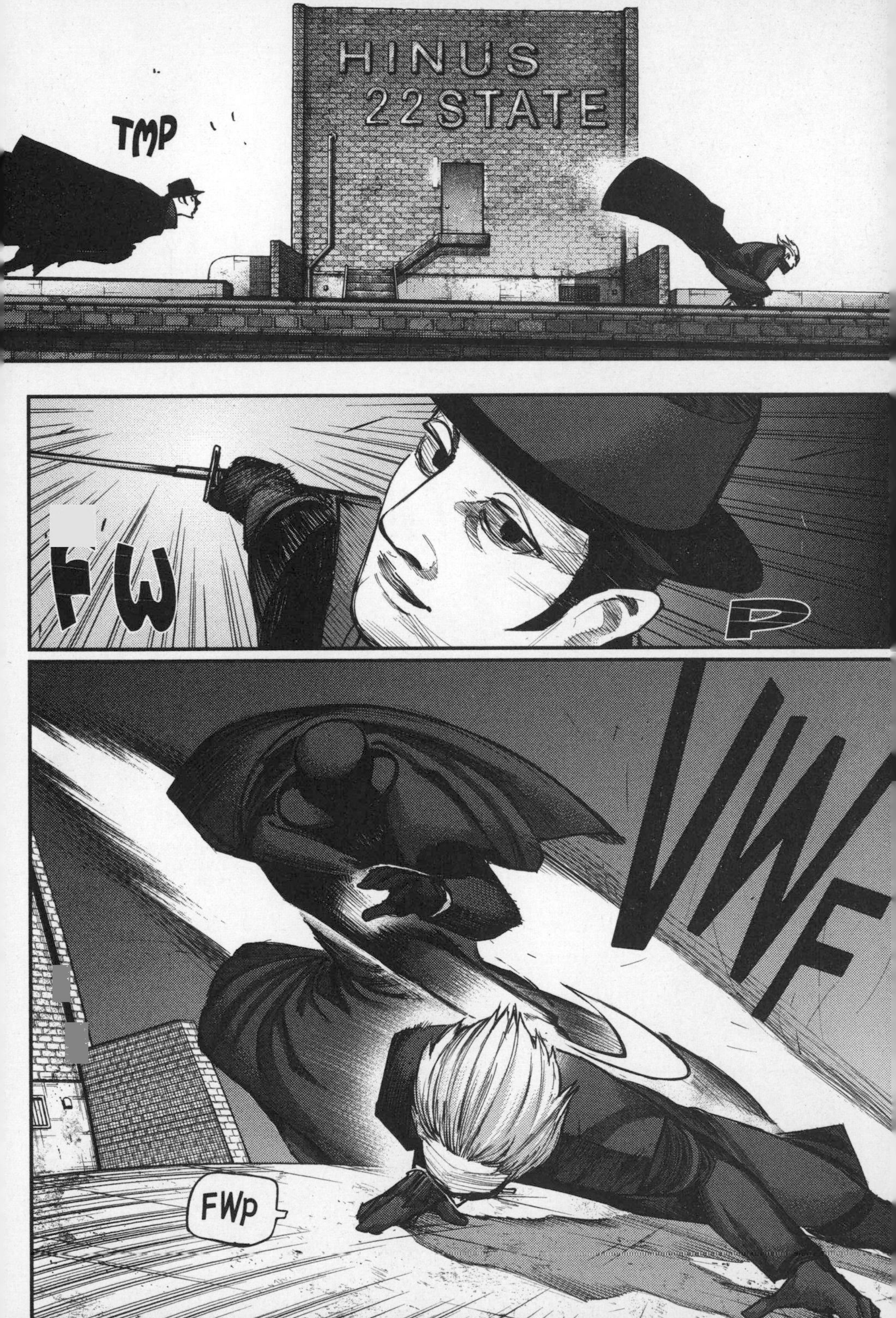
HINUS
22STATE
TMP
P
FW
VWF
FWp

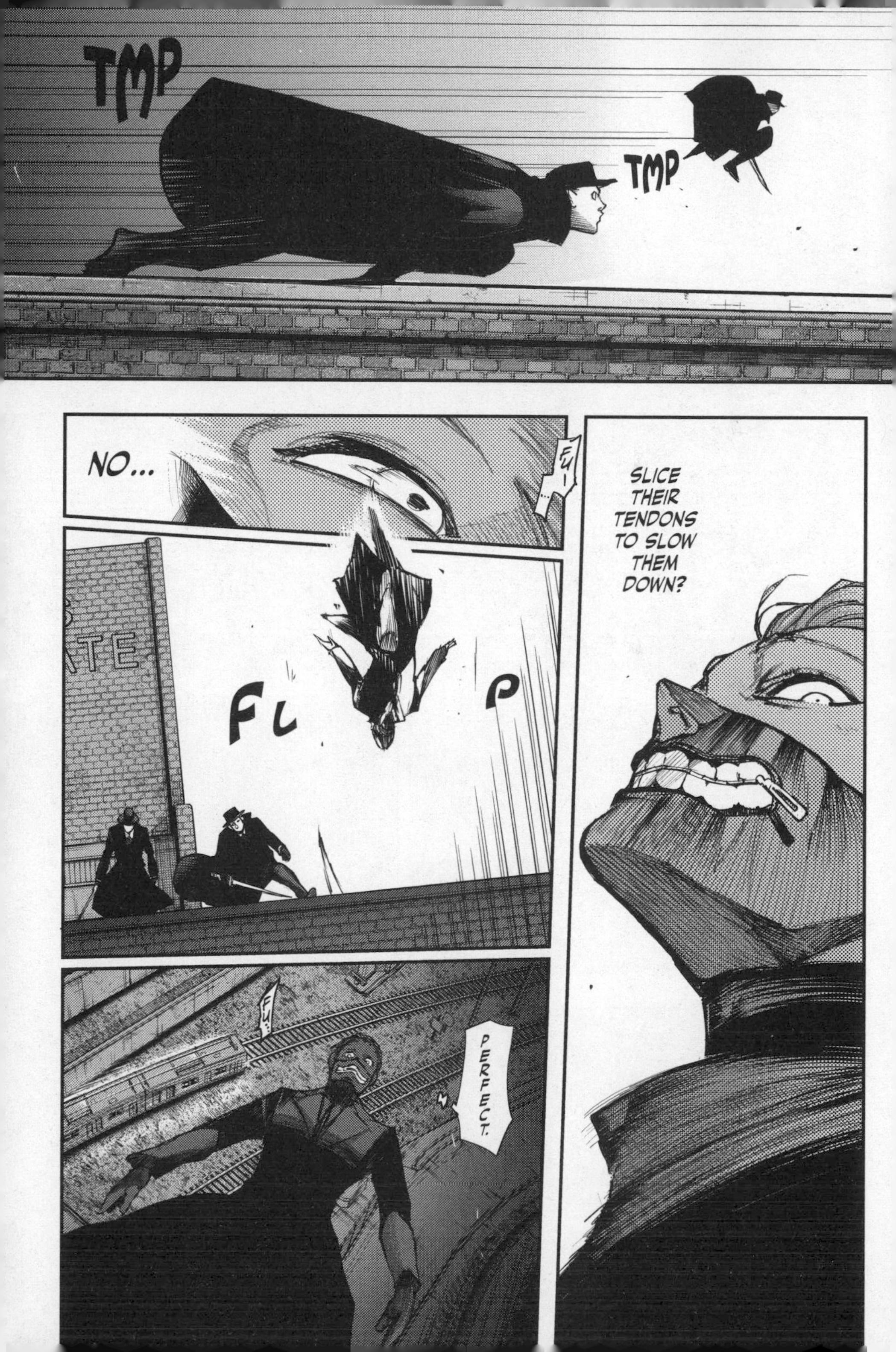
TMP
TMP
SLICE THEIR TENDONS TO SLOW THEM DOWN?
NO...
FU-I...
FLIP
FU...
PERFECT.

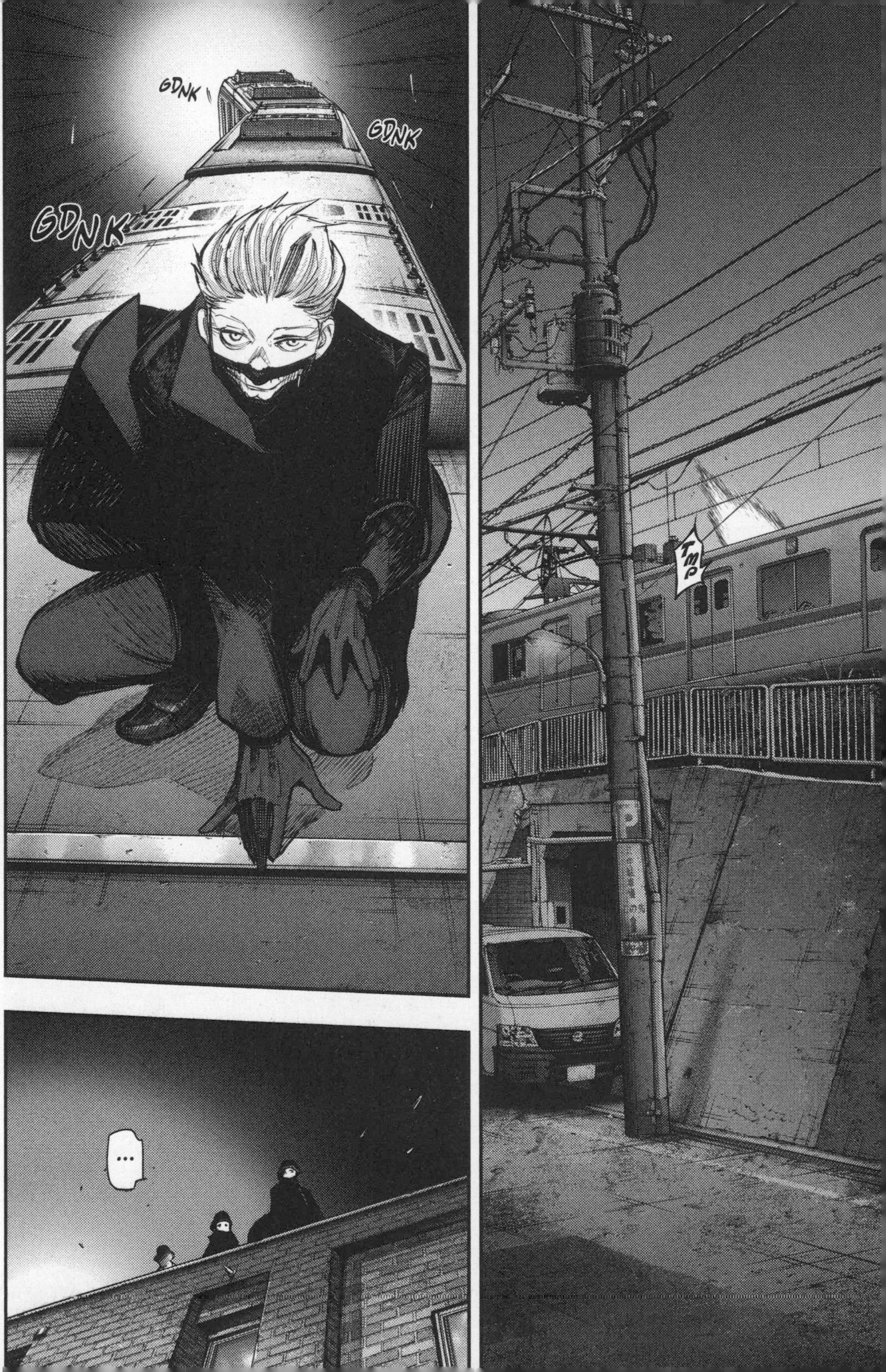
TMP
GDNK
GDNK
GDNK
...

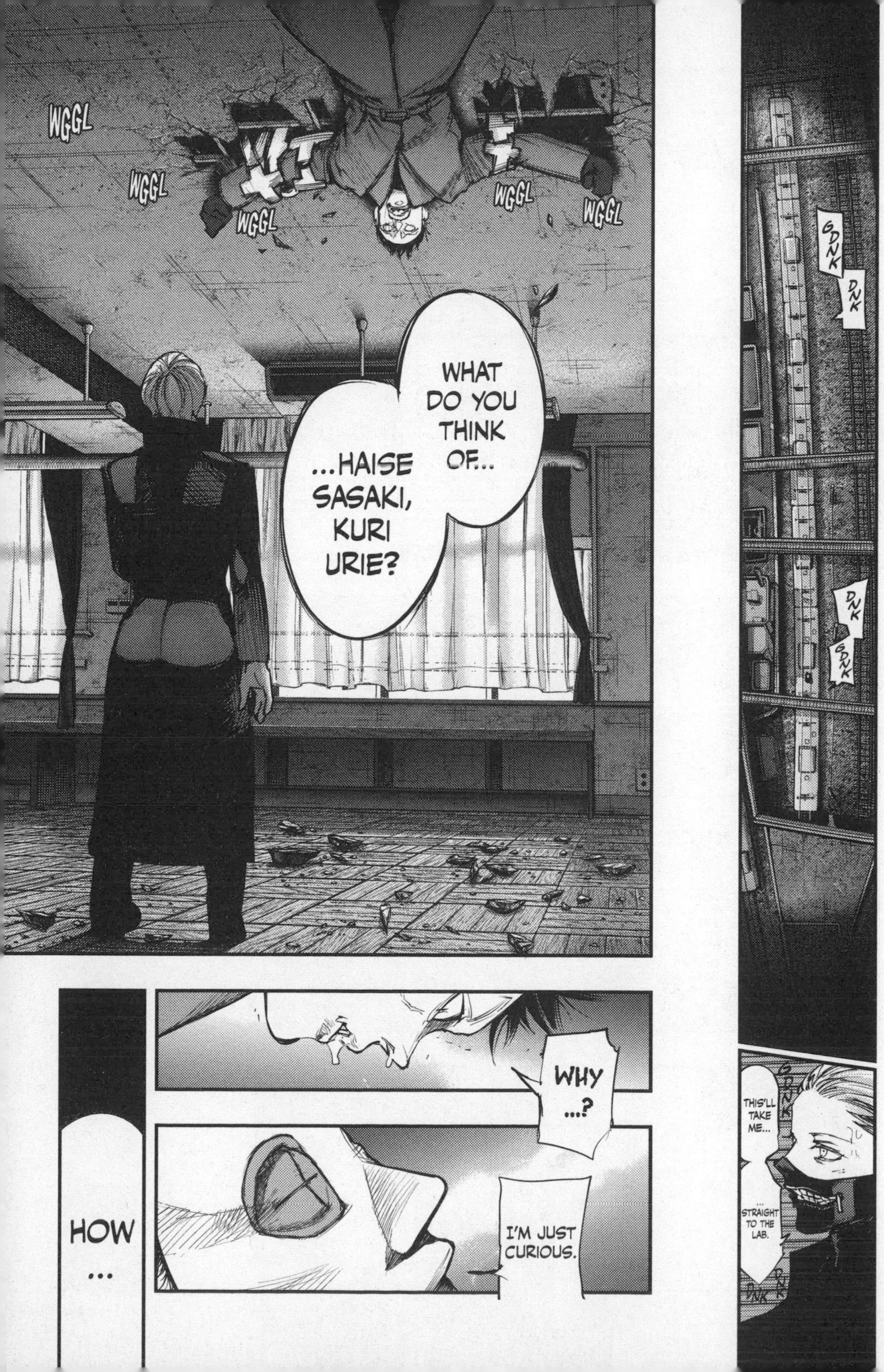
GDNK
DNK
DNK
GDNK
GDNK
THIS'LL TAKE ME...
...STRAIGHT TO THE LAB.
DNK
DNK
WGGL
WGGL
WGGL
WGGL
WGGL
WHAT DO YOU THINK OF...
...HAISE SASAKI, KURI URIE?
WHY ...?
I'M JUST CURIOUS.
HOW ...

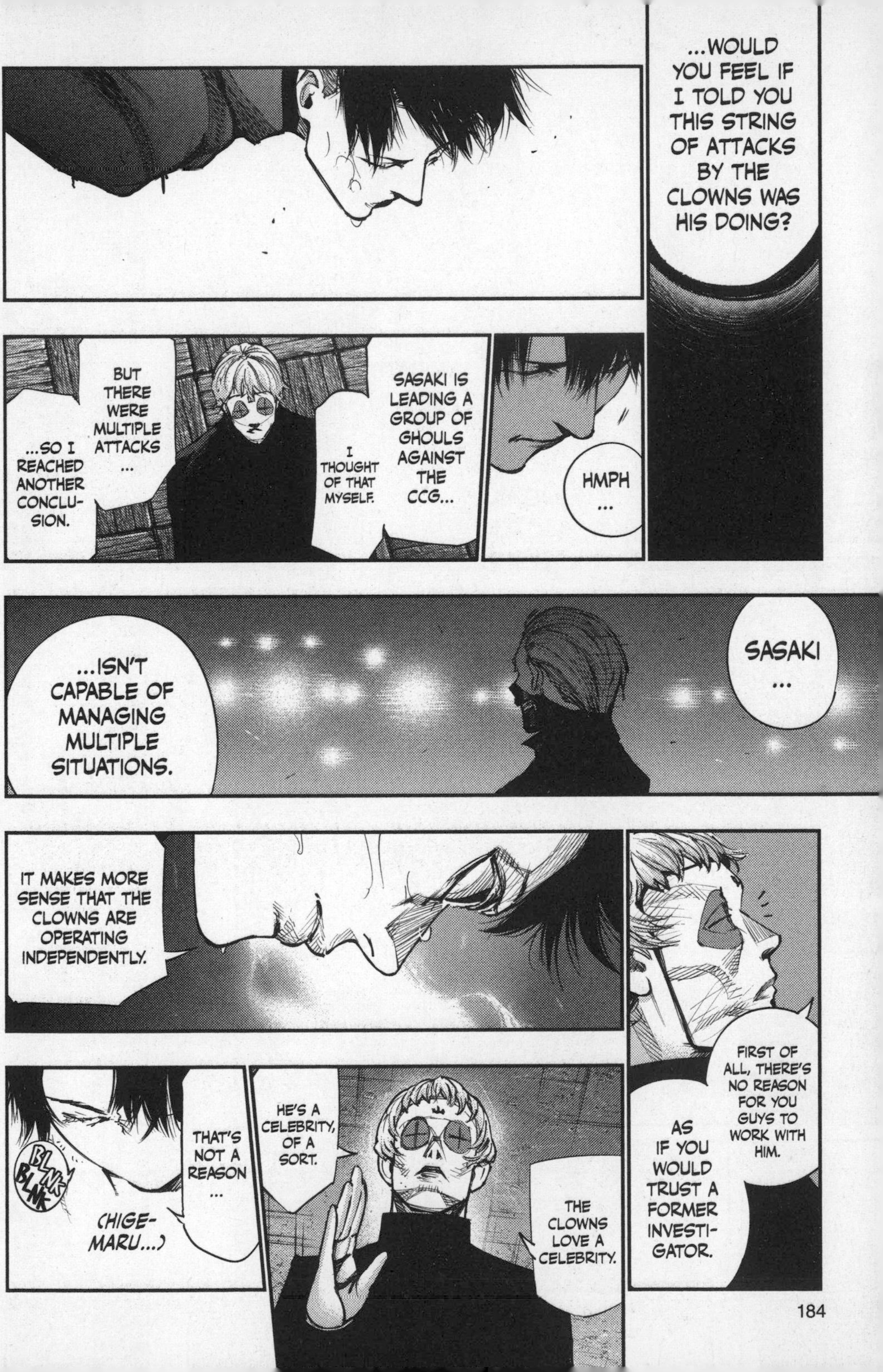

...WOULD YOU FEEL IF I TOLD YOU THIS STRING OF ATTACKS BY THE CLOWNS WAS HIS DOING?
HMPH ...
SASAKI IS LEADING A GROUP OF GHOULS AGAINST THE CCG...
I THOUGHT OF THAT MYSELF.
BUT THERE WERE MULTIPLE ATTACKS ...
...SO I REACHED ANOTHER CONCLUSION.
SASAKI ...
...ISN'T CAPABLE OF MANAGING MULTIPLE SITUATIONS.
FIRST OF ALL, THERE'S NO REASON FOR YOU GUYS TO WORK WITH HIM.
AS IF YOU WOULD TRUST A FORMER INVESTIGATOR.
IT MAKES MORE SENSE THAT THE CLOWNS ARE OPERATING INDEPENDENTLY.
THE CLOWNS LOVE A CELEBRITY.
HE'S A CELEBRITY, OF A SORT.
THAT'S NOT A REASON ...
(CHIGE-MARU...)
BLNK BLNK

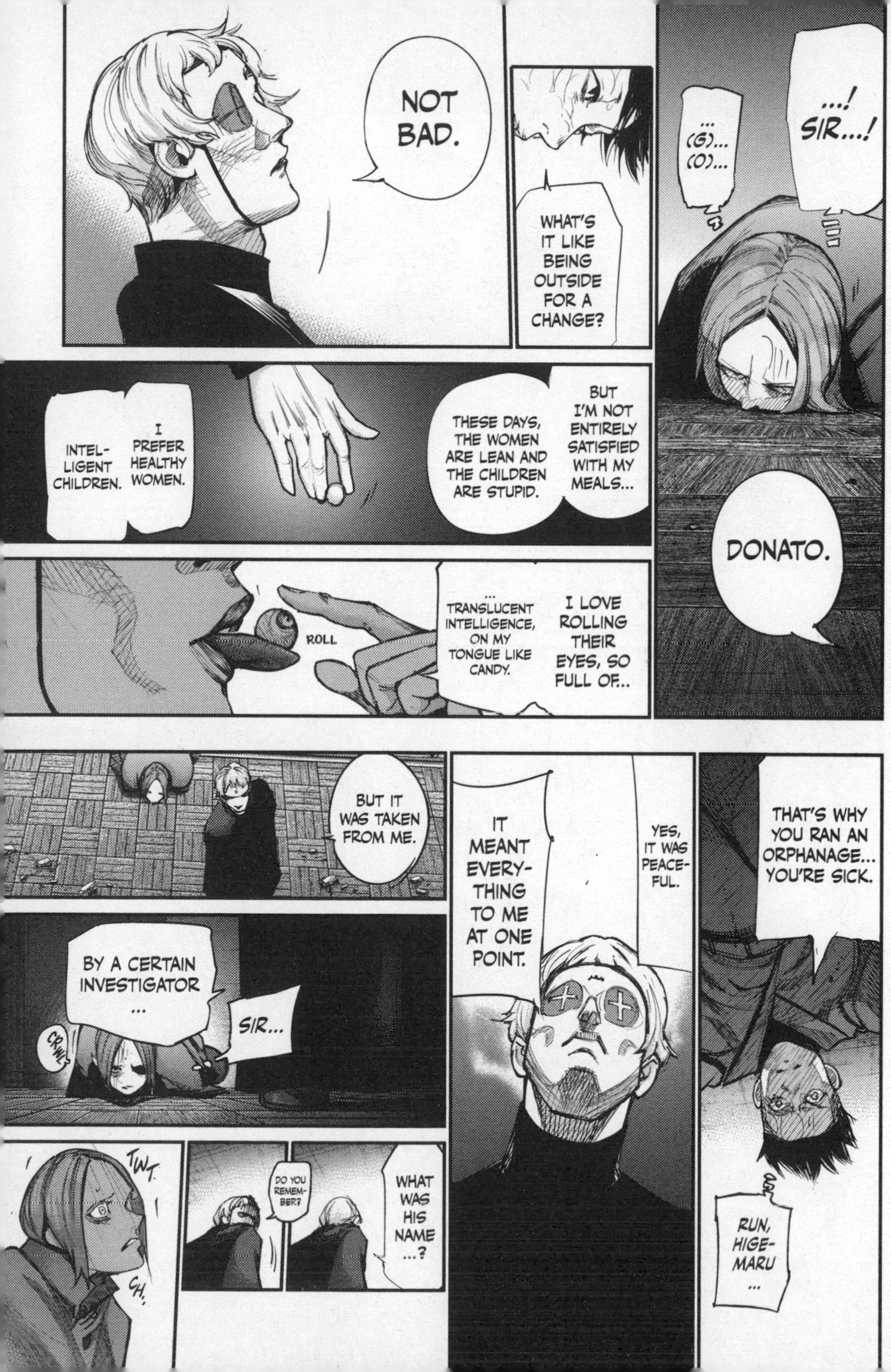

...! SIR...!
... (G)... (O)...
DONATO.
WHAT'S IT LIKE BEING OUTSIDE FOR A CHANGE?
NOT BAD.
BUT I'M NOT ENTIRELY SATISFIED WITH MY MEALS...
THESE DAYS, THE WOMEN ARE LEAN AND THE CHILDREN ARE STUPID.
I PREFER HEALTHY WOMEN.
INTEL-LIGENT CHILDREN.
I LOVE ROLLING THEIR EYES, SO FULL OF...
... TRANSLUCENT INTELLIGENCE, ON MY TONGUE LIKE CANDY.
ROLL
THAT'S WHY YOU RAN AN ORPHANAGE... YOU'RE SICK.
RUN, HIGE-MARU ...
YES, IT WAS PEACE-FUL.
IT MEANT EVERY-THING TO ME AT ONE POINT.
BUT IT WAS TAKEN FROM ME.
SIR...
BY A CERTAIN INVESTIGATOR ...
CRWL
WHAT WAS HIS NAME ...?
DO YOU REMEM-BER?
TWT.
CH.

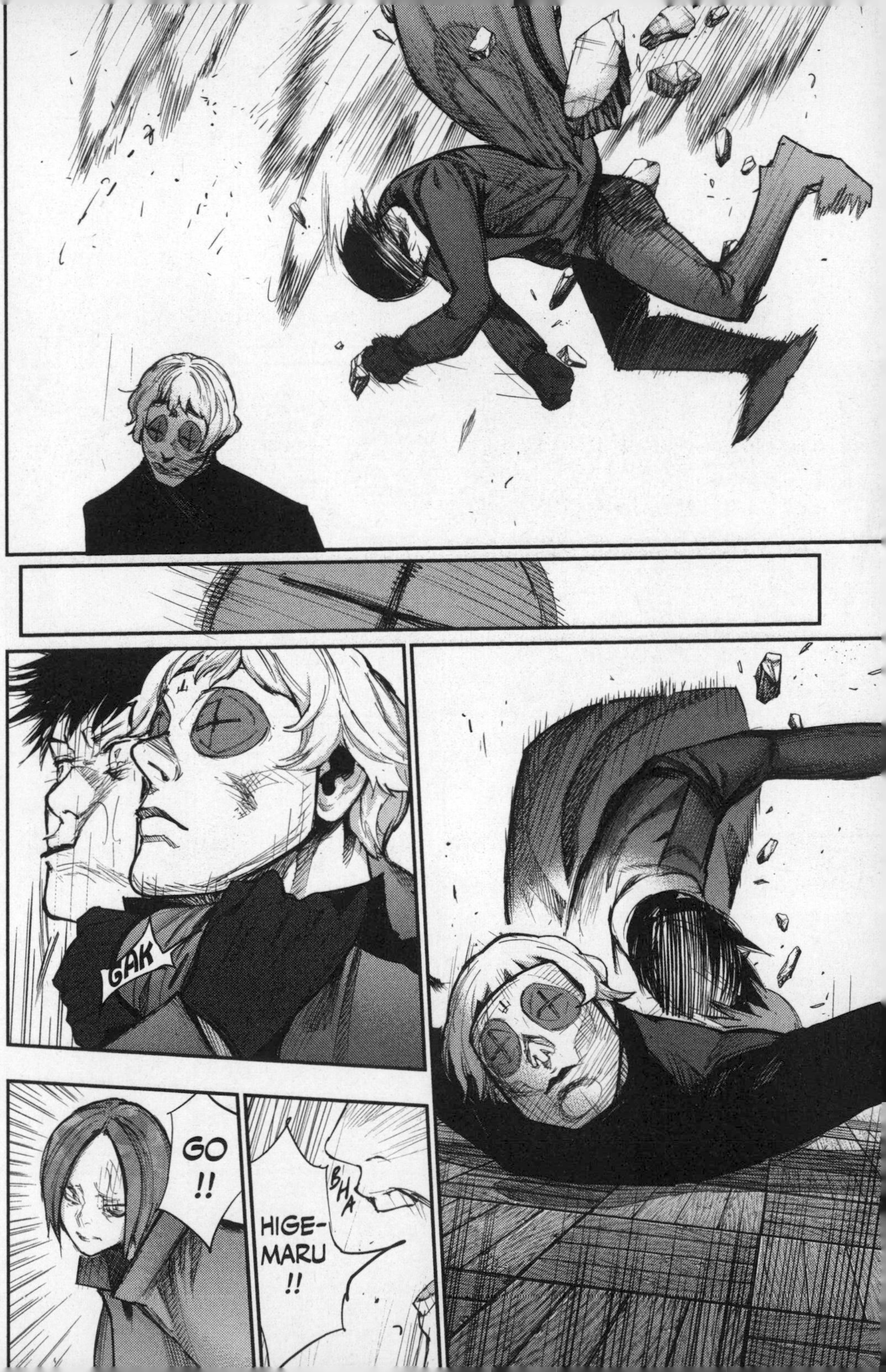
GAK
BHA
HIGE-MARU!!
GO!!

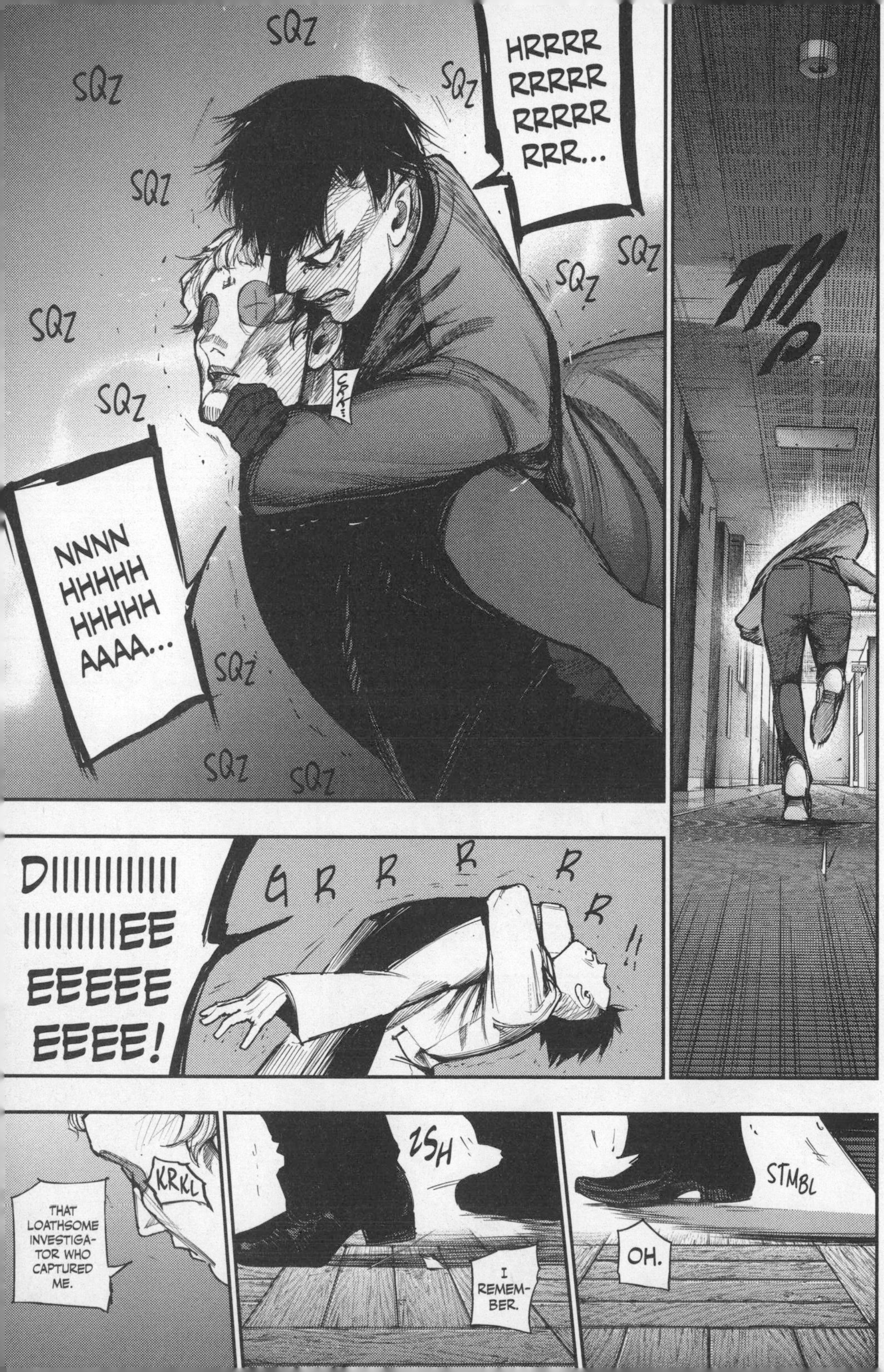
TMP
SQZ
SQZ
SQZ
SQZ
SQZ
SQZ
SQZ
SQZ
SQZ
SQZ
SQZ
HRRRR RRRRR RRRRR RRR...
NNNN HHHHH HHHHH AAAA...
DIIIIIIIIIIIIIIIIIIIIIIEE EEEEEE EEEEE!
GRRRRR
STMBL
OH.
ZSH
I REMEMBER.
KRKL
THAT LOATHSOME INVESTIGATOR WHO CAPTURED ME.

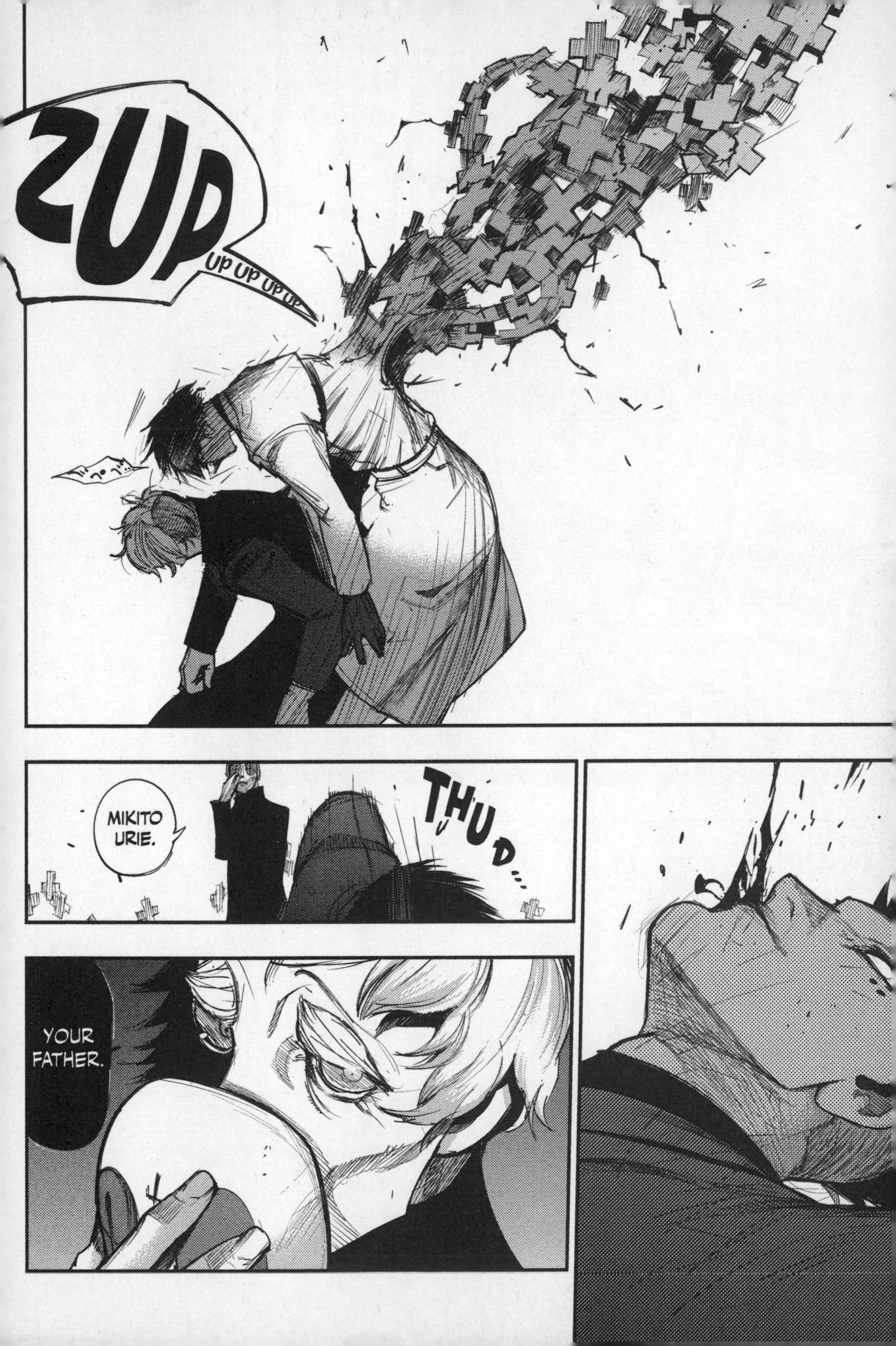
ZUP
UP UP UP UP
THUD...
MIKITO URIE.
YOUR FATHER.

To the Pen :109

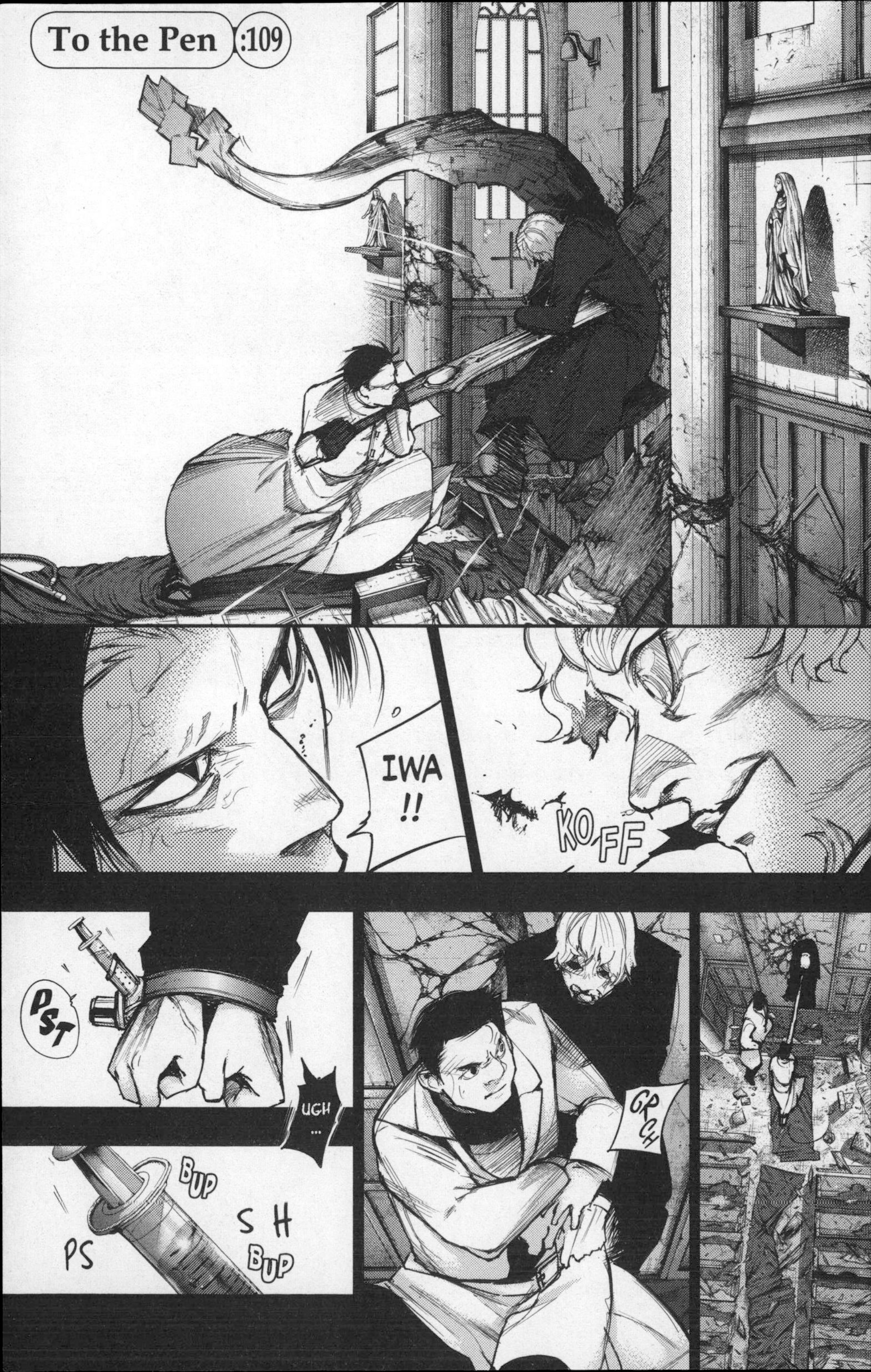
KOFF
IWA !!
GRCH
PST
UGH ...
BUP
S H
BUP
PS

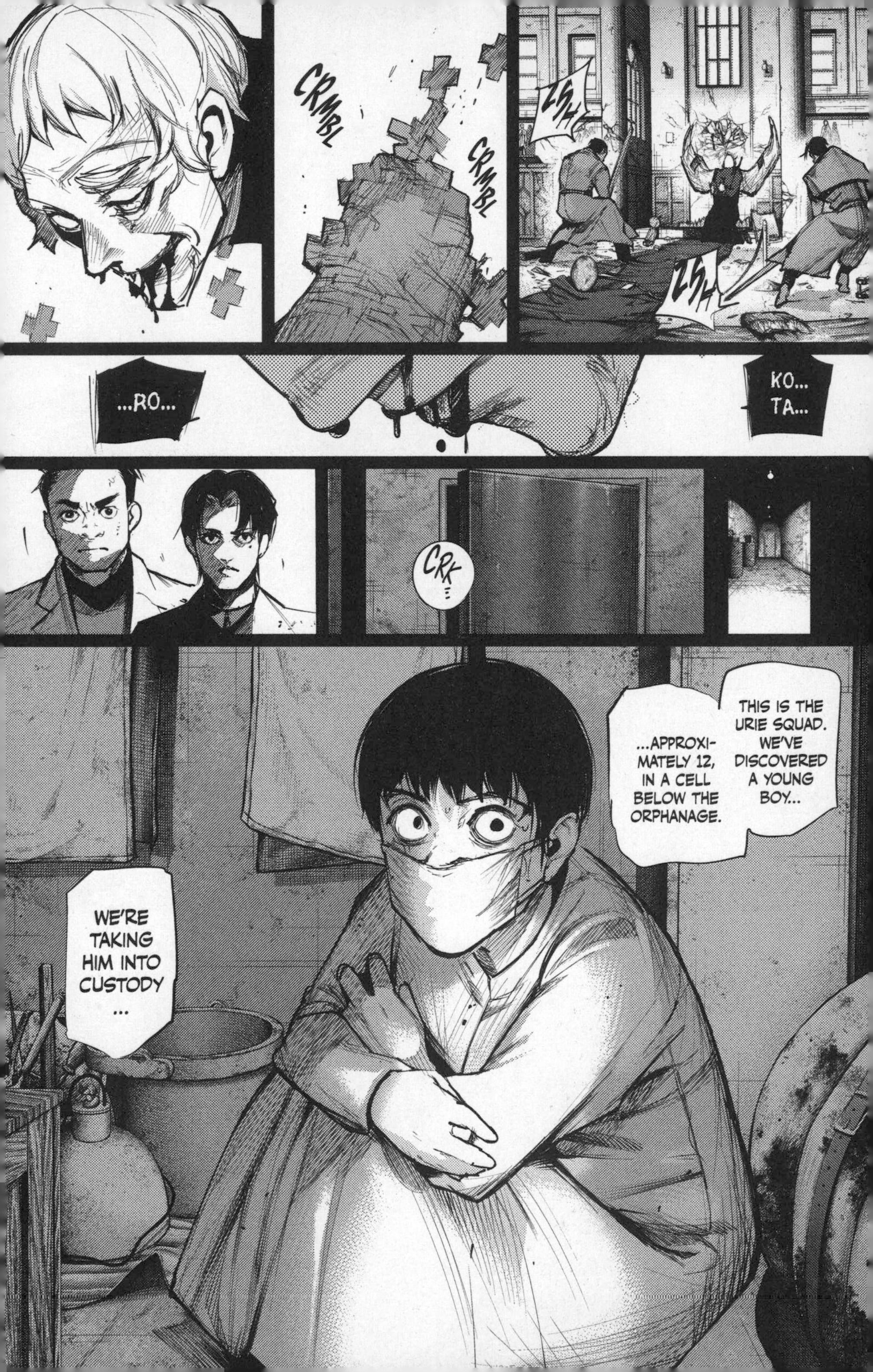
ZSH
ZSH
CRMBL
CRMBL
KO... TA...
...RO...
CRK
THIS IS THE URIE SQUAD. WE'VE DISCOVERED A YOUNG BOY...
...APPROXI-MATELY 12, IN A CELL BELOW THE ORPHANAGE.
WE'RE TAKING HIM INTO CUSTODY ...

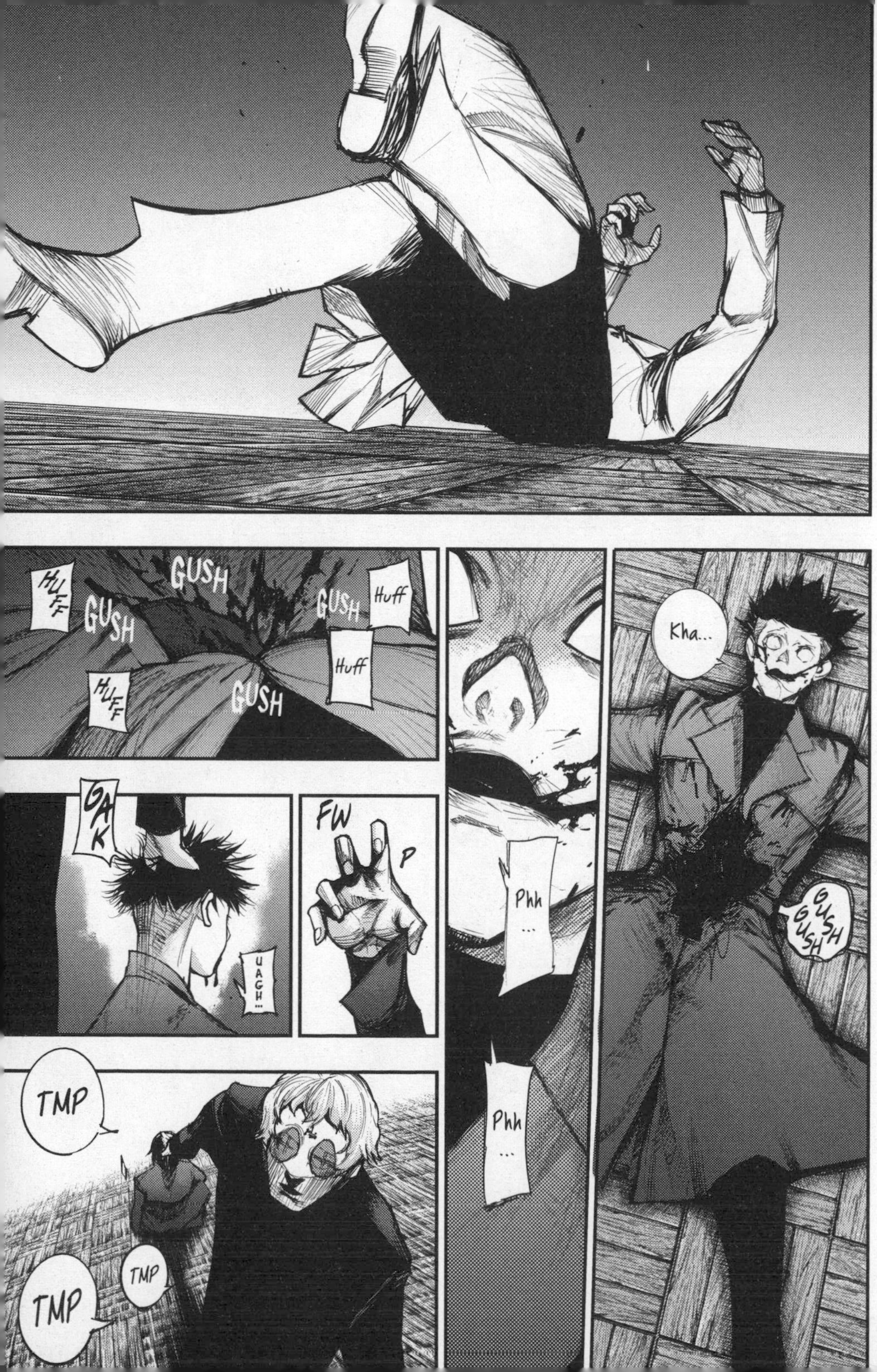
Kha...
GUSH GUSH
Phh...
Phh...
Huff
GUSH
GUSH
Huff
HUFF
GUSH
GUSH
HUFF
FWP
GAK
UAGH...
TMP
TMP
TMP

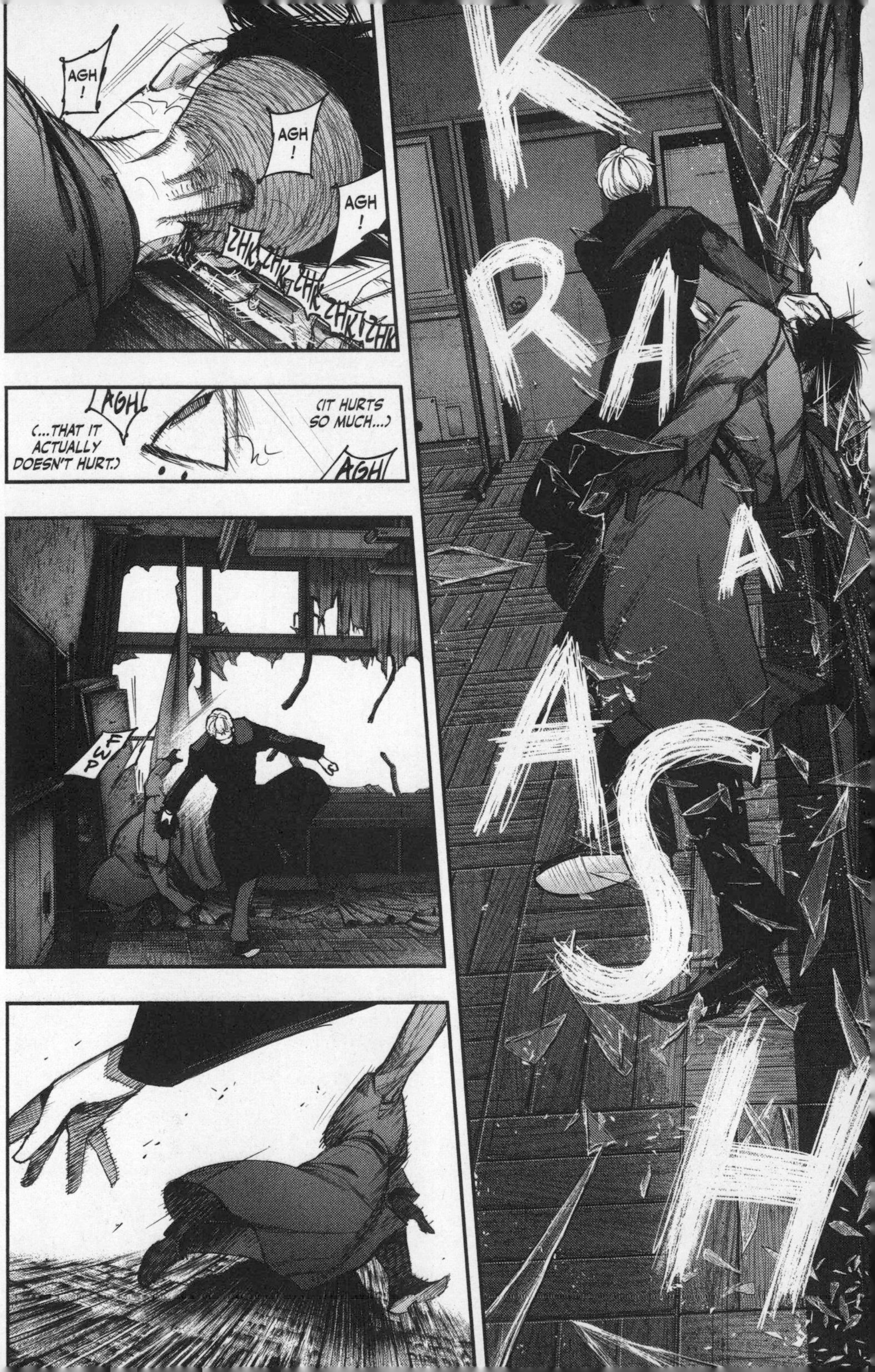
KRAAASH
AGH!
AGH!
AGH!
ZHK ZHK ZHK ZHK ZHK ZHK
(IT HURTS SO MUCH...)
AGH
(...THAT IT ACTUALLY DOESN'T HURT.)
AGH
FWP

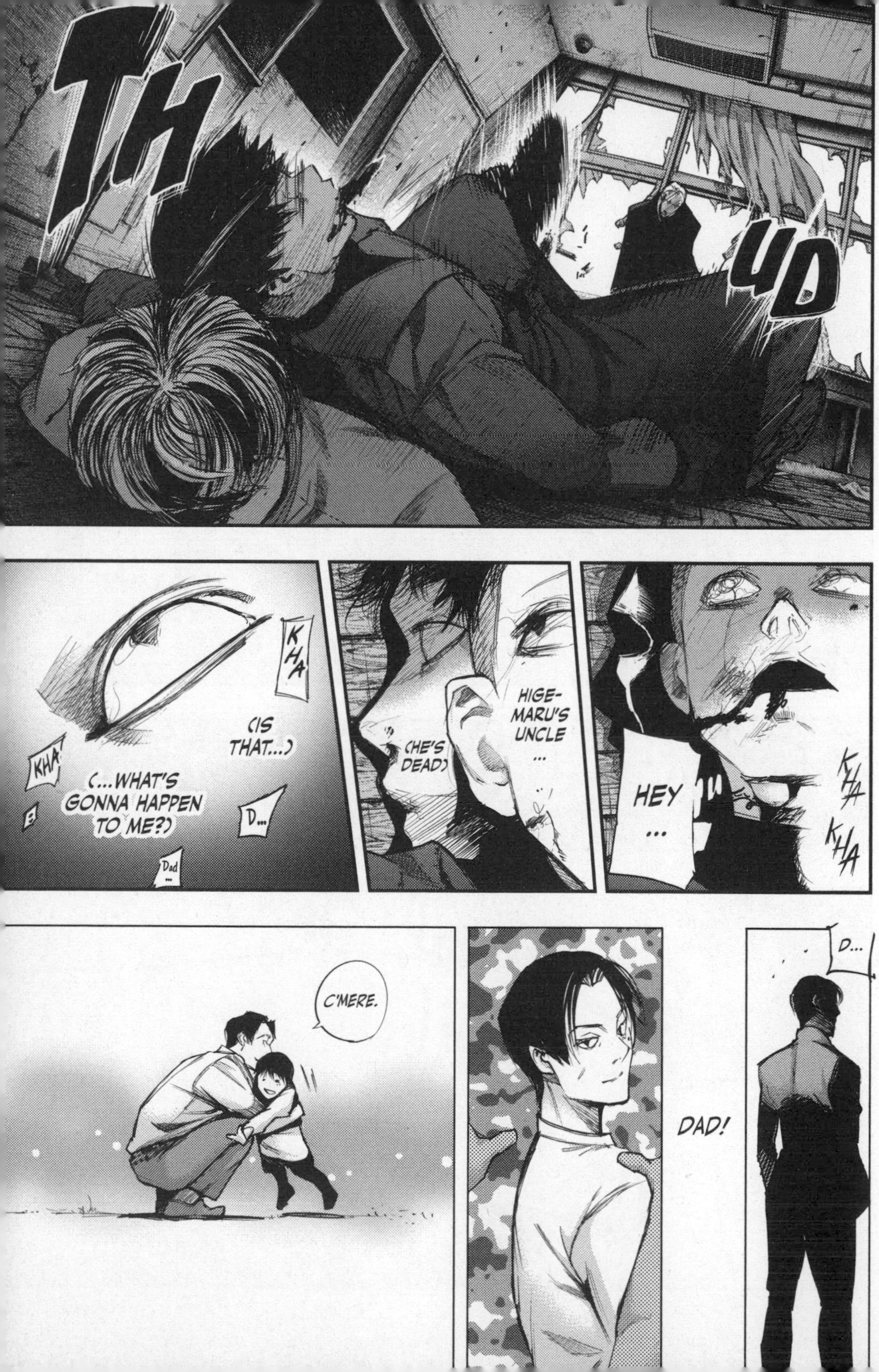
TH
UD
HEY...
KHA
KHA
HIGE-MARU'S UNCLE...
(HE'S DEAD)
KHA
(IS THAT...)
KHA
(...WHAT'S GONNA HAPPEN TO ME?)
D...
Dad...
D...
DAD!
C'MERE.

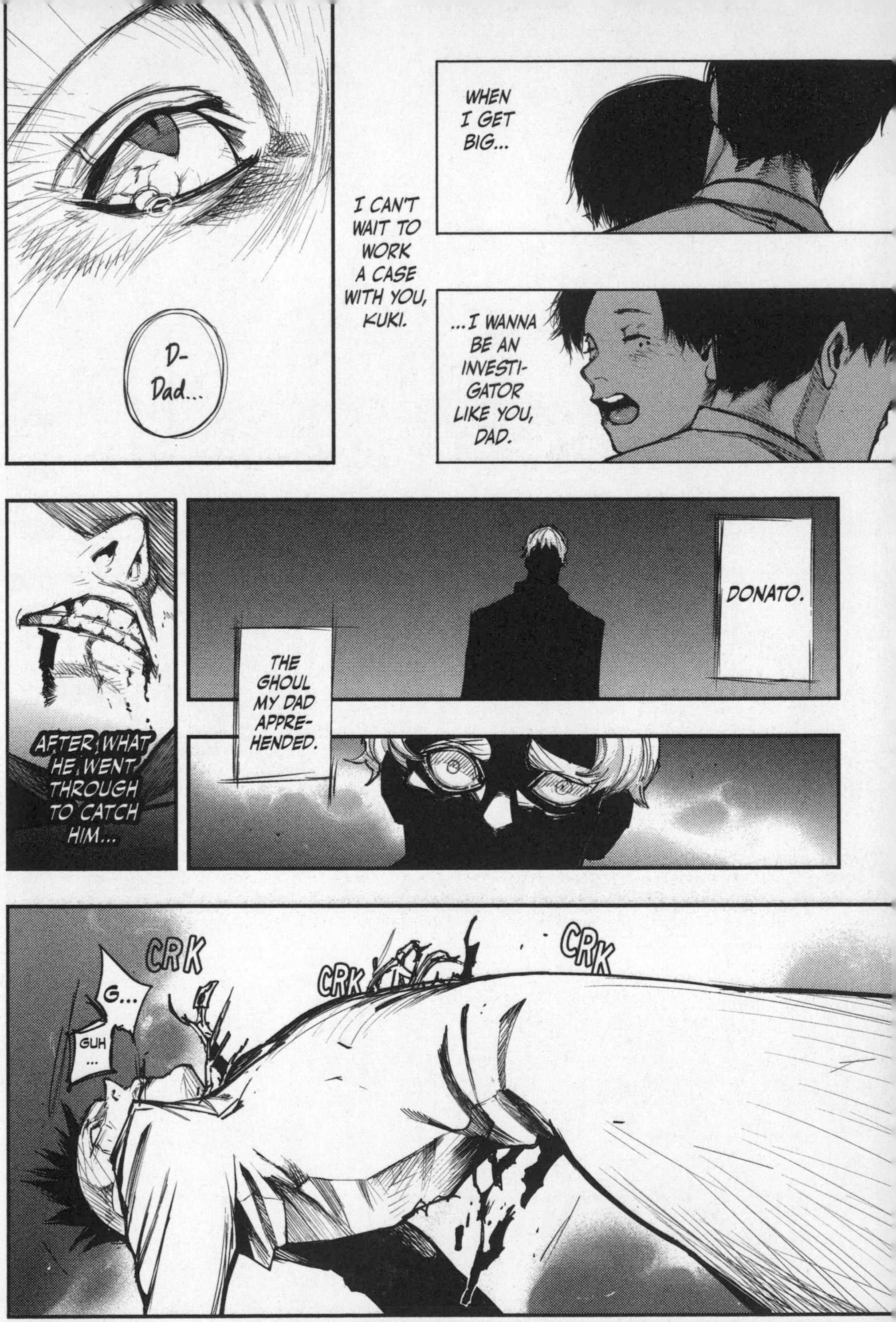

WHEN I GET BIG...
...I WANNA BE AN INVESTIGATOR LIKE YOU, DAD.
I CAN'T WAIT TO WORK A CASE WITH YOU, KUKI.
D-Dad...
DONATO.
THE GHOUL MY DAD APPREHENDED.
AFTER WHAT HE WENT THROUGH TO CATCH HIM...
CRK
CRK
CRK
G...
GUH...

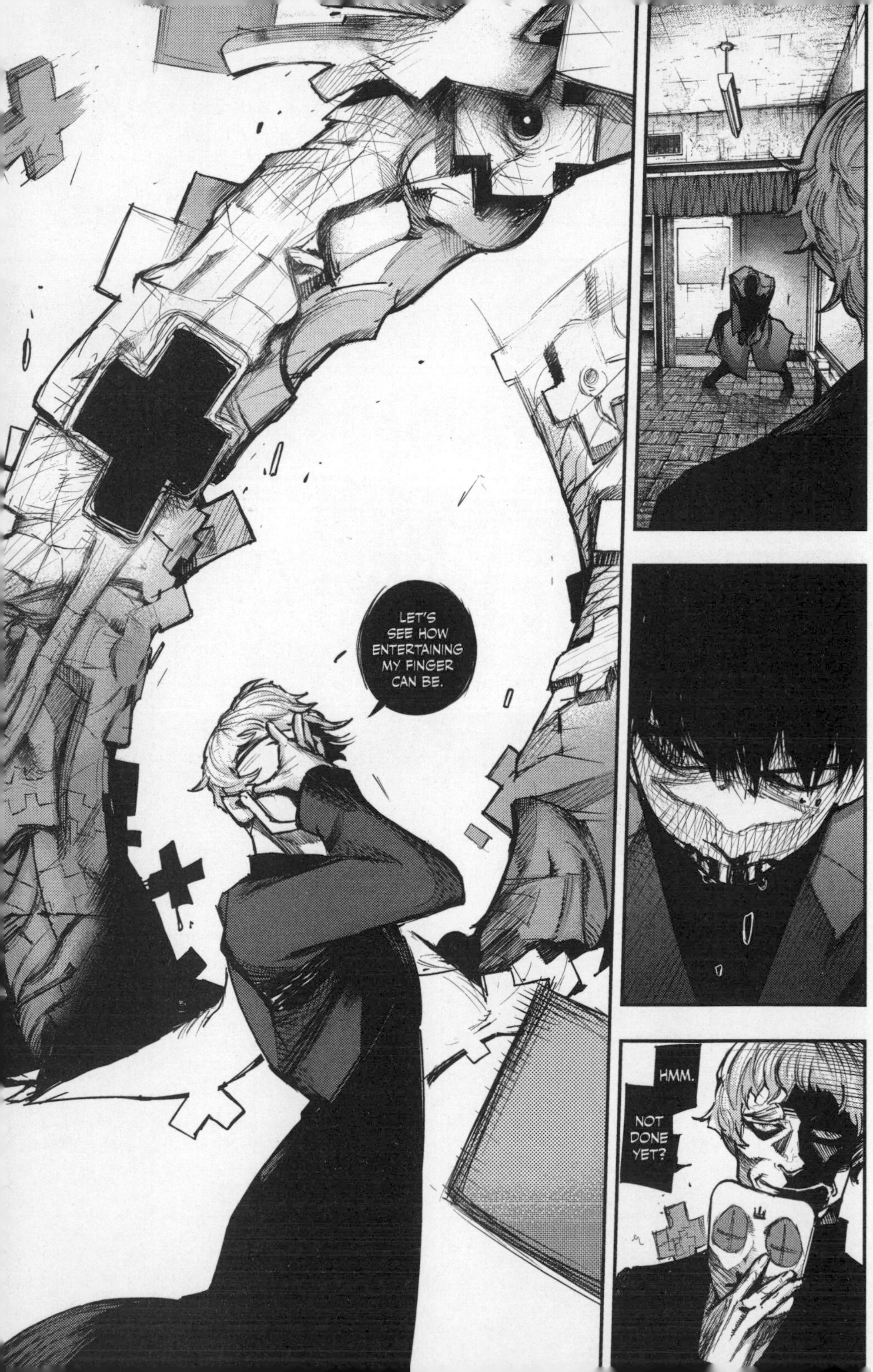
HMM.
NOT DONE YET?
LET'S SEE HOW ENTERTAINING MY FINGER CAN BE.

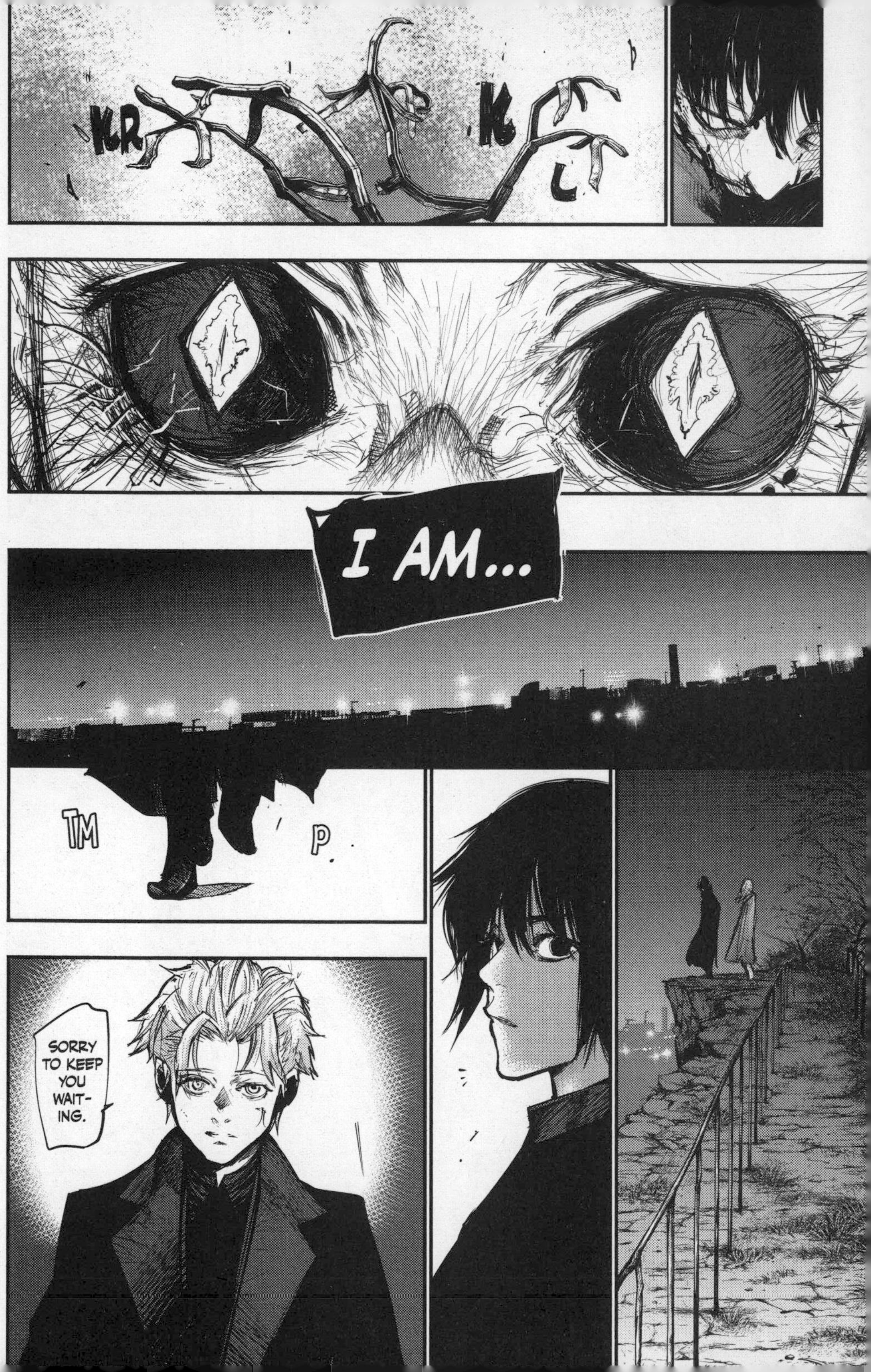

KRR
KK
I AM...
TMP
SORRY TO KEEP YOU WAIT-ING.

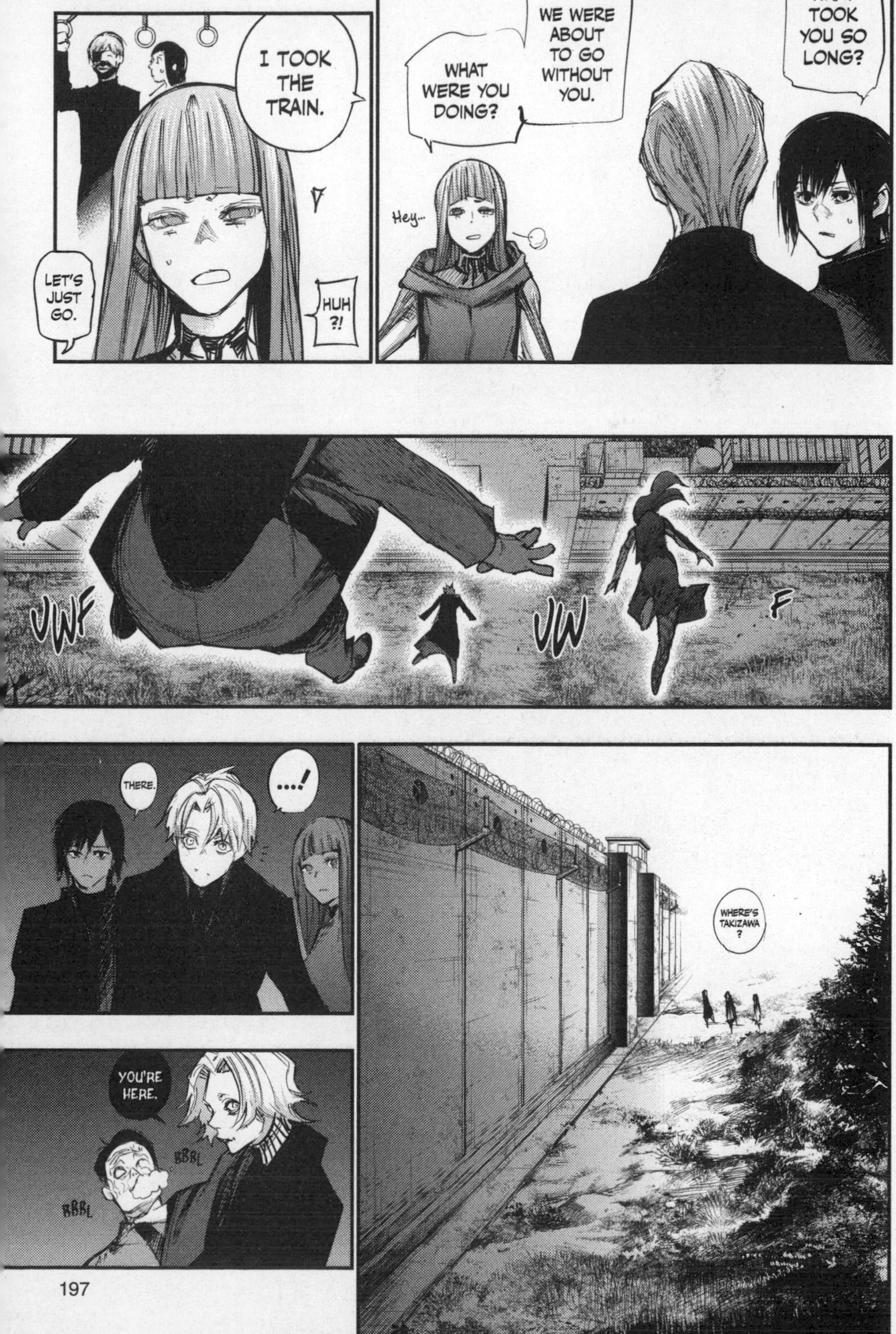

WHAT TOOK YOU SO LONG?
WE WERE ABOUT TO GO WITHOUT YOU.
WHAT WERE YOU DOING?
Hey...
I TOOK THE TRAIN.
HUH?!
LET'S JUST GO.
F
VW
VWF
WHERE'S TAKIZAWA?
...!
THERE.
YOU'RE HERE.
BBBL
BBBL

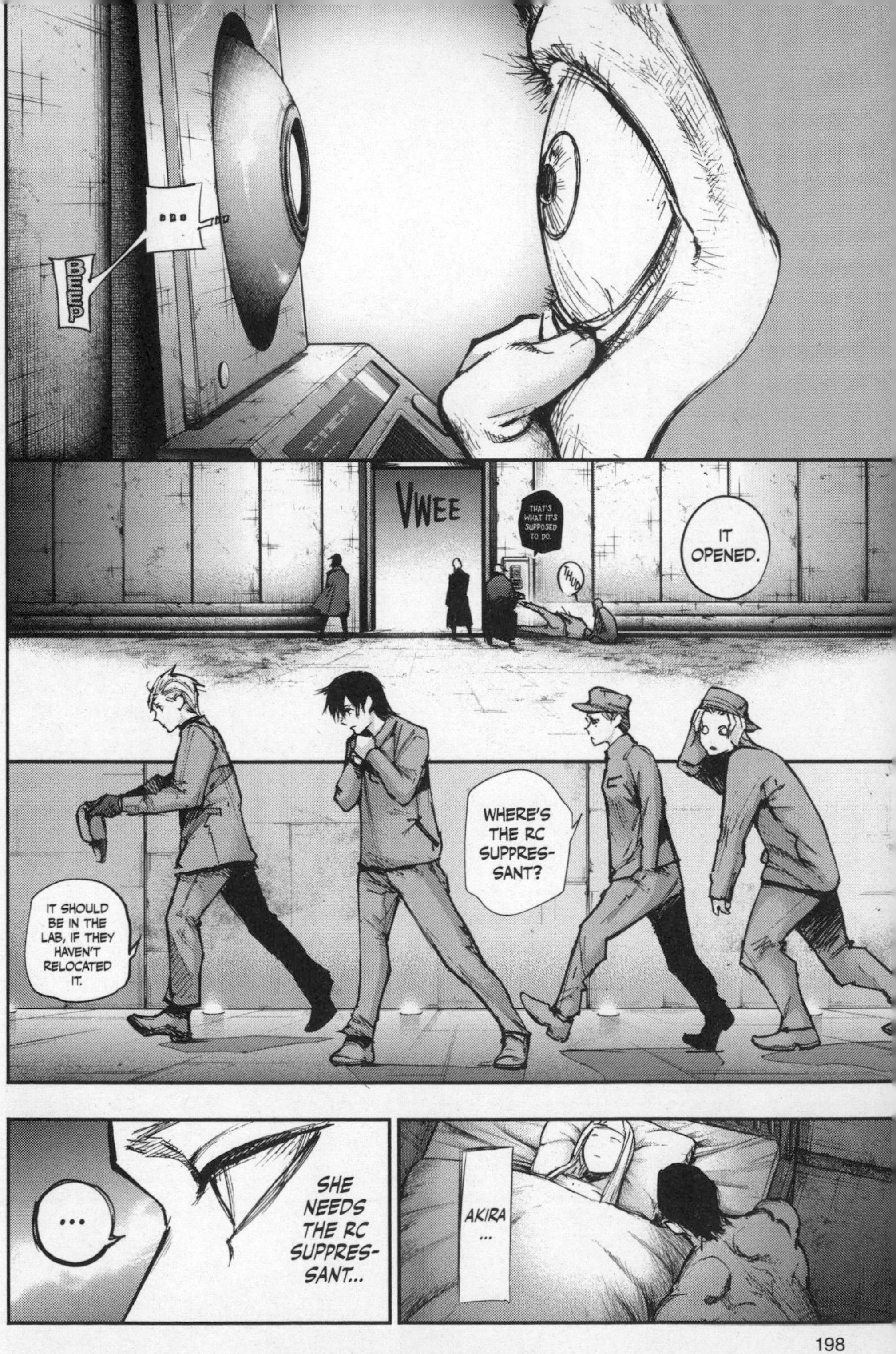
BEEEP
IT OPENED.
THUD
THAT'S WHAT IT'S SUPPOSED TO DO.
VWEE
WHERE'S THE RC SUPPRES-SANT?
IT SHOULD BE IN THE LAB, IF THEY HAVEN'T RELOCATED IT.
AKIRA...
SHE NEEDS THE RC SUPPRES-SANT...
...

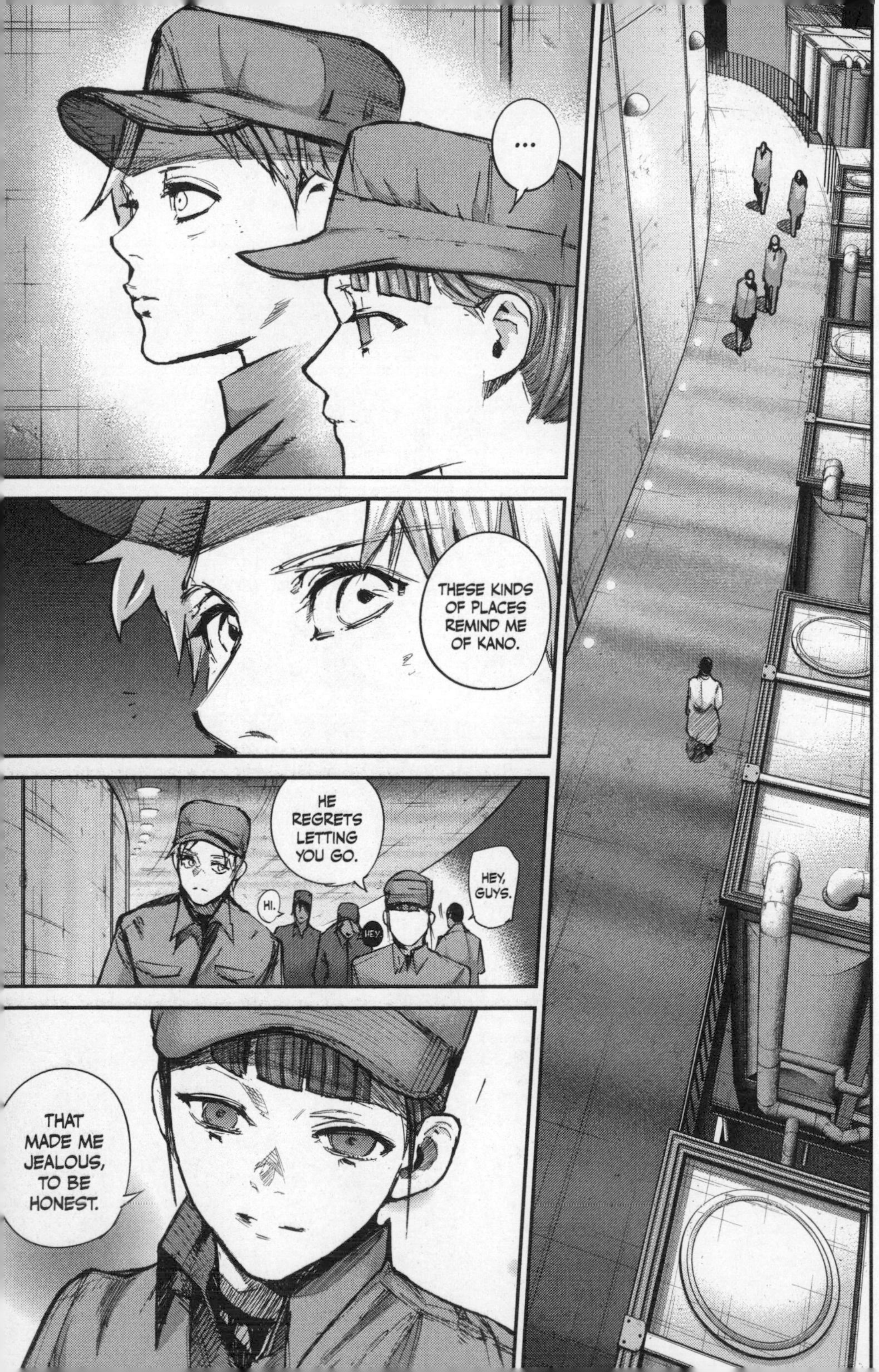
...
THESE KINDS OF PLACES REMIND ME OF KANO.
HE REGRETS LETTING YOU GO.
HEY, GUYS.
HEY.
HI.
THAT MADE ME JEALOUS, TO BE HONEST.

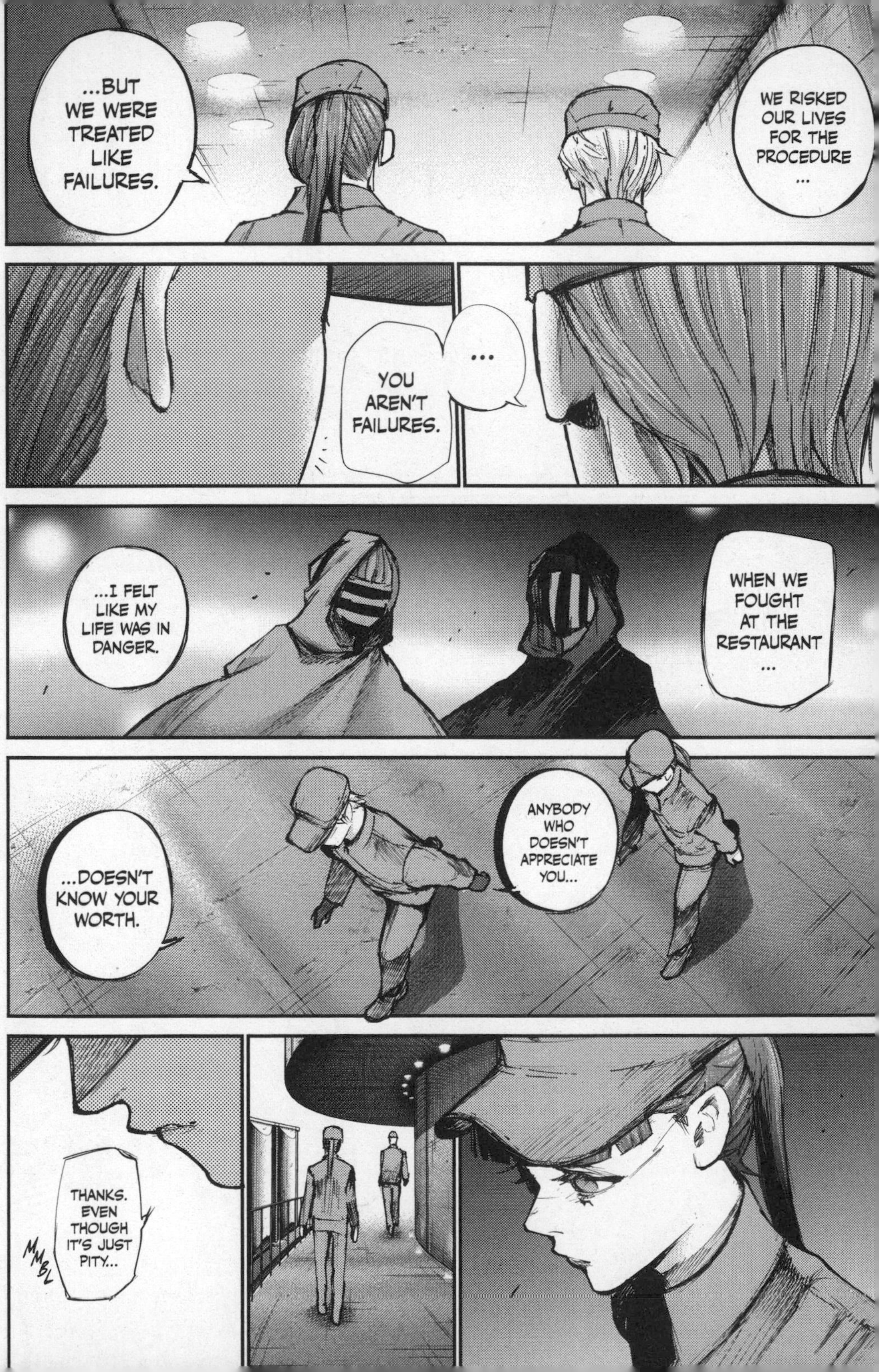
WE RISKED OUR LIVES FOR THE PROCEDURE ...
...BUT WE WERE TREATED LIKE FAILURES.
...
YOU AREN'T FAILURES.
WHEN WE FOUGHT AT THE RESTAURANT ...
...I FELT LIKE MY LIFE WAS IN DANGER.
ANYBODY WHO DOESN'T APPRECIATE YOU...
...DOESN'T KNOW YOUR WORTH.
THANKS. EVEN THOUGH IT'S JUST PITY...
MMBL

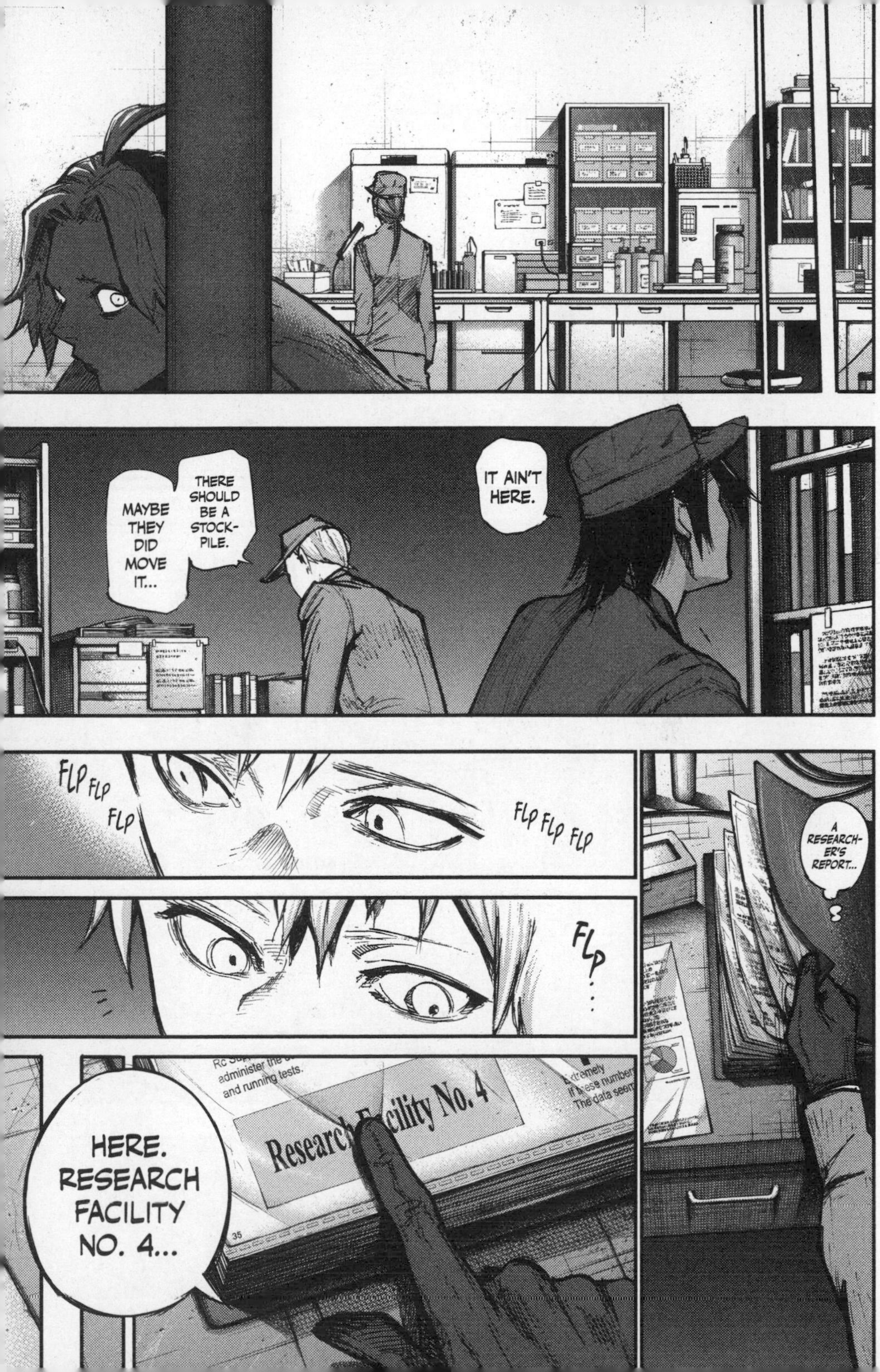
IT AIN'T HERE.
THERE SHOULD BE A STOCKPILE.
MAYBE THEY DID MOVE IT...
A RESEARCHER'S REPORT...
FLP FLP FLP
FLP FLP FLP
FLP...
HERE. RESEARCH FACILITY NO. 4...

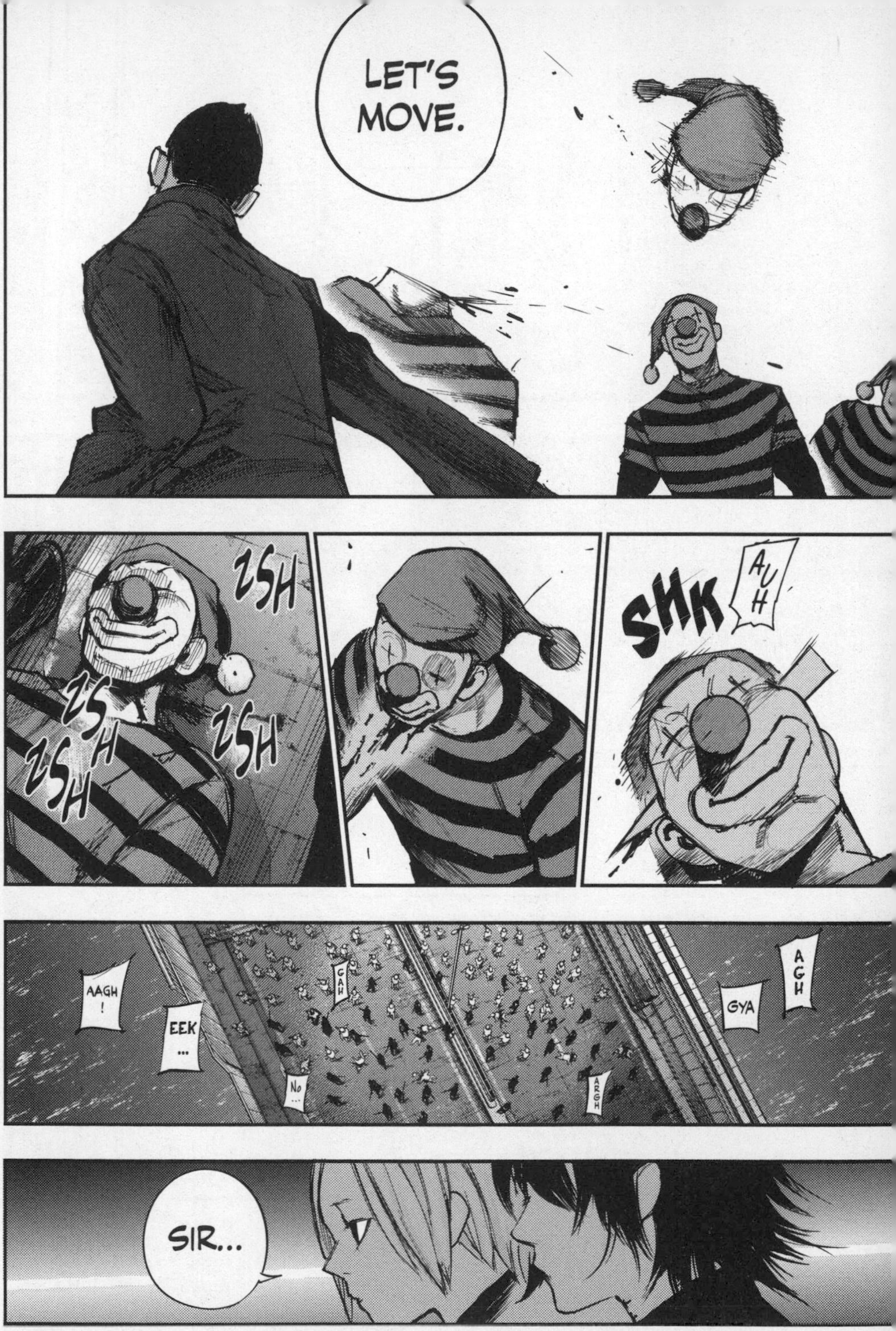
LET'S MOVE.
SHK
AUH
ZSH
ZSH
ZSH
ZSH
AGH
GYA
ARGH
No...
GAH
EEK...
AAGH!
SIR...

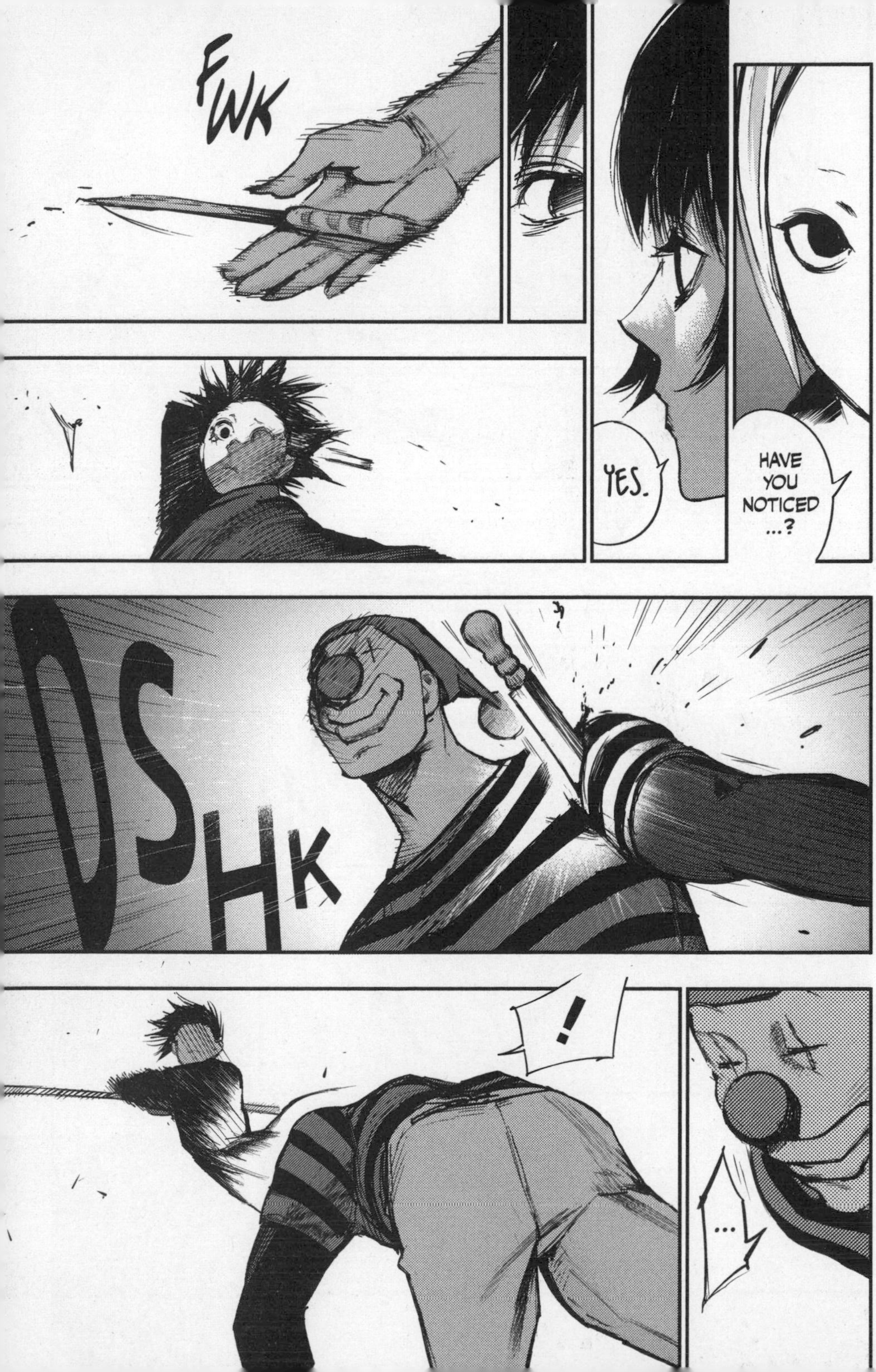
HAVE YOU NOTICED ...?
YES.
FWK
DSHK
...
!

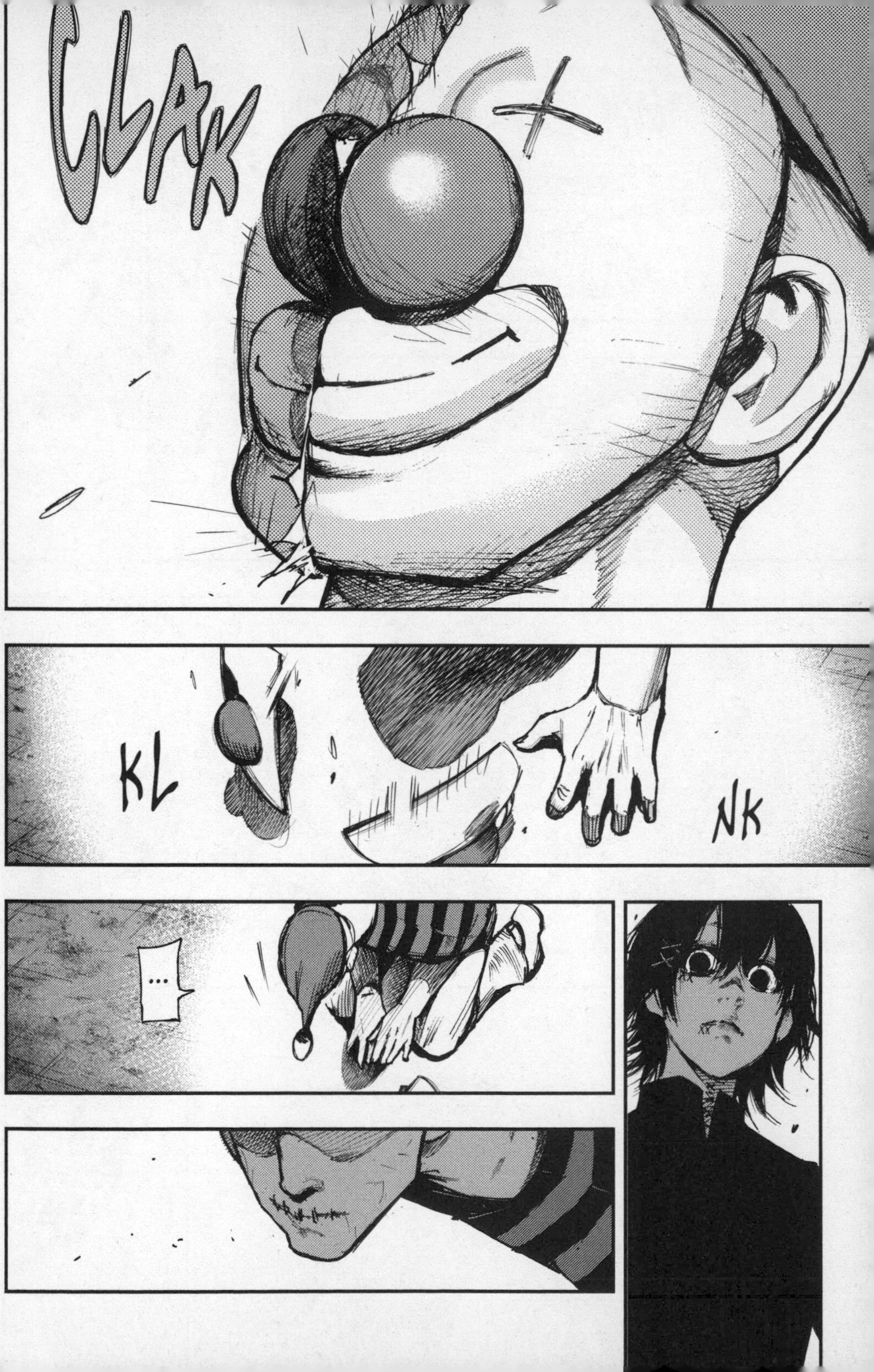
CLAK
KL
NK
...

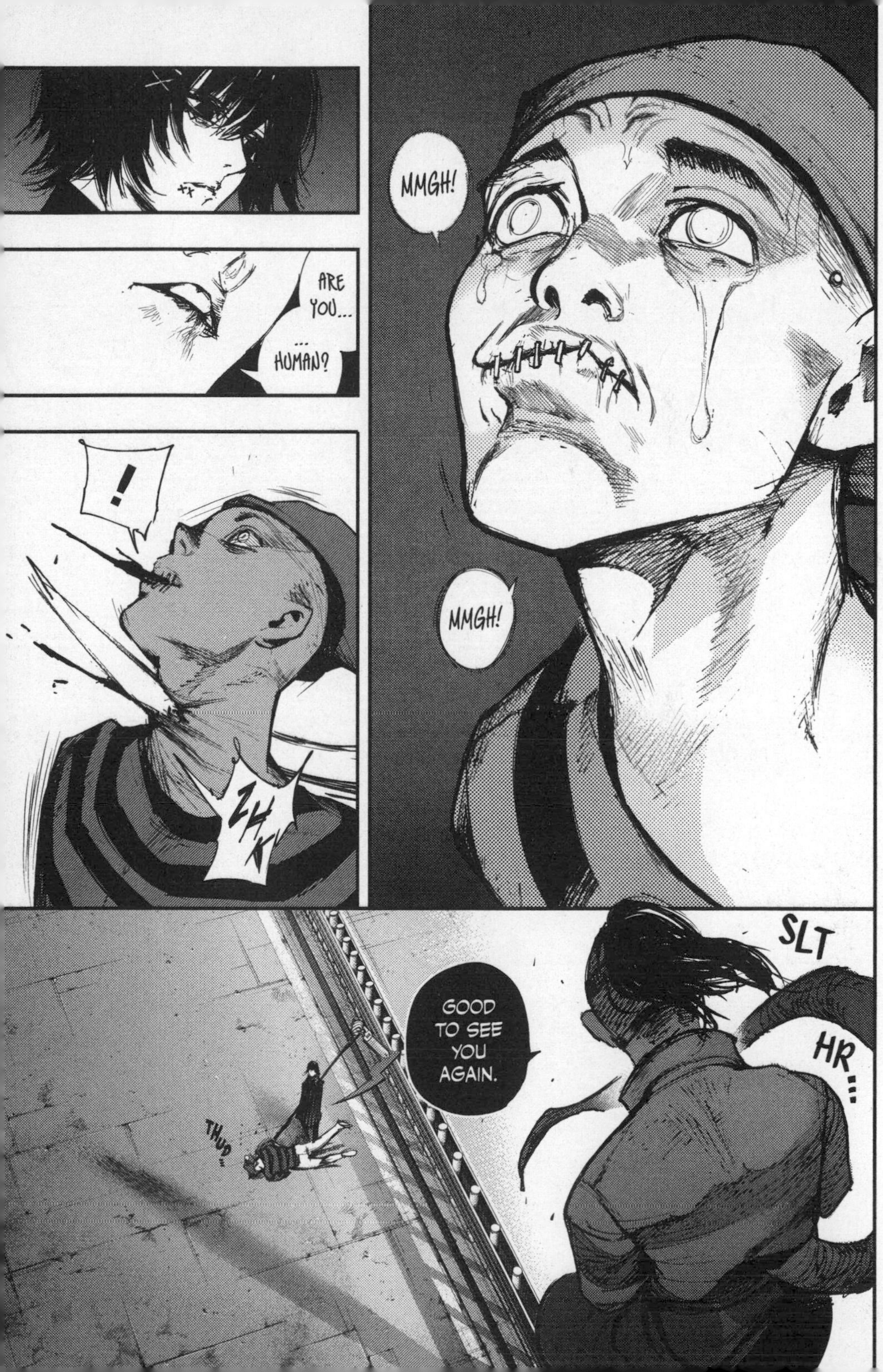
MMGH!
MMGH!
ARE YOU...
...HUMAN?
!
SLT
HR...
GOOD TO SEE YOU AGAIN.

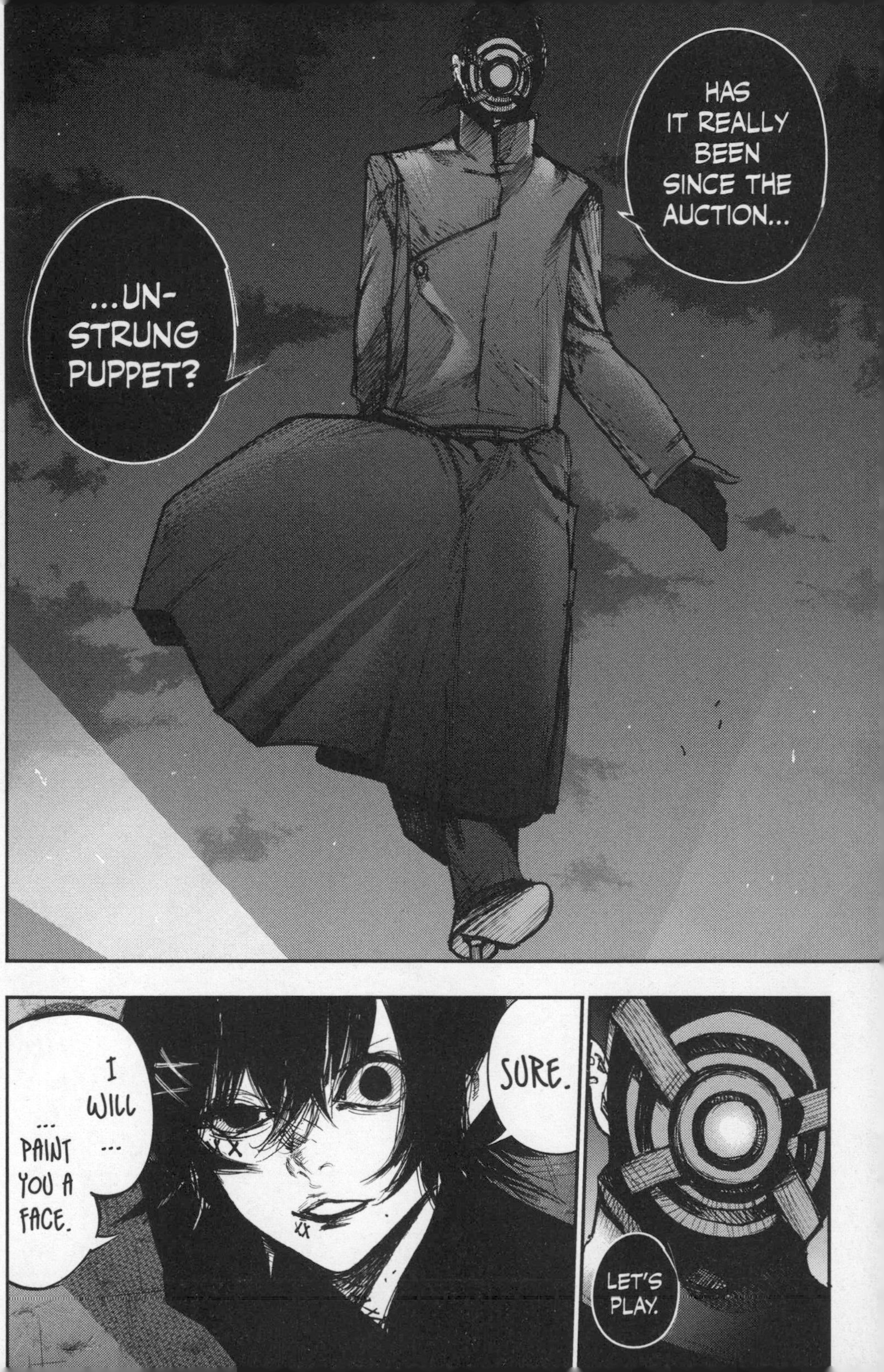
HAS IT REALLY BEEN SINCE THE AUCTION...
...UN-STRUNG PUPPET?
LET'S PLAY.
SURE.
I WILL ... PAINT YOU A FACE.

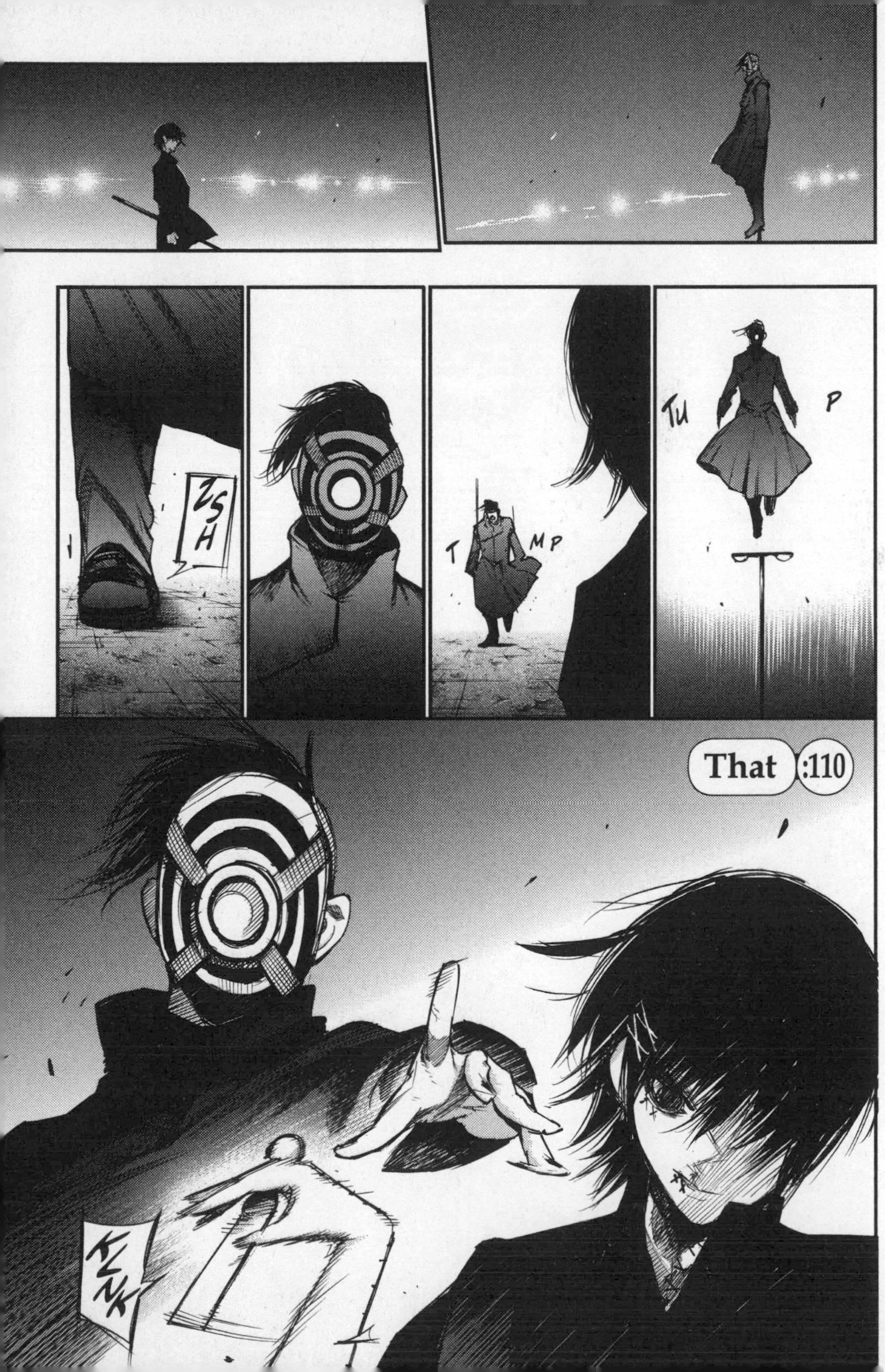
TU P
T MP
ZSH
That :110
KLNK

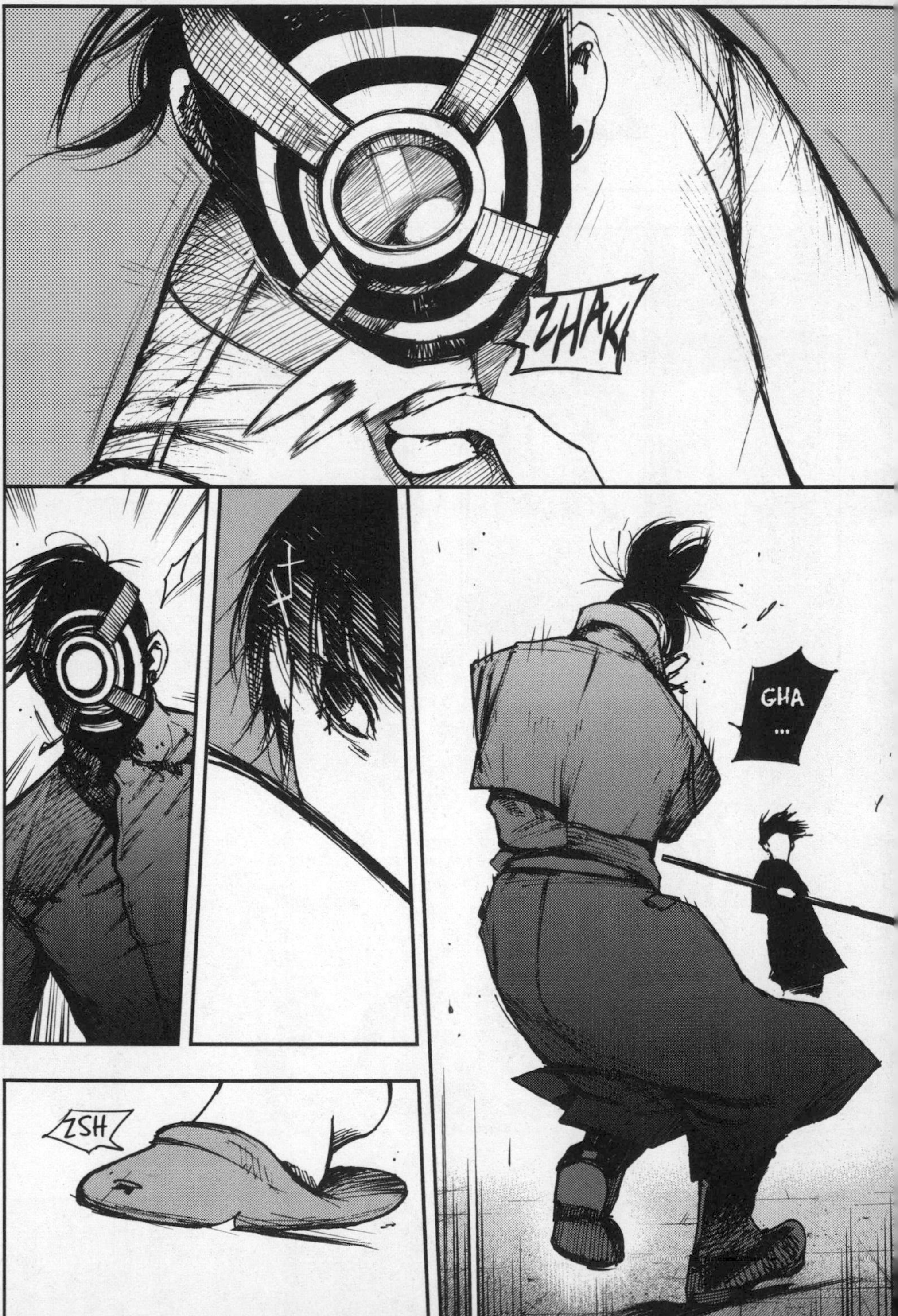
ZHAK
GHA ...
ZSH

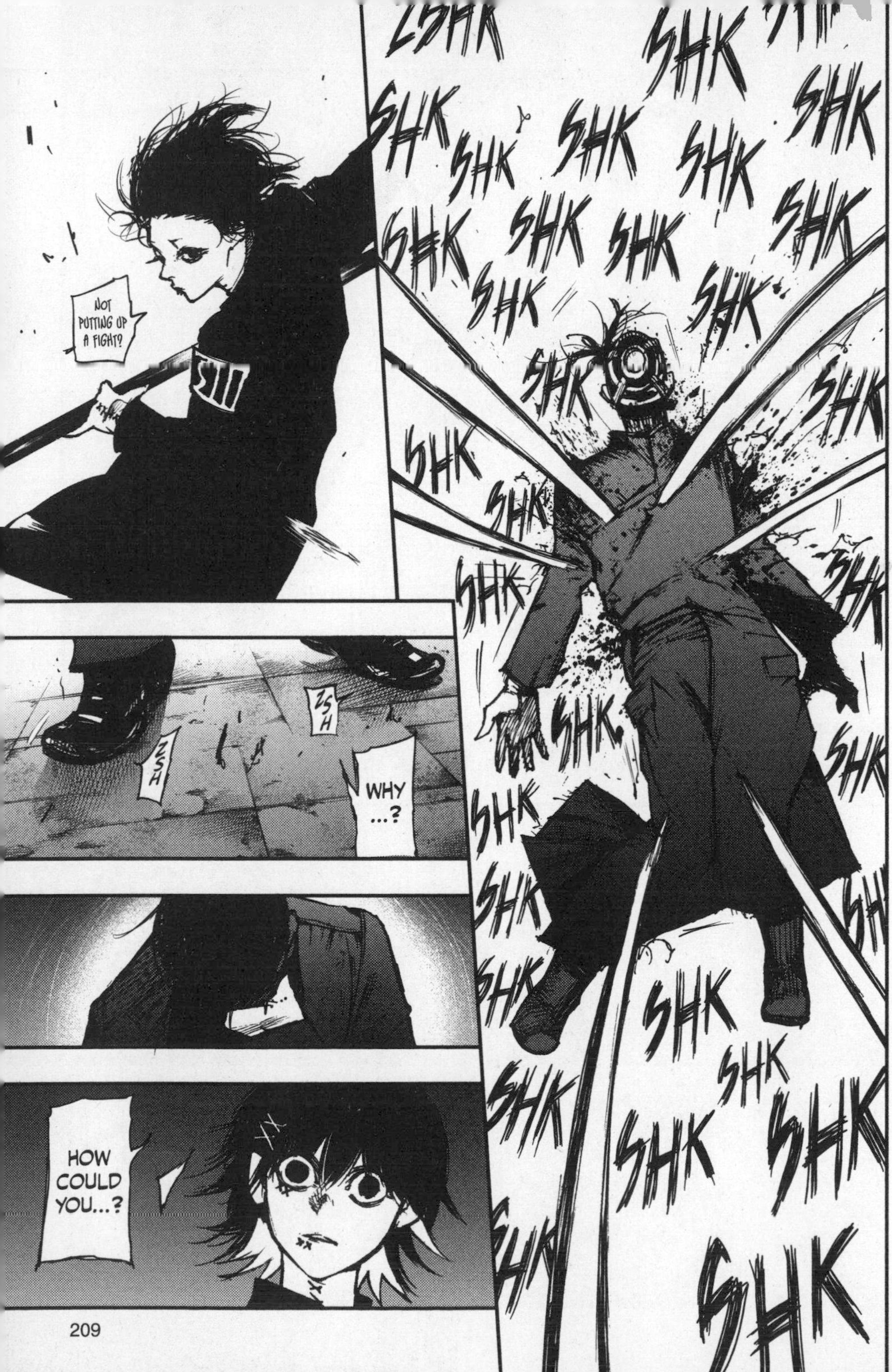
ZSHK
SHK
SHK
SHK
SHK
SHK
SHK
SHK
SHK
SHK
SHK
SHK
SHK
SHK
SHK
SHK
SHK
SHK
SHK
SHK
SHK
SHK
SHK
SHK
SHK
SHK
SHK
SHK
SHK
NOT PUTTING UP A FIGHT?
ZSH
ZSH
WHY...?
HOW COULD YOU...?

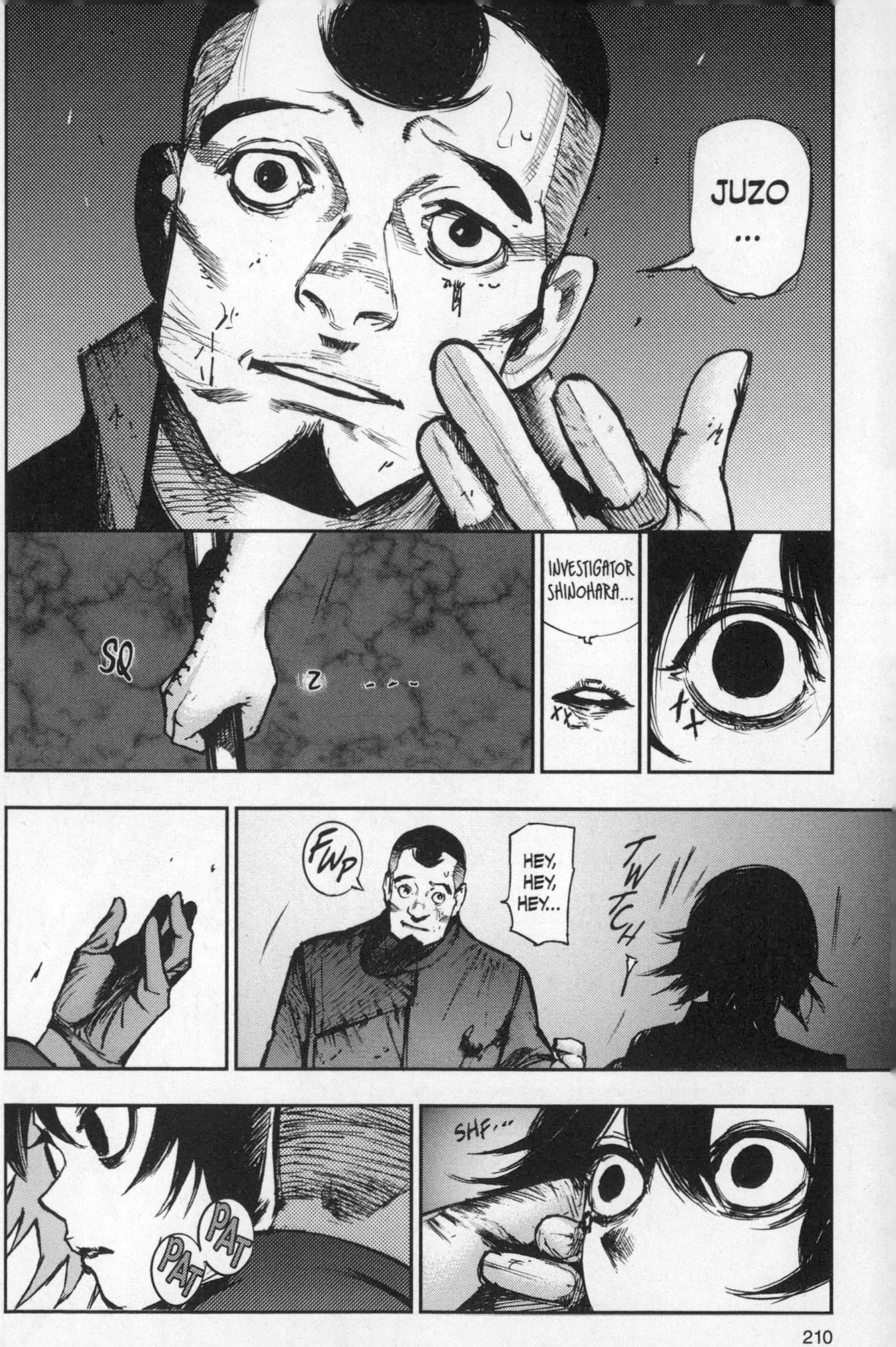
JUZO ...
INVESTIGATOR SHINOHARA...
SQ
TWTCH
HEY, HEY, HEY...
FWP
SHF...
PAT
PAT

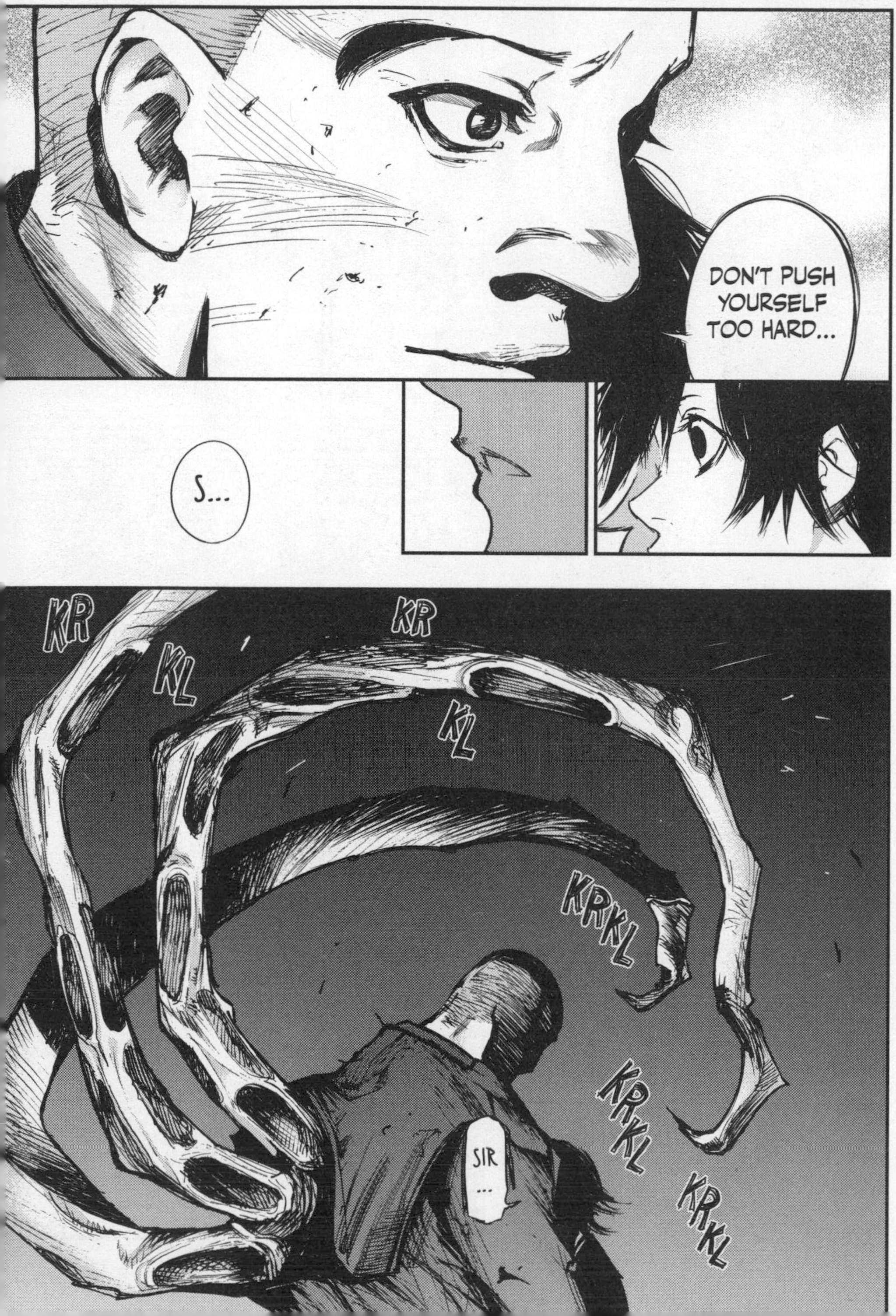

DON'T PUSH YOURSELF TOO HARD...
S...
KR
KL
KR
KL
KRKL
KRKL
KRKL
SIR ...

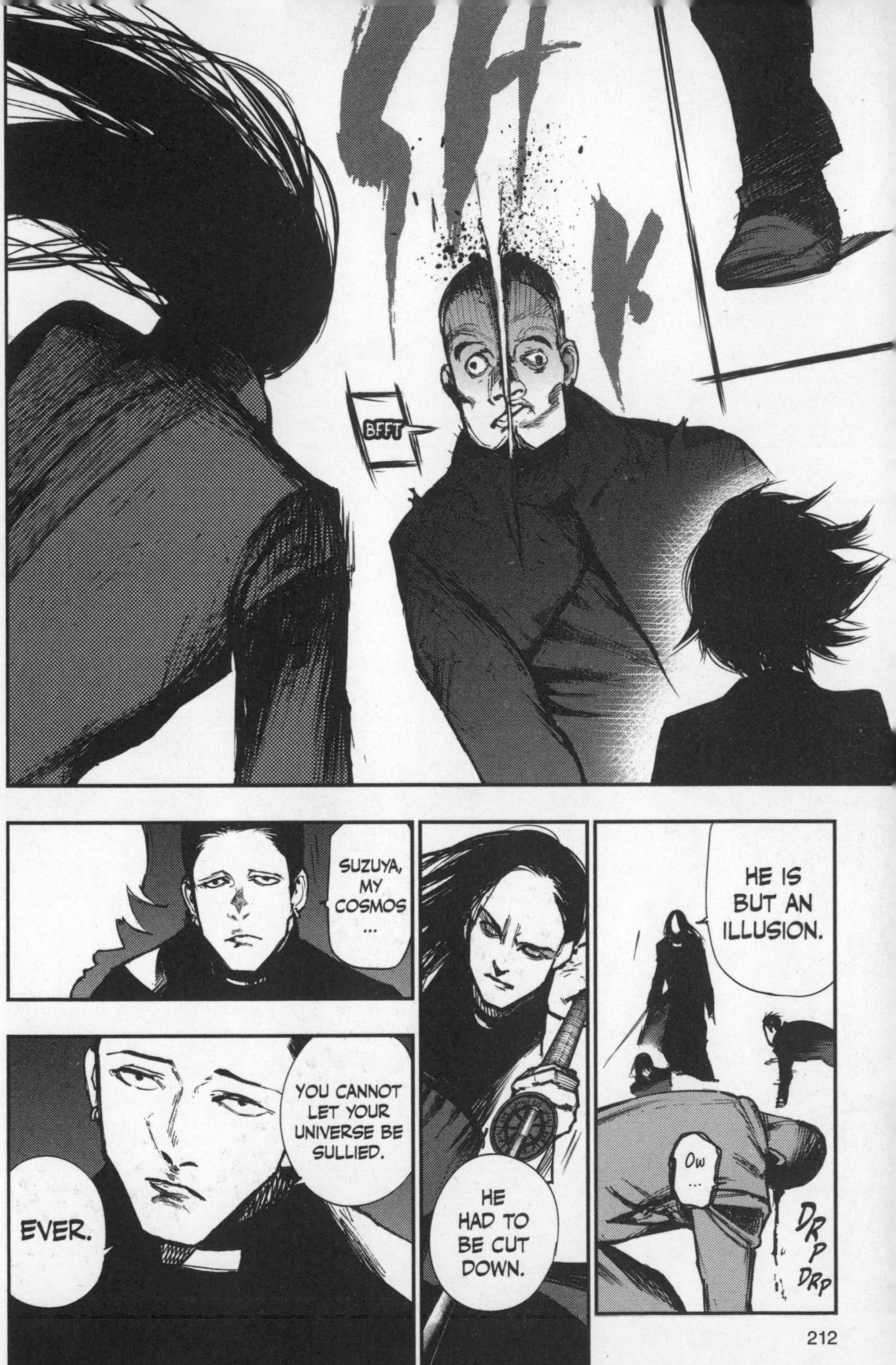
BFFT
HE IS BUT AN ILLUSION.
Ow ...
DRP DRP
HE HAD TO BE CUT DOWN.
SUZUYA, MY COSMOS ...
YOU CANNOT LET YOUR UNIVERSE BE SULLIED.
EVER.

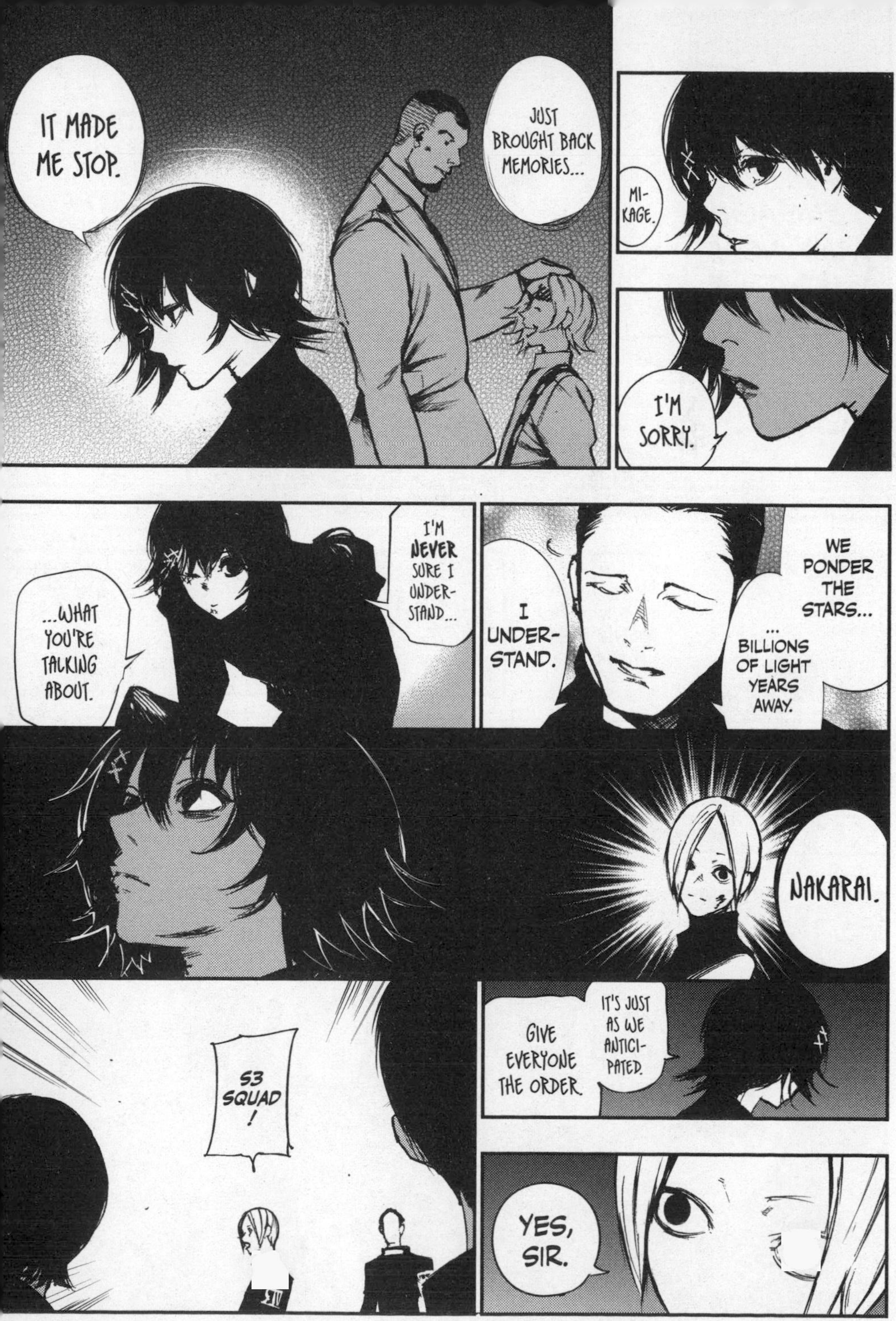
MI-KAGE.
I'M SORRY.
JUST BROUGHT BACK MEMORIES...
IT MADE ME STOP.
WE PONDER THE STARS...
...BILLIONS OF LIGHT YEARS AWAY.
I UNDER-STAND.
I'M NEVER SURE I UNDER-STAND...
...WHAT YOU'RE TALKING ABOUT.
NAKARAI.
IT'S JUST AS WE ANTICI-PATED.
GIVE EVERYONE THE ORDER.
YES, SIR.
S3 SQUAD!

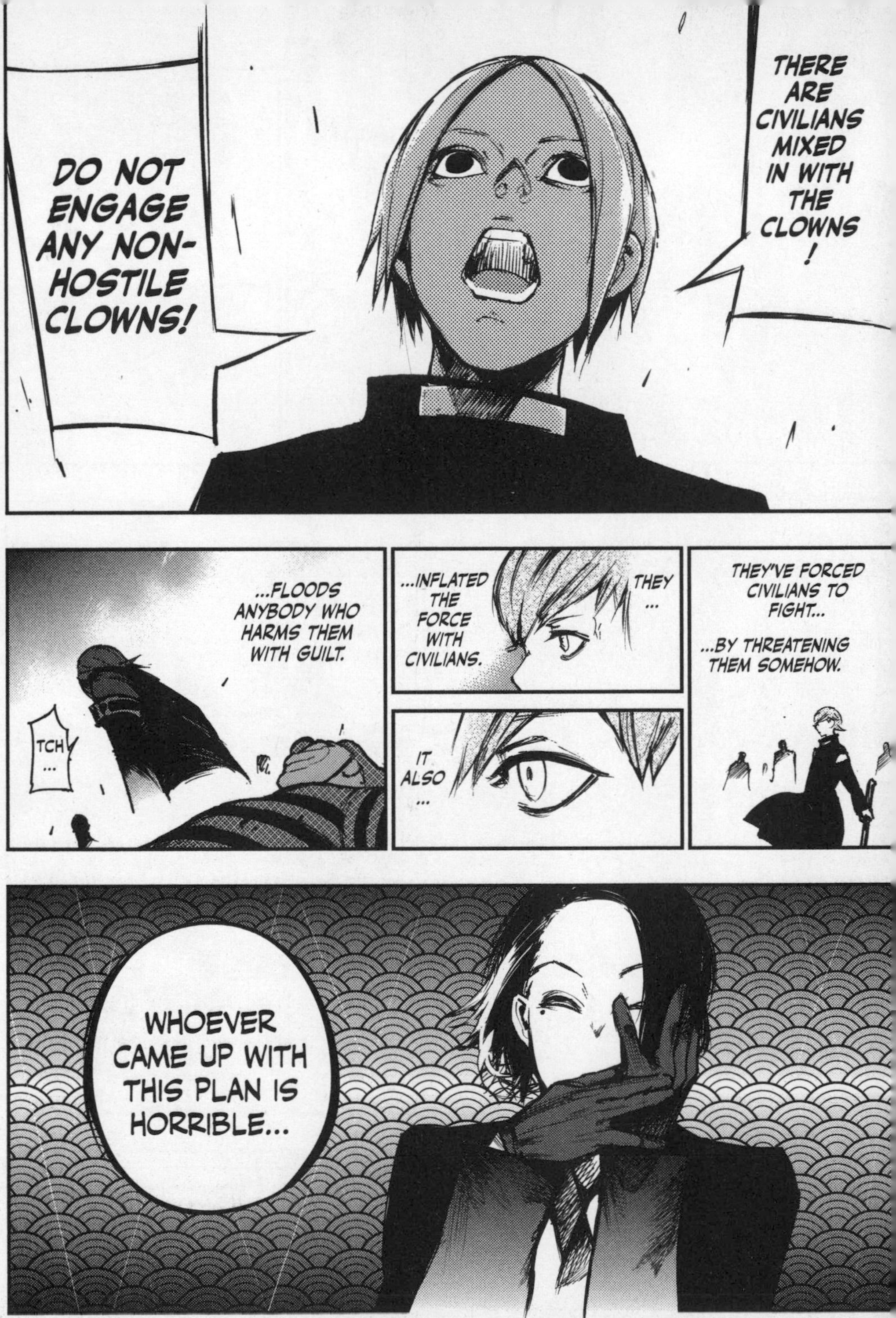
THERE ARE CIVILIANS MIXED IN WITH THE CLOWNS!
DO NOT ENGAGE ANY NON-HOSTILE CLOWNS!
THEY'VE FORCED CIVILIANS TO FIGHT...
...BY THREATENING THEM SOMEHOW.
THEY...
...INFLATED THE FORCE WITH CIVILIANS.
IT ALSO...
...FLOODS ANYBODY WHO HARMS THEM WITH GUILT.
TCH...
WHOEVER CAME UP WITH THIS PLAN IS HORRIBLE...

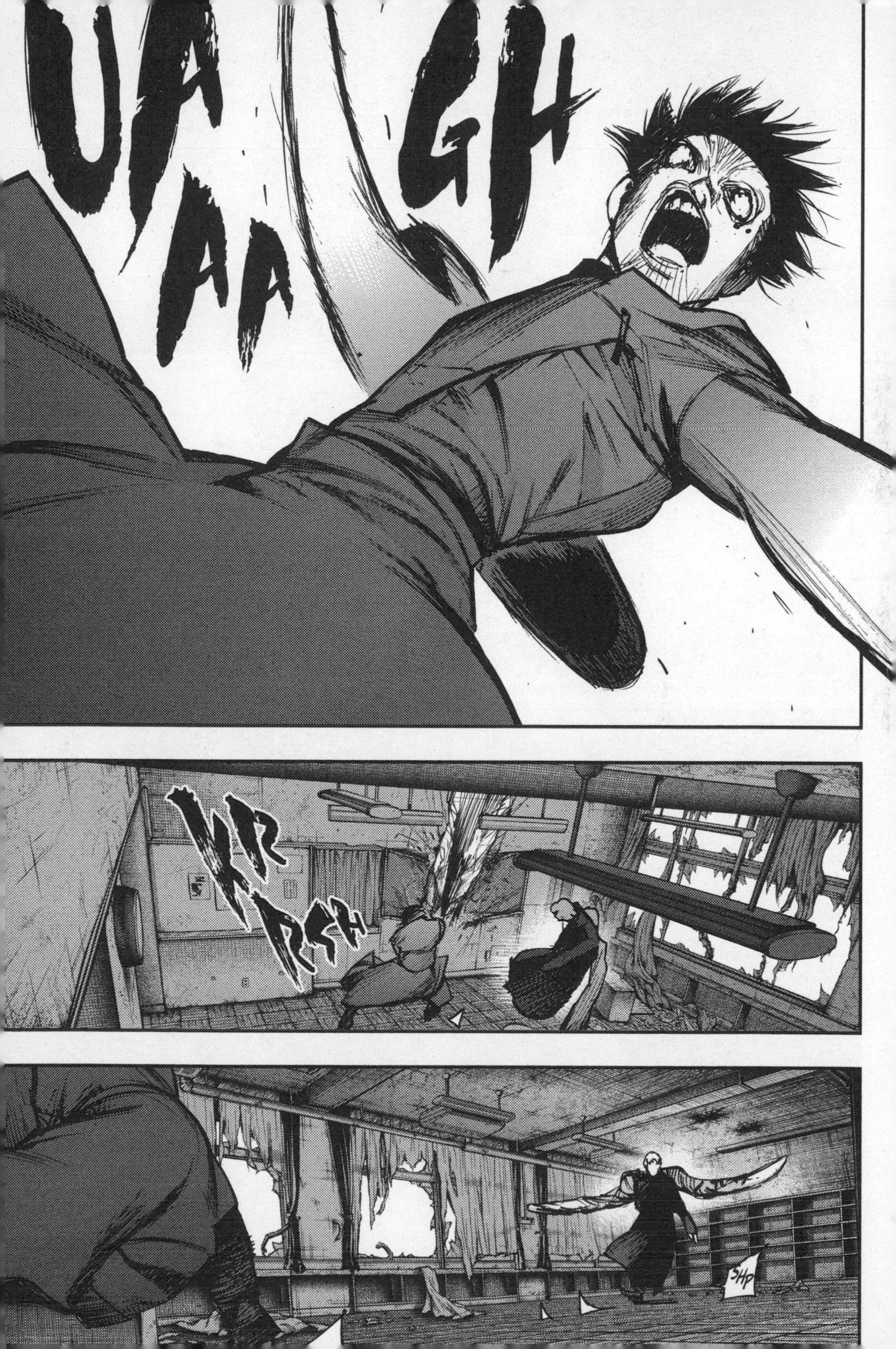
UAAAGH
KRRSH
SHP

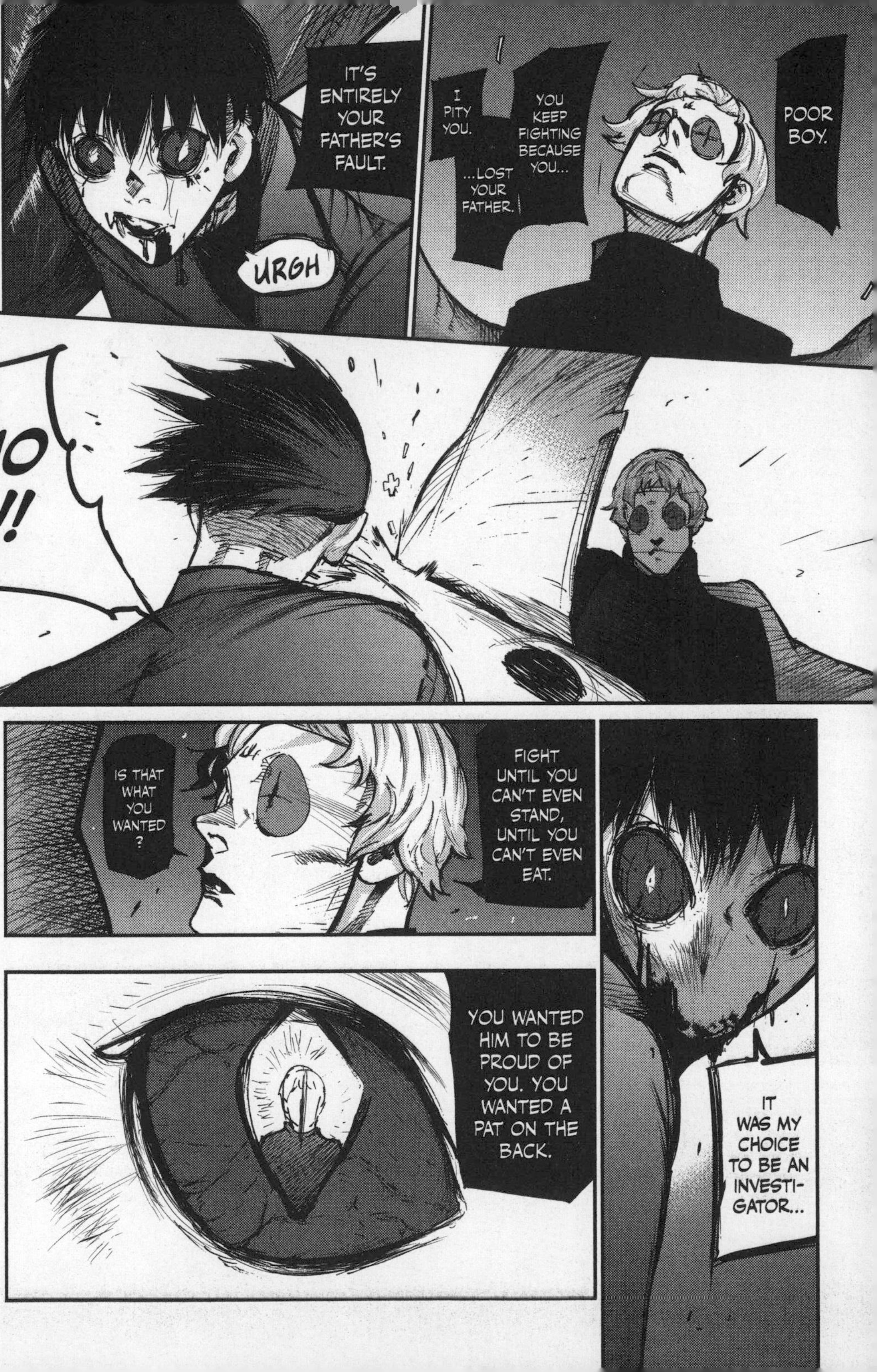
POOR BOY.
YOU KEEP FIGHTING BECAUSE YOU...
...LOST YOUR FATHER.
I PITY YOU.
IT'S ENTIRELY YOUR FATHER'S FAULT.
URGH
NO!!
IT WAS MY CHOICE TO BE AN INVESTI-GATOR...
FIGHT UNTIL YOU CAN'T EVEN STAND, UNTIL YOU CAN'T EVEN EAT.
IS THAT WHAT YOU WANTED?
YOU WANTED HIM TO BE PROUD OF YOU. YOU WANTED A PAT ON THE BACK.

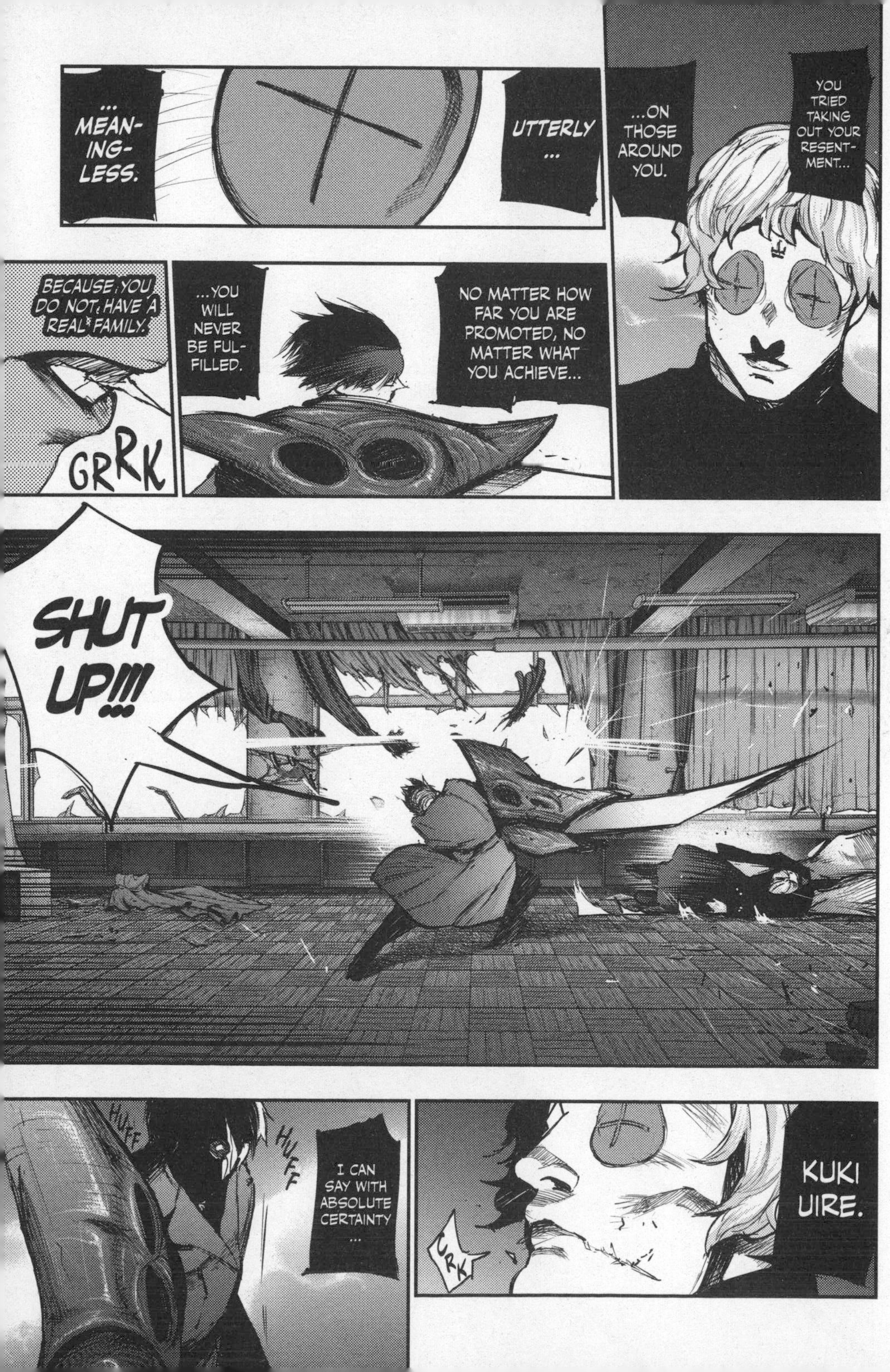
YOU TRIED TAKING OUT YOUR RESENT-MENT...
...ON THOSE AROUND YOU.
UTTERLY...
...MEAN-ING-LESS.
NO MATTER HOW FAR YOU ARE PROMOTED, NO MATTER WHAT YOU ACHIEVE...
...YOU WILL NEVER BE FUL-FILLED.
BECAUSE YOU DO NOT HAVE A REAL FAMILY.
GRRK
SHUT UP!!!
KUKI UIRE.
CRK
I CAN SAY WITH ABSOLUTE CERTAINTY...
HUFF
HUFF

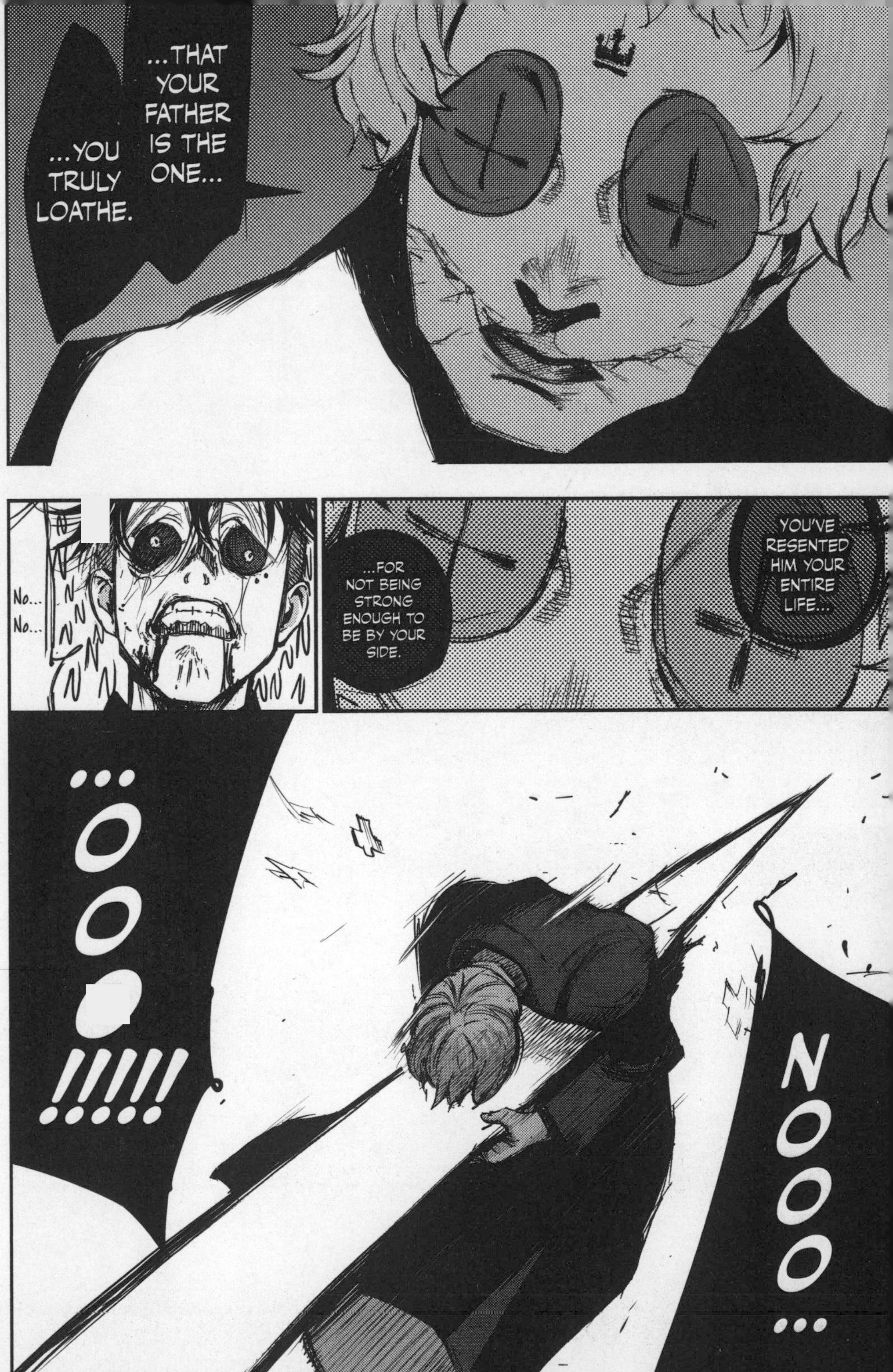

...THAT YOUR FATHER IS THE ONE...
...YOU TRULY LOATHE.
YOU'VE RESENTED HIM YOUR ENTIRE LIFE...
...FOR NOT BEING STRONG ENOUGH TO BE BY YOUR SIDE.
No... No...
NOOO...
...OOO!!!!!

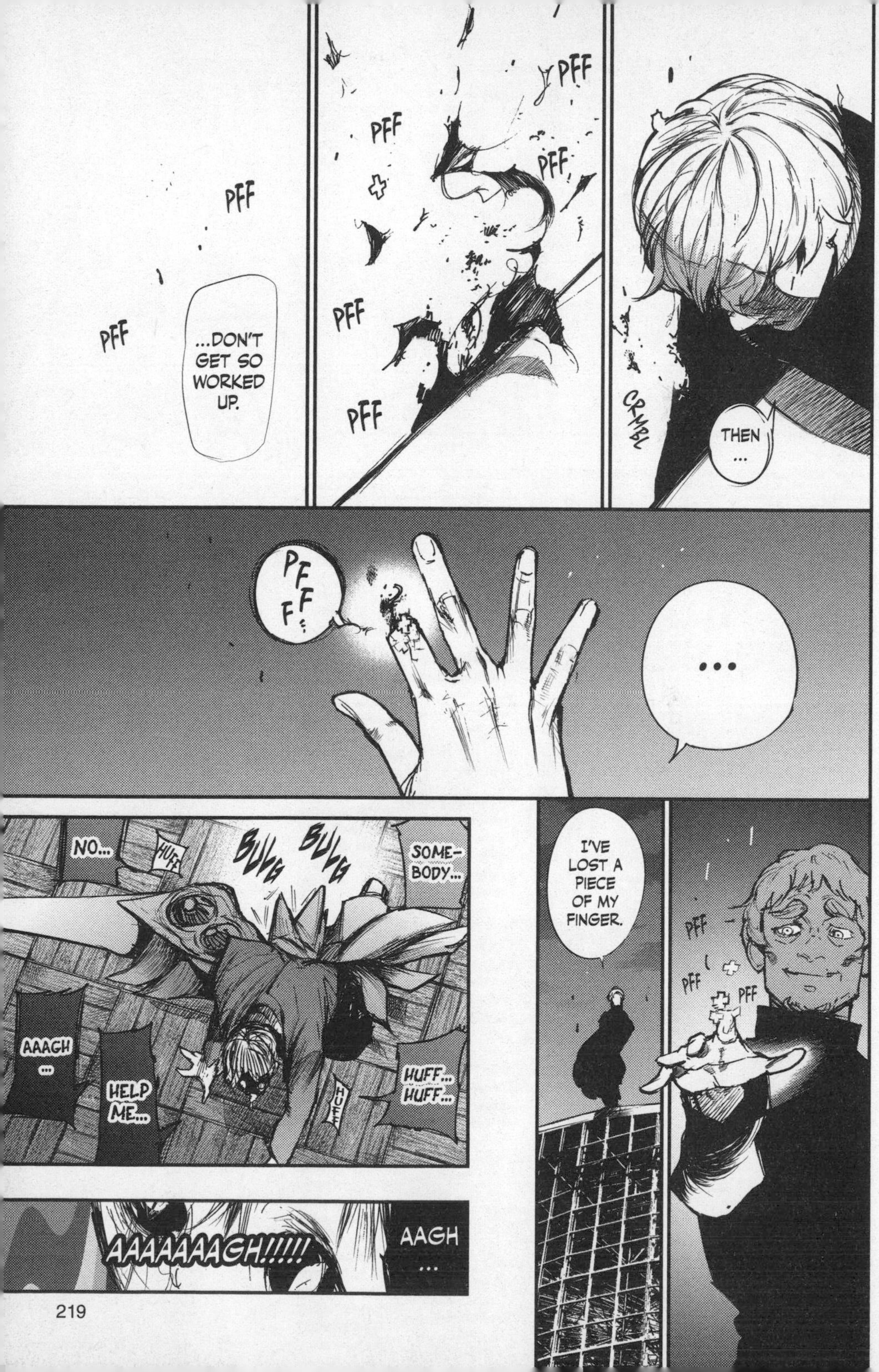
CRMBL
THEN ...
PFF
PFF
PFF
PFF
PFF
PFF
PFF
PFF
...DON'T GET SO WORKED UP.
...
PFFF
PFF
PFF
PFF
I'VE LOST A PIECE OF MY FINGER.
SOME-BODY...
BULG
BULG
HUFF
NO...
HUFF... HUFF...
HUFF
HELP ME...
AAAGH ...
AAGH ...
AAAAAAAGH!!!!!

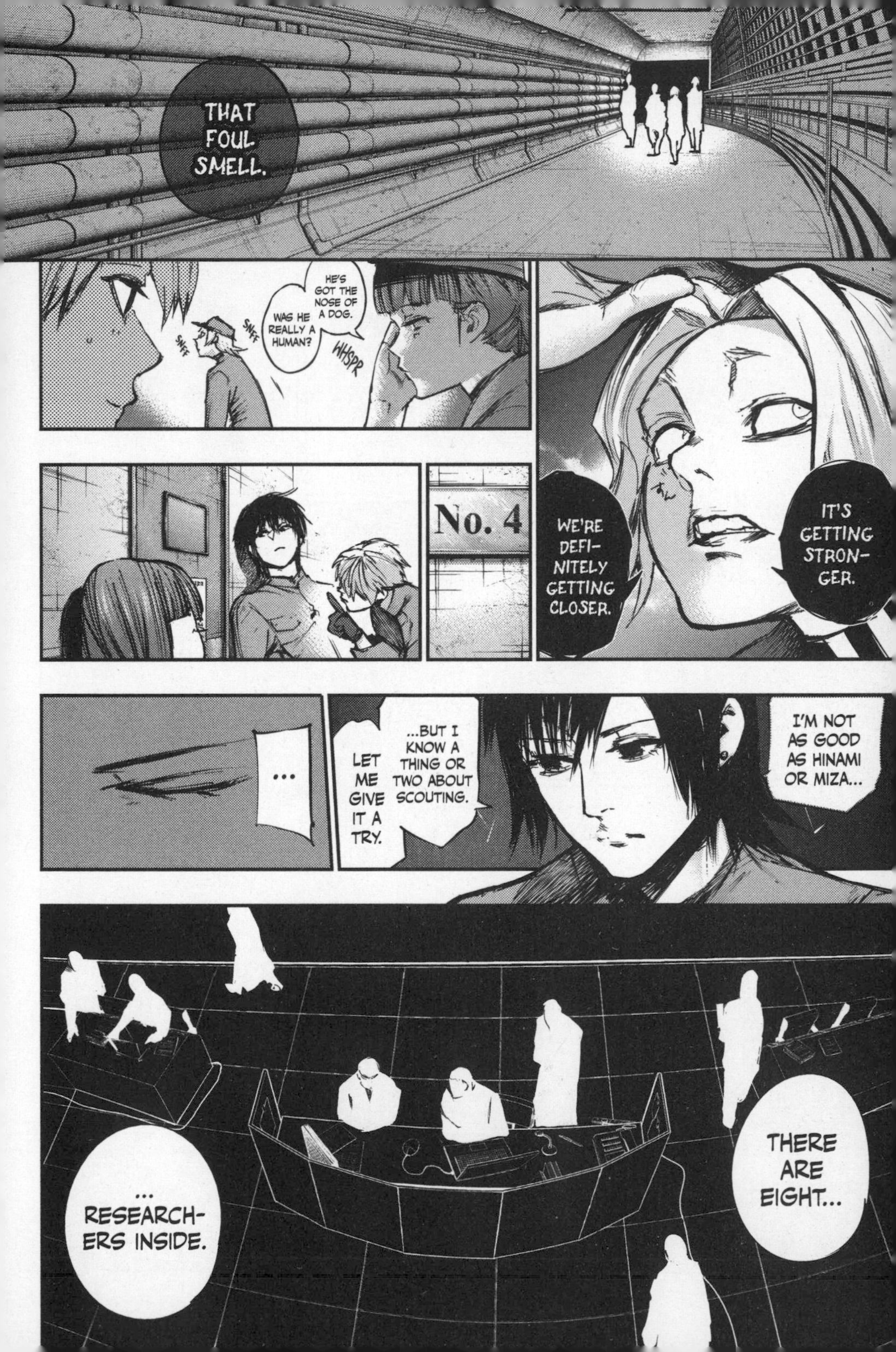
THAT FOUL SMELL.
IT'S GETTING STRON-GER.
WE'RE DEFI-NITELY GETTING CLOSER.
HE'S GOT THE NOSE OF A DOG.
WAS HE REALLY A HUMAN?
WHSPR
SNFF
SNFF
No. 4
I'M NOT AS GOOD AS HINAMI OR MIZA...
...BUT I KNOW A THING OR TWO ABOUT SCOUTING.
LET ME GIVE IT A TRY.
...
THERE ARE EIGHT...
...RESEARCH-ERS INSIDE.

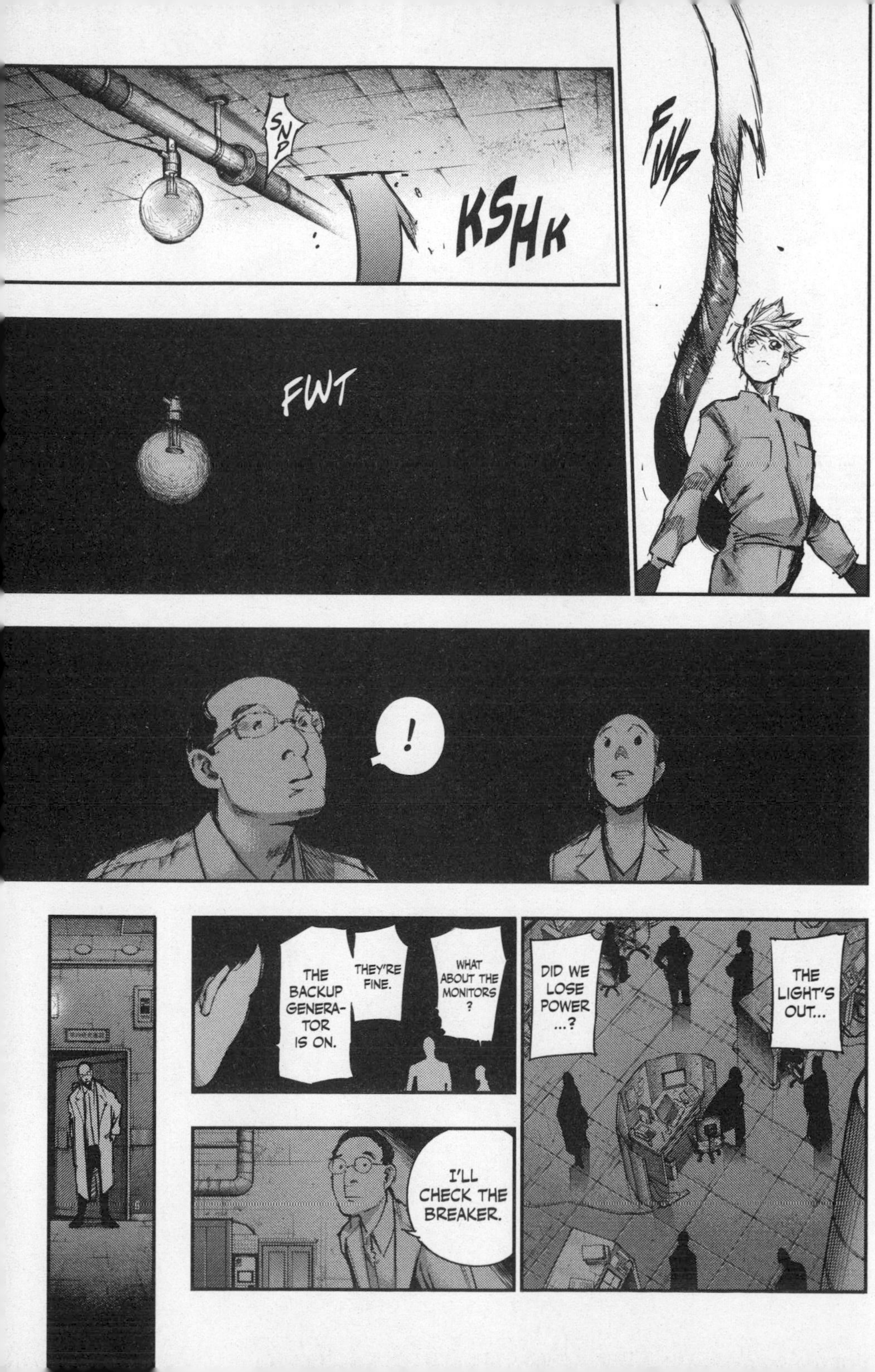
FWP
SNP
KSHK
FWT
!
THE LIGHT'S OUT...
DID WE LOSE POWER ...?
WHAT ABOUT THE MONITORS ?
THEY'RE FINE.
THE BACKUP GENERATOR IS ON.
I'LL CHECK THE BREAKER.

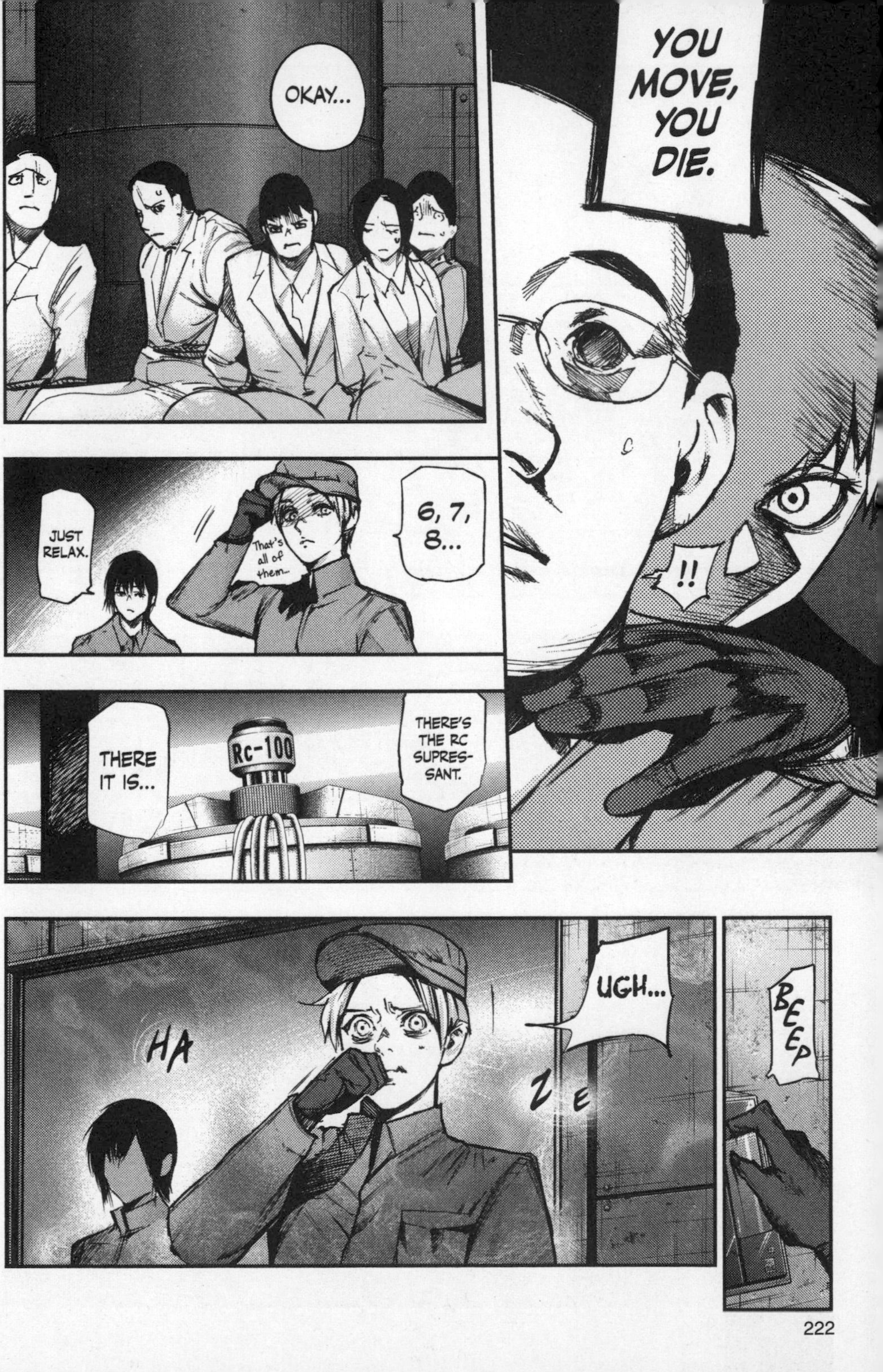
YOU MOVE, YOU DIE.
!!
OKAY...
6, 7, 8...
That's all of them...
JUST RELAX.
THERE'S THE RC SUPRES-SANT.
Rc-100
THERE IT IS...
BEEP
UGH...
ZE
HA

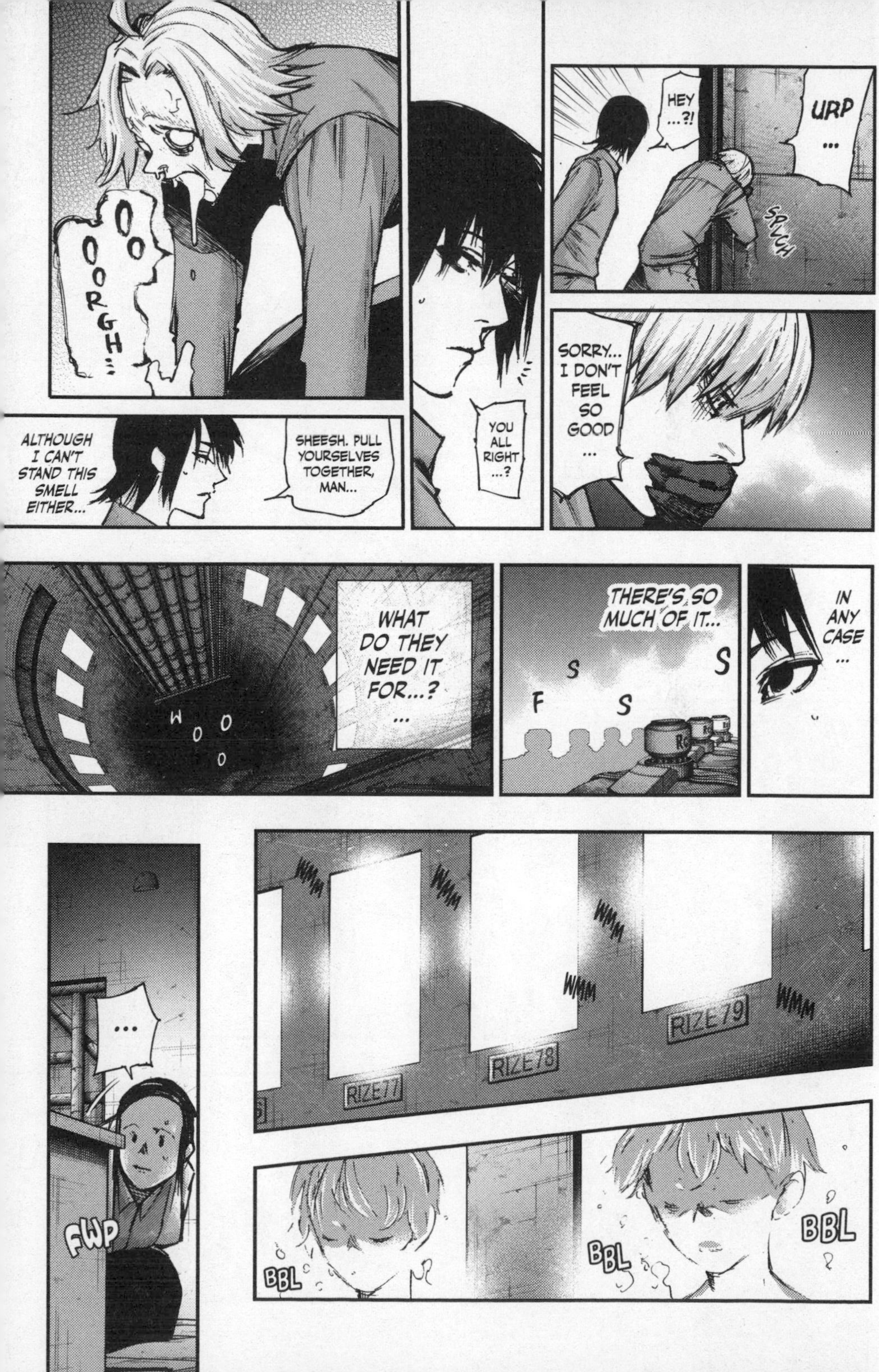
URP ...
SPLCH
HEY ...?!
SORRY... I DON'T FEEL SO GOOD ...
YOU ALL RIGHT ...?
OOOORGH...
SHEESH. PULL YOURSELVES TOGETHER, MAN...
ALTHOUGH I CAN'T STAND THIS SMELL EITHER...
IN ANY CASE ...
THERE'S SO MUCH OF IT...
S
S
S
F
WHAT DO THEY NEED IT FOR...? ...
WOOO
WMM
WMM
WMM
WMM
WMM
RIZE79
RIZE78
RIZE77
BBL
BBL
BBL
...
FWP

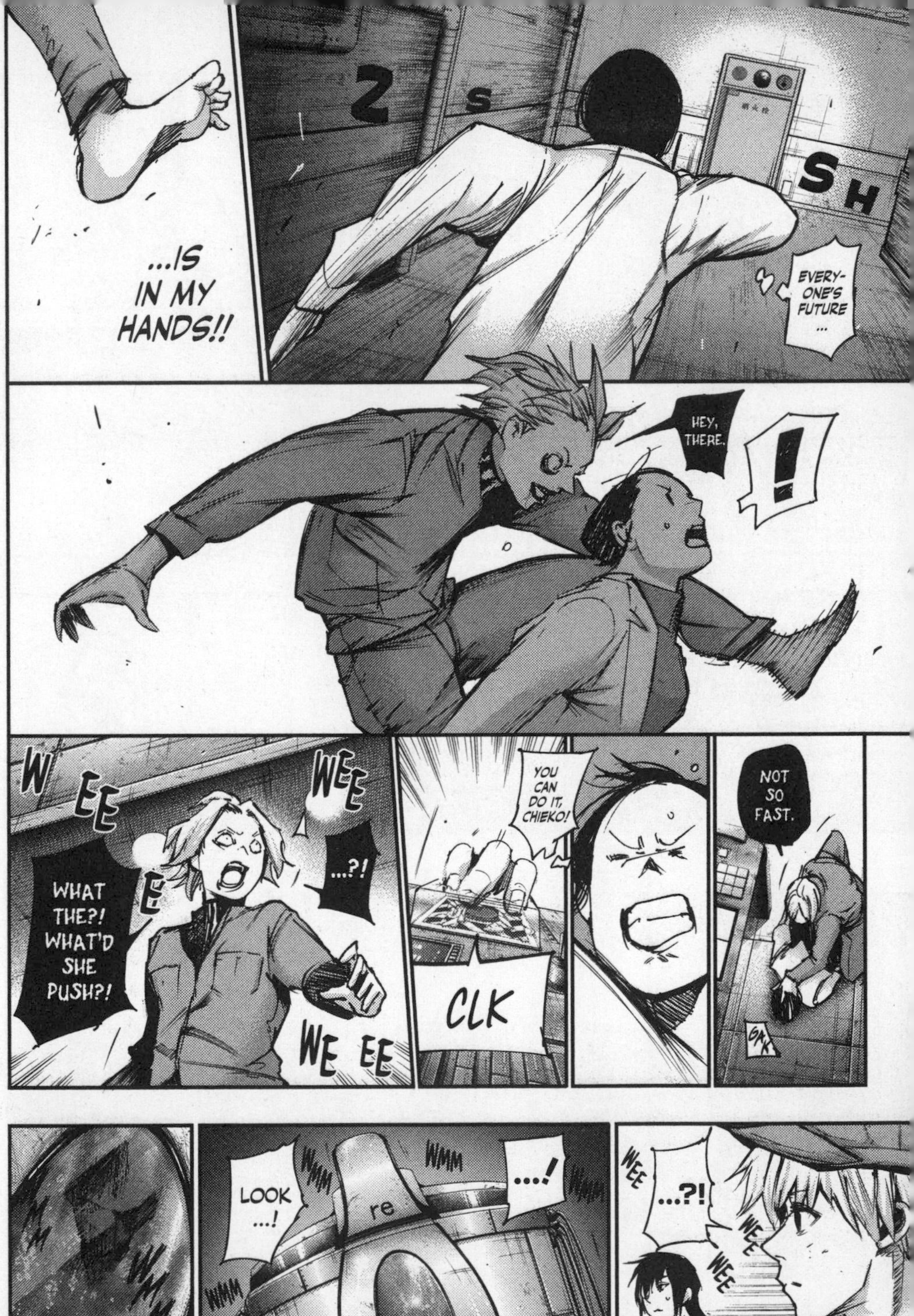
SH
ZS
EVERY-ONE'S FUTURE ...
...IS IN MY HANDS!!
HEY, THERE.
!
NOT SO FAST.
GAK
YOU CAN DO IT, CHIEKO!
CLK
WEE
...?!
W EE
E
WHAT THE?! WHAT'D SHE PUSH?!
WE EE
WEE
...?!
WEE
WEE
...!
WMM
WMM
LOOK ...!
re
WMM
WMM
WMM
WMM

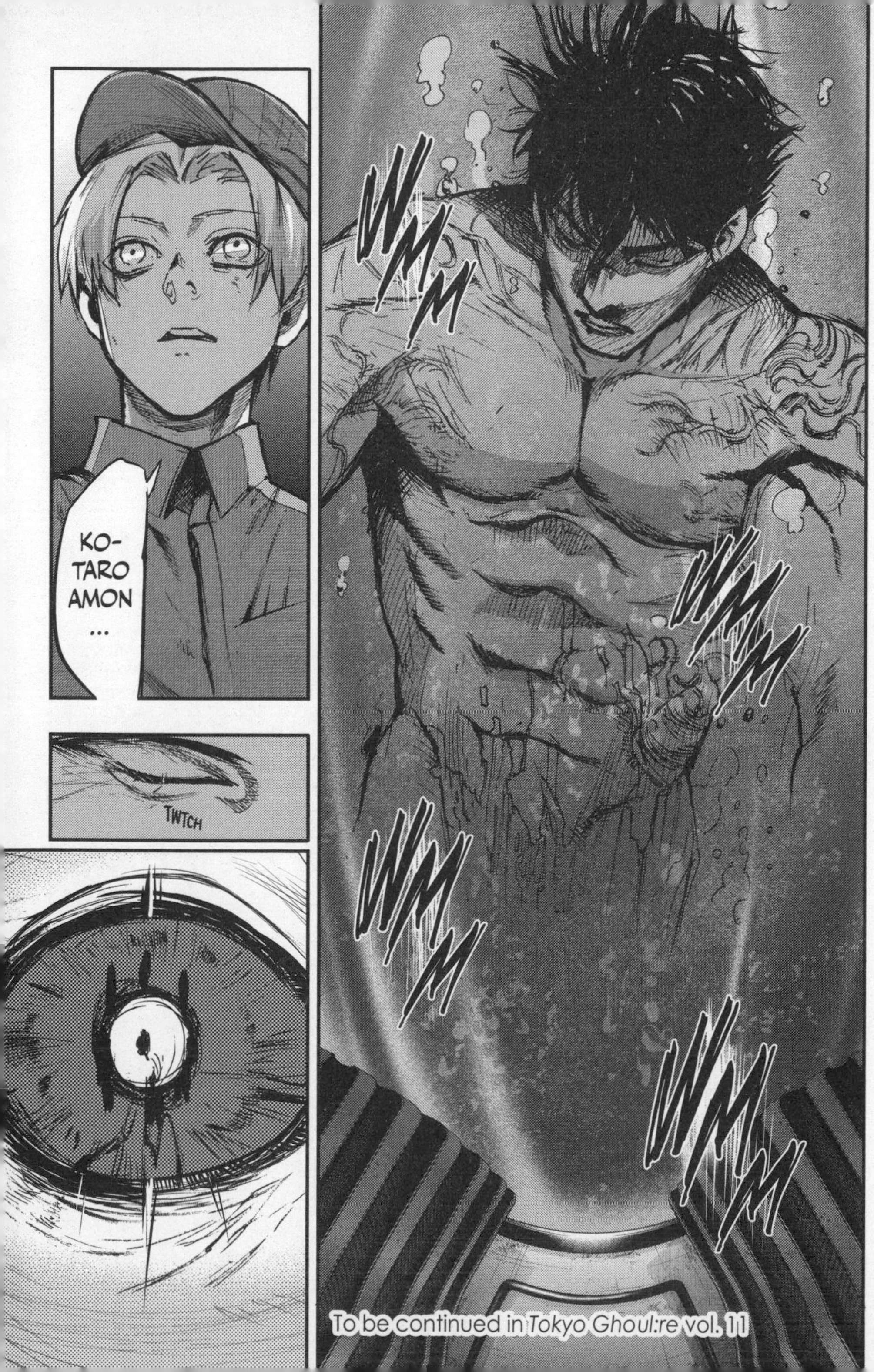
WMMM
WMMM
WMMM
WMMM
KO-TARO AMON...
TWTCH

To be continued in *Tokyo Ghoul:re* vol. 11

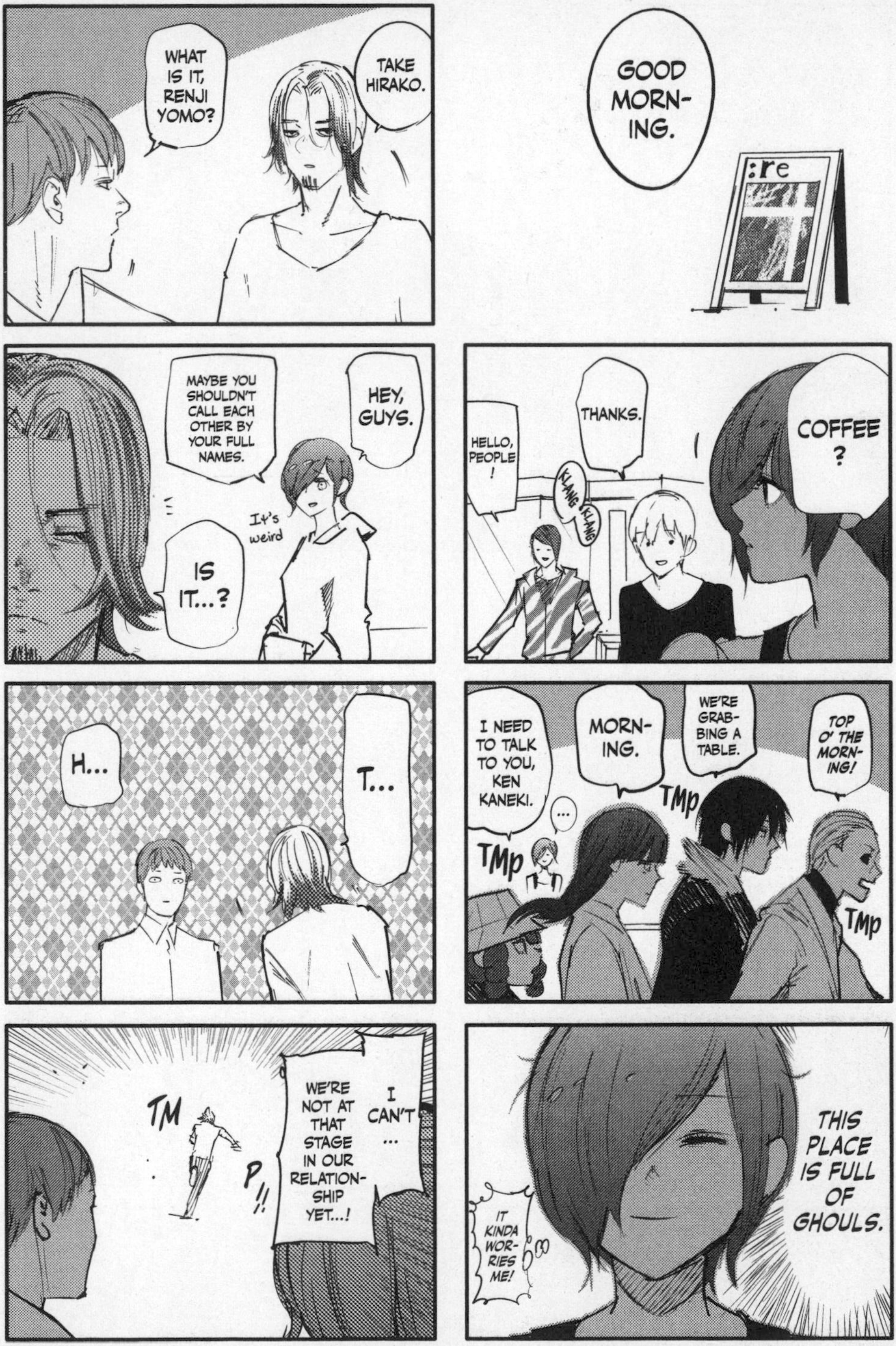
GOOD MORNING.
:re
TAKE HIRAKO.
WHAT IS IT, RENJI YOMO?
COFFEE?
THANKS.
KLANG KLANG
HELLO, PEOPLE!
HEY, GUYS.
MAYBE YOU SHOULDN'T CALL EACH OTHER BY YOUR FULL NAMES.
It's weird
IS IT...?
TOP O' THE MORNING!
WE'RE GRABBING A TABLE.
MORNING.
TMp
I NEED TO TALK TO YOU, KEN KANEKI.
...
TMp
TMp
T...
H...
THIS PLACE IS FULL OF GHOULS.
IT KINDA WORRIES ME!
I CAN'T...
WE'RE NOT AT THAT STAGE IN OUR RELATIONSHIP YET...!
TM
P!!

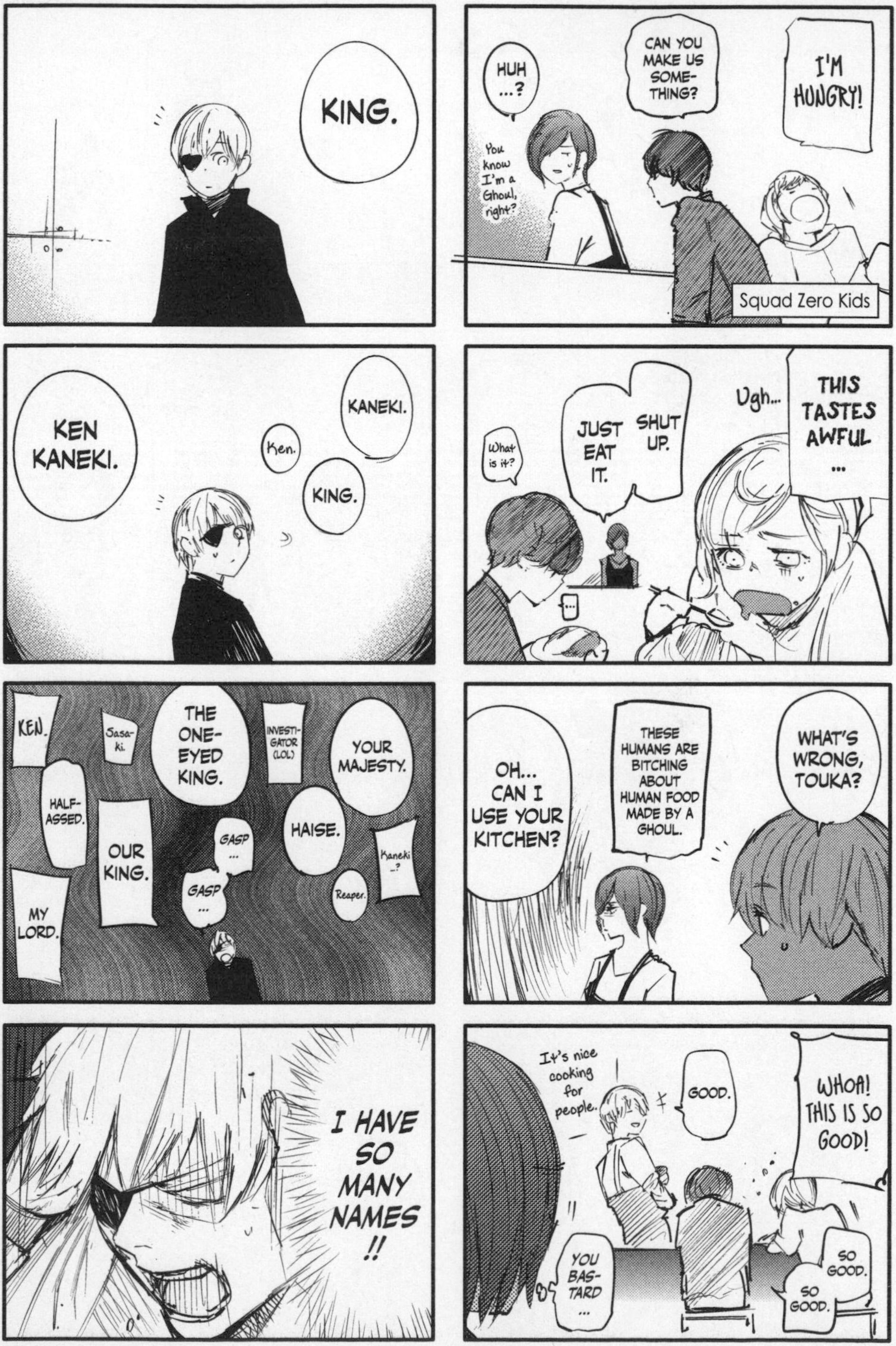
I'M HUNGRY!
CAN YOU MAKE US SOME-THING?
HUH ...?
You know I'm a Ghoul, right?
Squad Zero Kids
THIS TASTES AWFUL ...
Ugh...
SHUT UP.
JUST EAT IT.
What is it?
...
WHAT'S WRONG, TOUKA?
THESE HUMANS ARE BITCHING ABOUT HUMAN FOOD MADE BY A GHOUL.
OH... CAN I USE YOUR KITCHEN?
WHOA! THIS IS SO GOOD!
GOOD.
It's nice cooking for people.
SO GOOD.
SO GOOD.
YOU BAS-TARD ...
KING.
KANEKI.
Ken.
KING.
KEN KANEKI.
YOUR MAJESTY.
INVESTI-GATOR (LOL)
THE ONE-EYED KING.
Sasa-ki.
KEN.
HAISE.
Kaneki ...?
Reaper.
GASP ...
GASP ...
OUR KING.
HALF-ASSED.
MY LORD.
I HAVE SO MANY NAMES !!

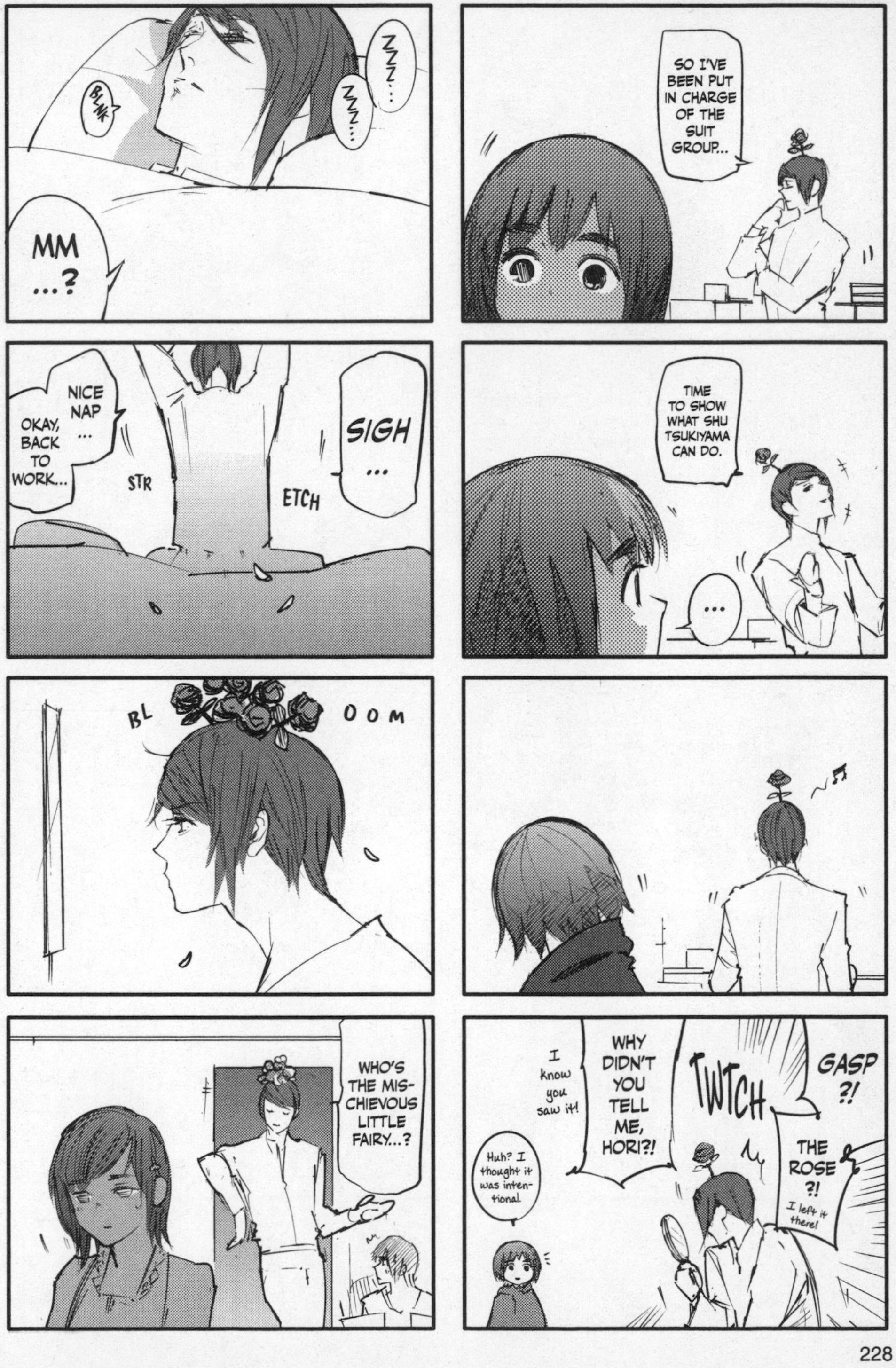

SO I'VE BEEN PUT IN CHARGE OF THE SUIT GROUP...
ZZZ...
ZZZ...
BLINK
MM ...?
TIME TO SHOW WHAT SHU TSUKIYAMA CAN DO.
...
SIGH ...
ETCH
STR
NICE NAP ...
OKAY, BACK TO WORK...
BL OOM
GASP ?!
THE ROSE ?!
I left it there!
TWTCH
WHY DIDN'T YOU TELL ME, HORI?!
I know you saw it!
Huh? I thought it was inten-tional.
WHO'S THE MIS-CHIEVOUS LITTLE FAIRY...?

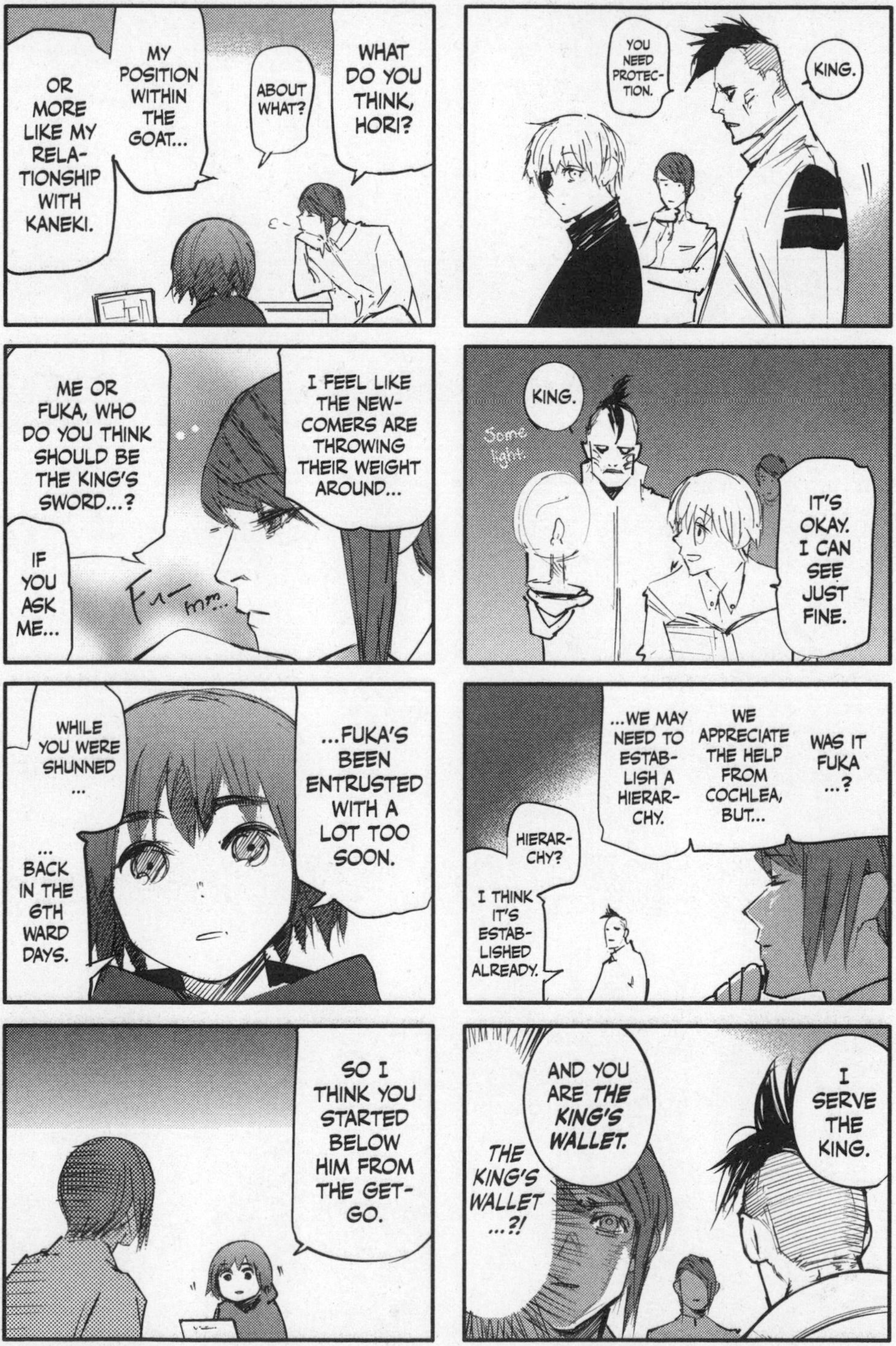
KING.
YOU NEED PROTECTION.
KING.
Some light.
IT'S OKAY. I CAN SEE JUST FINE.
WAS IT FUKA ...?
WE APPRECIATE THE HELP FROM COCHLEA, BUT...
...WE MAY NEED TO ESTABLISH A HIERARCHY.
HIERARCHY?
I THINK IT'S ESTABLISHED ALREADY.
I SERVE THE KING.
AND YOU ARE THE KING'S WALLET.
THE KING'S WALLET ...?!
WHAT DO YOU THINK, HORI?
ABOUT WHAT?
MY POSITION WITHIN THE GOAT...
OR MORE LIKE MY RELATIONSHIP WITH KANEKI.
I FEEL LIKE THE NEWCOMERS ARE THROWING THEIR WEIGHT AROUND...
ME OR FUKA, WHO DO YOU THINK SHOULD BE THE KING'S SWORD...?
IF YOU ASK ME...
...FUKA'S BEEN ENTRUSTED WITH A LOT TOO SOON.
WHILE YOU WERE SHUNNED ...
... BACK IN THE 6TH WARD DAYS.
SO I THINK YOU STARTED BELOW HIM FROM THE GET-GO.

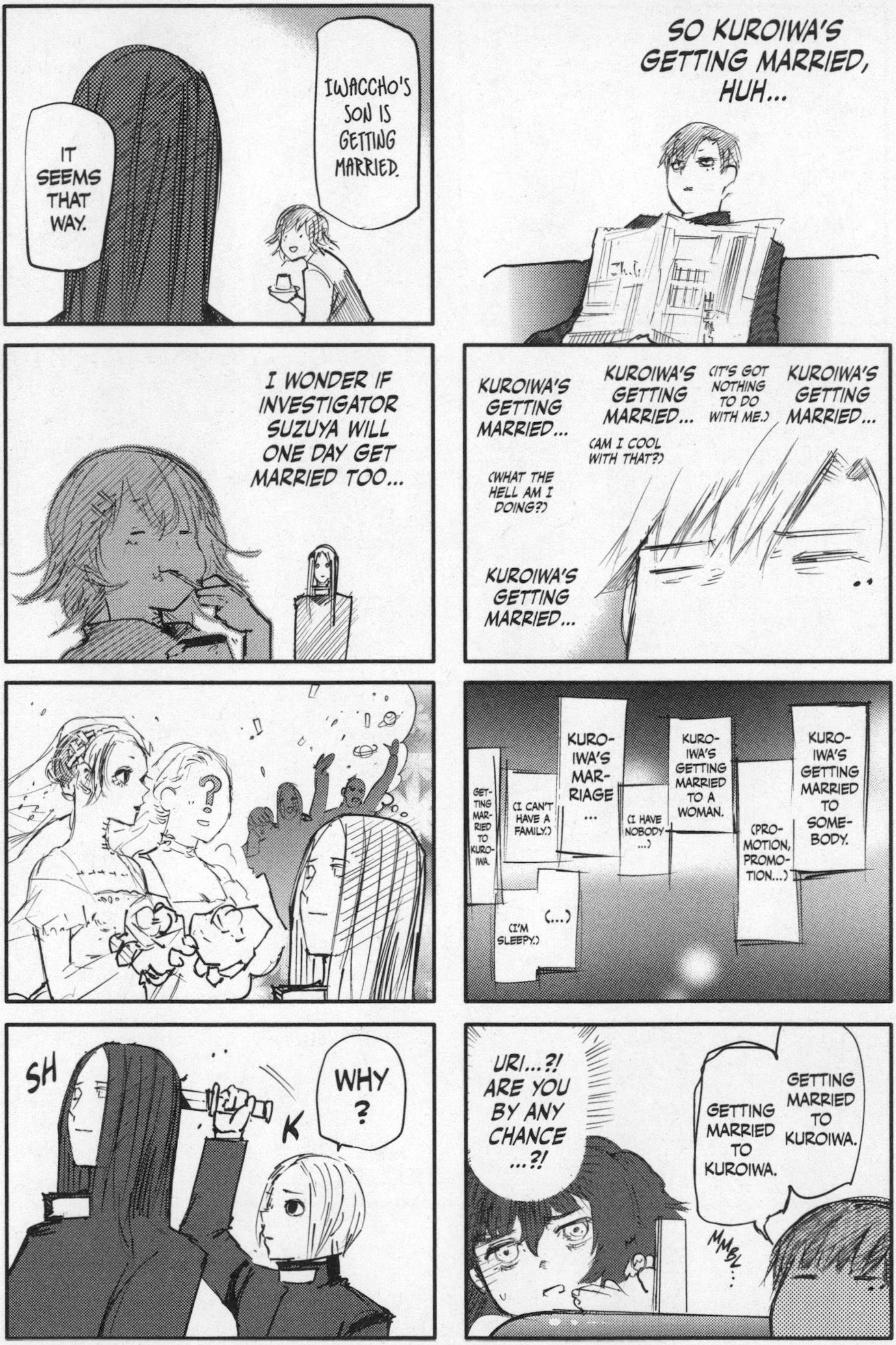
SO KUROIWA'S GETTING MARRIED, HUH...
IWACCHO'S SON IS GETTING MARRIED.
IT SEEMS THAT WAY.
KUROIWA'S GETTING MARRIED...
(IT'S GOT NOTHING TO DO WITH ME.)
KUROIWA'S GETTING MARRIED...
(AM I COOL WITH THAT?)
KUROIWA'S GETTING MARRIED...
(WHAT THE HELL AM I DOING?)
KUROIWA'S GETTING MARRIED...
I WONDER IF INVESTIGATOR SUZUYA WILL ONE DAY GET MARRIED TOO...
KURO-IWA'S GETTING MARRIED TO SOME-BODY.
(PRO-MOTION, PROMO-TION...)
KURO-IWA'S GETTING MARRIED TO A WOMAN.
(I HAVE NOBODY...)
KURO-IWA'S MAR-RIAGE...
(I CAN'T HAVE A FAMILY.)
(...)
GET-TING MAR-RIED TO KURO-IWA.
(I'M SLEEPY.)
GETTING MARRIED TO KUROIWA.
GETTING MARRIED TO KUROIWA.
URI...?! ARE YOU BY ANY CHANCE ...?!
MMBL...
WHY?
SH
K

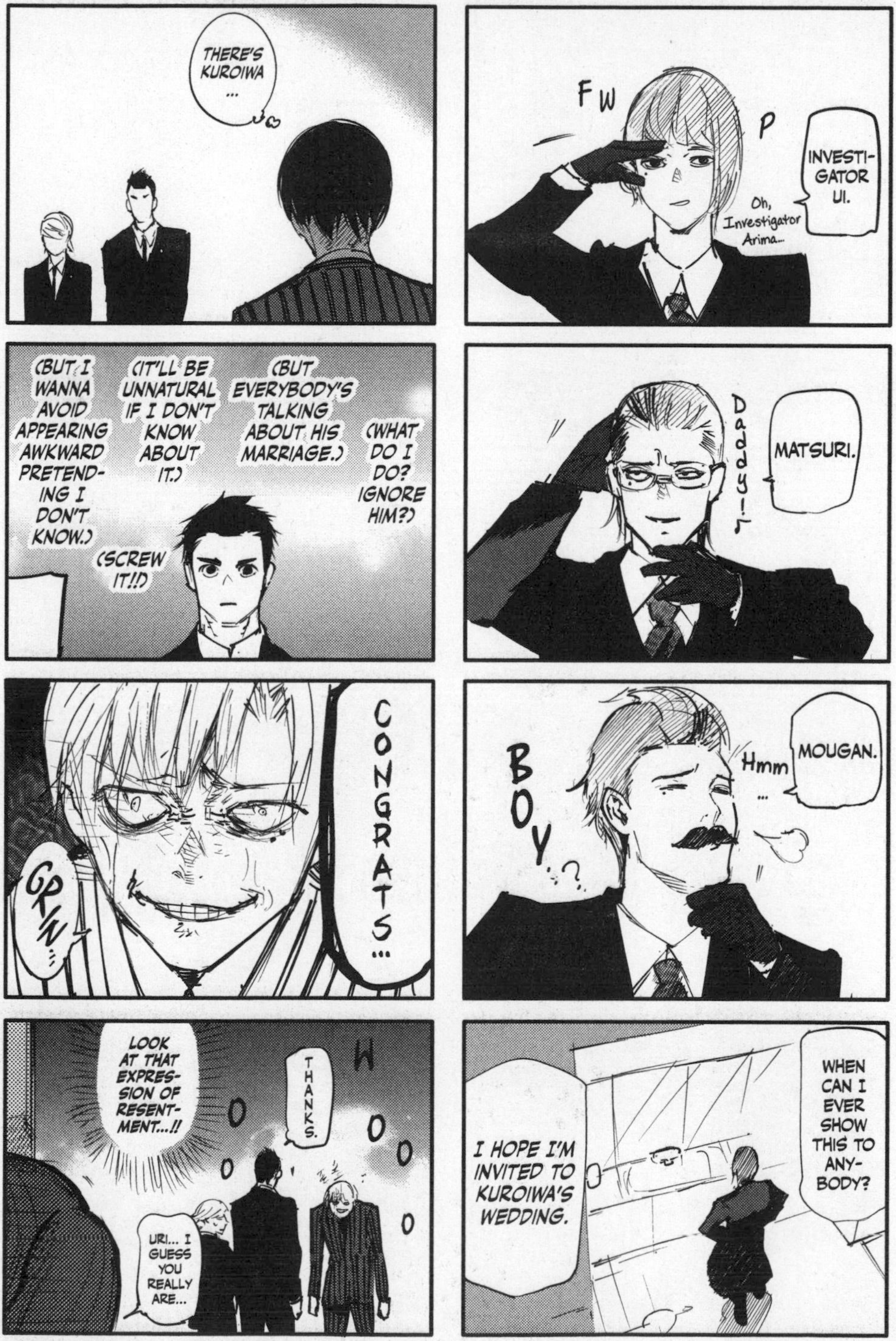
INVESTIGATOR UI.
Oh, Investigator Arima...
FW P
THERE'S KUROIWA...
MATSURI.
Daddy!♪
(WHAT DO I DO? IGNORE HIM?)
(BUT EVERYBODY'S TALKING ABOUT HIS MARRIAGE.)
(IT'LL BE UNNATURAL IF I DON'T KNOW ABOUT IT.)
(BUT I WANNA AVOID APPEARING AWKWARD PRETENDING I DON'T KNOW.)
(SCREW IT!!)
MOUGAN.
Hmm...
BOY...?
CONGRATS...
GRIN...
WHEN CAN I EVER SHOW THIS TO ANYBODY?
I HOPE I'M INVITED TO KUROIWA'S WEDDING.
WOOOOOO
THANKS.
LOOK AT THAT EXPRESSION OF RESENTMENT...!!
URI... I GUESS YOU REALLY ARE...

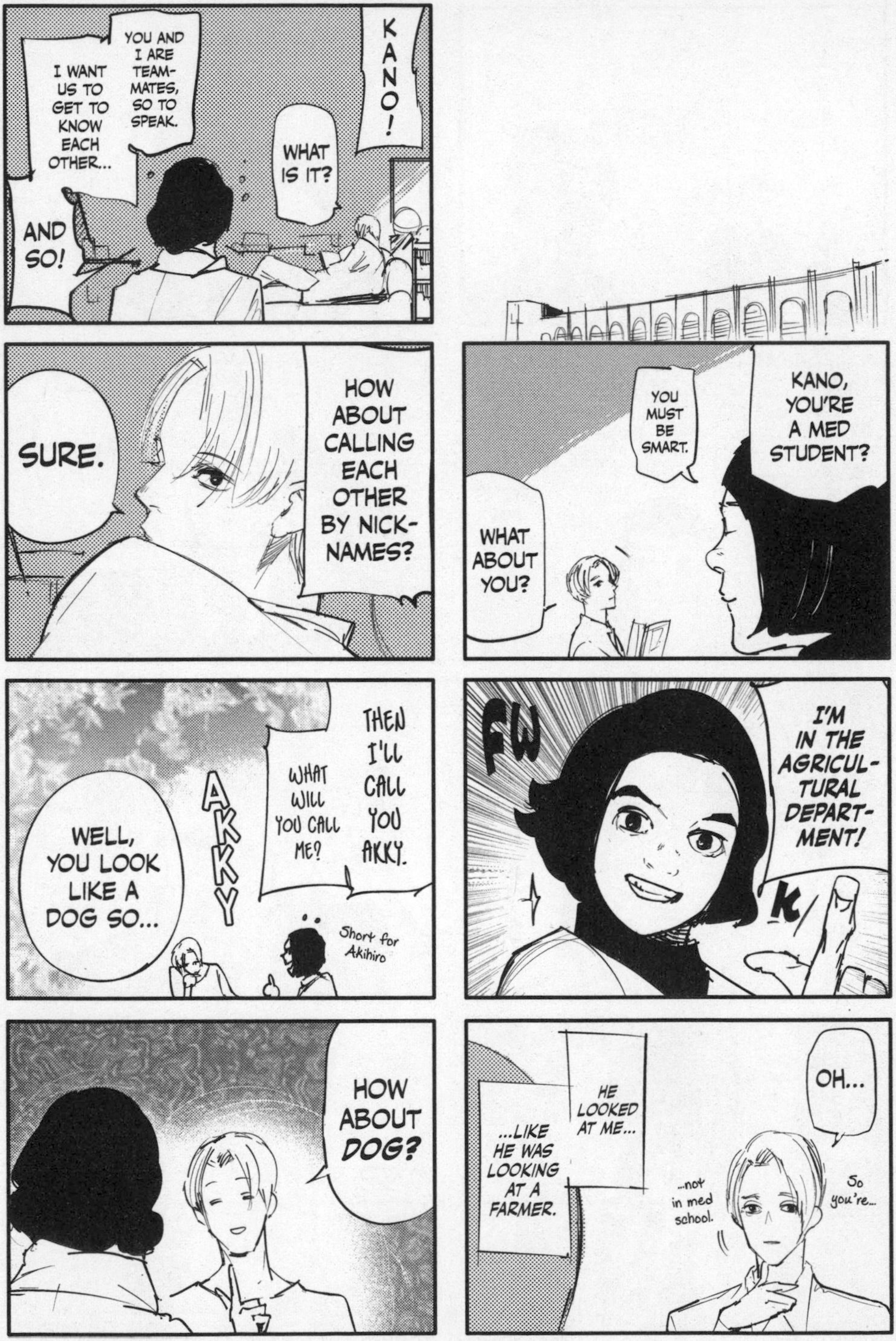
KANO!
WHAT IS IT?
YOU AND I ARE TEAM-MATES, SO TO SPEAK.
I WANT US TO GET TO KNOW EACH OTHER...
AND SO!
KANO, YOU'RE A MED STUDENT?
YOU MUST BE SMART.
WHAT ABOUT YOU?
HOW ABOUT CALLING EACH OTHER BY NICK-NAMES?
SURE.
I'M IN THE AGRICUL-TURAL DEPART-MENT!
FW
K
THEN I'LL CALL YOU AKKY.
WHAT WILL YOU CALL ME?
AKKY
Short for Akihiro
WELL, YOU LOOK LIKE A DOG SO...
OH...
HE LOOKED AT ME...
So you're...
...not in med school.
...LIKE HE WAS LOOKING AT A FARMER.
HOW ABOUT DOG?

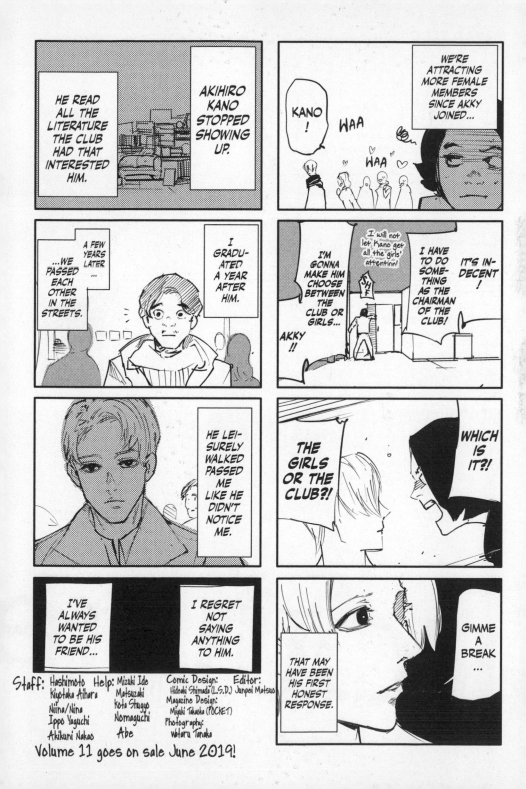

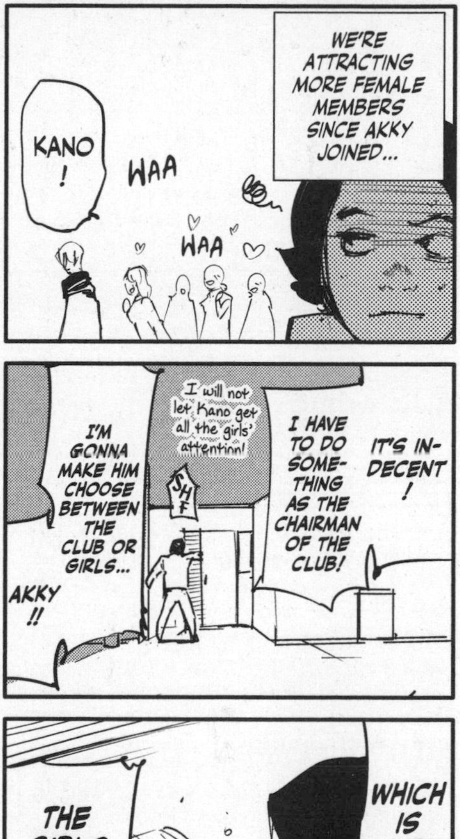
WE'RE ATTRACTING MORE FEMALE MEMBERS SINCE AKKY JOINED...
KANO!
WAA
WAA
IT'S IN-DECENT!
I HAVE TO DO SOME-THING AS THE CHAIRMAN OF THE CLUB!
I will not let Kano get all the girls' attention!
I'M GONNA MAKE HIM CHOOSE BETWEEN THE CLUB OR GIRLS...
SHF
AKKY!!
WHICH IS IT?!
THE GIRLS OR THE CLUB?!
GIMME A BREAK...
THAT MAY HAVE BEEN HIS FIRST HONEST RESPONSE.

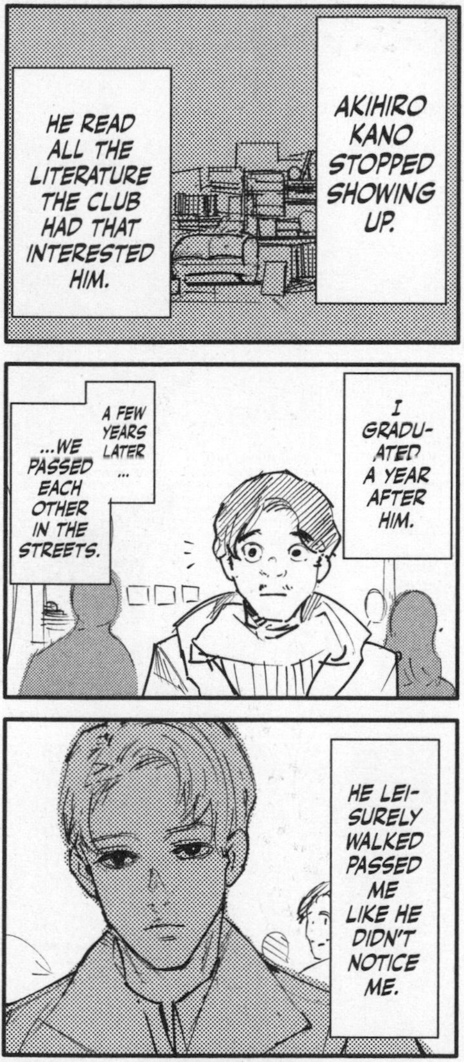
AKIHIRO KANO STOPPED SHOWING UP.
HE READ ALL THE LITERATURE THE CLUB HAD THAT INTERESTED HIM.
I GRADU-ATED A YEAR AFTER HIM.
A FEW YEARS LATER...
...WE PASSED EACH OTHER IN THE STREETS.
HE LEI-SURELY WALKED PASSED ME LIKE HE DIDN'T NOTICE ME.
I REGRET NOT SAYING ANYTHING TO HIM.
I'VE ALWAYS WANTED TO BE HIS FRIEND...

Staff: Hashimoto, Kiyotaka Aihara, Niina/Nina, Ippo Yaguchi, Akikuni Nakao
Help: Mizuki Ide, Matsuzaki, Kota Shugyo, Nomaguchi, Abe
Comic Design: Hideaki Shimada (L.S.D.)
Magazine Design: Miyuki Takaoka (POCKET)
Photography: Wataru Tanaka
Editor: Junpei Matsuo

Volume 11 goes on sale June 2019!

SQUAD ZERO

● Rikai Sozu
層頭 理界（そうず りかい）

- Age: 16 ● Blood type: AB ● Height/weight: 164cm/59kg
- Member of the Sozu family, a branch of the Washu family.
- Withdrawn, but becomes attached to those with whom he's familiar.
- Skilled with club- or spear-type Quinques.

● Yusa Arima
有馬 夕乍（ありま ゆさ）

- Age: 16 ● Blood type: B ● Height/weight: 160cm/60kg
- A quiet, mild-mannered boy.
- Likes to daydream and has a secret fascination with the world beyond fighting.
- There are several Arima branches in the Washu family, and he is not Kisho Arima's brother.
- Skilled with long sword-type Quinques.

● Shio Ihei
伊丙 士皇（いへい しお）

- Age: 14 ● Blood type: B ● Height/weight: 153cm/46kg
- A distant relative of Hairu Ihei.
- A cheerful and innocent boy.
- The youngest member of Squad Zero, but he has eradicated the most Ghouls.

SUI ISHIDA is the author
of the immensely popular
Tokyo Ghoul and several
Tokyo Ghoul one-shots,
including one that won
second place in the *Weekly
Young Jump* 113th Grand
Prix award in 2010. *Tokyo
Ghoul:re* is the sequel to
Tokyo Ghoul.

TOKYO GHOUL:re

**Story and art by
SUI ISHIDA**

TOKYO GHOUL:RE © 2014 by Sui Ishida
All rights reserved.
First published in Japan in 2014 by SHUEISHA Inc., Tokyo.
English translation rights arranged by SHUEISHA Inc.

Translation Joe Yamazaki
Touch-Up Art & Lettering Vanessa Satone
Design Shawn Carrico
Editor Pancha Diaz

Printed in the U.S.A.

Published by VIZ Media, LLC
P.O. Box 77010
San Francisco, CA 94107

10 9 8 7 6 5 4 3 2 1
First printing, April 2019

VIZ MEDIA
viz.com

VIZ SIGNATURE
vizsignature.com

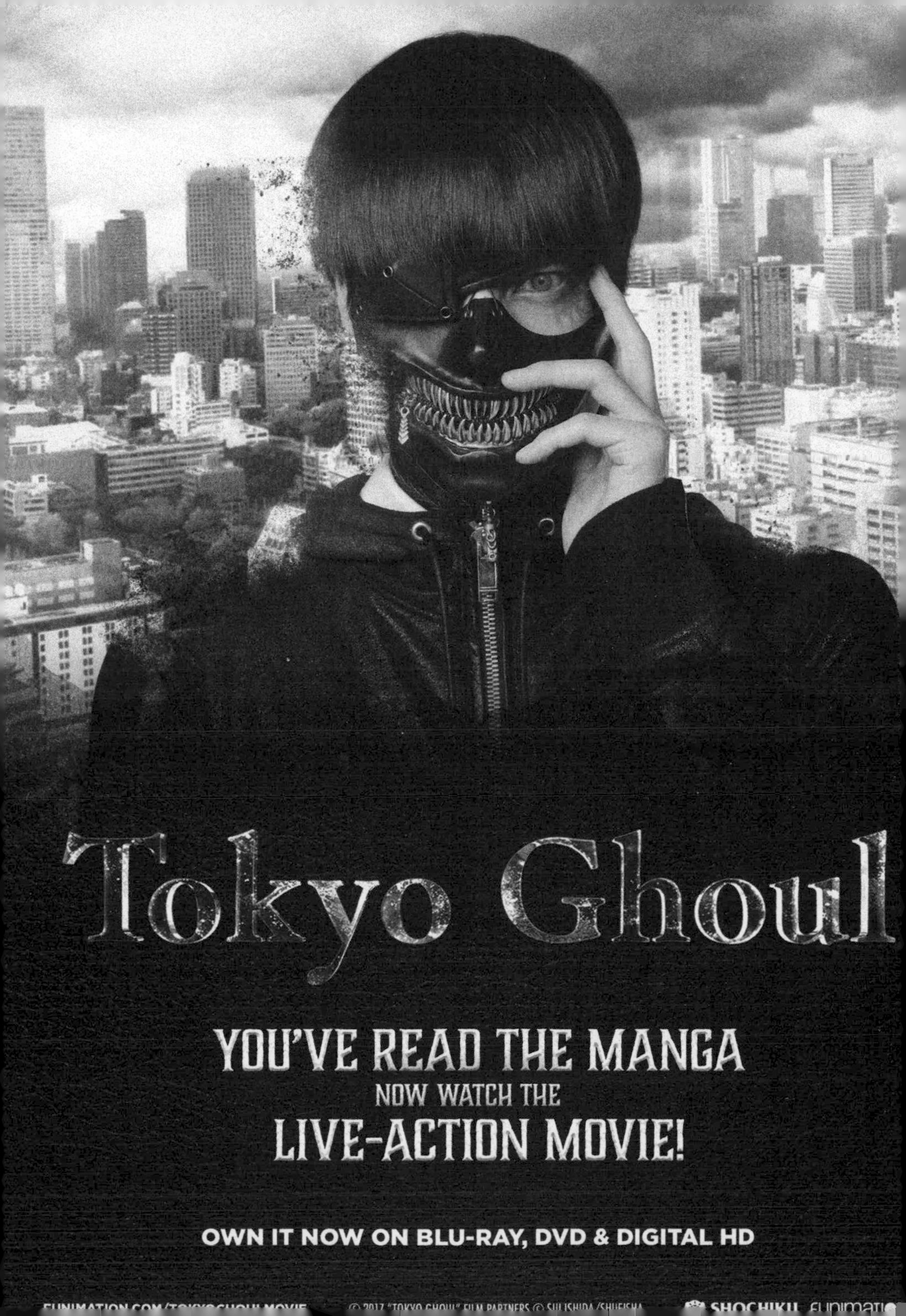
Tokyo Ghoul
YOU'VE READ THE MANGA
NOW WATCH THE
LIVE-ACTION MOVIE!
OWN IT NOW ON BLU-RAY, DVD & DIGITAL HD
FUNIMATION.COM/TOKYOGHOULMOVIE
© 2017 "TOKYO GHOUL" FILM PARTNERS © SUI ISHIDA/SHUEISHA
SHOCHIKU funimation

MOBILE SUIT GUNDAM THUNDERBOLT

In the Universal Century year 0079, the space colony known as Side 3 proclaims independence as the Principality of Zeon and declares war on the Earth Federation. One year later, they are locked in a fierce battle for the Thunderbolt Sector, an area of space scarred by the wreckage of destroyed colonies. Into this maelstrom of destruction go two veteran Mobile Suit pilots: the deadly Zeon sniper Daryl Lorenz, and Federation ace Io Fleming. It's the beginning of a rivalry that can end only when one of them is destroyed...

STORY AND ART
YASUO OHTAGAKI

ORIGINAL CONCEPT BY
HAJIME YATATE
AND YOSHIYUKI TOMINO

MOBILE SUIT GUNDAM
THUNDERBOLT

RATED
T+
FOR OLDER
TEEN

viz media
viz.com

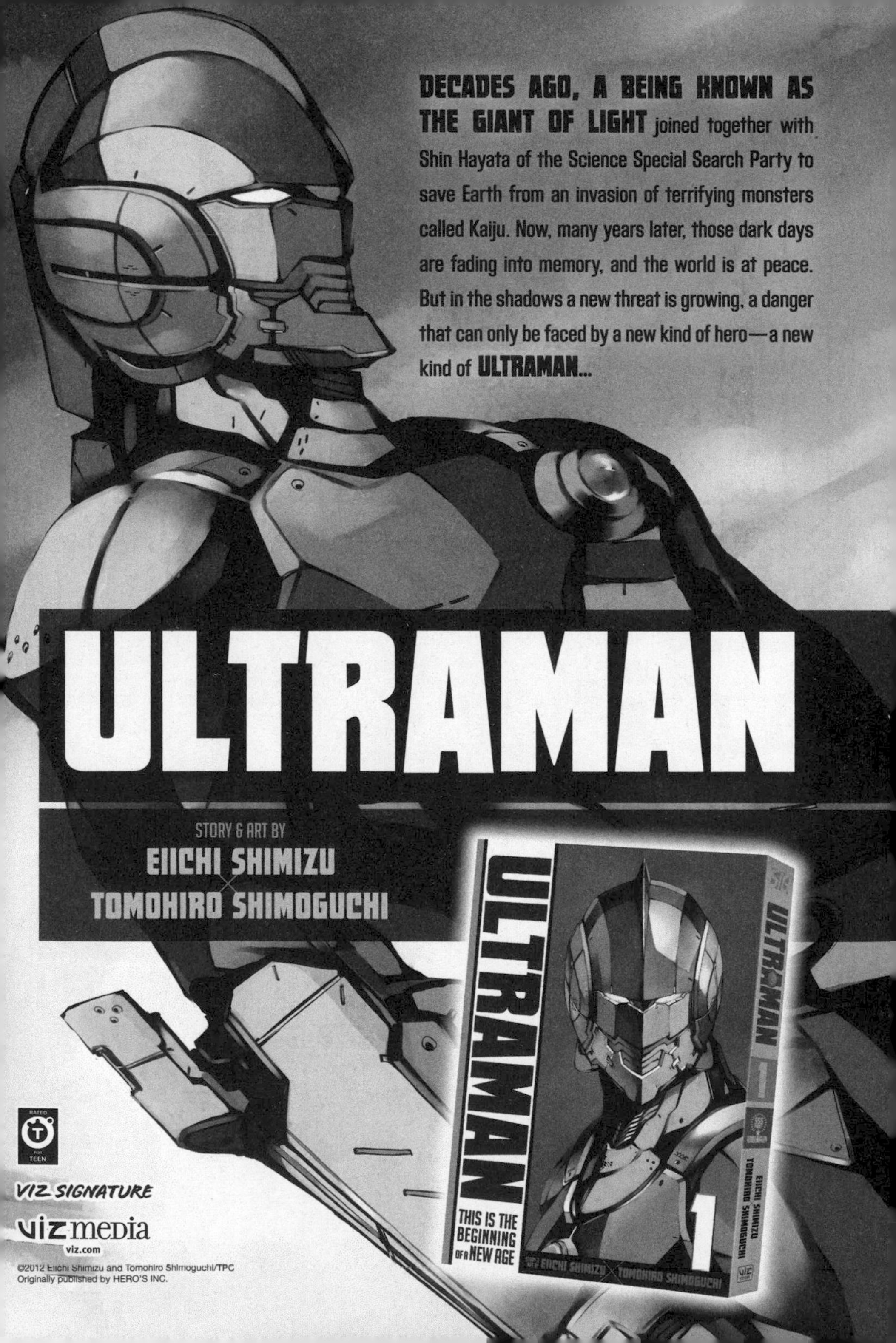

DECADES AGO, A BEING KNOWN AS THE GIANT OF LIGHT joined together with Shin Hayata of the Science Special Search Party to save Earth from an invasion of terrifying monsters called Kaiju. Now, many years later, those dark days are fading into memory, and the world is at peace. But in the shadows a new threat is growing, a danger that can only be faced by a new kind of hero—a new kind of **ULTRAMAN...**

ULTRAMAN

STORY & ART BY

EIICHI SHIMIZU
TOMOHIRO SHIMOGUCHI

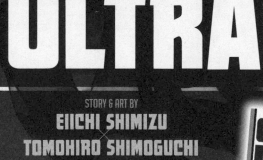

TOKYO GHOUL:re

This is the last page.
TOKYO GHOUL:re reads right to left.